Learning Windows
Server 2003

Other Microsoft Windows resources from O'Reilly

Related titles   Windows Server Hacks™   Securing Windows Server
Windows Server Cookbook™   2003
Windows Server 2003   Active Directory
Network Administration   Active Directory Cookbook™

Windows Books   *windows.oreilly.com* is a complete catalog of O'Reilly's Win-
Resource Center   dows and Office books, including sample chapters and code
examples.

oreillynet.com is the essential portal for developers interested in
open and emerging technologies, including new platforms, programming languages, and operating systems.

Conferences   O'Reilly brings diverse innovators together to nurture the ideas
that spark revolutionary industries. We specialize in document-
ing the latest tools and systems, translating the innovator's
knowledge into useful skills for those in the trenches. Visit *con-
ferences.oreilly.com* for our upcoming events.

Safari Bookshelf (*safari.oreilly.com*) is the premier online reference library for programmers and IT professionals. Conduct
searches across more than 1,000 books. Subscribers can zero in
on answers to time-critical questions in a matter of seconds.
Read the books on your Bookshelf from cover to cover or simply flip to the page you need. Try it today for free.

SECOND EDITION

Learning Windows Server 2003

Jonathan Hassell

Beijing · Cambridge · Farnham · Köln · Paris · Sebastopol · Taipei · Tokyo

Learning Windows Server 2003, Second Edition
by Jonathan Hassell

Published by O'Reilly Media, Inc., 1005 Gravenstein Highway North, Sebastopol, CA 95472.

O'Reilly books may be purchased for educational, business, or sales promotional use. Online editions are also available for most titles (*safari.oreilly.com*). For more information, contact our corporate/institutional sales department: (800) 998-9938 or *corporate@oreilly.com*.

Editors: Robbie Allen and John Osborn	**Cover Designer:** Ellie Volckhausen	
Production Editor: Matt Hutchinson	**Interior Designer:** David Futato	
Production Services: GEX, Inc.	**Illustrators:** Robert Romano, Jessamyn Read, and Lesley Borash	

Printing History:

December 2004:	First Edition.
February 2006:	Second Edition.

RepKover™ This book uses RepKover™, a durable and flexible lay-flat binding.

ISBN: 0-596-10123-6
[M]   [4/06]

Table of Contents

Preface

Microsoft's server-oriented Windows operating systems have grown by leaps and bounds in their capabilities, complexities, and sheer number of features since the release of Windows NT Server in the early 1990s. With each release, system administrators have found themselves grappling with new concepts, from domains, directory services, and virtual private networks to client quarantining, disk quota, and universal groups. Just when you've mastered one set of changes, another comes along and suddenly you're scrambling once again to get up to speed. A vicious cycle this IT business is.

One source of help for the beleaguered administrator has always been the technical book market and its communities of authors, publishers, and user groups. Major releases of popular operating systems have always been accompanied by the publication of books written to support them, often encouraged by the software manufacturers. Some tout themselves as complete guides to their software compadres, while others approach their subject gingerly, as though their readers were of a questionable intellectual capacity. But over the years many of these books have become complex and have accumulated as much detritus as the operating systems they explain. You now see on the shelves of your friendly local bookstores 1,200-plus-page monstrosities that you might find useful, but only if you enjoy dealing with 30 pounds of paper in your lap or on your desk, and only if you find it productive to wade through references to "how things worked" in Windows NT four versions ago. After all, there's a limit to how many times you can revise something before it's best to simply start from scratch. Do you need all of that obsolete information to do your job efficiently?

I'm wagering that you don't (my luck in Las Vegas notwithstanding), and it was in that spirit that I set out to write *Learning Windows Server 2003*, Second Edition. I wanted to trim down the content of this volume so that I included just enough theory on a subject for you to understand how different features and systems work in *this* version of Windows. I wanted you to come away with a firm understanding of what's happening under the hood of the system, but without the sense that you've just completed a graduate course in OS theory. Most of all, I wanted this book to be a practical guide that helps you get your work done—"here's how it works, here's how to do it."

The result is the book you're either holding in your hands right now or reading online: a book with a more compact presentation, a lower price, and a tighter focus on tasks than other books on the market. And in this new second edition, I've strived to maintain that focus on efficiency and density while still providing a detailed introduction and walkthrough of Windows Server 2003 R2's new features.

I hope that this work meets your expectations, and I hope you turn to this book again and again when you need to understand some feature of the massive product that is Windows Server 2003.

Audience

Beginner to intermediate system administrators most certainly will find this book a helpful guide for learning how Windows Server 2003 and its follow-up release, R2, works and the different ways to administer machines running that operating system. This book has step-by-step procedures and discussions of complex concepts such as Active Directory replication, DFS namespaces and replication, network access quarantining, and server clustering. Although I've eliminated material that isn't relevant to day-to-day administration, you still will find the chapters full of useful information for understanding the "why" as well as the "how" of a given operation.

Advanced system administrators also might find this book useful for discovering new concepts and components outside of their realm of expertise. I've found that senior system administrators often focus on one or two specific feature sets of a product and are less familiar with other elements of the OS. This book provides a stepping stone for further exploration and study of less well-known parts of the operating system.

One other item to mention: throughout the book I've tried to highlight the use of the command line in addition to (or in some cases, as opposed to) graphical ways to accomplish tasks. Command lines, in my opinion, are fabulous for quickly and efficiently getting things done, and they provide a great basis for launching into scripting repetitive tasks. Microsoft has done an excellent job of integrating command-line functions into the R2 revision of Windows, and I've attempted to do the effort justice within the text. In fact, a new addition to the second edition is the inclusion of a "Command Line Utilities" section at the end of each applicable chapter. But none of this should cause you to shy you away from this book if you are a GUI aficionado: you'll still find everything you're accustomed to within this volume.

Organization and Structure

In structuring the contents of this book, I have tried to make a logical progression through the product, from a high-level overview through complete discussions and treatments of each its major components. Let's walk through the Table of Contents a little more thoroughly.

Chapter 1 provides a very general overview of Windows Server 2003 from Microsoft's approach to its design and packaging and the different versions that are available, to an overview of the features in this release that are new or otherwise improved. In short, this chapter is designed to give the administrator a complete and systematic overview of the product.

Chapter 2 provides a detailed guide to installing Windows Server 2003 in a variety of different environments. I've included scenarios for upgrade and new installations, and considerations with regard to security, user requirements, hardware necessities, and distributed installation (mass deployment). I also cover the System Preparation tool (Sysprep), which allows mass duplication of a single OS image on deployment to multiple computers, and Remote Installation Services (RIS), another tool for installing the OS over the network.

Chapter 3 discusses the basic file and print services built into Windows Server 2003. The chapter begins with an overview of sharing, and a guide to creating shares, publishing them to Active Directory, mapping drives, using the My Network Places applet, and accessing shares from the Start → Run command and from within Internet Explorer. Then I dive into a detailed discussion of the Windows permission structure, including permission levels, "special" permissions, inheritance, and ownership. Here, you'll also find a guide to settings permissions. Also covered in this chapter is an overview of the Distributed File System (DFS), how to set it up, and how to manage it.

Chapter 4 covers the domain name system, or DNS. Because DNS is such a fundamental component of Active Directory, I wanted to include a separate treatment of how it works, including a discussion of the different types of resource records and zone files supported, integration with Active Directory, the split DNS architecture, and backup and recovery of DNS data.

Most installations of Windows Server 2003 include Active Directory because so many products that require the server OS are tightly integrated with this technology. Chapter 5 provides a complete guide to the technical portion of Active Directory, including its logical and physical structure, hierarchical components (domains, trees, forests, and organizational units), scalability, and replication. Coverage of the LDAP standards is included, as well as a discussion to migration and security considerations. Then I move into planning strategies, installing Active Directory onto Windows Server, and the day-to-day administrative tools.

Group Policy (GP) is one of the most underappreciated management technologies in any server product. Chapter 6 is dedicated to introducing GP and its structure and operation. I begin with a survey of GP and Active Directory interaction, objects, and inheritance. Then I provide a practical guide to implementing GP through user and computer policies and administrative templates, installing software through GP, administration through scripting, and redirecting folders and other user interface elements. I also discuss IntelliMirror, a cool technology for application distribution (similar to ZENworks from Novell).

Chapter 7 helps ensure that you are well versed in locking down your systems to protect both your own computers and the Internet community as a whole. I cover security policy, including ways to manage it using predefined templates and customized policy plans, and an overview of the Security Configuration and Analysis Tool, or SCAT. Then I provide a complete procedural guide to locking down both a Windows network server and a standard Windows client system. (Despite the fact that this is a server book, administrators often are responsible for the entire network, and client and server security go hand in hand.)

IIS received a major revamp in this release, and Chapter 8 covers the details. In Version 6, IIS is ready for primetime hosting. I cover the architectural improvements and new features in this release, and then move on to a practical discussion of daily IIS administration. Guides include administering basic web sites, the SMTP listener, the new POP3 service, the NNTP service, and the FTP server.

Chapter 9 covers the .NET Framework services introduced in this server revision. I discuss their purpose and then provide a guide to administering the .NET Framework on a standard server. A complete list of references to other works that cover these services in more detail is provided as well.

Chapter 10 provides a guide to Terminal Services, including an overview from the server administrator's perspective and a similar overview from a typical user's point of view. Then I cover how to install both Terminal Services itself *and* applications such as Microsoft Office and other tools inside the Terminal Services environment. A guide to configuring Terminal Services follows, including procedures for general configuration, remote control options, environment settings, logons, sessions, and permission control. Concluding the chapter is a guide to daily administration using Terminal Services Manager, the Active Directory user tools, Task Manager, and command-line utilities.

Chapter 11 covers the standard networking architecture of the operating system, including addressing and routing issues. Then I move into a discussion of the various network subsystems: the Domain Name System (DNS), the Dynamic Host Configuration Protocol (DHCP), and a discussion of VPN connectivity, the different phases of VPN, tunneling and encryption, and the RADIUS server bundled with .NET Server, the Internet Authentication Service (IAS). Finishing up the chapter, I discuss

IPSec, its support from within the OS, and how to install, configure, use, and administer it. Coverage of client quarantining is also included.

The penultimate chapter, Chapter 12, covers Windows clustering services. First, a discussion of the different types of clustering services is provided, and then I cover successfully planning a basic cluster and its different elements: the applications, how to group the machines, capacity and network planning, user account management, and the possible points of failure. A treatment of Network Load Balancing clusters follows, and I round out the chapter with a guide to creating and managing server clusters, as well as an overview of the administrative tools bundled with the OS.

Finally, Chapter 13 discusses the other elements of Windows Server 2003 not covered elsewhere, including the Indexing Service and the Microsoft Message Queue. Tips for managing each are discussed.

The Appendix provides a peek at the upcoming, revolutionary revision of the operating system, currently known as Longhorn Server.

Conventions Used in This Book

The following typographical conventions are used in this book:

Plain text
> Indicates menu titles, menu options, menu buttons, and keyboard accelerators (such as Alt and Ctrl).

Italic
> Indicates new terms, URLs, email addresses, filenames, file extensions, pathnames, directories, and command-line utilities.

Constant width
> Indicates commands, options, switches, variables, attributes, keys, functions, types, classes, namespaces, methods, modules, properties, parameters, values, objects, events, event handlers, XML tags, HTML tags, macros, the contents of files, or the output from commands.

Constant width bold
> Shows commands or other text that should be typed literally by the user.

Constant width italic
> Shows text that should be replaced with user-supplied values.

 This icon signifies a tip, suggestion, or general note.

 This icon indicates a warning or caution.

Using Code Examples

This book is here to help you get your job done. In general, you can use the code in this book in your programs and documentation. You do not need to contact O'Reilly for permission unless you're reproducing a significant portion of the code. For example, writing a program that uses several chunks of code from this book does not require permission. Selling or distributing a CD-ROM of examples from O'Reilly books *does* require permission. Answering a question by citing this book and quoting example code does not require permission. Incorporating a significant amount of example code from this book into your product's documentation *does* require permission.

O'Reilly appreciates, but does not require, attribution. An attribution usually includes the title, author, publisher, and ISBN. For example: "*Learning Windows Server 2003*, Second Edition by Jonathan Hassell. Copyright 2006 O'Reilly Media, Inc., 0-596-10123-6."

If you feel your use of code examples falls outside fair use or the permission given above, feel free to contact O'Reilly at *permissions@oreilly.com*.

We'd Like to Hear from You

Please address comments and questions concerning this book to the publisher:

> O'Reilly Media, Inc.
> 1005 Gravenstein Highway North
> Sebastopol, CA 95472
> (800) 998-9938 (in the United States or Canada)
> (707) 829-0515 (international or local)
> (707) 829-0104 (fax)

O'Reilly has a web page for this book, where it lists errata, examples, and any additional information. You can access this page at:

> *http://www.oreilly.com/catalog/lwinsvr20032*

To comment or ask technical questions about this book, send email to:

> *bookquestions@oreilly.com*

For more information about our books, conferences, Resource Centers, and the O'Reilly Network, see the O'Reilly web site at:

> *http://www.oreilly.com*

As the author of this book, I also have created a comprehensive resource web site as its companion, located at the following URL:

> *http://www.learning2003.com*

There you will find regular updates to the book, extended contact information, code samples from the book, and information on when and where you can find me speaking and conducting seminars. I invite you to visit today and become a regular reader.

Safari® Enabled

 When you see a Safari® Enabled icon on the cover of your favorite technology book, that means the book is available online through the O'Reilly Network Safari Bookshelf.

Safari offers a solution that's better than e-books. It's a virtual library that lets you easily search thousands of top tech books, cut and paste code samples, download chapters, and find quick answers when you need the most accurate, current information. Try it for free at *http://safari.oreilly.com*.

Acknowledgments

I've always liked the fact that the acknowledgments in technical books are typically in the front. That way, when you read the remainder of the book, you already know who to thank for it, unlike in a movie. So, without further ado…

John Osborn at O'Reilly was instrumental in getting this process organized and off the ground and provided very welcome guidance and feedback during the initial stages of writing this book. My sincere appreciation also is extended to Robbie Allen, who spent many (painstaking, I'm sure) hours combing through the manuscript and providing very helpful, precise feedback. Robbie is an excellent editor, author, and tech head simultaneously, and this book is all the better for his involvement in its creation and production.

Special thanks are due to Jacob Morgan for sharing his expertise in .NET services and his contribution to Chapter 9.

Errors and shortcomings were dutifully found by the technical review team for both editions, which consisted of IT professionals Abigail Cooke, Dan Green, Laura Hunter, Rick Kingslan, Carlos Magalhaes, Eddie Phillips, Dan Stolts, and Mitch Tulloch.

Of course, my family is also to thank: particularly my fiancée, Lisa, who patiently accepted the insufficient answer of "not yet" repeatedly to her reasonable question of "Aren't you done with that book?" My parents deserve credit as well; thanks for your support throughout the project.

Finally, I'd like to dedicate this book to my grandfather, John Broughton. He has taught me much in life, but perhaps most significantly, he showed me the value of hard work and his confidence in my ability to achieve what I dreamed. My success today is in no small part directly associated with his love and encouragement. Thank you, Papa, for all that you have done for me.

CHAPTER 1

Introducing Windows Server 2003

It all started with Windows NT, Microsoft's first serious entry into the network server market. Versions 3.1 and 3.5 of Windows NT didn't garner very much attention in a NetWare-dominated world because they were sluggish and refused to play well with others. Along came Windows NT 4.0, which used the new Windows 95 interface (revolutionary only to those who didn't recognize Apple's Macintosh OS user interface) to put a friendlier face on some simple yet fundamental architectural improvements. With Version 4.0, larger organizations saw that Microsoft was serious about entering the enterprise computing market, even if the product currently being offered was still limited in scalability and availability. For one, Microsoft made concessions to NetWare users, giving them an easy way to integrate with a new NT network. The company also included a revised security feature set, including finely grained permissions and domains, which signified Microsoft considered enterprise computing an important part of Windows.

After a record six and one-half service packs, NT 4.0 is considered by some to be the most stable operating system ever to come out of Redmond. However, despite that, most administrators with Unix experience required an OS more credible in an enterprise environment—one that could compare to the enormous Unix machines that penetrated that market long ago and had unquestionably occupied it ever since. It wasn't until February 2000, when Windows 2000 Server was released, that these calls were answered. Windows 2000 was a complete revision of NT 4.0 and was designed with stability and scalability as first priorities.

However, something still was lacking. Sun and IBM included application server software and developer-centric capabilities with their industrial-strength operating systems, Solaris and AIX. Windows 2000 lacked this functionality. In addition, the infamous security problems associated with the bundled Windows 2000 web server, Internet Information Services (IIS), cast an ominous cloud over the thought that Windows could ever be a viable Internet-facing enterprise OS. Given that many saw Microsoft as "betting the company" on a web services initiative called .NET, it was critical that the company save face and do it right the next time. It wasn't too late, but customers were very concerned about the numerous security vulnerabilities and the lack of a convenient patch management system to apply corrections to those vulnerabilities. Things had to change.

From stage left, enter Windows Server 2003. What distinguishes this new release other than a longer name and a three-year difference in release dates? That's a difficult question to answer. Microsoft is slowly but surely raising the standard it sets for itself in creating a server OS: it's transformed a departmental fileserver system into an enterprise-class, centrally managed OS and then into an application server platform designed to interoperate using open standards. Along with this transition has come improved hardware support, redesigned directory services, management tools designed in a role-based paradigm, and a host of security enhancements.

Changes from Windows 2000 Server

Windows Server 2003 provides scores of new features that most administrators have been hoping for since the release of Windows 2000 Server, as well as critical bug fixes, tool improvements, management refinements, and enhancements to the general fit and finish of the product. In this section, I'll take a look at the major changes in the product from Windows 2000 Server.

Security

Windows Server 2003 is fairly secure after the installation process is complete, as Microsoft promised. The product also benefited from the month-long halt of new development in March 2002, referred to by Microsoft as the beginning of the Trustworthy Computing Initiative, wherein all developers and product managers did nothing but review existing source code for security flaws and attend training on new best practices for writing secure code.

But it's not only in the actual code that security takes front seat. Perhaps the most welcome improvement in the eyes of network administrators with large Windows XP deployments is Windows Server 2003's native understanding and support for the expanded feature set of Group Policy (GP) found in XP. Windows 2000 Server was unaware of the new XP support for software execution restrictions and remote desktop support tools and thus required a bit of handholding to get it all working together. Windows Server 2003 knows about these XP tools out of the box.

Windows Server 2003 also debuts new secure wireless LAN support, and as an added bonus, this support can extend to wired networks, too. This allows you to keep unauthorized hosts off any part of your network, wired or wireless. 802.1X clients can authenticate to Windows Server 2003 machines using the Internet Authentication Service (IAS). For added security, you can add dynamic key exchange and WEP support as well. This is a great boon to both wireless and wired security. I'll explore Windows security features and configurations in greater detail in Chapter 7, and IAS in Chapter 11.

Performance and Scalability

Changes designed to improve both performance and scalability received attention from the development team. When the product was released in early 2003, VeriTest, an independent testing organization, ran benchmarks and custom-designed tests that demonstrated that Windows Server 2003 outperformed Windows 2000 and Windows NT 4.0 by a dramatic margin of anywhere from 100–200%, depending on the task, using the same hardware. That's impressive for any follow-up release and bucks the all-too-familiar trend of needing to upgrade hardware and software simultaneously. Compared with NT 4.0, Windows Server 2003 is about twice as fast when operating as a fileserver, three times as fast as a dynamic web application server, and up to 400% faster at just plain web-page hosting. VeriTest ran all the tests using the same server, but during the battery it alternated the number of processors in the machine at any given time, using one, two, four, and eight processors interchangeably.

In fact, performance is so good that a lot of companies might want to consider adopting Windows Server 2003 for the purposes of server consolidation. Improvements to the underlying operating system, coupled with a complete rewrite of IIS, make it possible to increase the duties of a single machine. If you find your datacenter is growing by leaps and bounds, by giving each Windows Server 2003 machine more responsibility—which it can handle—you can reduce the number of servers you have to support. Having fewer servers can make managing those servers easier, too, and it can provide the primary benefit of reducing the total cost of ownership (TCO), a frequent measure of the progress and success of IT projects.

As far as scalability is concerned, most notably Windows Server 2003 offers the ability in the 32-bit versions to use computers that scale to 32 processors. On 64-bit platforms with the Windows Server 2003 native 64-bit versions, operation can scale to 64 processors.

Management Tool Enhancements

Improvements to GP, including the new Group Policy Management Console (GPMC), as well as a task-oriented suite of management tools, helps administrators control and administer more servers with much less effort than Windows 2000 required.

The Microsoft Management Console (MMC) is a central location where various parts of Windows subsystems come together in a single, consistent, and integrated user interface. Windows Server 2003 includes the MMC, first introduced in parts of Windows NT and by default in Windows 2000, and integrates nearly all administrative components into it.

The GPMC is an MMC snap-in that introduces easier ways of working with Group Policy Objects (GPOs). In the past, an administrator had to view GPOs not with one tool, but with several, depending on where a GPO was applied. This required different snap-ins, such as Active Directory Users and Computers, Active Directory Sites and Services, the Delegation of Control Wizard, Resultant Set of Policy (RSoP), and Access Control List (ACL) editors. Needless to say, it was not as simple as it should have been. Fortunately, Microsoft realized this pain-in-the-neck way of administering GP and released the GPMC, which offers a centralized view of all GPOs. Perhaps the largest benefit of the GPMC is that it reduces the amount of clicking you have to do to find the GPO you need to modify. If you've used GP with Windows 2000 before, you are all too familiar with this.

The GPMC makes it a lot easier to:

- Import, export, copy, and paste GPOs
- Manage GP security
- Generate file- and printer-based GPO reports
- Examine GPO and RSoP data
- Back up and restore GPOs
- Script GPO operations that you can perform with the GPMC (i.e., you can't script individual policy settings, only GPO operations such as template GPO importing)

Additionally, if you are running Windows XP on your desktop, you'll be pleased to know that Microsoft has the Administrative Tools Pack available to install on Windows 2000 and Windows XP workstations. However, note that the Windows 2000 version of the Administrative Tools Pack does not install properly on XP. Windows Server 2003 comes with a new, released version of the administrative tools compatible with XP that you also can use to manage Windows 2000 servers.

These management tools and their enhancements are covered in their respective areas throughout the book. Specifically, Chapter 6 is a core reference to GP in general using the GPMC as a key management interface.

Trans-Forest Active Directory Trusts

Having multiple domains in a forest is a neat way to gain some significant management and security advantages, primarily the ability to do away with the old, inflexible, and difficult-to-manage Windows NT 4.0–style trusts. As well, with Active Directory there's a beneficial feature known as the *global catalog*, which serves as a sort of "superdirectory," responding to queries with a more efficient but smaller database than the full Active Directory. But what happens when your corporations merge? What do you do with two Active Directory forests that need to share things with each other?

Windows Server 2003 introduces forest root transitive trusts, wherein you click two forest root domains and tell Windows that they ought to trust one another, and everything just automatically works. To tell the truth, you can create the end result of these transitive trusts in Windows 2000, but you need to create multiple trusts between all domains, a process that is tedious and ripe with room for error. As with all good things, though, this functionality has limitations. First off, there's the somewhat prohibitive limitation that all domain controllers in both forests must be running Windows Server 2003 for this to work. I'll explore these types of trusts, including additional limitations, in more detail in Chapter 5.

Remote Office Domain Controller Creation Improvements

The standard process to create a Windows 2000 domain controller was to run the DCPROMO Wizard, enter your login information, and download a copy of the Active Directory database. If you spot a problem with this scenario, chances are you've run into said problem yourself. If your branch office is in an extremely remote location—say, a location with no broadband Internet connectivity or nothing higher than 28.8kbps dial-up connectivity—and your Active Directory database is, perhaps, larger than 500MB, the third step in the process is going to take quite a long time. On top of that, if your connection is faulty and drops in the middle (or worse, right at the end) of the download process, you have to start all over. Obviously that can make for a very frustrating and nonproductive upgrade session.

Windows Server 2003 enables you to create a copy of the Active Directory database on removable media at your central office, or at least at a branch office with good connectivity to the domain. You then can carry this copy to the remote office with the flaky and slow connection, run DCPROMO, and tell the wizard that you have the Active Directory database on removable media. The wizard will copy that database onto the computer, and at that point, the wizard needs only to replicate any changes made to directory information between that time and the point at which you made the copy of the directory database. It's a really clever and simple solution.

I'll also cover these domain controller feature enhancements in Chapter 5.

Replication Control

Active Directory replication to branch office domain controllers has always been a touchy subject for administrators. At what point do the disadvantages outweigh the benefits? Windows 2000 tried to make it a bit easier on flaky WAN links by enabling traffic compression by default, and by using a "least-cost" algorithm that calculates how and when it would be cheapest to send the data over the link. Microsoft improved the replication algorithm in Windows Server 2003 significantly. With Windows 2000 it wasn't uncommon for branch-office domain controllers to experience high CPU loads while trying to decompress hundreds of megabytes of replication data; in the new edition, you can turn off compression and save some CPU cycles.

In addition, you can now selectively replicate information between a set of domain controllers, not just all domain controllers, using a new feature called *application partitions*. In the previous version of Windows 2000, if you had information that you wanted to pass along to other controllers in a domain, you had to send it to all of them. Active Directory-integrated DNS zones are a popular example of this. But if your DNS servers are only in Seattle and Boston, why would your domain control-lers in Tokyo—at the other end of an expensive WAN link—care about receiving new DNS server information? They don't, but they had to get it anyway. In Win-dows Server 2003, it is possible for only Active Directory-integrated DNS servers to receive replicated information; it's not mandatory that other domain controllers do so. Kudos to Microsoft on this one.

I will discuss replication in more depth in Chapter 5.

Domain Renaming

In these days riddled with corporate investing, mergers, acquisitions, and divesti-tures, administrators can find that their business name, or the name of the network that they're responsible for supporting, can change rapidly. In Active Directory implementations this can be embarrassing, because with Windows 2000, once you have created and named a domain, you cannot rename it. Four years later, some businesses are still logging on to networks with names that ceased to exist many years before.

Windows Server 2003 introduces the ability to rename existing domains. That's about all I can say on that issue because "ability to do" does not equate to "simple to do." There are several restrictions on the process, not the least of which is that all domain controllers in the domain must be running Windows Server 2003. That can be an expensive proposition for large companies, some of which might need Win-dows Server 2003 only for that very ability. You also have to reboot all the domain controllers in that domain twice and each member server once. So, you can rename domains, but not easily or cost-effectively in most cases.

Chapter 5 contains detailed information on how domain renaming works and the limitations thereof.

Volume Shadow Copies and Shadow Copy Restore

Some of the most exciting ground being broken in server technology today has to do with increasing storage capacity and availability, and Windows Server 2003 is taking part in the movement. Virtual disk services, volume shadow copy, dynamic disks, and storage area network (SAN) management technologies abound in Windows Server 2003.

One of the most useful features of Windows Server 2003 is its support for shadow copies. This allows an administrator to configure the operating system so that it will make copies of files identified by an administrator from a disk volume at regular intervals—sort of like taking a snapshot of the disk at specific times—and store them in a protected area on a volume. By installing a client extension on Windows XP machines, an end user can simply click the option to "view previous versions" inside the folder view of any volume in Windows Explorer, and Windows will bring up a list of all saved versions. This is absolutely fantastic when, at 3:45 p.m., a user realizes that before lunch, she accidentally overwrote the final draft of her proposal that is due during a meeting that begins at 4:00 p.m. She can grab the snapshot taken before lunch and all is well. Administrators who routinely restore user data from backups after "accidents" or "unfortunate and inadvertent data misplacements" (to use politically correct terminology) will appreciate the ability to recover files at the user level. I cover shadow copies in Chapter 3.

Volume shadow copy services also enable administrators to periodically take snapshots of their disk volumes, which provides a great way to perform backups on critical databases that can never be taken down for traditional offline backup procedures. The snapshot of the database is taken and stored in a special folder on the disk, and that folder can be backed up at leisure. This reduces a lot of headaches and (at least somewhat) assuages the tediousness of performing backups.

Virtual disk services (VDS) also enable administrators to configure SAN hardware directly from Windows, bring volumes online and offline, format them, and use them without intermediary software. This also increases the availability of backup products because third-party providers of these products are spared the task of writing their own custom drivers. Those products can interface with the native Windows support for these types of tasks, thereby decreasing the cost of that software to make, sell, and buy.

There's more, too. VDS is the foundation of two new command-line utilities that pack a lot of power:

DiskRaid

> DiskRaid, part of the Windows Server 2003 Deployment Guide and the Windows Server 2003 Resource Kit, is a utility that you can use to manage RAID subsystems. With it, you can script disk operations, list disks, create, delete, unmask, and extend logical units, and manage a RAID array or container from the command line. It's a great tool for automated server provisioning.

DiskPart

> DiskPart is a command-line version of the Disk Management snap-in that ships with the operating system. It's completely scriptable and enables you to control any aspect of disks, partitions, and volumes without the GUI.

There is more on both of these tools in Chapters 3 and 13, but the important thing to notice is that both of these tools take advantage of the underlying VDS systems in Windows Server 2003. Expect many more third-party disk management tools in the coming years as well.

Terminal Services and Remote Administration

An idea first introduced with Windows NT 4.0 Terminal Server Edition, Terminal Server has consistently improved with each release. Those of you with Windows 2000 Server machines on your network have appreciated the remote administration capabilities included with that OS for some time. And for years, a third-party software company, Citrix, has been making its MetaFrame software, going above and beyond the quality and support of Microsoft's integrated terminal offering.

With Windows Server 2003, the free Terminal Server part gets even better. Support for increased color depth, automatic redirection of sound and printer ports, and lower bandwidth requirements makes it easier to use Terminal Server to access your servers from home, even over dial-up connections. As well, Windows Server 2003 includes the Remote Assistance feature, which places a helpful user interface over a raw Terminal Server connection. (The Remote Assistance feature is exactly like that found in Windows XP.)

Windows Server 2003 also includes native support for *headless servers*, or servers without a keyboard, video card, or mouse. Now you can have machines in your server room without these bulky items and Windows will run normally, without a lot of software hacks. In addition, the OS also includes a new set of functionality called Emergency Management Services (EMS), which enables administrators to perform disaster recovery and server-down maintenance over a network from a location away from the broken machine.

The .NET Framework

The Microsoft .NET Framework is the programming model that developers use for writing, publishing, and executing web applications, smart client applications, and XML services. These applications allow network access to their features via SOAP, XML, and HTTP. With the .NET Framework fully integrated into the Windows Server 2003 operating system, developers are freed from writing "plumbing" code: the framework handles code integration and management details seamlessly.

The .NET Framework itself has not changed with the integration into Windows Server 2003. In fact, the default install looks as if Microsoft just slapped the .NET Framework

1.1 install on top of it. Nevertheless, its presence is a benefit to developers who write applications for you to host on your systems. Some key points include the following:

- IIS 6 radically improves the hosting environment for ASP.NET web applications. The new concepts of application pools and web gardens enhance the stability, scalability, and performance of applications. The new security measures further pull ASP.NET into the leading technology for enterprise web application development.

- Integrated Universal Description, Discovery, and Integration (UDDI) provides the management and organization of web services within secure company boundaries.

- COM+ adds features that align it with .NET. These include application pooling, application recycling, partitioning, and SOAP support.

I discuss the .NET Framework in depth in Chapter 9.

IIS 6

Improvements to security, reliability, and interoperability enhancements in IIS 6 are possibly the most improved part of Windows in this release.

Most noticeably, IIS is not installed out of the box, and when it is installed, it's locked tight. If you've been around Windows server editions for a while, you'll recall that ever since NT 4.0 shipped, IIS has been available and has been installed by default in Windows 2000 prior to Service Pack 4. The security vulnerabilities in IIS that caused the outbreaks of Melissa, Code Red, and Nimda (do these names ring a bell?) have convinced most administrators that IIS is suitable only for internal web sites and those applications that absolutely require ASP support.

But what a difference a release makes. Some improvements in IIS 6 include the following:

- For the first time, you must explicitly install IIS.

- You have to specifically enable scripting support, server extensions, and the dynamic page-generation language you plan to use.

- In its default configuration, IIS will handle only static HTML pages. This is a welcome relief to anyone who has tried to install Windows 2000 and been infected with a nasty virus in the five minutes it takes to boot the server and then turn off the service.

- On a lower level, IIS has been completely rewritten, and the HTTP generation module (*http.sys*) is now a kernel-level driver, which provides Windows Server 2003 with the ability to isolate separate sites on a box and protect each separately from a program crash. That means no more high-load applications taking down an entire server.

- In addition, by being a kernel-level driver, IIS performance is greatly improved in a number of situations. IIS 6 is three times as fast as IIS on Windows 2000 at serving dynamic web pages. Eat your heart out, Apache.

I explore IIS 6 in Chapter 8.

Command-Line Integration

Windows is a popular hate target of Unix system administrators. Unix people claim that Windows depends too much on the GUI. You might have heard these complaints:

- "Windows isn't customizable enough."
- "Windows hides the directness, the inner workings of the operating system, making it difficult to fix it when things go wrong."
- "Things go wrong too often with Windows."

That is, until Windows Server 2003, of course. By my estimation (because Microsoft has not released any official numbers), more than 95% of features that can be managed through the GUI have an associated command-line utility that enables them to be controlled from a prompt, and therefore more easily scripted. On top of that, some functions, such as relocating the volume on which shadow copies are stored, are accessible only through a command-line utility.

Why is the command line so important? For one, it's often a great deal easier to perform simple administrative tasks through one command line. Take adding a user as an example. With the GUI, you need to click several different menu items, do some right-clicking, use the keyboard, tab through some fields, click OK a couple of times, and then close everything. But adding a user through the command line is simple: one line of net user /add, or even dsadd user, with all the options specified, is a lot simpler than clicking through all the graphical screens. Now of course, the GUI has its place, but when it comes to quick-and-dirty system administration, Windows is closing the gap with Unix and its brethren.

I've made a special effort in this second edition to highlight the most useful command-line tools and programs that pertain to a certain topic at the conclusion of each corresponding chapter in a section called "Command-Line Utilities." You'll find this beginning with Chapter 2 and continuing through until Chapter 12. I hope this is a useful addition.

DNS Improvements

Windows Server 2003 creates a great new way to support multidomain-based, Active Directory-integrated DNS systems, called *conditional DNS forwarding*. This feature enables you to instruct Windows to access a specific DNS server if requests are made for a specific domain.

Let's say your company, with the domain widgetsinc.com, has its own DNS service running internally. However, Widgets, Inc. purchased Whatzits Ltd., an English company, which needs to use whatzits.co.uk internally, and people within widgetsinc.com need to be able to log on to whatzits.co.uk resources. You want to keep the domain separate for logistical reasons. But that need to keep your domains distinct creates its own issues because domain controllers handle logons, and widgetsinc.com users need to contact a domain controller for whatzits.co.uk to access that domain's resources. When your Widgets users ask for DNS information, they are sent to the public-facing DNS servers for Whatzits, which of course don't know what a domain controller is. Windows Server 2003 enables you to tell the DNS service running for widgetsinc.com that if clients request information on whatzits.co.uk, they need to be sent to the actual internal domain controllers for the latter. Now, everyone is happy because domain controller information is available, you still can maintain separate sets of public- and private-facing DNS servers for each domain, and users can log on to each domain from the other. This is a big feature and a security enhancement, and I'll cover this more in Chapter 4.

Windows Server 2003 also creates a new feature called *stub zones*, which are basically small scraps of a DNS zone file that are ideal for transferring between DNS servers. The process in which they're used is quite complex and is covered in depth in Chapter 4 as well.

Licensing

Yes, licensing rears its ugly head again. The corporate accounting folks will be pleased to learn that Microsoft has decided to keep the price of the Standard and Enterprise editions of Windows Server 2003 at their Windows 2000 levels. However, there is another change that might be somewhat surprising—and disheartening: as soon as you add a system running Windows Server 2003 to your network, you must purchase brand-new client access licenses (CALs). However, do note that if you decide to purchase Windows Server 2003 R2, you do not need additional client-access licenses if you've already upgraded those CALs upon installation of Windows Server 2003. The only additional expense is the server license in that particular scenario. In addition, Software Assurance (SA) customers will receive R2 as part of their agreement and can install it at no additional charge.

What doesn't make sense in this is that the upgrade from 2000 to Windows Server 2003 isn't a major revision of the Windows server product. In keeping with history,

Microsoft has consistently required new CALs for seats or devices on your network with every major revision of NT. However, with the NT 3.5 to 3.51 upgrade, which was a minor release, one of the main selling points was that your NT 3.5 CALs were still legal. Now I'm not attempting to argue that the new features and fit-and-finish improvements in Windows Server 2003 aren't important, or necessary, or even desired. But I suspect those who have tested and evaluated the product would argue that it's more of a Windows 2000 upgrade than a new product (one might note that in any window, choosing About from the Help menu denotes Windows Server 2003 as being Version 5.2). Of course, Microsoft could remove this requirement at any time, but it's definitely a cog in the wheel to the en masse deployments the company is hoping to see.

Although Windows Server 2003 boasts numerous other minor features, those features give you the idea that while Windows Server 2003 is not a revolutionary upgrade, it's definitely several steps in the right direction.

What Service Pack 1 Adds

Windows Server 2003 Service Pack 1 was released in April 2005 and consists of several must-have updates. Essentially, SP1 brings the new security features, improvements to the built-in firewall and Windows Explorer, and the overall better user experience found in Windows XP Service Pack 2 over the fence to the server side. You'll find the following:

- The Security Configuration Wizard makes it its debut. The SCW is perhaps the biggest security enhancement to any version of Windows on the server since the initial release of Windows NT Server. The SCW takes into account the functional roles a machine is performing and adjusts the configuration and operation of its installed services, Registry, filesystem, and auditing policies to significantly reduce the attack surface of the machine. It does this with a wonderfully easy-to-use interface that includes the ability to save created policies, apply existing policies to other machines, and roll back misapplied policies. I cover the SCW in great detail in Chapter 7.

- The Internet Connection Firewall is renamed Windows Firewall and is improved to work almost exactly like its Windows XP counterpart. A major difference, however, is the default state: unlike XP, the firewall is turned off by default on the server. You'll need to specifically enable it if you want its protection.

- The Automatic Updates interface has been completely redesigned, again to resemble the XP interface.

- Security for the DCOM and RPC subsystems of the product, both of which have been exploited by several pieces of malware over the past few years on other Windows operating systems, has also been significantly improved.

- Microsoft has increased the speed at which IPSec connections between trusted nodes are made by moving code into kernel mode for faster SSL connections and other secure transmissions. Now the performance hit of using secure channels for communication has been lessened.

- IIS start-up times have also been optimized. I cover other, more specific (and less obvious) improvements to IIS in SP1 in Chapter 8.

- Finally, don't discount the convenience of having all security updates issued between the initial "gold" release of the product in April 2005 all rolled into one easily executable package. Patching is a big headache these days, and service packs are great ways to leap ahead to the most secure installation possible if you're a bit behind on your updating.

The bottom line is that Service Pack 1, in my opinion, is a critical upgrade that you should install as soon as you've done due diligence (making sure your applications will run with the updates, ensuring the new security features don't interfere with legacy communications, and generally giving the service pack a thorough once-over). There have been some Windows commercial upgrades in the past that didn't offer the level of improvements and new features that this freely available service pack contains. Recommendation: download and install Service Pack 1 as soon as you can.

What R2 Adds

Alas, Windows Server 2003 R2, released in late 2005, is a less obvious upgrade: it's the first deliverable in Microsoft's newly adopted server update schedule. The idea is that a new version—that is, what most of us would characterize as a major release—will be offered every four years. Two years after each major release, Microsoft will issue an incremental version upgrade that will refresh the product and bring it more in line with other out-of-band software releases the company may have made. (Case in point: Windows SharePoint Services [WSS] was released after the original version of Windows Server 2003 hit the commercial channels. Windows Server 2003 R2 includes WSS, thus adding a fresh face to the original release.) If you do the math, you'll see that the next major version of the core Windows server product, which is codenamed Longhorn at this point, is due in 2007, with Longhorn Server R2 supposedly due in 2009. As you probably know, though, forward-looking statements, when made about Microsoft products and release dates, are hardly ever very precise. At any rate, R2 ships as a second CD in the Windows Server 2003 product, and that product includes an integrated version of Service Pack 1 so that you're automatically at the latest service pack level when you install.

From a more general standpoint, R2 includes a lot of upgrades to already released technologies. There's an update to the Microsoft Management Console, improvements to Active Directory Application Mode, and an integrated version of Windows

SharePoint Services with its second service pack. Specifically, though, the most useful enhancements to R2 are as follows:

- Upgrades to the Distributed File System (DFS). There's great new functionality involved in replicating files, folders, and software out to branch offices over sometimes unpredictable links. And if you're an NT veteran and are familiar with the instability and limitations of the old File Replication Service (FRS), take heart: R2 has a completely new DFS replication engine that handles huge files and huge numbers of files effortlessly. You can use the new engine to maintain real-time replicas of large data volumes in a central location, which makes multiple-targeted DFS links completely possible. I'll cover these updates in Chapter 3.

- The introduction of Active Directory Federation Services. If you do cross-site business that involves managing the identity of business partners, you need ADFS now. ADFS lets you automatically and securely share identity information with business partners electronically, reducing the headaches caused when users forget passwords or leave companies. ADFS could also be considered a security enhancement. Check out Chapter 5 for more information.

- The release of the new Print Management Console. The PMC is what print management in Windows should have been a long time ago: you sort your printers into various categories based on name, location, number of jobs in the queue, and so on, or let the PMC detect all the network print servers in a subnet and automatically add them to the console as managed printers. Once all printers are managed, you can see every single printer and its queued jobs, and you can easily access the web interface of network print servers. All of this is a big improvement over using three or four different interfaces in a mixed environment of tens or hundreds (or even thousands) of network print servers. Chapter 3 has full details.

- Easier management of hard disks and other media with the Storage Resource Manager (SRM). Microsoft licensed storage management technology from Veritas and with it comes improved quota support, among other things. You can assign quotas to individual folders or sets of folders and limit folder size regardless of who created the files. There's even an AutoQuota where applying a quota to the top folder above the user home folders limits the size of each user folder to a specific maximum, with intermediate settings that trigger email and administrative updates and alerts. You'll also find a file screening utility with which you can block storage of music, videos, and ripped DVDs, and a great reporting facility where you can get statistics by file size, owner, least recently used files, duplicate files, and more. SRM can generate reports automatically every night so you keep yourself informed when things go awry storage-wise. Look in Chapter 3 for a detailed walkthrough of this as well.

R2 includes quite a few other, more minor improvements that, due to time constraints, I was unable to cover in detail in this edition. However, the four major features outlined above are covered in depth in this book. And if you're wondering whether R2 is a good investment for you personally, continue reading; I'll address that at the end of the chapter.

Windows Server 2003 Editions

Microsoft has increased the number of versions of Windows Server 2003 it offers over what was offered in Windows 2000 Server. Windows 2000 Server was sold in three editions: Server, Advanced Server, and Datacenter Server, each requiring increasingly faster processors and more memory. Windows Server 2003 is available in the following editions:

Web Edition (WE)
> This version of Windows Server 2003 is optimized to host web sites using IIS and is therefore limited in its support of hardware and in its feature set. It cuts the addressable memory in half from 4 GB to 2 GB, restricts Internet Connection Sharing, network bridging, and Terminal Services (although you can still use the XP-like Remote Desktop feature for Remote Administration), and does away with DHCP and fax services. In addition, WE can be a member server of a domain, but it cannot be an Active Directory domain controller. Windows Server 2003 WE is available only through OEMs; you can't purchase it through traditional retail channels.

Standard Edition (SE)
> This is the plain-vanilla version of Windows that most corporations likely will deploy. Included with it is support for up to four processors and 4 GB of memory. SE includes most of the features and support of the other editions, including the .NET Framework, IIS 6, Active Directory, the distributed and encrypting filesystems, and various management tools. You also receive Network Load Balancing (a feature previously reserved for the "premium editions" of the NT server product) and a simple Post Office Protocol 3 (POP3) server which, coupled with the existing Simple Mail Transfer Protocol (SMTP) server bundled with IIS, can turn your Windows Server 2003 machine into an Internet mail server.

Enterprise Edition (EE)
> Aimed squarely at more demanding environments, EE adds Metadirectory Services support, high-level memory management features, and some session management features for Terminal Services. It also includes support for eight-node clustering and booting directly from a SAN. Plus, you can add memory to EE while the system is running, without needing to reboot.

Datacenter Edition (DE)
> This performance- and scalability-enhanced Windows Server 2003 edition supports from 8 to 32 processors and features 64 GB of memory and from two to

eight node clusters. With the exception of more extensive firewalling features, DE is identical to EE. You can obtain DE only on a Microsoft-certified computer preinstalled by the OEM, much like the Web Edition.

Windows Server 2003, Enterprise Edition for 64-Bit (Itanium and Extended)

For some time now, this flavor of Windows Server 2003 has been available as the only 64-bit Windows operating system. Recently, Microsoft added support for Intel's second-generation Itanium 2 and the AMD 64 chip. This version isn't as well known as its more common cousins, largely because the OS and the hardware necessary to run it are still rather uncommon. However, Microsoft has made a commitment to 64-bit Windows and is indeed developing the Longhorn versions of Windows on both x86 and x64 platforms simultaneously.

Hardware Requirements

Table 1-1 lists Microsoft's minimum and recommended system requirements for running Windows Server 2003 Standard and Enterprise, the most commonly purchased editions.

Table 1-1. Minimum and recommended system requirements

Requirements	Standard edition	Enterprise edition
Minimum CPU speed	133 MHz	133 MHz for x86-based computers; 733 MHz for Itanium-based computers
Recommended minimum CPU speed	550 MHz	733 MHz
Minimum RAM	128 MB	128 MB
Recommended minimum RAM	256 MB	256 MB
Maximum RAM	4 GB	32 GB for x86-based computers; 64 GB for Itanium-based computers
Multiprocessor support (MPS)	Up to 4	Up to 8
Disk space for setup	1.5 GB	1.5 GB for x86-based computers; 2 GB for Itanium-based computers

However, anyone with prior experience with Windows operating systems is likely familiar with the simple fact that Microsoft's minimum system requirements (and often, the recommended requirements as well) are woefully inadequate for all but the most casual serving duties. Based on price and performance considerations as of this writing, I recommend the following specifications for any Windows Server 2003 version available through traditional channels. I'll refer to these as the "realistic minimums" from this point on in the book.

- A Pentium III 1 GHz processor
- A server machine capable of using dual processors
- At least 512 MB of RAM
- At least 9 GB of disk space

In this day and age, PC hardware changes in value, speed, and availability on what seems like a daily basis. Unless your sole job is to continually specify the hardware platforms and configurations on which your client and server computers will run, it only takes missing a week's worth of developments to miss out on new processor speeds, chipset replacements or introductions, and hard-drive enhancements.

The good news is that Windows Server 2003 runs faster than Windows 2000 on the same hardware. This marks the first time a follow-up release performs as well on the same hardware as the old release and doesn't require a hardware upgrade to switch platforms. Of course, the methodology for selecting hardware for your servers remains true regardless of the operating system—disk speed is the single most prominent bottleneck in a fileserver, whereas an application server has performance obstacles in the processor and memory.

The Last Word: Assessing the Release

Two camps of people and their organizations will find compelling reasons to immediately upgrade to Windows Server 2003 and R2:

Those still running a version of Windows NT
> The official Microsoft decree of end of life for NT Workstation 4.0 was on July 1, 2003, well before this book and this edition were published. NT Server 4.0 reached the end of its supportable life on December 31, 2004, so it's really not prudent to continue to bet your company's IT assets and policy on what is now a dead, deprecated, and fundamentally unsafe operating system. Windows Server 2003 provides a good jump, and it's a stable jump, too. A new server version of Windows will not be released at current estimates for at least two years, and more likely three. Upgrading now—as soon as possible—makes sense if you're running NT, and as a bonus for waiting, you'll get Windows Server 2003 R2 as well with new SKU purchases.

Those with current Microsoft Select, Software Assurance, or Open License agreements that allow them to upgrade to the latest release at no additional cost
> If there's no fee or additional monetary outlay for your upgrade, you can get the benefit of Windows Server 2003 R2 for little overall cost. Windows Server 2003 requires about the same hardware as Windows 2000 Server, so if you're currently on that level, you can keep the machines you already have and enjoy the fit, finish, and new features Windows Server 2003 R2 offers you.

If you are not a member of either group, the value of upgrading to Windows Server 2003 and R2 is less clear. Traditionally, Microsoft operating system upgrades offered at least somewhat compelling reasons to move to the newest edition: improved user interfaces, performance enhancements, the migration from 16- to 32-bit, and so on. That's not as much the case anymore, at least until the next paradigm shift at Microsoft, which again won't be for a couple of years. If you're happily chugging away with Windows Server 2003 and don't have an update agreement with Microsoft, you're forced to determine if the license expense is worth the added features and benefits that R2 brings to the table. It probably isn't worth it unless your organization has a lot of branch offices, has a critical storage resource management crisis, or requires the identity management improvements of ADFS.

For most corporations, it's a question of timing. Consider that the next radically different revision of Windows, codenamed Longhorn, is about a year and a half away on the desktop and two to three years away on the server. So, whatever you choose, you have some time to live with it before facing upgrade pressures again. For others, it's a question of finances: if you can't afford to upgrade to Windows Server 2003, you are not missing much. If you are satisfied with Windows 2000, and have secured it properly, nothing in Windows Server 2003 is absolutely mandatory. The same goes with those running the original release of Windows Server 2003 with Service Pack 1 without a complimentary upgrade route to R2. If you're on NT, however, it's (past) time to move to Windows Server 2003 R2. (Although I am familiar with several IT shops that have done so, it doesn't make practical sense to go to Windows 2000 from NT at this point.)

CHAPTER 2

Installation and Deployment

Now that you've been thoroughly introduced to what's new, what's hot, and what's not in Windows Server 2003, the time has come to install the operating system on your machines. Installing Windows Server 2003 is easy: the fun comes in configuring and customizing the operating system. I begin this chapter by covering the installation options and how you can install the operating system using a CD-ROM, including the additional components located on the second disc as part of the R2 release. Then I devote a large part of this chapter to unattended installations, automated deployment, and batch machine imaging, because you can gain a significant time savings by letting your computer handle as many of the tedious installation tasks as possible. So let's jump in and get started.

Preparing to Install Windows Server 2003

As with any operating system, Windows Server 2003 comes with optional components that add or extend functionality in addition to the components that are required for everyday use. In this section, I'll outline these optional components, explain their function, and guide you as to whether you should install them.

Choosing Windows Components

An unwritten rule of system administration is to never install any components unless they are required. Although that might seem really basic at first, the point to take from this is that systems that operate only with the components required for their daily work are far easier to manage and considerably reduces your attack surface. There's less to go wrong, less to secure, and less to administer. Microsoft has embraced this maxim in a lukewarm sort of way by eliminating the ability to customize components (including adding them) at the time of a standard installation; you can add and remove Windows components only after installation is complete. (I'll cover ways around that limitation later in this chapter, but for now be aware that you can't customize an installation while it is in progress.)

However, even before you install the operating system, you should spend some time looking over its components to figure out which ones you need. Use Table 2-1 as a guide, which lists the components available for installation on machines with Windows Server 2003 loaded. Some of these options have submenus that deserve a look as well.

Table 2-1. Windows Server 2003 installation components

Option	Purpose
Accessories/Utilities	A collection of small applications and utilities such as WordPad and Paint
Certificate Authority	Secure authentication support for email, web site access, smart cards and LDAP directory services (among others) using X.509 authenticity certificates
Cluster Services	Provides for real-time failover in the event that one or more servers in a group stops working (*only in EE and DE editions*)
Indexing Services	Enables searching on both the text and properties of documents stored across the filesystem
Internet Information Services (IIS)	Provides support for web, FTP, news, and outgoing mail services
Management and Monitoring Tools	Tools to use with, among other things, the simple network management protocol (SNMP) to monitor systems and networks; Network Monitor is included within this group
Message Queuing	Provides a system for application developers to pool and queue messages across a diverse network
Microsoft Scripting Debugger	The development environment for scripts
Network Services	Networking components including DNS, DHCP, RADIUS (IAS), TCP/IP, and WINS
Other Network File and Print Services	Provide file and print services for Macintosh and Unix systems on the network
Remote Installation Services	Allows for remote installation of Windows 2000, XP, and Windows Server 2003 machines from the server
Remote Storage	Migrates local storage to remote and auxiliary storage devices
Terminal Services	Allows clients to run applications using a virtual session hosted by the server
Terminal Services Licensing	Automated licensing for Terminal Services (see preceding option)
Windows Media Services	Internet extensions to support server-side streaming media

Although actually installing Windows Server 2003 on your machines might be on the lighter side of your duties as an administrator, you still need to do some planning about both the architecture and organization of the computer and of your company's network. This section introduces you to the most common aspects of server installations and how you can make the appropriate decisions.

Partitioning Disks and Allotting Disk Space

You have a number of options when it comes to slicing and dicing the disk space on a machine that will run Windows Server 2003. You can, of course, create a new partition on either a nonpartitioned portion of a disk or by deleting an existing partition to make room for a new one. You also can install Windows Server 2003 on an existing disk partition if there's enough free disk space.

A single partition is the most common option for new Windows Server 2003 installations and is the simplest to use. However, some administrators like to create a separate partition, ranging from 4 to 10 GB in size, to hold the operating system files, and then another partition for the remainder of the disks in the server to hold user or application data. Additionally, if you choose to run Active Directory, Microsoft recommends keeping the Windows Server 2003 operating system separate from the Active Directory database and log files by using either a different disk or a different partition. During the Active Directory setup process you can specify an alternate location to store the Active Directory files. Finally, many administrators also like to create a separate partition that contains only the "page" file, the area of disk used by Windows Server 2003 to swap in and out pages of memory depending on server load and memory usage. In any case, segregating the operating system from your data makes it easier to perform upgrades to the operating system and to apply security updates and service packs without worrying about how it might affect the integrity of user data stored on the machine. You also might want to create other partitions to use Remote Installation Services, covered later in this chapter.

How much disk space? A general guide is that the partition on which Windows Server 2003 resides ought to be at least 1 GB in size, and preferably much larger. Always consider that your page file (if stored on the same partition as the Windows Server 2003 install files) might grow if managed by Windows Server 2003 and adequate space must be allocated to avoid virtual memory errors. Luckily, disk space these days is fairly cheap, so this shouldn't be too big of a hurdle to overcome. Most administrators also recommend that you keep the system files separate from user data files—at the very least, user data should be on a separate partition, and even better, on a separate disk. Having separate partitions ensures that user data won't be lost if the operating system ever becomes corrupted, whereas having separate physical disks affords that security as well as increased I/O performance because of less wear and tear on the disk controllers.

Along with partitioning comes the choice of filesystems. Windows Server 2003 supports three: NTFS, FAT, and FAT32. NTFS is the filesystem native to Windows NT-based operating systems, and it supports the full range of built-in security features, automatic file compression, disk space quotas, and file encryption. FAT and FAT32, although venerable standards that have a place in systems where legacy compatibility is crucial, do not offer NTFS security features and therefore should be used only if required. You can convert an existing FAT or FAT32 system to NTFS at a later time, but you cannot convert to either FAT filesystem from NTFS.

Table 2-2 shows the comparative advantages and disadvantages of the three filesystems.

Table 2-2. Comparison of supported filesystems

Feature	FAT	FAT32	NTFS
Granular security			✗
Compatibility	Can read FAT32; cannot read NTFS	Can read FAT; cannot read NTFS	Can read both FAT and FAT32
Support for Recovery Console in emergencies			✗
Support for becoming a domain controller			✗
Can be converted	To FAT32 or NTFS	To NTFS	No conversion supported

The remainder of this book assumes that you have installed Windows Server 2003 on a disk or partition formatted with NTFS.

Assigning Licenses

Windows Server 2003 offers two licensing options for clients, and each has specific advantages depending on the computing environment in which the OS will be installed:

- In *per-seat* mode, each connecting computer must have a CAL. However, any number of clients with CALs can connect to the server at any time.

- In *per-server* mode, only clients with licenses can connect to the server simultaneously. For smaller businesses without roaming employees, however, per-server mode saves money on CALs because it's relatively easy to determine a peak load.

Those familiar with NT and Windows 2000 licensing schemes will note that Windows Server 2003 licensing hasn't changed much from earlier versions.

Per-server licensing almost always is the better choice among the two options, for a couple of reasons. First, the Windows Licensing Service will take care of enforcing the number of licenses you tell it you have in per-server mode. So, if you have 25 CALs, and user 26 tries to access a file on your machine, Windows will reject the connection. This takes away a big headache of license enforcement as long as you've configured the license service with accurate information. After you configure the license service, Windows takes care of policing the connections for you automatically. Second, it's a better way of tracking how your employees use the network. Under per-seat licensing, you need a license for your vice president of finance's home computer because he sometimes checks email there at night. You'd also need a license for desktop, laptop, and PDA devices if any of them use a server resource.

Per-server licensing eliminates the need to go overboard with license purchases, and it doesn't make you distinguish and prioritize between licenses.

In some situations, per-client licensing makes sense, however. If you have a lot of Windows servers, buying a client license for each workstation eliminates the need to license clients for each server. If you also use Terminal Services in application mode, you'll probably find that per-client licensing is less expensive. However, if you're in doubt as to which licensing method to choose, you should pick per-server. Windows allows you to change once from per-server to per-seat licensing, but not from per-seat to per-server licensing.

Another issue also needs to be noted: as soon as you add a system running Windows Server 2003 to your network, you must purchase brand-new CALs to remain in compliance with the Windows Server 2003 license agreement. If you read Chapter 1, you'll be familiar with this requirement. That's really unfortunate from my point of view, mainly because traditionally, NT upgrades that require new licenses involve significant changes to the underlying operating system code; in many opinions, Windows Server 2003 just doesn't offer enough change to justify that expense. But regardless of whether any of us agree with the license terms, it is a necessary condition of using Windows Server 2003.

You can purchase CALs at any major vendor, including Computer Discount Warehouse (CDW) and PC Connection. You also can purchase CALs directly from Microsoft through an enterprise agreement. You can discuss how best to acquire licenses by speaking with a Microsoft licensing representative. They're more than happy to discuss options with you.

Joining Domains Versus Joining Workgroups

During the second half of the installation process, you'll be asked whether you want to create or join an existing workgroup or make this machine a member of an existing domain. A *workgroup* is a decentralized collection of computers designed to facilitate resource sharing among a handful of computers. There is no common security database, and all user files and folders, as well as profile information, are stored locally on each computer. A *domain* is a group of network resources delineated by the network administrator with a centralized and shared security database. Domains allow for a central logon and easier management of their member clients and servers. In Windows Server 2003, domains are administered as part of Active Directory forest. To join a new machine to a domain, that domain must already exist and a domain controller for that domain must be reachable (via the network) by the new machine. You can also create a new Active Directory domain after you've installed Windows Server 2003.

Installing Windows Server 2003

It's a fairly effortless procedure to install Windows Server 2003 onto new systems. Here are the steps:

1. Turn the system power on and insert the Windows Server 2003 CD into the drive. If you receive a prompt asking you to select from what location to boot, choose the option to boot from the CD. The system will boot a minimal, text-only version of Windows Server 2003 into main memory and will begin the initial installation procedure. Figure 2-1 shows the beginning of this phase.

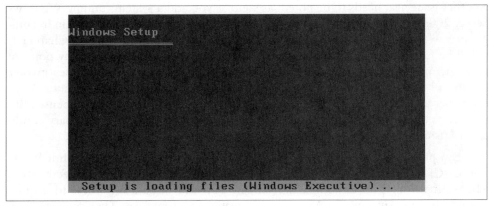

Figure 2-1. The character-based Setup process

2. The Welcome to Windows Setup screen will appear. Press Enter to continue.

3. Read the terms of the license agreement. If you accept (which, of course, you have to do to continue installation), press F8 to continue.

4. A screen listing your current disk partitions will appear. You can simply move around the menu and select an existing partition on which to install by pressing the arrow keys and then Enter to confirm your selection. You also can delete partitions (be sure you have backed up your data first!) by selecting the partition and pressing the D key. Lastly, you can create a new partition by selecting the Unpartitioned space selection in the menu and then pressing the C key. Figure 2-2 shows the disk partitioning screen.

   Choose the best option for you, and then press the appropriate key.

5. You'll now be prompted to choose a filesystem. Select the filesystem with which you want the partition formatted and press Enter to start the format. The formatting process can take up to one hour to complete, depending on your drive's size and speed, and then large amounts of files will be copied to the newly formatted partition. Now's a good time to catch up on your email backlog or to take a coffee break.

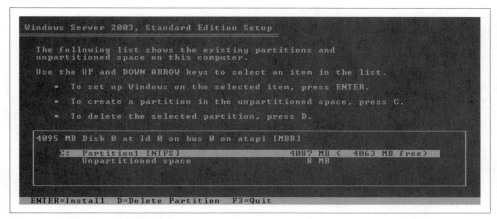

Figure 2-2. The disk partitioning screen

6. Once the format and file copy processes are complete, the system will reboot, and the next portion of the installation will commence in graphical mode. The process starts with the Regional Settings screen, which pops up soon after the reboot. On this screen, you can change the language, locale, and keyboard settings depending on your geographical location. Click Next to continue.

7. Enter your name and organization. Click Next to continue.

8. Choose your licensing mode, as explained earlier in this chapter. Figure 2-3 shows the options you are presented. Click Next when you're finished.

9. Choose a unique name for this server (using alphanumeric characters), which can be up to 15 characters long. Click Next to continue.

10. Enter a password for the administrator account. Windows will alert you if you choose what it considers to be an insecure password. You'll need to enter your password twice for verification. Once you're finished, click Next.

11. Adjust the time zone and server time and date on the next screen. Click Next to continue.

12. If Windows detects a modem, it will present the Dialing Locations screen. Here, input your area code and any dialing-related configurations (including a prefix digit for an outside line or a required area code). Click Next to continue.

13. The network components of Windows Server 2003 are installed next. Windows will first detect the network adapter or adapters installed in the machine. It will then prompt you to confirm the selection of network protocols. On modern networks, you will typically want the Client for Microsoft Networks, File and Print Sharing for Microsoft Networks, and the TCP/IP protocol. The "typical" setting, as shown in Figure 2-4, will install these automatically. Click Next to proceed.

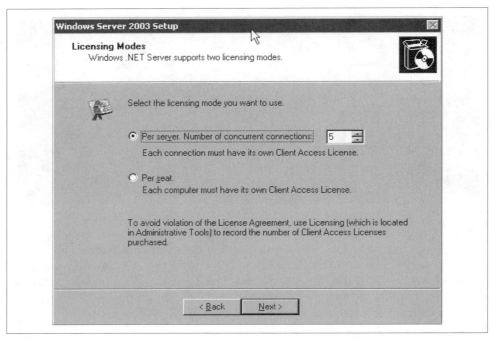

Figure 2-3. Choosing the Windows Server 2003 licensing mode

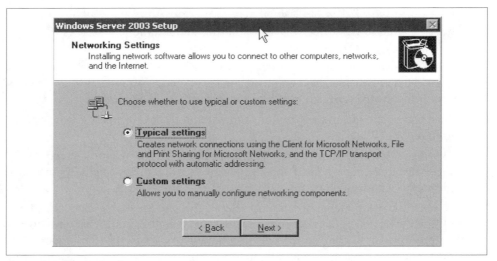

Figure 2-4. The networking options selection screen

14. If you want to specify your own configuration, choose the Custom option and click Next. Otherwise, a screen prompts you to create or join an existing workgroup or domain. To create or join a workgroup, select the first option and input the name of the workgroup. To join a domain, click the second option and type

in the name of the domain. To create a new domain later, choose the work-group option for now. If you choose to join an existing domain now, a box will pop up asking for a username and password of someone who is authorized to join computers to the domain. I cover this process in detail in Chapter 5. Click Next to continue.

15. Finally, files are copied and settings are finalized. This step can take an additional 20 minutes, enough time for perhaps another coffee break.

Your installation will be complete once the system restarts. It's important that you immediately visit Microsoft Windows Update, at *http://www.windowsupdate.com*, to apply the latest security fixes and service packs before placing the machine into production.

 In today's hostile Internet environment, I strongly encourage you to perform your installation on a machine that is at least protected by a firewall, and preferably on a machine that is completely disconnected from the network. You can complete step 14 after you initially boot, so you lose no functionality, but you reduce the risk of penetration and infection by viruses and worms to nearly zero by taking these protective steps.

Understanding Product Activation

Retail copies of Windows Server 2003 have a feature known as *activation*, which is an anti-piracy measure instituted by Microsoft. In essence, when you install Windows with a specific license key on a computer, a hash is created using the key and several attributes of hardware on the computer, including the network card's MAC address. (The exact way this hash is created is, of course, secret.) This hash can't uniquely identify a computer, but it identifies a specific installation of Windows. This hash is sent to Microsoft during the activation procedure. The theory is that if you later try to use the same product key for an installation on different hardware (for example, another computer), the hash created would be different, and activation would fail because it's likely you are trying to use more than one copy of Windows when you're licensed for only a single installation.

You have 30 days to activate the product upon initial installation with a retail-purchased copy of Windows Server 2003. When you reach this deadline, you won't be able to log on to the system, though it will continue to run without console access until you reboot it.

The catch to activation is this: if you change enough hardware in the same system to change the hash, Windows will complain that you need to activate the software again. You might need to actually telephone a toll-free number to speak with a representative in this case to explain why your hardware changed. This service is available 24 hours a day, 7 days a week, but it's a pain to spend time pleading your case. The service is fast and many users have reported the staff that runs the activation service is very helpful and usually quite accommodating, but it's really the principle of the situation.

To avoid the hassle of activation, you can buy the volume license versions of Windows Server 2003 and other operating systems and applications. Special license keys and CDs are distributed as part of the volume license program that don't require activation.

Default Post-Installation Behavior

If you perform a clean install of Windows Server 2003 with Service Pack 1 integrated, the new Windows Firewall is activated during Setup and during the first boot process. When the administrator logs on after Setup completes, Windows Server 2003 SP1 launches a new feature called Post-Setup Security Updates, shown in Figure 2-5.

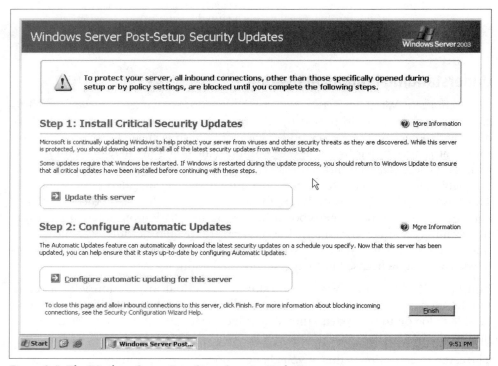

Figure 2-5. The Windows Server Post-Setup Security Updates screen

This new Post-Setup Security Updates feature simply shuts off any incoming network traffic except those that you might have configured through group policy objects that apply to this new machine, until you download any critical updates from

Windows Update or, alternatively, forcibly cancel out the window. You can't get this screen to reappear after first boot, as the idea is simply to make sure the administrator is aware that patches are available, to allow him to turn on Automatic Updates, and to give him the opportunity to update that system before external hosts can access it. This screen is also not available from the Start menu. A one-shot deal, if ever there were one.

You won't see this screen if you install the RTM copy of Windows Server 2003 and later apply the service pack separately; Microsoft probably figures that by that time you've already made the necessary security updates and configurations and won't need the default out-of-the-box protection. However, it is available to upgrades from Windows NT 4.0 to Windows Server 2003 SP1.

Upgrading Previous and Existing Installations

Most organizations and businesses have extensive investments in previous versions of server operating systems. In this section, I'll cover issues you'll run into when upgrading from Windows NT and Windows 2000 to Windows Server 2003.

Upgrading Windows NT

A lot of companies are jumping the sinking NT ship—end of life for the NT Workstation product was mid-2003 and NT Server's death has reached us as well—and so it's highly possible you have some machines running NT that are worth upgrading. It's remarkably easy to upgrade any type of Windows NT installation—be it a primary domain controller (PDC), a backup domain controller (BDC), or a regular member server—to Windows Server 2003. Microsoft has taken great pains to ensure the upgrade to Windows Server 2003 is as painless as possible. The installation procedure follows a clean install reasonably closely, and in fact requires less hands-on work. The program doesn't prompt you at all after the inception of the installation, and at the beginning, you're asked only for the CD Key and to acknowledge any compatibility issues.

NT upgraders should, however, note the following points:

- The Windows NT installation must be running Service Pack 5 or greater. You can download the most recent update, Service Pack 6a, from *http://www.microsoft.com/ntserver/nts/downloads/recommended/SP6/allSP6.asp*. Other acceptable Windows NT versions include NT Terminal Server Edition with SP5 or later, and NT Server Enterprise Edition, also with SP5 or later.

- Little to no reconfiguration is required with an upgrade installation because existing users, settings, groups, rights, and permissions are saved and automatically applied during the upgrade process. You also don't need to remove files or reinstall applications with an operating system version upgrade.

- Before the upgrade, you should evaluate the hardware on which Windows Server 2003 will run. Does it require an upgrade based on the minimum or recommended hardware requirements covered in Chapter 1?

- On a machine that's a candidate for Windows Server 2003, insert the Windows Server 2003 CD and run *winnt32.exe* with the /checkupgradeonly switch. (If you don't have AutoRun disabled, the splash screen that pops up will allow you to run the upgrade tester directly from there—without the need for a command prompt.) This will present a report to you with issues that the Setup program detects that might cause problems with an upgrade to Windows Server 2003. It is important that you do not skip this step as it could save you some major headaches. There are literally thousands of things that are reported with this tool. With this version of Windows, Microsoft has made some fundamental changes that may interfere with applications you have installed. Even many of Microsoft's business applications, such as SQL Server, will not run in Windows Server 2003 natively. (If you run SQL Server on a Windows Server 2003 machine, you will need to upgrade SQL Server to at least Service Pack 3.)

- In an environment with domain controllers running both Windows NT and Windows 2000, it's highly recommended that you upgrade the Windows NT domain controllers as soon as possible. You get better security for your client-to-server transmissions and you can take full advantage of Active Directory features that I discuss in Chapter 5.

- Make sure you have a good backup and it has been tested. This is not a simple application upgrade—you're changing the entire OS and there is the possibility of a lot of issues cropping up.

The upgrade procedure for an NT domain, although relatively straightforward, is involved. First, you must choose the first server to upgrade in your Windows NT domain. As you upgrade different machines, depending on their existing role in the domain, features and capabilities become available with Windows Server 2003 on the upgraded machine.

In particular, upgrading an NT primary domain controller (PDC) enables Active Directory, as well as the other capabilities inherent in any Windows Server 2003 server (such as improved Routing and Remote Access service features), no matter the role. Note that you can upgrade Windows NT *member servers* at any time during your migration plan; most migration plans specify that member servers are last on the list to receive the upgrade. However, when you begin upgrading NT domain controllers to Windows Server 2003, you must upgrade the PDC before any other domain controller machines.

 Chapter 5 contains quite a bit of detailed information on moving from NT to Windows Server 2003. It's a complex procedure that deserves an in-depth discussion.

Additionally, if you have a member server functioning as a remote access server (RAS) machine, you should upgrade it to Windows Server 2003 before the last domain controller is upgraded. The RAS machine has certain security requirements that are incompatible between the different operating system versions. This means that if you have only one domain controller in your domain, you need to upgrade your RAS machine before beginning any domain controller upgrades.

Regarding storage, you might want to examine the following disk issues before upgrading:

Partition sizes

On machines being upgraded from NT to Windows Server 2003, ensure that the system partition of each machine has plenty of disk space. This is especially true of domain controllers because converting a SAM database to an Active Directory database can increase the SAM's size by as much as 10 times.

Filesystems

Domain controllers require their system partitions to be formatted with the NTFS filesystem. Although as a general procedure I recommend formatting all partitions on all server machines with NTFS, you are not required to do so unless the machine in question is a domain controller.

Volume, mirror, and stripe sets

Upgrading to Windows Server 2003 Enterprise Edition from NT on a system with volume, mirror, or stripe sets (including stripe sets with parity) that were created under NT requires some modifications of those sets. Because Windows Server 2003 includes new dynamic disk technologies, support for older enhanced disk features has been removed—and this is indeed a change from Windows 2000. You will need to do the following before you upgrade to Windows Server 2003 from NT, depending on your current disk situation.

Break any mirror sets

Before running Setup, simply break the mirror. It's wise to back up the filesystem first, but the mirror-breaking procedure will not erase any data on either drive.

For all other media sets, back up any data on the set, and then delete the set

Before running Setup, you'll need to back up any data on the set, and then delete the set. The backup step is crucial in this case because deleting the set also will delete any data on the drives. When Setup is complete, you can replicate your existing disk configuration using native Windows Server 2003 tools and then restore any data required.

For more information on using native Windows Server 2003 tools to replicate your existing NT fault-tolerant functionality, consult Chapter 12.

Evaluating NT-based Windows Server 2003 interoperability issues

As with any complex upgrade, issues exist concerning interoperating with the various operating system revisions, levels, and versions that currently reside on your network.

By default, Windows Server 2003 domain controllers will sign all network communications and verify the authenticity of parties to a transaction. These settings help prevent communications between machines from being hijacked or otherwise interrupted. Certain older operating systems are not capable of meeting these security requirements, at least by default, and as a result are unable to interact with Windows Server 2003 domain controllers. These legacy operating systems are Windows for Workgroups, Windows 9x machines without the Directory Services client pack, and Windows NT 4.0 machines prior to Service Pack 4.

Windows Server 2003 domain controllers by default require all clients to digitally sign at a minimum just their server message block (SMB) communications. The SMB protocol allows Windows systems to share files and printers, and enables various remote administration functions, as well as logon authentication over a network. If your clients are running one of the operating systems mentioned in the previous paragraph and upgrading them to a later revision is not an option, you'll need to turn off the SMB signing requirement. The most efficient way to do this is by disabling the following security policy in the Default Domain Controller GPO on the Domain Controllers OU:

```
Computer Configuration\Windows Settings\Security Settings\Local Policies\
Security Options\Microsoft Network Server:
Digitally sign communications (always)
```

If you are certain you want to disable secure signing, follow these steps:

1. Log on to a machine that has the Active Directory Users and Computers snap-in installed.
2. Click Start, then click Run…, and enter **DSA.MSC** into the Open box and click OK.
3. Expand the domain that contains your domain controller machines by clicking its icon.
4. Right-click the Domain Controllers organizational unit and then click Properties.
5. Click the Group Policy tab, select Default Domain Controller Policy, and then click Edit.
6. Expand Computer Configuration, Windows Settings, Security Settings, Local Policies, and Security Options.
7. In the result pane, double-click the security option you want to modify, as indicated previously.
8. Check the Define this policy setting checkbox.
9. Disable or enable the security setting, as desired, and click OK.

Additionally, Windows Server 2003 domain controllers similarly require that all secure channel communications be either signed or encrypted. *Secure channels* are encrypted *tunnels* of communication through which Windows-based machines interact with other domain members and controllers, as well as among domain controllers that have a trust relationship. Windows NT 4.0 machines prior to Service Pack 4 are not capable of signing or encrypting secure channel communications. If NT 4.0 machines at a revision earlier than SP4 must participate in a domain, or if a domain must trust other domains that contain pre-SP4 domain controller machines, you can remove the secure channel signing requirement by disabling the following security policy in the Default Domain Controller GPO:

```
Computer Configuration\Windows Settings\Security Settings\
Local Policies\Security Options\Domain Member:
Digitally encrypt or sign secure channel data (always)
```

You risk exposing your domain controller transmissions to so-called "man in the middle" attacks by disabling these security settings. Therefore, it is highly recommended that you upgrade your clients instead of disabling this security setting. You can obtain the DS Client Pack, necessary for Windows 9x clients to perform SMB signing, from the *\clients\win9x* subdirectory of the Windows server CD.

If you are certain you want to disable secure channel signing and encryption, follow the steps outlined in this section.

Upgrading Windows 2000 Server

Upgrading from Windows 2000 to Windows Server 2003 is a straightforward process. You simply insert the CD, perform the in-place upgrade, and wait for Setup to process some data. Then, out comes your Windows Server 2003 server. You might think this section is ridiculously short, but in reality, 2000 Server and Windows Server 2003 are so alike that upgrades to the base operating system are really simple, almost akin to applying a service pack. (If you involve Active Directory, the process becomes a little more complicated than that, but I discuss those issues in Chapter 5.)

The only key to an even smoother installation is to ensure that your 2000 Server system is configured exactly as you want it before the upgrade, and that all third-party software installed on the system, be it application software or drivers, is compatible with Windows Server 2003. It can be a nasty surprise to launch the newly upgraded system and see a blue screen before ever logging on. To ensure application compatibility on a machine that's a candidate for Windows Server 2003, insert the Windows Server 2003 CD and run *winnt32.exe* with the /checkupgradeonly switch (or select Check System Compatibility from the CD splash screen if you don't have AutoRun disabled). This will present a report to you with issues that might cause problems with an upgrade to Windows Server 2003.

Other than those issues, Windows 2000 Server to Windows Server 2003 migrations are defined.

Installing the R2 Components

For the first time in the history of Windows on the server, Microsoft is shipping additional, optional components on a second CD inside the actual Windows Server 2003 R2 product box. Most of these components are enabled for future installation by running a separate Setup process, which you can launch directly from the desktop after you finish the base install of Windows Server 2003 SP1 from the first disc (Setup places a shortcut on the desktop for you for easy access). You use the same product key for both the initial installation of Windows Server 2003 and the R2 components. It's a very simple Setup program that copies some libraries and descriptive files to your computer, and it shouldn't take more than a couple of minutes.

By running that Setup process, you populate the existing Windows Components dialog within Add/Remove Programs in Control Panel with more options that correspond to the R2 components. You can choose single components to install at any time. Most of the R2 components reside as subcomponents of the larger feature categories within the Windows Components screen—for example, the Print Management Console is located within the Management and Monitoring Tools category. Other components, such as Windows SharePoint Services 2.0, are located within the first set of categories.

Table 2-3 shows the relative locations of all R2 components with the Windows Components section of Add/Remove Programs.

Table 2-3. Relative locations of all R2 components

Top-level components	Level 1 components	Level 2 components	Level 3 components
Active Directory	Active Directory Application Mode (ADAM)		
	Active Directory Federation Services (ADFS)	Federation Service Proxy	
		Federation Service	
		ADFS Web Services Agent	Claims-Aware Applications
			Traditional Applications
	Unix Identity Management	Administration Components	
		Password Synchronization	
		Server for NIS	
Distributed File System	DFS Namespaces		
	DFS Replication Service		

Table 2-3. *Relative locations of all R2 components (continued)*

Top-level components	Level 1 components	Level 2 components	Level 3 components
Management and Monitoring Tools	ACS Forwarder		
	File Server Management Console		
	Hardware Management		
	MMC 2.1 Managed Framework		
	Print Management Console Component		
	Storage Management for SANs		
	Storage Resource Manager		
Microsoft .NET Framework 2.0			
Other Network File and Print Services	Common Log File System		
	File Server Migration Toolkit 1.1		
	Microsoft Services for NFS	Mapping Server	
		NFS AdminUI	
		NFS Client	
		NFS Server	
		Portmap	
		RpcXdr	
		Server for NFS Authentication	
Windows SharePoint Services 2.0			
Subsystem for Unix-Based Applications			

Note that it's Microsoft's recommendation that you use the two product CDs that are bundled with the R2 product and not a separate copy of Windows Server 2003 in conjunction with the second R2 component CD. This can avoid problems with product keys and product activation.

Troubleshooting an Installation

Although the vast majority of the time Windows Server 2003 installs without a hitch, some issues (a piece of malfunctioning hardware, a power failure during installation, or a faulty download of a dynamic update) can cause the installation process to fail.

Luckily, you can recover from a bugged-out installation in at least two ways: starting over or using the Recovery Console.

Starting Over

Sometimes it can be easier to cut your losses and restart an installation from the beginning, particularly if an error early in the process is preventing you from proceeding. The installation process changes three things on your drive, all of which you need to reverse to restart the installation (unless, of course, you want to format the hard drive and therefore aren't concerned with data loss):

- Setup constructs the *win_nt.~bt* directory to store *boot files*, which instruct your computer to boot into Setup's post-first phases (that is, all phases after the initial reboot). Remove this directory.

- Setup modifies your *boot.ini* file with a line such as this, that needs to be removed as well:

    ```
    Multi(0)disk(0)rdisk(0)partition(2)\$win_nt$.~bt="Microsoft Windows
    Server 2003 Setup"
    ```

- Setup creates the *win_nt.~ls* directory and copies all files in this directory to the system to have data to work with if it cannot access the setup CD. Remove this as well, if it exists. (Some installation scenarios don't require its creation, such as ones initiated from a network share or a hard disk and not on a CD.)

Once you've removed these three items, no traces of the previous setup attempt remain on the machine, and you are free to restart the installation process.

Using the Recovery Console

For dealing with serious installation problems that don't allow you into the standard graphical interface, or for a once-functional installation that seems to have failed, Microsoft provides a tool that might help you rescue a system from the jaws of certain death. Available since Windows 2000, the Recovery Console is a text-based operating system extension that allows you direct access to the disk on which Windows Server 2003 is installed, and similar access to key configuration files and data. It also provides a convenient way around DOS's inability to read NTFS-formatted drives, which is an issue any administrator with troubleshooting experience has come up against.

Setting up the Recovery Console

To use the Recovery Console, first you must set it up. If you are using a working Windows Server 2003 system, it's prudent to go ahead and set up the console; that way, if it fails, using the console is as simple a procedure as selecting it from the start up menu at first boot. To do so, simply run `winnt32 /cmdcons` from within Windows. Setup will copy files and modify your boot configuration file to list the console within its options. Now you're prepared for disaster, should it ever strike. It's a good idea to make a habit of installing the console when you first install Windows Server 2003; it's not a difficult process and you can automate it using the /firstboot option in a preinstall script, which I cover later in this chapter.

If, on the other hand, you're working on the failed system, you still can set up the console; you'll just have to delve into Windows Setup to do so. Boot from the Windows Server 2003 CD-ROM, select the option to repair an existing installation, and choose to do so using the Recovery Console. Windows will copy the files, make the boot modifications for you, and launch the console. Note that if you use this method, and if you have oddball hardware that Windows doesn't support natively, you'll need to invoke the driver install utility by pressing F6 at the first appearance of Setup's blue-tinted screens (watch for the prompt at the bottom of the screen) so that the console knows how to access any drives that might be attached to a controller that Windows can't communicate with out of the box. Once you've pressed F6, simply insert the driver disk and press Enter, and Windows will detect and load the driver.

Working with the Recovery Console

Once the console has launched, it's a two-step process to access the command line:

1. Select the installation to repair.
2. Enter the administrator credentials for that installation.

Figure 2-6 shows the main Recovery Console screen.

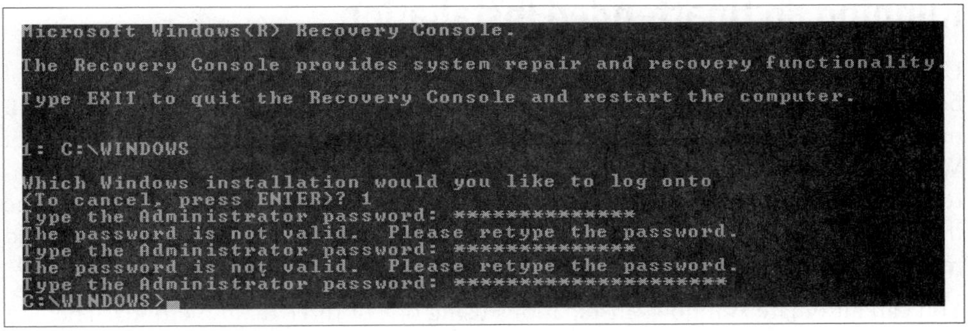

Figure 2-6. The Recovery Console

Windows will approve your password and then leave you at a DOS-like prompt. You can move around the filesystem with common DOS commands such as CD, DEL, FORMAT, and the like, but you also can use the commands detailed in Table 2-4 that control special functions peculiar to the console.

Table 2-4. Selected commands for the Recovery Console

Command name	Function
DISABLE	Prevents a service, named in the argument syntax of this command, from starting up on a normal boot.
DISKPART	Executes a disk partitioning utility much like that used in the initial text-based phase of Setup.
ENABLE	Explicitly instructs a service named in the argument syntax of this command to start up on a normal boot.
FIXBOOT	Like the old `fdisk /mbr` command from DOS days, this will restore boot sector information and make the drive contained in the argument syntax the default drive for booting.
FIXMBR	This command is like FIXBOOT, but it will touch only the master boot record of the drive; it won't alter default boot drives or create *BOOT.INI* files.
HELP	Lists all commands available in the Recovery Console.
LISTSVC	For use with the DISABLE and ENABLE commands, this lists all available services that can be started and stopped.
LOGON	Logs you out of an existing console and enables you to select another installation on which to perform recovery functions.
SYSTEMROOT	Goes to the default Windows directory without grappling with unwieldy "CD" (change directory) commands.

The Recovery Console makes it easy to correct simple errors, such as boot record misfires and incomplete driver or service installations, which used to require reinstallation. It is a good idea held over from Windows 2000, but yet still unknown to many.

Running an Unattended Installation

Unless you have only two or three servers, it's likely that you tire fairly quickly of being a high-paid installation babysitter, shoving disks and CD-ROMs in and out of machines while telling them all what country you live in. For all but the smallest of Windows shops, it is a good idea to use the Windows *unattended installation* feature—that is, installations run by files constructed by an administrator ahead of time that answer all of Setup's questions. This will save you time and make deploying and rolling out the operating system less tedious.

You can automate Windows installations using one of three main methods. The first is through the use of unattended installation scripts, which are simple to configure and use but lack some flexibility in deploying to machines that are configured with different hardware. Scripts are best when you have a uniform hardware base.

The second method is through the use of Remote Installation Services (RIS), a very useful feature that enables you to boot from the network and install Windows without any sort of distribution media. With this method, you have a lot of upfront configuration, but on the other hand, you can deploy to nearly any base of hardware, and you can customize certain aspects of the user experience during the installation, too. RIS is most appropriate when you have a diverse hardware base, plenty of network bandwidth, and computers that can boot from the network.

The third and final method to use unattended installations is through the deployment of system images. It requires quite a bit of upfront installation, but it's a great timesaver when you need a computer reformatted and reinstalled in less than 30 minutes.

Let's discuss each method.

Using Scripts

Perhaps the simplest method of automating a Windows Server 2003 deployment is to use scripts, or more specifically, unattended setup answer files. These files use a syntax not unlike that found in Windows 3.1 *INI* files, providing answers for questions such as computer name, your CD key, your name, where you live, and the like.

Windows is instructed to read these files using an argument switch on its main setup program executable file, *winnt32.exe*. Table 2-5 lists all the switches this program will accept.

Table 2-5. winnt32 command-line switches

Command-line switch	Function
/checkupgradeonly	Verifies that Setup can run and perform an upgrade on the current system.
/cmd:[command]	Launches the command specified before Setup completes, giving you an opportunity to customize an installation by running an additional program.
/cmdcons	Installs the Recovery Console and modifies the boot configuration so that it appears on the boot menu.
/copydir:[folder]	Copies a file or folder to the local system where it can be accessed during Setup; useful for copying files that reside on a network that are used to install drivers or the like in the OS.
/copysource:[folder]	Similar to the /copydir option, but will delete the specified folder after Setup completes.
/debug[level][:filename]	Logs error messages and/or activity to the specified file. The levels available are—in increasing comprehensiveness: 0 for serious errors; 1 for common, non-fatal errors; 2 for warnings; 3 for any informational prompts or messages; and 4 for detailed activity reports on every aspect of the installation. These logging levels are cumulative, so choosing 1 gets you logging level 0 plus common, non-fatal errors, and so forth.
/dudisable	Disables Setup's Dynamic Update feature.
/duprepare:[folder]	Prepares a given directory for the installation of private dynamic updates by downloading said updates from a Microsoft site. You can find more information on this feature later in this chapter.
/dushare:[folder]	Instructs Setup to download Dynamic Update files from the folder specified in the argument syntax.
/m:[folder]	Specifies an alternate location for all installation files; useful for applying hotfixes or using alternate versions of files in multiple installations.

Table 2-5. winnt32 command-line switches (continued)

Command-line switch	Function
/makelocalsource	Copies all installation files locally to the *win_nt.~ls* directory to ensure availability during the installation process.
/noreboot	Performs all functions within Setup's text-based phase but does not automatically reboot the machine. To be honest, I'm not quite sure why you would use this option, but it's there if you need it.
/s:[folder]	Enables you to specify multiple source paths from which Setup can download files; useful over slow links or on slow hardware.
/syspart:[drive]	Starts Setup, marks the drive active, and then prepares the installation so that you can physically transplant that drive between systems.
/tempdrive:[drive]	Specifies an alternate location for temporary, or "scratch," files.
/unattend	Specifies a hands-off upgrade installation using all configuration data from a previous installation.
/unattend:[file]	Specifies a hands-off installation, but using an answer file that allows direction of a clean installation without an existing reference installation.
/udf:[id][,file]	Instructs Setup to use a specific UDF file; you can find more information on this later in this section.

As we continue, you'll find that one of the simplest ways to control an unattended setup using a script is to call *winnt32.exe* from the command line using the following, assuming your script is in *C:\Deploy*:

```
Winnt32 /unattend:c:\deploy\winnt.sif
```

If you want to create a boot floppy for your unattended scripts so that you can simply truck it around to each workstation, just copy your script to the floppy and name it *WINNT.SIF*. Then, use the distribution CD-ROM to install Windows Server 2003 and boot directly from it, and Setup will automatically look for a file on a floppy in the A: drive named *WINNT.SIF*. If it finds one, Setup will read the instructions from it; if it doesn't, Setup will continue along a normal, user-interactive process.

Regardless of how you instruct Setup to use an unattended script file, you must create one. The next section details this process.

Constructing unattended setup scripts

It's easy to create the setup files used by an unattended setup in Windows Server 2003. Microsoft has included a utility called the Setup Manager, which is a graphical utility that asks you most of the questions Setup would ask during an installation, notes your answer, and constructs a *WINNT.SIF* answer file based on your inputs. Although the file that's created is very basic, it certainly works, and it's a great starting point for further customizations on your own. You'll see some of these options in action as we step through this process. To access the Setup Manager program, follow these steps:

1. On the Windows Server 2003 distribution CD, navigate through the *Support\Tools* folder hierarchy.

2. Double-click the *deploy.cab* file.

3. From the Edit menu, select all files inside the new folder, and select Copy to Folder.

4. Copy the files to a directory on your hard disk. You might need to create this directory using the Make New Folder button. Use any convenient path, as long as you can get to it easily to rename, copy, and edit your scripts.

5. Inside the new folder, launch Setup Manager by double-clicking *setupmgr.exe*.

Once Setup Manager has started, you'll be prompted to either create a new answer file or edit an existing one. Choose to create a new one, and click Next. Now, you're presented with several options, depending on the particular application for which your new answer file will be used. You can create a basic unattended setup answer file, one that can automate the Mini-Setup program inside an installation that has been SYSPREPed, or a file that will control installations started with RIS. I cover the latter two options later in this section. For now, select to create a normal, basic, unattended setup answer file, and click Next.

The next screen prompts you to choose the operating system for which you're creating an unattended install. You can create files for all editions of Windows XP and all editions of Windows Server 2003 except Datacenter, too, so the Setup Manager utility is more useful than it might otherwise appear. Choose to install Windows Server 2003 Standard Edition and click Next. At this point, you can now choose what level of "hands-off" you want to achieve: a completely hands-on installation with customized defaults read from the answer file, a fully hands-off installation that is started from the command line and not finished until Windows Server 2003 is completely installed, and most options in between. Choose Fully Automated to get the full breadth of options that Setup Manager can configure, and click Next.

Here, Setup Manager offers to assist you in creating on your network a *distribution share*, or a file share that contains an entire copy of the Windows distribution files for the purposes of kicking off network-based automated installation sequences. For our purposes, click Set up from a CD because we just need to create an answer file, not generate an infrastructure for more complex rollouts. Click Next, accept the End-User License Agreement, and click Next once more. You have completed the wizard portion of the Setup Manager process, and the screen shown in Figure 2-7 is displayed.

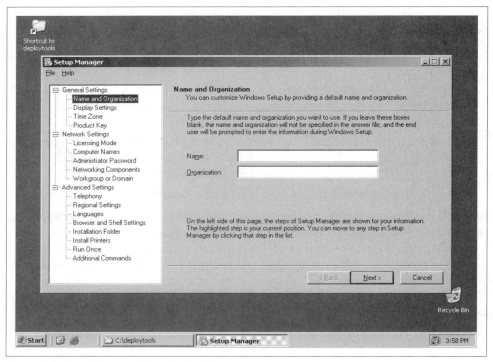

Figure 2-7. Setup Manager's detailed configuration screen

The remaining portion of Setup Manager involves customizing the many details of a Windows Server 2003 installation:

1. The first section, General Settings, enables you to enter your name and organization, display settings such as color depth and resolution, your time zone, and your Windows product key. Enter the appropriate values and click Next in each section.

2. In Network Settings, select per-seat or per-server licensing, and click Next.

3. The Computer Names screen appears. You have some options as far as assigning names to newly deployed computers: you can type the names directly into Setup Manager, import names from a text file, or tell Setup to automatically generate them based on the values entered for the name and organization earlier in the process. Click Next to proceed.

4. Now, you need to generate an administrator password. Because you've chosen the fully automated type of answer file, the option for the user to provide a password is not available. Instead, enter one yourself. The news of note on this screen is the option to encrypt the administrator password in the answer file. With Windows 2000, the only truly secure way to use answer files was to use a dummy password for the administrator and then manually change it later after

the installation completed—obviously that wasn't very convenient. Now you can use a real password without fear of unauthorized viewing of your answer file by password snoops. Click Next to move on.

5. You're prompted on the next screen to select the appropriate networking components for these systems. The Typical option's settings configure the computer to use DHCP to get an IP address; it also installs file-sharing capabilities. You can opt to use a static IP address by selecting the appropriate option and entering the address. Click Next once you've configured the relevant options.

6. On the Workgroup or Domain page, choose whether to be a part of a workgroup or to join an existing NT or Active Directory domain. Also specify the names of either the workgroup or the domain to join. Click Next.

7. You're now in the Advanced Settings portion of Setup Manager, and the first screen is very useful: it enables you to determine exactly what parts of Windows are installed on a machine. Now (again) you can get rid of WordPad on all your machines by default, a useful ability to have that Microsoft inexplicably removed first in Windows 2000 Professional and then in all later versions. Select the appropriate Windows components to include or not install, and click Next.

8. The Telephony settings page appears. Enter your area code and outside dialing preferences, and then to proceed, click Next.

9. On the next page, adjust any regional settings, such as keyboard, currency, time zone, and the like. Click Next, and again, specify your region-specific language settings. Click Next when you are finished.

10. The Browser and Shell Settings page appears next. Using this feature, you can customize Internet Explorer's home page, security, and personalization settings so that these are automatically set up during installation. Click Next once you've configured these options appropriately.

11. Specify the name of the folder where the Windows system files should reside (the default is *C:\Windows*). This also is known as the SYSTEMROOT for other purposes, as in the context of the Recovery Console. Click Next to continue.

12. The Install Printers screen appears. Here, you can specify the names of network printers (not local) that will be automatically configured and available to the new installation. You can specify any number of network printers. Click Next once you've entered your list of printers.

13. The Run Once page enables you to specify commands and programs that will run after the first boot of the newly installed operating system—that is, just after it's finished. This is useful if you want to kick off the domain controller installation program, DCPROMO. These settings are stored in the Windows Registry. Click Next.

14. The Additional Commands screen appears. These commands are executed at the end of Setup, but before the first restart (whereas in the previous step you're

specifying commands that run after the first restart). This feature is great if you're interested in installing the Recovery Console automatically after an installation is completed. To continue, click Next.

15. Finally, you'll be prompted to select a location for the answer file. Select one and click OK. You have successfully created your answer file.

 Before using your unattended installation script, you'll need to rename it from *UNATTEND.TXT* to *WINNT.SIF*. Not doing so will result in a nonfunctional script. Understand that these are essentially the same file: *UNATTEND.TXT* is used when *winnt32.exe* is called from a script. *WINNT.SIF* is used when an unattended install is required and needs to be run from the CD.

Privatizing the dynamic update process

Microsoft has begun releasing updated system and setup files that can be accessed by Setup for new installations. The net benefit of this initiative is the immediate updating of a newly deployed machine: many problems with the installation and upgrade process are eliminated with updated Setup executables.

Although Microsoft allows these updates to be downloaded directly from their Windows Update service, you might want to run the dynamic update feature directly from your own network to control what updates are applied to which workstations or servers. To internalize this process, you must first download the dynamic update package, expand the files onto a network share, and then instruct the Setup program to use the localized version of the updated files and not those on the Windows Update web site. Here are the steps involved:

1. Surf to the WindowsUpdate Catalog at *http://windowsupdate.microsoft.com/catalog*.

2. Click Find Updates for Microsoft Windows Operating Systems.

3. Select Windows Server 2003 under Operating System.

4. You need to display additional search criteria to filter the dynamic update package; to do so, click Advanced Search Options.

5. Under Update Types, check the Service Packs and Recommended Downloads checkbox. Clear the remaining checkboxes, and proceed by clicking Search.

6. Under Your Search Returned *n* Results, click Service Packs and Recommended Downloads.

7. Under Dynamic Setup Updates, click Add, and then click Go to Download Basket.

8. Select the path to the network share that contains the update package and click Download Now.

Once the download has completed, navigate through your filesystem to the place where you downloaded the update package. Double-click to open it. This will open a window that contains the package's contents, which should consist of a few cabinet (.*CAB*) files in a structure similar to that shown in Figure 2-8.

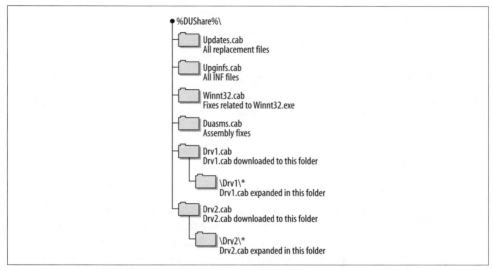

Figure 2-8. Relative folder structure of a dynamic update package

To use the package, you must prepare the network share where the update package currently resides. Use the following command to complete this preparation, substituting the path to your network share for [path]:

```
Winnt32 /DUPrepare:[path]
```

Your share is now ready to use. For manual installations, you can use the /DUShare switch, specifying the path to the private dynamic update network share as an argument much like the /DUPrepare switch. But by default, in unattended installations dynamic update is disabled. You must include a line in the answer file to direct Setup to enable Dynamic Update and to specify a location where the updated packages can be found. Insert the following line into *WINNT.SIF*, in the [Unattended] section:

```
DUShare = "Path to privatized update package share"
```

Understanding and creating UDF files

You might be wondering how to deploy several computers using one file when one crucial requirement remains unaddressed: how do you assign unique names to each installation? The answer lies in a single file: the uniqueness database file (UDF), which provides a method for Setup to select values for variables that are unique to each individual system deployed. Some of the settings you can customize with UDFs include computer names, descriptions, and administrator passwords. The UDF files themselves are very simply constructed: like an old *.INI* file, they contain a list of identification values and pointers to full sections for each value later in the file. Here is a sample:

```
;SetupMgrTag
[UniqueIDs]
MERCURY=UserData
VENUS=UserData
EARTH=UserData
MARS=UserData
[MERCURY:UserData]
ComputerName=MERCURY
[VENUS:UserData]
ComputerName=VENUS
[EARTH:UserData]
ComputerName=EARTH
[MARS:UserData]
ComputerName=MARS
```

Note that under the UniqueIDs section, each value is identified along with the specific section in the standard unattended answer file to replace with the information in the UDF. Then, Setup reads the files, and in each individual computer's section it identifies the key to be replaced as defined in the file, and uses the replacement value given to actually make the change. How does it all come together in the end? Setup reads this file as instructed from the command line with an argument that tells it which value the current deployment is; that is, computer MERCURY, VENUS, EARTH, or MARS from my sample UDF. Once Setup reads in the value, it looks in the individual section and replaces the standard responses to the prompts given in the standard answer file with the specific ones listed in the UDF file. Issue the following command to kick off this process for computer EARTH, assuming this UDF file is called UNIQUE.UDF:

```
Winnt32 /unattend:c:\deploy\winnt.sif /udf:EARTH,unique.udf
```

Using RIS

If you have a larger network in which you might receive 5 or 10 new machines a week to deploy initially, or in which you might need to completely reformat and reinstall some computers, you'll probably be longing for a more hands-off procedure than simple unattended scripts can give you. Microsoft, answering the call, has combined the convenience and features of unattended scripts with a tool that will allow your computers to boot from the network, select a preconfigured operating system image, and transfer that image to the hard drive of the target computer, all with just a few short answers at the beginning of the process.

And it's not too good to be true, I promise. RIS makes it simple to install hundreds of machines by booting them off the network. It's remarkably flexible. You can perform three types of installations with RIS:

A simple installation
> In this scenario, the files in the *I386* directory of the distribution CD are copied to a network share and subsequently used for normal, user-interactive setups.

A scripted installation
> In scripted installations, the computers boot off the network and are tossed into an installation using a specific unattended install script (which can make Setup completely hands-off).

A disk image transfer
> In this scenario, a computer is completely set up with OS and applications, an image of that computer is created and uploaded to the RIS server, and then clients can retrieve that image and copy it to their local computer.

RIS limitations

RIS has a few key hardware limitations that you should be aware of. They are detailed as follows:

All client machines must support the Pre-boot eXecution Environment (PXE) boot feature. This is the tricky part here. PXE allows a computer's BIOS to hand off boot control to the Ethernet card installed on the computer. The Ethernet card searches for an Active Directory-authorized DHCP server, applies the address assigned by that server, and then launches a TFTP transfer client that downloads the necessary files to boot into the Client Installation Wizard—the first step of an RIS installation. If your network card doesn't support PXE booting, you can't get on the network, and therefore can't take advantage of RIS.

> However, if you own one of 32 specific models of network cards that don't support PXE booting, you are in luck: Microsoft provides a network boot disk that takes care of the PXE logic for the network card, enabling you to use RIS on a machine that otherwise would not qualify. Microsoft has made many promises to expand this boot disk's coverage of network cards—claims of such modifications exist back before the release of Windows 2000—but as of yet, Microsoft has made no additions.

Laptops must be able to boot off the network. The aforementioned boot floppy works with only two PC card-based Ethernet adapters, and those are fairly old. So, most likely, if your laptop is newer and it doesn't have PXE capability built in, you still will need to deploy it manually, or at least without RIS. However, notebook manufacturers have begun to include built-in Ethernet connections using the miniPCI standard, and these commonly are PXE-compliant. If it's time to reevaluate your baseline corporate laptop configuration, you would do well to ensure that your laptops are PXE-compliant.

RIS imaging, using either a scripted install or a flat image installation, can install only the system root (all the operating system's core files) to the C: drive. If you have a computer with multiple physical disks, RIS will only transfer an image *of* a C: drive *to* a C: drive, and nothing else. RIS will only build images of C: drives, and it will only service C: drives on the client side. This works similarly for partitions, too; however, you should be careful about partitioning because RIS tends to reformat the entire hard disk (although a warning is provided, it's easy to overlook), which will blow away your existing partitions as well. Either pay careful attention when performing RIS deployments to computers with many partitions or use another scheme to organize your computers.

You must have a separate partition or physical disk on the server to use for the RIS subsystem. RIS cannot cope with having Windows system files on the same volume where flat images and RIPrepped images are located. This is mainly because of interactions between critical copies of active Windows system files and the Single Instance Storage (SIS) Groveler service, which allows one copy of one file to be placed on a disk, and links to be placed in all other locations on the disk where a copy of that file resided. It's like mail aliasing, in that small links to one copy of one file save space that otherwise would be wasted with multiple copies of the same file. Enterprises with eight different Windows Server 2003 images available to RIS obviously have eight copies of many files. SIS reduces the disk space usage almost eightfold.

Some people have reported that it's not possible to install an RIS server on a machine that is functioning as a DHCP or DNS server. I'm happy to explain that that is false. In my test lab, I have two domain controllers, the first of which is also a DHCP server, a DNS server, and the RIS server for my network. I have no problems delivering any sort of image to any compatible client on the network. So, for the server consolidation advocates among you, I don't see any problems with using a server acting in multiple roles and as an RIS server as well.

The software requirements for using RIS on your network are a little less stringent than the hardware RIS needs. You must have a DHCP server on your network, and you must be conducting RIS deployments in an Active Directory-based domain. RIS cannot handle static IPs, mainly because the PXE protocol has no such provision for them. RIS also uses DHCP as a mechanism to control the entry of unauthorized RISs to your network: before an RIS server can be used for deployments, it must be authorized within Active Directory.

Activating an RIS server

To begin using RIS on your network, you must first authorize the RIS server as a DHCP server in your network. Then you install the RIS component onto your server, reboot, and add images. The process is outlined here:

1. Go to a DHCP server, and log in with an account that has Enterprise Administrator privileges.

2. Select Start → All Programs → Administrative Tools → DHCP.

3. Select Manage Authorized Servers from the Action menu.

4. The Manage Authorized Servers dialog box appears. Click the Authorize button, enter the IP address of the RIS server you want to authorize, then click OK.

5. You will be prompted to confirm the decision. Click Yes to confirm or No to change your entry.

6. The newly entered address will appear in the white box. Click OK to close the box.

Now it's time to actually install the RIS component on the server:

1. Navigate to the Add/Remove Programs applet in the Control Panel.

2. Choose Add/Remove Windows Components in the left menu bar.

3. After a short wait, the Windows Components Wizard will appear. A list of optional Windows components will be displayed. Scroll to Remote Installation Services, check the checkbox, and click Next. The wizard will copy necessary files and then prompt you to reboot.

Finally, you must configure RIS and install an image to be used with RIS. In this example, we'll use a basic Windows XP Professional image that can be used to deploy on new computers later in the chapter. To get started, follow these steps:

1. Run *RISETUP* from a command prompt to launch the Remote Installation Services Setup Wizard. Click Next on the splash screen.

2. The wizard will determine the best place to put image files. The default drive and directory will be the largest non-system, non-boot, NTFS-formatted partition. Remember that this must be either a separate partition or a separate physical drive from the system boot partition and it must be formatted NTFS. You also can change the name of the directory the wizard will create. Click Next to continue.

3. The next screen asks you if you want to begin accepting new clients for deployment immediately. By default, RIS will not answer requests for network booting until you configure it to do so. To override this default, select Respond to Client Computers Requesting Service and click Next.

4. The Installation Source Files Location screen appears. Insert your Windows XP Professional CD-ROM into the server, or find a location on the network where XP's *I386* directory can be found, and click Browse to show Windows where it is. Click Next when you've finished.

5. Here you're prompted to select a name for the folder where the basic XP image will be installed. Because you likely will have many images, it's advisable to use a specific name for the folder, such as *XPPRO-BASIC* or *XP-SP1*. Click Next when you've typed an appropriate name.

6. The Friendly Description and Help Text screen appears. Type a one-line description to identify the image; this will appear in the Client Installation Wizard text-based setup files during network booting as a menu option. Then, in the Help text box, enter a short description of the image. This is for your records only. Click Next once you've done so.

7. The Review Settings screen enables you to ensure the wizard has obtained the inputs that you want. Click Finish if everything looks right, and Windows will begin copying the image.

The image copying procedure takes awhile—on the order of 15 to 20 minutes per image, usually, depending on the speed of your server and CD-ROM. When you come back, though, the image will be installed into RIS and available for deployment. A reboot is not required.

> You can manage your RIS server after installing and configuring it using the Active Directory Users and Computers applet. You can review and change your settings by logging into Active Directory Users and Computers or running dsa.msc. Expand your domain, click Domain Controllers in the left pane, and in the right pane, right-click on your RIS server and select properties. Select the Remote Install tab and give it a look. Even if you do not need to make any changes, you should take a look at this page as it gives you some options that can't be set at installation time.

Deploying an image to a client

Once you've activated your RIS server and added images to deploy, you can then network-boot your client computers and transfer the images to them. The process to do so depends somewhat on the client computer. Some corporate-targeted PCs have options in the machine's BIOS to boot from the network, usually found in the area that determines the boot order of the storage devices. Other computers offer an option directly during the POST process to press F12 or some similar key to perform a network service boot. (The Compaq Armada E550 I'm using to write this now uses the latter method, whereas the Dell Precision Workstation that is my main desktop computer uses F10.)

However, some older computers—and yes, some newer computers as well—don't have the option to boot to the network in their BIOS or during POST. In this case, you'll need to use the RIS remote boot disk, mentioned earlier in this chapter as the saving grace for some machines. The Windows Server 2003 RIS disk supports 32 network adapters, all of which are PCI cards. If your Ethernet card is on that list, RIS will work even if the machine doesn't support PXE directly. To generate the network boot disk, navigate to the *\RemoteInstall\Admin\i386* directory on your RIS server machine, and double-click *RBFG.EXE*. It will prompt you to insert a disk, which it will then format and reconstruct as the RIS remote boot disk.

On to actually performing the deployment: insert the boot floppy or select the option to boot from the network, whichever applies in your case. If you use the boot floppy, you will see text similar to the following:

```
Microsoft Windows Remote Installation Boot Floppy
Copyright 2001 Lanworks Technologies Co., a subsidiary of 3Com Corporation
All rights reserved.
3Com 3C90XB / 3C90XC Etherlink PCI
Node: 00115A5E3E12
DHCP....
TFTP..........
Press F12 for network service boot
```

During that process, no matter which method you used to activate the network boot, the computer contacted a DHCP server and requested an address. That address was sent in a packet, containing a pointer to a server which has files needed to continue the RIS boot process. These files were transferred using the TFTP protocol, a cousin of the commonly used FTP protocol. Once the boot files were transferred, the program prompts you to confirm that you want to boot from the network. Press F12 to confirm this, and the blue background, text-based Client Installation Wizard appears.

The first screen prompts you to enter your username, password, and account domain membership information. Then, you will be prompted whether to do an automatic or custom setup, or if you'd like to restart a previously failed setup attempt. Here is the difference between the two: automatic setups generate the computer name from a combination of your username and the computer's MAC address and set up an unattended installation with all the defaults. They also can retrieve existing data from Active Directory with regard to computer name and identification if you're redeploying a machine already configured in Active Directory. On the other hand, custom setups enable you to define a specific computer name for each RIS installation regardless of whether the machine is already set up in AD. Restarting a failed setup attempt is as functional as it is obvious; it begins either back at the text-based portion of Setup or at the graphical portion, depending on where in the process Setup stopped.

If you get an error message stating that the operating system image you selected does not contain the necessary drivers for your network adapter and that Setup cannot continue, don't panic: refer to the OEM section a bit later in this chapter to take care of this problem.

 When using the Custom Setup option, you will be expected to know where in Active Directory the computer account should be located. If you do not specify a location, the default *<domainname.com>/Computers*, the Computers container, will be the home of the newly deployed machine.

Slipstreaming service packs

Because deployment and initial installation are now so convenient, you likely will find yourself longing for a streamlined post-Setup process. One of the most common tasks that must be performed before you can hand off a computer to an employee is installing the latest service pack and security updates. This is especially important in light of the latest wave of worm attacks, where newly installed machines can be infected with these worms before you even have a chance to install patches!

All hope is not lost, however. Using a special command-line function of the service pack executable, you can instruct all versions of Windows 2000-, Windows XP-, and Windows Server 2003-based service packs to replace old files in a central distribution share with updated ones. This process, known as *slipstreaming*, works very well with RIS images because you already have the requisite distribution share. Let's walk through the process. You'll need the network/administrative (in other words, the full) version of the service pack for your respective platform, not the regular user version. To create the slipstreamed installation, follow these steps:

1. Create a directory called *c:\winsp*, and copy the downloaded service pack file there. I'll assume the service pack file is named *ws2k3sp3.exe*.
2. Extract the service pack to that directory by executing the following command from the command line or from Start, Run: `ws2k3sp3.exe -x`.
3. Now, update the files from the regular Windows distribution CD with the new service pack files by executing the following command from the command line or from Start, Run: `D:\wins2k3sp3\i386\UPDATE\UPDATE.EXE -S:C:\windist`.

The files are then updated, and the process is complete. Slipstreaming is an easy way to make sure that new systems are updated before they're ever put into production.

Using the OEM option for further customization

System builders and solution integrators have a wonderful set of tools at their disposal to customize the first-use, or "out-of-box" experience. Manufacturers such as Dell and Gateway can use OEM installation options to install software, add support information, and generally make a plain-vanilla Windows installation their own. So, if they can do it, why can't you, the system administrator? After all, you're creating your own "brand" of computer, specifically for your company. Using the OEM folder, you can apply hotfixes during Setup so that your machines are as updated as possible, customize a browser, and add support information to the System applet in the Control Panel.

 You can use the instructions in this section with plain, non-RIS unattended installations as well. I note the differences in processes between the two methods of deployment where applicable.

The Setup program is hard-coded to perform special actions when it finds certain files and folders within an *OEM* folder in the installation directory or CD-ROM. To use this folder, create it at the same level as *I386* in your RIS distribution share. (If you're using these instructions to create a special CD-ROM for computers that can't use RIS, create the *OEM* folder inside *I386*. For some reason, the *OEM* folder for RIS installations needs to be at the same level as the *I386* folder.)

Next, open your RIS script, RISTNDRD.SIF, which you can find at *RISServerName\Reminst\Setup\English\Images\imagename\I386\templates*, and find the [Unattended] section. There should be a line called OEMPreinstall with a value of No. Change this to Yes and save the file. This instructs Setup to look for the *OEM* directory.

First, let's add some updated drivers to our installation. Although Windows Server 2003 likely has reasonably up-to-date drivers for the most common hardware available, as time goes on new hardware obviously comes out for which Windows Server 2003 doesn't have native support. You can instruct Setup to look inside the *OEM* directory for updated drivers and install them before the machine ever finishes the installation. The procedure we're about to go through works not only with Windows Server 2003, but also with any NT-based client operating system, including Windows 2000 and Windows XP. To make this work, follow these steps:

1. Create a directory called *$1* inside *$OEM$*.

2. Create individual directories inside *$1* for each peripheral for which you have updated drivers. I'll assume you're installing new audio drivers, so for the purposes of this example, create a directory called *SOUND* inside *$1*. Place the driver files for the audio card within *OEM\$1\SOUND*. Make these names as short as possible, for reasons described in the next step.

3. In RISTNDRD.SIF or your alternative unattended installation script, add the line OEMPnPDriversPath="SOUND" and save your work. Note that you describe directories in this command only by their location under *OEM\$1*. It's also important to limit the length of the path portion of this command to more than one character but fewer than 40 characters; otherwise, Setup will fail.

If you have multiple new drivers to install, separate each directory in the preceding command with a comma and a space. Make sure to enclose the paths in double quotation marks.

Next, let's describe installing hotfixes using the *OEM* options. When the OEMPreinstall option is set to Yes inside your unattended installation script, Setup looks for a file called *CMDLINES.TXT* inside the *OEM* directory. If it finds one, it executes the commands listed in the file near the end of setup, before the first reboot. There are two catches to this: one, the programs that those commands listed in this file execute must reside in the *OEM* directory, not in subdirectories above or below it; and two, the file *CMDLINES.TXT* itself must be inside the *OEM* directory.

Now, the hard part of this tip is actually finding the hotfixes and transporting them to the correct location for use within Setup. Microsoft recently reorganized the way hotfixes are obtained outside of the automated, user-blind Windows Update process. To obtain these "network administrator"-style patches, you must connect to the Windows Update service at *http://windowsupdate.microsoft.com*. Click Windows Update Catalog in the left bar. Then, follow these steps:

1. Click Find Updates for Microsoft Windows Operating Systems.
2. Select Windows Server 2003 under Operating System.
3. You need to display additional search criteria to filter the hotfixes; to do so, click Advanced Search Options.
4. Under Update Types, click Security Patches and Hotfixes.
5. Under Your search returned *n* results, click Security Patches and Hotfixes.
6. Click Add for each hotfix, and then click Go to Download Basket.
7. Select the path to the network share that contains update package and click Download Now.

The really frustrating part about this process is that when you download these hotfixes, the Download Manager creates this supremely convoluted directory structure in which each particular hotfix resides in its own directory, with the executable file and an HTML document describing the fix. Because using *CMDLINES.TXT* requires that all the executable files to be run reside in the same directory, you have to manually extract the executables from this directory structure and copy them to the *OEM* directory. Although it's not much of a problem with Windows Server 2003 hotfixes, if you happen to be deploying Windows XP without Service Pack 2 with this process, the 60-odd files you must drag and drop out of this structure will either drive you mad, put you into the advanced stages of carpal tunnel syndrome, or perhaps both. If any Microsoft people are reading this, give us the option to put all these executables into one directory!

Simplifying Hotfix Catalogs

Technical reviewer Eddie Phillips provided me with the following method that might make the process of sorting out these downloaded hotfixes a bit less tedious.

Simply put the following in a batch file, and called it *WUFix.bat*:

```
for /F "tokens=1 delims=!" %%i in ('dir %1\*.exe /s /b') do @copy %%i %2
for /F "tokens=1 delims=!" %%i in ('dir %1\*.exe /s /b') do %%i /?
```

Now, if *D:\Temp\WU\WUpdate* is the directory where you saved the hotfixes you downloaded from the Microsoft web site, and you want the meat of those packages to go to *D:\Temp\WU*, run the batch file you just created with the following parameters:

```
WUFix.bat D:\Temp\WU\WUpdate D:\Temp\WU
```

You should have all your patches in one directory now.

Thanks again to Eddie for this tidbit.

The next frustrating part of this process is actually using the updates. Microsoft has said repeatedly that patch management would be quite a bit easier in the future, and the first step, it said, was to create patches with standard nomenclature and standard methods of execution and application. The news is—not surprisingly—that this utopia hasn't been reached yet. When you download hotfixes from Windows Update, some are named using one system, such as *Q823980_WXP_SP3_ENU.exe*, and others are named using some other system, such as *WindowsXP_Q329834_ENU.EXE*, and still others are named using what seems like no convention at all. Further, the switches that control the installation and execution of these hotfixes are not standard either. Some require /q and /z to install silently without reboots, while some require -q and -z, some need /noreboot, and others don't have switches at all. This is a sad state of affairs, and at this point, the only workaround is to manually test each patch on a system, note their behavior, and adjust the line in *CMDLINES.TXT* that calls that patch accordingly.

You might think that with all these negatives, it's not worth the time it takes to create this *OEM*-based solution. But if you're installing machines using RIS and are not behind a firewall, the 45 minutes it takes to use Windows Update after the first reboot is more than enough time for a worm to infest your system before the applicable update is installed. These days, it's nearly a necessity to use this procedure. Hopefully, in the future there'll be a better way to perform these updates. But for now, once you've dragged the multiple hotfixes out of their individual directories, tested each one individually for its command-line behavior, and iced up your wrists, generate *CMDLINES.TXT* using the following formula:

```
[Commands]
"q823980_wxp_sp2_enu.exe -q -z"
"WindowsXP_Q329834_enu.exe -q -z"
```

Make sure the commands are fully surrounded in double quotes, and that the switches you use tell the hotfix to install silently and without a reboot. (If in doubt, run the executable with the /? argument: this will list the switches to which that program will respond.)

Deploying a System Image: RIPrep and Sysprep

If RIS and unattended installations are great for deploying operating systems and hotfixes to a varied hardware base, RIPrep and Sysprep are wonderful helpers to deploy a complete "image" of a system, including the operating system, applications, customizations, settings, and restrictions, to a base of hardware that is identical in every respect. This is great for lab environments, and even better if your organization has a standard hardware base for all its new purchases within a year or two. The process is simple, too. You first create a prototype system, with the operating system, any applications, any environmental customizations, and anything else you want to pass on. Next, you run RIPrep, the Remote Installation Preparation Wizard, which gets rid of personal and security-related information and copies the image to the RIS server. You then deliver the image to the appropriate systems using the regular RIS network boot process.

There is, however, a limitation to using RIPrep—you cannot image the following types of systems:

- A domain controller because security information is stripped out of any RIPrepped image
- A DHCP server because multiple rogue DHCP servers on a network can wreak havoc
- An RIS server because each RIS server is authorized to be a DHCP server and these are prohibited as mentioned previously

Let's pick up the step-by-step process after you've created your prototype system, the one you want to be duplicated. Install and configure a system exactly as you like. Then, follow these steps from your prototype workstation:

1. Navigate to the *REMINST* share on your RIS server and open up the *Admin\I386* folder.
2. Double-click *RIPREP.EXE*. The Remote Installation Preparation Wizard welcome screen appears. Click Next to continue.
3. Type the name of the RIS server where you want to store the image, and click Next.
4. Generate the name of the folder that will house the image, and click Next.
5. The Friendly Description and Help Text screen appears. Much like with a flat RIS image, select the text that will describe the image and a short statement about the image and enter it into the appropriate boxes. Click Next to continue.

6. The Report System Compatibility screen appears. Here, RIPrep will look over your system and tell you whether it's suitable to be imaged. You'll also note that multiple local profiles won't work because all security identifier information is stripped out of the image. Click Next.

7. RIPrep notifies you of its need to suspend some services, and then prompts you to confirm your choices on the Review Settings screen. Click Next to create the image.

Reboot the prototype once RIPrep is finished. You'll note that it looks like Setup is being performed all over again; this is again because of RIPrep scrubbing the security identifier information from the prototype. Basically, it's all of the graphical setup, without the Plug-and-Play installation process. Just proceed through it, including reactivating the installation after Setup is finished, and you'll have the machine back for use.

To deploy an image that was RIPrepped, simply go through the RIS boot process, and from the menus that allow you to select which image to deploy to the target computer, select the RIPrep image with the friendly description and help text that you specified in the previous procedure. The remainder of the process works exactly like a flat RIS installation.

Sysprep: the system preparation tool

Sometimes, though, using products such as Symantec Ghost and PowerQuest Drive-Image is the quickest way to lay down an image onto multiple systems at once. The difference is that Ghost and DriveImage take what amount to photographs of the drive, copying whole partitions and physical disks without regard to individual files. RIPrep and RIS, on the other hand, look at individual files, which sometimes make it a little difficult to exactly replicate advanced prototype images. There's a catch, though: although products such as DriveImage and Ghost contain security identifier (SID) generators, which scrub out security identifier information in an image and replace it with a fresh, randomly generated SID, Microsoft doesn't support SIDs created with these generators. The company wants you to use Sysprep, which does just that in Microsoft's fashion, and in such a way that the company will support if you ever need technical assistance. Because the price is right (Sysprep is shipped free with Windows Server 2003), and it could save some headache in the future, it's a smart move to use it instead of the SID generators in third-party products.

 Sysprep will not reimage a domain controller, a member of any cluster, or a machine functioning as a certificate server because of the inherent machine-specific characteristics of those services. However, after Sysprep has completed, these services are certainly supported and available to be installed.

Here's an overview of how Sysprep works:

1. You generate a prototype image, much like with RIPrep, and configure everything on that system as needed.

2. You put Sysprep on that image, in a separate directory, along with an ancillary program called *SETUPCL.EXE*.

3. You then copy the profile of the local administrator account, which likely has the settings and customizations you've been performing, to the Default User profile so that all future users of the system get those tweaks.

4. Then, you run Sysprep. This scrubs SIDs and personal information from your prototype and shuts down the machine.

5. Next, you boot the computer from a floppy disk and let your third-party imaging software take over, "photographing" the disk.

6. Finally, you reboot the computer without the floppy, and proceed through mini-Setup again so that all personal information can be restored and new SIDs can be generated. (You can script this process so that a mini-unattended installation is performed.)

To start Sysprepping a machine, follow these steps:

1. Install and configure a system as you like it, using the local Administrator account.

2. Create a new local administrator. See Chapter 5 for instructions on creating local users.

3. Log out of the local Administrator account and log on to the new account you created.

4. Navigate to the System applet inside the Control Panel. Click the User Profiles tab.

5. Select the one called Administrator that has the local machine's name in it, and click Copy To.

6. The Copy To dialog box is raised. Click Change in the Permitted to Use section.

7. Select Everyone from in the list that appears. This gives permission for anybody logged onto the computer to use the contents of the profile. Click OK.

8. Click OK to get out of the Copy To dialog box.

9. Finally, copy the contents of *Documents and Settings\Administrator* to *Documents and Settings\Default Users*. Ensure that you are displaying hidden files and folders so that you copy all configuration files.

10. Now, run Sysprep with the following command-line switches:

```
Sysprep -reseal -quiet -mini -pnp
```

Sysprep will strip the SIDs off the system, scrub any personal identifying information from the image, and then shut down the machine. This is where you need to take over with your third-party tools to deploy these images.

You also can run Setup Manager, as described earlier in this chapter, to create an unattended mini-Setup script that will make setup on newly deployed Sysprepped images a hands-off process. Setup Manager even includes an option whereby you are prompted to select the type of script to create to generate a Sysprep script. Set this, follow the screens using the guide presented earlier in this chapter, and copy the created file—renamed *SYSPREP.INF*—to *C:\SYSPREP* on your image.

The Last Word

In this chapter, I've covered quite a bit about the various methods need to install Windows, how activation works, ways to recover from a bungled Setup, and what to do when Windows Server 2003 just won't boot. I've also looked at automated rollouts of the product and its client brethren.

In the next chapter, we'll step through in detail the file and print service functionality of Windows Server 2003.

CHAPTER 3

File, Print, and User Services

One of Windows Server 2003's primary functions within a typical organization is to serve files and connect multiple machines to a smaller number of printers. Windows Server 2003 enables you to create any number of shared folders that contain documents and programs that your users can access via such methods as Windows Explorer, Network Neighborhood, or mapped drives. The operating system also enables you to create a hierarchy of shared folders stored across multiple machines that can appear to end users as though they're stored on a single server.

Print services are simple to configure and manage. Windows Server 2003 enables you to share a printer connected either physically to the server, or to a print server device that is attached directly to the network. It also can host drivers for multiple operating systems and automatically distribute the correct drivers to client systems.

You'll need to be familiar with the following terminology to get the most from this chapter. Feel free to skip to the next section if you've been working with Windows for a while.

Disk
> A *disk* is the actual, physical hard disk within the machine.

Drive
> A *drive* is a logical object formatted for use with Windows. This can be either an entire physical disk or a partition.

Partition
> A *partition* is a portion of a physical disk that can be used with volumes.

Volume
> A *volume* is either a drive or a partition within Windows—it's a common term for both.

In this chapter, I discuss in depth all the file and print services Windows Server 2003 provides.

New File and Print Server Features

Several new features have been added to Windows Server 2003 to enable faster, more seamless access to file and print services on your network. Although the infrastructure of the file and print systems has not been completely redesigned, it certainly has been modified to provide for ease-of-use enhancements, increased data integrity, automatic and assisted backup, and other key features, including the following.

Enhanced Distributed File System (DFS)

DFS is a feature, introduced in Windows NT but refined in Windows 2000 and nearly completely rewritten in Windows Server 2003 R2, which permits an administrator to create one logical filesystem layout despite the fact that shares can be scattered across the network on different servers. This makes it easier for clients to find and store files consistently, and it allows for better equipment utilization. Windows Server 2003 adds the ability for a server to host multiple DFS roots, which are "starting" points for a hierarchy of shared folders. A Windows Server 2003 server can also use Active Directory site topology to route DFS requests from clients to the closest available server, increasing response time. The brother to DFS, the File Replication Service (FRS), is also improved in that it's more resilient to transient network errors. Those of you using RoboCopy might find that FRS now fulfills that need.

Enhanced Encrypting File System (EFS)

Native encryption abilities are built into the NTFS filesystem used in this release of Windows. By simply checking a checkbox in the Properties sheet for a file, you can easily encrypt and decrypt files and folders to protect their integrity. This feature is particularly useful for mobile computers, which have a greater risk of data loss and capture than traditional corporate desktop machines.

Volume shadow copy

The volume shadow copy feature is perhaps one of the most beneficial additions to Windows Server 2003. The server will take snapshots of files at specific periods during the day, thereby making available a library of previous versions of a file. If a user accidentally overwrites a file, saves an incorrect version, or somehow destroys the primary copy, he can simply click Previous Versions in the Explorer view of the folder and access a shadow copy version.

Enhanced content-indexing services

The Indexing service catalogs and indexes the contents of server hard disks, enabling users to search in files in different formats and languages for the data they need. Interfaces to the search engine include the Search front end on the Start menu at the client side, or, on the server side, HTML pages to which the client can surf. The engine has been enhanced in Windows Server 2003 to accelerate the search process and to use less processor time when cataloging and indexing files.

I devote a third of this chapter to file services—folder sharing, permissions, shadow copies, Dfs, and backup strategies, techniques, and procedures—and another third to print server functionality, including separator pages, custom configuration, driver distribution, location tracking, and spooler services. The final third is concerned with a user service known as roaming profiles, which allows your users' preferred desktop settings to travel with them to any workstation in the network they might be using.

Setting Up File-Sharing Services

To configure a machine as a file server, open the Manage Your Server Wizard from the Start menu. Adding a file server role to a machine involves the following tasks.

Configuring the machine as a file server
> This process involves turning on file sharing and creating the first shared folder. Windows also creates a few of its own shares by default, which I'll discuss in more detail as the chapter progresses.

Establishing disk space limits by enabling disk quotas, if necessary
> Disk quotas are a simple way to limit and control the amount of disk space your users take up with their data. Quotas monitor and limit a user's disk space on a per-partition or per-volume basis; quotas do not stretch across multiple disks. The wizard can configure Windows to apply default quota settings that you select to any new users of any NTFS filesystem. This is not required to set up file sharing services, but you might find the feature useful. And if you are running Windows Server 2003 R2, there is a totally new way of managing quotas—through the File Server Resource Manager, where you can enable per-folder quotas and further limiting by file-type filters.

Turning on the Indexing Service, if necessary
> The Indexing Service reads the contents of most files on the server and makes a catalog of their contents for easy search and retrieval at later points in time. Because the user interface for the Manage Your Server Wizard presents this option, I mention it here, but I cover it in detail in Chapter 13.

Installing the File Server Management MMC console
> This console snap-in provides an easy way to create, modify, edit, and generally administer shared folders, and I'll talk about it in this chapter.

Creating shared folders and setting share permissions for each folder
> Finally, you'll want to create the shared folders and apply permissions to them. After all, that's why you started the process, right?

Start up the Manage Your Server utility from the Start menu and click Add or remove a role. On the Server Role page, select File server and click Next. The Configure Your Server Wizard appears, as shown in Figure 3-1.

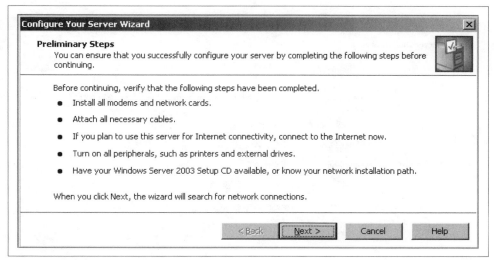

Figure 3-1. The Configure Your Server Wizard

The following procedure steps you through the rest of the process.

1. To assign disk space to a user on a particular disk, use disk quotas. The wizard will first ask you if you want to configure user disk quotas.

   To let users know when they have exceeded their disk quota and to prevent them from using additional space, set a warning, or *soft quota*. This writes an error to the event log when the user exceeds a certain amount of space to let him know he's approaching his quota limit. Also, configure the final quota, or *hard quota*.

   Check the Deny disk space to users exceeding disk space limit checkbox to enable disk quotas; otherwise, Windows will simply track disk usage by user but will not enforce the limits you configured.

   You also can set Windows to write to the event log when a user exceeds his hard or soft quota, or even when he exceeds both. Figure 3-2 shows the quota configuration process.

2. Next, decide whether to enable the indexing service. If you turn on the service, users can search in files in different formats and languages, through either Search on the Start menu or the HTML pages they view in a browser. (More on that in Chapter 13.) Turn on the indexing service only if users will need to frequently and consistently search the contents of this particular server. The service requires a good bit of CPU horsepower and memory resources despite the enhancements made in Windows Server 2003, and it can slow network request performance if you leave it on. It's best to use it only if you need it.

   Figure 3-3 shows the indexing service configuration screen.

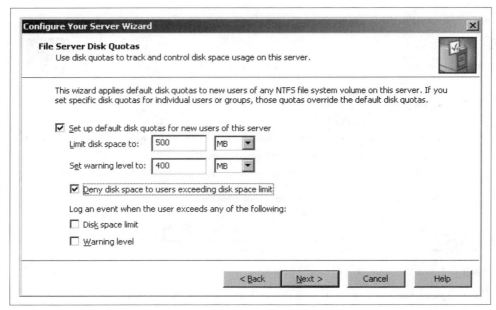

Figure 3-2. Configuring disk quotas

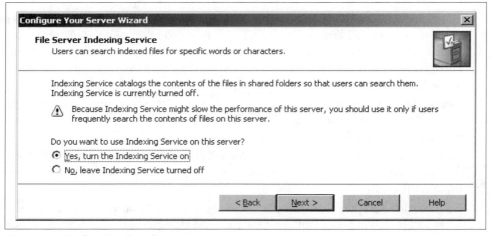

Figure 3-3. Configuring the indexing service

3. At this point, the wizard will summarize your selections thus far. Acknowledge this by clicking Next. Windows will install the File Server Management console, where you can access information on open shares, open files, and connections to the server, disk fragmentation analysis, and disk volume management tools. Then, the Share a Folder Wizard will be started to enable you to add your first

shared folder to the new file server. I explain the procedure for using this wizard later in this section.

4. Once the Share a Folder Wizard finishes, you will see the This Server Is Now a File Server page. Click the Configure Your Server log link to view the changes the wizard made to the machine. (Alternatively, you can find this file at *%systemroot%\Debug\Configure Your Server.log*.) Click Finish to finalize all the changes.

Creating a Share Manually

Only members of the Administrators, Server Operators, or Power Users groups can share folders by default. However, you can configure network-based GP settings to restrict other users and groups from doing so as well. Shares created using Windows Server 2003 are, by default, configured to allow the Authenticated Users group—all users who logged into the machine or network—read-only access. This is a result of the new security consciousness at Microsoft; in previous releases, all users were allowed full control of a share by default, which made for some sticky situations on compromised machines.

Share permissions are different from file- and folder-level permissions, which are more granular. File- and folder-level permissions (also known as NTFS permissions) are covered later in this chapter. If you have a smaller business with fewer employees and less emphasis on security, you might find simple share-level permissions sufficient for protecting content that should be confidential. However, in larger organizations, share-level permissions often don't provide enough manageability and flexibility. Also, the storage and shared folder hierarchies in a large organization are often more complex than in smaller businesses, which makes administering share-level protection on lots of shares very tedious and unwieldy.

 Some file-sharing options might be limited if simple file sharing is enabled. When this option is enabled on workstations running Windows XP Professional, creating, managing, and changing permissions on shares is impossible to do remotely because all remote connections authenticate to that computer using the Guest account. It is recommended that, in a business networking environment, you disable simple file sharing. Consult a good Windows XP book for more information on simple file sharing under Windows XP.

You can create a share in three ways: using the Share a Folder Wizard, using the Explorer GUI, and using the command line. To share a folder using the Share a Folder Wizard, follow these steps:

1. Launch the Share a Folder Wizard through the Manage Your Server utility.

2. On the Folder Path page, select the folder for sharing. Click Browse to access a directory tree. Then, click Next.

3. The Name, Description, and Settings page appears, as shown in Figure 3-4. Enter the following data for the new shared folder:

- In Share name (a required field), type the name you want to use for the shared resource. This should be short and descriptive, such as "ACCNTG" for accounting or "SCRATCHPAD," so users can quickly see a share's purpose.

- In Description (an optional field), type a description of the shared resource. Descriptions can assist you as an administrator as well as your users with understanding the purpose of a share. Use something clear, such as "Accounting documents for Q3 1999" or "Inactive Proposals."

- In Offline setting, specify how you want to make the contents of the shared folder available to users when they are not connected to the network. Click the button to make further tuning adjustments. The three options are fairly self-explanatory: the first option gives the user control over which documents are available offline, the second makes all documents available, and the third prevents any documents from being used offline. Note that checking the Optimized for performance checkbox automatically caches documents so that users can run them locally, which is helpful for busy application servers because it lowers overall traffic to and from the server. After you finish, click Next.

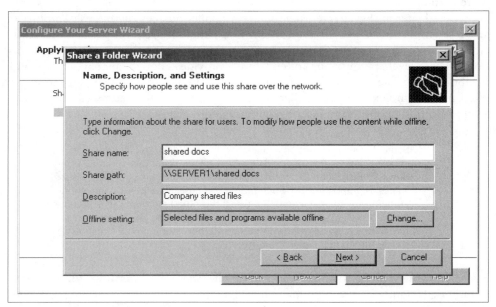

Figure 3-4. Creating a shared folder manually

4. On the Permissions page, configure the permissions for the shared folder. Share permissions apply only to users who access the share from the network; users at the console still will be able to look at the contents of the share unless file-level NTFS permissions restrict them from doing so.

The available permissions are as follows:

All users have read-only access
Both administrators and normal users will only be able to read files from this share; no writing or modification is allowed.

Administrators have full access; other users have read-only access
Members of the Administrators group retain full control over the share, including the ability to set new NTFS file permissions; everyone else has only read privileges. This is the best setting for a share that contains a program to be run over a network.

Administrators have full access; other users have read and write access
All users can read and write. Only members of the Administrators group retain the ability to change NTFS file permissions, however.

Use custom share and folder permissions
Using the custom permissions feature, you can assign specific permissions and deny permissions to users and groups. This is how a user would remove the default read-only access for all users, a wide-open door in effect that might not be desired for sensitive materials.

Figure 3-5 shows the shared folder permissions page.

5. Click Finish when you're done.

6. The wizard completes by showing the Sharing was Successful page. You can share another folder immediately by checking the When I click Close, run the wizard again to share another folder checkbox. Click Close to exit.

To share a folder using Windows Explorer, follow these steps:

1. Find the folder you want to share, and right-click it.

2. Select Sharing and Security from the context menu.

3. Fill in the form:

- In Share name (a required field), type the name you want to use for the shared resource. This should be short and descriptive.

- In Description (an optional field), type a description of the shared resource. Descriptions can assist you, as an administrator, and your users with understanding the purpose of a share.

- In User Limit, enter the maximum number of users that can simultaneously connect to this share, or check the Maximum allowed checkbox to permit as many connections as your OS license allows. The best choice really depends on the purpose of the share, its contents, the hardware of your server, and the bandwidth on your network.

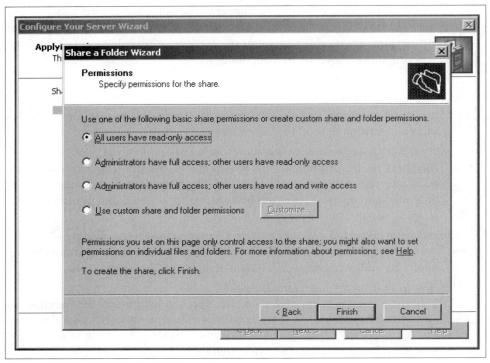

Figure 3-5. The shared folder permissions page

The completed form is shown in Figure 3-6.

4. Click the Permissions button to tune the restrictions users have on this share. On that screen, click Add to select the users to whom the permissions you assign will apply, and then click their names in the top pane and select the appropriate permissions using the checkboxes in the bottom pane. Click OK when you're done.

5. Click the Offline Settings button. Adjust the settings for how offline files are used for this share (see the descriptions later in this chapter), and then click OK.

6. Click OK to finish sharing the folder.

Default Shares

Upon installation, Windows Server 2003 creates several default shares that serve various purposes. You can examine these using the Computer Management tool inside the Administrative Tools applet in the Control Panel. Open that applet, and then navigate through System Tools and Shared Folders in the left pane. Click Shares, and in the right pane, you will see all the shares that currently exist on that machine. Figure 3-7 shows this screen.

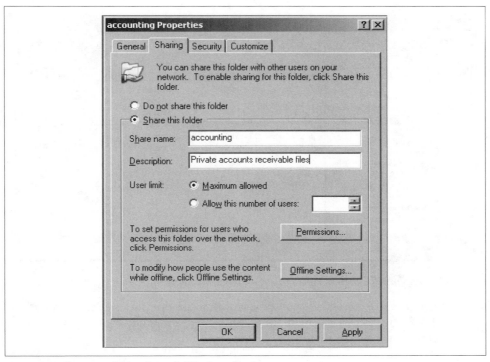

Figure 3-6. Sharing a folder through Windows Explorer

Creating a Hidden Share

You might need to share a resource but not make it publicly known. For example, the Payroll department might need its own file share, but the rest of the company doesn't require access to it, and in the interest of confidentiality, you might want to hide it from public display. You can do this by typing $ as the last character of the shared resource name. Users can map a drive to this shared resource by naming it explicitly (including the $ appended to the end), but the share is hidden in Explorer, in My Computer on the remote computer, and in the `net view` command on the remote computer.

Let's step through the default shares and list their function and purpose:

`C$` *and other similar drive letters*

These shares are known as administrative shares, and they provide a quick way for you to access a certain computer over the network and inspect the contents of the drive. Windows Server 2003 creates one of these administrative shares for each local drive in a system. You can't easily get rid of these shares permanently

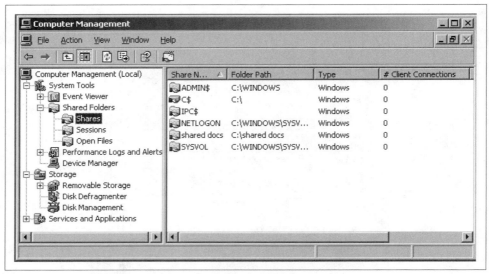

Figure 3-7. The Shared Folders portion of the Computer Management applet

because they are recreated upon reboot if they are not present. You can't adjust the share permissions on them either. Still, they're a handy tool in your toolbox for remote management and troubleshooting.

ADMIN$

This also is an administrative share that maps directly to the location of the Windows Server 2003 system files; this is the same as the %systemroot% environment variable. This is useful for spreading out operating system updates, especially across different operating systems. Recall that Windows 2000 used \WINNT, whereas Windows Server 2003 uses good old \WINDOWS. If you write a script to pass a file to all of these servers, you don't have to account for this difference if you use ADMIN$ on each machine as the location.

IPC$

This share is part of Windows Server 2003's method of sharing resources, not files, with other machines. Any type of remote management function other than sharing files uses this share.

NETLOGON

Mandatory on domain controllers, this share is a place to put logon and logoff scripts, programs, and profile information for users to read and access before they are logged on to the network. It's located at *%SystemRoot%\sysvol\domainname\SCRIPTS* on the filesystem of the server.

PRINT$

Print drivers that are shared to the network, usually for previous versions of operating systems, are stored in this share and requested by clients at the time of printer installation on the clients. It's located at *%SystemRoot%\System32\spool\drivers* on the filesystem of the server.

SYSVOL

This is used for internal domain controller operations and shouldn't be modified or deleted. It's located at *%SystemRoot%\Sysvol\Sysvol* on the local filesystem of the server.

Publishing Shares to Active Directory

By publishing shares to Active Directory, your users can use the Find feature on the Start menu on their Windows desktops to find remote shares based on their identifier or description. This is handy for using a new piece of simple software that's being run directly from the network. It is equally handy for retrieving an electronic PowerPoint presentation that might have been given earlier in the day. Note that you must use an account with domain administrator or enterprise administrator privileges to publish a share to Active Directory.

To publish a share, follow these steps:

1. From the Administrative Tools applet in the Control Panel, open Active Directory Users and Computers.
2. Right-click the appropriate organizational unit (OU).
3. Select Shared Folder from the New menu.
4. Enter a name and description of the share.
5. Enter the path (network location) to the folder you want to share, and then click Finish.

The share has now been added to the directory.

NTFS File and Folder Permissions

File- and folder-level permissions are one of the most dreaded and tedious tasks of system administration. However, they are significant in terms of protecting data from unauthorized use on your network. If you have ever worked with Unix permissions, you know how difficult they are to understand and set: complex CHMOD-based commands, with numbers that represent bits of permission signatures—it's so easy to get lost in the confusion. Windows Server 2003, on the other hand, provides a remarkably robust and complete set of permissions, moreso than any common Unix or Linux variety available today. It's also true that no one would argue how much easier it is to set permissions in Windows than to set them in any other operating system. That's not to say, however, that Windows permissions are a cinch to grasp; there's quite a bit to them.

Standard and Special Permissions

Windows supports two different views of permissions: standard and special. *Standard permissions* are often sufficient to be applied to files and folders on a disk, whereas *special permissions* break standard permissions down into finer combinations and enable more control over who is allowed to do what functions to files and folders (called *objects*) on a disk. Coupled with Active Directory groups, Windows Server 2003 permissions are particularly powerful for dynamic management of access to resources by people other than the system administrator—for example, in the case of changing group membership. (You'll meet this feature of Active Directory, called *delegation*, in Chapter 5.)

Table 3-1 describes the standard permissions available in Windows.

Table 3-1. Windows Server 2003 standard permissions

Type	Description
Read (R)	Allows user or group to read the file.
Write (W)	Allows user or group to write to the contents of a file or folder and to create new files and folders. It is possible to have read permissions without write permissions.
Read & Execute (RX)	Allows user or group to read attributes of a file or folder, view its contents, and read files within a folder. Files inside folders with RX rights inherit the rights onto themselves.
List Folder Contents (L)	Similar to RX, but files within a folder with L rights will not inherit RX rights. New files, however, automatically get RX permissions.
Modify (M)	Allows user or group to read, write, execute, and delete the file or folder.
Full Control (FC)	Similar to M, but also allows user or group to take ownership and change permissions. Users or groups can delete files and subfolders within a folder if F rights are applied to that folder.

The following key points should help you to understand how permissions work:

- File permissions always take precedence over folder permissions. If a user can execute a program in a folder, he can do so even if he doesn't have read and execute permissions on the folder in which that program resides.

- Similarly, a user can read a file for which he explicitly has permission, even if that file is in a folder for which he has no permission, by simply knowing the location of that file. For example, you can hide a file listing employee Social Security numbers in a protected folder in Payroll to which user Mark Evaul has no folder permissions. However, if you explicitly give Mark read rights on that file, by knowing the full path to the file, he can open the file from a command-line or from the Run command on the Start menu.

- Permissions are cumulative: they "add up" based on the overall permissions a user gets as a result of his total group memberships.

- Deny permissions *always* trump Allow permissions. This applies even if a user is added to a group that is denied access to a file or folder that the user was previously allowed to access through his other memberships.

Windows also has a bunch of permissions labeled special permissions, which, simply put, are very focused permissions that make up standard permissions. You can mix, match, and combine special permissions in certain ways to make standard permissions. Windows has "standard permissions" simply to facilitate the administration of common rights assignments.

There are 14 default special permissions, shown in Table 3-2. The table also shows how these default special permissions correlate to the standard permissions discussed earlier.

Table 3-2. Windows Server 2003 special permissions

Special permission	R	W	RX	L	M	F
Traverse Folder/Execute File			✗	✗	✗	✗
List Folder/Read Data	✗		✗	✗	✗	✗
Read Attributes	✗		✗	✗	✗	✗
Read Extended Attributes	✗		✗	✗	✗	✗
Create Files/Write Data		✗			✗	✗
Create Folders/Append Data		✗			✗	✗
Write Attributes		✗			✗	✗
Write Extended Attributes		✗			✗	✗
Delete Subfolders and Files						✗
Delete					✗	✗
Read Permissions	✗		✗	✗	✗	✗
Change Permissions						✗
Take Ownership						✗
Full Control	✗	✗	✗	✗	✗	✗

The default special permissions are further described in the following list:

Traverse Folder/Execute File
> Traverse Folder allows you to access a folder nested within a tree even if parent folders in that tree deny a user access to the contents of those folders. Execute File allows you to run a program.

List Folder/Read Data
> List Folder allows you to see file and folder names within a folder. Read Data allows you to open and view a file.

Read Attributes

Allows you to view basic attributes of an object (read-only, system, archive, and hidden).

Read Extended Attributes

Allows you to view the extended attributes of an object—for example, summary, author, title, and so on for a Word document. These attributes will vary from program to program.

Create Files/Write Data

Create Files allows you to create new objects within a folder; Write Data allows you to overwrite an existing file (this does *not* allow you to add data to existing objects in the folder).

Create Folders/Append Data

Create Folders allows you to nest folders. Append Data allows you to add data to an existing file, but not delete data within that file (a function based on file size), or delete the file itself.

Write Attributes

Allows you to change the basic attributes of a file.

Write Extended Attributes

Allows you to change the extended attributes of a file.

Delete Subfolders and Files

Allows you to delete the contents of a folder regardless of whether any individual file or folder within the folder in question explicitly grants or denies the Delete permission.

Delete

Allows you to delete a single file or folder, but not other files or folders within that folder.

Read Permissions

Allows you to view NTFS permissions on an object, but not to change them.

Change Permissions

Allows you to both view and change NTFS permissions on an object.

Take Ownership

Allows you to take ownership of a file or folder, which inherently allows the ability to change permissions on an object. This is granted to administrator-level users by default.

You also can create custom combinations of permissions, known as special permissions, other than those defined in Windows Server 2003 by default; I cover that procedure in detail later in this section.

Setting Permissions

Setting permissions is a fairly straightforward process that you can perform through the GUI. To set NTFS permissions on a file or folder, follow these steps:

1. Open My Computer or Windows Explorer and navigate to the file or folder on which you want to set permissions.

2. Right-click the file or folder, and select Properties.

3. Navigate to the Security tab.

4. In the top pane, add the users and groups for whom you want to set permissions. Then click each item, and in the bottom pane grant or disallow the appropriate permissions.

Figure 3-8 shows the process of assigning write rights to user Lisa Johnson for a specific folder.

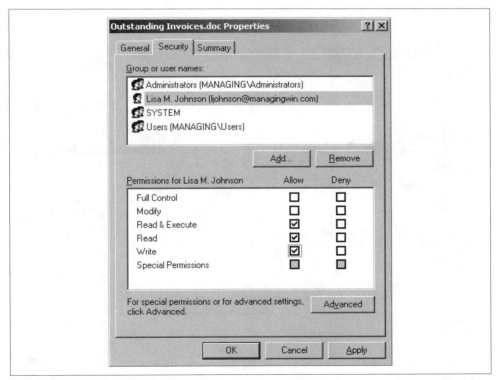

Figure 3-8. Granting permissions on a folder to a user

If a checkbox under Allow or Deny appears gray, this signifies one of two things: that the permissions displayed are inherited from a parent object (I discuss inheritance in more detail in the next section), or that further special permissions are defined that cannot be logically displayed in the basic Security tab user interface. To review and modify these special permissions, simply click the Advanced button. On this screen, by using the Add button you can create your own special permissions other than those installed by default with Windows Server 2003. You also can view how permissions will flow down a tree by configuring a permission to affect only the current folder, all files and subfolders, or some combination thereof.

Inheritance and Ownership

Permissions also migrate from the top down in a process known as *inheritance*. This allows files and folders created within already existing folders to have a set of permissions automatically assigned to them. For example, if a folder has RX rights set, and you create another subfolder within that folder, users of the new subfolder will automatically encounter RX permissions when they try to access it. You can view the inheritance tree by clicking the Advanced button on the Security tab of any file or folder. This will bring up the screen shown in Figure 3-9, which clearly indicates the origin of rights inheritance in the Inherited From column.

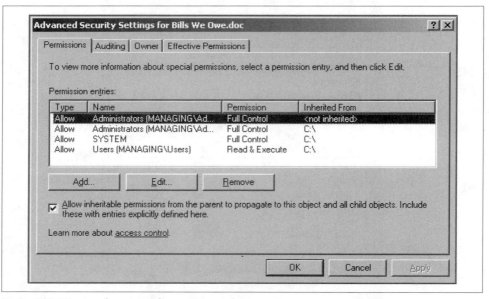

Figure 3-9. Viewing the origin of permissions inheritance

You can block this process by unchecking the Allow inheritable permissions from parent to propagate to this object checkbox on the screen in Figure 3-9. Any children of the folder for which you've stopped inheritance will receive their permission from that folder, and not from further up the folder tree. Also, if you ever decide to revert to standard permissions inheritance on an object for which you've blocked the process, simply recheck the checkbox. Custom permissions that you've defined will remain, and all other permissions will automatically trickle down as usual.

There also is a concept of ownership. The specified "owner" of a file or folder has full control over the file or folder and therefore retains the ability to change permissions on it, regardless of the effect of other permissions on that file or folder. By default, the owner of the file or folder is the object that created it. Furthermore, there is a special permission called Take Ownership that an owner can assign to any other user or group; this allows that user or group to assume the role of owner and therefore assign permissions at will. The administrator account on a system has the Take Ownership permission by default, allowing IT representatives to unlock data files for terminated or otherwise unavailable employees who might have set permissions to deny access to others.

To view the owner of a file, click the Owner tab on the Advanced Permissions dialog box. The current owner is displayed in the first box. To change the owner—assuming you have sufficient permissions to do so—simply select a user from the white box at the bottom and click OK. Should the user to whom you want to transfer ownership not appear in the white box, click Other Users and Groups, then click Add, and then search for the appropriate user. You also can elect to recursively change the owner on all objects beneath the current object in the filesystem hierarchy. This is useful in transferring ownership of data stored in a terminated employee's account. To do so, select the checkbox for Replace owner on subcontainers and objects at the bottom of the screen. Click OK when you've finished. (This operation can take a while.)

Determining Effective Permissions

As a result of Microsoft's inclusion of RSoP tools in Server 2003, you can now use the Effective Permissions tab on the Advanced Permissions screen to view what permissions a user or group from within Active Directory or a local user or group would have over any object. Windows examines inheritance, explicit, implicit, and default ACLs for an object, calculates the access that a given user would have, and then enumerates each right in detail on the tab. Figure 3-10 demonstrates this.

The Effective Permissions display has two primary limitations. First, it does not examine share permissions. It concerns itself only with NTFS filesystem-based ACLs, and therefore, only filesystem objects. And second, it functions only for users and groups in their individual accounts. It will not display correct permissions if a user is logged in through a remote access connection or through Terminal Services, and it also might display partially inaccurate results for users coming in through the local Network service account. Although these are reasonably significant limitations, using the Effective Permissions tool can save you hours of head scratching as to why a pesky Access Denied message continues to appear. It's also an excellent tool to test your knowledge of how permissions trickle down, and how allow and deny permissions override such inheritance at times.

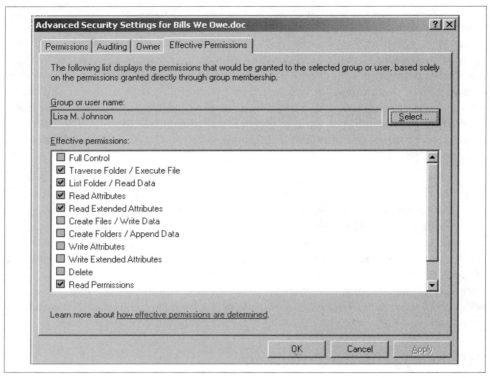

Figure 3-10. The Effective Permissions tab

Access-Based Enumeration

ABE is a great feature that (and I'm not sure why) hasn't been included in releases of Windows Server to date. Essentially this removes any access-denied errors for users by showing them only what they're allowed to access; if they don't have permission to use a file, browse a folder, or open a document, then it won't appear in whatever file management tool they're using at the time. This also closes an arguably moderately significant security hole, in that if users can see folders they're not able to access it might prompt hacking attempts or other tries to circumvent security, whereas one is less likely to hack what one doesn't know is there. Or so the theory goes.

It looks like the real drawbacks at this point are:

- ABE only works when you're connecting via UNC to a network share. It won't work for local files. Perhaps this will be fixed in Longhorn Server? Of course, this doesn't seem like a terrible drawback since not many users are browsing locally on Windows Server 2003 machines.

- You do need to be running Windows Server 2003 with Service Pack 1 installed. R2, however, is not required.

- It isn't bundled in the box. It's an out of band release, and as of this writing it is not included on the second CD in Windows Server 2003 R2. That's a minor setback, since it's freely available for download.

You can download the ABE installer from:

http://www.microsoft.com/downloads/details.aspx?FamilyID=04A563D9-78D9-4342-A485-B030AC442084&displaylang=en

or, if you'd rather not type in a URL that long, I've provided a link to the tool from my blog entry at:

http://www.learning2003.com/blog/2005/05/allow-users-to-see-only-what-they-can.html

It's easy to install. Simply download the tool and double-click on the resulting installable file. You'll be asked for the appropriate disk to install on, and then you can select whether you'd like to have ABE enabled on all shared folders on that particular system or if you'd rather enable it on a folder-by-folder basis.

 ABE needs to be installed on each server that hosts shared folders you'd like to protect with its services.

Once installation is complete, you can see the extremely simple ABE interface by right-clicking on any shared folder from within Windows Explorer, selecting Properties, and then clicking on the Access-Based Enumeration tab. This is shown in Figure 3-11.

To apply ABE to the current folder, click the first checkbox. You can also choose to apply the setting in the first checkbox to all other shared folders on that particular machine by selecting the second checkbox.

What will your users see? Nothing—that is, nothing that they don't have permissions to access. It's a seamless add-in.

Auditing

Object access auditing is a way to log messages concerning the successful or unsuccessful use of permissions on an action against an object. Windows Server 2003 writes these messages to the Security Event Log, which you can view using the Event Viewer in the Administrative Tools applet inside the Control Panel. First, though, you must enable auditing at the server level and then enable it on the specific files and folders you want to monitor.

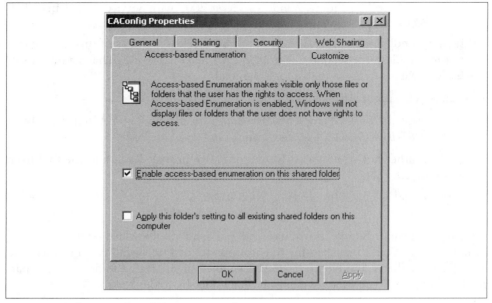

Figure 3-11. The Access-based Enumeration tab

You can enable auditing overall in one of two ways—either on a system-by-system basis by editing the local system policy, or on selected machines (or all machines) participating in a domain through GP. In this section, I'll focus on editing local system policies. To begin, follow these steps:

1. Select Start → All Programs → Administrative Tools, and click Local Security Policy.
2. Expand Local Policies in the lefthand navigation pane, and click Audit Policy.
3. Double-click Audit Object Access.
4. To enable auditing, select which events—a successful access of a file or folder, an unsuccessful attempt, or both—to audit, and then click OK.
5. Close the Local Security Policy box.

Audit events for the appropriate types of accesses will now be written to the Security event log as they happen.

Here is a quick summary of enabling auditing through domain-based GPs: create a new GPO linked to a selected container of machines, and navigate through Computer Configuration, Windows Settings, Security Settings, and Local Policies to Audit Policy. Select the appropriate events, and click OK. Give the domain controller a few minutes to replicate the policy to other domain controllers in the domain, and then refresh the policy on your client machines through gpupdate /force or by rebooting the machines.

Now, select the objects within the filesystem you want to audit and right-click them. Choose Properties and click the Security tab in the resulting dialog box. Then click Advanced and select the Auditing tab. You'll be presented with a screen much like the one shown in Figure 3-12.

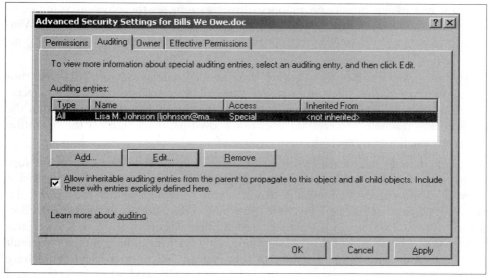

Figure 3-12. Enabling auditing on an object

Assigning audit objects in Windows is much like assigning permissions. Simply click Add, and a dialog will appear where you can enter the users to audit. Note that audit instructions work for both users and groups, so although you might not care what members of the Administrators group do, those in Finance might need a little more monitoring. Click OK there, and then select what actions—a successful object access or a failed use—of an event should be written to the log. You can easily specify different auditing settings between the various permissions, saying that you don't want to know when someone fails to read this object but you want to know whenever someone adds to it.

Auditing is a helpful way to keep track of what's happening on your file shares.

Limiting Use of Disk Space with Quotas

Windows 2000 first introduced the quota feature, allowing an administrator to define a limit or set of limits on the consumption of disk space by individual users. Up until Windows 2000, Windows quota support was available only through third-party software, which was typically very expensive.

Windows Server 2003's quota management features some interesting properties:

- Windows Server 2003 can distinguish between volumes, so you can set different quotas on different volumes to perhaps segregate types of data, or to offer a specific volume for one department's exclusive use.

- You can assign quotas on mapped drives as long as the physical volumes to which the mapped drives point were created with Windows 2000 Server or Windows Server 2003 or were upgraded to either of the later versions from Windows NT 4.0.

- Unlike some third-party software programs, Windows Server 2003 does not allow *grace writes*. That is, some software allows a user to continue an operation—say, a file copy process—even if during the middle of that operation the quota is reached. Server 2003 does not allow this; it will cut off the operation when the quota is reached.

As usual, though, neat features always contain weak points. First, quotas are supported only on disks formatted with the NTFS filesystem. This isn't too surprising because most progressive filesystem features aren't available under the various flavors of FAT. Second and perhaps more disturbing is that, due to an architectural limitation, filesystem-based quotas can be added only to individual users. This creates quite a headache, as most other network operating systems allow you to set a default quota based on group membership. In this manner, all normal users could have 500MB, power users and executives could have 1.5 GB, and administrators could have unrestricted space. Alternatively, payroll users could have 250 MB, while the sales team with their myriad PowerPoint presentations might need 1 GB a piece. Alas, Windows Server doesn't support this, but later in this section I'll show you a problematic but workable way around this limitation. And third, Windows Server 2003 doesn't provide any sort of messaging mechanism when users exceed their quota. The OS simply writes an event to the System event log, and although you can filter through these events via either the GUI or the command line, as described later, it still requires manual labor on your part. This certainly could be improved in future revisions.

Setting Default Quotas

To set up default quotas through Windows Explorer, follow these steps:

1. Open My Computer, right-click the drive for which you want to enable quota support, and select Properties.

2. Navigate to the Quota tab.

3. Make sure the Enable quota management checkbox is checked. If it's not, quota support is not enabled. If you want to continue, check this checkbox.

4. Choose one or more of the following selections based on your needs:

Deny disk space to users exceeding quota limit

If you check this checkbox, when users reach their usage limit, Windows returns an "insufficient disk space" error, thereby preventing them from writing more data until they either change or remove files to make more space available. To individual application programs where this behavior is handled in various ways it appears that the volume is full. If the checkbox is not checked, users can exceed their quota limit, which makes this an effective way to simply track disk usage by user and not enforce limits on storage space use.

Limit disk space to

Here, specify the amount of space newly created users of the disk can fill, and the amount of space that can be used before alerts are recorded in the event log (known as the soft quota, or warning level). You can use decimal values and varying units to fine-tune your settings.

Log event when a user exceeds their quota limit

If quotas are enabled, disk event entries are recorded hourly in the system event log when a user reaches his hard quota, or official limit.

Log event when a user exceeds their warning level

If quotas are enabled, disk event entries are recorded hourly in the system event log when a user reaches his soft quota, or warning level.

Configuring Individual Quota Entries

You might find it useful to set individual quotas for specific users which exempt them from a more limiting default quota you might have configured. This is useful in working around the limitation of being able to assign quotas to users and filesystems, but not to groups. You can set these individual quota entries through the GUI by clicking the Quota Entries button on the Quota tab under the Properties sheet of the disk in question. In the Quota Entries for Drive box, select Quota from the pulldown menu and click New Quota. Figure 3-13 shows this.

Select the user to which to apply the new quota, and in the box configure the restrictions on the user's space.

The File Server Resource Manager

Windows Server 2003 R2 includes the File Server Resource Manager, an integrated console that contains various tools and reporting functions so that you can determine, control, and administer the amount and kind of data stored on your file servers. FSRM provides a single and convenient place for you to configure quotas on folders and volumes, screen for unacceptable types of files, and generate comprehensive reports on exactly where your disk space is going.

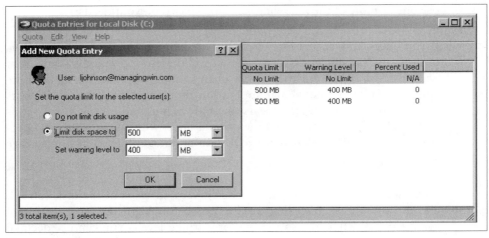

Figure 3-13. Entering a new disk quota entry

To install the FSRM, you'll need to install the R2 components on the accompanying product disc. Then, from Control Panel, use the Add/Remove Programs applet, choose Windows Components, and under Management and Monitoring Tools, choose the File Server Resource Manager. Click Next and then Finish, and Windows will install the tool for you.

 You can only manage resources on servers with the FSRM installed, which means that you're limited to servers running R2.

To launch the FSRM, simply choose it from the Administrative Tools menu. The default console looks like Figure 3-14.

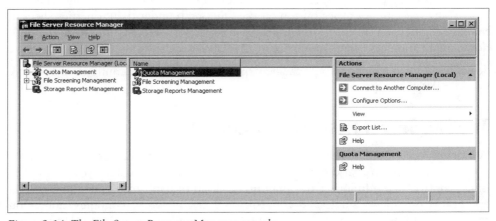

Figure 3-14. The File Server Resource Manager console

Configuring the FSRM

The first step in using the FSRM is configuring some options that will be used by the console. In the Actions pane, click the Configure Options link, and you'll see a screen like Figure 3-15.

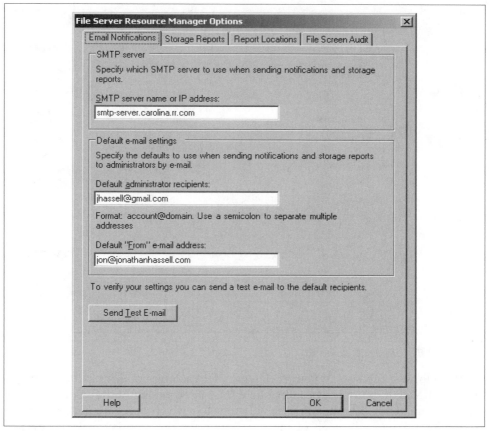

Figure 3-15. Configuring FSRM options

The FSRM is designed to send email alerts and reports via email; on the Email Notifications tab, enter the outgoing SMTP server (either through an installed SMTP service on the local machine or another mail server provided either by your organization or your ISP), and the To and

Figure 3-16 shows the Storage Reports tab.

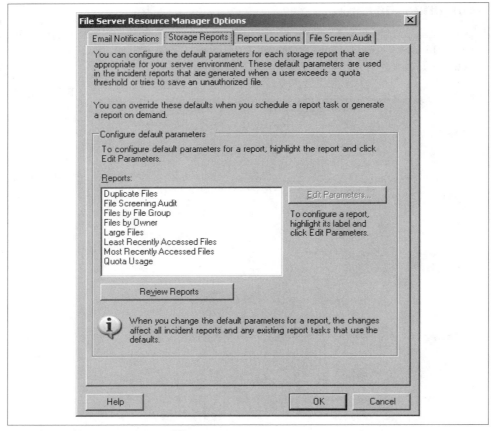

Figure 3-16. The Storage Reports tab

On this tab, you can specify your preferences for each report that can be generated by the FSRM. For example, if you highlight the File Screening Audit report and click the Edit Parameters button, you'll be able to select which users are included in the report. To take a look at all of the parameters for the reports, click the Review Reports button. The defaults work pretty well here, but as you'll see as we dig further into the FSRM, you may want to alter these slightly to customize the reports for your environment.

Figure 3-17 shows the Report Locations tab.

On this screen, choose where to save each type of report that the FSRM can generate. You can store them either on the local drive or on a network volume.

Figure 3-18 shows the File Screen Audit tab.

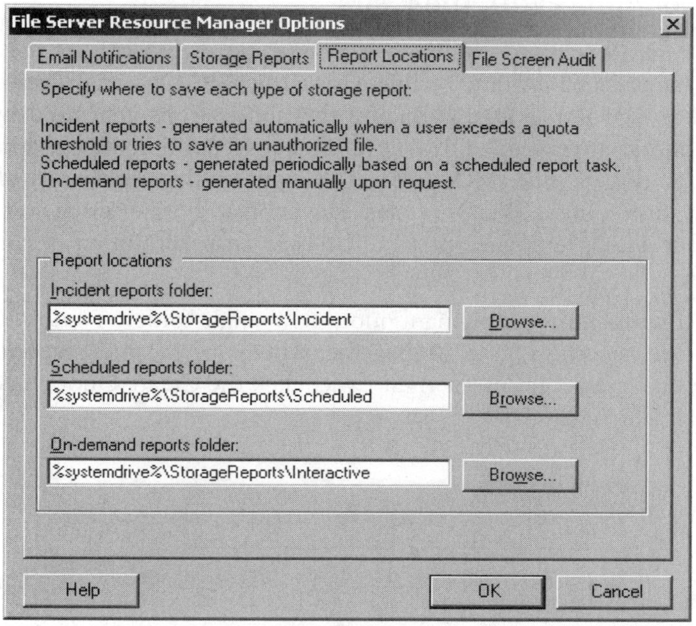

Figure 3-17. The Report Locations tab

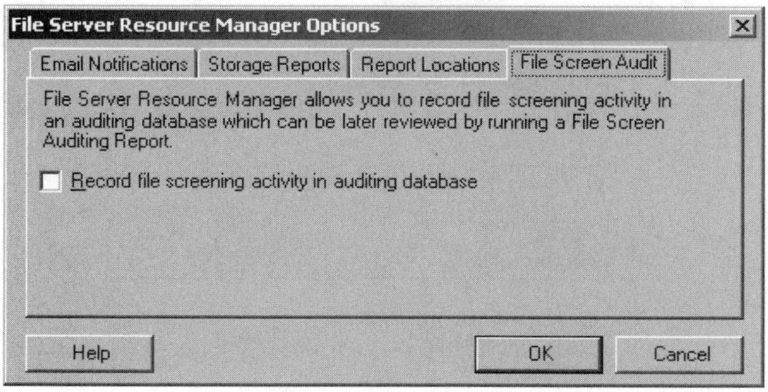

Figure 3-18. The File Screen Audit tab

Here, you can tell the FSRM whether or not to log screening activity in the auditing database. If you don't intend to use file screening reports, then clearing this checkbox will give you a slight performance improvement since the extra logging isn't required.

Configuring Quotas with the FSRM

It's more straightforward to configure quotas using the FSRM, as the interface is cleaner and the rules a bit more flexible. Using the FSRM, you can create quotas for specific folders or volumes and configure the notifications generated by Windows when those quotas are exceeded. I've covered that scenario in the previous section in this chapter on quotas. But FSRM takes it a couple of steps further by allowing you to customize "auto quotas" that automatically apply to both existing and future folders, and define quota templates that can be used anywhere in an organization's IT infrastructure.

Let's start off with simply applying a quota to a single folder. To do so, within the FSRM, double-click the Quota Management item in the middle pane, and then double-click on Quotas. From the right pane, click the Create Quota link. You'll see a screen much like Figure 3-19.

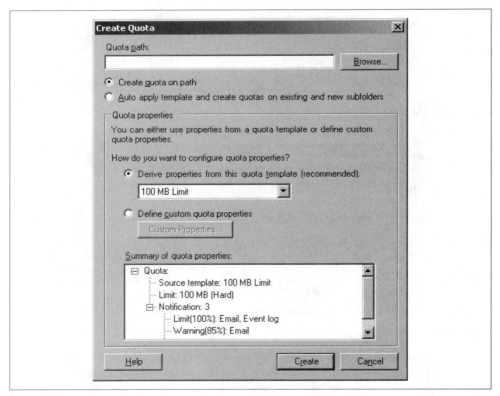

Figure 3-19. The Create Quota screen

Enter the path to the folder in the top box, or click Browse to find it graphically. Select Create quota on path, and then choose either a preexisting template, which offers some preconfigured limits, or choose the Define custom quota properties option and click the Custom Properties button. If you select the latter option, you'll be prompted with the Quota Properties screen, where you can enter the space limit, define whether the quota is hard or soft, and add different notification thresholds. Click OK when you're done, and the summary window on the Create Quota screen will show your selections. If all looks well, then click Create, and the quota placement is complete.

That process works well for one-off quota needs, but suppose that you want to centralize quota management across all folders and volumes. The best way to do that is to use the quota template facility with FSRM. By applying quota templates to folders, you can simply make one change to the template's configuration, and all folders to which that template has been applied will reflect the change. Think of it as having a "group" of quotas to make administration simpler.

To make a quota template, double-click the Quota Management item in the middle pane of the FSRM and then double-click on Quota Templates. From the right pane, click the Create Quota Template link. You'll see a screen much like Figure 3-20.

In the top drop-down box, you can select an existing template and copy the settings from it into the new template you're creating, which is a great timesaver when you need to make just a few minor changes. Otherwise, enter the template name, a friendly name if you wish, and then select the space limit and the severity of the limit. You can also configure the specific thresholds for notification when users hit a quota. Click Add to define a new notification; you will see the Add Threshold screen appear, as shown in Figure 3-21.

Note the first box, called "Generate notifications when usage reaches (%)." In this box, specify the actual threshold at which the action you're going to define on these screens will take place. Now, the most common notification administrators send is an email message, both to the user who exceeded the limit and to the administrator himself. On the E-mail Message tab, you can check to whom to send such messages, and also change the text of the message. On the Event Log tab, you can customize the text of a warning event that will be sent to the Event Log, and on the Command tab you can define a script or program that will be run when a user exceeds the threshold you set. Finally, on the Report tab, you can tell the FSRM to automatically generate a storage report (covered a bit later in this section) when the quota is exceeded. Each of these tabs has a straightforward interface. Click OK when you've finished, and then OK again to finish creating the template.

Once the template is in place, you can use it to apply quotas to specific folders. Then when you need to increase the quota on all folders using a given template, for example, you can simply edit the space limit field within the template definition, and all folders will then reflect the new limit.

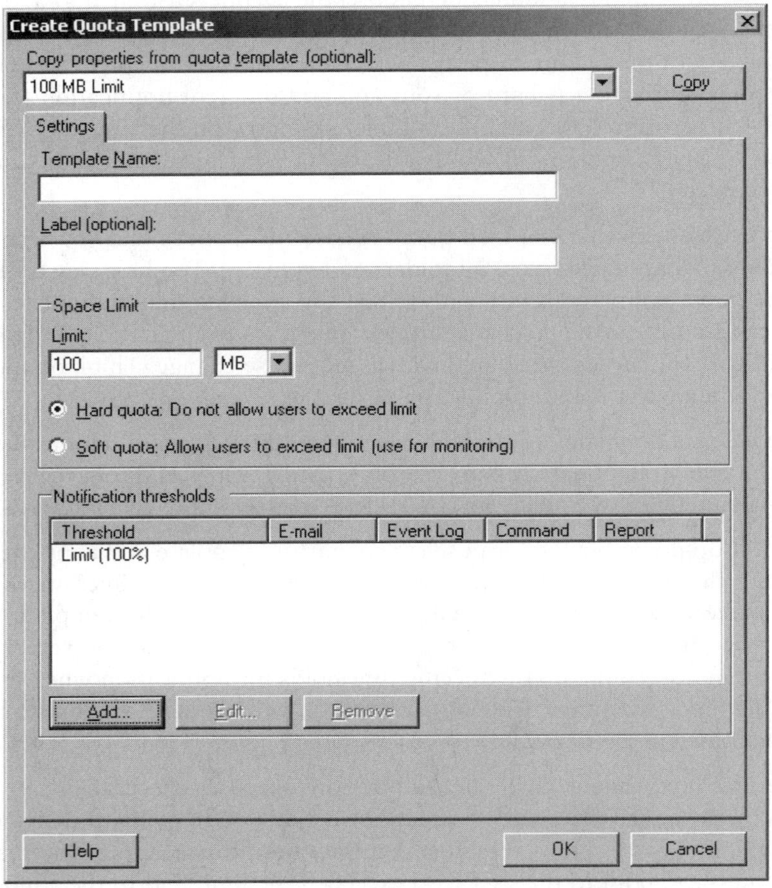

Figure 3-20. The Create Quota Template screen

Screening for File Types

Another useful capability of the FSRM is the ability to screen for certain file types and prevent them from being stored on your file servers. If your storage resources are limited and space is at a premium, there probably isn't a legitimate reason to store tons of MP3 and WMA files within your user's home directories. Even if you have plenty of "first line" space, these files are probably part of your backup set, and if they are you're likely needlessly wasting precious backup media storing the latest Mariah Carey CD in an off-site location in case disaster strikes. File screening can help keep this type of waste to a minimum.

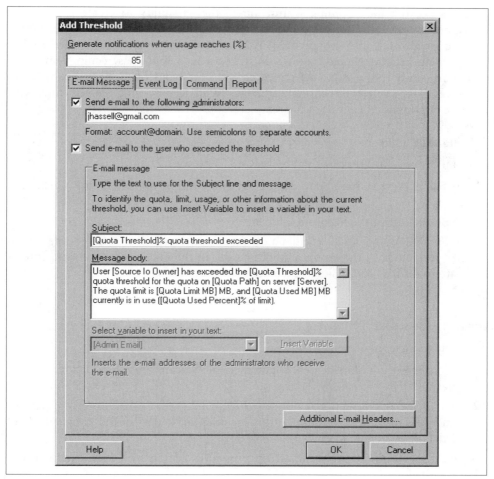

Figure 3-21. The Add Threshold screen

FSRM is pretty flexible. For example, it allows for the following scenarios:

- You can prevent all music files from being stored on a server, except for those files with specific file names (your marketing theme, or a media file relating to an upcoming commercial) or files placed on the server by a certain person or group within your company.

- You can get a pre-warning emailed to you whenever a suspicious script or EXE file is stored on a shared volume, thus alerting you to a possible security breach or virus infestation.

- You can write notifications of screening alerts to the event log, so if you have an event log consolidation program running on all of your servers, you can see the screening reports directly from them.

Like quotas, the file-screening feature offers the capability to create file groups, which are simply collections of file extensions with like characteristics (for example, a media file group would contain MP3, WMA, OGG, and others) that can be used to specify included or excluded files in a particular screen, and file screening templates, which are ready-to-use rules for screening different types of files. Again, by using templates extensively, you can make changes to all servers using file screening with just one or two modifications to the template.

Defining a File Group

You can define a file group within the FSRM. To do so:

1. In File Screen Management, right-click File Groups, and then click Create file group.
2. Type a name for the file group.
3. In the Files to include box, enter a file name pattern (such as *.exe*) for files you'd like to include in the group, and click Add. In the Files to exclude box, enter a pattern for files you'd like to exclude.
4. Click OK.

Creating a File Screen

To create a single file screen:

1. In File Screening Management, right-click File Screens, and then click Create file screen.
2. The Create File Screen box appears. Figure 3-22 shows this. Enter the path to which the file screen will apply (this includes subfolders of the specified folder by default).
3. Select the Define custom file screen properties option, and then click Custom Properties.
4. The File Screen Properties screen appears. You can elect to use an existing template, or create a custom screen.
5. Under Screening type, select whether to apply active screening, which prevents users from saving files that are members of blocked file groups and generates notifications of such actions, or passive screening, which sends notifications but does not prevent users from saving blocked files.
6. Under File Groups, select each file group that you want to include in the screen. To select the checkbox for the file group, click the file group label twice.

7. To configure email notifications for the file screen, set the following options on the E-mail Message tab:

- Select Send email to the following administrators in order to notify said persons when an attempt is made to save an unauthorized file, and enter the administrative accounts that will receive notifications. To enter multiple accounts, separate them with semi-colons.

- Select Send email to the user who attempted to save an unauthorized file if you want to alert the user that he or she almost breached policy.

- You can also edit the subject line and message body. To insert additional variables in the text, click Insert Variable and then choose the appropriate variable as listed on the screen.

8. On the Event Log tab, select the Send warning to event log checkbox, and edit the default log entry. Both of these tasks are optional. In addition, on the Command tab, you can tell Windows to run a program or script when a violation occurs, and on the Report tab, you can elect to automatically generate a report upon a violation.

9. Click Create to save the file screen.

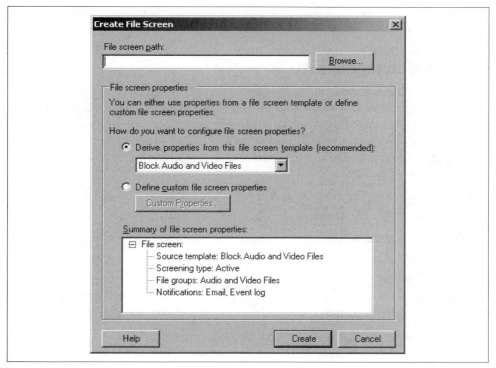

Figure 3-22. The Create File Screen dialog box

Note that when you're creating a "one-off" file screen, you have the option to save it as a file screen template, meaning that (a) it can be reused later if you need to apply the same settings to a different target and (b) FSRM remembers the link between the target of your one-off screen and the newly created template—in essence, it creates the template and *then* applies the screen, so you get the advantages of template use.

Creating an exception to a screen

A file screen exception essentially overrides any screening that would otherwise apply to a folder and its subfolders—it basically blocks rules derived from a parent folder. You can't, however, apply an exception to a folder that already has a file screen applied: you need to either apply the exception to a subfolder or make changes to the existing screen.

To create an exception to a screen:

1. In File Screening Management, right-click File Screens, and then click Create file screen exception.
2. This opens the Create File Screen Exception dialog box. Enter the path to which the exception will apply.
3. Under File groups, select each file group that you want to include in the exception.
4. Click OK.

Generating Storage Reports

The FSRM includes a great facility to get a picture of exactly how your storage is behaving. You can look at trends in how your disk space is being occupied and see alerts and notifications of users who are going over quota or attempting to save files that are in violation of your file screening policies. You can schedule these reports to be generated automatically on a time rotation that you specify, or you can create ad hoc reports as you see fit.

The following reports are available out of the box:

- Duplicate files
- File screening audit
- Files by file group
- Files by owner
- Large files
- Least recently accessed files
- Most recently accessed files
- Quota usage

To generate an ad hoc report:

1. Right-click the Scheduled Report Tasks node, and click Generate reports now.

2. The Storage Reports Task Properties dialog box appears as shown in Figure 3-23. Add each volume or folder that you want to report on to the Scope box, and in Report data, select and format each report that you want to include. To edit the parameters of any particular report, highlight the report label and click the Edit Parameters button. When you finish editing the parameters, click OK.

3. Back on the Storage Reports Task Properties screen, select each file format that you want to save the report in.

4. The Delivery tab allows you to elect to have the report emailed to administrators once it has been generated. To enable this, check the E-mail report to the following administrators box and then enter each email address that you want the report delivered to. To enter multiple accounts, separate each with semicolons.

5. Click OK when you're finished, and then choose whether to open the reports when they're finished or to look at them later.

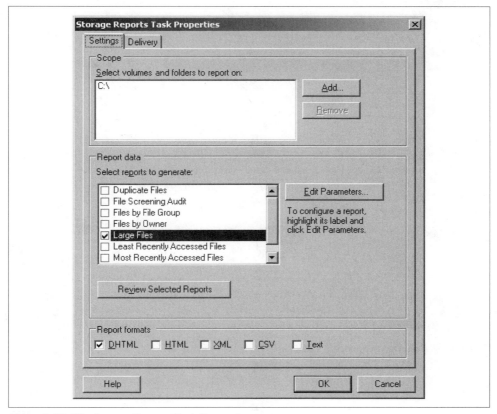

Figure 3-23. The Storage Reports Task Properties screen

You can also schedule reports to be created, which allows you to monitor your storage resources on a regular schedule. To create a scheduled report:

1. Right-click the Scheduled Report Tasks node, and click Schedule a new report task.

2. Follow steps two through four above to define the properties of the report.

3. Click the Schedule tab, and then click the New button to define a schedule. This is shown in Figure 3-24.

4. Select the interval at which to generate the report (daily, weekly, monthly, and one-time reports are supported).

5. The options below the interval box morph themselves depending on your selected interval. Enter this information as necessary.

6. Enter the time of day to generate the report under Start time.

7. Click OK to save the schedule.

8. Click OK to save the task.

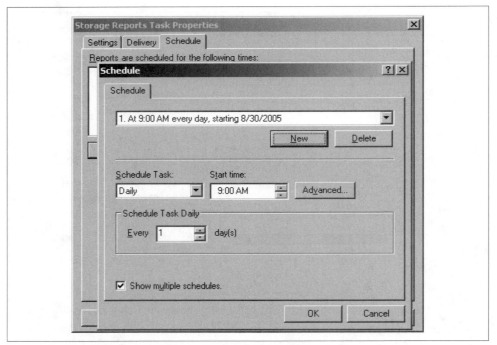

Figure 3-24. Creating a scheduled report task

Using Offline Files and Folders

Offline Files and Folders is a neat feature, offered for the first time in Windows 2000 Professional, which synchronizes files and folders when you connect to and disconnect from the network. Similar to the Windows 95 Briefcase, except much more versatile and automated, Offline Files and Folders caches a copy of selected files and folders on a computer's hard drive. When that computer becomes disconnected from the network for any reason, Windows reads the cache on the machine and intercepts requests for files and folders inside the cache. To the end user, he or she still can open, save, delete, and rename files on network shares because Windows is fooling him or her into thinking that everything is still on the network and not in the cache. Windows records all changes, and the next time an appropriate network connection is detected, the changes are uploaded to the network and the cache and the actual network file store are synchronized.

 What happens when a common network share—call it Contracts—is modified by two different users while they're offline? In this instance, it's really a case of who gets connected first. User A will synchronize with the network, and his modified version of the file will be the one now stored live on the network volume. When User B attempts to synchronize, Windows will prompt him to choose whether to keep the existing version (the one that User A modified) or to overwrite it with the one that User B has worked on.

This has obvious advantages for mobile users. In fact, as I write this, I am sitting at a rest stop on Interstate 20 outside Augusta, Georgia, taking an extended break from a road trip. To open this file, I navigated through Windows Explorer to my regular network storage location for this book and its assorted files. I noticed no difference between being in my office and being in this car right now, at least as far as Windows' interface to the network was concerned. However, tomorrow, when I am back in my office, I will plug the Ethernet cable into my laptop, and Windows will synchronize any files I modified in that folder with the files on my servers in the office. Using this feature, I always have the latest file with me wherever I am, be it in the office or on the road, and I don't really have to consciously think about it. But there's also a plus side that you might not have considered: if you enable Offline Files on regular desktop machines, not just mobile laptops, you create a poor man's fault-tolerant network. (The price you pay for such fault tolerance is bandwidth.) That is, when the network connection disappears, Windows doesn't care if you are using a big mini-tower system or an ultra-thin notebook. So, your desktop users still can safely and happily use network resources, even if the network has disappeared, and you as the administrator can rest assured in knowing whatever the users do will be updated safely on the network when it reappears. Now, of course, this is no substitute for a well-planned network with quality components, but in a pinch, offline folders do well to reduce user panic and wasted help-desk calls.

Enabling Offline Files

To make a server's share contents available offline using the Control Panel, follow these steps:

1. Open the Control Panel and double-click Computer Management.
2. In the left pane, expand Computer Management, System Tools, and Shared Folders and select Shares.
3. On the right pane, right-click the share in question and select Properties.
4. Navigate to the General tab and click the Offline Settings button.
5. Select the appropriate settings (described shortly), and then click OK when finished.

To make a share's contents available offline using Windows Explorer, follow these steps:

1. Open Windows Explorer.
2. Right-click the shared folder in question, and select Sharing and Security.
3. Click the Offline Settings button.
4. Select the appropriate settings, and then click OK when finished.

In both of these processes, the individual offline availability configuration settings are as follows:

- The first option gives the user control over which documents are available offline.
- The second option makes all documents available.
- The third option prevents any documents from being used offline.

You can enable Offline Files and Folders on Windows 2000 and Windows XP clients by opening any folder and selecting Folder Options from the Tools menu. Then click the Offline Files tab, and select the checkbox called Enable Offline Files.

Points to Remember

Be careful to note that offline access is allowed by default when creating a new share. If you have sensitive data which is stored on a share that is accessible by mobile computers, that data can represent a real business intelligence risk if a mobile user's laptop is stolen or compromised. Consider disabling offline access for shares that contain potentially private corporate information not suitable for storage on computers that leave the corporate campus.

Also, beware of the false sense of security that Offline Files and Folders gives the user. If I were to go to the airport without plugging my laptop into the network right before I left, I certainly did not get the latest version of any files I have modified since I last connected the laptop to the network; I'm potentially missing many more files that perhaps had been added since that time as well. A good rule of thumb, even though it's low-tech, is to plug in the laptop right before you leave the office, and then disconnect the laptop and reboot. This enables you to synchronize for a final time and to verify that the utility is working correctly. It's a lot better than arriving at a conference without the PowerPoint slides that derived a significant portion of your talk. (Not that I know from experience....)

Note that checking the Optimized for Performance checkbox in the Windows GUI automatically caches documents so that users can run them locally, which is helpful for busy application servers because it lowers overall traffic to and from the server.

Using Shadow Copies

Shadow copies are a new technology within Windows products that enables a server to take snapshots of documents on a disk to record their states at certain points in time. If a user accidentally deletes or otherwise overwrites a file, he or she can open a version the server saved earlier in time, thereby eliminating the need to either recreate his or her work or contact the help desk to get them to restore the file from the most recent backup. When shadow copies are enabled on a disk, clients connecting to a share on that disk will be able to view and access previous point-in-time copies of either individual files or entire directories.

Further benefits lurk beneath the surface of this feature, however. The service behind shadow copies, called the Volume Shadow Copy Service (VSS), is actually responsible for a newly developed application programming interface (API) that allows server-based applications such as Exchange, SQL, and backup programs to take advantage of the benefits of shadow copies. Perhaps the most famous example is a backup that skips open files, either because they are currently open by a user or because they are locked by another process. In the past, this resulted in incomplete backups, either because the backup process halted in midstream because of this unrecoverable error, or because the process skipped the open file. If the open file is, say, your Exchange email database, that's not necessarily a good thing. But now, with volume shadow copies, the backup application can simply use an API to take a snapshot of any open files and back up that snapshot. Now you have an instant backup of a database at any point in time, with no interruption in availability to the user. This is a very nice feature.

You definitely can take advantage of shadow copies in the user realm as well. Part of the volume shadow copy service is a piece of client software that can be pushed out to any computer in your domain through Group Policy. (This software is located on the Windows Server 2003 CD and can also be downloaded from Microsoft's web site.) Once the user has this client, Windows adds a tab to the Properties sheet for any document. This is shown in Figure 3-25.

Figure 3-25. The Previous Versions add-on for the Volume Shadow Copy Service

To restore a previous version of a file, all the user has to do is select the appropriate version and either copy it to a different location using the Copy button, or restore it to its location at the time the snapshot was taken by using the Restore button. (This will overwrite the newer version because it's assumed that when a user wants to restore a previous version, he doesn't want the current version.) Note that viewing an executable file will run that file.

To reduce user confusion, when a user accesses the Previous Versions link in the Explorer view (in Windows XP, the only client version of Windows that currently supports Previous Versions) of a particular share, he or she is presented only with a list of unique copies—that is to say, a list of versions that differ from each other, a condition that indicates the file or folder changed. In addition, shadow copies are read-only, in that users can copy, drag-and-drop, and perform any other function on them as usual except for overwriting or deleting them.

Some restrictions on shadow copies from an administrator standpoint are noted as follows:

- Local views of folders on a disk do not permit accessing shadow copies. For the Previous Versions link to appear in a folder's view, you must be accessing that folder from a network share.

- The Windows XP clients that require the Previous Versions update can find it (on any Windows Server 2003 system) inside the *%systemroot%\system32* folder; its name is *TWCLI32.MSI*. It is installed by default on all Windows Server 2003 machines. It also can be pushed out, as discussed earlier, through a GPO.

Enabling Shadow Copies

To enable shadow copies on the server, follow these steps:

1. Open the Control Panel and double-click Computer Management.
2. Expand Computer Management, System Tools, and Shared Folders.
3. Right-click Shared Folders, select All Tasks, and click Configure Shadow Copies.
4. Select the disk on which to enable shadow copies, and click Enable.

When you enable shadow copies on a volume, the system creates a folder on that volume called System Volume Information, where the actual snapshots and log files of the operations are stored. By default, this folder is allocated 10% of the volume's total disk space, much like the Recycle Bin default in Windows.

When you first enable shadow copies, a current snapshot of the volume is taken so that Windows can store a picture of the "state" of files on the disk. This state data is used to determine if files have changed from the time at which the state information was recorded. For example, an administrative assistant is performing rudimentary formatting functions on an Excel spreadsheet and she leaves for the day. Overnight, the Windows Server 2003 machine on which the file share resides is configured to take a snapshot of all files—for this example, I will use 5:30 a.m. When this snapshot is taken, the state information for this Excel spreadsheet is copied into the System Volume Information folder. Now, when the administrative assistant arrives at work and begins to work on the spreadsheet, she is using the same version as the one she saved the previous night; remember that this is also the one on which the snapshot is based. When she finishes with some formatting, she saves the spreadsheet before she attends the Tuesday morning meeting of all employees. The VSS service detects that the Excel file is one which already has state data, and it realizes that it has changed, so it immediately makes available the 5:30 a.m. version of the file—the previous version—under the appropriate tab in the Properties sheet for the Excel file. So now, when the administrative assistant comes back and realizes that she unintentionally removed an entire page from the workbook while she was formatting the file, she can retrieve the version from the previous night, and likely save her job.

You should, however, note three very important items concerning how shadow copies might and (most notably) might not rescue you or your users from catastrophe:

- You can only restore the shadow copy of a file that consisted of the oldest modification since the most recent snapshot. Even if multiple changes are made to a file throughout the day, the only previous version available for rollback is the one that was made directly after the most recent snapshot. This can be somewhat counterintuitive to understand, but it's crucial that your users not rely on the previous versions feature as a crux and learn to use it only when a major disaster strikes.

- If you rename a file, you lose all access to previous versions of that file, even if some exist. VSS tracks exclusively by filename and state, so if the filename changes, VSS (at least at this stage) isn't smart enough to follow the rename.

Altering the Shadow Copy Schedule

Shadow copies are scheduled by default to be made at 7:00 a.m. and at noon on weekdays. Server performance can be adversely affected if you schedule shadow copies to be taken more frequently than once every 60 minutes.

 Because the times at which shadow copies are made can be a good ways apart in the work day, it's best to remind users that the shadow copy functionality is not a crutch and that the best way to ensure that no data is lost is to save early and often.

Additionally, as soon as 64 shadow copies per volume are stored, the oldest will be deleted and become irretrievable as new shadow copies are made to replace them.

To change the shadow copy schedule, follow these steps:

1. Open the Control Panel, and double-click Computer Management.
2. Expand Computer Management → System Tools → Shared Folders.
3. Right-click Shared Folders, select All Tasks, and click Configure Shadow Copies.
4. Select the disk on which to modify the shadow copy schedule, and then click the Settings button.
5. Click the Schedule button in the box that appears next.
6. Change the schedule as appropriate.

Backing Up Your Machines

The oft-neglected process of backing up your machines and the critical data they contain is perhaps the most effective insurance policy you can take out for your business. It's like exercise: although nearly everyone knows that it's an excellent idea and vital to health, not everyone does it. Fortunately, Windows Server 2003 includes a backup utility in the box which performs this function at a basic level. This section will discuss how to use the GUI front end, and how to access the same features from the command line using the core NTBACKUP program for enhanced automation possibilities.

NTBACKUP can perform several different types of backups:

Copy

Copies all selected files but does not mark each file with a cleared archive attribute. Copy backups can be performed completely independently of other backup procedures without affecting their sets.

Daily

A daily backup backs up all files modified since the last day. With a daily backup, the archive attribute is not cleared.

Differential

A differential backup copies new files and other files modified since the last normal or incremental backup. It does not mark files as having been backed up. To restore a complete backup, you'll need the last normal backup (covered later) in addition to the last incremental backup.

Incremental

An incremental backup backs up files created or modified since the last normal or the last incremental backup. It does mark files as having been backed up. To restore a complete backup, you'll need the last normal backup (covered next) in addition to the last incremental backup.

Normal

A normal backup (sometimes called a full backup) copies all selected files and marks each file as backed up. You create these to start a backup scheme, and they're used in conjunction with differential and/or incremental backups, depending on what you choose. Normal backups can be used independently; they don't require another accompanying set.

 The files that NTBACKUP creates are very large, even when compared with an eye for price to commercial products such as Veritas BackupExec. Keep that in mind when justifying the cost of sticking with the built-in product versus investing the money in a third-party backup product.

Using Backup from the GUI

To back up the contents of your server to a file or to another removable media device using the GUI, follow these steps:

1. From the Start Menu, select All Programs → Accessories → System Tools → Backup. The wizard starts by default. You can use the wizard if you'd like, but I'll describe a more direct and flexible method, so click the Advanced Mode link.

2. Navigate to the Backup tab, and then select New from the Job menu.

3. Click the box to the left of a file or folder to select the files and folders you want to back up.

4. In Backup Destination, choose File (the default selection) if you want to back up to a file on disk. Choose another device if you want to back up to a tape or something similar.

5. In Backup Media or File Name, choose a location for the backup (*.bkf*) file if you are backing up to a file. Otherwise, choose the tape you want to use.

6. Make sure you've configured this backup operation the way you want by selecting Options from the Tools menu and verifying the choices there.

7. Click the Start Backup button, and then make any changes to the Backup Job Information dialog box.

8. Click Advanced to configure options such as compression and verification. Then click OK.

9. Click Start Backup.

 You should note the following considerations if you use either Removable Storage or Remote Storage. You should make a note to back up the contents of:

    %systemroot%\System32\Ntmsdata

and:

    %systemroot%\System32\Remotestorage

on a regular basis. If you don't, it's possible (although somewhat unlikely) that Removable/Remote Storage data could be lost and unrestorable.

Using the Encrypting File System

Windows 2000 introduced the Encrypting File System (EFS), a way to scramble the contents of documents, other files, and even programs so that they become unreadable by anyone other than the person who encrypted them. Although EFS has merits in environments consisting of corporate desktop computers, the real boon is for laptops: because theft of laptops has been on the rise for almost a decade, there is a real risk in storing sensitive information on these mobile systems. If a laptop from a research and development representative were to fall into a competitor's hands, the cost of that loss would far exceed the retail price of a new laptop; indeed, the damage would be almost immeasurable. So, EFS is definitely an asset.

How does EFS appear to the end user? It's nearly transparent in operation, though not as much in presentation. When you encrypt a document, Windows doesn't attempt to hide the document's presence on the disk. In fact, encrypted documents are outlined in blue with a normal default folder view. The real transparency comes when you open the document. The process goes as follows: from each individual file on a server's disk, Windows calculates a unique file encryption key. When a user selects to encrypt a file, the file encryption key is encrypted too, using the public key stored on the user's EFS certificate. (This public key is generated the first time a request to encrypt an object is submitted.) To decrypt a file, the file encryption key must first be decrypted, which happens when a specific user has a private key that corresponds with the public key. These private keys are not stored in the SAM; rather, they are held in a protected key store. Note that other users can be authorized to decrypt the file encryption key by using their own private key. If the keys match up correctly—that is, if the expected result is obtained from the mathematical processes—the filesystem object is decrypted transparently. If there is an error, and unexpected results are returned, the user is denied access and the object remains encrypted. The object is encrypted again when the user closes it.

There are some limitations to note when using automatic encryption in the filesystem. For one, you can encrypt files and folders only on disks formatted with NTFS. Two, compressed files and folders cannot be encrypted; they will be uncompressed before the procedure. Three, you cannot encrypt files marked with the System attribute, as well as files in the system root folder.

If you encrypt the parent folder when encrypting a single file or a single folder, all future additions to that folder will be encrypted automatically. But if you encrypt the folder only, objects in the folder at that point are not encrypted, though any future additions will be encrypted automatically. Additionally, when decrypting, if you select to decrypt a single file within an encrypted folder, future additions to that folder will not be encrypted.

 There are performance implications when using EFS. Because of the nature of encryption and decryption, opening files that are subjected to those processes takes longer.

Encrypting Files and Folders

To encrypt a file or folder using the GUI, follow these steps:

1. Right-click the file or folder to encrypt, and then select Properties.
2. Navigate to the General tab, and then click the Advanced button.
3. Check the Encrypt contents to secure data checkbox, and then click OK.
4. In the Properties dialog box, click OK. You'll be prompted if the file or folder you want to encrypt is contained within another folder that is not encrypted. Select one of the following options:
   - Encrypt the file and the parent folder
   - Encrypt the file only
5. Next, the Confirm Attribute Changes dialog box appears. To encrypt a folder only, select Apply Changes to This Folder Only. To encrypt a folder and all its contents, select Apply Changes to This Folder, Subfolders, and Files.

To decrypt a file or folder, follow these steps:

1. Right-click the file or folder to encrypt, and then select Properties.
2. Navigate to the General tab, and then click the Advanced button.
3. Uncheck the Encrypt contents to secure data checkbox, and then click OK.

Recovering Encrypted Objects

It can be somewhat disconcerting that, in emergency or recovery situations, encrypted files can be decrypted by a user other than the user who encrypted the file originally. This is actually a feature, and it really is quite secure. Designated user accounts, called *recovery agent accounts*, are issued recovery agent certificates with public keys and private keys upon their creation that are used for EFS data recovery operations. The Windows user accounts that function as recovery agent accounts are designated by a GPO or a local security policy object, depending on the machine's participation in a domain. By default, they are the highest-level administrator account available. Depending on the network environment of a particular machine, this is either the local administrator or the domain administrator. The private key from the appropriate agent certificate must be located on the computer where recovery operations are to be conducted.

When a recovery agent certificate is issued, the certificate and private key are installed in the user profile for the user account that requested the certificate. An EFS file can contain more than one recovery agent account, and each EFS file can have a different private key. However, data recovery discloses only the encrypted data, not the user's private key or any other private keys for recovery. This ensures that no other private information is revealed to the recovery agent administrator unintentionally.

 Windows Server 2003 no longer requires a file recovery agent (FRA). Anyone can begin playing around with this feature in a test lab, for example, and because there is no default FRA on the network, that user's files will never be able to be accessed by anyone other than him. Ack!

To view the recovery agents for an object, log in as the owner of the encrypted object. Then, right-click the object and select Properties. Click the Advanced button, which opens the Advanced Attributes dialog box. Click the Details button to bring up the Encryption Details box. The recovery agents for the specified object are listed in the bottom box. Figure 3-26 shows this.

But what is in the top box of the Encryption Details dialog? This is a new feature of Windows Server 2003 which makes it quite a bit easier to enable other users to decrypt a file without them being recovery agents. By designating their user accounts in the top list, the users can access and use the file transparently. Simply click Add and select the users from the local computer or from a domain that should be able to access the file transparently.

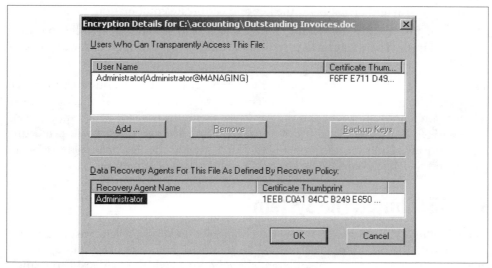

Figure 3-26. An object's recovery agents

Protecting User Certificate Integrity

Microsoft recommends that, to protect a user's certificate from thievery, users should export their personal certificate, save it to some sort of removable media, and then remove it entirely from the local computer. This is because although the encryption/decryption methods EFS uses are quite secure, if someone happens to make off with a machine and is able to log on with administrator credentials, he or she could modify the certificate configuration to allow him- or herself the ability to decrypt any files. Obviously, this is a problem. To perform this recommended procedure, take these steps:

1. Open the Certificates snap-in to the MMC.

2. Navigate through the Personal folder to Certificates.

3. In the righthand section of the console, right-click the certificate to export, and select Export from the All Tasks menu.

4. The Certificate Export Wizard begins. Select to export the private key along with the certificate and click Next.

5. On the Export Options screen, select what file type the exported certificate should take, the level of encryption that should be used, and the action you want to be performed with the local key once the export is complete. Click Next once you've selected appropriate options.

6. By exporting the private key, you need to encrypt it with a password of your choosing. Select the password carefully, as the certificate and private key will be irretrievable if you forget it.

7. Select a path and filename for the key and certificate combination.

8. On the final step in the wizard, double-check your selections carefully, and then click Finish. The wizard will trundle and notify you if the operation was successful.

The certificate will no longer reside on the computer from which you removed it. To reimport it to the same or a different computer, right-click inside the Certificates folder again, choose Import from the All Tasks menu, browse for your exported certificate file from the preceding list of steps, enter any necessary passwords protecting that certificate, choose a location for the key (usually the Personal folder is sufficient), and then click Finish. The key now resides on that computer.

The Distributed File System

The Distributed File System (DFS) is a technology that allows several distinct filesystems, potentially on multiple servers, to be mounted from one place and appear in one logical representation. The different shared folders, which likely reside on different drives in different server machines, can all be accessed from one folder, known as the *root node*. Link nodes serve to point from shared folder to shared folder to mimic a directory tree structure, which can be rearranged and altered according to a particular implementation's needs. DFS also allows the clients to know only the name of the share point and not the name of the server on which it resides, a big boon when you field help-desk calls asking, "What server is my last budget proposal located on?"

DFS root nodes come in two basic flavors: *standalone root nodes*, which store the folder topology information locally, and *fault-tolerant root nodes*, which store the topology structure in Active Directory and thereby replicate that information to other domain controllers. In this case, if you have multiple root nodes, you might have multiple connections to the same data—it just so happens that they appear in different shared folders. You even can set up two different share points to the same data on two different physical servers, because DFS is intelligent enough to select the folder set that is geographically closest to the requesting client, saving network traffic and packet travel time. (The redundant share points also replicate around the network, which is another layer of backup protection.) In either case, you can replicate a DFS root by creating root targets on other servers in the domain. This provides file availability when the host server becomes unavailable.

First, let's look at some definitions used in DFS. A *DFS root* can exist either as a standalone entity or as a member of a domain. In either case, the root collects links to all shared paths in the network and publishes those links to users. The childlike *links* maintain a mapping of a friendly name to a concrete path in a server's filesystem. When a user accesses the DFS link, the service navigates the mapping and points the user to the destination path. A *DFS target*, also known as a replica, refers to either roots or links and serves to combine two identical shares on different servers into one link automatically, with synchronization and replication all a part of it.

The major difference between domain-based roots and standalone roots is that of replication. By default, fault-tolerant roots publish their information in Active Directory into the Partition Knowledge Table (PKT). The PKT is distributed to all domain controllers in a domain, which makes it easier for users to connect to shares. In a standalone root environment, only a single server can keep track of the DFS topology, so if that server is unavailable for any reason, user interruption will occur.

You can expand a DFS topology by adding a link to the root. There's no functional limitation on the number of levels your topology can have, although Windows permits no more than 260 characters in any file path. A new DFS link can refer to a target (with or without subfolders) or to an entire disk. If you have adequate permissions, you also can access any local subfolders that exist in or are added to a target.

DFS clients, as mentioned earlier, get referrals to the closest server that houses a copy of the data they request. These referrals are "sticky," meaning that they persist until the next system restart. This is done to protect data integrity in environments where replication takes place over great geographic distances—because it can take hours or even days before all DFS changes are replicated to all servers within a domain. If a user had a referral to data stored on a server in Chicago, and then caught a flight home to New York and plugged his laptop back in, the most up-to-date data might not be available to him if changes to DFS in Chicago had not replicated back to New York at that point. The bottom line is that it's safer for the client to go back from where he came from to get data, at least until system reboot.

Windows Server 2003 Standard Edition supports only one DFS root per server. Other editions, namely the Enterprise and Datacenter editions, support multiple DFS roots on the same machine.

Adding a DFS Root and Link

The following procedure creates a simple DFS share (which consists of a root node and a child link):

1. Click Start, and then select All Programs → Administrative Tools → Distributed File System.

2. Select the Action... menu and select New DFS Root Volume. The Create New DFS Root Wizard appears; click Next.

3. Select the Create a standalone DFS root radio button, and enter the server name on which the DFS root should be located.

4. To make an existing share participate in the DFS system, select the Use Existing Share button and select the share from the list. To construct a new share that

will use DFS, select the Create New Share option, and complete the path to the share and the share's official name. Click Next.

5. Enter the name for the DFS root volume on this screen. (Note that if you selected Use Existing Share on the previous screen, this option will be grayed out, and you'll be able to enter only a comment.) Click Next.

6. Verify the settings on the screen, and click Finish to create the new DFS root.

7. To create the child link, highlight the root node and press the New Child button.

8. Enter the friendly name you want users to see for this link in the Link Name box. Enter the path to the folder in the Send the user to this shared folder link, and add an optional comment for the users in the Comment box.

9. Click OK to finish.

Adding DFS Links and Targets

You should not use the steps I outlined earlier for adding a target in a DFS system: that is added when you first create the DFS link.

The folder you specify as the target in step 3 of the following procedure must be an existing shared folder. Additionally, if a link points to another domain's DFS, it cannot point to any other targets. To add a target in this case, you must add it to the targeted DFS system, and not to the link itself.

To add a DFS link, follow these steps:

1. Click Start, and then select All Programs → Administrative Tools → Distributed File System.

2. Click an existing DFS root node, and then from the Action menu, select New Link.

3. Enter a name for the link, and then enter the path for the new link. Use the Browse button to navigate through a list of your existing shared folders.

4. Enter a comment for administrative purposes to help identify the purpose of this link.

5. Enter a value for the length of time this link should be cached on the client side, and then click OK when finished.

To add a target to a DFS link, follow these steps:

1. Click Start, and then select All Programs → Administrative Tools → Distributed File System.

2. Click an existing DFS root node, and then from the Action menu, select New Target.

3. Enter the path to the target. Use the Browse button for a list of existing shared folders.

4. If you are using a domain-based DFS system, to enable Windows to automatically replicate files for the target, check the Add this target to the replication set checkbox. (If you do not check this checkbox, you need to manually migrate files to your target from other targets.)

5. Click OK when complete.

The Basics of DFS Replication

During the previous wizard, you might be prompted to configure replication. By clicking Yes, the Configure Replication Wizard is opened. Hold that thought for a moment while we look at how DFS replication works; then we'll come back to the wizard and step through it.

If you have a nondomain-based DFS system, replication is purely a manual exercise for the administrator, pushing files from a master to slaves in a single-master fashion. (One link replica is designated the master.) On the other hand, in a domain-based DFS system, if your data resides in shares on servers running Windows 2000 Server or Server 2003 with NTFS drives, replication is automatic and is multimaster. This means changes are pushed from all servers to all servers, and are orchestrated by an algorithm that takes into account server load, geography, and network link costs.

Now, back to the wizard. Bypass the welcome screen and come to the master selection page. Here, you choose a temporary "master" share to start replication—temporary because, as I just described, all subsequent replications within Server 2003 are a multimaster process, much like domain controllers. Click Next, and the next screen enables you to choose the replication strategies available. You can choose from the following:

- Ring
- Hub and spoke
- Full mesh
- A custom topology of your construction, where you map connections yourself at a later point

DFS automatically configures the first three for you, so they're simple and likely to work better with DFS than any other custom topology. You should use the fourth strategy only if you really know what you're doing. Click Finish once you've made your selection, and you will return to the DFS Management console screen.

Managing DFS Systems

You might need to perform a few common administrative tasks on your DFS structure. This section will describe the procedure for each task.

Connecting to different roots

Inside the DFS management console, click the Action menu, and then select Show Roots. The Show Root dialog box will open. You can either directly type in the name of the DFS root or the name of the server that hosts it, or you can browse in the bottom box through a list of the current domain and all domains that trust your current domain to find the server or root.

Checking DFS node status

From within the management console, open the root and expand it so that you can see the shares under it. Right-click the share in which you're interested, and select Check Status. The icon in the right pane will change depending on the status; you also can look in the table under the Status field for an update as well. The two possible values are Online and Offline, represented by a green checkmark icon and a red "X" icon, respectively.

Removing child nodes

If you have a failed node, you can remove the link from your DFS system so that clients will not get a faulty referral. This does not remove the actual data or the physical share from the server; in effect it just takes the share out of the DFS table of contents so that users aren't pointed to a broken link. To do so, just right-click the share in the left pane from within the management console and choose Delete Link.

Downing replica members

You can enable and disable DFS referrals so that users aren't pointed to a server that's unavailable or malfunctioning. This is useful for server maintenance periods when you don't want users to have their own connections terminated, but you don't want to remove the entire replica set from the DFS and readd it when your maintenance window is complete. To disable referrals to a replica, just right-click the share and select Enable/Disable Referral. This action will set the status to whatever is the opposite of the current setting.

DFS in Windows Server 2003 R2

DFS in Windows Server 2003 R2 is broken up into two components:

- DFS Namespaces, which is basically everything you knew of DFS before R2 came along, minus replication. With DFS namespaces, you can group shared folders stored on different servers and present them to users in one coherent tree, making the actual location of the files and folders irrelevant to the end user.

- DFS Replication, which revolutionizes replication in the original version of DFS and is almost a complete and total rewrite of the File Replication service (FRS) introduced in Windows 2000 Server. DFS Replication is a multimaster replication engine that supports scheduling, bandwidth throttling, and compression. Most notably, DFS Replication now uses an algorithm known as Remote Differential Compression (RDC), which efficiently updates files over a limited-bandwidth network by looking at insertions, removals, and rearrangements of data in files, and then replicating only the changed file blocks. There is substantial savings to this method.

Figure 3-27 shows a basic flow that DFS transactions proceed through in R2.

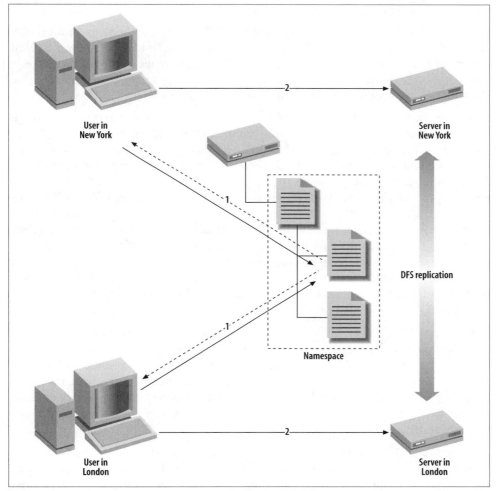

Figure 3-27. The basic flow of DFS in Windows Server 2003 R2

Let's walk through this. When an end user wants to open a folder that's included within a DFS namespace, the client sends a message to the namespace server (which is simply a machine running the R2 version of DFS). That machine will then refer the client to a list of servers that host copies of those shared folders (these copies are called folder targets). The client machine stores a copy of that referral in its cache and then goes down the referral list in order, which is automatically sorted by proximity so that a client is always using servers within his Active Directory site before traversing to machines located outside of his current location. That's mostly DFS as you know it now, with some improvements in terminology and target selection.

But let's crack the nut a little further and see the sparkling technology in R2 that is DFS replication. At first it seems normal: you can store a folder on a server in New York and the same folder on a server in London, and replication will take care of keeping the copies of the folders synchronized. Users, of course, have no idea that these folders are kept in geographically disparate locations.

However, the replication mechanism is incredibly optimized: it determines what has changed about two files and then, using remote differential compression, only sends the differences between the files and folders over the wire. Over slow WAN links and other bandwidth-metered lines, you'll see a real cost savings. You really see the benefits when relatively minor changes to large files are made. According to Microsoft, a change to a two megabyte PowerPoint presentation can result in only 60 KB being transmitted across the wire—which equates to a 97% percent savings in terms of amount of data sent. Delving a bit further: according to the product team, they "ran a test on a mix of 780 Office files (*.doc*, *.ppt*, and *.xls*) replicating from a source server to a target server using DFS Replication with RDC. The target server had version n of the files and the source server had version n+, and the two versions differed with significant edits. The percent savings in bytes transferred was on average 50 percent and significantly better for large files."

Of course, with DFS you also get the fault tolerance benefit of "failing over" to a functional server if a target on another server isn't responding. Prior to R2, there wasn't a simple way for you to instruct clients, after a failure, to resume back to their local DFS servers once the machines came back online. A new hotfix, which works in conjunction with R2 and Windows XP and Windows Server 2003 as a client, allows you to specify that clients should fail back to a closer, less costly server when services are restored.

Although R2's DFS components are two separate technologies, when they're used in tandem they solve some real problems companies face. Take branch office backup, for instance. Instead of tasking your administrators in these offices with tape drive maintenance, backing up, storing data off site, and everything else associated with disaster avoidance, simply configure DFS to replicate data from the servers in the branch office back up to a hub server in the home office or another data center. Then, run the backup from the central location. You are more efficient in three ways:

- You save on tape hardware costs.

- You save time through the efficiencies in DFS replication.

- You save manpower costs because your IT workers at the branch offices can move onto other problems and not spend their time babysitting a backup process.

What about software distribution? The new version of DFS really excels at publishing documents, applications, and other files to users that are separated geographically. By using namespaces in conjunction with replication, you can store multiple copies of data and software at multiple locations throughout the world, better ensuring constant availability and good transfer performance while still making it transparent to users where they're getting their files from. DFS replication and namespaces automatically look at your AD site structure to determine the lowest cost link to use in the event that a local namespace server isn't available to respond to requests.

The UI for managing DFS has also improved over the more clunky and less put-together MMC snap-in in Windows 2000 and the original version of Windows Server 2003. The new snap-in offers you the ability to configure namespaces and other abilities that previously only existed through the command-line interface.

 DFS Replication is not supported for SYSVOL replication in Windows Server 2003 R2, so don't try to disable FRS and create replication group for SYSVOL. At this point, FRS and DFS Replication can coexist on the same member server or domain controller.

Creating a namespace

In the MMC snap-in for DFS in R2, the Namespaces node in the left pane contains any namespaces you may create as well as any existing namespaces you add to the console display. Beneath each namespace in the tree you'll find a hierarchical view of folders. Folders with targets use a special icon to differentiate them from ordinary folders without targets. We'll use this UI to create a new namespace, add some folders and folder targets, and then eventually set up replication between two machines to demonstrate the functionality.

In order to create a new namespace, the following conditions must be met:

- You need at least two servers, both running Windows Server 2003 R2. You'll need the DFS system installed, which you can do through Add/Remove Windows Components as described earlier in this chapter.

- If you want an AD-integrated topology, you will need to have deployed Active Directory on your network. For the purposes of this exercise, I'll assume that you have NOT deployed AD yet, and we will focus on the non-AD specific DFS features.

To deploy a new namespace, launch the DFS Management snap-in, and then right-click on the Namespace node in the left pane and select New Namespace from the context menu. Then:

1. On the Namespace Server page, shown in Figure 3-28, enter the name of the server which will host the namespace. Then click Next.

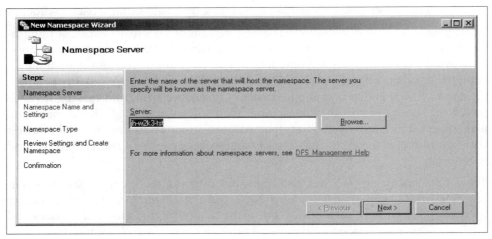

Figure 3-28. The Namespace Server screen

2. On the Namespace Name and Settings page, enter a name for your new namespace. I've named my new namespace Files, as you can see in Figure 3-29.

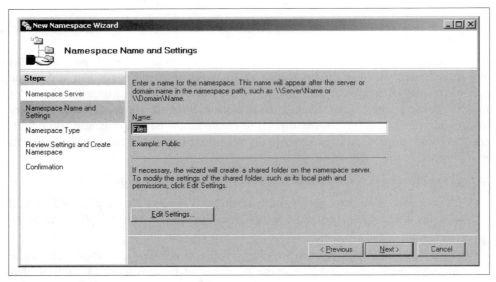

Figure 3-29. The Namespace Name and Settings screen

3. The Namespace Type screen appears, as shown in Figure 3-30. Choose Standalone namespace from the list, and then click Next.

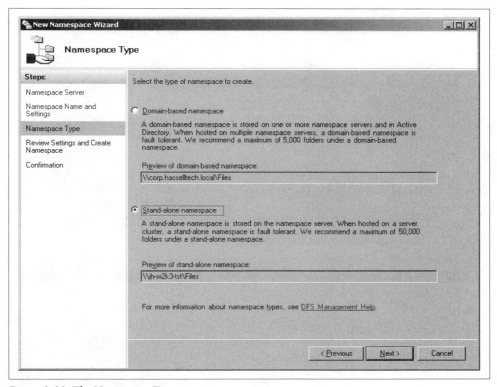

Figure 3-30. The Namespace Type screen

4. On the Review Settings and Create Namespace screen, depicted in Figure 3-31, verify the settings you've chosen and then click Next.

5. The Completion screen appears; this is shown in Figure 3-32. Close the wizard after confirming that there were no errors during the completion process.

Adding and managing folders and folder targets in a namespace

It's very simple to add a folder to an already existing namespace. In the left pane, right-click on the name of the namespace and choose New Folder. You'll see the New Folder screen, as shown in Figure 3-33. Enter the name of the folder you'd like to add in the Name box.

If you'd like, you can go ahead and add some folder targets to this folder at the same time you're creating the folder. Recall that folder targets allow you to redirect a specific DFS namespace folder to a physical location on a shared folder structure. For example, if I wanted to have the "Office" folder appear in my DFS namespace

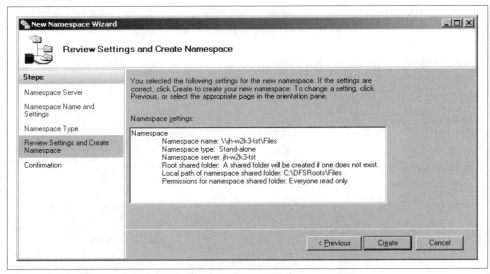

Figure 3-31. The Review Settings and Create Namespace screen

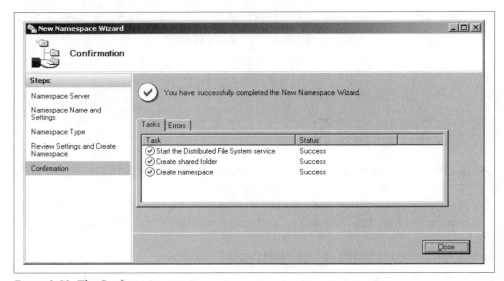

Figure 3-32. The Confirmation screen

structure, I could create a folder target, attached to a DFS folder, that pointed to the actual location where Office resides. Folder targets are just a way to clean up and simplify the appearance of files and folders within your network.

If you want to move or rename a particular folder, simply right-click on the folder within the left pane in the console and select Move or Rename and complete the appropriate action. The DFS service handles the rest; moving is a particularly seamless action.

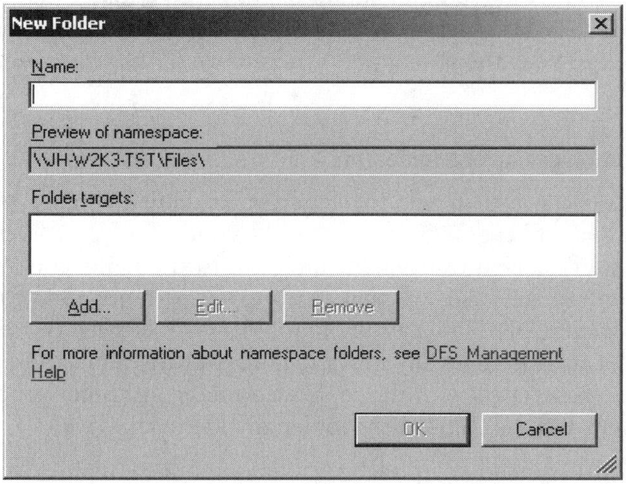

Figure 3-33. Adding a folder

To add a folder target, click the Add button, and then the Add Folder Target screen will appear, as shown in Figure 3-34. Enter the correct path to the location you want to folder target to reference, and then click OK.

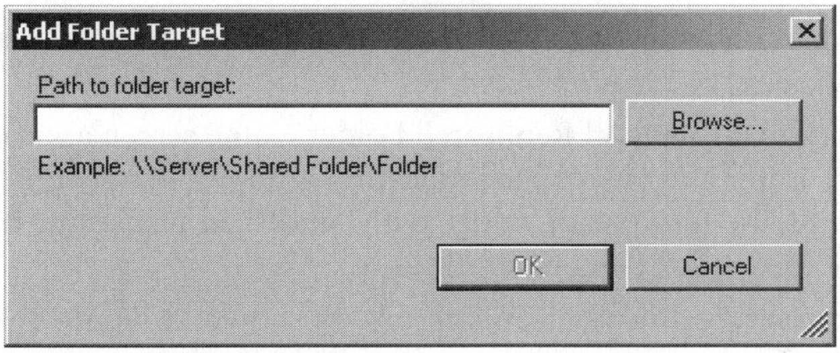

Figure 3-34. Adding a folder target

You can add multiple folder targets to any one folder as a way of maintaining fault tolerance. That way, if a user is directed to a particular machine that is down, the client will work down the referral list it received from the namespace server and try another server that hosts a copy of the folder target. You can adjust how this referral is done, within or outside of a site, by right-clicking on the name of the namespace in the left pane of the console and selecting Properties. Navigate to the Referrals tab, and then select the appropriate option from the Ordering Method box. You can choose "lowest cost," which takes into account sites and site links as configured within Active Directory, "random order," which does exactly as it sounds, or "exclude targets outside of the client's site," which simply removes the ability for clients to access targets exterior to their current site.

Note that when you try and add an additional target to a folder that already has just one target, the DFS MMC snap-in will prompt you and ask if you'd like to create a replication group to keep the two targets synchronized. And that's what the next section is all about.

Creating a replication group for a folder

Again, if you have more than one folder target for fault tolerance purposes, you'll want to configure a replication group so that the contents of the folders are kept synchronized and users have a transparent interface to the items contained therein. A replication group is a set of servers that sends or receives updates of replicated folders. When you enable DFS Replication on a folder with targets, the servers that host the folder targets are automatically made members of the replication group, and the folder targets are associated with the replicated folder. All other properties, like the name of the group and the name of the folder, are identical as well.

You can use DFS Replication in both stand-alone and domain-based namespaces. Therefore, you can complete this task regardless of the type of namespace you created in "Task 1: Create a Namespace." You do, however, need to have Active Directory deployed and you need to be a member of the Domain Administrators group. (I'll cover AD in Chapter 5; if you want to wait until you've read there before continuing with this section and procedure, that's not a problem.)

To create a replication group for a folder:

1. In the left pane of the console, right-click on the folder in the namespace you created, and select Replicate Folder.

2. The Replication Group and Replicated Folder Name screen appears, as shown in Figure 3-35. Enter a name for the replication group (most people keep this as the same name as the namespace folder path) and then also enter the name of the replicated folder. Click Next to continue.

3. The Replication Eligibility screen appears, as shown in Figure 3-36. In this step, the Replicate Folder Wizard determines which, if any, folder targets are able to participate in replication. Make sure that at least two of these targets, located on different servers, are eligible, and then click Next.

4. The Primary Folder Target screen appears, as shown in Figure 3-37. Here, specify the folder target that will be used as the primary member of the replication group—i.e., the member whose content is authoritative; the master copy of the content. Click Next to continue.

5. The Topology Selection screen appears, as shown in Figure 3-38. On this screen, you can choose how the connections among the server members of the replication group will be deployed. If you have three or more members in your replication group, you can choose the hub and spoke methodology, in which hub members are connected to other members and data originates from the center and moves outward to the spokes. Your other choices are full mesh, in which

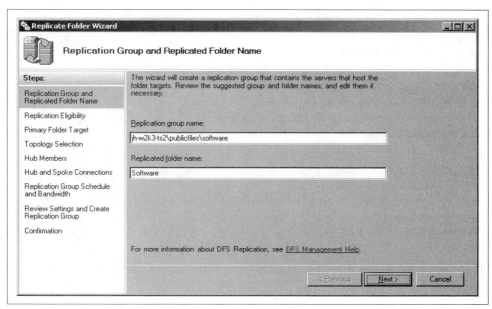

Figure 3-35. The Replication Group and Replicated Folder Name screen

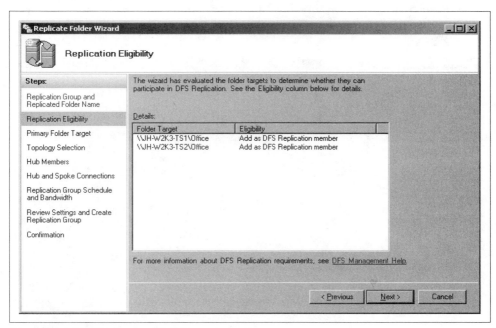

Figure 3-36. The Replication Eligibility screen

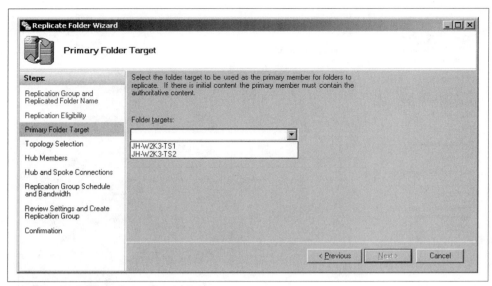

Figure 3-37. The Primary Folder Target screen

each member replicates all data with all other members; and no topology, where you can create your own topology. For this example, choose full mesh, and then click Next to continue.

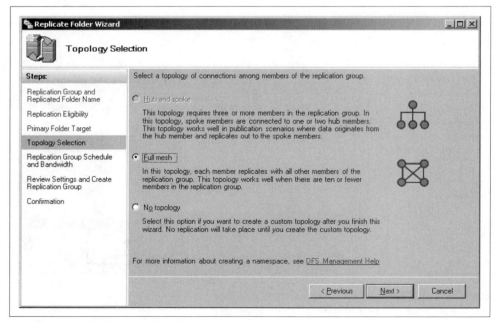

Figure 3-38. The Topology Selection screen

6. The Replication Group Schedule and Bandwidth screen appears, as shown in Figure 3-39. Here, you can choose whether to replicate full-time (24/7) or on a specific schedule. To set the schedule, click the Edit Schedule button. You can also choose how much bandwidth to use during replication, which helps keep more bandwidth available for regular usage. You can choose Full from the list to drop all bandwidth concerns and replicate everything as fast as possible. Click Next to continue.

Figure 3-39. The Replication Group Schedule and Bandwidth screen

7. The Review Settings and Create Replication Group screen appears, as shown in Figure 3-40. Verify all of the settings you have chosen; if you need to change something, click the Back button. Otherwise, click Next, and the wizard will set off creating your replication group.

8. The Confirmation screen appears. Make sure there are no errors, and then click Close.

9. The Replication Delay screen appears, as shown in Figure 3-41. This message appears to let you know that there may be an initial delay while the configuration of the replication group is propagated among all of the members of the group. Click OK to acknowledge.

Your replication group is now set up. If you add a file or make other changes to the folder target location on one machine, DFS Replication will pick up the change and replicate it to all of the other folder targets on the other machines within the replication group, thus enabling a seamless interface to files and folders for your users as long as they use Explorer to find files through the namespace you created.

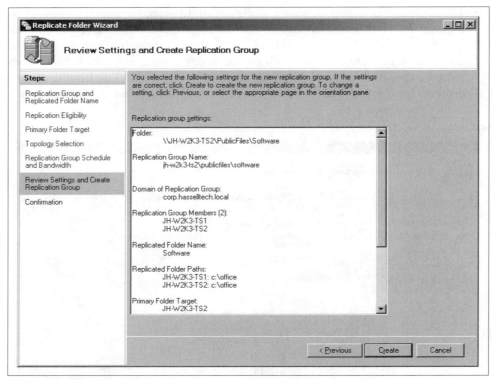

Figure 3-40. The Review Settings and Create Replication Group screen

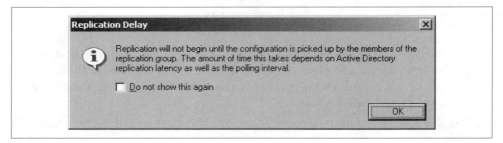

Figure 3-41. The Replication Delay screen

From the Replication node, you can manage all of the properties and settings of DFS Replication, such as the schedule, bandwidth throttling, the topology, and others. On the Replicated Folders tab in the details pane of the MMC console, you can also view the namespace path that corresponds to the replicated folder or folders.

Understanding Print Sharing Services

Printers and printing services are areas of Windows Server 2003 that haven't changed very much in the migration from Windows 2000. Given that, let's take a brief look at the relevant terminology associated with printing services and how Windows treats printing in general.

To Windows, a *printer* is the machinery that actually puts ink or toner on a page. There is also such a thing as a *logical printer*, which refers to the interface between the physical printer and the software that is instructing the printer to print. Think of the logical printer as the printer driver; you can indeed use the two terms interchangeably.

Some important points to consider:

- It is possible and practical in some instances to have multiple logical printers for every physical printer. I cover some of the scenarios in which such a configuration would be useful in this section.

- Conversely, you can associate one logical printer with multiple physical printers, creating a "printer cluster" of sorts. The technical term for this is a *printer pool*, and it's most commonly used when print jobs need to be directed to the first available printer. I also discuss that a bit later in this part of the chapter.

- Different types of drivers are available for use in Windows Server 2003. Level 2 drivers are older drivers that were written for Windows NT which run in kernel mode, a function of the OS that makes the entire OS vulnerable to any instability on the part of the driver. Fortunately, this becomes an issue only when you upgrade NT systems to Windows Server 2003. Level 3 drivers, which are newer and are meant for Windows 2000, XP, and Server 2003, run in protected user mode, which separates them from the kernel and isolates them from the rest of the operating system in the event they crash.

Internet Printing

There's also a feature introduced in Windows 2000 but retained in Windows Server 2003 known as *Internet printing*, which enables you to print directly to the printer over an intranet or the Internet using the HTTP protocol. You do this either by using an Internet-enabled printer, which some of the more expensive printers are, or by using Windows Internet printing services, which involves using IIS.

Although the technology sounds neat and useful in theory, think about it in practice. All of us remember junk faxes and fax attacks: taping a sheet of paper completely covered in black ink to itself so that it would continually transmit and waste paper and ink on the receiving end. Think about a cracker compromising your Internet-attached printer and the wasted paper and toner there. Also, some of the more expensive printers retain the last few print jobs in memory in case they need to be repeated—a sort of spooler cache. A cracker who penetrates the Windows Internet printer server could access the printer's memory and make off with copies of sensitive documents.

The bottom line is that this feature just isn't safe and isn't practical in today's hostile Internet environment. I strongly recommend against using this feature. Standard printing services are flexible enough for most of your needs, and if you really need to print over the Internet, do it to a Kinko's printer and have them deliver the job to you.

Setting Up Print Sharing

To configure a print server, use the Manage Your Server Wizard. Click Add or Remove a Role, and on the Server Role page, select Print Server and click Next. Then follow these steps:

1. Select the appropriate versions of operating systems that are running on client workstations on your network, and then click Next.

2. The wizard will summarize the choice you just made, in a ridiculously repetitive manner. Click Next to continue.

3. The Add Printer Wizard is started. Here, you'll actually add the printer drivers to your system. If your printer supports Plug and Play, click Cancel on this wizard—your printer and Windows will communicate without you having to go through the wizard.

4. On the Local or Network Printer page, choose whether to send print jobs directly to the printer, or to a secondary print server on another machine. If you want to send print jobs directly to a printer connected to the machine on which the wizard is running, or to a printer with its own network adapter, choose Local Printer. Otherwise, choose Network. Click Next when you're finished.

5. If the wizard can't detect a Plug-and-Play printer, the New Printer Detection screen will appear. Choose the printer port (most likely it's LPT1 for a directly connected printer). If you have a printer with its own network adapter, click the Create a New Port button, and follow the instructions that came with your printer. This commonly involves setting up a standard TCP/IP port and specifying the printer's IP address as the destination for print jobs. Click Next to continue.

6. If you selected a network printer or a printer attached to another computer, the Specify a Printer page appears. You can browse for a shared printer, type in the explicit pathname to the shared printer (e.g., \\printsrv\flr1-printer), or connect using TCP/IP to the remote printer. It's important to note that by selecting a network printer in this wizard, the print server role will not be fully installed on your server—you must have a local printer attached to be an official Windows print server. To proceed, enter the appropriate information where requested, and click Next.

7. On the Install Printer Software page, select the appropriate printer manufacturer and model. If it's not listed, find the appropriate drivers for the printer from the manufacturer, and click the Have Disk button to install those drivers. Click Next.

8. The Name Your Printer page appears. The default name is the manufacturer and model of the printer, but you might want to consider changing it to make it easier for users to recognize what printer it is and where it's located. Also, on this screen, determine if you want to use this printer as the default printer, and select Yes or No accordingly. Note that this doesn't set this printer as the one that clients use by default. It simply sets it as the default printer from the print server console. Click Next to proceed.

9. On the Printer Sharing page, Share Name is selected by default. Note that you must share a printer for this machine to act as a print server. The default share name is the first eight letters of the printer manufacturer and model, without spaces; you might change this name as well to something more meaningful to your users.

10. On the Location and Comment page, type a description of the print server location, and then, in the Comment box, type a general notation about the printer's capabilities and features. This step is optional. After you finish, click Next.

11. You can print a test page from the next screen to ensure you've configured the printer correctly. (The page prints when you finish the wizard, not immediately upon clicking Next.) Click Next when you're ready to proceed.

12. Click Finish to complete the wizard, or select the box to restart the wizard so that you can add more shared printers.

13. When you click Finish, the wizard installs the printer driver files. Then, if you chose to print a test page, the wizard attempts to print that page. If you selected All Windows clients in step 1, the Add Printer Driver Wizard starts after you complete the Add Printer Wizard. You can use the Add Printer Driver Wizard to install client printer drivers onto the print server, which then can distribute them to clients automatically. See later in this section for this procedure.

14. After you complete the Add Printer Wizard and, if necessary, the Add Printer Driver Wizard, you see the This Server is Now a Print Server page. Review the logs to see what changes were made, and then click Finish.

You can remove the print server role through the Manage Your Server Wizard by clicking Add or Remove a Role, selecting Print Server, and clicking Remove. This will unshare and then remove any shared printers on that server, making them unavailable for use over the network.

The Print Management Console

The Print Management Console, a feature in Windows Server 2003 R2, unifies all printer and print server management tasks into one convenient, efficient interface. The PMC can manage all network printers on print servers running Windows 2000 Server, Windows Server 2003, or Windows Server 2003 R2, making it a great tool to get an all-encompassing picture of the printers in your organization.

To install the PMC, use the Add/Remove Programs applet within Control Panel. Select Windows Components, and under Management and Monitoring Tools, check the Print Management Console component. Click OK, and Windows will install the PMC for you.

Figure 3-42 shows the Print Management Console when you first load it.

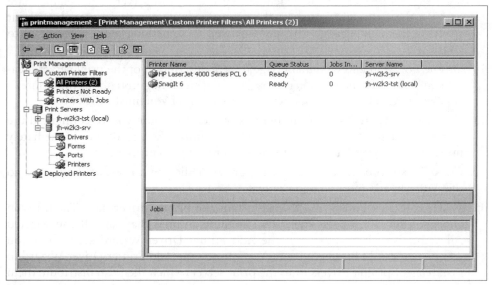

Figure 3-42. The Print Management Console

You can add various print servers on your network to the list on the left side of the console by right-clicking on Print Servers and selecting Add/Remove Servers. Either type the name of the server or browse to it. Repeat as necessary.

Adding and viewing printers

Using the PMC, you can automatically add all printers located on the same subnet as the print server—a task that involves detecting the printers, installing the appropriate drivers, creating and configuring the queues, and enabling sharing. This is all done by the PMC without any intervention from you, with the exception of being prompted for drivers for some more obscure printers. All you need is to (1) be on the subnet as the printers you want to autodetect and (2) have administrator credentials for the print server. Just right-click on the local print server within the PMC and select Automatically add network printers. Click Start, and you're done.

To give yourself a more organized view of the printers on your network, you can add printer filters, which restrict a view to only printers which meet a certain criteria. The PMC comes with three built-in filters—all printers (which isn't really a filter after all), printers that have a status of "Not Ready," and printers that currently have an active job. You might find it useful to create specific views of all printers in a building, printers that have the capability to print in color, or all printers out of paper. With each filter, you can specify that an email or script be run or sent when there are printers that satisfy the filter's criteria—useful for those problem printers.

To set up a filter:

1. Right-click on the Custom Printer Filters folder, and then select Add New Printer Filter.
2. The New Printer Filter Wizard will appear. Type a name and a description for the filter. You can also choose to include the number of printers that satisfy the criteria of the filter beside its name in the PMC by clicking the checkbox. Click Next to continue.
3. The Define a Printer Filter screen appears.
4. The Set Notifications (Optional) page appears. Choose either to set an email notification (which requires a destination email address and an outgoing SMTP server) or a script to run.
5. Click Finish.

Performing mass administration tasks

By using the All Printers view of the PMC, you can perform some mass actions on all the printers listed, including pausing printing, resuming printing, canceling all jobs on all printers, listing all of the printers in Active Directory, or removing all printers from Active Directory. Just select the All Printers view in the PMC, and then select all printers in the righthand pane. Right-click anywhere in the pane, and then select the bulk action you'd like to perform.

Device drivers

The PMC can list, by server, each printer driver installed on your print servers. This is useful for seeing which print servers support which types of printers, and you also have a convenient interface to add, remove, or reinstall print drivers. You can perform all of these actions by expanding the particular print server in question in the left pane, right-clicking on the Drivers section of the tree, and selecting Manage Drivers. From there, you can:

- Click Add to launch the Add Printer Driver Wizard.
- Select a printer driver from the list and click the Remove button to clear it from that server.
- Select a driver and click Reinstall to reinstall the driver.
- Select a driver and click Properties to view the details for a particular driver.

Custom Printing Configurations

In this section, I'll look at some custom printing configurations and scenarios which you might encounter in your organization.

Controlling the print spooler service

The print spooler service controls all parts of printing in Windows, taking documents from applications that request printing services and distributing them to the correct printer drivers as needed. You can control the service through both the GUI and the command line.

To view the print spooler service status through Windows, follow these steps:

1. Open the Computer Management snap-in.
2. Expand the Services node.
3. Find the Print Spooler service in the righthand pane, right-click it, and select Properties from the context menu.
4. Click Start or Stop to perform either task on the service.

To start or stop the printer spooler from a command line, follow these steps:

1. Open a command prompt.
2. Execute the following commands, depending on your intent: `net start spooler` to start the spooler, or `net stop spooler` to stop it.

The spooler service can have dependencies from other services. If other services need the spooler to be running, you'll be prompted with a list of those services that need to be stopped before Windows will allow you to stop the service.

Also note that the print spooler service is authenticated through the Local Computer system account by default, not through a specific user account.

Configuring default printer settings

By using the Printing Defaults section of the properties page, you can set the default settings, such as paper size, layout orientation, tray selection, and number of copies printed, for all users who connect to that specific printer. Individual users can further customize these settings by using the properties page for the printer as listed on their client workstation, but those settings will apply only to that installation, not to all users who connect to the networked printer.

In security-sensitive environments, you might want to set the default paper source to Manual. This ensures that a document will not print until the user feeds the paper to the printer, so confidential information is not left on a printer tray. You also might consider purchasing a printer that supports a password authentication feature, which holds a print job from actually being printed until the user enters a password at the printer console. You usually find this feature on the more expensive network printers from HP, Tektronix, and others.

To configure default settings for a printer, follow these steps:

1. Open the Printers and Faxes Control Panel applet.
2. Right-click the printer you want to use and select Properties.
3. Navigate to the Advanced tab and click Printing Defaults.
4. Click the Layout and Paper/Quality tabs and the Advanced button on each to see the available choices and to specify the new default settings.
5. Click OK to apply the new settings.

Choosing a separator page

A *separator page* is simply a piece of paper that follows a job to acknowledge a switch in printer language. It's useful for a high-volume shared network printer, where many people's jobs go, so that the users don't get confused about printer languages.

You need the Manage Printers permission—set via your user account properties in Local Users and Groups inside the Control Panel for nondomain machines or Active Directory Users and Computers for domain computers—to adjust the settings for the separator page. Note that in smaller networks or individualized security groups, it might be easier to assign the Manage Printers or Manage Documents permissions to the group that is associated with a particular printer. For example, if the accounting department has their own printer (called ACCTG1) that no one else uses, by granting the Manage Printers right to all members of the ACCTG1 Users group, you can delegate a good bit of administrative responsibility. Any member of the group can then add and delete documents from, modify, or otherwise manage the print queue itself.

To enable and choose a separator page, follow these steps:

1. Open the Printers and Faxes Control Panel applet.
2. Right-click the printer you want to use, and select Properties.
3. Navigate to the Sharing tab and click Separator Page.
4. Click Browse and find your *C:\Windows\System32* folder or equivalent.

5. Specify one of the following separator page files that Windows provides in the *System32* folder:

   - The file *pcl.sep* prints a page after switching the printer to PCL printing.
   - The file *sysprint.sep* prints a page after switching the printer to PostScript printing.
   - The file *pscript.sep* does not print a page after switching the printer to Post-Script printing.

Adding printer drivers for other operating systems

Take, for example, this scenario: you have clients running other operating system versions that need to connect to the same shared printer, and you want to automate driver installation for those clients.

Especially in larger organizations, it's generally a good idea to install drivers for other operating systems on the server to facilitate printer setup, deployment, and management. If the drivers for a particular printer are on a server on your network, it's easy to construct a login script or other GP-based automated install utility to deploy a new network printer to a group of users and desktops.

Storing drivers on the server also makes pushing updated revisions of the driver a lot easier. NT 4.0, Windows 2000, and XP Home clients check printer drivers on the print server each time the connection to the server is reestablished. NT 3.1, 3.5, and 3.51 clients look for an updated driver each time the client spooler service is started. New copies of the drivers are downloaded at each of these times if newer versions of the drivers are available from the server. Windows 9x-based print drivers are not capable of being kept current automatically, so you must manually update the drivers on these clients when you do a server-based update for other platforms.

To install printer drivers for other operating systems, follow these steps:

1. Open the Printers and Faxes Control Panel applet.
2. Right-click the printer you want to publish into the directory, click Properties, and navigate to the Sharing tab.
3. Click Additional Drivers.
4. Check the checkboxes for the additional operating systems your clients are running, and click OK.

Publishing shared printers into Active Directory

Publishing a printer to Active Directory accomplishes much the same effect as publishing a file share: your users can search for it within Start/Find or Start/Search (depending on the operating system) without needing to call the help desk to find the closest printer.

Of course, you must share a printer before you can publish it to the directory. If you add a printer to a server running Server 2003, it is shared by default. However, printers attached to computers running client operating systems—Windows XP, Windows 2000, Windows NT, and the like—are not shared by default. You must share them manually. As well, the user account you use to share and publish a printer into the directory must have the Manage Printers permission on the user account. Note that to publish a printer shared using a computer running Windows NT, you must use the Active Directory Users and Computers snap-in.

If you have Active Directory domains and your GP settings are still at their default configuration, the options to Automatically publish new printers in Active Directory and Allow printers to be published still are enabled. Therefore, the printer will be published by default.

The full name of a shared printer (for example, \\SERVER\LASER_PCL) should contain no more than 32 characters, for maximum legacy application compatibility.

To publish a printer to Active Directory, follow these steps:

1. Open the Printers and Faxes Control Panel applet.
2. Right-click the printer you want to publish into the directory, and navigate to the Sharing tab.
3. Click Share This Printer, and enter a name for the printer share.
4. Check the List in the Directory checkbox.
5. Click OK.

Setting up alternate/restricted printing times

Printers are always available by default, but for various reasons you might want to restrict their availability. For example, if you have an expensive printer that is used only for producing camera-ready proofs and the proofs are due by 1:00 p.m. each day, you might want to set the printer as available only between 6:00 a.m. and 1:00 p.m. to help prevent wasting the expensive resources it uses for jobs other than those proofs.

To restrict printing to certain times of the day, follow these steps:

1. Open the Printers and Faxes Control Panel applet.
2. Right-click the printer you want to configure in this manner and select Properties.
3. Navigate to the Advanced tab, and then click Available From.
4. To set the time period that the printer will be available, click the up or down arrows, or alternatively, type a start and end time, such as "9:00 a.m. to 5:00 p.m."
5. Click OK to finish the wizard.

Controlling print priority between groups

Let's say you want to give a user or a certain group priority access to a printer. How do you do that?

The process is simple, if non-intuitive: create two logical queues for the same physical printer, one with a higher priority than the other, and restrict the higher-priority queue to the members of the group that require it. Note that setting a priority on a single printer with only one print queue is effectively doing nothing. You must have two or more logical print queues for one physical printer to take advantage of the priority feature.

To control print priority between groups, follow these steps:

1. Open the Printers and Faxes Control Panel applet.
2. Right-click the printer you want to configure in this manner and select Properties.
3. Navigate to the Advanced tab. In the Priority box, click the up or down arrows and click OK when you reach the priority level you want. Alternatively, you can type in a priority level between 1 and 99 and click OK (1 is the lowest priority, and 99 is the highest priority).
4. Add another printer, configured exactly the same, using the Add Printer Wizard. This creates a second print queue for the same physical printer.
5. Right-click New Logical Printer, select Properties, and navigate to the Advanced tab.
6. Set a priority higher than that of the first printer queue, as defined in step 3.
7. Configure the permissions on the higher-priority print queue to allow only certain groups to print to it. Leave the regular print queue open to all if you want.
8. Instruct the regular group of users to use the first logical printer name and the group with higher priority to use the second logical printer name.

Using PostScript and PCL

If you want users to print to a printer that supports both PostScript and PCL, create two different print queues, one for each language. Users can then print to the appropriate queue, depending on the language they need.

 You also can use this procedure for any printer that supports multiple languages—it is not restricted to just PostScript and PCL.

To print to a printer that supports both PostScript and PCL, follow these steps:

1. Open the Printers and Faxes Control Panel applet.
2. Double-click Add Printer and click Next.

3. Follow the wizard until it prompts you to choose the make and model of the printer. Click the appropriate model under the respective manufacturer, with either PostScript (PS) or PCL as indicated. For example, for an HP LaserJet 8100 series printer, click HP LaserJet 8100 Series PS to configure a PostScript queue.

4. Continue the wizard until that queue is created.

5. Begin the wizard once again, this time to add a second logical queue (for the other printer language) for the same physical printer.

6. When the wizard asks you to choose the make and model of the printer, click the appropriate model under the respective manufacturer and select the other language that's supported that you didn't configure in step 3.

7. Continue the wizard until that queue is created.

 It is highly recommended when you create a PCL print queue and a PostScript print queue that they both have the same name with the exception of adding a "_PS" on the end of the PostScript queue name. This way, when you sort your printers, it will be easy for you to tell which printers have an associated PS queue, as they will all sort together. It's a useful method for when you are deleting or performing maintenance on old printer queues.

Retaining all print jobs

For regulatory reasons, you might want to keep a copy, inside a print queue, of everything that is printed from that queue.

To retain documents in a print spool, follow these steps:

1. Open the Printers and Faxes Control Panel applet.

2. Right-click the printer you want to configure in this manner, and select Properties.

3. Navigate to the Advanced tab, and check the Keep Printed Documents checkbox. Click OK to finish.

When retaining copies of the documents you print from a queue, you need to carefully monitor the disk space on the server that hosts the queue. To clear out the disk space occupied by the copies of the documents, uncheck the Keep Printed Documents checkbox as described in step 3.

Configuring printing to multiple physical printers

Printer pooling enables you, as the administrator, to create a set of printers that print multiple copies of documents when they are sent to the queue. This is useful in law or customer service applications, in which printed document review must be completed in a timely fashion.

To use printer pooling, you must have identical printers with identical drivers.

To set up a printer pool, follow these steps:

1. Open the Printers and Faxes Control Panel applet.
2. Right-click the printer you've set up and select Properties.
3. Navigate to the Ports tab and select Enable Printer Pooling.
4. Finally, select the ports to which the printers you want to pool are connected. Click OK to finish.

Adding color profiles

Color profiles help users of publishing software synchronize colors between their client computer's monitor and the color printer. Often, colors are mismatched and painted differently between each device, which can result in substandard output from the printer. By associating a color profile with a printer, publishing software on the client computer can use the profile to ensure the colors that are displayed on the screen are the colors that will be printed on the document itself.

Native to Windows is a color profile that is compatible with any device that supports the Image Color Management 2.0 specification. This file is: *%SystemRoot%\ System32\Spool\Drivers\Color\sRGB Color Space Profile.icm.*

Logically, it follows that color profiles are supported only on color printers, and the Color Management tab within a printer's properties page is found only on printers that the driver installed on the server specifies as color printers.

To associate a color profile with a printer, follow these steps:

1. Open the Printers and Faxes Control Panel applet.
2. Right-click the color printer with which you want to associate a profile and click Properties.
3. Navigate to the Color Management tab and click Add.
4. Browse for the profile file. You typically can find them in the *System32\Spool\ Drivers\Color* folder under the Windows root folder.
5. Select the file and click Add to associate the profile with the printer.

Tracking the location of printers

If you have more than one Active Directory site, you can enable printer location tracking to help your users identify the geographic location of printers within the directory. To use printer location tracking, you need to have an IP address assignment system that corresponds closely to the physical layout of your sites, and a subnet object within Active Directory for each site.

Active Directory sites—as well as other Active Directory parlance—are covered in detail in Chapter 5, and Group Policy is discussed thoroughly in Chapter 6.

To enable printer location tracking, you must first create a subnet object for each site, which is named based on a common pattern that you determine. Configure a Group Policy object to preconfigure a printer search location for each user. Enter the printer's location (based on the naming convention assigned in the first phase of this procedure) inside its properties page and publish that information to the AD.

The following instructions step you through this process:

1. Open the Active Directory Sites and Services snap-in.

2. Right-click the subnet (under Sites and Services, choose Sites, and then Subnets), and choose Properties.

3. On the next screen, click the site with which to associate the subnet and click OK. Figure 3-43 demonstrates this.

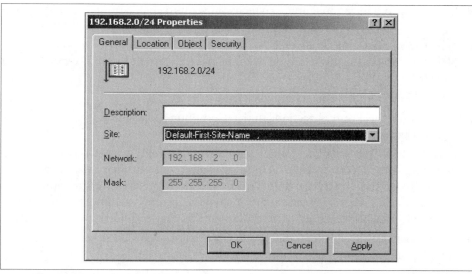

Figure 3-43. Associating a site with a subnet

4. Repeat as necessary for all subnets and sites.

5. Once you've associated all sites in your tree with a subnet, right-click once more on each subnet, and navigate to the Location tab.

6. Enter a descriptive location based on a common pattern. For example, many companies might want to consider using a consistent pattern such as *country/ state/city*. Using this example, a subnet in the sales office in Charlotte might be identified as US/NC/Charlotte. Figure 3-44 shows this step.

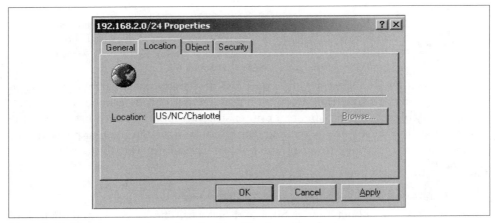

Figure 3-44. Entering a consistent location identifier for each subnet

7. Repeat as necessary for all subnets and sites.

8. Open Active Directory Users and Computers.

9. Identify the organizational unit to which you want to enable printer location tracking, right-click it and select Properties.

10. Navigate to the Group Policy tab, and click New... to create a new policy object. Name the object (in this example, we'll name it Printer Location Pre-population) and click OK.

11. Select the new policy object, and click Edit.

12. Navigate to the Printers section, under Computer Configuration and Administrative Templates.

13. Double-click "Pre-populate printer search location text" within the policy template list. When you do this, Windows clients will automatically detect their subnet (based on their site within AD) and populate this information in the Search field, so when clients search for available printers geographically close to them, they will be presented with a complete list. Figure 3-45 shows this step.

14. Now, open up the Printers and Faxes Control Panel on each server that hosts shared printers. Right-click a printer and select Properties.

15. Type the printer location (alternately, click Browse to find it). Enter the location based on the naming convention used earlier and on the printer's location. For example, the color laser on the third floor of the Chicago office, as described earlier in this section, might be named *US/IL/Chicago/Sales/Col-Laser-3*.

16. Repeat for all printers in the directory.

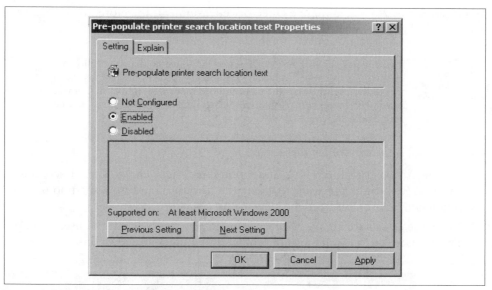

Figure 3-45. Enabling the printer prepopulation policy

Roaming User Profiles

Do you have a very mobile local user base? Do your users tend to move between machines in your location, and if so, do they often complain to you that their personalized settings and desktop customizations don't travel with them? If you are nodding your head in the affirmative, then roaming user profiles may make your phone ring a bit less.

Roaming user profiles are simply collections of settings and configurations for each user that are stored in a network location. Once you perform some fairly simple configuration, every time a user logs on to a machine in your domain with his or her domain credentials, that user's settings will follow them and automatically be applied to their logon session at that particular machine.

In this section, I'll show you how to create a baseline profile that will be used by default for new users wherever they log in, and then I'll share some tips on how to make a mass deployment of roaming profiles—particularly for users who already have customized their working environments—a bit easier for you.

Creating a Basic Profile

Before you begin creating a roaming profile, you need to create a temporary user on your machine, and then configure that temporary account's profile however you would like it. For the remainder of this section, I will assume that you're running

Windows Server 2003 in an Active Directory environment; therefore, to create a new user, you will need to load Active Directory Users and Computers.

 If you're not running Active Directory yet, have no fear: the following instructions can apply to local users and groups as well. You just need to add the user through the Computer Management applet in Control Panel. For more information on Active Directory, including creating users and groups in AD, see Chapter 5.

Once the tool is loaded, follow these steps:

1. Within Active Directory Users and Computers, right-click on the Users folder (or wherever you might want to create the test user), and from the pop-up context menu, select User from the New menu.

2. Enter the details for this temporary user. In my case, I'll call the user Example Profile User with a logon name of profiletest. Figure 3-46 shows this.

Figure 3-46. Creating a test user

3. Click Next, and then give this temporary user a secure password.

4. Finish out the wizard, and then log off of the machine.

5. Now, log into the machine using the temporary account you just created.

What just happened? Essentially, creating the temporary account allows you to create a "template," and within the environment of that template you can customize the settings and appearance that will make it into the future roaming profile. All of these settings are stored in a directory on the local computer, which is called something like this:

```
C:\Documents and Settings\<username>
```

Once you've logged into the machine using the temporary account, configure everything how you would like it: add shortcuts to the desktop, change the format of the Start menu, change the colors, font, and size of windows and title bars, and so forth. Remember: we want this profile to be the default for all users, so create the profile's configuration with that baseline in mind. Once you have finished your customization, log off of the machine, and then log in again with an administrator account.

Making Profiles Available on the Server

You might be wondering at this point what is actually stored within a user profile. A profile is actually made up of several different folders:

- The Application Data folder contains program-specific settings and user security settings that correspond with applications that person has used.
- The Cookies folder contains all of the web cookies a user has encountered and chosen to allow during his or her travails on the web.
- The Desktop folder, as obvious as it might sound, contains files, folders, shortcuts, and data regarding the appearance of the desktop on the user's screen.
- The Favorites folder contains shortcuts to the user's preferred web sites and other frequently visited locations.
- The Local Settings folder contains application data, history, and temporary files.
- The My Documents folder contains files for the user, music, pictures, and other things the user tends to store in his home directory.
- The Nethood folder contains shortcuts to sites in My Network Places.
- The Printhood folder contains printer shortcuts.
- The Recent folder shows the most recently accessed files and folders.
- The Send To folder is where the Send To menu, a popular "right-clicking" destination, is obtained. This folder can contain shortcuts to popular target destinations, like a floppy drive, My Documents, a printer, and so on.
- The Start Menu folder contains items on the user's Start menu.
- The Templates folder holds templates for applications, like Microsoft Word and Excel.

If you can't see all of these folders, don't worry; they're most likely still hidden. To see them, select Folder Options from any Explorer window's Tools menu, click the View tab, and select the option to Show Hidden Files and Folders.

With that said, the next task is to actually send the profile to your network server. To do this, create a folder on the network drive that will hold roaming profiles. In my case, I'll create a share on my Windows Server 2003 machine called Profiles. Then, on the client machine where your new baseline profile is stored, go into the Control Panel and double-click on System. Then follow these steps:

1. Navigate to the Advanced tab.
2. Under the User Profiles section, click the Settings button.
3. The User Profiles screen appears.
4. Select your temporary user, and then click the Copy To button. The Copy To screen appears, as shown in Figure 3-47. Enter the path to the network profile folder in the Copy Profile To box. (Windows will automatically create a folder underneath the Profiles folder with the appropriate username.)

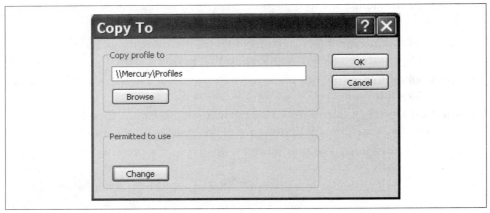

Figure 3-47. Copying the profile to the network server

5. Under the Permitted to Use section, click the Change button.
6. Enter the name of the temporary user you created earlier in this procedure, and then click OK.
7. Click OK on the Copy To screen, and then click OK on the User Profiles screen.

 When you're determining where to put the shared location for user profiles, try to put them on a member server as opposed to a domain controller. Domain controllers have their own issues to deal with, and there's no need to bog them down with profile processing as well as authentication, replication, authenticating, emulating, and so on. While you're at it, make sure that the server you choose is regularly backed up so you don't lose all of your user profiles to a machine failure.

You should be back out to the desktop now. Now, load Active Directory Users and Computers again, right-click on your temporary user and select Properties from the pop-up context menu. Navigate to the Profile tab, and then in the Profile Path box in the User Profile section, enter the full network path to the profile you just copied, including the username. Figure 3-48 shows this.

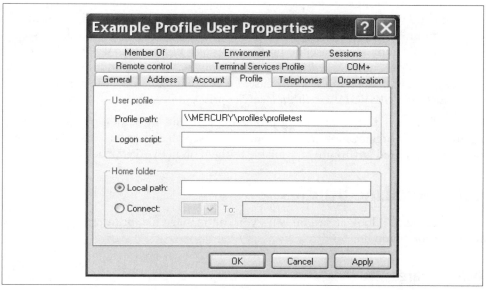

Figure 3-48. Specifying the path for the user's roaming profile

Click OK, and you're done. The temporary user can now use the profile stored on the network, and whenever he logs onto a machine that is a member of the domain with his domain credentials, he will receive a copy of his profile, including any changes he makes at any time.

On Deploying Profiles En Masse

If this worked successfully for you, you can repeat this procedure for other users as needed. Here are a few tips, tricks, and "from-the-streets" experiences to hopefully make the repetitive process a bit easier:

- If you are selecting multiple accounts in Active Directory to configure a profile path for each, you can use the %USERNAME% variable in the profile path. Windows will sort out the correct username for each user.

- If your users already have profiles that have been created on their individual machines, you don't necessarily have to copy their profiles to the server. The simple act of specifying a profile path in the user's account properties tells Windows that if no profile exists on the network, it needs to automatically copy the locally stored profile to the server the next time the user logs out. The bottom line here is that if you want to save some time, specify the profile path in your users' account properties, and then tell them to log in to the machine that has their desktop and appearance configured how they like it. Then, have them log off, and their profile will automatically be copied.

- If you are creating a brand new user that has no profile data anywhere on your network, you'll probably want him or her (and any other new users you create in the future) to automatically receive a default roaming profile. To do this, you need only copy your baseline profile to \\<SERVERNAME>\SYSVOL\<yourdomainname>\Scripts\Default User. Replace your server name and domain name as appropriate. For example, in my case, I would configure my baseline profile to \\MERCURY\SYSVOL\hasselltech.local\Scripts\Default User.

That's all there is to basic roaming profile deployment. By setting up roaming user profiles in your organization, your mobile user base will always have their customizations and preferred environment available to them on networked machines.

Command Line Utilities

In this section, I'll look at several ways you can manage file, print, and user services from the command line.

Using Shares

Sometimes it's inconvenient to use the Windows GUI to map a drive—this is a problem particularly in logon scripts. How do you use a batch file to tell the mouse pointer to move over to My Network Places? Instead, there's a better way. The net use command enables you to map any drive to any server on your network, and in some cases, outside networks, too. The syntax is:

```
net use drive \\server\share
```

Here are some common examples that you should find useful.

To map drive H to Lisa Johnson's home directory on server MERCURY:

```
net use H: \\mercury\users\lmjohnson
```

To map the first available drive letter to the same directory:

```
net use * \\mercury\users\lmjohnson
```

Sometimes you might need to connect to a share on a domain that isn't trusted by your home domain. If you have an account on that domain, you can use it to connect, like so:

```
net use H:
\\foreignmachine\sharename
  /user:foreigndomain\username
```

(If you need to use a password, you'll be prompted for it.)

If you need to terminate a connection or map to a server, use the /d switch:

```
net use \\mercury\users\lmjohnson /d
```

To disconnect all drive mappings on the local machine maps:

```
net use * /d
```

To connect to a foreign machine (152.1.171.133 in this example) over the Internet or an intranet without relying on name resolution:

```
net use H: \\152.1.171.133\c$
```

You also can use a different account with the IP address:

```
net use H:
\\152.1.171.133\c$
/user:hasselltech\hassell
```

And you can specify that this mapping be for the current session only and not be restored upon logon. This is a feature that I call *map persistency*—keeping the same mappings across login sessions, a big timesaver for your users. To do so:

```
net use H:
\\152.1.171.133\c$
/persistent:no
```

FSUTIL

To set up default quotas and modify them using the command line, type the following at the prompt:

```
fsutil quota modify [VolumeOrDrive] [warninglevel] [hardquota] [username]
```

replacing the text in brackets with the appropriate information as specified in the following list:

VolumeOrDrive
> The drive letter or volume name of the disk on which you want to modify a quota. Volume names are tricky to specify because you must do so using the globally unique identifier (GUID), which can be a long string of seemingly random numbers.

warninglevel
> The amount of space at which warnings will be recorded in the system event log.

hardquota
> The amount of space at which users will reach their maximum allowed disk space.

username
> The user to which this quota specification applies.

Using *fsutil.exe*, you can create scripts to automatically set quota entries upon new-user creation to work around the limitation of assigning quotas to groups, as described earlier in this chapter. *fsutil.exe* can help you access functionality more quickly and efficiently than you can by using the GUI interface. The following examples, designed to run from a command line, illustrate the quota functionality available through *fsutil.exe*.

To disable quota support on drive C:

```
fsutil quota disable C:
```

To enable quota support on drive E:

```
fsutil quota enforce E:
```

To set a 250MB quota for Lisa Johnson (user ID *lmjohnson*) on drive C:

```
fsutil quota modify C: 250000000 lmjohnson
```

To list the current quotas set on drive D:

```
fsutil quota query D:
```

To track the disk usage—in other words, to list which users are taking up what amount or portion of space—on drive F:

```
fsutil quota track F:
```

To list all users over quota on any volume on the server:

```
fsutil quota violations
```

ABECMD

ABECMD is the command-line counterpart to the access-based enumeration add-in to Windows Server 2003. You can enable access on a specific shared folder, on all shared folders on the current computer, or on shared folders on another machine. The syntax works like this:

`abecmd /enable "Users Folder"`
Enables ABE on the "Users Folder" shared folder

`abecmd /enable /all`
Enables ABE on all shared folders on the current machine

`abecmd /disable "Users Folder"`
Disables ABE on the "Users Folder" shared folder

`abecmd /enable 192.168.0.2 "Common"`
Enables ABE on the "Common" shared folder residing on the machine at IP address 192.168.0.2

Managing Offline Folders

To make a share's contents available offline from the command line, at a prompt type:

```
net share
nameofshare
   /CACHE:[manual | documents | programs | none]
```

/CACHE:manual enables manual client caching of programs and documents from this share. /CACHE: documents enables automatic caching of documents from this share /CACHE:programs enables automatic caching of documents and programs (distinguished by their file extension) from this share. /CACHE:none disables caching from this share.

VSSADMIN

The GUI for managing shadow copies is somewhat complete; however, it lacks the ability to specify on what disk or volume shadow copies are stored. Also, an administrator cannot delete specific shadow copy files using the GUI. This might be needed if a user creates an incorrect version of a file, then leaves and another worker comes back the next day. An administrator might need to delete the previous version as soon as possible so that the new user doesn't inadvertently work from the incorrect version.

The *vssadmin.exe* command-line utility was created to offer administrators the ability to control these factors. I'll now walk through several examples.

This command specifies that storage for shadow copies (known as an *association*) of drive *C:* will be stored on drive *D::*

```
vssadmin Add ShadowStorage /For=C: /On=D: /MaxSize=150MB
```

The maximum space the association can occupy on the shadow copy storage volume is 150 MB. If a value is not specified, there is no limit to the amount of space shadow copies can use. Shadow copies require at least 100 MB of space, and you can specify the maximum amount in KB, MB, GB, TB, PB, and EB, although it's assumed if you don't use a suffix, the value is in bytes.

This command creates a new shadow copy of drive *E::*

```
vssadmin Create Shadow /For=E: /AutoRetry=2
```

The /AutoRetry switch dictates that if another process is attempting to make shadow copies at the same time vssadmin is attempting to make them, the utility will keep trying for two minutes.

This command deletes the oldest shadow copy on drive *C::*

```
vssadmin Delete Shadows /For=C: /Oldest
```

You can use the /all switch to instead delete all shadow copies that can be deleted. You also can specify a specific shadow copy to delete by using /Shadow=ID, where ID is the hexadecimal number you obtain through the List Shadows command, covered later in this section.

This command deletes the storage space on drive *D:* that is used to store shadow copies of drive *C:*:

```
vssadmin Delete ShadowStorage /For=C: /On=D:
```

If you leave off the /On switch, all shadow copy storage associations for drive C: will be deleted.

This command modifies the maximum size for a shadow-copy storage association between drives *C:* and *D:*:

```
vssadmin Resize ShadowStorage /For=C: /On=D: /MaxSize=150MB
```

Again, the maximum size has to be 100 MB or more. If you decrease the maximum size, older shadow copies can be deleted to make room for more recent shadow copies.

Here are some other useful commands:

This command lists registered volume shadow copy providers:

```
vssadmin List Providers
```

This command lists existing volume shadow copies and their ID numbers, for use with the Delete Shadows command:

```
vssadmin List Shadows
```

This command shows the disks that are eligible to support shadow copy functionality:

```
vssadmin List ShadowStorage
```

NTBACKUP

To back up to a file or tape from the command line, use:

```
ntbackup backup [systemstate] "@FileName.bks"/J "JobName" [/P "PoolName"] [/G
"GUIDName"][/T "TapeName"] [/N "MediaName"] [/F "FileName"][/D "SetDescription"] /DS
"ServerName"][/IS "ServerName"] [/A] [/V:yes | no] [/R:yes | no][/L:f | s | n] /M
"BackupType"][/RS:yes | no] [/HC:on | off] [/SNAP:on | off]
```

Table 3-3 explains the various options.

Table 3-3. NTBACKUP command-line options

Option	Explanation
@*FileName*.bks	Specifies the name of the backup selection file (*.bks* file) to be used. The @ character must precede the name of the backup selection file. The *.bks* file must be created using the GUI version of NTBACKUP, and is essentially a summary of what set of files a particular job is supposed to back up.
	Alternatively, you could supply the path to the drive or file to back up—for example, D:\.
/J "*JobName*"	Specifies the job name to be filled in the post-backup report.
/F "*FileName*"	If you back up to a file, this specifies the path of that file.
	You *cannot* use the /P, /G, and /T switches when using /F.
/T "*TapeName*"	If you back up to a tape, this specifies the tape to which to overwrite or append data.
/P "*PoolName*"	If you back up to a tape, this specifies the media pool to use. This is usually a subpool of the media specified with the /N switch.
	You *cannot* use the /A, /G, /F, and /T switches when using /P.
/G "*GUIDName*"	If you back up to a tape, this specifies the tape to which to overwrite or append data.
	You *cannot* use the /P switch when using /G.
/N "*MediaName*"	If you back up to a tape, this specifies the new tape name.
	You *cannot* use the /A switch when using /N.
/A	If you back up to a tape, this specifies to perform an append operation.
	You *must* use either the /G or /T switch when using /A. You *cannot* use the /P switch when using /A.
/D "*SetDescription*"	Specifies a label for each backup.
/DS "*ServerName*"	Backs up the directory service information and contents for an Exchange Server machine.
/IS "*ServerName*"	Backs up the Information Store on an Exchange Server computer.
/V:yes | no	Specifies whether to perform a verification pass when the backup is complete.
/R:yes | no	Restricts access to the tape to members of the Administrators group only.
/L:f | s | n	Specifies the type of log file to be written. "f" indicates a full file, "s" indicates a summary, and "n" instructs NTBACKUP not to write any logs.
/M "*BackupType*"	Specifies the type of backup. Replace BackupType with one of the following: copy, daily, differential, incremental, or normal.
/RS:yes | no	Backs up the migrated data files located in Remote Storage. (This also is backed up when you select the system root folder to be included in a job.)
/HC:on | off	If available, uses hardware compression for the job.
/SNAP:on | off	Specifies whether to use a volume shadow copy for the backup.
Systemstate	Includes system state data (registry and other critical system information) in the backup.

Using NTBACKUP from the command line has two important limitations. One, you cannot restore files, and two, you cannot back up system state data on a remote computer.

Actually, you can back up system state data on a remote computer—check out Hack 93 in Mitch Tulloch's book *Windows Server Hacks* (O'Reilly).

Switches /V, /R, /L, /M, /RS, and /HC default to the setting in the GUI version of Backup unless you explicitly set them on the command line.

Sample scenarios

In this section, I'll offer some possibilities for automating backups using the command line. You should find that it's easy to modify the examples provided here (if they don't fit your needs as-is) to extend their capabilities.

The first example executes a normal backup named "Nightly" of the network share \\winsrv-1\c$. This example selects media from the Tapes pool and names the tape "Nightly NTBACKUP 1." The description of the backup job is "Standard evening backup." A verification pass is done, access to the tape is open to all, and only a summary log will be produced, Remote Storage data is not backed up, and hardware compression will be used.

```
ntbackup backup \\winsrv-1\c$ /m normal /j "Nightly" /p "Tapes" /n
"Nightly NTBACKUP 1" /d "Standard evening backup" /v:yes /r:no /l:s
/rs:no /hc:on
```

The next example starts a copy backup named "Lunchtime" of the E: drive on the server itself. The backed-up files and folders are appended to the tape named "Nightly NTBACKUP 1." Because no other switches are present, the default settings in the GUI version of Backup are used.

```
ntbackup backup e:\ /j "Lunchtime" /a /t "Nightly NTBACKUP 1" /m copy
```

The following example performs a backup using the GUI Backup program's current setting. The program looks at the file *weekend-backup.bks*, located in the *C:\Program Files\Windows NT\ntbackup\data* directory, to select the particular data to back up. The backup job is named "Weekend" and it overwrites the tape named "Weekend NTBACKUP 1" with the new name "Weekend NTBACKUP 2." It also includes System Statesystem state information.

```
ntbackup backup systemstate "@C:\Program Files\Windows NT\ntbackup\data\
weekend-backup.bks" /j "Weekend" /t "Weekend NTBACKUP 1" /n "Weekend
NTBACKUP 2"
```

The final example backs up a remote share to a file named *backup.bkf* using the Backup program's default values for the backup type, verification setting, logging level, hardware compression, and access restrictions:

```
ntbackup backup \\win-srv2\acctg$ /j "To File on MWF" /f "E:\backup.bkf"
```

When running this command again, if you want to append another backup to the existing file, simply add the /a switch as shown. Otherwise, you will overwrite the existing file automatically.

```
ntbackup backup \\ntsrv-5\sales-execs$ /j "To File on TH" /f "E:\
backup.bkf" /a
```

CIPHER

You can control encryption from the command line using the CIPHER utility, located in *%SystemRoot%\System32*:

- To encrypt a folder using the command line, run cipher /e foldername.
- To decrypt a folder using the command line, run cipher /d foldername.
- To encrypt a folder and all its subdirectories recursively, run cipher /e /s:foldername.
- To encrypt a single file within a directory, run cipher /e /a filename.
- To decrypt a single file within a directory, run cipher /d /a filename.
- To create a user's file encryption key before the first encryption request is submitted, run cipher /k.
- To generate an EFS recovery agent, allowing a user other than the one who encrypted a file or folder to decrypt it in emergency situations, run cipher /r:filename.
- filename represents the name of a file without its extension, because the command will generate both a *.PFX* file containing the certificate and private key and a *.CER* file containing only the certificate.

You also can decrypt files and folders quickly from the command line if you are the recovery agent for those folders or the user who originally encrypted the objects. Use the cipher command with the /u and /a switches. For example, to decrypt a file called *man_ch3r3.doc*, issue the following command:

```
cipher /u /a man_ch3r3.doc
```

Table 3-4 lists other command-line arguments for the CIPHER utility.

Table 3-4. Miscellaneous command-line CIPHER switches

Argument	Function
/F	Forces an encryption function to encrypt all files, regardless of whether they are encrypted already.
/H	Displays hidden and system files, which are left out by default, in the listing of files that are affected by an action.
/I	Ignores errors that normally stop an encryption function.
/N	Prevents keys from being updated. Used mainly to locate all encrypted files on a specified volume. Works only with /U.
/Q	Displays only essential information when an action is completed.

Table 3-4. Miscellaneous command-line CIPHER switches (continued)

Argument	Function
/U	Hits all encrypted files on a volume and updates the user's encryption key if it has changed. Works only with /N.
/W	Removes any data from available, noncommitted portions of a volume. This is an exclusive option. No other switches are acknowledged when /W is used.

Printing from the Command Line

You can accomplish some of the more basic printing functions through the command line, which makes it easier for an administrator to script printer configuration and mapping for logon/logoff scripts and other batch automation procedures.

The following example commands perform a variety of printing functions:

- To print a text file called *employees.txt* to a printer on LPT1:

  ```
  print /d:LPT1 employees.txt
  ```

- To print a text file called *phonelist.txt* in the HR directory to the front office laser printer on the server Lisa:

  ```
  print /d:\\lisa\frnt-laser c:\public\hr\phonelist.txt
  ```

- To view the current jobs in the print queue for the front office laser:

  ```
  net print \\lisa\frnt-laser
  ```

- To view information on job 902 (based on the output of the preceding command):

  ```
  net print \\lisa 902
  ```

- To hold, release, or delete job 902:

  ```
  net print \\lisa 902 /hold (or /release or /delete)
  ```

- To manually assign physical port LPT1: to a network printer:

  ```
  net use lpt1: \\lisa\frnt-laser
  ```

- To view information on a network printer mapped to the physical port LPT1:

  ```
  net use lpt1:
  ```

- To start or stop the printer spooler:

  ```
  net start spooler or net stop spooler
  ```

The Last Word

In this chapter, you've learned about all of Windows Server 2003 and R2's file, print, and user services. We began with an overview of sharing and a guide to creating shares, publishing them to Active Directory, and mapping drives, and then moved into a detailed discussion of the Windows permission structure, including permission levels, "special" permissions, inheritance, and ownership. You also saw an overview of the Distributed File System (DFS), how to set it up, and how to manage it, and how offline files and folders and the Encrypting File System operate. Rounding out the chapter, you saw how to manage printing services, use roaming profiles, and administer most of these services from the command line.

In the next chapter, I'll talk about the foundation of Windows Server 2003's Active Directory service—the domain name system, or DNS.

CHAPTER 4

Domain Name System

The Domain Name System (DNS) is a staple of the public Internet and is the name resolution system of choice for both large and small networks. DNS is a directory of IP addresses and their corresponding hostnames, much like a phonebook in functionality. However, DNS is more complex than a phonebook and it stores many types of mappings, as well as information on services provided by servers on your network.

Whereas Windows NT relied on the Windows Internet Naming Service (WINS) and NetBIOS for name resolution, Windows 2000 and Windows Server 2003 depend on DNS. In fact, DNS is required for anyone who wants to use Active Directory—DNS lies at the heart of Active Directory, and they're inseparable. WINS is obsolesced, at least in terms of pure Windows infrastructure if you have an Active Directory network with all machines running Windows 2000 or later and DNS-aware applications.

In this chapter, I'll discuss the fundamentals of DNS, its structure, and the various types of data it supports and requires, then I'll proceed through installing and configuring a Windows DNS server and describe how you can integrate it with Active Directory.

Nuts and Bolts

Let's go through the basic building blocks of DNS first before we break into more advanced concepts. I'm going to provide you with a very fundamental, introductory look at DNS, and then in the following sections I'll break down each part with more detailed explanations and examples. Think of this as an abstract or executive summary, just so we're all on the same page before I move on to more technical topics.

The main premise of DNS is to provide name resolution services—that is, to resolve friendly textual hostnames to their associated IP addresses. DNS is the *de facto* standard for name resolution on the Internet and in modern networks that use TCP/IP as the transmission protocol. DNS is based on domains, which are simply textual names that refer to logical groupings of computers There are top-level domains (TLDs), including some that are probably familiar to you: .COM, .NET, .ORG, and the like. There are also second-level domains, which are less inclusive and usually take the form of *name*.tld. For example, my domain is jonathanhassell.com. O'Reilly has a domain name of oreilly.com. CNN's domain is cnn.com.

Politically, there is an organization called ICANN, short for the Internet Consortium of Assigned Names and Numbers, which keeps track of all the top-level domains. This keeps utter confusion from breaking out when thousands upon thousands of top-level domains might be issued. Individuals and businesses are allowed to register second-level domain names beneath top-level domains—hasseltech.net, for example.

DNS resolves names based on zones. Zones contain information on computers, services, and IP addresses for a collection of computers. Zones typically correspond to DNS domains, but they certainly do not have to. The DNS server or servers in a zone that contain a readable and writeable copy of the zone file (which contains all that information on computers, services, and addresses) is considered to be *authoritative*. You must have at least one authoritative server per zone for DNS to function. Any other DNS servers within this zone are considered to be secondary servers, meaning they hold a read-only copy of the DNS zone file.

Finally, there are two types of zones: *forward lookup zones*, which resolve hostnames to IP addresses, and *reverse lookup zones*, which do the opposite and resolve IP addresses to hostnames. Reverse lookup zones fall under a special top-level domain named in-addr.arpa, which ordinary users and clients never see in the course of their day-to-day work.

Now, let's take a closer look at these elements of DNS.

Zones Versus Domains

As you learned in the previous section, a DNS domain in its simplest form is a second-level name coupled with an ICANN-sponsored top-level domain—hasselltech.net, for example. In DNS parlance, a zone is the range of machines and addresses that a specific nameserver needs to be concerned about. Zones don't necessarily need to correspond to DNS domains, meaning that I can have multiple DNS zones for the single hasselltech.net domain. For example, I can have one zone for sales.hasselltech.net, another zone for billing.hasselltech.net, and yet another for hosting.hasselltech.net, all with separate nameservers but all within the control of the hasselltech.net domain.

Why would you want multiple DNS zones for a single DNS domain? To delegate administration is a common reason. If your organization is spread all over the country and you have an administrator for each office around the country, that administrator is likely best equipped and skilled to handle DNS configuration for his office—after all, he works with the individual computers more than a higher-level administrator at the home office does. So, the home office nameserver is configured to hold a few names and addresses for servers and machines there, and the branch office nameservers hold zones for their respective computers. In this configuration, when a computer comes to their servers and requests a name for an IP address associated with a branch office, the nameservers at the home office will refer the requesting computer to the nameserver at that branch office that holds the names and addresses for that zone, a process known as *delegating* name resolution to other servers. Additionally, the branch office server is *authoritative* for its zone, meaning that it holds the definitive name-to-address correspondence for computers in its zone.

Of course, domains aren't limited to just a second-level name plus an ICANN-approved extension. You also can have multiple levels of names: for example, customers.extranet.microsoft.com is a valid name, as is payjon.corp.hasselltech.net. You'll see as you read further into the chapter where situations in which a longer, more extended domain name would be appropriate.

Zone Files

Zone information is stored in zone files which, by default, are stored as ASCII test files in *%SystemRoot%\system32\dns*. The files are stored in the format *<domain>.dns* (e.g., *hasselltech.net.dns*). These ASCII files contain the different types of information contained within forward and reverse lookup zones, which we'll look at in just a bit.

DNS also can store zone information within Active Directory (as an application partition), an option I'll discuss in more detail later in this chapter. For now, we'll proceed on the assumption that zone files are stored in this location in ASCII format.

Forward and Reverse Lookup Zones

DNS handles forward lookups, which convert names to IP addresses, and the data is stored within a forward lookup zone. But DNS also handles reverse lookups, which convert IP addresses to names. There's also something called a reverse lookup zone, which does the opposite of a forward lookup zone—it catalogs all machines within a certain network range. You construct the name of a reverse lookup zone in a rather odd way. The easiest way to construct a reverse lookup zone name is to look at the range of IP addresses you've been assigned, drop the last dotted quad that contains the numbers you control, reverse the order of the remaining dotted quads, and then add `.in-addr.arpa`. For example, if your IP address is 64.246.42.130, the name of the associated reverse lookup zone is 42.246.64.in-addr.arpa.

Reverse lookup zones are constructed a bit differently, depending on whether you have a class A, B, or C IP address. Table 4-1 shows the respective ways to generate a reverse lookup zone name.

Table 4-1. Generating a reverse lookup zone name

Address class	Resulting zone name and method
Class A (12.0.0.0/8)	12.in-addr.arpa. Only the first quad is set, so only one quad needs to be in the reverse zone.
Class B (152.100.0.0/16)	100.152.in-addr.arpa. Because only two dotted quads are included, only two need to be noted in the reverse zone.
Class C (209.197.152.0/24)	152.197.209.in-addr.arpa. All dotted quads set in the IP address range need to be included in the reverse lookup zone name.

In practice, it's very likely that you don't need a reverse lookup zone for public-facing DNS servers, and it's equally likely that you would be prevented, on a technical basis, from creating one. (Internal DNS servers are another matter, which you'll see in a bit.) Although forward lookup zones concern hostnames and DNS domain names, which are under your control and management because you buy them from an accredited registrar, reverse lookup zones deal mainly with IP addresses and their owners, which probably are not under your control. Unless you have contacted the Internet Assigned Names Authority (IANA) and obtained a block of IP addresses specifically from them, it's probable that your ISP actually owns the addresses and therefore is the one tasked with maintaining reverse lookup zones.

There are really only a few reasons why it's advantageous to control your own reverse lookup zone. First and foremost, some mail servers will refuse to exchange Internet mail with your servers if their reverse lookups reveal that you're using a dynamically assigned IP address block of typical ISPs. This can be a real problem, but your ISP usually can help you out with this. Second, the Nslookup command can return a nasty but harmless error message about being unable to find a server name for your current IP address, depending on how you are connected to the Internet. Although this is annoying, it's simply saying no appropriate reverse zone is configured for the current computer. So when you've just installed Active Directory and you run Nslookup to check things out, and you get no results, this is most likely because you haven't yet configured a reverse lookup zone.

Resource Records

A DNS zone contains various types of entries, called *resource records*. Resource records are the meat of a DNS zone, providing information about hostnames, IP addresses, and in some cases the services offered by a particular machine. There are several different classes of record types, the most common of which I'll define now.

 Don't use "-" or "_" as the first character in any DNS name, as they are not compliant with the DNS standard. Confusingly, Windows DNS systems will accept these entries, but it's best to stay away from them. Even better, stay away from using underscores at all.

Host (A) Records

Host records, or A records, simply map a hostname to an IP address. You generally create host records for each machine in your network.

A sample A record looks like this in a zone file:

```
colossus A 192.168.0.10
```

Using host records, you can implement a load-balancing technique known as *round-robin DNS*. Round-robin DNS involves entering multiple A records, all configured with the same hostname, but with different IP addresses that correspond to different machines. This way, when computers contact a nameserver for a certain hostname, they have an equally proportionate chance of receiving any one of the number of machines with A records. For example, if I have a web site at www.hasselltech.net and I have three web servers at 192.168.0.50, 192.168.0.51, and 192.168.0.52, I can configure three A records, all named "www," but with the three IP addresses mentioned earlier. Now, when client computers come to the nameserver and ask for the IP address of www.hasselltech.net, they have a 33% chance of receiving 192.168.0.50 as the web server of choice, a 33% chance of receiving 192.168.0.51, and a 33% chance of receiving 192.168.0.52. It's a poor-man's load-balancing system.

 Let's get a bit more technical: in this scenario, Windows 2000 and Windows XP clients will continue to attempt a connection to the first web server that was originally resolved. A DNS cache timeout value on the client is set to 86,400 seconds (one day) by default. If you change this value on the client to one second, you have better odds of reaching your server. You can change this value in the registry with the following key:

> HKEY_LOCAL_MACHINE\SYSTEM\CurrentControlSet\Services\
> Dnscache\Parameters

Change the MaxCacheEntryTtlLimit to the number of seconds desired.

If the group of machines that serve web sites are on different subnets, the DNS system can return the "proper" address from a round-robin record set—that is, the one that is closest to the client requesting it. This functionality is enabled by default. For example, if you have one A record set up for www.hasselltech.net on IP address 192.168.0.51, and another A record set up for the same hostname on IP address 10.0.0.25, a client computer located on the 10.0.0.0 subnet will receive the 10.0.0.25 A record from his request, and a client computer located on the 192.168.0.0 subnet will receive the 192.168.0.51 A record from his request.

Some advantages to round-robin DNS balancing include the following:

- The price is right—it's free with any nameserver.
- It's less complex than other, proprietary balancing systems.
- It's easy to maintain. You simply can add and delete A records in the zone file for each host as they come and go to and from production service.

The disadvantages include the following:

- It's less complex than other, proprietary balancing systems. Yes, this is an advantage and a disadvantage because a less complex system is less flexible than a proprietary solution.
- If a web server goes down, DNS isn't aware of it. It simply will continue to dole out IP addresses regardless of whether the server is available.
- It doesn't take into account the various capabilities and capacities of each system—it distributes the load fairly equally, whether your group of machines includes a Pentium 2 or a dual Pentium IV Xeon machine.

Canonical Name (CNAME) Records

CNAME, or canonical name, records allow you to give multiple host names to one IP address. Using CNAMEs, you can have a machine answering on one IP address but listening to several different hostnames—www.hasselltech.net, ftp.hasselltech.net, and mail.hasselltech.net all might be on one IP address, 192.168.1.2. CNAMEs effectively work as aliases.

However, there is a caveat to these records: you cannot have multiple identical CNAMEs. For example, if you have a record for www-secure.hasselltech.net on 192.168.1.2, you can't have another CNAME record named www-secure.hasselltech.net for a different IP address. CNAMEs are only for multiple names to one IP address, not for multiple IP addresses to one name. Note that these names are zone dependent, not server dependent.

 Sometimes Windows will refer to CNAME records as *aliases*, in a confusing mix of technical accuracy and common parlance.

A sample CNAME record in zone file format looks like this:

```
ftp CNAME colossus.hasselltech.net
```

Mail Exchanger (MX) Records

Mail exchanger, or MX, records identify the mail server or mail servers for a specific zone or domain. Very simply, they instruct connecting computers to send all mail destined for a domain to a specific machine configured to receive Internet email.

In practice, a specific DNS zone can have multiple MX records. Each MX record also is assigned a preference number, which simply indicates what steps the respective machines listed should take when receiving Internet email. Lower preference numbers have higher priority. For example, let's say I have the following MX records:

- Hasselltech.net, MX preference 10, to mail.hasselltech.net
- Hasselltech.net, MX preference 100, to queue.perigee.net

This instructs connecting computers to send Internet email destined to hasselltech. net to the machine mail.hasselltech.net. However, if that machine isn't answering requests, connecting computers are instructed to try the machine queue.perigee.net and deliver mail there because the preference number is higher (100) than that of the first machine, which is 10. MX preference numbers provide a bit of failover protection if your organization's mail server is on a flaky or nonpermanent connection.

 Entering two MX records with the same preference number distributes the load between the two hosts roughly equally, much like round-robin DNS balancing using multiple A records.

A sample MX record in zone file format is similar to this:

```
@ MX 10 mail.hasselltech.net
@ MX 100 queue.perigee.net
```

Nameserver (NS) Records

Nameserver (NS) records define the nameservers that can answer queries for a specific domain. They also delegate the resolution duties for various subdomains to other zones. For example, you might configure an NS record for the "sales" subdomain to delegate name resolution duties to the salesns.hasselltech.net machine, which handles that zone, or an NS record for the "billing" subdomain to delegate duties to the billing-dns.hasselltech.net computer.

A sample NS record in zone file format looks like this:

```
@ NS colossus.hasselltech.net.
@ NS ns2.hasselltech.net.
```

Start of Authority (SOA) Records

The start of authority, or SOA, record for a zone names the primary nameservers that are authoritative for a particular zone and provides contact information for the primary administrator of the zone. It also controls how long a nonauthoritative nameserver can keep the information it retrieved in its own cache before needing to verify the data with the authoritative server again.

There are three important intervals to discuss at this point when it comes to SOA records:

Refresh interval
> The refresh interval indicates to secondary nameservers how long they can keep their copies of the primary nameserver's zones before being required to request a refresh of the zone.

Retry interval
> The retry interval indicates how long the secondary nameserver must wait before attempting to contact the primary nameserver again after a failed attempt to refresh its zones after the refresh interval has lapsed.

Minimum (default) TTL
> This value indicates to other nameservers how long they can use information they've previously retrieved from this authoritative nameserver before being required to consult the authoritative server again for updated or refreshed information. This is, by default, 60 minutes. You also can set TTL values for individual records that override this minimum default setting for a zone.

A sample SOA record in zone file format looks like this:

```
@ IN SOA colossus.hasselltech.net. admin.hasselltech.net. (
200509171203; serial number
100; refresh
50; retry
86400 ; expire
3600 ) ; default TTL
```

Pointer (PTR) Records

Pointer (PTR) records work very similarly to A records, except they perform the function in reverse—PTR records point IP addresses to hostnames and reside in reverse lookup zones.

A sample PTR record in zone file format looks like this:

```
61.130.98.66.in-addr.arpa. IN PTR alpha.enablehosting.com
```

Service (SRV) Records

Service (SRV) records indicate the range and availability of services in a particular zone or domain. They catalog the protocols and services running on specific ports in a zone, creating a "Yellow Pages" of sorts for connecting computers to find machines in the zone that will handle their specific types of requests. Like MX records, SRV records have a preference number, so you can perform a kind of poor man's load balancing and fault tolerance with these as well.

SRV records require a bit more explanation because they are so important to Active Directory. Here is an example SRV record in zone file format:

```
_kerberos._tcp._sites.dc._msdcs 600 SRV 100 88 colossus.hasselltech.net.
```

The service—in this case, Kerberos—is the leftmost part of the record, and the _tcp refers to whether the service operates on the TCP or UDP transmission protocols. The rightmost part of the record identifies the machine that is listening for requests for the service named in the record, in this case *colossus.hasselltech.net*. The first number in the middle, 600, indicates the time to live (TTL) for that record, recorded in seconds. The rightmost number, 88, refers to the port number on which the service is listening. Finally, 100 refers to the preference number for the record—these work exactly like MX record preference numbers as described in the previous section.

Why are SRV records crucial to Active Directory? Because they indicate which domain machines are running what Active Directory services. Active Directory really looks for only four services to be advertised within SRV records:

_kerberos
> To provide user and computer authentications using Kerberos Key Distribution Center (KDC) servers

_kpasswd
> To provide a mechanism for changing Kerberos passwords securely

_ldap
> For the Lightweight Directory Access Protocol, the way external programs communicate and exchange data with Active Directory

_gc
> For the Global Catalog, which contains a subset of attributes for all the objects in an Active Directory forest

 A warning that applies from this point forward: even though Microsoft has set up these entries with a leading underscore, you do not want to use "-" or "_" as the first character in a DNS name, as they are not RFC-compliant. This will cause problems for you if you ever need to integrate or operate in conjunction with Unix-based BIND DNS servers.

Using Primary and Secondary Nameservers

DNS has built-in redundancy by allowing for multiple primary and secondary nameservers for a particular domain or zone. Each server, whether identified as primary or secondary, holds a copy of the zone file and acts on its contents. Secondary nameservers can answer queries without any sort of architectural limitation, just as primary nameservers can. However, the secondary nameservers must retrieve updates to zones from the primary nameserver on a regular basis to ensure their records are up to date.

Each zone can have only one primary nameserver, but can have as many secondary nameservers as is practical. All changes, deletions, and other modifications to a zone are made on the primary nameserver. However, nameservers designated as secondary nameservers hold read-only copies of the zone contents from their associated primary nameservers—zones can't be directly modified on secondary nameservers. The secondary nameserver will automatically determine the primary nameserver for a zone by examining the SOA records for that zone and will contact that machine on a regular basis to force a zone file refresh.

 Secondary nameservers are not limited to zone transfers from only a primary nameserver; they can accept transfers from other secondary nameservers as well.

Several mechanisms exist to force a zone transfer. For one, all of the secondary nameservers will query the primary nameserver for updates: these refreshes are generally "pull"-style updates, whereby machines fetch zones from a particular computer, rather than "push"-style updates. In addition, when a nameserver identified as secondary for any zone is rebooted or its DNS service is restarted, it will automatically query the primary server on record for an update. You also can force a zone transfer by simply right-clicking the zone inside the DNS Management snap-in on the secondary server and selecting Transfer from Master or Reload from Master, to either refresh changes or refresh the entire zone file, respectively.

Transfers also are triggered by the expiration date and refresh interval, and, indirectly, by the retry interval for a particular zone. The secondary nameserver will query the primary at the time indicated by the refresh interval—this is generally 15 minutes by default, but you might find a compelling reason to change this depending on your network traffic and needs. If the serial number on the SOA record for a zone is higher on the primary nameserver than on the secondary nameserver's zone record, the transfer will take place. However, if the secondary nameserver can't contact the primary nameserver at the time the refresh interval has elapsed, the secondary nameserver will wait for the amount of time specified in the retry interval and then try again. If further attempts fail, upon the time listed in the expiration date section of the record, the secondary nameserver will simply stop answering DNS requests, lest it give inaccurate and obsolete information to clients.

Full and Incremental Zone Transfers

A relatively new DNS RFC, 1995, now allows for incremental zone transfers (known in shorthand as IXFRs), which remove one of the largest stumbling blocks of DNS administration. It used to be that when a zone refresh was needed, DNS couldn't discriminate the changes made on the primary server: even if only one line of a 6,000-line zone file had changed, the entire zone needed to be transferred to the secondary machines in a process commonly referred to as a full zone transfer (or AXFR).

Although that process wasn't a big deal if you had only one secondary nameserver, it became a large headache for organizations with tens or hundreds of secondary nameservers spread across the country or world. With the advent of RFC 1995, nameservers now have the ability to detect the differences between two zone files and transfer only the changed information, saving bandwidth, transfer time, and CPU power.

Building a Nameserver

In this section, I'll guide you through the process of actually creating a nameserver, and then in the remainder of the chapter I'll add to the functionality of the nameserver to prepare it for use with Active Directory.

Nameservers need a constant connection to the Internet and a non-changing IP, either set statically on the server itself or delivered consistently through a DHCP reservation. The machine you're building out as a nameserver doesn't need to be that powerful; a fast Pentium III machine with 512 MB or so of RAM will be more than sufficient.

> In the following examples, I will use the fictitious domain name has-selltech.net, with the also fictitious machine name colossus and IP address 192.168.0.5. You can, of course, replace these as appropriate when following along with your own computer.

The first step is to install the nameserver software onto your Windows Server 2003 computer. To do so, follow these steps:

1. Open Add/Remove Programs inside the Control Panel.
2. Click the Add/Remove Windows Components button on the left side of the window.
3. Select Network Services in the list box, and then click the Details button.
4. Check the Domain Name System (DNS) checkbox, and click OK to return to the previous screen.
5. Click Next to proceed with the DNS software installation.
6. Click Finish, and then Close, to finish the procedure.

> If you have your computer set up to receive an IP address via DHCP, the nameserver installation will complain loudly that DNS isn't intended to work on dynamically assigned IP addresses. For this example, click OK three times to acknowledge these warnings. As mentioned previously, make sure nameservers have a consistent, unchanging IP address.

Next, point your new nameserver to itself for name resolution so that when you run tests, you're not querying your ISP's nameservers. In fact, most nameservers point to themselves, rather than to other nameservers, for name resolution. I recommend setting this through the command line using the `netsh` command, like so:

```
netsh int ip set dns "Local Area Connection" static 192.168.0.5 primary
```

You can replace `Local Area Connection` with the name, as appearing in your network connection properties, of your network connection. Also, replace `192.168.0.5` with the local nameserver's IP.

Of course, you also can change the nameservers to use for name resolution through the Windows interface by following these steps:

1. Inside the Control Panel, double-click the Network Connections applet.
2. Inside the Network Connection dialog box, right-click the name of your network connection and choose Properties from the context menu.
3. Navigate to the General tab, and then select Internet Protocol (TCP/IP).
4. Click the Properties button.
5. Click the Use the following DNS server address radio button, and then enter the nameserver's IP address into the box.
6. Click OK.

Now that the DNS server software is installed, you need to start the DNS service. Select Start, then click Administrative Tools and select DNS. The DNS Management Snap-in will appear, as shown in Figure 4-1 (although it will not have all of the forest lookup zones shown in the figure).

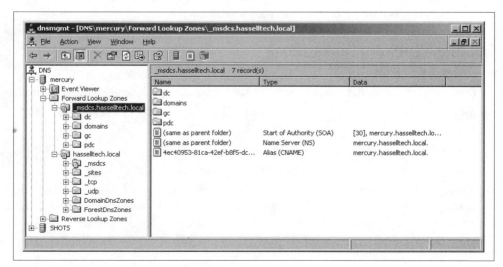

Figure 4-1. The DNS Management Snap-in

We'll manually set up DNS later in this chapter, so ignore the message to use the Configure Your DNS Server Wizard. At this point, you have a functional nameserver, which performs "caching-only" functions—that is, it doesn't hold any DNS information unique to itself, but it does know how to contact the 13 root servers as held by ICANN, the master of DNS on the Internet, and it can resolve Internet addresses by contacting them. Windows Server 2003's DNS software knows how to do this by default, without any configuration on your part.

Enabling Incremental Transfers

Windows Server 2003's DNS component is compliant with RFC 1995 and can do incremental transfers (known as *IXFRs* in DNS parlance) with other Windows 2000 or Windows Server 2003 servers supporting the feature. It also still can do the old-style full zone transfers, referred to as *AXFRs*, with noncompliant nameservers and with non-Windows 2000 or non-Windows Server 2003 machines. There is not a way to instruct Windows Server 2003 to always send full zone files to all servers, regardless of whether they are compliant. You can, however, tell Windows to send incremental zone transfers to all supporting servers, regardless of whether they run Windows 2000 or Windows Server 2003. Here's how:

1. Open the DNS Management snap-in.
2. Right-click your server and select Properties from the context menu.
3. Navigate to the Advanced tab, and *un*check the box labeled BIND Secondaries.
4. Click OK to finish.

Now the server will use incremental zone transfers to all supporting servers, not just to those running Windows 2000 or Windows Server 2003.

Creating a Forward Lookup Zone

Now, to further configure your server, let's create a forward lookup zone file. Inside the DNS snap-in, expand the server name in the lefthand pane. Then do the following:

1. Right-click Forward Lookup Zones and select New Zone. The New Zone Wizard appears.
2. Choose Primary Zone, and then click Next.
3. Enter the zone name. In this example, I'll use *hasselltech.net*. Click Next to continue.
4. Enter a name for the new zone file, which is stored in ASCII format. The default name is your domain with *.dns* appended to the end—*hasselltech.net.dns*, for example. The zone files are stored in *%SystemRoot%\system32\dns*. Click Next.

5. On the Dynamic Update screen, choose to allow both insecure and secure dynamic updates. I'll discuss dynamic DNS updating in a later section. Click Next.

6. Click Finish to complete the zone creation process.

The *hasselltech.net* zone has now been created.

Entering A Records into a Zone

Inside the DNS snap-in, right-click the *hasselltech.net* node in the lefthand pane and choose New Host (A) from the context menu. The New Host dialog box appears, as shown in Figure 4-2.

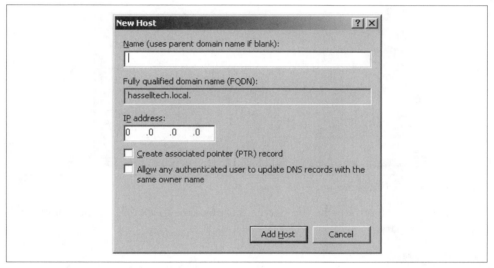

Figure 4-2. Entering a new A record

Enter the hostname of the machine for which you're entering the record, and then enter the IP address of the machine. As you enter the hostname, the fully qualified domain name (FQDN) will adjust to show the full hostname, including the domain, to check your work. You also can check the Create associated pointer (PTR) record checkbox, which enters a PTR record into the reverse lookup zone, if one is currently configured. (If none is set up, the process will throw an error.) Click OK.

Controlling Round-Robin Balancing

You can enable or disable round-robin DNS balancing using the nameserver's Advanced Properties screen, which you'll find by right-clicking the nameserver name in the DNS Management snap-in's lefthand pane and selecting Properties from the context menu. Figure 4-3 shows this screen, on the Advanced tab of the Properties sheet.

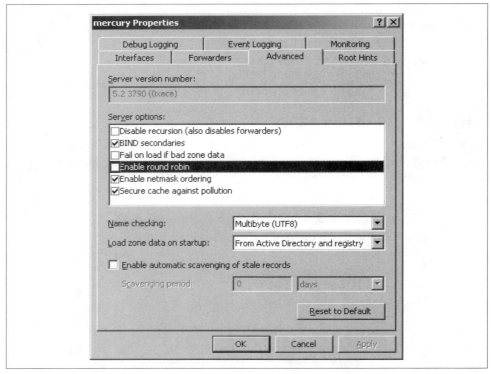

Figure 4-3. Advanced properties of a DNS server

Check Enable round robin in the Server options box to enable round robin, and uncheck it to disable it.

 DNS round-robin functionality is enabled on a per-server level, not on a per-zone level.

Also, if you want to turn off the subnet mask ordering feature, on the Advanced Properties screen shown in Figure 4-3 uncheck Enable netmask ordering in the Server options box.

Entering and Editing SOA Records

A default SOA record is created when you create a new zone in Windows Server 2003. To modify an SOA record, double-click it in the DNS Management snap-in. The screen will look something like Figure 4-4.

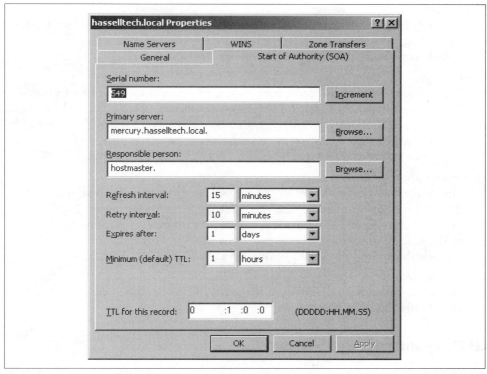

Figure 4-4. SOA record properties for a zone

Here are descriptions of the various fields on this tab:

Serial number

The serial number indicates whether the SOA record has changed since the last update on the part of a nonauthoritative nameserver. If you want to change this number, click the Increment button; you can't simply edit the field.

Primary server

This field denotes the primary, authoritative nameserver for this zone.

Responsible person

This field indicates the administrator responsible for configuring and editing this zone. This is the administrator's email address, but with a period in place of the normal at sign (@) and a period appended to the end of the string. For example, if your administrator is hostmaster@hasselltech.net, in this field you would enter **hostmaster.hasselltech.net**.

Refresh interval

The refresh interval indicates to secondary nameservers how long they can keep their copies of the zones before being required to request a refresh.

Retry interval

> The retry interval indicates how long the secondary nameserver must wait before attempting to contact the authoritative nameserver again after a failed attempt to refresh its zone after the refresh interval has lapsed.

Expires after

> This value essentially indicates how long a zone file is valid for use in production environments. It dictates how long a secondary nameserver will continue attempting a zone transfer from its primary nameserver. When this expiration date is reached, the zone on the secondary nameserver expires and that server stops responding to queries.

Minimum (default) TTL

> This value indicates to other nameservers how long they can use information they've previously retrieved from this nameserver before being required to consult the authoritative server again for updated or refreshed information. This is, by default, 60 minutes. You also can set TTL values for individual records that override this minimum default setting for a zone.

TTL for this record

> This value overrides the minimum (default) TTL as described earlier and is limited to only this SOA record.

Creating and Editing NS Records

NS records, as you learned earlier in this chapter, link the hostnames of nameservers to their IP addresses. To create these records, inside the DNS Management snap-in right-click the zone file in question and select Properties. Then, select the Name Servers tab. You'll be greeted with the screen shown in Figure 4-5.

The primary NS record is displayed, as it was created by default when you first constructed the zone. Click the Add button to insert a new NS record—for example, for a secondary nameserver. In the box that appears, type in the new machine's fully qualified domain name and click the Resolve button. Windows Server 2003 uses a reverse lookup to determine the IP address of the hostname you entered. If you agree with its finding, click the Add button beside the IP address and the NS record will be entered. Click OK twice to close.

Creating and Editing CNAME Records

Recall that CNAME records map different hostnames to preexisting A records, allowing multiple DNS names for a host. To create these records, right-click the hasselltech.net node in the lefthand pane of the DNS Management snap-in and choose New Alias (CNAME) from the context menu. The New Resource Record dialog box appears, as shown in Figure 4-6.

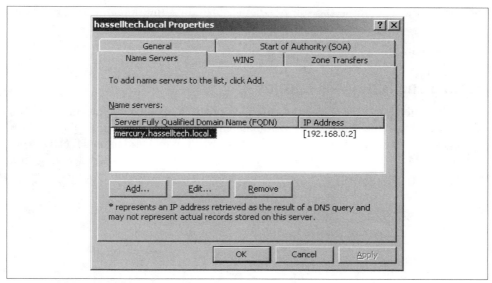

Figure 4-5. Editing NS records for a zone

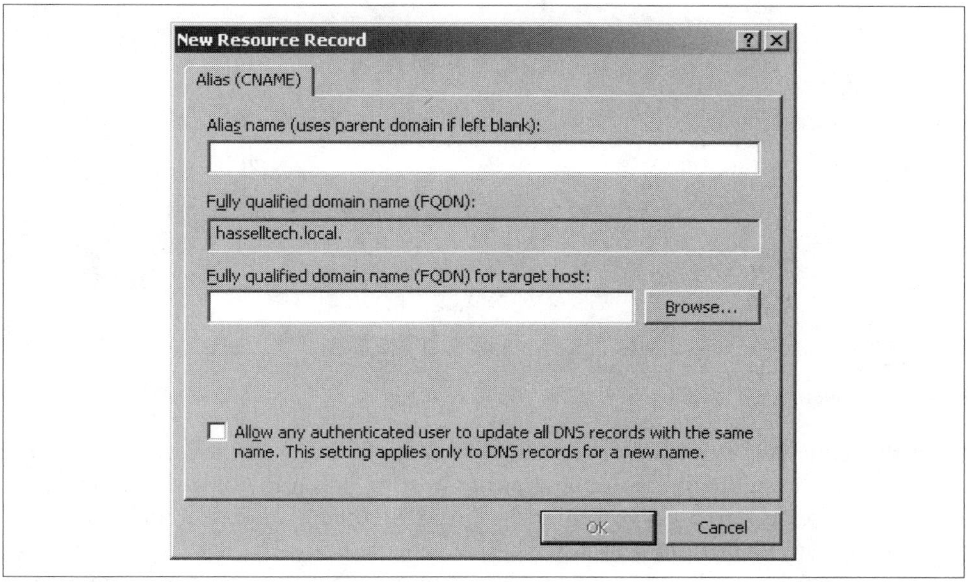

Figure 4-6. Entering a new CNAME record

Enter the aliased name of the machine for which you're entering the record (this is the canonical name), and then enter the fully qualified domain name of the host you're aliasing. As you enter the CNAME, the fully qualified domain name field just below will adjust to show the full hostname, including the domain, to check your work.

Click OK to finish.

Creating and Editing MX Records

As you'll remember from earlier in this chapter, MX records dictate how mail is delivered to a specific DNS zone. To create these records, inside the DNS snap-in right-click the *hasselltech.net* node in the lefthand pane and choose New Mail Exchanger (MX) from the context menu. The New Resource Record dialog box appears, as shown in Figure 4-7.

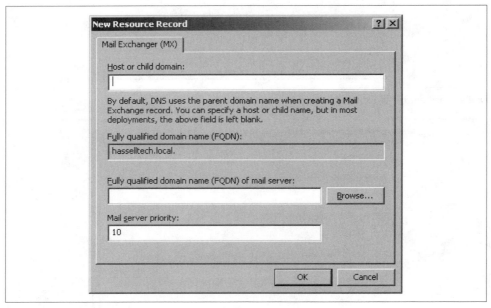

Figure 4-7. Entering a new MX record

Enter the name of the domain or zone for which you're entering the record, and then enter the fully qualified domain name of the host to which mail for that domain or zone should be delivered. As you enter the CNAME, the fully qualified domain name field just below will adjust to show the full hostname, including the domain, to check your work. Finally, in the Mail server priority box, type the MX preference number that should apply to this record.

Click OK to close.

Generating a Reverse Lookup Zone

You learned earlier in this chapter that reverse lookup zones map IP addresses to their corresponding hostnames. To create these records, inside the DNS Management snap-in, right-click the Reverse Lookup Zones folder and choose New Zone from the context menu. You'll be presented with the New Zone Wizard. Click Next to bypass the introductory screen and you'll see Figure 4-8. Then follow these steps:

1. Choose Primary zone, and click Next.

2. Enter the network numbers for your network in the Network ID field—for example, 192.168.0.0—and then click Next.

3. The Dynamic Updates page appears. Select to allow both insecure and secure updates, and then click Next.

4. Click Finish to complete the wizard.

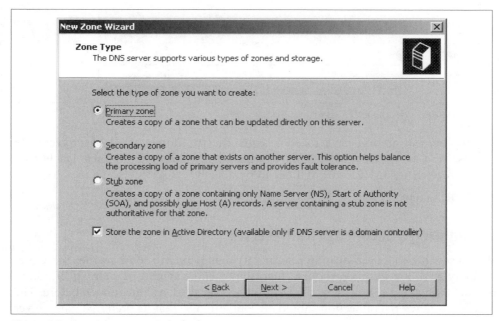

Figure 4-8. Creating a new reverse lookup zone

Your reverse lookup zone has been created.

Creating and Editing PTR Records

Remember that PTR records map IP addresses to their hostnames and are vital within a reverse lookup zone. To create these records, right-click the appropriate reverse lookup zone within the DNS Management snap-in and select New Pointer

(PTR) from the context menu. The New Resource Record dialog box will appear, as shown in Figure 4-9.

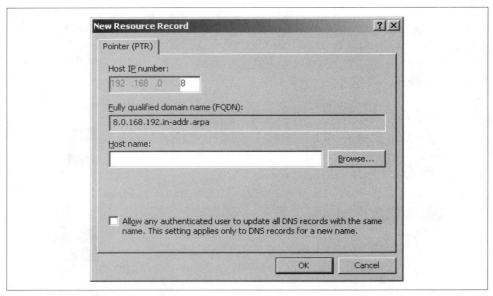

Figure 4-9. Entering a new PTR record

On this screen, all you need to do is enter the last dotted quad of a specific IP address, and then enter the hostname to which that address should refer. The FQDN for the reverse lookup record will fill in automatically.

Click OK to finish.

Configuring a Secondary Nameserver

In this section, I'll cover creating a secondary nameserver to serve a zone. Some preliminary steps are in order, though: first, the machine should be running Windows Server 2003, and it should have the DNS service installed, as I mentioned before. The machine's network connection should be configured so that its preferred nameserver is itself. (Also, for the purposes of this section, the secondary nameserver will be called *ns2.hasselltech.net* at IP address 192.168.0.6.)

To proceed:

1. Open the DNS Management MMC snap-in.

2. Right-click Forward Lookup Zones and select New Zone from the context menu. The New Zone Wizard will appear; click Next to skip the introductory screen.

3. Choose Secondary to create a secondary lookup zone, which will indicate to Windows that this should be a secondary nameserver. Click Next.

4. Enter the name of an existing zone on the Zone Name screen, and click Next.

5. Specify the nameservers from which Windows can fetch the existing zone files. Simply enter the primary nameserver in the box, click Add, and then click Next, as shown in Figure 4-10.

6. Click Finish to create the zone.

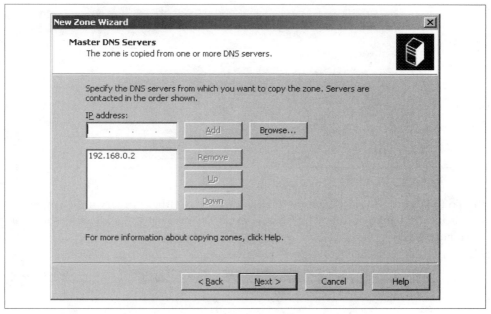

Figure 4-10. Specifying a primary DNS server for a secondary DNS zone

Upgrading a Secondary Nameserver to Primary

Perhaps you decide, upon acquiring a new business into your organization, that you need more horsepower in responding to DNS queries. Or perhaps eventually you'd like to cluster your DNS servers. In these cases, you would want to promote some secondary nameservers to primary status. It's an easy process to promote an existing secondary nameserver to a primary nameserver.

1. Open the DNS Management snap-in.

2. Right-click the zone folder that you want to convert, and select Properties from the context menu.

3. Navigate to the General tab, as shown in Figure 4-11.

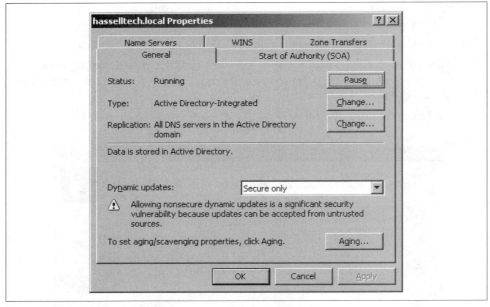

Figure 4-11. Promoting a DNS server

4. To the right of the Type entry—it should now say either Primary or Secondary—click the Change button. The Change Zone Type screen will appear, as shown in Figure 4-12.

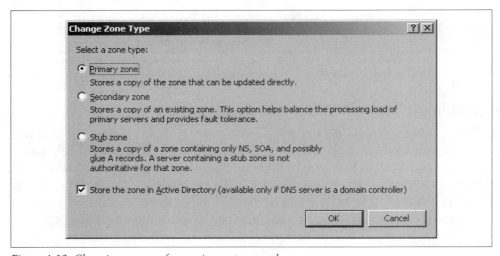

Figure 4-12. Changing a server from primary to secondary

5. Click the Primary zone radio button to perform the promotion.

6. Click OK.

The server will now be a primary server for that zone.

Manually Editing Zone Files

All zone files are stored in *%SystemRoot%\system32\dns*. The files are stored in the format *<domain>.dns* (e.g., *hasselltech.net.dns*). You can edit them with your favorite text editor or with a script that you can write to perform large-scale and/or automated machine rollouts.

 When you directly edit zone files, make sure you manually increment the serial number value in the zone's SOA record. You can increment by any value. Otherwise, the changes are likely to be missed by any secondary nameservers during a zone transfer.

Controlling the Zone Transfer Process

For obvious reasons, you'll find it necessary to control which machines can perform a zone transfer from nameservers—after all, users at large on the Internet have no legitimate need to retrieve a full copy of your zones, and having a full record of your connected machines is a huge security breach. Unfortunately, Microsoft didn't lock down this process, so by default your Windows Server 2003 nameserver will transfer its zone files to any machine upon request. This is locked down, however, in Service Pack 1.

To lock this down, open the DNS Management snap-in and expand the nameserver's name. Find a zone under Forward Lookup Zones, right-click it, and choose Properties. Click over to the Zone Transfers tab. You'll see the screen depicted in Figure 4-13.

You see that you can disallow zone transfers wholesale by unchecking the box labeled Allow zone transfers. However, if you choose to enable them to have secondary nameservers, you can lock down the access to those zone files a bit more granularly. The first option, To any server, leaves the transfer process wide open—this is the default setting on machines that haven't been upgraded to Service Pack 1. The second option, Only to servers listed on the Name Servers tab, seems to be the most reasonable option by restricting transfer to the servers identified as authoritative for the domain on that tab. The third option, Only to the following servers, can lock down that list even further. Simply select the option, enter an IP address into the box, and click Add when you're done. Make the list as long or short as it needs to be, and then finish the process by clicking OK.

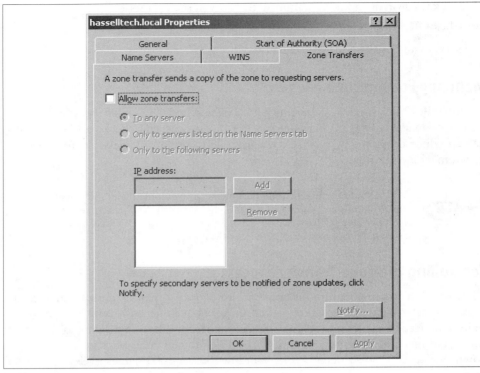

Figure 4-13. Controlling zone transfers

Windows Server 2003 also supports a feature listed in RFC 1996 known as zone modification notification, which nearly contradicts what I wrote earlier about the zone transfer process being primarily a pull, rather than a push, process. Click the Notify button on the Zone Transfer tab to explore this feature; you'll be greeted with the screen in Figure 4-14.

The notification feature will contact the servers listed on this Notify screen when changes are made to the zone file on the primary nameserver. You can have the server contact the authoritative nameservers for a zone or domain as listed on the Name Servers tab, or contact only the servers in the list that you create on this screen. (To create this list, simply enter an IP address and click Add. Repeat as necessary to build the list.) Click OK when you've configured or disabled this feature as you wish.

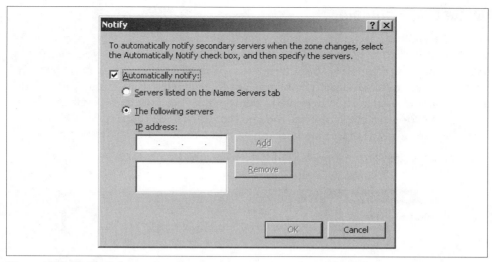

Figure 4-14. Notify dialog screen

Subdomains and Delegation

It's rare to find an organization running its own DNS that is small enough to not take advantage of subdomains and delegation. By delegation, I mean letting one group, whether logical or physical, administer a section of an organization's network. Let's take a look at an example.

Perhaps my company has two offices: one in Boston and the other in Charlotte, North Carolina. Although I have an overarching domain name, mycompany.com, I might want to delineate these two locations within my network—I can call all machines in Boston with the *north.mycompany.com* domain suffix and all machines in Charlotte with the *south.mycompany.com* domain suffix. Because the respective IT groups at each location have a better sense of which machines are going in and out of the network at their own offices than a central group of administrators at the headquarters site, the decision was made to let each office's group administer DNS within each subdomain. To make this happen, there are three steps to follow: first, the overarching domain's DNS zone needs to be told there will be a subdomain that will be administered elsewhere. Second, the overarching (in technical terms, the "root" but not the ultimate TLD-root) nameserver needs the address of the subdomain's nameserver for its records. And finally, the subdomain's nameserver needs to be installed and configured.

Delegating a Domain

Inside the DNS Management snap-in, right-click the zone that is the parent of the subdomain you want to create (e.g., *mycompany.com*), and select New Delegation from the pop-up menu. The New Delegation Wizard appears; click past the introductory screen to the Delegated Domain Name Screen. Here, simply enter the subdomain you want to create and delegate in the top box. The bottom box will expand to show the full domain name of what you entered. Click Next to move on. On the next screen, enter the name of the subdomain you'd like to delegate, and click Next.

The Name Servers screen appears, as shown in Figure 4-15.

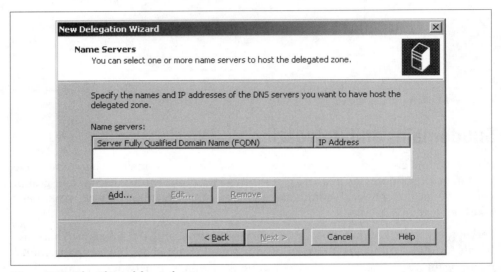

Figure 4-15. Identifying delegated nameservers

On this page, insert the fully qualified domain name and IP address of the nameservers, which will be responsible for the new domain. Just click Add to enter these on the New Resource Record screen which will appear. When you're finished, click OK, and then click Next. Click Finish to complete the wizard. The newly delegated domain will appear in the DNS Management snap-in, but it will be grayed out to indicate its delegated status.

How does this process modify the actual zone files within the DNS service? For one, it adds new NS records to the parent domain to indicate the server responsible for a particular subdomain. For example, if I were delegating the fully qualified *subdomain north.mycompany.com* with a nameserver at *dns1.north.mycompany.com*, the resulting record would look like this:

```
north NS dns1.north.mycompany.com
```

Next, the delegation wizard adds an A record to the parent zone so that it can find the new nameserver via its IP address, like this:

```
dns1.north A 192.168.1.105
```

This A record is known as a *glue record* because that A record is the only way DNS and requesting clients would know the IP address of the delegated nameserver—after all, the primary zone no longer holds information on and controls that zone. The A record eliminates that problem and provides a direct way to get in touch with that delegated nameserver.

When Delegation Goes Lame

Lame delegation is the condition when an NS record points to an incorrect machine. This can be caused when a zone is delegated to a server that has not been properly configured as an authoritative nameserver for that zone, or an authoritative nameserver for a zone has an NS record that points to another machine that is not authoritative for the zone.

When lame delegation occurs, these nameservers direct queries to servers that will not respond authoritatively, if at all. This causes unnecessary network traffic and extra work for servers. According to the Domain Health Survey, 25% of all zones have lame delegations.

I'll talk about a utility later in this chapter, called DNSLint, that can help you detect lame delegations and fix them.

Creating the Subdomain

Logically, creating the subdomain you've just delegated is very simple. From the delegated server, inside the DNS Management snap-in, you can right-click the Forward Lookup Zones folder and choose New Zone. From there, just follow the instructions in the "Creating a Forward Lookup Zone" section earlier in this chapter.

Dynamic DNS

Dynamic DNS is Windows 2000 and Windows Server 2003's way of bringing together the one good feature of WINS—automatic machine registration and record updating—with the resiliency and open standards advantage of DNS, a staple of the Internet. With dynamic DNS, machines running Windows 2000, Windows XP, and Windows Server 2003 can register their presence automatically with the nameserver that controls the zone associated with their connection's DNS suffix. In the case of the examples so far in this chapter, if I have a machine named sales1.north.mycompany.com, this computer would automatically register an A record for that hostname and

IP address with the nameserver that controls north.mycompany.com—a handy feature, indeed.

Figure 4-16 shows the actual flow of dynamic DNS registration when a workstation needs to register itself.

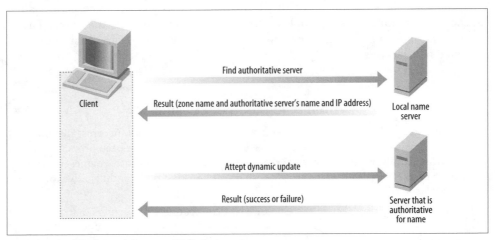

Figure 4-16. The flow of dynamic DNS registration

The process works a bit different when IP addresses are assigned by a Windows DHCP server. The client, when it receives its IP address from the DHCP server, only registers an A record in the nameserver's forward lookup zone. The DHCP server by default is responsible for registering the PTR records in the nameserver's reverse lookup zone, if one exists.

> If you want to alter this behavior, you can configure the DHCP server to take care of both parts of the registration by looking on the properties sheet for the DHCP scope in question within the DHCP snap-in.
>
> Open the DHCP snap-in, expand your machine in the left pane, and then click Scopes. In the right pane, select the scope you want to alter and then right-click it and select Properties. Now, navigate to the DNS tab and select Always Update DNS. The DHCP server will register A records in the forward lookup zone and PTR records in the reverse lookup zone for all clients leasing an address.

When does this registration take place? Five possible actions will trigger a DNS registration on the part of the client:

- The computer has been restarted.
- The computer's DHCP lease, if the machine uses a dynamic IP address, has just been renewed.

- The computer's statically assigned IP address has been changed.
- A full 24 hours have passed since the last DNS registration on record.
- An administrator issues the `ipconfig /registerdns` command from the command line.

Although the default period for reregistering DNS dynamically is 24 hours, you can change this value inside the Registry on the client. On the key:

> *HKEY_LOCAL_MACHINE\SYSTEM\CurrentControlSet\Services\ Tcpip\Parameters*

add a new REG_DWORD entry called `DefaultRegistrationRefreshInterval` and give it a value in seconds. (For reference, there are 86,400 seconds in a day.)

Scavenging

Obviously, with multiple machines registering DNS information periodically throughout the day, you need to clean up that information when it expires. The Windows Server 2003 DNS scavenging process finds the dynamically registered records that haven't been updated for some time, and then simply deletes them to ensure that after a delay for propagation between servers, the zone information contains the most up-to-date data on the machines and addresses therein.

Let's take a look at how scavenging is presented in the user interface and how you can best control it. To control scavenging for all zones on a particular nameserver, right-click the server's name from the DNS Management snap-in and select Set Aging/Scavenging for All Zones. The Server Aging/Scavenging Properties screen appears, as shown in Figure 4-17.

At the top of the screen, you see the master switch to enable or disable scavenging. Additionally, you see two options. One of them is for the no-refresh interval, which is simply the time a dynamically registered record should be allowed to stay registered in a "read-only" fashion before the scavenger can take a look at it. This means client computers cannot reregister themselves during this period. The other option is for the refresh interval, which is the amount of time a record should remain and be allowed to be refreshed after the no-refresh interval has passed before the scavenger should remove it. In essence, the scavenger process is not allowed to touch a record unless both the no-refresh and the refresh intervals have passed in full.

To enable scavenging, check the top checkbox and click OK. If you have Active Directory–integrated zones, you'll be asked to confirm your choice for those as well. Click OK once again, and scavenging will be enabled. Another step remains—you need to enable scavenging on the nameserver, which you can do by right-clicking the server name inside DNS Management, selecting Properties, and clicking the Advanced tab. This is shown in Figure 4-18.

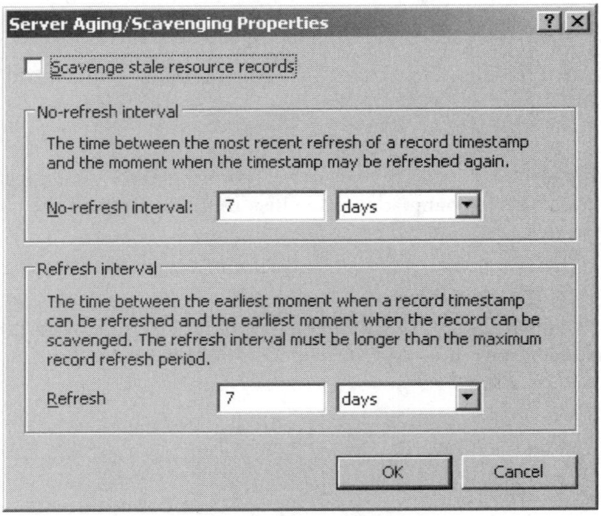

Figure 4-17. Setting dynamic DNS scavenging

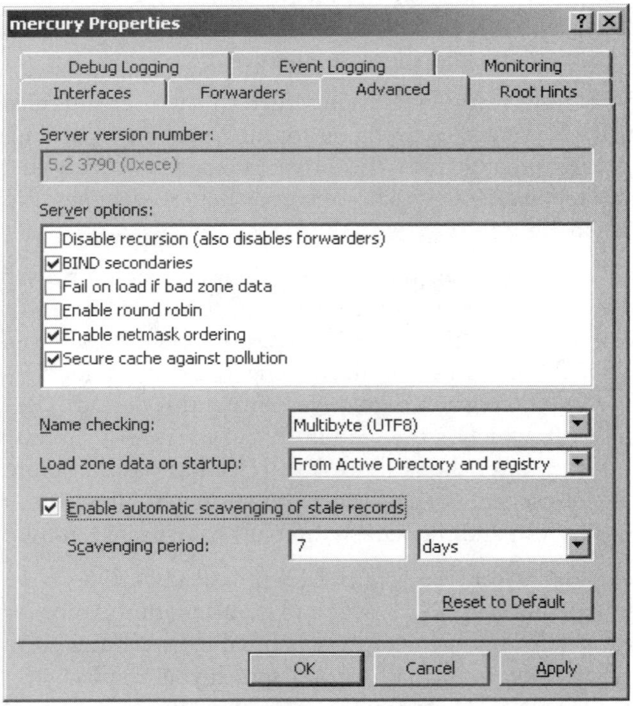

Figure 4-18. Setting up scavenging on the server

At the bottom of the screen, check the checkbox labeled Enable automatic scavenging of stale records, and then enter a period of time after which the scavenger can automatically engage.

If you want to control scavenging and its associated intervals for an individual zone, right-click the zone inside DNS Management and select Properties. Then, navigate to the General tab and click the Aging button. The screen is identical to the server-wide scavenging control screen shown in Figure 4-17.

For the scavenging service to do the mathematics required to calculate these intervals, the DNS service adds a nonstandard bit of information to a resource record's zone information. For instance, an A record on a server or zone with scavenging enabled might look like this:

```
colossus [AGE:47363030] 36400 192.168.0.5
```

The AGE portion is the inception point of the record, measured in some small interval since a certain date. How that number is determined is unimportant; what matters is that with scavenging enabled, the AGE information is added to a DNS record so that the no-refresh and refresh intervals can be honored correctly. You can see that timestamp in a human-readable format by right-clicking any record in the DNS Management snap-in and selecting Properties. The Record timestamp field will show the date and time the record was created in DNS, as shown in Figure 4-19.

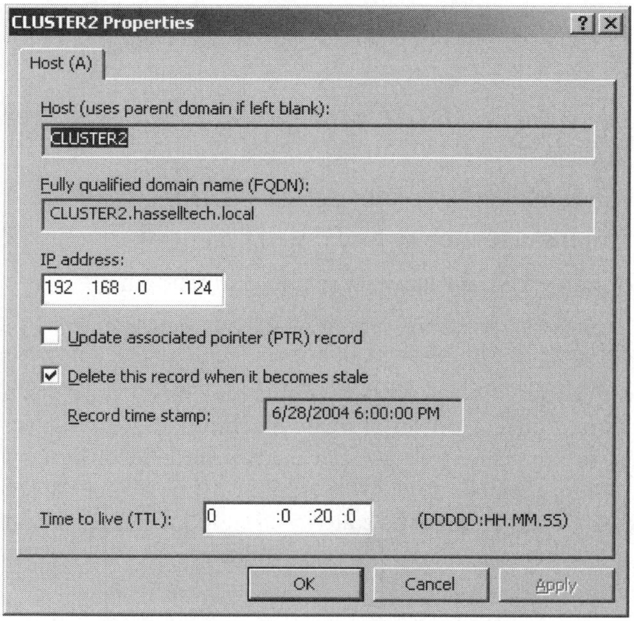

Figure 4-19. Viewing a record's timestamp in the GUI

To view the record timestamp, select Advanced from the View menu of the console.

Preventing Dynamic DNS Registration

If your organization hasn't deployed Active Directory yet, the dynamic DNS registration default settings that modern Windows client operating systems have can be aggravating to IT groups—your nameservers will be pelted, sometimes forcefully, with registration attempts from Windows systems that *believe* that for an Active Directory in your organization, they need to register themselves. Of course, that's not necessarily true, but it's the default behavior.

Fortunately, you can turn this off, either through a registry change (to make the modification on a larger scale) or through the GUI. To do so through the GUI, follow these steps:

1. Open the connection's properties.
2. On the Network tab, select TCP/IP, and then click the Properties button.
3. Navigate to the DNS tab.
4. Uncheck Register this connection's addresses in DNS.
5. Click OK.

To do so through the Registry, open the Registry Editor, and then take the following steps:

1. Navigate through *HKEY_LOCAL_MACHINE\CurrentControlSet\Services\TcpIp*.
2. Click the Parameters key.
3. Add a new value, of type `REG_DWORD`, called `DisableDynamicUpdate`.
4. Set the value of the new entry to 1.

Alternatively, you can type the following at the command line:

```
reg add hklm\system\currentcontrolset\services\tcpip\parameters /v
DisableDynamicUpdate /t REG_DWORD /d 1 /f
```

You also can use Group Policy (GP) to deploy a policy that disables this to all machines in a domain or to a subset of those machines. GP, in this case, necessitates Active Directory. In any case, the proper object is under Computer Configuration/ Administrative Templates/Network/DNS client. The object is called Dynamic Update, and to turn it off, change the state to Disabled. Chapter 6 covers GP in more detail.

Active Directory–Integrated Zones

Up to this point, I've treated the Windows Server 2003 DNS service as a traditional nameserver, mostly compliant with the relevant RFCs, which can act in both primary and secondary "modes" for a zone. However, Windows Server 2003 offers a third mode specific to Windows that, although not listed in an RFC, offers some distinct advantages if you've made an infrastructure investment in Active Directory and Windows.

The third mode, Active Directory–integrated DNS, offers two plusses over traditional zones. For one, the fault tolerance built into Active Directory eliminates the need for primary and secondary nameservers. Effectively, all nameservers using Active Directory–integrated zones are primary nameservers. This has a huge advantage for the use of dynamic DNS as well: namely, the wide availability of nameservers that can accept registrations. Recall that domain controllers and workstations register their locations and availability to the DNS zone using dynamic DNS. In a traditional DNS setup, only one type of nameserver can accept these registrations—the primary server, because it has the only read/write copy of a zone. By creating an Active Directory–integrated zone, all Windows Server 2003 nameservers that store their zone data in Active Directory can accept a dynamic registration, and the change will be propagated using Active Directory multi-master replication, something you'll learn about in Chapter 5. All you need to do to set up this scenario is install Windows Server 2003 on a machine, configure it as a domain controller, install the DNS service, and set up the zone. It's all automatic after that. Contrast this with the standard primary-secondary nameserver setup, where the primary server is likely to be very busy handling requests and zone transfers without worrying about the added load of dynamic DNS registrations. Active Directory–integrated zones relieve this load considerably. And to add to the benefits, Active Directory–integrated zones support compression of replication traffic between sites, which also makes it unnecessary to use the old-style "uncompressed" zone transfers.

 As you read in the previous section, part of the dynamic DNS functionality provided in Windows Server 2003 is the scavenger process. Recall the no-refresh interval function, which was created to eliminate exorbitant amounts of traffic being passed between domain controllers for each DNS re-registration.

Active Directory–integrated zones also afford a big security advantage, in that they provide the capability to lock down dynamic DNS functionality by restricting the ability of users and computers to register records into the system—only computers that are members of the Active Directory domain that hosts the DNS records can add and update records dynamically to these zones. However, to have an Active Directory–integrated zone, your nameservers must be domain controllers for an Active Directory domain. If other nameservers are used that are not domain controllers, they can act as only traditional secondary nameservers, holding a read-only copy of the zone and replicating via the traditional zone transfer process.

If you're already running a nameserver that is a domain controller with an active zone in service, it's easy to convert that to an Active Directory–integrated zone. (And for that matter, it's easy to revert to a primary or secondary zone—this isn't a be-all and end-all.) Here's how to go forward:

1. Open the DNS Management snap-in.
2. Right-click the zone folder you want to convert, and select Properties from the context menu.
3. Navigate to the General tab, as shown in Figure 4-20.

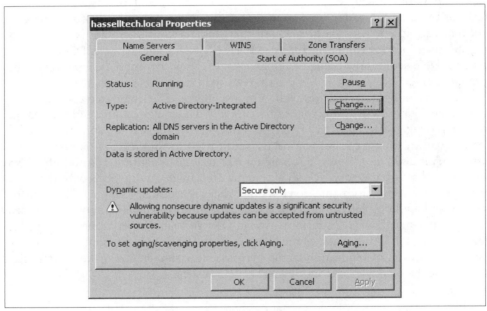

Figure 4-20. Converting a zone to Active Directory–integrated mode

4. To the right of the Type entry—it should now say either Primary or Secondary— click the Change button. The Change Zone Type screen will appear, as shown in Figure 4-21.
5. Check the Store the zone in Active Directory checkbox.
6. Click OK.

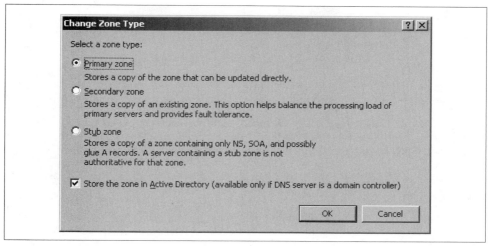

Figure 4-21. Storing a zone in Active Directory

You'll note that your options expand once you've converted to Active Directory–integrated zones. Go back to the zone's properties, and on the General tab, note a couple of things:

- The Dynamic Updates field now allows Secure Only updates.
- You have options for replicating zone changes throughout all domain controllers in Active Directory.

Let's focus on the latter for a moment.

Replication Among Domain Controllers

Windows Server 2003 introduces a new feature that allows you to tune how Active Directory replicates DNS information to other domain controllers. (While I'll present AD in all of its glory in Chapter 5, I'll go ahead and cover this here.) Click the Change button beside the Replication field on the zone properties, and you'll be presented with the Change Zone Replication Scope screen as shown in Figure 4-22.

The default setting is "To all domain controllers in the Active Directory domain," which instructs Windows to behave exactly as it did in Windows 2000 Server: replicate DNS information to all domain controllers in Active Directory, regardless of whether they're actually running the DNS service. Obviously, if you have 20 domain controllers in your domain, but only three domain controllers that run DNS, this is a lot of replication traffic that is just wasted. On this screen, you can select to replicate the DNS information only to domain controllers running DNS in either the forest or the domain. This is very helpful, and for large organizations, it should cut down on WAN traffic.

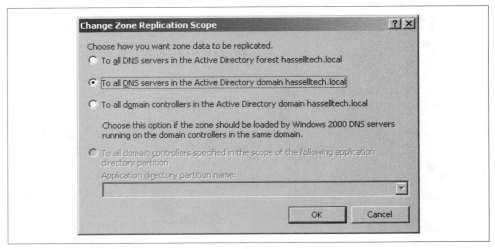

Figure 4-22. Controlling DNS replication in Active Directory

Forwarding

Forwarding, in the simplest terms, is the process by which a nameserver passes on requests it cannot answer locally to another server. You can make forwarding work to your advantage so that you effectively combine the resolver caches for many nameservers into one. By doing this, you allow clients to resolve previously retrieved sites from that "mega-cache" before requiring a true refresh lookup of the information from authoritative nameservers on the public Internet.

Here's how it works. DNS behavior by default is to consult the preferred nameserver first to see if it has the necessary zone information for which the client is searching. It doesn't matter to the client if the preferred nameserver has the zone information but isn't authoritative; having the information is enough for the client, and it takes the returned results and makes the connection. But if the server doesn't have the zone recorded in its files, it must go upstream, to the public Internet, to ask other nameservers for the zone information that's needed. This takes time because it adds a delay to the initial resolution while the preferred nameserver is searching the Internet for the answer. However, after the nameserver looks up the information once, it stores it in its cache of resolved names so that the next user looking for the same resolver information doesn't incur that delay: the preferred nameserver can simply answer out of its cache and return the data nearly instantaneously.

Forwarding takes this cache and expands it to multiple nameservers. Consider an organization with four or five nameservers. Clients likely will have different preferred nameservers, set to one of each of those four or five. So, when one client wants information that's not in his nameserver's cache, his preferred nameserver will search it out and return it, and all future users of that particular preferred nameserver will get information for that zone returned out of its cache. But the other users in the organization won't be able to take advantage of that cached entry because they're likely using other machines as their preferred nameservers.

A forwarder comes in and adds an extra step to this process: if the preferred nameserver doesn't have zone information in its cache, it will ask a separate server, known as the forwarder, if it has information on the requested zone. The forwarder is simply another nameserver that looks up zone information on the Internet and stores it in its own cache for easy reference. So, if all nameservers in an organization are configured to ask the same forwarder for cached information if it has some, all of those nameservers are taking advantage of the forwarder's cache and the near-instantaneous response the forwarder can give to resolution requests. Again, the forwarder acts like a regular nameserver in all respects; it's just that other nameservers in an organization are configured so that they can use the forwarder's cache. If, however, the forwarder machine takes too long to respond to a request, the original preferred nameserver can take over and make a request to the Internet itself, so you don't lose the ability to resolve DNS requests—you're only making it more efficient. You also can have more than one forwarder for your organization if you're worried about a single point of failure, but you lose a bit of the advantage because you're again using more than one cache database.

Now, to set up forwarding: *

1. Open the DNS Management snap-in on the machine you want to set up to forward requests elsewhere.

2. Right-click the server name and choose Properties from the context menu.

3. Navigate to the Forwarders tab, and then in the Selected domain's forwarder IP address list, enter the IP address to which requests should be forwarded. This is shown in Figure 4-23.

4. Also as shown in the previous figure, enter 5 in the Number of seconds before forward queries time out field. Five seconds is a standard number that ensures efficient name resolution if the forwarders somehow fail at their task.

5. Click Apply to complete the process.

Slaving

Slaving is a logical extension to the forwarding process. Servers slaved to a specific nameserver forward requests to that server and rely entirely on that server for resolution; in plain forwarding, on the other hand, the original nameserver can resolve the request itself after a timeout period by querying the root nameservers. With slaving, the upstream nameserver becomes the proxy through which all slaved nameservers make their requests.

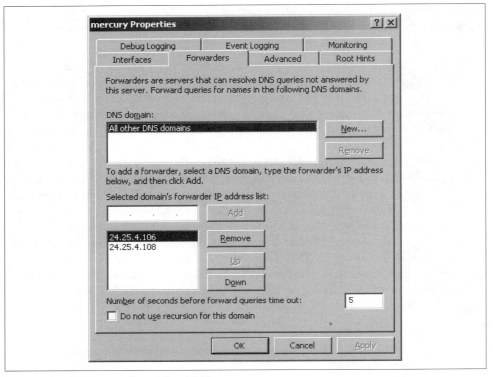

Figure 4-23. Setting up a forwarding DNS system

This is useful mainly in situations where you need multiple nameservers within your organization to handle Active Directory– and internal-related tasks, but you want outside requests to stay outside the firewall. You can set up one very secure nameserver and place it outside your firewall and internal network, allowing it to service requests from the inside to the outside and from the outside to certain machines within the network. Then, you can slave the internal machines to the one machine outside the firewall, making them depend entirely on the machine in the hostile environment but keeping that environment out of your internal network and away from the many nameservers you administer locally. Because most firewalls are stateful inspection machines that only allow packets inside the firewall that are in response to communications initiated internally, and because your internal nameservers query only the external nameserver and not the Internet itself, the public has no reason to know that your internal nameservers exist, and no ability to get to them, either.

Setting up slaving, as opposed to forwarding, involves only one extra checkbox. To enable slaving, follow these steps:

1. Open the DNS Management snap-in on the machine you want to set up to slave to another server.

2. Right-click the server name and choose Properties from the context menu.

3. Set up forwarding first. Navigate to the Forwarders tab, and then in the Selected domain's forwarder IP address list, enter the IP address to which requests should be forwarded. This is shown in Figure 4-24.

4. Also as shown in the previous figure, enter 5 in the "Number of seconds before forward queries time out" field. Five seconds is a standard number that ensures efficient name resolution if the forwarders somehow fail at their task.

5. Now, check the Do not use recursion for this domain box at the bottom of the screen. This slaves the server to the forwarders listed in the box above.

6. Click Apply, and then OK, to complete the process.

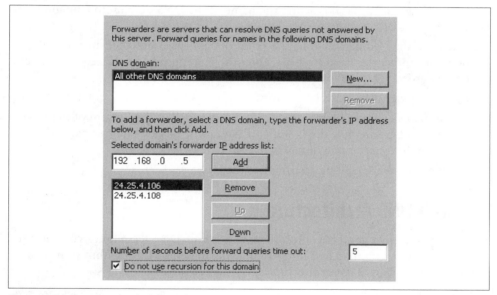

Figure 4-24. Setting up a slaved DNS system

Conditional Forwarding

There might be occasions, especially when using the split DNS architecture technique that I'll cover in the next section, where you want to assign certain nameservers to answer queries for specific domains that your users ask for. Conditional forwarding can be useful for many reasons, including increasing in the speed of name resolution for clients, to effect a structural DNS change in a case of company acquisitions or divestitures.

 Conditional forwarding is supported only in Windows Server 2003.

The Forwarders tab inside the DNS Management snap-in holds multiple lists of domains and their associated forwarders specifically to accommodate the conditional forwarding feature. To set up conditional forwarding, follow these steps:

1. Open the DNS Management snap-in on the machine you want to set up for conditional forwarding.
2. Right-click the server name and choose Properties from the context menu.
3. Navigate to the Forwarders tab, and then click the New button to the right of the DNS domain box.
4. In the New Forwarder box, enter the name of the DNS domain to configure forwarding for, and then press OK.
5. Click the new domain within the DNS domain list, and then in the Selected domain's forwarder IP address list, enter the IP address to which requests should be forwarded. This is shown in Figure 4-25.
6. In the Number of seconds before forward queries time out field, enter 5.
7. Leave the Do not use recursion for this domain box at the bottom of the screen unchecked because you don't want to slave your nameserver permanently to a forwarder for only certain domains.
8. Click Apply, and then OK, to complete the process.

The Split DNS Architecture

Now that you have a good background on the special DNS techniques you can use, let's discuss a very common and fairly secure way to deploy DNS within your organization: using the split DNS architecture.

As I've briefly mentioned previously in this chapter, the split DNS architecture scenario consists of a set of internal nameservers that are used within the corporate computing environment in daily operations. There are also one or more nameservers facing externally to the Internet that outsiders use to connect to your corporation's electronic services, but that are separated from the internal nameservers for security purposes. Outsiders who query for information from your external nameservers won't be able to obtain information on your internal network structure and composition because the external nameserver is completely separate from the internal nameservers that hold this data. The external nameservers hold records only for externally facing

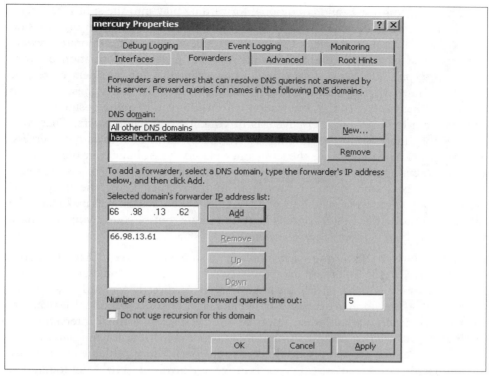

Figure 4-25. Setting up a conditionally forwarded DNS system

servers and not for your entire internal domain. This technique is called the split DNS architecture because DNS information is split between the inside and the outside of an organization.

 Split DNS is a great way to deploy Active Directory-compatible DNS services within your organization, but it isn't the only way to deploy DNS.

Stub Zones

Now is the time to introduce a new type of zone, introduced in Windows Server 2003, called the *stub zone*. Stub zones contain only a subset of the information contained in a regular forward or reverse lookup zone. Specifically, a stub zone contains the SOA record, any pertinent NS records, and the A records for the nameservers that are authoritative for that zone, and nothing more. Stub zones are useful for creating split DNS infrastructures, where internal DNS requests are serviced by internal machines and external DNS requests are serviced elsewhere, perhaps at a data center or Internet service provider.

Now, how do stub zones and conditional forwarding play into the split DNS architecture? In a couple of ways: for one, you might do business with an organization that occasionally needs to access systems that reside within your corporate firewall, not outside of it. Because the external nameservers have no information on your internal systems, there's no default way using split DNS for outsiders to resolve canonical names within your firewall. To resolve this, you use stub zones, placed on the internal nameserver of the corporation with whom you're doing business, which again contain only NS and SOA records of your internal nameservers. That way, when people query for resources that you host, they go to their local nameservers, and their local nameservers see the stub zones placed there about your organization with the proper name and IP address for your nameservers. In essence, any organization that hosts a stub zone for your domain always will know the names and addresses of your nameservers. Best of all, regular zone transfers will make sure the information inside these stub zones is kept up to date, but of course you must have permission to conduct these zone transfers.

Conditional forwarding operates very similarly to stub zones, except that where stub zones simply contain information about a foreign domain's nameservers, conditional forwarding is used on the local nameserver to directly forward requests for information to the foreign nameserver. Unlike stub zones, conditional forwarders don't automatically update when information changes, so manual intervention is required if you need to change the addresses or names of the foreign nameserver; however, you don't need any special permissions on the foreign nameserver to use conditional forwarding because no zone transfers are involved. (I have not found that this process is scriptable, but this issue might be fixed in a future service pack or in Longhorn Server, due in 2007.) Some overhead is involved with conditional forwarding, however, if you have a large list of names to forward; the server has to check each and every request against this list, and if you have a large load on the server, this can slow down response time considerably for everyone hitting that particular server. For just a few zones, however, conditional forwarding can be the best solution, and it can be done without the foreign DNS hostmaster or administrator knowing or approving.

Both of these techniques are a major part of the split DNS architecture strategy. Let's take an example corporation—one that is intending to use Active Directory and is deploying DNS with that in mind—with a primary and secondary nameserver for the external side of the infrastructure and a second set of primary and secondary nameservers for the internal side. A basic diagram of this infrastructure is shown in Figure 4-26.

Note that the first set of primary and secondary nameservers is outside the corporate firewall, and they take care of any external requests that come for the domain. In fact, the registrar that has the corporation's domain registration lists these two nameservers as authoritative for that domain. However, the zone files on these servers are static—they list only a few, rarely changing items, which could be web, FTP, and mail servers. This is really all the public needs to know.

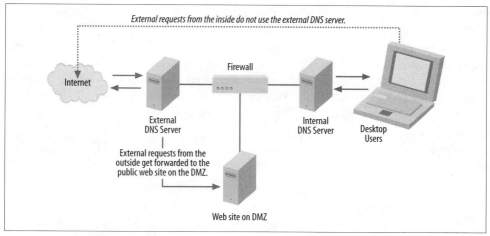

Figure 4-26. How split DNS architecture is laid out

There are two points to note about this portion of the scenario:

- The external nameservers are *not* authoritative for the internal, Active Directory–based DNS structure. They are authoritative only for external, Internet-based requests.

- If your ISP has been providing hosting for your nameservers, there's no reason it can't continue doing so. In fact, this is simpler to administer than hosting both sets of nameservers on your own premises.

Now let's focus on the internal nameservers for this corporation. The primary nameserver on the internal side is configured as the primary nameserver for the internal zone and is instructed to accept dynamic DNS updates from internal workstations and servers. However, these internal servers are blind (at this point) to the fact that outside the firewall, another set of nameservers is holding the same zone name with different records. In addition, the workstations within the business are configured to think of the authoritative nameservers for the domain as the internal servers; this is where they will register themselves via dynamic DNS, and also where they will first look to resolve Internet names.

So, how do internal users resolve names on the Internet if they can't see the external set of nameservers? It's easy—the internal primary and secondary nameservers are configured to forward Internet requests to the external primary nameserver. So, if the address being requested by the client isn't in the internal nameserver's cache (meaning it hasn't been requested recently by another client), it will ask the external nameserver for the answer. No zone transfers are involved—it's just straight forwarding, as I covered earlier in this chapter. But how might external users resolve internal DNS names? The short answer is: they won't. That's a security feature. Because the external users know only about the external nameservers, and the external nameservers know only about themselves and not the internal nameservers, there's no way for the external nameservers to report any information about internal DNS records inside the firewall.

The only problem you might run into is when internal users attempt to access the company's own resources on the external side of the firewall; to allow this, simply add a static record to the internal nameservers that points to the correct external resource. You don't introduce any security problems that way because there's still no "window" for external users to see into your internal structure.

So, in essence, you have a DNS architecture "split" between internal and external nameservers. If you're looking to reproduce this architecture, the following summarizes the correct procedure:

1. Create two sets of servers—one for in front of the firewall, and one for behind it. Install the DNS service on both.

2. Make every nameserver point to itself for its own DNS information; you do this within the network card properties where you indicate the IP address. There's no need to configure a secondary nameserver for each of these.

3. Copy any external records your internal users might need to the internal zone. This includes web, mail, and FTP servers. Remember, if you don't do this, your users won't be able to resolve the names of anything outside the firewall.

4. Configure external forwarders—these are the machines to which your internal nameservers will forward requests so that your internal users can resolve Internet names.

5. Slave the internal set of nameservers to these external forwarders you created in the previous step. This shields them from the Internet's blinding eye.

6. Configure all machines on the internal network to use only the internal nameservers. This allows them to register with Active Directory if appropriate and to find internal resources, which they couldn't find if directed to the external nameservers outside the firewall.

Security Considerations

Split DNS architecture is implemented with security in mind, but you can always take more steps to harden those DNS systems. You've already taken two steps in this process: for one, slaving the internal nameservers to the external forwarders eliminates the possibility that if the firewall of some other transmission problem prevents the external forwarder from responding, the internal nameserver will conduct its own search of the Internet. You obviously don't want your internal nameservers touching anything on the outside of the firewall except those external forwarders.

The other step is the use of the firewall to separate the two sets of nameservers from each other. You need to ensure that the firewall that protects the perimeter of your corporate network from the Internet is configured correctly and locked down as tightly as possible. I recommend the book *Building Internet Firewalls*, Second Edition (O'Reilly) for detailed and thorough guidance on this topic. You'll especially want to ensure that only a few ports, such as the DNS port, 53, are open.

Other than that, this architecture is fairly secure right after implementation.

Backup and Recovery

If you thought configuring DNS in the first place was difficult, you'll find the backup and recovery procedures refreshingly simple. There are two locations in the Registry to back up the DNS service and one directory on the physical filesystem.

 The following procedure won't work with Active Directory–integrated zones, as the zone files are within the directory service and are not available on the filesystem.

To back up a server that's hosting one or more primary or secondary DNS zones, follow these steps:

1. On the nameserver, stop the DNS service using the Services applet in the Control Panel or through the command line.
2. Open the Registry Editor (select Start/Run, type **regedit**, and press Enter).
3. Navigate to the key:

    HKEY_LOCAL_MACHINE\System\CurrentControlSet\Services\DNS

4. Right-click the DNS folder, and from the context menu, choose Export.
5. When prompted for a filename, enter **DNS-CCS** and choose an appropriate location that is off the server.
6. Now, navigate to the *HKEY_LOCAL_MACHINE\SOFTWARE\Microsoft\Windows NT\CurrentVersion\DNS* server key.
7. Right-click the DNS Server folder, and from the context menu, choose Export.
8. Name this file **DNS-CV** and again choose a location that is not on the current server. These two files will be *DNS-CCS.REG* and *DNS-CV.REG*.
9. Now, using Windows Explorer, navigate to the *%SystemRoot%\System32\dns* directory on the boot drive.
10. Find all files with the *.DNS* extension, select them, and then copy them to the same location that you exported *DNS-CCS.REG* and *DNS-CV.REG*.

Your DNS service is now completely backed up. Restart the DNS service to continue using it.

To restore a set of DNS configuration files, install a Windows Server 2003 machine and use the same computer name, DNS suffix, and IP address. Be sure to install the DNS service. Then, copy all of the *.DNS* files from your backup to the *%SystemRoot%\ System32\dns* directory and stop the DNS service. Double-click *DNS-CCS.REG* and confirm that you want its contents imported into the registry; do the same for *DNS-CV.REG*. Finally, restart the DNS service, and your replacement server should function normally.

 If you want to move only the primary role for a particular zone from one nameserver to another, simply copy the *.DNS* file for that zone to the target computer. Run the New Zone Wizard as described earlier in this chapter, and then instruct it to use a preexisting zone file.

Command-Line Utilities

In this section, I'll describe some useful programs designed to be run from a command line that you can use to automate your DNS setup and configuration processes.

DNSCmd

The Windows Server 2003 Support Tools collection, described earlier in the book, contains the DNSCmd utility, which is a great way to access some command DNS configuration-related functions through the power and speed of the command prompt. To get to DNSCmd, look in the *Support\Tools* directory on the Windows Server 2003 distribution CD for the file *support.cab*. Inside, copy and paste DNSCmd to a convenient location.

DNSCmd displays and changes the properties of DNS servers, zones, and resource records. Some operations of this tool work at the DNS server level while others work at the zone level. You can use DNSCmd on any Windows 2000 or XP computer as long as the user that is running the application is a member in the Administrators or Server Operators group on the target computer. Both the user account and the server computer must be members of the same domain or reside within trusted domains.

DNSCmd can be used in any of the following situations:

- You want to retrieve information about a DNS server.
- You want to begin the scavenging process.
- You want to view information and contents of a DNS zone.
- You want to create, remove, or "pause" zones.
- You want to change the properties of a zone.
- You want to add, delete, or enumerate records in a zone.

You use DNSCmd simply by specifying attributes and their values as part of a command. For example, to create a new standard primary zone called corp.hasselltech.local on a server named dc1.corp.hasselltech.local and stored in corp.hasselltech.local.dns files, use the following syntax:

```
dnscmd dc1.corp.hasselltech.local /ZoneAdd corp.hasselltech.local /Primary /file
corp.hasselltech.local.dns
```

I could have also chosen to make corp.hasselltech.local a secondary zone by replacing the */Primary* switch with */Secondary*.

To create a new A record, I could issue the following command, which adds a record for a machine named www to the zone with an IP address of 192.168.1.23 to the same DNS server as the previous example:

```
Dnscmd dc1.corp.hasselltech.local /RecordAdd corp.hasselltech.local www A
192.168.1.23
```

You can see all of the zones on a target server by entering the following command:

```
dnscmd dc1.corp.hasselltech.local /enumzones
```

If you're experiencing some problems with replication and want to trigger the process manually, you can start it with the following command (assuming you want to use the same server to begin the process as in the previous examples):

```
Dnscmd dc1.corp.hasselltech.local /ZoneRefresh corp.hasselltech.local
```

Likewise, you might find yourself needing to manually age all of the records on a particular machine. You can easily do so through DNSCmd using the following:

```
dnscmd corp.hasselltech.local /ageallrecords dc1.corp.hasselltech.local
```

You'll need to confirm your choice, and then the current time will be applied to all records on that machine.

You might also need to clear the DNS cache on a target server, which can be done using this command:

```
Dnscmd dc1.corp.hasselltech.local /clearcache
```

To quickly stop and start the DNS process on the target computer, use the following command:

```
Dnscmd dc1.corp.hasselltech.local /restart
```

If you want to export a particular zone to a file, you can issue the following command:

```
dnscmd /zoneexport corp.hasselltech.local corp.hasselltech.local.dns
```

And, finally, to delete a zone from a target server, use the following command:

```
dnscmd dc1.corp.hasselltech.local /zonedelete corp.hasselltech.local
```

DNSLint

Also on the distribution CD in support tools is DNSLint. DNSLint is a utility born out of the desire to automate the process of troubleshooting lame delegation issues and problems with AD replication because of faulty DNS records. DNSLint is a great tool to make sure that every DNS server that has records on your services has *correct* records and that there are no issues with those DNS servers' data. (And in case you're wondering, the name "DNSLint" comes from the idea that lint is something you find in your blue jeans after they come out of the dryer. When you find lint, it is useless and perhaps even embarrassing, meaning you probably quickly discard it. You should do the same with outdated or inaccurate DNS records for critical machines on your network.)

The best thing to do from the start is to create a standard report on any given DNS domain, using the following:

```
dnslint /d hasselltech.local /v
```

DNSLint produces an HTML-based report and then starts Internet Explorer to display the result. The results are color-coded with warnings in amber and errors in red for easy scanning. (You can elect to get a text-based report, if you prefer.) The report generated by the previous command will show a detailed listing of each DNS server for the corp.hasselltech.local domain and indicate whether or not the server responds to a query on port 53, which is the standard DNS port. It will tell you how it found each server, and it will also list each server that reports authoritatively. You will also see Mail Exchanger (MX) records in the zone, which is a useful addition to help with troubleshooting SMTP routing problems.

If you are specifically having email difficulties, you can use DNSLint to determine whether a designated email server listens on the correct port. Use the following command:

```
dnslint /d domainname.tld /c
```

The report generated by that command will list whether a server indicated in an MX record is listening for SMTP, POP3 and IMAP4 requests, and will also show the SMTP header returned by the server to help in diagnostics.

To assist in troubleshooting, the following functions are available in DNSLint:

dnslint /d domainname

> This diagnoses potential causes of "lame delegation," covered earlier in this chapter, and other related DNS problems. You'll receive an HTML-based report once the diagnosis is complete. Add /v for more information about how the DNS servers listed in the report were found. If you get errors saying that the domain specified is not listed with InterNIC, simply add the /s option.

dnslint /ql mylist.txt

> This verifies a user-defined set of DNS records on multiple DNS servers. You can specify in a simple text file the sets of records you'd like to test. For example, the

following tests A, PTR, CNAME, and MX records for the domain name and IP address of a fairly well-known company:

```
microsoft.com,a,r          ;A record
207.46.197.100,ptr,r       ;PTR record
microsoft.com,cname,r      ;CNAME record
microsoft.com,mx,r          ;MX record
```

```
dnslint /ad localhost
```

This verifies the DNS records on a specific host (in this case, the current machine) specifically used for Active Directory replication. If you get errors saying that the domain specified is not listed with InterNIC, simply add the /s option.

The Last Word

In this chapter, you saw how DNS is crucial to network communications among machines, and particularly to those who participate in Windows domains. DNS is such a core component of Active Directory that it was important to learn about it in depth before introducing Active Directory itself. In the next chapter, I'll look at how Active Directory works and how it relies on DNS as its foundation.

CHAPTER 5
Active Directory

In Windows NT, administrators were introduced to the concept of domains. Active Directory builds on that concept by creating a dynamic, easily accessible structure through which directory and management information can be stored and accessed centrally throughout an organization. By using Active Directory, you create a structure for managing your equipment, and the people who use that equipment, which is a helpful feature for all but the smallest of operations.

By using Active Directory you have access to several cool management tools, including Group Policy (GP), the ability to put groups inside groups multiple times, and an online directory of users, computers, printers, and contacts that you can access easily through the Windows user interface. Although you certainly can operate a Windows-based network without Active Directory, you lose out on a lot of functionality. You will learn about these tools in this chapter and the next.

In this chapter, I'll introduce you to Active Directory and its concepts, walk you through the process of building an Active Directory domain and tree structure, guide you through the process of managing domain users and groups, and discuss in detail the process of directory content replication. I'll also discuss different roles that domain controllers take in an Active Directory environment, the importance of time synchronization and how to accomplish it, and how to keep your Active Directory in tip-top shape through regular maintenance.

There's a lot to cover in this chapter, so let's dig in.

Active Directory Objects and Concepts

First it's important to learn that you can divide Active Directory components into two "states of being"—physical components, which include domain controllers, sites, and subnets; and logical components, which include forests, trees, domains, and organizational units. Physical and logical components of Active Directory don't necessarily have to correlate with each other: for example, a domain controller can be a member of a forest based in Rome, while actually sitting in a machine room in Chicago.

Keep that frame of reference in mind. Now, before diving in any further, let me introduce a few common terms:

Directory

A *directory* is a single repository for information about users and resources within an organization. Active Directory is a type of directory that holds the properties and contact information for a variety of resources within a network so that users and administrators can find them with ease.

Domain

A *domain* is a collection of objects within the directory that forms a management boundary. Multiple domains can exist within a forest (defined later in this list), each with their own collection of objects and organizational units (also defined later in this list). Domains are named using the industry-standard DNS protocol, covered in detail in the previous chapter.

Domain controller

A *domain controller* holds the security information and directory object database for a particular domain and is responsible for authenticating objects within its sphere of control. Multiple domain controllers can be associated with a given domain, and each domain controller holds certain roles within the directory, although for all intents and purposes all domain controllers within a domain are "equal" in power. This is unlike the primary and backup labels assigned to domain controllers in Windows NT.

Forest

A *forest* is the largest logical container within Active Directory and encompasses all domains within its purview, all linked together via transitive trusts that are constructed automatically. This way, all domains in a particular forest automatically trust all other domains within the forest.

Organizational unit

An *organizational unit* (OU) is a container with objects (discussed next) contained within it. You can arrange OUs in a hierarchical, tree-like fashion and design them in a structure that best fits your organization for boundary delineation or ease of administration.

Object

Within Active Directory, an *object* is anything that can be part of the directory—that is, an object can be a user, a group, a shared folder, a printer, a contact, and even an OU. Objects are unique physical "things" within your directory and you can manage them directly.

Schema

The *schema* in Active Directory is the actual structure of the database—the "fields," to use a not-quite-applicable analogy. The different types of information stored in Active Directory are referred to as *attributes*. Active Directory's schema also supports a standard set of classes, or types of objects. *Classes* describe an object and the associated properties that are required to create an instance of the object. For example, user objects are "instances" of the user class, computer objects are "instances" of the computer class, and so on. Think of classes as guideline templates describing different types of objects.

Site

A site is a collection of computers that are in distinct geographical locations—or at least are connected via a permanent, adequate-speed network link. Sites are generally used to determine how domain controllers are kept up to date; Active Directory will select its methodology for distributing those updates (a process called *replication*) based on how you configure a site to keep traffic over an expensive WAN link down to a minimum.

Tree

A *tree* is simply a collection of domains that begins at a single root and branches out into peripheral, "child" domains. Trees can be linked together within forests as well, and trees also share an unbroken DNS namespace—that is, hasselltech. local and america.hasselltech.local are part of the same tree, but mycorp.com and hasselltech.local are not.

Trust

A *trust* in terms of Active Directory is a secure method of communicating between domains, trees, and forests. Much like they worked in Windows NT, trusts allow users in one Active Directory domain to authenticate to other domain controllers within another, separate, distinct domain within the directory. Trusts can be one-way (A to B only, not B to A), transitive (A trusts B and B trusts C, so A trusts C), or cross-linked (A to C and B to D).

Domains

When examining Active Directory for the first time, it's easiest to examine the domain first because so much of the basis of Active Directory is derived from the domain. It's adequate to boil down the function of domains into three basic areas:

- Consolidating lists of usernames and passwords for all machines within a domain and providing an infrastructure for using that consolidated list
- Providing a method of subdividing objects within a domain for easier administration (into OUs, as described earlier)
- Offering a centralized, searchable list of resources within the domain so that users and administrators can easily query that list to find objects they need

Domains, at a minimum, keep a list of all authorized users and their passwords on a machine or groups of machines called domain controllers. This list is stored in Active Directory. However, many other objects are stored within the directory—which is actually a file on a domain controller's hard drive called *NTDS.DIT*—including sites, OUs, groups of users, groups of computers, GPOs (described in Chapter 6), and contacts, just to name a few.

The engine that drives this database of information is the same engine within Microsoft's powerhouse Exchange Server product, and it supports the transmission of database contents to multiple domain controllers over network links—a process called replication. Replication answers the question of how multiple domain controllers within a domain can contain the same information. For example, if you have a domain controller in Seattle and another in Charlotte, and you were to add a user in Charlotte, what if that user tried to log on to a computer in Seattle? How would the Seattle domain controller know about the user added in Charlotte? Replication allows Active Directory to transmit changed data across a domain to all relevant domain controllers so that the contents of the directory are always up to date on each domain controller.

Astute readers at this point who are familiar with the domain structure of Microsoft's Windows NT products surely are asking, "What about PDCs and BDCs?" For the most part, Microsoft has removed that designation from domain controllers in Active Directory environments, meaning that with only a couple of minor exceptions, all domain controllers are equal. This is referred to as a *multimaster* environment.

Because a domain controller holds a large database of information, Active Directory has some interesting characteristics that weren't necessarily true of NT 4.0's Security Accounts Manager (SAM)-based list of accounts. For instance, programmers can write code to interface directly with Active Directory and run queries to pull data from the database. These programmers can use either the Lightweight Directory Access Protocol (LDAP), an industry-standard protocol for accessing any sort of directory, or the Microsoft-specific Active Directory Services Interface (ADSI) for taking advantage of Active Directory features not supported directly within the LDAP specification. Additionally, Active Directory doesn't have the same size limitations that the SAM had. Active Directory easily can handle up to a few million objects, as compared to the SAM's ability to handle no more than about 5,000 accounts.(That's scalability, folks!) Active Directory is also fast when handling large amounts of data, so you won't get bogged down when your directory grows.

Organizational Units

A domain can be an awfully big, comprehensive unit to manage, and most environments would benefit from some mechanism to separate that large, unitary domain into smaller, more manageable chunks. An organizational unit is Active Directory's way of doing that. Organizational units, or OUs, act like folders on a regular client's operating system, containing every type of object that Active Directory supports. You might choose to separate your domain into OUs in one of the following ways:

- A university might create a domain with a name corresponding to the entire university (ncsu.edu, for example), with each college in that institution getting an OU (biology, physics, mathematics, etc.).

- A medium-size business might use one domain for all of its Active Directory needs, but segregate objects into their geographical locations—an OU for the Los Angeles office, an OU for the Birmingham office, and an OU for the Richmond office.

- Larger corporations might want to divide their domain by department. Within business.com, for example, an OU could be created each for Sales, Support, Marketing, Development, and Q/A.

- An administrator also could decide to create OUs based on the type of objects contained therein—for example, a Computers OU, a Printers OU, and so on.

A particularly interesting feature of OUs is the ability to delegate administrative control over them to a subset of users in Active Directory. Take, for instance, the third example in the previous list. Perhaps you, as the domain administrator, want to designate one technically savvy person in each department as the official Password Change Administrator, to reduce your administrative load. You can delegate the authority to modify users' passwords to each user over only their respective OU, thereby both allowing them power but finely controlling it over certain areas of your Active Directory infrastructure. This ability is called delegation, and you'll find an entire section devoted to it later in this chapter.

OUs are designed to be containers in Active Directory, meaning that their point is to hold objects and to have contents. You can apply GPs to the objects within a specific OU (as you'll see in Chapter 6), controlling users' desktops, locking them out of potentially dangerous system modification settings, and creating a consistent user experience across your domain.

Sites

Sites are great ways to manage the use of bandwidth for Active Directory replication across WAN links. All domain controllers in an Active Directory domain must stay in contact with each other at regular intervals to acquire and transmit the changes that have occurred to their databases since the last update. Otherwise, information becomes "stale" and the directory is no good to anyone. However, this replication traffic can be costly if you have domain controllers in different countries and you use slow WAN links to keep in contact with your various offices.

By designating different sites with Active Directory, a process we'll cover later in the replication section of this chapter, you can tell Active Directory to compress the replication traffic to allow it to be transmitted more quickly, and you can give preferences to certain WAN links over others by using the "cost" feature, specifying a higher value for a connection you want used less often and a lower value for a connection you'd like to use the most often. It's a great way to manage your telecommunications expenses while still taking advantage of the better management features of Active Directory.

In a domain environment, the Distrubuted File System, which you learned about in Chapter 3, also uses Active Directory's site structure to control file replication traffic.

Groups

The point of groups is to make assigning attributes to larger sets of users easier on administrators. Picture a directory with 2,500 users. You create a new file share and need to give certain employees permissions to that file share—for example, all accounting users. Do you want to take a hard-copy list of all members of the accounting department and hand-pick the appropriate users from your list of 2,500? Of course you don't. Groups allow you to create an object called Accounting and insert all the appropriate users into that group. So, instead of selecting each individual user from a large list, you can pick the Accounting group, and all members of that group will have the same permissions on the file share.

There are four different scopes of groups within Windows Server 2003 and Active Directory, and each scope can nest groups differently. Let's outline the group scopes first, and then bear with me as I explain the concepts of each:

Machine local groups
> *Machine local groups* contain objects that pertain only to the local computer (or more specifically, to objects contained within the local computer's SAM database). These types of groups can have members that are global groups, domain local groups from their own domain, and universal or global groups from their own domain or any other domain that they trust.

Domain local groups
> *Domain local groups* can be created only on a domain controller, so ordinary client computers or member servers of a domain cannot host domain local groups. Domain local groups can be put inside machine local groups within the same domain (this is a process called *nesting*). They can contain global groups from a domain that trusts the current domain and other domain local groups from the same domain. As you will see later in the chapter, they are of limited utility unless you are working in a larger, multi-domain environment.

Domain global groups
> Like domain local groups, *domain global groups* can be created only on a domain controller, but domain global groups can be put into any local group of any machine that is a member of the current domain or a trusted domain. Domain global groups can also be nested in other global groups, however all nested

domain global groups must be from the same domain. Domain global groups are great tools that contain all the functionality of domain local groups, and more, and they are the most common type of group used across a domain.

Universal groups

> *Universal groups* are a sort of "do-it-all" type of group. New to Active Directory in Windows 2000 and Windows Server 2003, universal groups can contain global and universal groups, and those nested groups can be from any domain in your Active Directory forest.

Briefly, I'll also mention that there are two types of groups: a *security group* is used for the purposes of assigning or denying rights and permissions, and a *distribution group* is used for the sole purpose of sending email. A security group, though, can also act as a distribution group.

Nesting

Nesting is a useful ability that has been around in limited form since Windows NT. By nesting groups you achieve the ability to quickly and painlessly assign permissions and rights to different users. For example, let's say you have a resource called COLORLASER and you want all full-time employees to be able to access that resource. You don't have a group called FTEs that contains all your full-timers throughout your organization, but your departmental administrators have set up a structure wherein full-time employees are put into groups and part-timers are in another. To quickly create your overall FTE group, you can take your different groups of users from each department (ACCTG_FTE, ADMIN_FTE, PRODUCTION_FTE, and SALES_FTE, for example) and put them within a new group you create called ALL_FTE. Then, you can quickly assign access rights to COLORLASER by giving the ALL_FTE group permission to use the resource. You have "nested" the departmental groups within one big group.

Different types of groups, as you saw in the previous list of groups, support different methods of nesting. Table 5-1 shows the relationships between the types of groups and the respective abilities to nest.

Table 5-1. Nesting by group type

Type of nesting	Machine local	Domain local	Domain global	Universal
Within themselves	Yes	Yes (from the same domain)	Yes (from the same domain)	Yes
Within other types	None	Machine local	Machine local Domain local Universal	Machine local Domain local Domain global

You should remember a couple of important issues regarding backward compatibility with Windows NT 4.0 and Windows 2000 and the types of group capabilities available:

- Active Directory cannot support universal groups until you operate at least in Windows 2000 Native functional level, as NT 4.0 supports only one level of group nesting.

- A group cannot have more than 5,000 members until your forest is operating in the Windows Server 2003 forest-functional level. Functional levels are covered later in this chapter, but for now, be aware of this limitation.

Trees

Trees refer to the hierarchies of domains you create within Active Directory. The first Active Directory domain you create is automatically designated the root of your first tree, and any domains after that are considered child domains unless you choose to create a domain at the root of a new tree. Child domains always have the root domain in their name—for example, if I create the hasselltech.local domain, any child domains must be in the format of newdomainname.hasselltech.local. In effect, you are creating what are referred to as subdomains in DNS parlance. You can create as many child domain levels as you need; children can be children of other children of other children, and so on, as long as it makes sense to you.

A neat feature of Active Directory is that it automatically creates two-way trust relationships between parent and child domains, so you don't need to manually trust the domains you create. As such, my new child domain from our earlier example will automatically trust its parent domain, hasselltech.local, and the parent will trust the child—the transitive trust is created automatically. This type of trust is passed along the child domain chain, so a domain such as charlotte.eastcoast.us.northamerica. enterprise.com will automatically trust eastcoast.us.northamerica.enterprise.com, us. northamerica.enterprise.com, northamerica.enterprise.com, and enterprise.com.

Forests

Forests, in the simplest terms, are just groups of trees. All trees in a forest trust each other automatically. Think of a forest as an extended family, and individual domain trees as brothers. If you have five brothers in a family, each child of those brothers trusts their immediate brothers, and (usually!) each brother's family trusts the other brother's family—cousins typically get along. Forests just refer to collections of domain trees that trust each other.

There are two caveats, though, that are fairly significant and bear mentioning:

- The only way to add a domain to a tree is to create it completely from scratch, adding it to an existing tree at that time. It's the same with trees—you can't directly add an existing tree to an existing forest without deleting and subsequently recreating it.

- Likewise, two existing, separate domains can't be linked together as parent and child. For example, hasselltech.local created on one network and charlotte.hasselltech.local created on another, separate network cannot be joined later as parent and child. The child would need to be recreated or migrated.

Transitive forest root trusts

The latter of the preceding two limitations might be frustrating for you, and you're not alone. Fortunately, what experts might term an "official hack" is available to effectively graft existing domains together into a tree-like structure so that trusts are established. Although it's not as easy and not as flexible as a forest—Active Directory makes things slick and easy when you do things its way—it will work, with effort and maybe a bit of luck. The tool is called a *transitive forest root trust*, and with it, you can make two disparate forests trust each other.

Let's say I have a forest called businessone.com. Business One purchases another organization with an Active Directory forest created already, known as businesstwo.net. Recall that I can't just graft businesstwo.net onto the already existing forest at Business One. However, with a transitive forest root trust, I can make it so that businessone.com trusts businesstwo.net, achieving some of the benefits of one unified forest. However, there are limitations and disadvantages:

- Each forest must be operating in the Windows Server 2003 forest functional level. Although I will cover this later, suffice it to say that all domain controllers in each domain in each forest must be running Windows Server 2003. This might be a prohibitive expense.

- You'll learn more about this feature later in this chapter, but keep this in mind for now: a transitive forest root trust does not automatically make one, unified global catalog. Two separate forests still equals two separate global catalogs.

- Transitive forest root trusts do not flow through. For example, businessone.com and businesstwo.net trust each other. But if businessone.com buys businessthree.org and a trust is set up there, businesstwo.net will not trust businessthree.org automatically—another trust will need to be set up. With that, we're back to the kludgy trust process found in Windows NT 4.0.

So, transitive forest root trusts aren't the answer to everything, but they are a reasonably effective way to create a "pseudo-forest" within already existing trees.

The dedicated forest root model

You also can create a hedge against future Active Directory changes if you are deploying Active Directory for the first time. If a department in your organization deploys Active Directory ahead of other departments, as the other groups come on board, they effectively become subordinates of that first domain. How does a smart administrator get around that problem? The dedicated forest root model provides a way to maintain the autonomy of multiple domains that you create. Figure 5-1 shows how this is achieved.

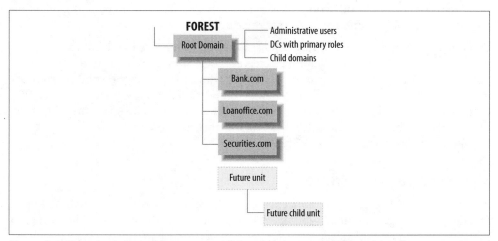

Figure 5-1. How the dedicated forest root model enables separate NT domains to be separate in Active Directory

A dedicated forest root domain can be either an "empty domain," which contains only a small number of universal users and resources, or a normal production domain that just happens to be at the root of a forest. The latter is not recommended. An empty forest root domain that does *not* serve as a production domain is advantageous for several reasons. For one, the domain administrators group in the root domain has power over the forest, which is something you might not want. Keeping the root empty allows you to delegate administrative authority to individual domains without giving everything away, a security protection that keeps honest administrators honest. It also helps you to structure your Active Directory environment; a constant root makes further changes logical and easy to implement and manage—for instance, if you acquire a new company or build a new office. The forest root domain, if kept empty, is very easy to replicate and to back up. And if you ever make changes to the administrative authority in your business, you can transfer the keys to the kingdom to others without affecting the administrators' autonomy of your child domains.

You can name the empty forest root domain anything you want—even emptyroot.local. It is only a placeholder. However, most clients use a domain name based on their company's domain name.

However, the key to the empty root strategy is to keep the root empty: have it contain only one administrative account—the Enterprise Administrator, which is, of course, created by default when you create the first domain in a new forest—and use that only when absolutely necessary. Then, create all the domains you need under that first domain and you won't have one particular domain in your organization unnecessarily holding Enterprise Admin-style accounts.

Of course, this method has its downsides. Costs definitely are involved: for one, you need a separate license of Windows Server 2003 for your dedicated forest root domain controller, and you have the burden of administrative responsibility in ensuring that the root domain is kept up, patched, and the like. However, if you are in a high-growth industry and your organization is likely to make acquisitions and divestitures within the near future, it's best to use this method to hedge against major changes to Active Directory structure.

Shared Folders and Printers

As you saw in Chapter 3, the concept of shared folders and printers within Active Directory merely relates to a "pointer" residing within the directory, guiding users to the real location on a physical filesystem of a server for a particular shared directory, or the location of a print share on a print server. This process is known as publishing a share (or publishing a printer).

The point of publishing shares and printers in Active Directory is to make them available for searching, either through Active Directory Users and Computers for administrators or through Start → Search or Start → Find for client users. You can search for shared folder or printer names containing target keywords, and their locations will be populated within the results box.

Contacts

Contacts are simply objects in the directory that represent people and contain attributes with indicators as to how to contact them. Contacts neither represent users of any directory, nor convey any privileges to log on to the network or use any network or domain resources.

The point of the contacts object is to create within Active Directory a phonebook of sorts, with names of vital business contacts that reside outside your organization—partners, customers, vendors, and the like. Because Active Directory as a directory can be queried by the LDAP protocol, which most groupware applications support, the contents of contacts objects likely can be accessed directly within that application.

Global Catalog

The global catalog, in an Active Directory environment, acts as a sort of subset directory that is passed among all domains in a particular forest. Consider that Active Directory gives you the ability to connect to any computer in your particular Active Directory tree. If you have a small organization, this isn't much of a problem, but in a large organization with many domains, can you imagine the performance lag while Active Directory tries to (a) find the correct domain where your account resides, then (b) communicate with it, and finally (c) log you in? You would be waiting for a significant amount of time for all the pieces of the puzzle to come together in a complex Active Directory implementation.

For that reason, Active Directory constructs a subset of all the domains in a forest and puts it into what's called the *global catalog* (GC). The GC contains a list of all domains in the forest and a list of all the objects in those domains, but only a subset of the attributes for each object. This is a fairly small bit of information compared to the rest of the directory, and because of its reduced size, it is easy to pass on to given domain controllers in the forest. So, now when a user connects to a computer in any given domain in a forest, the nearest domain controller checks the username against the GC and instantly finds the correct "home" domain for a user and the authentication process can begin. Think of the GC, therefore, as an index of your directory, much like the index of this book helps you to see which pages cover a topic in which you're interested.

The GC also contains the name of each global group for every domain in the forest, and it contains the name and the complete membership list of every universal group in the forest. (Recall that universal groups can contain users and other groups from any domain in the forest.) So, limit your use of universal groups, lest you decrease the performance of your users' logins.

Building an Active Directory Structure

To get the best foundation for the rest of this chapter, much as we did in Chapter 4, let's actually build an Active Directory forest, tree, and domain. In this section, I'll walk through the process of creating a domain, promoting a domain controller, adding another domain controller to the domain, adding a second child domain, and then adding a few users and groups to the mix.

The First Domain

The first domain in an Active Directory setup is special for a few reasons. For one, the setup process for a new domain automatically adds the first domain controller to that domain—the machine on which you run the Active Directory Wizard becomes the first domain controller for the new domain. Second, this new domain becomes the root of the entire forest, meaning it has special powers over other domains you create within the forest, even if their names aren't the same. We'll go over that in a bit.

To start the process, from the machine you want to become the first domain controller for the new domain, select Run from the Start menu, type **DCPROMO**, and click OK. The Active Directory Installation Wizard starts, as shown in Figure 5-2.

Figure 5-2. Beginning Active Directory installation

Click Next to continue and you'll see the Operating System Compatibility screen. This screen is simply informing you that Windows 95 clients and Windows NT clients running Service Pack 3 or earlier, by default, will be effectively locked out of participating in the domain and using resources within Active Directory. This is because of more stringent communications requirements in Windows Server 2003—clients must electronically "sign" their transmissions to the server to make sure those transmissions aren't intercepted and modified on their way to the server—and Windows 95 doesn't have logic to perform this signing process. You can choose to relax these requirements later, but I don't recommend that. (It's 2006. It's definitely time to move to at least Windows 98, which can sign its communications with the Active Directory Client software.) Click Next to continue.

The Domain Controller Type screen appears, as shown in Figure 5-3.

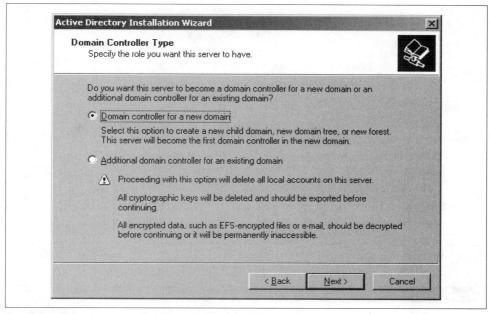

Figure 5-3. Selecting a new domain controller installation

You can create a new forest, a new domain tree, or a new domain by selecting the first option: Domain controller for a new domain. Select the second option to simply promote the current machine to domain controller status within an existing domain, something I'll walk through in just a bit. Click Next.

The Create New Domain screen appears, as shown in Figure 5-4.

Here, you can create a brand-new domain with the first option, a new child domain for an existing domain tree (such as *main.jonathanhassell.com* under an existing *jonathanhassell.com* domain), or a completely separate domain tree that is *not* a child to any other domain but that is located within the same forest. For this demonstration, select the first option, and click Next.

The New Domain Name screen appears, as shown in Figure 5-5.

On this screen, type the full DNS canonical name of the domain you're creating. In this example, I'll use the domain for the web site of this book, *learning2003.com*, as shown in the figure. Enter the name, and click Next to continue.

The NetBIOS Domain Name screen appears. This is shown in Figure 5-6.

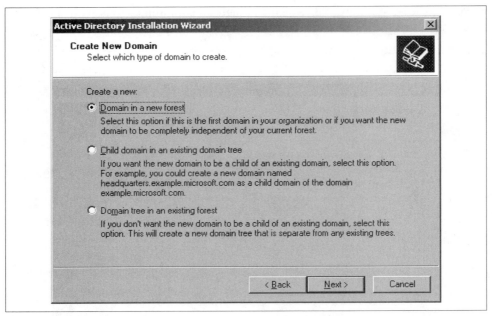

Figure 5-4. *Creating a new domain*

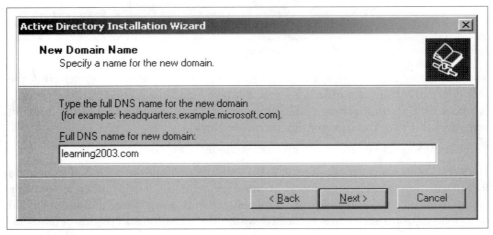

Figure 5-5. *The New Domain Name screen*

The NetBIOS name allows down-level compatibility with Windows NT and Windows 9x clients. NetBIOS names are restricted to 15 characters or fewer and should consist of letters and integers only. The Active Directory Wizard selects a NetBIOS name from the full DNS name you selected in the previous step, simply taking the leftmost part of the name. You can change this if you want. This name is what your users will see when they are logging on to their machines, if they have chosen to look at the advanced options in the logon dialog box.

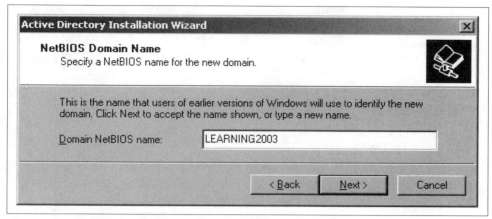

Figure 5-6. Choosing a NetBIOS name

 Do not use a period in the NetBIOS name. This will completely confuse both the NetBIOS and DNS subsystems (because they look for periods in names to separate the different elements of a canonical name) within Active Directory and Windows Server 2003.

Click Next once you've chosen a NetBIOS name.

The Database and Log Folders screen appears, prompting you to choose where you want the Active Directory database (recall that this is the *NTDS.DIT* file on all domain controllers' hard drives) and where you want the transaction log that keeps track of changes to the directory. This is shown in Figure 5-7.

If possible, place the database on one drive and the log file on another drive. This ensures the best performance in production environments. You can use the Browse buttons to choose a location on the physical filesystem, or you can simply type a path into the boxes. Once you've finished choosing a location, click Next to continue.

The Shared System Volume screen appears, as shown in Figure 5-8.

The SYSVOL share is akin to NT 4.0-style NETLOGON shares, in that the contents of the share are replicated automatically to all domain controllers within a domain. SYSVOL contains user logon scripts, system policy files, default profiles, and other configuration-related files. The SYSVOL location must be on an NTFS volume. You can use the Browse button to choose a path, or you can type in a path. Click Next to continue.

DNS health checks and configuration are next. If your DNS servers aren't fully healthy, you'll receive a screen such as that shown in Figure 5-9.

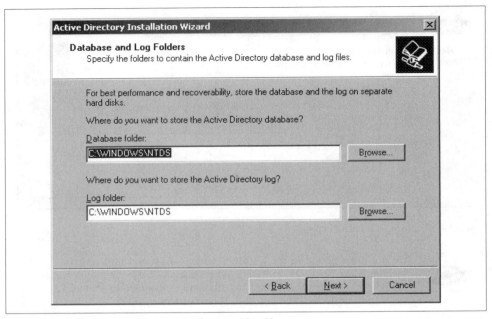

Figure 5-7. Choosing a location for database and log files

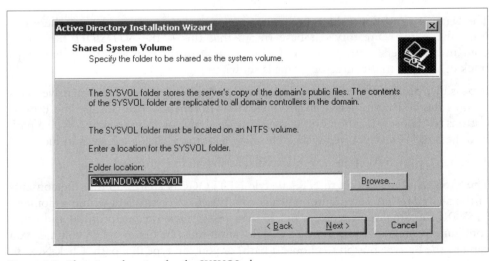

Figure 5-8. Choosing a location for the SYSVOL share

Here, Active Directory is complaining that it can't contact DNS servers. If you encounter this screen, it's almost certainly because of one of the following problems: either (a) the DNS servers can't be found because they're unavailable or your current machine is not on the network; or (b) the DNS servers that were found during the

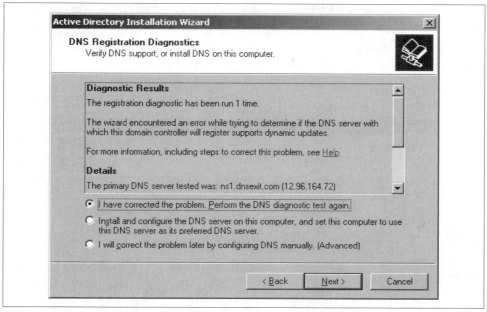

Figure 5-9. A DNS system health check

check don't support dynamic updates. For more information on taking care of either of those problems, consult Chapter 4, which explains DNS in detail with an eye to Active Directory.

You have three options at this point: you can rerun the test if you've identified your specific problem and want to retest; you can instruct Active Directory to go ahead and install the DNS service on this computer, configure it correctly, and change this computer's LAN connection properties so that it points to itself for DNS services; or you can tell Active Directory, "To hell with DNS! Go ahead!" and proceed without having verified that DNS is installed and accessible. Let me offer a caution: do *not* use the second or third options. Take the time, armed with the information you learned in Chapter 4, to get DNS right *before* using DCPROMO to create a domain. You'll save yourself a lot of heartache, hassle, and time by ensuring DNS is as hard as a rock ahead of time. Why? For a few reasons. For one, your organization can often benefit from a solid DNS system even before Active Directory is rolled out. Second, Active Directory DNS systems can interfere with another DNS system you might have in place, and letting the wizard handle this part isn't smart—you need to evaluate your current environment and integrate DNS first before introducing Active Directory to the mix. Also, a solid, functionally efficient DNS system makes deploying additional domain controllers and creating new trees very efficient, as Active Directory "piggybacks" a lot of its internal functionality onto the DNS structure.

Why would you want to trust to a wizard a system that is that fundamental to Active Directory?

At any rate, once you're satisfied with your DNS structure and you want to proceed with the remainder of the Active Directory installation, click Next.

The Permissions screen will appear, as seen in Figure 5-10.

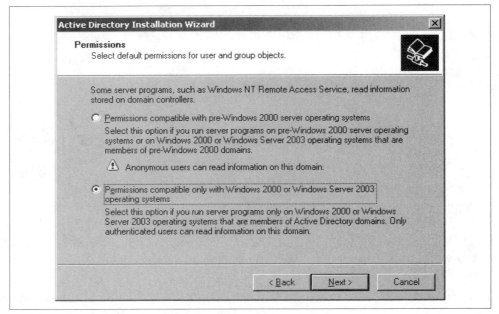

Figure 5-10. Determining default Active Directory client permissions

On this screen, you can choose the default permissions for new objects to either allow anonymous access for the purpose of reading information stored on a domain controller, or deny that access. As the screen says, the main culprit behind this choice is the Remote Access Service in NT. To make a long story short, for an NT-based RAS server (which could be only a member server) to figure out if an account has permission to dial into the network, it has to query a domain controller about the properties of the account. But because this hypothetical RAS server is only a member server, it doesn't have the necessary permissions to just ask about user properties that a domain controller does, so it needs another "back door" into the domain controller to find out about this permission. Hence, the ability to anonymously access a few details about user accounts on an NT domain controller. Of course, these days, this is a *huge* security hole, so please upgrade your NT RAS servers as soon as possible.

All this option does is either remove or add the Everyone group into the Pre-Windows 2000 Compatible Access Group, found in the Built-in container in Active Directory Users and Computers. To deny anonymous access after you finish installation, remove Everyone from this group. To reallow this access, add Everyone back to this group.

Of course, you also can include other objects for more specific access without using the Everyone group.

Make the appropriate choice, and then click Next.

The Directory Services Restore Mode Administrator Password screen appears. This is shown in Figure 5-11.

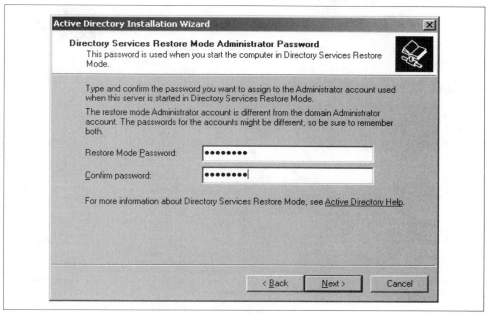

Figure 5-11. Setting the directory restore mode password

On this screen you can choose the password that will be required of anyone attempting to access the Active Directory restore mode tools before Windows boots. Set this password to something that is secure and different from all your other administrator passwords, and then lock it away in a safe place. You probably won't need it very often. Once you've set the password, click Next.

Let me explain a bit about this special password. The Active Directory Restore Mode password is actually a password that is stored in the SAM database for a domain controller, accessible only through specific methods, one being Active Directory Restore Mode. Even more interesting, Active Directory Restore Mode is in fact a single-user mode of Windows Server 2003 (and Windows 2000). So, the password for a directory services restore is not stored in the directory at all, meaning it is not replicated to other domain controllers.

The Summary screen appears, as displayed in Figure 5-12.

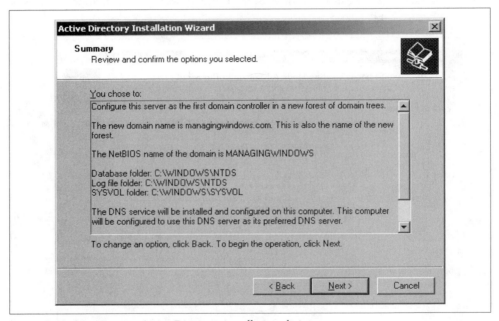

Figure 5-12. Summarizing Active Directory installation choices

Ensure the choices you selected are the correct ones you wanted, and then click Next to begin the procedure to install Active Directory and promote the current machine to a domain controller within your new domain. The installation process will trundle along, until you receive the success notification pictured in Figure 5-13.

Congratulations! You've built a new domain and promoted your machine to a domain controller. You'll need to restart your machine to continue.

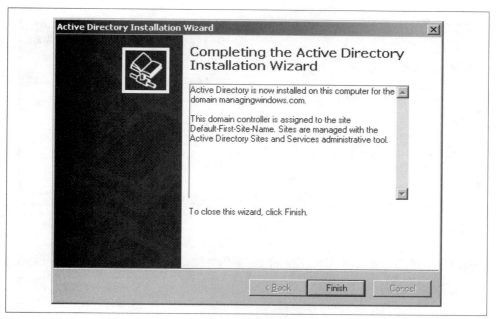

Figure 5-13. Successful Active Directory installation

Using Active Directory Tools

Before we go any further, I'd like to discuss the three most common tools you will find yourself using as an Active Directory administrator. The first of these tools is Active Directory Users and Computers, the tool that allows you to create your Active Directory structure within a domain, add users and groups, adjust account properties, and generally administer the day-to-day operations of your directory. Figure 5-14 shows the default screen for Active Directory Users and Computers.

Next, there's Active Directory Domains and Trusts, a utility you can use to create trusts between domains and to eventually raise the domain functional level to enable new features for Active Directory. Figure 5-15 shows the default screen for Active Directory Domains and Trusts.

Finally, let's briefly glance at Active Directory Sites and Services, a graphical tool that allows you to design your Active Directory structure around how your business is geographically dispersed, making Active Directory replication traffic go across links that cost the least and are the fastest. You also can delineate how your organization's computers are addressed via outlining different subnets, thereby increasing the likelihood that clients will log on to domain controllers that are the closest distance to them. Figure 5-16 shows the default screen for Active Directory Sites and Services.

We'll use each tool in time as we proceed through the remainder of this chapter. For now, let's move on.

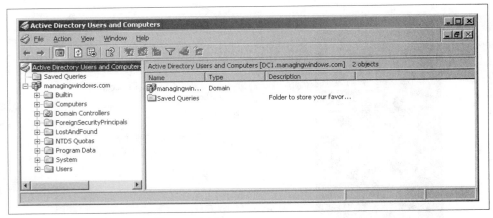

Figure 5-14. Active Directory Users and Computers

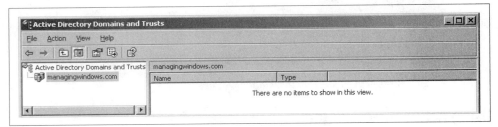

Figure 5-15. Active Directory Domains and Trusts

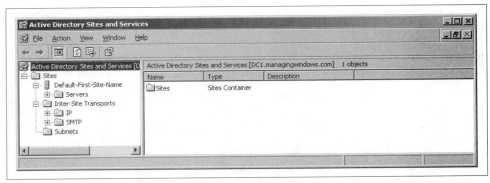

Figure 5-16. Active Directory Sites and Services

Adding Another Domain Controller to a Domain

Promoting another machine to domain controller status within an existing domain is even easier than promoting the first machine in a new domain. You can use the DCPROMO Wizard to do the job for you in this case, as well.

To begin, start DCPROMO as before, and on the screen asking you what action you want to perform, select Additional domain controller for an existing domain, and click Next. The Network Credentials screen will appear, asking you to type in the username and password for a domain administrator account. Do so, and then click Next. Enter the full DNS canonical name of the domain for which you want this machine to become a domain controller, and then click Next. From there, proceed through the wizard starting from the Database and Log Files screen as indicated in the previous section. Once the wizard is finished and your machine has restarted, it is an official domain controller for your domain.

Adding Another Domain

Adding a child domain is equally simple: you use DCPROMO and you tell it to create a new domain, but not a new tree. This will add a "subdomain" to the existing domain tree. Then the Network Credentials screen will appear, asking for a domain administrator account. After that, the Child Domain Installation screen will appear, as shown in Figure 5-17.

Here, you can select to install a domain controller into a new domain. Click Next, and then you will be prompted to provide a name for the domain, as shown in Figure 5-18.

Next, you need to tell Active Directory which domain you want to add on to, and then the name of the child domain to add on to the parent tree. You can use the Browse button to scroll around the directory or simply type the name in. In the second box, enter just the first portion of the new child domain's name. The box at the bottom will adjust automatically to show the full name of the new child domain.

Now you can proceed through the wizard, as shown in the previous section. One note of interest, though: if the domain has a lot of information to replicate out to its new domain controller, this promotion process can take a long time. An option is available on the final screen of this wizard that allows you to finish replication later, and you might be tempted to take advantage of this option. Although it does decrease the amount of time it takes to bring a new domain controller in an existing domain online, I prefer to let replication happen immediately. The only instance in which I wouldn't want to do this is if I were bringing up a new domain controller in a branch office with a very slow connection to the home office. In that case, it's OK to wait until off hours and let the replication happen then. In all other cases, I recommend moving ahead with replication and simply waiting it out.

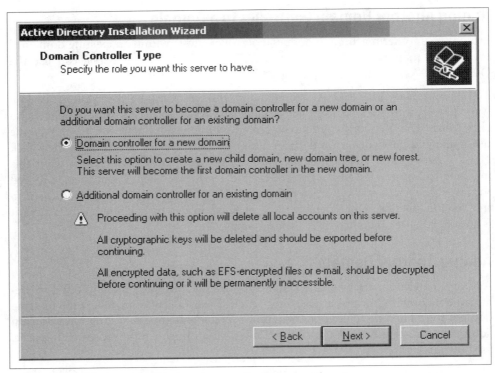

Figure 5-17. Selecting to install a domain controller into a new domain

Managing Users and Groups

Of course, critical to a multiuser system are user accounts and groups, which you can create within Active Directory using the Active Directory Users and Computers tool, which we previewed two sections ago. (In this section I'll use the acronym ADUC to refer to this tool to save me from having to type out "Active Directory Users and Computers" over and over.) Within ADUC, you can create, change, and delete user accounts, manage groups and their members, and configure Group Policies—the latter being a topic I will save for Chapter 6.

Creating users and groups

Let's look at creating users and groups within ADUC. It's a simple process to create a user or a group. First, you ought to decide on a username or group name. You can

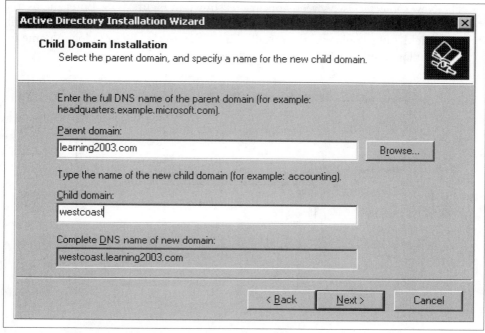

Figure 5-18. Providing a name for the new child domain

select almost any username or group name for a particular person or group in Windows Server 2003, but you must keep the following restrictions in mind:

- The name must be unique within a domain (if you are creating a domain user) or on a machine (if you are creating a local user).
- The name can be a maximum of 20 characters.
- The name cannot contain any of the following characters: " / \ [ ] : ; | = , + * ? < >.
- The name cannot consist of all spaces or all periods, though individual spaces or periods within a name are acceptable.

 Group names have the same restrictions.

So, to create a user, follow these steps:

1. Open ADUC.
2. In the left pane, select the container in which you want the new user to reside. Right-click it and select User from the New menu.

3. The New Object - User screen appears, as shown in Figure 5-19. Enter the user's first name, middle name, and last name in the appropriate boxes and the Full name field will populate automatically. Enter the user's preferred logon name in the User logon name box, and then click Next.

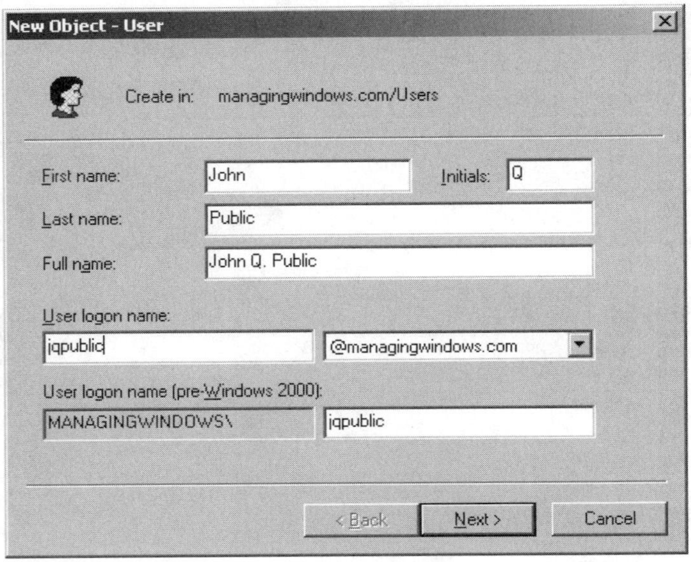

Figure 5-19. Entering a new user

4. The next screen is where you enter the user's initial password and a few properties for his account. This is shown in Figure 5-20. Enter and confirm the password, and then decide whether the new user will be prompted to change this password when he logs on, whether he can change his password at all, whether the password will follow the domain's expiration policy, and finally, whether the account is disabled. (Disabled accounts cannot log in.) Click Next.

5. Confirm the information you have just entered, and click OK to create the user.

To create a new group, follow these steps:

1. Open ADUC.

2. In the left pane, select the container in which you want the new user to reside. Right-click it and select Group from the New menu.

3. The New Object - Group screen appears, as shown in Figure 5-21. Enter a name from the group, its scope as a domain local, global, or universal group, and the type of group (either security or distribution). Click OK.

That's it! You've created a new group.

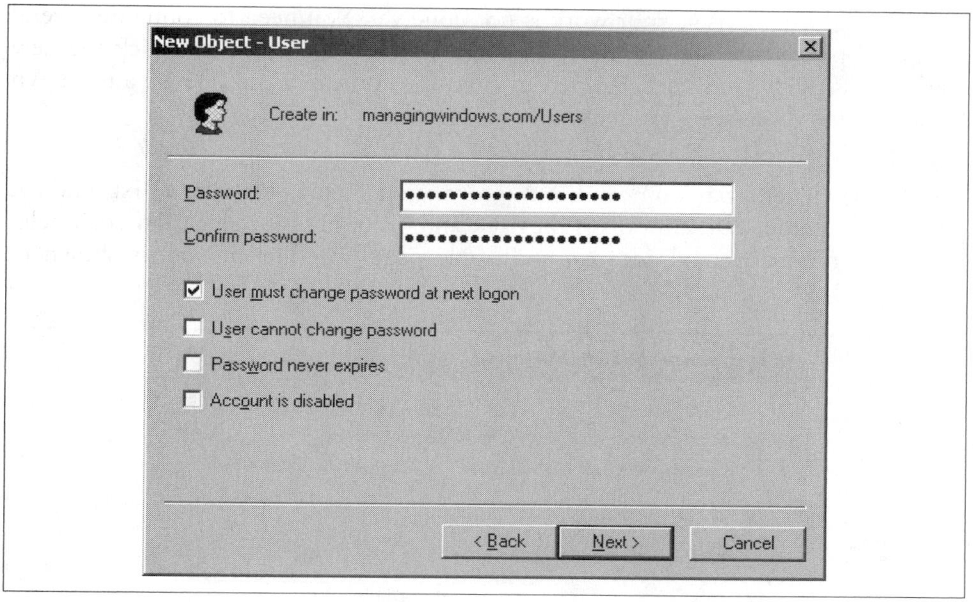

Figure 5-20. Entering a new user's password

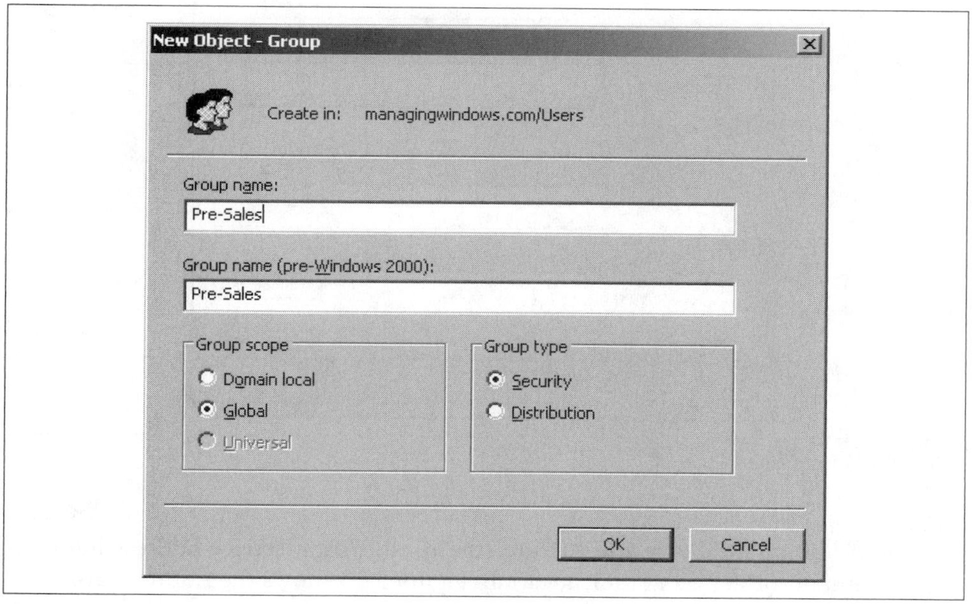

Figure 5-21. Creating a new group

If you are creating a user, your work is not done yet. You need to configure several additional properties before the user account is ready for use. Right-click the new user within ADUC and select Properties from the context menu. Here's a rundown of each option on the properties sheet's various tabs:

General

On the General tab, you can input information such as the user's first, middle, and last name, a description of the user, and his or her office location, main telephone number, email address, and home page. The General tab is shown in Figure 5-22.

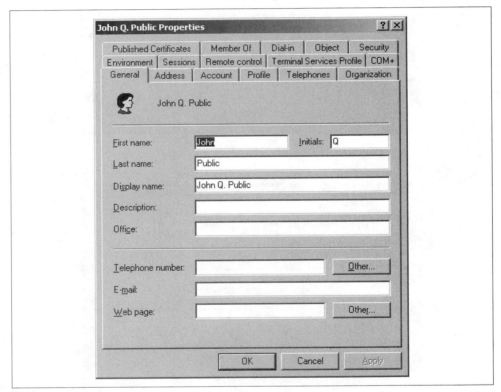

Figure 5-22. The General tab

Address

The Address tab allows you to enter the user's postal service address information and his or her geographic location. Figure 5-23 shows the Address tab.

Account

On the Account tab, you can modify the user's logon name, the suffix for his or her principal name (a concept which I'll explain in a bit), logon hours, and the workstations he or she is permitted to use. To set logon hours, click the Logon

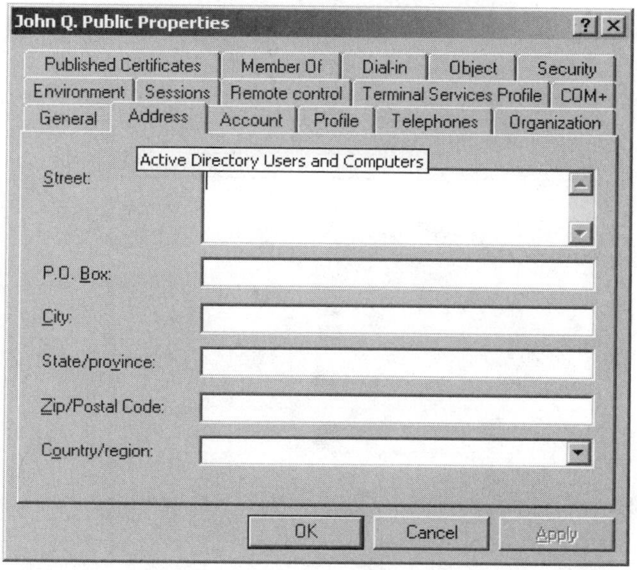

Figure 5-23. The Address tab

Hours button and then select the block of time you want to either permit or deny. To set permitted workstations, click the Logon To button—but note that you need to have the NetBIOS protocol on your network for that restriction to be enforced.

You also see several options. You can specify that a user must change his password the next time he logs in, that he cannot change his password, that his password never expires, that Windows should store his password using a weaker, reversible encryption scheme, that his account is disabled, that a smart card must be used in conjunction with his password to log on, that the account is to be used for a software service such as Exchange and ought to be able to access other system resources, that the account is not trusted, that DES encryption should be used for the account, or that an alternate implementation of the Kerberos protocol can be used.

The Account tab is shown in Figure 5-24.

Profile

On the Profile tab, you can specify the path to the user's profile. A user's profile contains the contents of his or her Desktop and Start menu and other customizations (such as wallpaper and color scheme). You can specify where that profile is stored with the Profile Path option. You also can designate the path to the user's home folder, which is the default location within most Windows applications for a particular user's data to be stored. Plus, you can choose to automatically map a specific drive letter to the user's home folder that you have set up. Figure 5-25 shows the Profile tab.

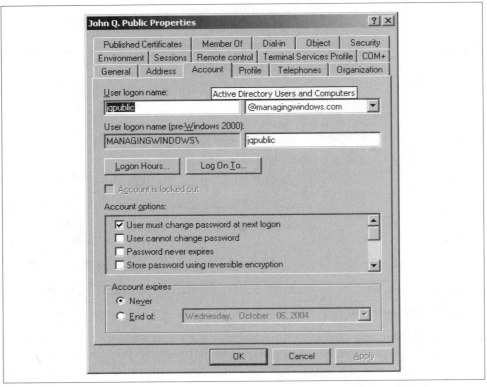

Figure 5-24. The Account tab

Telephones

On the Telephones tab, you can enter different numbers corresponding to this particular user's home, pager, mobile, fax, and IP telephones. The Telephones tab is shown in Figure 5-26.

Organization

The Organization tab gives you a place to specify the user's official title, the department in which he works, the name of the company where he works, his direct reports, and his manager's name. The Organization tab is shown in Figure 5-27.

Remote control

This tab specifies Terminal Services properties. See Chapter 9 for a detailed walkthrough of the options on this tab. The Remote control tab is shown in Figure 5-28.

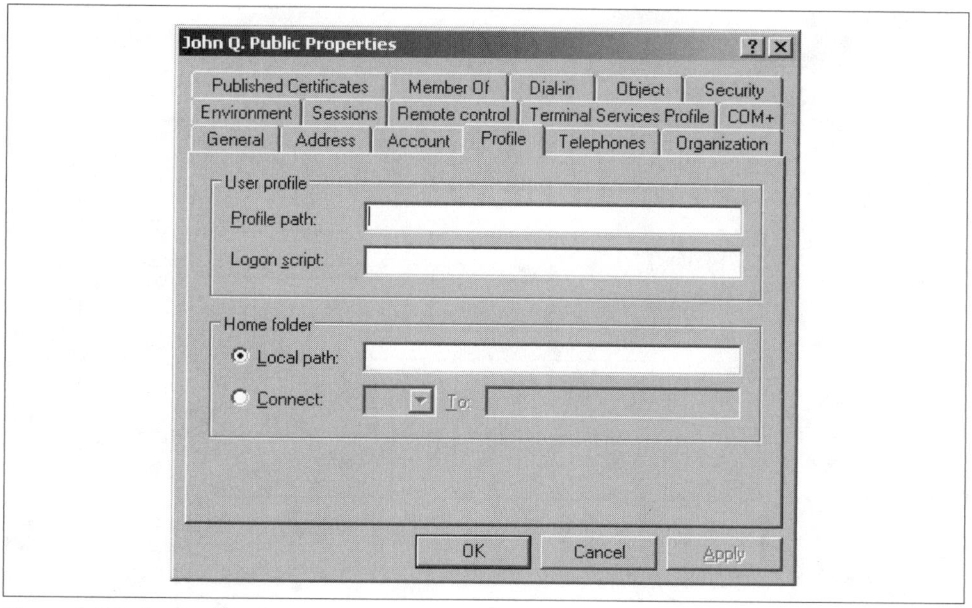

Figure 5-25. The Profile tab

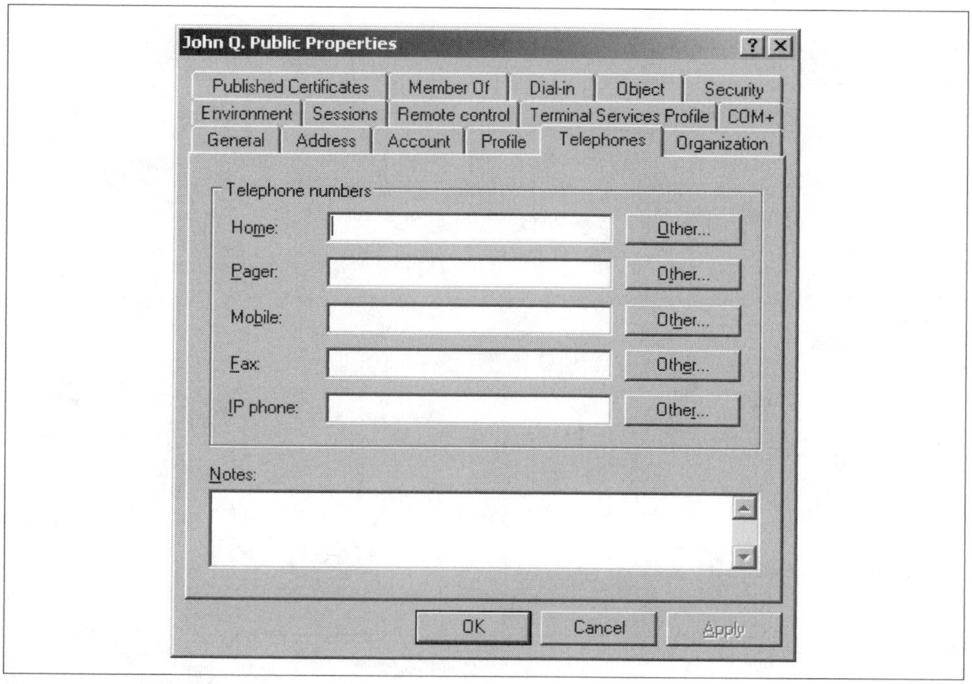

Figure 5-26. The Telephones tab

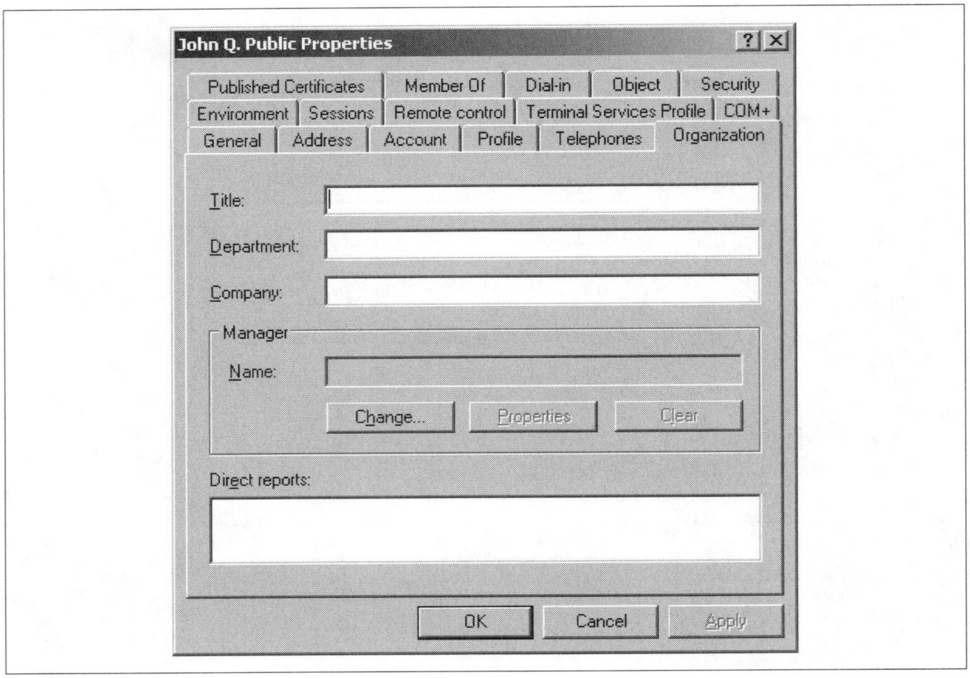

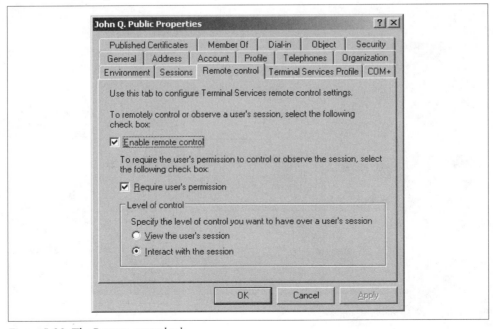

Figure 5-27. The Organization tab

Figure 5-28. The Remote control tab

Terminal Services Profile

This tab specifies Terminal Services properties. See Chapter 9 for a detailed walkthrough of the options on this tab. The Terminal Services Profile tab is shown in Figure 5-29.

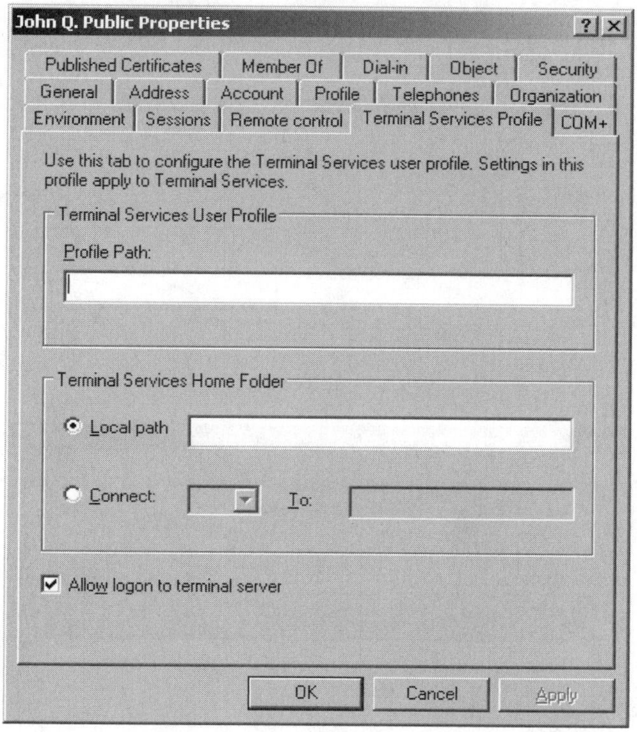

Figure 5-29. The Terminal Services Profile tab

COM+

On the COM+ tab, you can assign users to applications on COM+ partitions that you have set up on different servers. The COM+ tab is shown in Figure 5-30.

Member Of

The Member Of tab shows a user's group memberships. All users by default are a member of the Domain Users group. You can click the Add button to add groups of which this user is a member. To remove a user from a current group membership, click Remove. The Member Of tab is shown in Figure 5-31.

Dial-in

The Dial-in tab is where you configure several remote access options and properties for the user. Routing and remote access are covered in detail in Chapter 11. The Dial-in tab is shown in Figure 5-32.

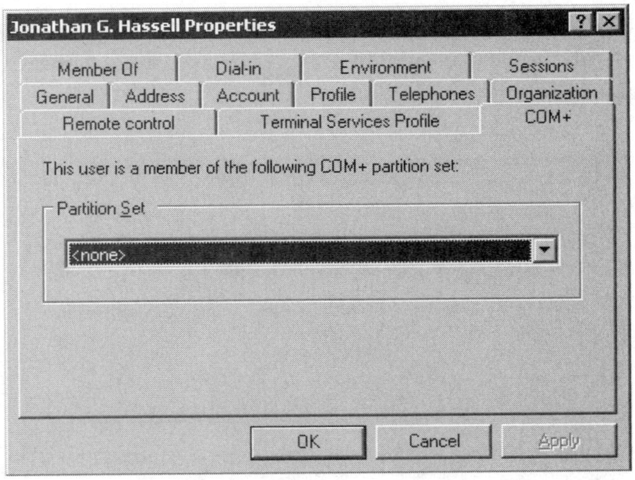

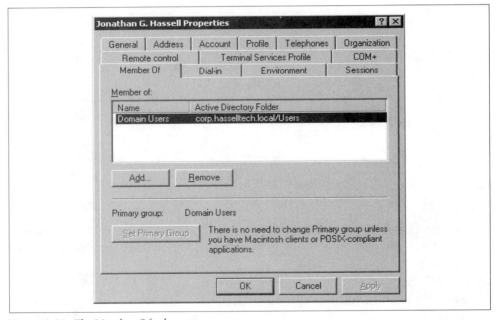

Figure 5-30. The COM+ tab

Figure 5-31. The Member Of tab

Environment

This tab specifies Terminal Services properties. See Chapter 9 for a detailed walk-through of the options on this tab. The Environment tab is shown in Figure 5-33.

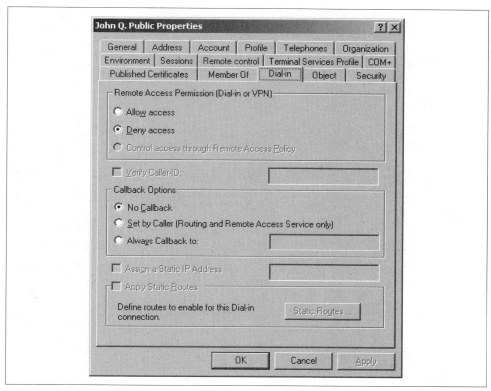

Figure 5-32. The Dial-in tab

Sessions

This tab specifies Terminal Services properties. See Chapter 9 for a detailed walk-through of the options on this tab. The Sessions tab is shown in Figure 5-34.

You have fewer properties to configure when you create a new group. Those group-specific properties are profiled in the next section.

General

On the General tab, you can specify the name of the group, a friendly description of the group, the group's email address, the group's scope and type, and any notes you want to write to yourself or to other administrators. Figure 5-35 shows the General tab.

Members

The Members tab shows the current members of the group. Click the Add and Remove buttons to add and remove members from the group, respectively. Figure 5-36 shows the Members tab.

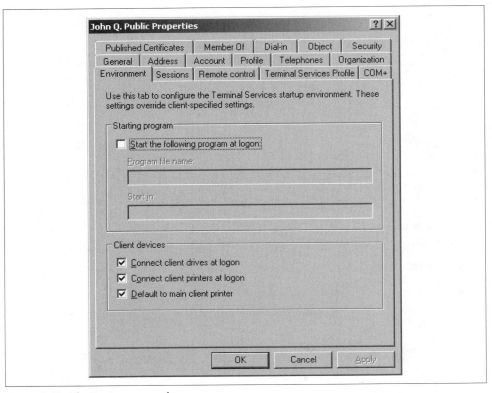

Figure 5-33. The Environment tab

Member Of

On the Member Of tab, you specify the groups of which this current group is a member—this is an example of the "nesting" feature profiled earlier in this chapter. You can click Add and Remove to change this group's membership. The Member Of tab is shown in Figure 5-37.

Performing common administrative tasks

You can accomplish a couple of neat tricks using ADUC on multiple accounts at once, reducing some of the tedium involved in making repetitive changes. For one, you can select multiple accounts within ADUC by clicking one account and doing one of the following:

- Holding down the Shift key and selecting another account to completely select the range of accounts within your two initial selections

- Holding down the Ctrl key and clicking individual accounts to select them independently

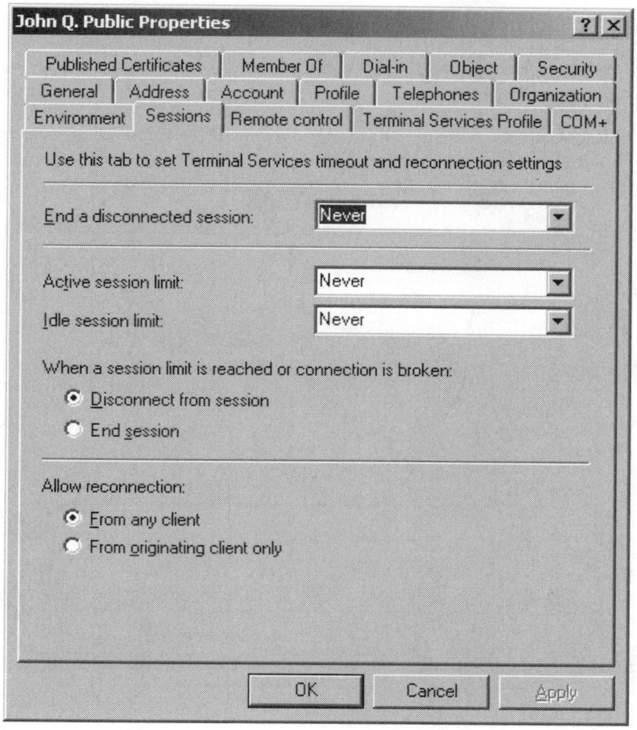

Figure 5-34. The Sessions tab

Then you can right-click the group of accounts and perform actions such as changing common properties or sending email. When you right-click multiple accounts and select Properties, the screen in Figure 5-38 appears.

On this screen, you can make changes to multiple accounts at the same time. A subset of the options available on individual accounts is accessible, but such common tasks as changing the UPN suffix of an account, specifying that a user must change his or her password, or requiring a smart card for logon are easy to make with this screen.

Using LDAP to create users

LDAP is the foundation protocol for accessing and modifying the contents of Active Directory. You can use LDAP-style strings in conjunction with a couple of command-line tools to automate the creation of users and groups.

First let's look at what makes an LDAP identifier. For instance, let's say my full name is Jonathan Hassell, and I'm in the container SBSUsers within the hasselltech.local domain. My LDAP name, therefore, is:

```
Cn="Jonathan Hassell",cn=SBSUsers,dc=hasselltech,dc=local
```

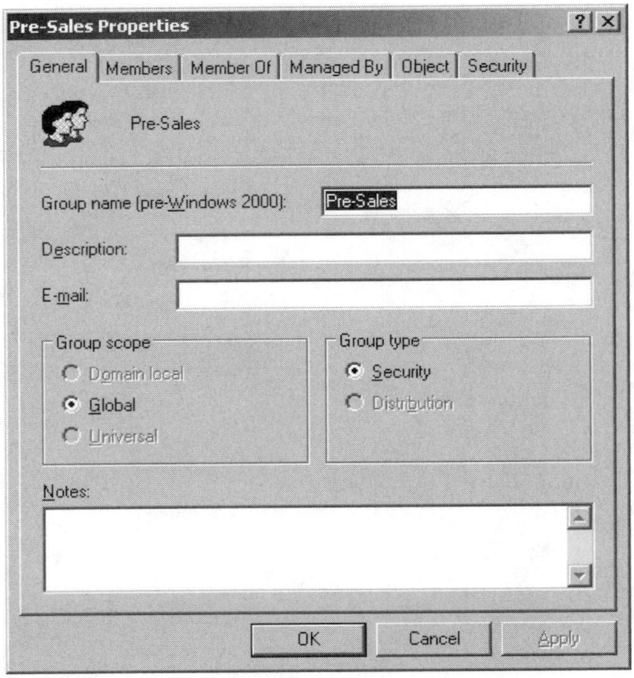

Figure 5-35. The General tab

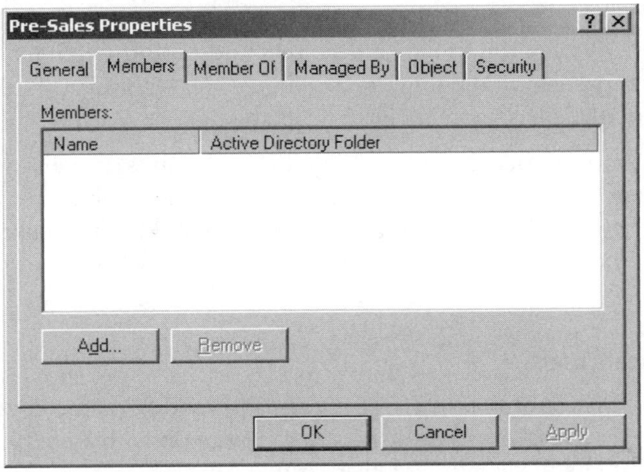

Figure 5-36. The Members tab

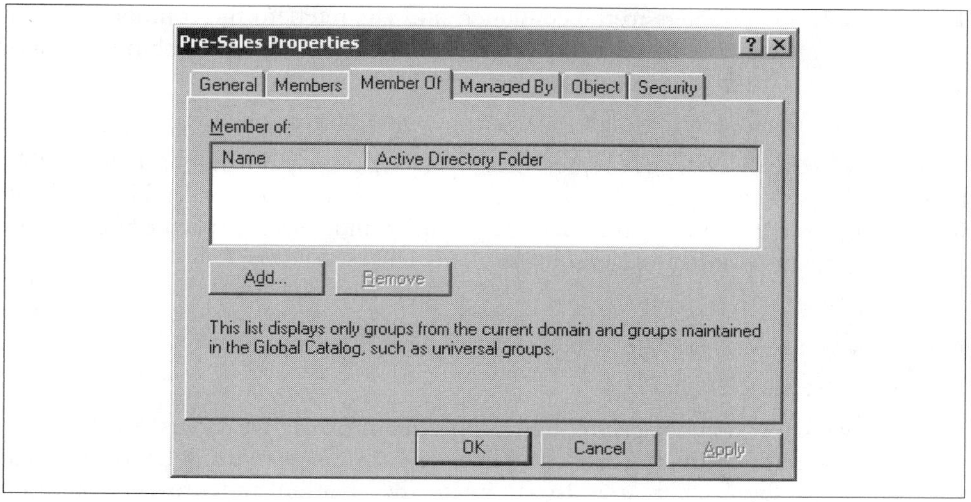

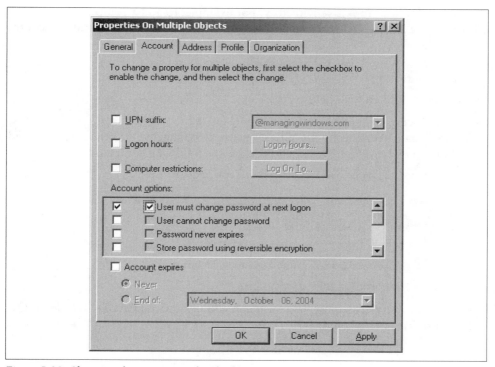

Figure 5-37. The Member Of tab

Figure 5-38. Changing the properties of multiple accounts

The abbreviation CN refers to the container, and DC refers to the components of a domain name. Likewise, Lisa Johnson in the Marketing container within the Charlotte container of enterprise.com would have an LDAP name of:

```
Cn="Lisa Johnson",cn=Marketing,cn=Charlotte,dc=enterprise,dc=com
```

Usernames in the directory are represented by a user principal name, or UPN. UPNs look like email addresses, and in some cases actually can be email addresses, but within the context of LDAP they serve to identify and select a specific user in the directory. So, if my username were jhassell, my UPN would be:

```
jhassell@hasselltech.local
```

And if Lisa Johnson's username were ljohnson, her UPN would be:

```
ljohnson@hasselltech.local
```

Now that we know how to specify some properties in LDAP, we can use the DSADD utility to create users from the command line. The advantage to using DSADD is that you can script these commands to automate the creation and provision of user accounts.

DSADD adds a user to Active Directory. For example, to add a computer named JH-WXP-DSK to the Admin OU while authenticating as the domain administrator account, enter the following:

```
dsadd computer CN=JH-WXP-DSK,OU=Admin,DC=hasselltech,dc=local -u
administrator -p
```

You will be prompted for a password.

Here's another example: to add user sjohnson (for Scott Johnson, email address sjohnson@hasselltech.local with initial password "changeme") to the Sales OU and make him a member of the Presales group, use the following command:

```
dsadd user cn=sjohnson,ou=sales,dc=hasselltech,dc=local -upn

sjohnson@hasselltech.local
 -fn Scott -ln Johnson -display
"Scott Johnson" -password changeme -email
sjohnson@hasselltech.local

-memberof cn=presales,ou=sales,dc=hasselltech,dc=local
```

Again, you will be prompted for a password.

You're getting the picture now. You also can add OUs with DSADD. To add an OU called support, use this command:

```
dsadd ou cn=support,dc=hasselltech,dc=local
```

Delegation

One of the absolute best features within Active Directory is the ability to allow other users to take partial administrative control over a subset of your directory—a process known as delegation. By delegating administrative authority, you can take some of the IT person's burden and place it elsewhere. For example, you might want to give one person in your department the power to reset passwords for other employees in a department. Or you might want to employ some part-time college students to staff a helpdesk and you want to give them the ability to create new users and to help other employees with lost passwords. You can accomplish this easily through Active Directory delegation.

And there's even a wizard to help you do it, too. The entire process works something like this:

1. You choose an Active Directory container over which you want to delegate administrative authority.
2. You create a group of users (or identify an already existing one) that will have those new, delegated administrative powers.
3. You use the Delegation of Control Wizard to actually grant the powers.

Let's get started. Within ADUC, select the organizational unit over which you want to delegate powers to others. Right-click it, and select Delegate Control from the pop-up context menu. The Delegation of Control Wizard appears. Click Next off the introductory screen, and the Users or Groups screen appears, as shown in Figure 5-39.

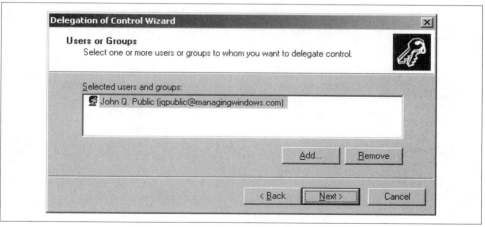

Figure 5-39. The Users or Groups screen

On this screen, click Add and identify the users or groups to which you want to have the powers assigned. Click Next when you've added the users, and the Tasks to Delegate screen appears, as shown in Figure 5-40.

This screen lists the most common tasks you want to delegate, including such options as managing user accounts, resetting passwords, managing groups, and administering GP. For our example, let's select the second option (to reset user passwords), and click Next.

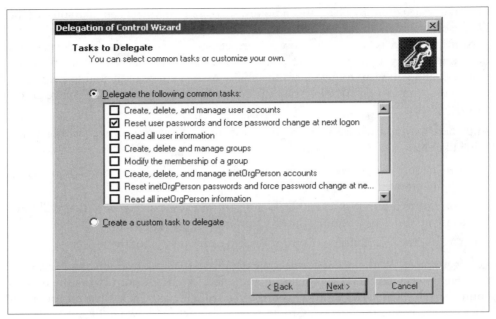

Figure 5-40. The Tasks to Delegate screen

On the final screen of the wizard, you're asked to confirm your choices. Click Finish to do so, and the delegation is complete.

Unfortunately, there is no mechanism to log what delegations have been configured. Be sure to keep a very detailed and accurate journal of the delegations you create, as there is no way to track this within the user interface.

However, the new DSREVOKE tool can offer a bit of assistance. This tool can report all permissions for a particular user or group on a set of OUs and, optionally, remove all permissions for that user or group from the ACLs on those OUs. This effectively provides the ability to revoke delegated administrative authority, though it's not as intuitive as a graphical utility might be. You can find more information at:

http://download.microsoft.com/download/b/1/f/b1f527a9-5980-41b0-b38e-6d1a52a93da5/Dsrevoke.doc

Understanding Operations Master Roles

As I mentioned earlier, all domain controllers are nearly equal in Active Directory—that is, any one of them can be updated and can replicate changes to the others. This decentralization is in direct contrast to Windows NT 4.0-style domains, which had only one PDC that accepted directory object modifications and any number of BDCs that held read-only copies of the accounts database. BDCs could authenticate users, but any changes to any attributes of domain accounts had to take place in direct communication with the PDC. Because the PDC pushed out copies of the accounts database, known as the SAM database, to the BDCs for a domain, this sort of replication was known as *single-master replication* because one master computer communicated changes to slaved, less-capable computers.

Enter Active Directory onto the scene, where there are effectively no distinctions between domain controllers in most operations. Unless your domain is functioning at the NT interim functional level (more on that in the migration section later in this chapter), all domain controllers for a domain can accept changes for data in their domain, and domain controllers have peers to which they replicate changes to those objects. This sort of setup typically is called *multimaster replication* because each domain controller acts as a master, passing changes to other domain controllers until those changes are replicated fully.

Replication is covered in detail in the next section, but that introduction serves as an adequate segue to this fundamental issue: this decentralized approach has problems. Some actions taken within forests and domains could cause havoc if performed simultaneously on two separate domain controllers before replication has occurred. What if:

- Two people made changes to the attributes of the Active Directory schema on two separate domain controllers and created an attribute named CC—one person wanted that attribute to be for credit card numbers, and another meant wanted it to be for calling card numbers. Which would be which, and under what circumstances?

- An administrator in one location, geographically separate from his company's headquarters, created a new domain, and then eight hours later at the headquarters complex (before replication took place) someone else created the same domain, thinking it hadn't been done yet. Which domain wins?

- Two distinct domain controllers were doling out security IDs (SIDs) to new objects, and by chance one object on one domain controller was assigned the same SID as another object on the other domain controller. How would Active Directory keep track of these two unique objects if they have the same SID?

- You still have NT domain controllers acting as BDCs on your network. (This is very, very common now.) As you know, those NT domain controllers aren't capable of multimaster replication, so all of them need to agree on one place from which they can get updates to their SAMs. Which Windows Server 2003 or Windows 2000 Server-based domain controller would perform this role?

- You renamed a user or made a user a member of a certain group, and you were attached to one domain controller but that change needed to replicate to the domain controller that's local to the user whom you're administering. How might you speed up replication for those essential attributes—how can they take priority over, say, changes to phone numbers for a user in Active Directory?

Clearly, some domain controllers need to have greater control over others, simply because sometimes, all computers need a bit of authority. Active Directory is not entirely self-governing. Microsoft took care of this problem by implementing special roles for some domain controllers in Active Directory, called *operations master roles*. (These roles also can be called flexible single master of operations roles, pronounced *fizz-moh*, but the proper term is *operations masters*.) There are five specific operations master roles, and each is listed here in the order in which it corresponds with the scenarios discussed earlier:

- Schema master (one per forest)
- Domain naming (one per forest)
- RID pool (one per domain)
- PDC emulator (one per domain)
- Infrastructure (one per domain)

These roles are distributed one per domain, except for the schema and domain-naming roles, which are allotted one per forest. After all, schema changes affect the forestwide Active Directory, and you shouldn't have two domains named exactly the same within the same Active Directory forest. However, RIDs are specific to domains, PDCs are specific to individual domains, and infrastructure masters account for changes within domains only, not the whole forest.

 The first domain controller in a forest assumes all five roles simultaneously. The first domain controller in the second domain of a forest assumes all three domain-specific roles simultaneously. Organizations with only one domain controller have all five roles on that one domain controller.

Schema Master

The schema master in a forest carries out a very important function—ensuring that changes to the schema, or to the actual structure of the Active Directory database, are made in a consistent manner. The schema master prevents change collisions across the forest, which is a bigger problem than you might imagine and one that grows with the size of your Active Directory–based network. Although you might not think the schema would change often, a few operations actually do this: for one, installing Exchange 2000 or 2003 into a domain will extend the forestwide schema even if some domains are not using Exchange. Other Active Directory–aware applications are likely to modify the schema as well, such as Microsoft's ISA Server firewall and some network and user management applications, such as those from NetIQ.

Also recall that the forest Active Directory schema and the global catalog are intertwined. Recall also that the global catalog contains a subset of information from all domains within a forest. If you added new attributes to the schema and wanted to include those in the global catalog, all your domain controllers that act as global catalog servers will need to receive the change. For Windows 2000-based domain controllers, the entire global catalog must be flushed and rebuilt on each domain controller; for Windows Server 2003-based domain controllers, only the change needs to be propagated. For large organizations, this is a big bandwidth saver if most of your GC-based domain controllers are on Windows Server 2003. It is just something to keep in mind.

To identify the schema master on Windows 2000 Server and Windows Server 2003, computers use the Schema Management console. You will find the DLL that enables the Schema MMC snap-in—called *schmmgmt.dll*—under the *\WINDOWS\system32* directory. Open a command-line window, navigate to that directory, and then do the following:

1. Register the COM object by running `regsvr32 schmmgmt.dll`. Once this has completed, Windows should raise a dialog box to notify you.
2. Open the MMC—using the Run option on the Start menu and typing **mmc** always works if you don't have a shortcut handy.
3. Select Add/Remove Snap-In from the File Menu.
4. In the resulting dialog box, click Add. The list of available MMC snap-ins will appear.
5. Select Active Directory Schema, and then click Add.
6. Close the dialogs to apply changes.
7. Right-click the root node of the MMC in the left pane, and then select Operations Master from the context menu.
8. The Change Schema Master dialog box will appear, and on the first line the full name of the current schema master is revealed. In smaller domains, this will be the first domain controller installed, but in larger domains, someone could have moved the role to another domain controller. This is shown in Figure 5-41.

To change the schema master (you must be a member of the Schema Admins group to do this), from within the Schema Management console you loaded in the previous procedure, right-click the root node labeled Active Directory Schema in the left pane, and select Change Domain Controller from the context menu. In the dialog box that appears, type the name of the domain controller to which you want to move the schema master role, and then click OK. Then, proceed from step 7 in the previous exercise, and click the Change button in the Change Schema Master dialog box. Confirm your choice, and once the processing is complete, click Close. The schema master role has been moved.

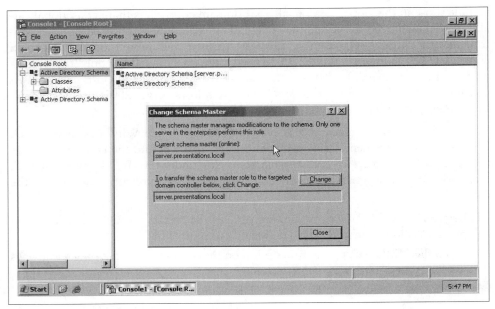

Figure 5-41. The Change Schema Master dialog box

Domain-Naming Master

The domain-naming master role is one of the forest-specific roles, meaning that only one domain controller in the entire forest has this role. This role protects against the creation of identically named domains in the same forest—if this were to happen, Active Directory could not cope with the same names and panic would result.

Keep in mind that this role is designed to be placed on a global catalog server, and not just a standalone server. It would seem that this role uses some information contained in the GC (excerpts of the directories of other domains in the forest) to fulfill its responsibilities. However, if you are operating in the Windows Server 2003 forest functional level, this placement is unnecessary.

To change the domain-naming master role (you must be a member of the Enterprise Admins group to do this), use the Active Directory Domains and Trusts tool. Open it from the Administrative Tools menu and then right-click the root node in the left pane of the window and select Change Domain Controller from the pop-up context menu. Type the name of the domain controller to which you want to move the role, and then click OK. The focus of the management console will switch to this domain controller. Then follow these steps:

1. Right-click the root node in the left pane, and select Operations Master.

2. Click Change to move the role.

RID Master

The RID master role handles the assignment and distribution of the latter portion of SIDs for objects within Active Directory. You know that when objects are created in Windows, a unique SID is assigned to it. The SID comes in the form of *S-1-5-21-A-B-C-RID*, where the S-1-5-21 is common to all SIDs. The "A," "B," and "C" parts of the number are randomly generated 32-bit numbers that are specific to a domain, or to a particular machine (if Active Directory is not installed on the server or if a work-station isn't joined to a domain). The RID, or relative identifier, part of the SID is another 32-bit number that is the unique part of the SID and identifies a distinct object in the directory.

The domain controller with the RID master role distributes groups of 500 unique RIDs to its brother and sister domain controllers with the domain, so that when they create unique objects, the SIDs they assign to those unique objects should also be unique. Much like DHCP ensures that no two workstations have the same IP address, distributing pools of RIDs in this way ensures that no two domain control-lers have the same groups of RIDs to assign.

To move the RID master role to another domain controller in a domain, follow these steps:

1. Open ADUC.
2. In the left pane, right-click the domain name, and then select Connect to Domain Controller.
3. Enter the name of the domain controller to which you want to switch the role.
4. Then, right-click the domain name in the left pane again, and select Operations Masters from the context menu.
5. Click the RID tab, and note the name of the RID master. This is shown in Figure 5-42.
6. Click Change to move the role.

PDC Emulator

The PDC emulator operations master role serves a very important function for mixed Windows NT Server, 2000 Server, and Windows Server 2003 domains. As I men-tioned at the beginning of this section, NT domain controllers—whether primary or backup—don't support multimaster replication, so if your PDC has been upgraded to Windows 2000 or Windows Server 2003, obviously there is no computer from which your BDCs can get updates, or at least none they can understand. Those of you familiar with Microsoft's older networking protocols know that the Master Browser service, the utility that populates Network Neighborhood and My Network Places on workstations and servers, typically runs on the PDC in an NT domain. Sys-tem policies for Windows 95 are stored on the PDC, not on any BDCs. And trusts

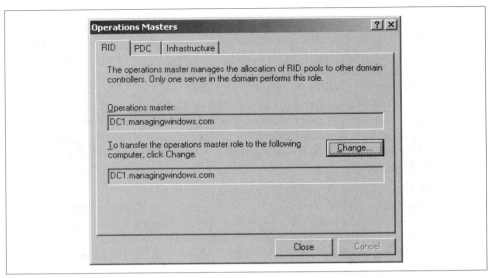

Figure 5-42. Identifying the RID pool master

between NT domains and Active Directory domains require a PDC, or a PDC emulator, because NT thinks only one computer has the read/write copy of the SAM database.

The PDC emulator runs on one domain controller in a domain to perform these functions. It also helps speed up propagation and replication of changes to two specific attributes of a user object in Active Directory: the password and the account lockout attribute. Think about large organizations, and the time it can take for changes made at one domain controller to filter out. (I'll cover replication in a lot more detail in the next section, but know for now that replication can involve a considerable amount of time if you have many domain controllers handling Active Directory responsibilities in your environment.) If a user called to reset a password and the help desk personnel responding to that call were in another site, the password change would take effect first on the domain controller local to the help desk personnel, not necessarily local to the person whose password was being changed. Do you really want to wait the hours it might take for that change to take effect? Of course not, so the domain controller for the help desk personnel immediately contacts the domain controller holding the PDC emulator role for the domain, and it gets that updated password, thus avoiding replication delays. So, although the local domain controller for the user might not have the new password, the local domain controller will look at the PDC emulator domain controller to check if the password matches there. If it does, the user gets a green light to log in. (Of course, password changes aren't actually immediate—there is still lag time.)

This policy stretches to one other attribute as well. If you use account lockouts— when a password is entered incorrectly for X number of times, the account becomes temporarily disabled for a period of time—it probably wouldn't do a lot of good for only the password to be passed quickly to the PDC emulator role. The user would have the right password, but neither the PDC emulator nor the local domain controller for the user would know the account actually wasn't locked out anymore. So, the account lockout attribute is passed at the same time as a password reset, to make sure users aren't sitting, twiddling their thumbs without access to their domain user accounts while the domain controllers wait for replicated changes to arrive.

Finally, the PDC emulator handles time synchronization in a domain.

Ideally, the PDC emulator role should be on the same domain controller as the RID master role. To move the PDC emulator role, use ADUC, as follows:

1. Open ADUC.
2. In the left pane, right-click the domain name, and then select Connect to Domain Controller.
3. Enter the name of the domain controller to which you want to switch the role.
4. Then, right-click the domain name in the left pane again, and select Operations Masters from the context menu.
5. Click the PDC tab, and note the name of the PDC emulator master. This is shown in Figure 5-43.
6. Click Change to move the role.

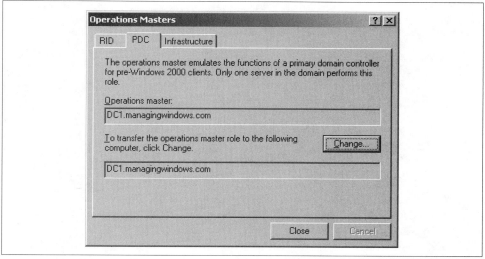

Figure 5-43. Identifying the PDC emulator master

Infrastructure Master

The infrastructure master also helps to speed up propagation and replication of certain pieces of information among domain controllers. The infrastructure master role is designed to *not* be on a domain controller functioning as a GC server—that is, unless every domain controller in your domain is a GC server as well, or if you have only one domain.

To find out and change which domain controller holds the infrastructure master role, use the ADUC tool. As before, if you have only one domain controller in your domain, that is obviously the infrastructure master. In larger domains, to identify and/or change this machine, follow these steps:

1. Open ADUC.
2. In the left pane, right-click the domain name, and then select Connect to Domain Controller.
3. Enter the name of the domain controller to which you want to switch the role.
4. Then, right-click the domain name in the left pane again, and select Operations Masters from the context menu.
5. Click the PDC tab, and note the name of the infrastructure master. This is shown in Figure 5-44.
6. Click Change to move the role to the domain controller of focus.

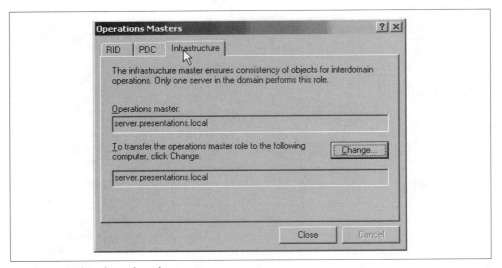

Figure 5-44. Identifying the infrastructure master

Transferring and Seizing Roles Manually

Sometimes you might need to change the operations master roles that domain controllers are playing without necessarily using the graphical interface. It might be that you inadvertently unplugged and reformatted your first domain controller in your domain too early, without transferring its roles elsewhere. Or maybe your specific server is temporarily offline but you really need a role transferred as soon as possible.

If your PDC emulator domain controller or infrastructure masters are offline, it is OK to transfer these roles through the GUI using the aforementioned procedures. You'll need to confirm the offline transfer a couple of times before it will go through, but eventually it will succeed.

Windows Server 2003 comes with the NTDSUtil tool, a command-line utility that allows you to perform Active Directory maintenance that goes above and beyond what the GUI tools allow. In this case, you might need to transfer the schema master, domain-naming master, or RID master roles—or you might need to force that transfer if the original holder of those roles is unavailable.

To transfer a role using NTDSUtil, open a command prompt and run NTDSUTIL. Then follow these steps:

1. Enter **roles** to switch into FSMO Maintenance mode.

2. Enter **connections** to enter the Server Connections context.

3. Enter **connect to *<targetcomputer>***, where *<targetcomputer>* is the computer to which you want to transfer the role.

4. Enter **quit** to leave the Server Connections context.

5. Enter **transfer schema master**, **transfer domain naming master**, or **transfer rid master**, whichever is appropriate, to transfer the role you want. NTDSUtil will attempt to contact the current holder of that operations master role. If it can, and that machine approves the transfer, your operation is complete. However, if for some reason the utility can't contact that computer, error messages will result.

If you find error messages when you're simply attempting a transfer, you can force the role transfer by using the SEIZE command. After step 4 in the previous procedure, start the following.

Once you have seized a role, *never* let the previous holder of that role back onto the network unless you've reformatted the machine. I repeat: *never, ever do this*. The previous holder doesn't know the roles were transferred and is not able to figure it out for itself. Picture a bitter custody battle.

1. Enter **seize schema master**, **seize domain naming master**, or **seize rid master** to force the transfer of the role to the target computer.

2. Type **quit** to leave NTDSUtil once the seizure is complete.

Understanding Directory Replication

At its foundation, the replication process is simply an effort to keep the copy of the Active Directory database identical on all domain controllers for a particular domain. For example, if an administrator removes a user from a group, the change is made on the domain controller that the administrator is currently logged into. For those few seconds after the change, that domain controller alone has the most current copy of the database. Eventually, though, after replication takes place, all domain controllers will have exact replicas of the database, including the change in group membership.

Within a Site: Loops and Meshes

Active Directory replicates information between domain controllers using different methods, depending on the topology of your network—in particular, how many sites you have configured within Active Directory. In a single-site situation, all domain controllers in a domain will discover each other through published records in both Active Directory and the DNS system for the domain. But to cut down on network traffic, not every domain controller needs to actually replicate with every other domain controller. Active Directory uses a "loop" method. Take, for instance, four domain controllers—A, B, C, and D, as shown in Figure 5-45.

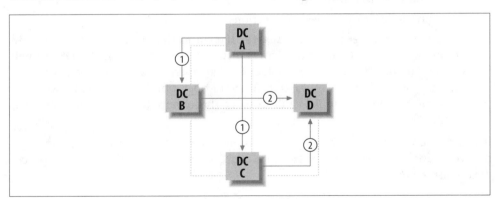

Figure 5-45. Looking at all replication topologies in a forest

In this example, Active Directory will replicate using two loops. Let's assume that a change was made on domain controller A. A will tell B and C that it has new information, and eventually B and C will ask A for that information. Once the information is received, both B and C will attempt to tell D about their new information. D will ask for the new information from the first domain controller that reaches it—there isn't a good way to determine if that would be server B or C in our case—but when the second "message" telling D that it has new information arrives, server D will simply respond, acknowledging that it already has that information, and that will be the end of the transmissions because all domain controllers now have the most up-to-date information. In contrast, consider using only one loop and not two. In that case, A would tell B, B would tell C, C would tell D, and D would tell A again. That doesn't happen. In the actual case, news is spread more quickly and network traffic is reduced, making the entire process more efficient. In fact, this entire process triggers every five minutes, and if there's new information, the process will engage. If there is no new information, the domain controllers won't transmit anything; however, if 60 minutes pass without any new information, each domain controller will send a message to its partners, making sure there's no new information.

 In simple networks, you usually find each domain controller has two replication partners. However, in more complex environments, domain controllers can have more than two partners. To see a domain controller's replication partners, open Active Directory Sites and Services, expand the site in question in the left pane, and expand each domain controller's node. Click NTDS Settings in the left pane, and in the right pane, note the two servers listed in the From Server column.

You might wonder how this loop is designed. The Knowledge Consistency Checker, or KCC, wakes up approximately every 15 minutes and tries to detect changes in its idea of how many domain controllers there are and where they're located. The KCC will look at any changes that have occurred—you might have taken a domain controller offline for maintenance, for example, or even added a new domain controller for load control purposes. Then it adjusts the loop for best performance.

In larger sites, the KCC might find it necessary to add more than two replication partners for each domain controller, or it might do so for traffic control purposes. In still larger sites, even those with only two replication partners per domain controller, it can take more than three hops to transmit replication information completely. The KCC looks for this situation and, if it detects it, simply adds more links between domain controllers, changing the simple "loop" structure into more of a "mesh" structure.

Time Synchronization

For replication to function properly, it is crucial for all domain controllers in a domain and/or forest to be in sync in terms of the current time. The reason points to Kerberos, the underlying authentication scheme for the entire Active Directory: if any domain controller is more than five minutes out of synchronization, authentication will fail.

The Windows Time Service is the tool Microsoft provides to consistently keep your entire domain or forest at the same moment in time. Windows Time Service offers a hierarchy for members of Active Directory domains and forests, with the machine holding the PDC emulator operations master role being the "big kahuna" of sorts, holding the trusted time. The trusted time at the very top level does not need to be synchronized from anywhere—synchronization matters only within the domain, as all members must think it is the same time, regardless of whether that time is the actual time. In other words, everyone has to be the same, but it doesn't matter if everyone is wrong.

From the bottom up, the rest of the hierarchy looks something like this:

- Workstations and servers that are not domain controllers will synchronize their time with the domain controller that logged them in.
- Domain controllers will contact the domain controller for their domain with the PDC emulator operations master role for the current time.
- Each domain in a forest with multiple domains will look to the PDC emulator operations master-holding domain controller in the forest root—the first domain in the forest—to keep the other PDC emulator domain controllers in other domains in check.

You can synchronize the domain controller at the PDC emulator operations master role in a few ways, through the command line. First, though, you must choose a time source. Microsoft provides the host time.windows.com, which is synchronized to the U.S. Army's Atomic Clock, which is as good a choice as any. Once you have selected a time source, run the following from the command line of the PDC emulator domain controller:

```
net time /setsntp:
<TIMESOURCE>
```

Replace <TIMESOURCE> with the full DNS name of the time source you have selected. For example, if I were using time.windows.com as my time source, I'd run:

```
net time /setsntp:time.windows.com
```

Once you have set the time source for the PDC emulator domain controller, it will attempt to synchronize its time with the time source. It will try once every 45 minutes until it has successfully synchronized three times in a row. Once it has done so, it pings the time server only once every eight hours. If you want to trigger time synchronization manually, run:

```
w32tm /resync
```

 The Windows Time Service requires outbound UDP port 123 to be open on your firewall for time synchronizations to occur.

Time zones also play a role. Windows operates internally at Greenwich Mean Time, and although each server can be set to a different time zone depending on either its physical location or the location of the administrator who manages the box, within Windows itself the current time is translated to GMT. Be wary of this, and ensure that time zones are set correctly on all your servers. The object is to get Windows' internal clocks to synchronize—even though the time might seem right to the naked eye, if the time zone is set incorrectly, Windows is unforgiving when it comes to Active Directory operations in that state.

Replication Topologies

Loops and meshes are just two examples of what Microsoft terms *replication topologies*—essentially, maps of the ways domain controllers replicate to each other. And to confuse things, almost always, more than one replication topology exists simultaneously within any particular forest. Let's take a closer look at that.

Four types of data need to be replicated among domain controllers:

- Updates that stay within a particular domain—username and password changes, and other user account information
- Updates to the schema naming context and configuration naming context, which are specific to all domains with a forest, as you saw previously in this chapter
- Updates to the GC, which replicate to all domain controllers that function as GC servers
- Updates to DNS partitions and custom application partitions

With many domain controllers in a forest, you can see where one replication topology might either not suffice or not be the most efficient way to transmit information between these selected subgroups of domain controllers. Figure 5-46 shows this scenario graphically.

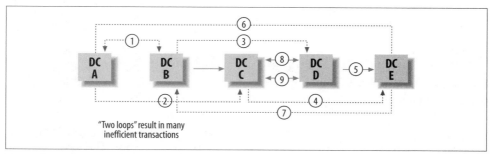

Figure 5-46. Creating a new site link

The Active Directory Sites and Services console again comes to your aid if you want to try to piece together all these replication topologies for your environment. Open the console, expand the site in question in the left pane, and expand each domain controller's node. Click NTDS Settings in the left pane, and in the right pane double-click the "<automatically generated>" objects.

If you see <Enterprise Configuration> in one of the fields at the bottom of the screen indicating replicated naming contexts, it shows that that particular link replicates the schema and configuration naming contexts. In the Partially Replicated Naming Context field, if you see a server name, this indicates that your server is a GC server and is receiving updates from the GC server listed in the field. It is perfectly acceptable for this field to be empty on servers not acting as GCs.

Handling Update Conflicts

Replication is great in and of itself, but there is one major, inherent problem—each domain controller is using its own copy of the database and, no matter how often each copy is updated, for a few moments in time each copy is unaware of actions taken on other copies of the database around the network. How might this design situation manifest itself as a problem?

Consider a large site, with branch offices in Sydney, Australia, Boston, and Los Angeles. An employee, Robert Smith, is being transferred to the Sydney office from L.A. because of personnel reorganization. The company uses groups within Active Directory, SYDUSERS and LAUSERS, for distribution list purposes and other security boundary assignments. On Robert's last day in the LA office, his manager changes Robert's group membership, moving him from LAUSERS to SYDUSERS in anticipation of his transfer. The Los Angeles domain controller notes this change and creates a record looking roughly like this:

```
Object: LAUSERS
Change: Remove RSMITH
Version: 1
Timestamp: 30 June 2004 5:30:01 PM GMT
Object: SYDUSERS
Change: Add RSMITH
Version: 1
Timestamp: 30 June 2004 5:30:02 PM GMT
```

Look closely at these records. They are denoting changes to *attributes* of objects—in this case, the member list is an attribute of a particular group object—not changes to the entire object. This is important for network traffic reduction reasons; if the LAUSERS group is composed of 2,000 members, it's good to transmit only the removal of RSMITH and not the entire membership list. Also, note the version numbers: the field is very simple and is designed to be used whenever domain controllers update an attribute for a particular object. Each time a change is made to a particular object attribute, the numeral in the version number field is incremented by 1. So, one object can have many version numbers, each representing the attributes of that object.

With that background out of the way, let's return to our fictional situation. Perhaps there was a miscommunication between Robert's old manager in Los Angeles and his new manager in Sydney, and each incorrectly thought they were supposed to make the change in group membership with Active Directory. So, at almost exactly the same time (we'll ignore time zone differences for the purposes of this demonstration), Robert's new manager makes the previously described change, which is recorded on the Sydney domain controller as follows:

```
Object: LAUSERS
Change: Remove RSMITH
Version: 1
Timestamp: 30 June 2004 5:32:08 PM GMT
Object: SYDUSERS
Change: Add RSMITH
Version: 1
Timestamp: 30 June 2004 5:32:10 PM PT
```

There are two things to note about this record: one is the closeness of the timestamps. This would seem to indicate that the L.A. and Sydney domain controllers haven't replicated yet. The second item of interest is the version number field in each record, which does not appear to have been incremented. The reason for this is simple: version numbers are incremented on the local domain controller. If a domain controller doesn't know about any changes to an attribute, there is no need to further increment the version number on that record. Because L.A. and Sydney haven't passed changes between each other yet, the Sydney domain controller doesn't know that a similar change has processed on the L.A. domain controller and therefore doesn't know to increment the version number field from 1 to 2.

This might seem like a harmless situation now because even though the changes are different only in time, their net effect is the same—on both domain controllers, RSMITH is a member of the correct group and not a member of the former group. But in reality there *are* two changes. So, which one is really the change accepted by Active Directory? And to ask a more specific question, when both the L.A. and Sydney domain controllers replicate to their partner, the Boston domain controller, which change will Boston accept?

The tie is broken in two ways when changes to the same object compete:

- First, the attribute change with the highest version number is the change formally accepted.

- If the version number of each attribute change is the same, the change made at the most recent time is accepted.

In our case, the change made on the Sydney domain controller would be the one formally accepted in Active Directory, and the L.A. manager's modification, although its intent was the same, would be rejected because it was made at 5:30 p.m. and not at 5:32 p.m.

Update Sequence Numbers

Version numbers have siblings, called update sequence numbers (USNs), which measure the increments of every change to every attribute of every object within Active Directory. That is to say, whenever any change is made within Active Directory, a domain controller increments its current USN by 1. For example, if you have a pristine domain controller and you add a user with an initial password (update 1), change his password (update 2), add another user (update 3), create a new group (update 4), and put the first user in that group (update 5), the USN for that domain controller would be 5. Keep in mind that version numbers coexist with USNs; let's look at the information in Table 5-2 to see how USNs and version numbers interact in the preceding example. (Note that the table assumes we're talking about a domain with only one domain controller; it gets a bit more complicated when you add more domain controllers, and I'll discuss that later in this section.)

Table 5-2. Examining version numbers and USNs in Active Directory

Action	Attribute version number	Update sequence number (USN)
Create New User	All attributes are 1 because the operation is seen as one cohesive change.	0
Change Password	Password attribute for that user is 2.	1
Create New User	All attributes are 1.	2
Create New Group	All attributes are 1.	3
Add User to Group	Group membership attribute is 2.	4

From this table, you can glean that version numbers are incremented only when attributes change. We changed the password for our first user, so the version number for that attribute became 2, and we added that user to our newly created group, so the version number for the attribute containing the member list for that group increased to 2. But all the while, the USNs were incrementing because USNs measure every individual change. Our USNs went from 0 to 4 because (a) USNs start at 0, not 1, and (b) five individual changes were made.

Note that earlier I said this scenario revolved around a single domain controller. Let's change that now: if we were to add a domain controller to this example domain, the domain controllers would attempt to replicate with each other. Let's assume that once a domain controller is added, our two accounts and one group are transmitted immediately. The version numbers and USNs, as seen on the new domain controller, would shape up as shown in Table 5-3.

Table 5-3. Examining version numbers and USNs with two domain controllers

Object	Attribute version number	Update sequence number (USN)
User 1	All attributes are 1 except for the Password attribute, which is 2.	0
User 2	All attributes are 1.	1
Group	All attributes are 1 except for the membership list attribute, which is 2.	2

We learn two things from this table:

- Version numbers of attributes are retained across replications, so around the directory, no matter which domain controller you access, version numbers for attributes are the same. This is critical to the functioning of replication in Active Directory.

- USNs are independent to each domain controller. In our first example, there were five changes because we were adding and changing things individually on that first domain controller. Because the second domain controller was brand new, it created the user accounts and group from the up-to-date and already changed information on the first domain controller, so it needed to denote only three changes (the creation of each account and the creation of the group).

USNs really act as "signatures" showing the timeliness of information in each domain controller's copy of the directory, and essentially guide a domain controller's replication partners as to exactly how much updating is needed to fully replicate. Each domain controller tells its replication partners the USNs it has assigned to each piece of data, and the partner domain controllers keep track of this. The partners then know that the last piece of data they received—for example, from domain controller X—had a USN of 6093, and they can then tell domain controller X upon the next replication to start transmitting data with a USN of 6094 (one number higher than the last USN) or more. There is no need to send USNs 1-6093 again, as they already possess that data. If the USNs haven't changed on domain controllers during the regular five-minute breaks from replication, domain controllers assume that no new information is available, and they go back to "sleep" for another five minutes. On the other hand, if domain controller X's replication partners contact domain controller X and ask for its highest USN, and it replies with 7000, the partners know they need the last six pieces of information, and those will then be replicated. Then the partners would make a note that domain controller X's highest USN is now 7000, and everyone is secure in the knowledge that they have the most current directory possible for at least the next five minutes.

So, let's return to the example and see where we are with version numbers and USNs. Table 5-4 will sum that up.

Table 5-4. USNs and version numbers

| | Domain Controller 1 | | | Domain Controller 2 | |
Object	Attribute version numbers	Highest USN	Object	Attribute version numbers	Highest USN
User 1	All attributes are 1 except for the Password attribute, which is 2.	4	User 1	All attributes are 1 except for the Password attribute, which is 2.	2
User 2	All attributes are 1.		User 2	All attributes are 1.	
Group	All attributes are 1 except for the Membership List attribute, which is 2.		Group	All attributes are 1 except for the Membership List attribute, which is 2.	

Now consider this scenario: an administrator changes the password for User 2, and that administrator is currently using domain controller 1. That change would be assigned USN 5 because it's the sixth change that domain controller has seen. Five minutes later, replication is initiated, and domain controller 2 queries domain controller 1 for its highest USN, which it tells domain controller 2 is 5. Because domain controller 2 thinks the highest USN for domain controller 1 is 4, it knows it has missed a change, so it asks for the new information. The new password is pushed along, and the change on domain controller 2 is assigned a USN of 3 (it *is* a unique change, after all). Then domain controller 2 makes a note of domain controller 1's new highest USN, domain controller 2 is up to date, and everyone is happy.

They're happy, that is, until a few minutes later, when domain controller 1 asks domain controller 2 what its highest USN is. Domain controller 2 will faithfully reply that it is 3, and domain controller 1 will know that figure is higher than its recorded high USN for domain controller 2 (which is 2, as shown in Table 5-4). However, that change is the original change pushed through from domain controller 1 to domain controller 2. The domain controllers don't know that, however, just from looking at USNs, so they push through the replication, and domain controller 1's highest USN now becomes 6 because of this "change." Five minutes later, the entire process starts again, with this one change being propagated over and over and over again, in an infinite loop.

Breaking the loop: originating USNs and UTD vectors

How does one cure this? Microsoft identified this problem and introduced two other values to the mix, called *originating USNs* and *up-to-date vectors*, specifically to prevent this situation from occurring. Originating USNs simply keep track of the domain controller from which a change was initially transmitted, and the USN on that domain controller. So, when we first introduced the brand-new domain controller into our example domain and a copy of the directory was first replicated, more information was transmitted than I discussed earlier. Table 5-5 contains a more detailed representation of the results of that replication than Table 5-4 does because it includes originating USNs.

Table 5-5. Examining version numbers, USNs, and originating USNs

Object	Attribute version number	Update sequence number (USN)	Originating domain controller	Originating domain controller's USN
User 1	All attributes are 1 *except* for the Password attribute, which is 2.	0	Domain controller 1	All attributes *except* for Password 0; Password 1.
User 2	All attributes are 1.	1	Domain controller 1	All attributes 2.
Group	All attributes are 1 *except* for the Membership List attribute, which is 2.	2	Domain controller 1	All attributes *except* for membership list 3; membership list 4.

In essence, originating USNs tell all domain controllers where information first came from and what USN that first domain controller assigned to each piece of data. But just as domain controllers keep track of the highest USNs for their replication partners, they also keep track of the highest originating USN they have ever come across from any and all domain controllers. This table of maximum originating USNs is known as the up-to-date vectors. Let's look at this more closely.

Our situation now is shown in Table 5-6.

Table 5-6. Example USNs, originating USNs, and UTD vectors

Domain controller	Highest USN	Partner's highest USN	Up-to-date vectors	
			Self	Partner
1	4	2	4 (from domain controller 1)	2 (from domain controller 2)
2	2	4	2 (from domain controller 2)	4 (from domain controller 1)

I just formulated the up-to-date vectors shown in Table 5-6 in my mind; all they represent is the latest originating USN that each domain controller knows from the other domain controller. Now, flip back a couple of pages and refresh yourself on the scenario that previously would have created an infinite loop: a change of User 2's password, made by an administrator attached to domain controller 1. Domain controller 1 gives this change a USN of 5, and consequently domain controller 1 updates its table of up-to-date vectors with the highest originating USN that it knows from itself—so, it changes from 1 (our arbitrary first number) to 5.

Replication is initiated once again, and domain controller 2 asks domain controller 1 if it has any new information higher than USN 4, which it knows is its partner's highest USN, *and* whether the originating USNs are higher than 1 for domain controller

1, and 1 for domain controller 2. Domain controller 1 checks its copy of the directory and finds the password change, and then sees that it originated the change itself, with an originating USN of 5. However, domain controller 2 asked for any information from domain controller 1 with an originating USN higher than 1, so now domain controller 1 knows that domain controller 2 has no idea of this new information and it passes it along. Domain controller 2 records the change and assigns a USN of 3, and then makes a note that its partner's highest USN is 5 and the highest originating USN it has seen from domain controller 1 is 5. Our values, after that process, are shown in Table 5-7.

Table 5-7. Example USNs, originating USNs, and UTD vectors after example replication

Domain controller	Highest USN	Partner's highest USN	Up-to-date vectors	
			Self	Partner
1	5	2	5 (from domain controller 1)	2 (from domain controller 2)
2	3	5	3 (from domain controller 2)	5 (from domain controller 1)

Let's go a bit further. Replication kicks off again, and this time domain controller 1 contacts domain controller 2 and asks if it has any new information higher than USN 2, which it knows is its partner's highest USN, *and* whether the originating USNs are higher than 5 for domain controller 1 and 2 for domain controller 2. Domain controller 2 checks its copy of the directory and sees that it has a change to which it assigned a USN of 3, but it also checks to see where that change came from—and it sees that the change came from domain controller 1 and that domain controller 1 assigned a USN of 5 to it. Domain controller 2 decides that even though the change was new to itself, domain controller 1 clearly already knows about it and therefore doesn't need that change replicated. Domain controller 2 tells domain controller 1 about its currently highest USN (3), and domain controller 1 makes a note of that. What does this entire process accomplish? It ensures that a change is replicated only between partners because each partner can figure out who knows about what changes and when they were made by looking at USNs and up-to-date vectors. So, now everyone is happy—really, this time—as shown in Table 5-8.

Table 5-8. Final replication results

Domain controller	Highest USN	Partner's highest USN	Up-to-date vectors	
			Self	Partner
1	5	3	5 (from domain controller 1)	2 (from domain controller 2)
2	3	5	3 (from domain controller 2)	5 (from domain controller 1)

In summary, domain controllers use this up-to-date vector table and the originating USN data fundamentally to construct a more specific replication request. So, instead of simply asking a replication partner for any data higher than the highest USN a requestor knows, it asks for any data higher than the highest USN it knows is also higher than the ones for each domain controller in its up-to-date vector table.

Managing Replication Using REPADMIN

Replication Administrator, or REPADMIN, is a command-line utility that can control a lot of aspects and behaviors of Active Directory replication. In case you're wondering why you've never seen the utility, REPADMIN is part of the Windows Server 2003 Resource Kit Tools—not the standard kit—and you can find it on the distribution CD within the *SUPPTOOLS.MSI* installer file in the *\SUPPORT\TOOLS* folder.

Running the KCC

Recall from earlier in the chapter that the KCC detects the network environment and adjusts the structure of replication partners among domain controllers. It does this by default every 15 minutes, but if you want it to update earlier, you can trigger the KCC manually from the command line by running repadmin /kcc.

Viewing up-to-date vectors

On production machines, you can view the up-to-date vectors on a particular machine using REPADMIN. From a command line, run repadmin /showutdvec servername <LDAP-naming-context>. To fill in the latter part of the command, examine the name of your Active Directory structure, and divide the parts from each other and include "DC=" in front of each. Separate the DC parts with commas. For example, if I have a domain jonathanhassell.com, I would use DC=jonathanhassell,DC=com, and my REPADMIN command looking at a machine named SERVER1 would be:

```
repadmin /showutdvec server1 dc=jonathanhassell.com,dc=com
```

A sample result looks like the following:

```
Caching GUIDs.
..
Default-First-Site-Name\SERVER3 @ USN 8404 @ Time 2004-06-10 12:24:30
Default-First-Site-Name\SERVER2 @ USN 8038 @ Time 2004-06-10 11:12:57
Default-First-Site-Name\SERVER1 @ USN 9374 @ Time 2004-06-10 12:27:23
```

Of course, the numbers after the USN constitute the up-to-date vector for each listed domain controller.

Viewing replication partners

REPADMIN gives you a way to view replication partners outside of the GUI method discussed earlier in this section. Use the command repadmin /showrepl servername <LDAP-naming-context> to do so. For example:

```
repadmin /showrepl server1 dc=jonathanhassell.com,dc=com
```

Viewing highest USNs

By simply adding the /verbose switch to the command to view replication partners, you can see what the current server thinks is the highest USN for each partner. For example:

```
repadmin /showrepl /verbose server1 dc=jonathanhassell.com,dc=com
```

For each replication partner, the number before the /OU indicator is the highest USN from that particular partner that the current server has encountered.

Pressing the "Big Red Button"

If you want to replicate now, not later, you can use one of two options with REPADMIN. To force replication among any two domain controllers, use the command repadmin /replicate targetcomputer sourcecomputer <LDAP-naming-context>. For example, to force replication from SERVER3 to SERVER2, issue this command:

```
repadmin /replicate server2 server3 dc=jonathanhassell.com,dc=com
```

To initiate replicate among all partners, use repadmin /syncall servername <LDAP-naming-context>. So, if I wanted to force replication among all SERVER2's partners in the jonathanhassell.com domain, I'd use the following command:

```
repadmin /syncall server2 dc=jonathanhassell,dc=com
```

Among Sites: Spanning Trees and Site Links

Although Active Directory uses loops and meshes to create and manage replication topologies within a particular site, using that many links across an expensive WAN connection can cost you dearly as well as take a lot of time. For that reason, when Active Directory replicates between sites, it uses a minimal spanning tree—in other words, a tree with as few branches as possible to span the link between multiple sites.

Let's use an example environment, with two servers in a site called MAIN (representing the headquarters in Charlotte) and a single domain controller in another site, called WEST (located in San Francisco). Recall that the KCC facility creates replication topologies within sites automatically—you, the administrator, do not have to intervene. Replication between sites isn't as simple; Active Directory needs to know several things about your individual sites before it can figure out how to replicate traffic among them.

Site links

By creating site links, you give Active Directory three key pieces of information it needs to know before it can determine the most efficient way to force replication traffic across your sites:

- Which connection, if there are more than one, to use for replication to the destination site
- The persistency of that connection
- How the replication should take place—either using RPC in real time, or through SMTP

Let's discuss the third bit of information first: Active Directory will allow you to create links based over IP (using RPC calls) or via SMTP for less reliable or less secure connections. Unfortunately, SMTP-based site links are extremely limited in functionality. For one, SMTP links will only transfer updates to the forest schema naming context and configuration naming context; it will not perform cross-site domain controller information updates. Also, you need a secure mail server, hardened against outside interception using encryption and certificates, to transfer even that bit of information. For these reasons, the vast majority of site links you create will be IP-based links.

Returning to our example, let's create a site link between MAIN and WEST. To do so, follow these steps:

1. Open Active Directory Sites and Services.
2. Expand the MAIN node in the left pane, and then expand the Inter-Site Transports folder.
3. Right-click IP, and select Site Link from the New menu.
4. The screen in Figure 5-47 appears.
5. Enter a friendly name for the site in the Name box.
6. Choose the sites you want to include in this link. A link must include two or more sites, and you can shift sites back and forth using the Add and Remove buttons in the middle of the screen. For our purposes, make sure MAIN and WEST are in the box labeled Sites in this site link. Click OK.

To further configure the site link, right-click the new link in the IP folder of the left pane of Active Directory Sites and Services. Choose Properties, and the screen in Figure 5-48 will appear.

This screen contains three critical items. First, the Cost field allows you to determine a cost quotient—in essence, an index of the expense of using a connection—for each site link you create. If you have more than one site link, Active Directory will choose the lowest-cost link to perform the replication. Unfortunately, Microsoft doesn't give

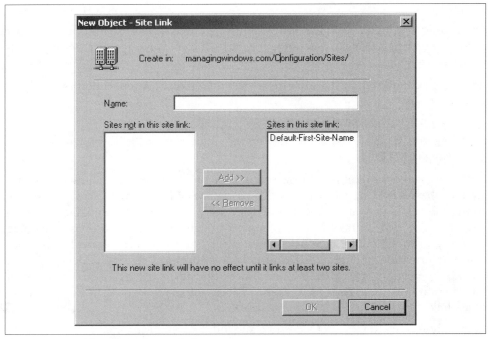

Figure 5-47. Configuring a new site link

you much guidance on how to arrive at your cost quotient figure; I recommend taking into account the base link cost, rates for prime and overnight periods, traffic limits, and link availability. Second, the Replicate every box allows you to specify how often Active Directory will attempt to initiate replication over this specific site link. You can set the shortest replication interval to 15 minutes, and there is no functional maximum value (although all Active Directory sites must replicate at least once every 60 days). Click the Change Schedule button to see the screen depicted in Figure 5-49.

Use the mouse to select the hours during which the link will not be available; Active Directory will use this information and not even attempt replication during that time period. Click OK to exit that dialog box, and then click OK to finish configuring the link.

Once you have specified the information for the site, the Sites and Services equivalent of the KCC, called the Inter-Site Topology Generator (ISTG), will begin developing the minimal spanning tree needed to pass replication traffic among sites.

And that's a basic but thorough treatment of Active Directory replication.

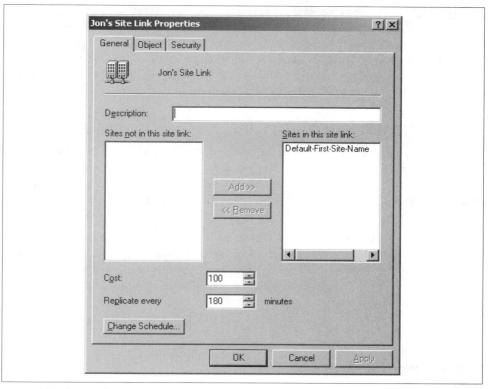

Figure 5-48. Setting the properties of a site link

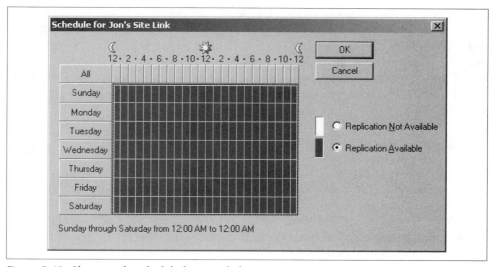

Figure 5-49. Changing the schedule for a site link

Migrating to Active Directory in Windows Server 2003

A primary reason businesses are purchasing Windows Server 2003 is to move away from other, older operating systems. In this section, I will look at moving to Active Directory from Windows NT and Windows 2000, including steps on planning, actually moving, and then keeping your systems running smoothly.

Moving from Windows NT Domains

A lot of companies are finding themselves jumping the sinking Windows NT ship and considering an upgrade to the latest server product from Microsoft, Windows Server 2003. After all, the end-of-life date for the NT Workstation product was in mid-2003 and NT Server's death is fast approaching as well, so it's very possible that your organizations have some machines running NT that are worth upgrading.

Microsoft released Windows Server 2003 in late April 2003, and since then the product has matured via various updates and out-of-band releases into a server product that is more stable, reliable, and secure than any previous version of Windows. It is usually not until after the first service pack of a new Microsoft operating system ships that companies really start looking to upgrade existing systems, and Service Pack 1 for Windows Server 2003 shipped in mid-2005. So, this would be an excellent time to consider upgrading.

Items to consider before migrating

If you have an NT domain and haven't investigated Active Directory, the new directory service Microsoft introduced in Windows 2000 Server, there's a lot in store for you. Active Directory is superior to NT-style domains in many ways, not the least of which is easier management. You can divide your directory into specific domains and OUs and manage like sets of objects with ease. Active Directory is more robust and fits better into more distributed environments, particularly in organizations with branch offices in multiple locations. Active Directory is more secure for your users and is also the foundation of many newer versions of Microsoft server products, including the new Microsoft Exchange Server 2003.

Moving from NT to Windows Server 2003 and Active Directory requires several steps. First, you'll want to analyze your current NT domain environment. Specifically, you'll need to find answers to these questions:

- Are you on a single domain, are you on a multiple domain model with accounts and computers located in each domain, or do you have a single master or multi-master domain model with separate domains each for user accounts and machine resources? The single domain model is the easiest to upgrade because the existing domain simply becomes the root of the Active Directory domain. However, if you have a particularly large domain or a network that might be restructured one day, you might want to consider a dedicated forest root model (sometimes called an empty root), in which you create a root domain within a forest and then create child domains off of that root, which allows you to change domains in the forest without scrapping your entire Active Directory structure. If you have a single master domain and child domains containing machines, you really don't need to continue that structure upon moving to Active Directory because you can create OUs to store specific types of objects within the directory. Multiple masters will want to use the dedicated forest root strategy because even in Active Directory, complex networks still should be broken up by domains for easier management.

- What sort of trust relationships have you built up with other domains in your environment? Trust relationships can make moving to Active Directory more complicated, but they don't have to be difficult. If you have trusts among a multi-master domain model, in that every domain trusts every other domain, you don't have to do anything if you put all these domains into a single forest— all of these trusts between domains are transitive automatically. If you have one-way trusts that you want to preserve for logistical reasons, you'll need to create multiple forests, which can be a headache; make sure this is the route you want to take before taking it. Figure 5-50 shows some sample trust relationships in Active Directory and how they fit together.

- How many PDCs and BDCs do you have, and where are they located—all at one location, or at separate sites? In Active Directory, the notion of the PDC and BDC has gone away (with a couple of minor exceptions). Plus, Windows Server 2003 is more robust than NT 4.0, so you can likely consolidate multiple domain controllers at a single location into a smaller number, depending on their load. Your main concern with domain controllers is their location. Part of Active Directory's technology is a replication algorithm that sends updated contents of the directory to all domain controllers within the forest, even at different sites. If you have offices in different locations with slow links, which you can define within Active Directory, this will affect your replication speed and how quickly those users at the remote offices can get authenticated and receive access to domain or forest resources. You'll want to look at how these locations will play into where you allocate domain controllers.

- If you have DNS deployed internally, what namespaces are you using and how are they assigned? You'll want to catalog all these internal domain namespaces and decide how they will "map" into your new Active Directory structure. Particularly of note are how you want DNS subdomains (for example, corp.acme.com) to map to actual Active Directory domains in a forest and if you want to have external DNS services separated from internal DNS services, as I described in Chapter 4 in the split DNS section. Of course, DNS is a major component of Active Directory and entire books are written about planning and using DNS in

Active Directory environments, so be sure to read up on best practices or bring someone experienced in DNS planning to assist you in your migration efforts.

- Do you have any NT 4.0 servers that are running the Routing and Remote Access Service (RRAS) or the LAN Manager Replication Service? The NT RAS machines, be they domain controllers or just ordinary member servers, really don't integrate well within an Active Directory environment. If you have a member server functioning as an RAS machine, you should upgrade it to Windows Server 2003 before the last domain controller is upgraded. The RAS machine has certain security requirements that are incompatible between the different operating system versions. Also, if you have only one domain controller in your domain, you need to upgrade your RAS server before beginning any domain controller upgrades. Plus, the LAN Manager Replication Service is incompatible with the new File Replication Service found in Active Directory, so disable that as well.

- Do you have any machines running versions of NT earlier than 4.0? You really need to simply rid yourself of these machines, as they're just not compatible with Windows Server 2003 or an Active Directory environment.

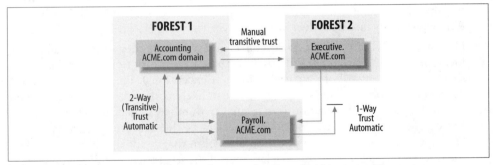

Figure 5-50. How trust relationships can be created and used within Active Directory

Migration strategies

Of course, any migration process is risky because your environment is changing. In this section, I'll take a look at some prudent strategies to mitigate that risk and ensure that the entire move from NT domains to Windows Server 2003 and Active Directory will go smoothly.

First, you'll want to make sure that your BDC and PDC are up to date for all NT domains you're touching with the migration. If the PDC fails to upgrade for some reason, the BDC can be promoted to PDC and nothing is lost but some time. If you have two BDCs, the best strategy is to leave one online during the migration, so users more or less don't notice that anything is going on, and take the other offline during the upgrade. This way, the offline BDC isn't touched by anything happening during the upgrade and can be plugged in, should everything go haywire. Figure 5-51 shows this procedure.

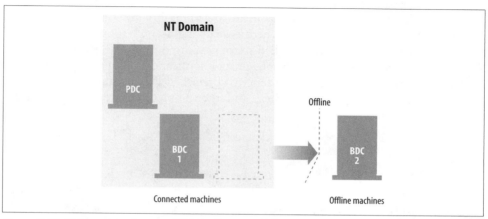

NT Domain

PDC

BDC
1

Offline

BDC
2

Connected machines

Offline machines

Figure 5-51. Taking a synchronized BDC offline as a failure recovery strategy

Also, synchronize your BDCs with their partner PDCs before proceeding. Out-of-date replication partners don't help anything when it comes to restoring service in the event of an outage. In the course of the migration, be sure to keep track of any changes you make after you take your BDCs offline—if your migration fails and you promote your BDC to a PDC, you will lose any changes you made since you took the BDC offline, and you'll need to manually redo any changes you made in that period.

Take some time to look specifically at the PDC for each domain and figure out if it's sufficiently powerful. When I said earlier that there are virtually no distinctions between domain controllers nowadays, I also said there were a couple of exceptions: the first domain controller upgraded into Active Directory will take on some roles that others don't have that will require a bit more operational horsepower. If you're in doubt as to whether your PDC is powerful enough, a common suggestion is to buy a new machine and load it with NT 4.0 and Service Pack 6 and configure it as a BDC. Promote it to a PDC and put it on the network for a bit to let the changes settle out and to let replication finish, and then take it offline and upgrade the machine to Windows Server 2003. This is the strategy closest to a clean install and usually gives you the best results. If you have more than one domain, do this for each domain. (Do note that if you decide to use the dedicated forest root strategy, you'll need to have a native Windows Server 2003 machine with Active Directory and create the forest and root domain *before* upgrading any PDCs.)

Performing the move

It's remarkably easy to upgrade any type of Windows NT installation, whether a PDC, BDC, or regular member server, to Windows Server 2003. Microsoft has taken great pains to ensure the upgrade to Windows Server 2003 is as painless as possible. The installation procedure follows a normal clean install of Windows Server 2003 reasonably closely, and in fact requires less hands-on work. The program doesn't prompt you at all after the inception of the installation; little to no reconfiguration is required with an upgrade installation because existing users, settings, groups, rights, and permissions are saved and applied automatically during the upgrade process. You also don't need to remove files or reinstall applications with an operating system version upgrade. So, at the beginning, you're asked for only the CD Key and to acknowledge any compatibility issues, and then sometime later the upgrade is complete.

There are, however, a few points of which to take note:

Service pack levels
> The Windows NT installation must be running Service Pack 5 or higher. You can download the most recent update, Service Pack 6a, from:
>
>> *http://www.microsoft.com/ntserver/nts/downloads/recommended/SP6/ allSP6.asp*
>
> Other acceptable Windows NT versions include NT Terminal Server Edition with SP5 or later, and NT Server Enterprise Edition, also with SP5 or later.

Evaluating immediate Setup issues
> On a machine that's a candidate for Windows Server 2003, insert the Windows Server 2003 CD and run *winnt32.exe* with the /checkupgradeonly switch. This will present a report with issues that the Setup program detects might cause problems with an upgrade to Windows Server 2003. A sample report is shown in Figure 5-52.
>
> Also, regarding storage, you might want to examine the following disk issues before upgrading.

Partition sizes
> On machines upgrading from NT to Windows Server 2003, ensure that there is plenty of disk space on the system partition of each machine. This is especially true of domain controllers because converting a SAM database to an Active Directory database full of the latter's capabilities can increase the size of the SAM by as much as 10 times.

Filesystems
> Domain controllers require that their system partitions be formatted with the NTFS filesystem. Although as a general procedure I recommend formatting all partitions on all server machines with NTFS, you are not required to do so unless the machine in question is a domain controller.

Volume, mirror, and stripe sets
> Upgrading to Windows Server 2003 Enterprise Edition from NT on a system with volume, mirror, or stripe sets (including stripe sets with parity) that were

created under NT requires some modifications of those sets. Because Windows Server 2003 includes new dynamic disk technologies, support for older enhanced disk features has been removed—and this is indeed a change from Windows 2000. You will need to break any mirror sets or, for all other media sets, back up any data on the set, and then delete the set. When Setup is complete, you can replicate your existing disk configuration using native Windows Server 2003 tools and restore any data required from the backups.

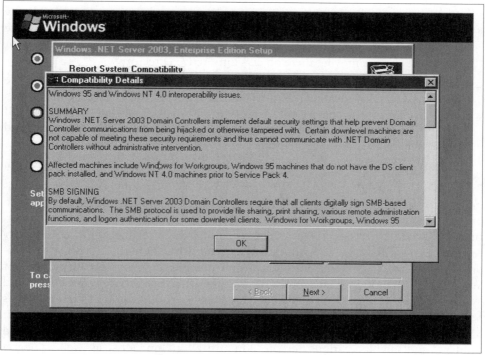

Figure 5-52. Using the Check Upgrade function of Windows Server 2003's setup to look for issues to correct

Moving domains to Active Directory

The upgrade procedure for an NT domain is relatively straightforward. Initially you must choose the first server to upgrade in your Windows NT domain. As you upgrade different machines, depending on their existing role in the domain, features and capabilities become available with Windows Server 2003 on the upgraded machine. In particular, upgrading an NT PDC enables all the included Active Directory features, as well as the other capabilities inherent in any Windows Server 2003 server, such as improved RRAS features, no matter the role. Note that you can upgrade Windows NT member servers at any time during your migration plan, and most migration plans specify that member servers are last on the list to receive the upgrade. However, no matter your order, when you begin upgrading NT domain controllers to Windows Server 2003, you *must* upgrade the PDC before any other domain controller machines.

Here's a checklist of some steps to take immediately prior to your move to ensure that your NT-to-Server-2003 migration goes smoothly:

- Make sure that all PDCs and BDCs are running Windows NT 4.0 with at least Service Pack 5, or better, Server Pack 6a.

- Clean up your domain account list, for both users and computers. We all know these lists can be cluttered with inactive users, multiple accounts for the same user, and so on. Take this opportunity to eliminate excess baggage from your directories before moving these objects into Active Directory.

- Remove any unused software via its uninstallation facility, and defragment the hard disk to take advantage of any unused space. Active Directory migrations can use a lot of disk space—sometimes upward of 10 times the size of the SAM database for an NT domain—and contiguous free areas of the disk can speed Active Directory query response time.

- Kill any trusts between domains that you don't want preserved over the migration.

By default, domain controllers in Windows Server 2003 digitally sign network communications and verify the authenticity of parties to a transaction, which helps to prevent communications between machines from being hijacked or otherwise interrupted. Certain older operating systems are not capable of meeting these security requirements, at least by default, and as a result are unable to interact with Windows Server 2003 domain controllers. Such operating systems are Windows for Workgroups, Windows 95 machines without the Directory Services client pack, and Windows NT 4.0 machines prior to Service Pack 4. You'll also find that Windows Server 2003 domain controllers by default require all clients to digitally sign their SMB communications. The SMB protocol allows Windows systems to share files and printers, and enables various remote administration functions, as well as logon authentication over a network. If your clients are running one of the operating systems mentioned previously and upgrading them to a later revision is not an option, you'll need to turn off the digital signing and SMB signing requirements by disabling the "Digitally sign communications" policy in the Default Domain Controller GPO that applies to the OU where the domain controllers are located. You certainly can turn this feature back on when the affected computers have been upgraded.

Additionally, Windows Server 2003 domain controllers similarly require that all secure channel communications be either signed or encrypted. Secure channels are encrypted "tunnels" of communication through which Windows-based machines interact with other domain members and controllers, as well as among domain controllers that have a trust relationship. Windows NT 4.0 machines prior to Service Pack 4 are not capable of signing or encrypting secure channel communications. If NT 4.0 machines at a revision earlier than SP4 must participate in a domain, or a domain must trust other domains that contain pre-SP4 domain controller machines, the secure channel signing requirement needs to be removed. This is also in the domain controllers' security policy, under the GPO setting titled "Digitally encrypt or sign secure channel data."

Moving from Windows 2000 Server

Although a move from Windows Server 2003's predecessor, Windows 2000, might seem simple, there are several issues that you need to address, and many strategies for doing so. In this section, I'll discuss the implications of and procedures to moving from Windows 2000 and an existing Active Directory environment to Windows Server 2003.

About forest and domain functional levels

The first issue to consider when moving to Windows Server 2003 is functional levels. Microsoft's Active Directory has several forest and domain functional levels that enable or disable certain features of the service depending on the makeup of the domain controllers within a domain. If you have a network mixed with Windows 2000 and Windows Server 2003 domain controllers, for example, the Active Directory forest will operate in one mode; if you have a pure Windows Server 2003 environment, the forest will function in another mode after you manually switch to a higher functional level. There are three forest functional levels:

Windows 2000 forest functional level
> This mode supports all types of domain controllers (NT, 2000, and Server 2003), supports only 5,000 members to a single, individual group, and only offers improved global catalog replication benefits when all domain controllers in the domain are running Windows Server 2003.

Windows Server 2003 interim forest functional level
> In this level, you lose support for Windows 2000 domain controllers, but you gain partial replication of group membership lists, complete improvements to global catalog replication (because all Active Directory domain controllers are running Windows Server 2003), and support for group membership to exceed 5,000 objects.

Windows Server 2003 forest functional level
> In this level, you lose support for Windows NT and Windows 2000 domain controllers, but you gain everything in the previous two levels and you add support for renaming existing domains, more efficient Active Directory replication, and transitive forest trusts.

The Windows 2000 forest functional level is the default for new forests, regardless of where you begin the forest or from where you upgrade. This mode will support a Windows 2000 or Windows Server 2003 domain controller or one or more Windows

NT 4.0 BDCs. You also can use any domain functional level. You can use the Windows Server 2003 interim functional level upon upgrade from Windows NT 4.0; it supports only NT or Windows Server 2003 domain controllers—no regular Windows 2000 domain controllers are allowed. In this forest functional level, you can use only Windows Server 2003 interim domain functional levels or higher. Finally, the Windows Server 2003 forest functional level is available when every last domain controller in the forest is running Windows Server 2003 and nothing below it—essentially, a pure "new" environment. This forest functional level requires the Windows Server 2003 domain functional level.

Which forest functional level should you use upon an initial migration from Windows 2000? I recommend using the Windows 2000 forest functional level, at least for 90 days or so after your migration. Because you can't revert to a previous functional level, don't throw the switch until you're sure all old servers that limit your functional level choices truly aren't needed.

Here's a list of domain functional levels and some of their primary benefits and drawbacks:

Windows 2000 mixed domain functional level
> This is useful for 20,000 accounts or less. You also get support for 300 sites per domain, multi-master replication (you're finally out of primarily NT land!), and support for Kerberos onto existing NTLM authentication support.

Windows 2000 native domain functional level
> With this level, you can store millions of accounts, create nested groups (groups within groups within groups, and so on), and receive support for cross-domain administration.

Windows Server 2003 interim domain functional level
> You do *not* have support for nested groups here, and you cannot use Windows 2000 domain controllers in this mode, but you do get the rest of the improvements discussed heretofore.

Windows Server 2003 domain functional level
> This is the Holy Grail, as it were. You get increased site support, improved replication, and better desktop management capabilities, among other things.

The Windows 2000 mixed functional level is the default for any new domain. All of your Windows NT 4.0, Windows 2000, and Windows Server 2003 machines can coexist peacefully at this level. The Windows Server 2003 interim functional level is meant for networks going directly from NT and Windows Server 2003, so your Windows 2000 domain controllers aren't permitted. The Windows 2000 native functional level allows domains to have more than 40,000 accounts and removes other limitations from NT-based domains, but NT domain controllers aren't allowed—only Windows 2000 and Windows Server 2003 can participate in this mode. Finally, the Windows Server 2003 domain functional level is meant for pure Windows Server 2003 environments.

Most likely you'll find yourself using the Windows 2000 mixed domain functional level, and I recommend the same timeframe for domain levels—wait 90 days before making a change. This will give you a chance to remove NT servers from your domain and find some way to allow any Samba servers you might have to connect to your domain.

Please do note that these functional modes dictate behavior between domain controllers in domains and forests in your Active Directory infrastructure: they have very little implication for client computers. Windows NT 4.0 client computers, with the appropriate security policy modifications, most certainly can operate in a Windows Server 2003 native mode, while Windows Server 2003 member servers can operate perfectly normally in Windows 2000 mixed mode domains. However, as a side note, WINS server deployment is affected by the presence of legacy clients: you definitely need WINS services for clients who need NetBIOS name resolution. Additionally, quite a few people mistake raising domain and forest functional levels as carte blanche to disable NetBIOS-over-TCP/IP traffic, but I advise against that: many, many legacy applications are still around—even some that you might not consider "legacy"—that rely on NetBIOS to resolve names. Disable that feature and you break your programs, which users don't particularly care for.

We'll come to what you actually do with these beasts after you've performed the upgrade. The next step is to massage your forests and domains to get ready for the upgrade.

Preparing existing forests and domains

To upgrade to Windows Server 2003 using an existing Active Directory structure, you need to make changes to the existing forest and any domains within them. To prepare a Windows 2000 domain for the upgrade to Windows Server 2003, you must use the Active Directory Preparation tool, ADPREP. The utility performs the following tasks:

- Updates the Active Directory schema
- Enhances the existing security descriptors
- Upgrades display specifiers
- Refines settings in ACLs on Active Directory objects and on files in the SYSVOL shared folder, mainly to permit access for domain controllers
- Creates new objects that COM+, Windows Management Instrumentation (WMI), and other such applications use regularly
- Creates new containers in Active Directory to signal successful completion of the preparation process

Let's focus a bit more on the fourth point. In previous Windows versions, the Everyone SID, when present on an ACL or in group membership, allowed authenticated users, guest users, and those logged in anonymously to access many resources. Windows 2000 domain controllers also use anonymous access to control a few Active Directory objects and files. In an effort to improve security, Windows Server 2003 no longer allows anonymous access with the Everyone SID. This inherently restricts Windows 2000 domain controllers from controlling particular objects. To compensate, ADPREP adjusts the ACLs on such objects so that the domain controllers in question can still use them.

ADPREP is a command-line-only tool. The program, *adprep.exe*, is located on the Windows Server 2003 operating system CD. When executed, ADPREP copies the files *409.csv* and *dcpromo.csv* from the *I386* directory on the installation CD to the local computer to prepare the Active Directory forest and domain. Then the *adprep.exe* tool updates the current Active Directory schema with new information contained in the template the tool provides, while at the same time keeping any modifications to the schema that you already made.

 You can reverse the changes ADPREP makes, but it is a difficult, time-consuming, and rather dangerous procedure that involves messing directly with the Active Directory schema. I don't recommend it, and it is too extensive to cover in this book.

Although a rare occurrence, ADPREP has corrupted the Active Directory database while preparing the forest on Windows 2000 domain controllers that are running any level of the operating system prior to Service Pack 2. Therefore, before running ADPREP, install at least SP2 on your Windows 2000 domain controllers to prevent this problem.

If you begin to encounter difficulty, note that ADPREP creates a log file each time it runs that can help you troubleshoot errors. The log file records each preparation step, as well as any errors found, while ADPREP is executing. The log files are separated into subfolders, identified by the date and time ADPREP was executed, under the *\Windows\system32\debug\adprep* directory.

Now that the background is out of the way, it's time to get started. To prepare Active Directory for the move, follow these steps:

1. Take the domain controller with the schema master offline.

2. Reconnect the schema master to a private network—just an empty hub with no uplink will suffice—and log on using an account with Schema Admin and Enterprise Admin credentials.

3. Run the following command from the *I386* directory on the Windows Server 2003 distribution CD:

```
adprep /forestprep
```

   Doing so will cause the following warning to pop up:

```
ADPREP WARNING: All Windows 2000 domain controllers in the forest
should be upgraded to Windows 2000 SP2 or higher before performing
Windows .NET forest preparation. This must be completed to avoid
```

> potential DC corruption. Type C and press Enter to continue, or
> type any other key and press Enter to quit.

4. Enter **C** and press Enter to acknowledge the warning and continue with the forest preparations. After the utility has finished, a message appears stating that all operations have completed successfully.

5. Verify that the changes were made successfully by running the following at the command prompt:

```
adsiedit.msc
```

Note that ADSIEdit is one of the Windows 2000 Support Tools, and one of the Windows Server 2003 Support Tools. You should install these on the computer from which you are verifying the changes. You can find these support tools on the Windows 2000 or Windows Server 2003 distribution CD.

6. Expand the Configuration container and ensure that CN=ForestUpdates exists. Also look in CN=ForestUpdates and make sure that CN=Windows2002Update has been created.

7. Examine the Event Log for any event messages that indicate that the domain controller is not functioning properly. Note that you can ignore error events involving the disconnection of the schema operations master.

8. Reintroduce the schema master into the production environment. The changes will replicate.

After you have prepared the forest for the upgrade, it's time to prepare each domain for the upgrade:

1. Log on to the infrastructure master using an account with Domain Admin or Enterprise Admin credentials.

2. At the command prompt, type:

```
adsiedit.msc
```

3. Expand the Configuration container and ensure that CN=ForestUpdates exists. Also look in CN=ForestUpdates and make sure that CN=Windows2002Update has been created.

4. Run the following command from the *I386* directory on the Windows Server 2003 distribution CD:

```
adprep /domainprep
```

After the utility has finished, a message appears stating that all operations have completed successfully.

To verify that ADPREP has completed all operations successfully, use one of the following procedures (it doesn't matter which):

- Using ADSIEdit, look in the Domain container, and explore down to DC=your-domain, DC=com, CN=System, and CN=DomainUpdates. Ensure that CN=-Windows2002Update is present. (You can find ADSIEdit in the Support Tools

MSI file that I discussed several times in this chapter; run it by executing `ADSIEDIT.MSC` from the command line.)

- In ADUC, select Advanced Features from the View menu. Look in the System container, and find and expand the DomainUpdates container. Make sure the Windows2002Update container exists.

Raising the forest and domain functional levels

Once you're ready to throw the switch and upgrade the forest and domain functional levels, do yourself a favor: simply unplug your legacy systems for a while and let any bugs in your network shake out. It's best to make sure you won't be disabling anything you need ready access to by increasing functional levels because, again, the upgrade is a one-way street: there is not a method to reverse the change.

When you have ensured that all legacy domain controllers are truly not necessary, log on to a domain controller with administrator privileges and do the following to change the domain functional level:

1. From the Start menu, choose Administrative tools, and then click Active Directory Domains and Trusts.

2. Click the applicable domain, and then select Raise Domain Functional Level. The screen will match at shown in Figure 5-53.

3. Select the appropriate functional level from the drop-down menu, and then click the Raise button.

4. Confirm your choice when prompted by clicking OK.

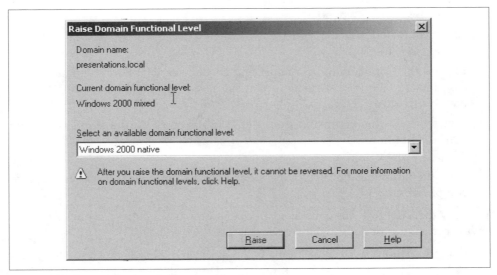

Figure 5-53. Raising the domain functional level

Windows will then upgrade the functional level of your domain. Keep in mind that switching to native mode is not reversible, so you will not be able to use any NT 4.0 domain controllers within that domain. Similarly, the move to Windows Server 2003 mode is final and will preclude the use of both NT and Windows 2000 domain controllers in the domain.

You can upgrade the forest functional level only after all the domains contained within the forest are operating in native mode. Once you upgrade the forest, you can only add domains that are living in the same mode or in a higher mode—for domains that need to operate in a lower mode, you'll need to create an entirely new forest just for them.

With that in mind, to raise the forest functional level, follow these steps:

1. From the Start menu, choose Administrative tools, and then click Active Directory Domains and Trusts.

2. Click the applicable domain, and then select Raise Forest Functional Level. The screen will match that shown in Figure 5-54.

3. Select the appropriate functional level from the drop-down menu, and then click the Raise button.

4. Confirm your choice when prompted by clicking OK.

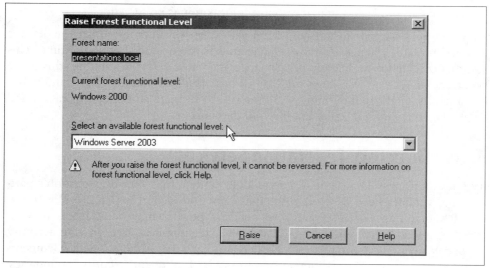

Figure 5-54. Raising the forest functional level

Tips for a smooth upgrade

Before you begin the upgrade from Windows 2000, install Windows Server 2003 on a computer and have it act as a simple member server of your domain. It doesn't matter in which domain you choose to have it participate: it can be any in the Active

Directory forest. Monitor the server's event and error logs, and ensure that it runs without problems for at least 10 days before proceeding.

Then, after you prepare the forest and domain for upgrade by using the ADPREP tool as described in the previous sections, install Active Directory on the member server and choose to make that machine an additional domain controller in the same domain. When you do this, the member server is converted into the first Windows Server 2003-level domain controller in the forest. This lets all existing services run uninterrupted while you are upgrading other domain controllers to Windows Server 2003.

Finally, you might be wondering about the merits of a clean installation—that is, formatting a drive and starting fresh with an initial installation of Windows Server 2003— or upgrading existing systems that are running Windows 2000. Traditionally, operating system upgrades have been rather tricky, with some settings and even possibly user data being lost in the process. However, Microsoft has expended a lot of effort to improve the reliability of the upgrade process and, as one colleague puts it, the results are "admirable." The benefits of performing an upgrade include the following:

- Your localized settings are preserved, including display, network, and other configurations.
- Your domain settings are preserved when upgrading a domain controller.
- All user accounts and shared resource information is preserved.

However, with upgrade installs you don't get the opportunity to remove the detritus that accumulates when a Windows system runs for an extended period of time. This assorted crud tends to degrade performance and cause errors at random; this is the syndrome known as "Windows rot." Clean installs afford you that opportunity, but in the end it might require more work for you to recreate all the configuration and data from your earlier installation. It's your decision.

Active Directory Federation Services

In today's business environment, you're likely finding that your organization's partners and vendors need to work with equipment and resources that cross organizational boundaries. For instance, your business partner may need access to your ordering system, your vendor has to have a way to submit invoices to your accounting department, and your alliance's R&D teams need to collaborate with documents and presentations across different platforms and different security boundaries. Today, it's not about being an information silo—it's about securely managing access to information, both internally and externally.

But with this new model of sharing information comes an interesting problem that's one of trust, particularly across security boundaries. Here, I'm digging at a core problem that's facing IT in larger organizations today. Let's look at this in terms of an example.

Let's say that TrinketBuild, Inc. sells trinkets, and TreasureBuild, Inc. sells treasures. To build a trinket, one needs to include a treasure, which is a core component of the trinket. TrinketBuild has come to an agreement with TreasureBuild to get treasures at a lower price in a large quantity. TreasureBuild uses an externally facing application to take orders and process payment for their orders, and their customers' employees (in this case, TrinketBuild's employees) have traditionally had accounts to be able to access this application.

When we introduce the concept of accounts into this example, we introduce an issue known as identity management. In a nutshell, how does one manage all of the accounts that one person has to his name? For example, TrinketBuild's employees probably have several accounts: one to log in to the network each day, perhaps a separate email account, accounts to access mainframe business applications, and—if they're like any other corporation—probably ten more accounts for various resources. Now upon the signing of this agreement with TreasureBuild, some TrinketBuild employees will have still one more account added to their load of usernames and passwords: the one used to access TreasureBuild's ordering and billing application.

But wouldn't it be great, from a lot of angles, if TrinketBuild employees could use their own Active Directory username and password—the one they use each day—to access TreasureBuild's extranet application? What if the two companies' IT departments could come to some sort of trust agreement, wherein the TreasureBuild department trusts certain Active Directory accounts (and more specifically, some attributes from those accounts) from TrinketBuild to access their application with their own credentials, without requiring a local TreasureBuild account? What benefits would this bring?

Here are just a few:

- For the user, it's one less additional username and password to remember. The TrinketBuild employee could log in as *john@trinketbuild.com* and receive all the access he was entitled to. If nothing else, it's a lot less confusing.

- For TreasureBuild, it means less of a headache in terms of administration. Authorized TrinketBuild employees won't need to have a local account created just so that they can access the extranet application.

- For TrinketBuild, it means their internal IT department will be getting fewer forgotten password calls. It also means that all of the user accounting calls can be passed, without cost, to TreasureBuild for them to handle.

- For the security team at TreasureBuild, it means that accounts for TrinketBuild employees who leave aren't left open indefinitely. Why? Since the TrinketBuild employees are using their AD accounts to log in, as soon as those accounts are disabled by TrinketBuild, those credentials are inherently invalid to log in anywhere else. This closes a significant security hole.

By integrating this sort of trust in their accounting and transactions, TrinketBuild and TreasureBuild are participating in federated identity management (FIM). FIM is a standards-based technology and process that enables identification, authentication, and authorization information to transcend traditional security boundaries. The idea of federation is one of heterogeneity: different companies use different technologies, identity storage and security approaches, and programming models, but they still need to interact with other companies with still different technologies, identity storage and security approaches, and programming models. Among these differences, there should be a standardized way of advertising the types of services one offers externally, but also of accepting trusts, credentials, and policy information from other organizations.

In Windows Server 2003 R2, Microsoft has included Active Directory Federation Services, a new component, which integrates the concept of FIM into Windows using Active Directory as the base identity store. By using ADFS, you can eventually enable secure access to web applications outside of a user's home domain or forest. ADFS uses all of the identity information in AD and "projects" that information outside of the local AD forest into the realm of the extranet, if there are applications out there, or to other organizations for their use. Doing so, of course, improves security, enables auditing and tracking (which is an important capability to have in today's regulatory environment), and increases end-user productivity.

Scenarios

ADFS supports a couple of scenarios natively: web single sign-on, and the traditional identity federation model.

Let's look at the single sign-on model first. If you use Windows Server 2003 R2 and IIS 6 for an externally accessible web application, you can use forms-based authentication and give users a single-sign on session cookie, which removes the need for them to log on to access any other resources in a trusted domain. In this way, users will log in once when they access the first web application, and then this cookie will be used to answer any future credential challenges by other resources in the domain. Since one web "application" is usually actually a collection of multiple applications, you remove the need for repeatedly requesting user credentials.

The second scenario involves regular identity federation. The difference here is fundamental: identity federation separates authentication (verifying an identity) from the access control, or authorization, decision, and places it squarely on the account side of the relationship rather than on the resource side. So instead of a user authenticating to an extranet site by entering his credentials, the user's home Active Directory—otherwise known as his "home realm"—authenticates the user and then automatically generates a security token for the end user. The user then presents that token to target application, and the application itself uses that token to grant access rights. The key to this process is the federated trust that the two partners set up, which includes exchange of keys and standardization on the types of information about users the application will require. (These pieces of information are called *claims*.) Thus, through the process of federation, the end user signs on once to all of their internal network applications through the regular Windows authentication process, but he also gets seamless access to partner applications without having to sign on again.

Architecture

ADFS is basically made up of four components: Active Directory, where the identity information is stored; a federation server, a federation server proxy, and an agent that runs on a web server. The AD component is simple—you have a repository of identity data that ADFS will make use of—so let's move to the other parts of the architecture.

The federation server is a service that handles and processes security tokens. The federation server also contains the tools needed to manage federated trusts between business partners. The server takes user information and claims and populates these security tokens with the claims. Common claims might include a user's job title, department, level of access to a particular function, a credit or purchasing limit, and approval requirements.

The federation server proxy is a machine to which the client will connect to request the security token. It also provides all the UI that the browser would potentially need to display for you—it basically acts as a front end for clients to all of the magic of ADFS.

The last component is an agent that runs on the web server that makes sure the end user is authenticated. Once this is done, the agent creates a context for the user. If you have a classic client-server application that requires an NTLM security context (one where you assign permissions based on ACLs and such), the agent will actually create that context after it decides the security token was valid. Windows SharePoint Services, among other applications, works really well with this type of context. If you have a claims-aware application—that is, one that recognizes roles and claims within its own processes—then you can use Authorization Manager for role-based access control.

The Flow of Applications and Claims

Let's step through the flow of a typical federation transaction.

1. A client will access the web server hosting the application.
2. The web server will look for the client's security token. If one isn't present, the user will be redirected back to the federation server on the resource side.

3. That resource federation server will then determine where the client is from; a drop-down list, an email address, or a persistent cookie will identify the client's origin.

4. The resource federation server, now knowing where the client is from, will redirect the client to the federation server on the account side.

5. The clients logs in, and subsequently authenticates to the account side federation server.

6. That server will then create a security token that will be sent back to the client.

7. The client presents the security token to the resource federation server.

8. The resource federation server will validate the security token (ensuring it came from a trusted partner, was signed appropriately, and hasn't been tampered with).

9. The resource federation server can make modifications to the security token, if necessary, to translate different claims into data the application can understand. (For example, if a Social Security number is being transmitted, the account-side federation server may term that data SocSecNum, while the resource side might need that data labeled SSN. More about this in a bit.) If no translation is necessary, then this doesn't occur.

10. The server will sign a new security token and send it back to the client.

11. The client will then go to the web server, which will allow him or her to access the application.

You can see this process depicted graphically in Figure 5-55.

Claims Transformation

The pieces of information being exchanged about a trusted partners' users—recall that these are called claims—have a flow all their own. Organizational claims are made by the user's home realm; most commonly, these organizational claims are simply attributes in Active Directory that each user possesses. It's just a standard way for your organization to think about the information that it stores about its users—what groups they belong to, their addresses, phone numbers, title, and identity information. The utility of ADFS is the capability to transform those claims into the label that the resource side of the trust is expecting. For example, TreasureBuild might expect a user's title to be Purchaser, but TrinketBuild uses the Purchasing Agent identifier internally. This is really the only point in which you need to fully understand and expect the format in which the resource side needs its claim information.

The same type of transformation can take place on the resource side. Different applications need different types of claims, so the order application might take Purchasing Agent, the ERP application might use Buyer, and the tracking application might use Purchases. The resource federation server knows about these peculiarities and can further transform these claims into what these applications and systems need. A

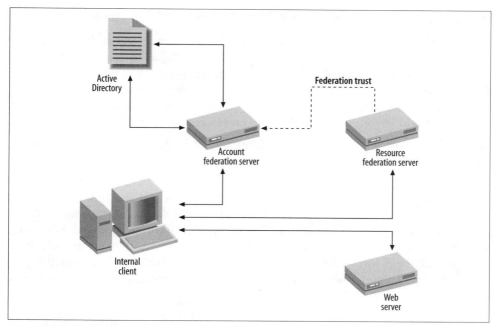

Figure 5-55. The ADFS application flow

key point here: this stuff doesn't matter to the account side. The account federation server only needed to know in what format the resource federation server expected the data; how the data is subsequently transformed is of no concern to the account side.

You can see this process diagrammed in a flowchart in Figure 5-56.

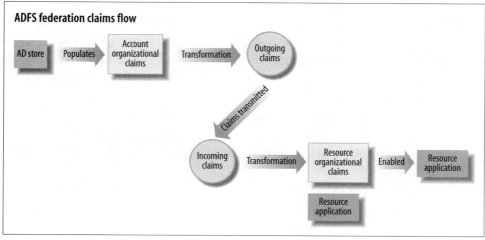

Figure 5-56. The ADFS claims flow

Demo: Collaboration with Windows SharePoint Services

So let's put all of this to use. It's difficult to put together an in-depth demo about ADFS within this book because where ADFS really shines is when claims-aware applications are used. Since there isn't a standard claims-aware application available to use for this demo (at least at the time of this printing), we'll demonstrate the concepts of federation using Windows SharePoint Services by setting up a trust between two distinct business units so that they can each access WSS and bring in new users.

To get started, you will need to install Windows Server 2003 R2 on three machines: one that will act as the SharePoint server; one as a federation server for the account side, and the third as the federation server on the resource side.

Once you have all three machines running, install ADFS and the Federation Server components on two of them. You can do this from the Windows Components section of Add/Remove Programs within Control Panel. On the third, install Windows SharePoint Services 2.0 and also select the ADFS Web Agent software, which is under the Active Directory Federation Services option. (Choose the traditional application option.) Then, to the third machine, add an administrator account which will be used to manage SharePoint.

The SharePoint machine needs some additional configuration. Step through the following process to get it ready:

1. Open the IIS Manager from the Administrative Tools menu.

2. In the left pane, navigate through Local Computer and Web Sites.

3. Right-click on Default Web Site and select Properties from the pop-up context menu.

4. The Add/Edit Filter Properties box appears. On the ISAPI Filters tab, click the Add button.

5. In the Filter Name text box, enter ADFS Filter and then click the Browse button.

6. Navigate to *C:\Windows\system32*, select *ifsfilt.dll*, and then click Open.

7. Click OK, and then make sure that the new ADFS Filter is the first filter listed.

8. Click the Home Directory tab, and under Application Settings, click the Configuration button.

9. In the Wildcard application maps tab, click the Insert button.

10. Next, click the Browse Button and navigate to *C:\Windows\system32* directory. Select *ifsext.dll*, and make sure that the Verify that file exists option is not checked. Click OK.

11. In the left pane, right click on Web Sites and select Properties from the context menu.

12. Click on the ADFS Web Service Agent tab.

13. In the Federation Service URL text box, type in the URL for the *FederationSer-verService.asmx* location for the local Resource Federation Service, and then click OK.

14. Right-click on the Default Web Site and select Properties.

15. Click on the ADFS Web Service Agent tab.

16. Check the Enable Active Directory Federation Service Web service agent box.

17. Set the Cookie path value to be "/".

18. Set Return Uniform Resource Locator (URL) to be https://*currentmachinename*.

19. Click OK.

On each of the federation servers, do the following:

- Create an application in the ADFS management tool. Open the tool from the Administrative Tools menu, and then in the left pane, expand Federation Service, Trust Policy, My Organization, and then right-click on Applications and select Application from the New menu. Create a traditional application, in which claims don't need to be sent. Note that the URL in the wizard should be the same as the URL that was entered as the Return URL in step 18 of the previous instructions.

- Choose to either set up your resource federation server as a local account federation server for your local administrative users—the ones that users will actually log in to in order to administer the SharePoint site—or set up a new federation between your resource federation server and your account federation server. Either option will work.

In terms of accounts, you also have a couple of options. You can, for example, create a local account for each user accessing the site. These local accounts will never actually be logged into a directory and the user will never need to know the password. As a matter of fact, the user will never even need to know the account exists. The advantage of this option is that you can control the access to each SharePoint site on a per-user basis, and you can go through the SharePoint invite process that's built into the product. The disadvantage is the Active Directory administrator will need to create a local AD accounts for each incoming user.

If that option doesn't appeal to you, your second option involves using a feature in ADFS called Group-to-UPN mapping. With this feature, the administrator creates one or more accounts locally that will have certain privileges in SharePoint. The user will also have a group claim that will be mapped to his or her local user account. The benefits for this method: you reduce the number of local accounts that a site will need to have; the account/ADFS administrator can now choose who has access to the SharePoint site, and the resource-side administrator can manage what groups have access. However, you lose the granular access control provided in the first option, and can't send standard SharePoint invitation messages.

If you choose option one, you should create local accounts for each user that will need to access the SharePoint Site. The UPN of the local account will need to be the same as the UPN coming across in the security token from the account federation server. Launch the Active Directory Domains and Trusts administrative tool to set up new UPN suffices. On the Active Directory Domains and Trusts node in the left pane, right-click and select Properties. In the Alternative UPN Suffixes text box, enter the UPN suffix of a federation-aware domain, then click the Add button. After all suffixes are entered, click the OK box and close the application. Then, to create new user accounts for accessing SharePoint, you can create a new OU to house the partner accounts, or they can be put anywhere else in your AD structure. Within ADUC, right-click the container you want to create the local account in, select New, and then select User. Proceed through the wizard as previously outlined in this chapter; however, in the User logon name box, enter the first part of the users UPN, then in the drop-down box on the left, select the user's UPN suffix. In the User logon name (pre–Windows 2000) box, make sure the name is unique. This unique name is not actually used, so you can enter whatever you want. Click the Next key after all the fields have been populated, And then enter a dummy password and finish the wizard. After all of these steps are accomplished, the standard SharePoint invitation messages will work.

If you choose option two, open the ADFS Management tool on the SharePoint server, and do the following:

1. Expand Federation Service, Trust Policy, Trusted Accounts, and click on Account Partners.

2. Click on the Account Partner that you will be using.

3. In the right pane, right-click on User Principal Name and select Properties.

4. Navigate to the Groups tab and type in the incoming claim from the account partner in the Group Field.

5. Click on the "…" button to the right of the UPN field.

6. Enter the username you want this group to map to, then click the Check Name button. If the name resolves correctly, click OK.

7. In the Incoming UPN Claim Transformation properties dialog box, click the Add button to add this mapping, and then click OK.

8. Finally, right-click on Trust Policy in the left pane and select Apply changes.

After that's complete, you're all set. Users from both the account and resource sides can use the WSS site, and if you chose option one, you can bring new people into the site by simply issuing a SharePoint invitation.

More Information

There are quite a few resources that Microsoft has made available for users interested in learning more about ADFS. For a more visual introduction to the concepts here, check out the .NET Show episode with David McPherson and Don Schmidt, where the two talk about ADFS' inherent capabilities. You can find that episode at:

http://www.microsoft.com/downloads/details.aspx?FamilyID=c82d1449-3239-40d7-954b-4cf8e763d785&displaylang=en

There is also a whitepaper on Microsoft's web site explaining scenarios, requirements, and terminology in further detail than what I've covered here. This paper is located at:

http://www.microsoft.com/WindowsServer2003/R2/Identity_Management/ADFSwhitepaper.mspx

And finally, for a step-by-step single sign-on lab setup, you can check out the document located at:

http://www.microsoft.com/downloads/details.aspx?FamilyID=062f7382-a82f-4428-9bbd-a103b9f27654&displaylang=en

Active Directory Troubleshooting and Maintenance

Things will inevitably break in your network—this is a given. Also, you'll need to perform a few fairly common tasks on a somewhat regular basis to keep your Active Directory installation running at maximum performance and efficiency. In this section, I'll take a look at troubleshooting and maintenance, and show you how to both keep your network in tip-top shape, and how to figure out what's wrong when things go wrong.

Troubleshooting AD with DNSLint

Recall DNSLint from Chapter 4? Well, since AD is based on DNS, there are some specific scenarios in which DNSLint can be a lifesaver in terms of identifying and solving a quirky problem with your AD infrastructure. In fact, DNS problems are the most common issue keeping AD from working correctly.

DNSLint can help you figure out when the following issues are occurring:

- A network adapter whose TCP/IP configuration doesn't refer to an authoritative DNS server for the zone that works with the AD domain.
- A DNS zone file wihout a CNAME record with the globally unique identifier (GUID) of each domain controller along with the A records that act as glue records. (Check out Chapter 4 for a refresher on what those terms mean.)

- Lame delegations to child zones where the NS records specified for the delegation either do not have corresponding glue records or point to servers that are offline or not responding.

- The DNS zone corresponding to an AD domain does not contain the necessary SRV records, including the _ldap service on TCP port 389, the _kerberos service on TCP and UDP port 88. GC servers need a SRV record for the _gc service on TCP port 3268.

- The PDC Emulator FSMO role master does not have a required SRV record for the _ldap service.

Even better, you can use DNSLint with Dcdiag, another program that can be found in the Support Tools on the Windows Server 2003 CD, to perform many tests and checks prior to promoting a machine to a DC role. You can also probe a current DC just to make sure it's configured correctly. Specifically, the /dcpromo switch for Dcdiag tests to verify that you have the correct DNS settings for promoting a machine to a DC, and it will list the problems and solutions if there are any.

To check the machine JH-W2K3-DC2 to ensure that it's ready to be promoted to a DC in the *corp.haselltech.local* domain, use the following command:

```
dcdiag /s:jh-w2k3-dc2 /dcpromo /dnsdomain:corp.hasselltech.local /replicadc
```

Offline Defragmenting of NTDS Database

Like a hard disk, the database containing all the objects and information within Active Directory can become fragmented at times on domain controllers because different parts of the directory are being written too often, and other parts are being rearranged to be read less often. Although you might think that defragging your hard drive will defragment the *NTDS.DIT* file on your domain controller's hard disk automatically, this just isn't the case.

Active Directory handles online defragmenting itself, and it does an adequate job. To really clean out the database, however, and defrag it for the maximum possible gain in efficiency, you need to take the domain controller offline so that the defragmenting process can have exclusive use of the database file. This requires four steps: first, reboot the domain controller in question and get it into directory services restore mode; second, perform the actual defragmentation; third, copy the defragmented database back into the production directory; and fourth, reboot the machine. (Replication to other domain controllers in Active Directory won't be affected, as Active Directory is smart enough to work around the downed domain controller. It will receive changes when it is brought back online.)

Let's step through these steps now:

1. Reboot your domain controller.

2. As the domain controller begins to boot, press F8 to make the Startup menu appear.

3. Select Directory Services Restore Mode.

4. When the system prompts you to log in, use the domain administrator account, but use the restore mode password you created when you first promoted this domain controller to a domain controller role.

5. Open a command prompt.

6. Enter **ntdsutil** at the command prompt to start the offline NTDSUtil tool.

7. Enter **file** to enter the file maintenance context.

8. Type **compact to <location>**, where *<location>* signifies the path to the place where you want the defragmented copy of the directory stored. When defragmented, Active Directory makes a copy of the database so that if something goes wrong, you haven't messed up the production copy of the directory.

9. Look for the line "Operation completed successfully in x seconds." If you see this, type **quit** to exit NTDSUtil.

10. At the regular command prompt, copy the file *NTDS.DIT* from the location you selected in step 8 to *\Windows\NTDS*. Feel free to overwrite the current file at that location—it is the fragmented version.

11. Delete any files with the extension *.LOG* in that same directory.

12. Restart your domain controller normally, and boot Windows Server 2003 as normal.

Your database is now defragmented.

Cleaning Directory Metadata

As your Active Directory implementation ages, you'll probably be left with some junk: old computer accounts that refer to PCs you dumped a long time ago, domain controllers you removed from service without first decommissioning them within Active Directory, and other detritus. Every so often, it's a good idea to clean out this old data so that bugs that are hard to track (and therefore are hard to troubleshoot) don't pop up, and so that future major Active Directory actions, such as renaming or removing a domain, aren't held up because of a junked-up directory.

Let's say we have a child domain, called cluster.hasselltech.local, which we want removed. To do this, we again will use the NTDSUtil tool and its *metadata cleanup* feature. To begin, go to a domain controller and log in as an enterprise administrator. Then follow these steps:

1. Open a command prompt.

2. Type **ntdsutil** to open the program.

3. Type **metadata cleanup** to enter that part of the program.

4. Type **connections** to receive the Server Connections prompt.

5. Enter **connect to server localhost** to initiate a connection with the current domain controller.

6. Type **quit** to exit that module.

7. Now type **select operation target** and press Enter.

8. Type **list domains** to get a list of domains.

9. NTDSUtil will bring up a list of domains in your system. In our example, cluster. hasselltech.local comes up as domain 2. So, to set the domain in our sights to destroy, type **select domain 2** and press Enter.

10. Next, you'll need to determine the site in which cluster.hasselltech.local resides. Type **list sites** to bring up a list like you saw in steps 8 and 9.

11. In our case, cluster.hasselltech.local resides in site CHARLOTTE, which comes up as site 3 in our list. So, type **select site 3** and press Enter.

12. Now you need to get rid of the domain controllers in that domain. Find out what those machines are by typing **list servers** for domain in site and pressing Enter.

13. There are two domain controllers, numbered 0 and 1. You need to get rid of both, so type **select server 0** and press Enter.

14. Type **quit**, and then type **remove selected server**. Confirm your choice.

15. Type **select server 1** and press Enter.

16. Type **remove selected server**, and again confirm your choice.

17. Finally, type **remove selected domain** and press Enter.

18. Type **quit** to exit NTDSUtil.

Conclusion

We've covered a lot of material in this chapter—perhaps the most complex component of Windows Server 2003, Active Directory. In the next chapter, we'll look at the wonderful component of Group Policy, which allows you to manage groups of systems with remarkable ease and consistency. GP's foundation is in Active Directory, as you will see.

CHAPTER 6

Group Policy and IntelliMirror

Windows Server 2003 offers a marvelous command and control system for your organization's computers called Group Policy (GP). With GP, you can manage user- and computer-based configurations, which you can apply en masse to computers in a particular Active Directory site, OU, or domain.

In this chapter, I'll introduce you to GP and its features and functions. I'll show you the differences between NT 4.0–style system policies and 2000-and-later-based GPs. I'll take you through creating and editing GPs and expanding or refining their scope. I'll show you how inheritance and overriding work, and I'll look at using the Windows Management Instrumentation (WMI) interface and the new Resultant Set of Policy (RSoP) tools in Windows Server 2003 to filter and further granulate policy application. Then you'll see the similarities and differences between local and domain GP. Finally, I'll review troubleshooting strategies and considerations for wide-scale GP deployment.

An Introduction to Group Policy

Group policies consist of five distinct components:

Administrative templates
> Configure registry-based policies. You'll see what this really entails in a bit.

Folder redirection
> Alters the target location of various elements in the UI, such as My Documents, to other places on the network.

Scripts
> Execute when computers are first booted and shut down. They also can run during user logon and logoff.

Security settings

Configure permissions, rights, and restrictions for computers, domains, and users.

Software policies

Assign application packages to users and computers.

The data for each component is stored in a Group Policy Object (GPO). In domain-based GPs, GPOs are stored at various levels in Active Directory, but they're always associated with a domain. GPOs are affiliated with a variety of objects within Active Directory, including sites, domains, domain controllers, and OUs, and they can be linked to multiple sites, to the domains themselves, and to OUs. For non-domain-based (i.e., local) GPs, you simply configure those settings on individual servers.

GPOs store their contents in two parts: as files as part of a Group Policy Template (GPT), and as objects inside a specialized container in Active Directory called a Group Policy Container (GPC). GPTs are stored in the *C:\WINDOWS\SYSVOL* directory on each domain controller and contain settings related to software installation policies and deployments, scripts, and security information for each GPO. The GPTs usually contain subfolders called Adm, USER, and MACHINE, to separate the data to be applied to different portions of the computers' registries—the USER portion is applied to keys in HKEY_CURRENT_USER, and the MACHINE portion is applied to keys in HKEY_LOCAL_MACHINE, while the Adm portion specifies other properties of the template itself. The GPCs simply contain information, such as version, status, or extensions for the policy itself, regarding the GPO's link to Active Directory containers. Each GPC is referred to by a string called a globally unique identifier, or GUID. Data stored in the GPC rarely needs to be modified and is used to indicate whether a specific policy object is enabled, as well as to control the proper version of the GPT to apply.

Local computer policies are stored in the *%SystemRoot%\System32\GroupPolicy* directory because they apply only to the computer on which they're stored and they need not be replicated. Local policies are also more limited in scope and ability, as you'll see later in this chapter.

When you first set up an Active Directory domain, two default GPOs are created: one that is linked to the domain itself, and therefore affects all users and computers within the domain; and one that is linked to the Domain Controllers OU, which affects all domain controllers within a domain.

A Comparison: Group Policies and System Policies

How do GPs compare to the old Windows NT 4.0 system policies? For one, with GPs, Active Directory handles pushing and synchronizing updates across domain controllers. With system policies, the file *NTCONFIG.POL* was pushed out, usually by the FRS, to all domain controllers from the *NETLOGON* share of the PDC. Sometimes, though, FRS simply would forget to actually replicate—quite a bit of manual intervention was involved. With GP, Active Directory handles replication itself.

Second, domain-based GPs have a reversal feature: if you remove a policy's application to an object within the directory, any changes made by that policy are undone. System policies under Windows NT were permanent changes to the registry: once a policy was applied, there was no way—short of manually changing back any modified keys—to "de-apply" the policy. This was called *tattooing*.

Third, it's easier to control the timing of GP deployment than of system policies. With NT system policies, the setting changes were applied only twice: during computer boot and during a user logon. By contrast, GPs are applied at regular intervals. Workstations poll the domain every one to two hours to see if there are new policies, and if there are, the workstations simply apply the policies without protest. In addition, you don't have to deal with NT's peculiarities regarding policy application and domains. Unlike NT, machines can obtain policies from the domain they are in, and users can obtain policies from the domain they are in, and there's no confusion between the two; NT had a nasty habit of applying policies from only one domain (the one the machine was in), which might be different from the user's machine.

Fourth, the registry entries written to by NT system policies and Windows 2000 or Windows Server 2003 GPs are different. GPs are written to four different trees of the registry, the first two of which are the default location:

- *HKEY_LOCAL_MACHINE\Software\Policies*
- *HKEY_CURRENT_USER\Software\Policies*
- *HKEY_LOCAL_MACHINE\Software\Microsoft\Windows\CurrentVersion\ Policies*
- *HKEY_CURRENT_USER\Software\Microsoft\Windows\CurrentVersion\Policies*

If Windows runs into problems writing to the first two keys, it will attempt to apply information to the latter two keys instead.

NT system policies can write to any part of the registry, but GPs simply delete and rewrite the four trees of the registry when changes are made. The four areas of the registry are secure and written to only by the operating system, whereas other parts of the registry can be modified by users and applications.

 That's not entirely the case, actually. You can indeed write to any part of the registry you want using GP with custom ADM templates, but that is beyond the scope of this book.

Additionally, it is very difficult to limit the scope of NT system policies. GP has the ability to granularly apply policies to specific objects.

Finally, one sour note: domain-based GPs work only with workstations and servers running Windows 2000 or later that are members of an Active Directory domain. Although you can apply local GP to non-domain machines, the functionality is more limited and replication of GPOs among non-domain machines is not automatic. If you have older machines running operating systems prior to Windows 2000, you'll need to stick with system policies until you migrate those systems to a later platform. You can, however, store NT and Windows 9x system policies on machines running Windows Server 2003.

Group Policy Implementation

Now that you know the components of GP, let's take a look at how they are implemented. Like NTFS permissions, GPs are cumulative and inherited—cumulative in that the settings modified by a policy can build on other policies and "amass" configuration changes, and inherited in that objects below other objects in Active Directory can have any GPs that are applied to their parent object be applied to themselves automatically.

GPOs are associated with, or *linked*, to any number of objects, either within a directory or local to a specific machine. To implement a GP on a specific type of object, follow these guidelines:

Local computer
> Use the Local Security Policy snap-in inside Control Panel → Administrative Tools. Or, for a more complete look, use Start → Run → gpedit.msc.

A specific computer
> Load the MMC, and then select Add Snap-in from the File menu. Browse in the list and add the Group Policy Object Editor to the console. On the Select Group Policy Object screen, peruse the list to find the specific object you want.

Entire domain
> Install and launch the Group Policy Management Console, and then right-click on the domain and create or edit a policy from there.

OU within Active Directory
> Install and launch the Group Policy Management Console, and then right-click on the OU, and create or edit a policy from there.

Active Directory site
> Launch Active Directory Sites and Services, right-click the site's name, and select Properties from the context menu. Navigate to the Group Policy tab, and create or edit a policy from there.

Windows applies GPs in the following order, which you can remember with the acronym "LSDOU":

1. Local GPOs
2. Site-specific GPOs, in an order that the site administrator configures
3. Domain-specific GPOs, in an order that the domain administrator configures
4. OU-specific GPOs, from the parent OU down through the ranks to the child OU

The only exception to this rule occurs when you're using NT 4.0 system policies that are created and set with the NT System Policy Editor. Recall from NT administration days that the system policies are called *NTCONFIG.POL*, so if Windows finds that file present, it applies these policies before the local GPO. Of course, these policies can be overwritten by policies that come farther down in the application chain.

 Here's an easy rule of thumb to remember: for domain-based GPs, the lowest-level Active Directory container has the last opportunity to override inherited policies. For example, a policy applied to a site will be overwritten by a policy applied to an OU, and a local policy will be overwritten by an Active Directory object-based policy.

Introducing the Group Policy Management Console

You'll find that GPOs themselves are much easier to create and edit using Microsoft's Group Policy Management Console (GPMC), a drop-in replacement for the more limited Group Policy Object Editor that ships installed with Windows Server R2. While it's certainly possible to perform the actions I'll describe in this chapter with the native Group Policy Object Editor, the tool has limitations: the biggest by far being the lack of ability to see the exact scope of a GPO's application, making troubleshooting very difficult. The GPMC fixes this and also offers a cleaner interface, scripting functionality, and enhancements to troubleshooting and modeling features.

It's very easy to get the GPMC: simply visit:

http://www.microsoft.com/windowsserver2003/downloads/featurepacks/default.mspx

and click on Group Policy Management Console. Follow the Download link and double-click on the resulting MSI file to install the GPMC. Once the installation wizard is finished, you can begin managing GP through the utility. Launch the Group Policy Management Console from the Administrative Tools menu off the Start menu; you'll see a screen much like Figure 6-1.

To navigate around in the GPMC, you need to expand the forest you want to manage in the left pane. Then you can select specific domains and sites within that forest, and OUs within individual domains. When you expand, for example, a particular domain,

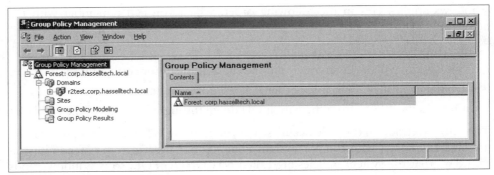

Figure 6-1. The Group Policy Management Console

links to the GPOs that exist are listed within their respective OUs. They also are listed under the Group Policy Objects folder. Clicking on a GPO brings up a four-tabbed screen in the right pane.

The first tab is the Scope tab, which examines how far-reaching the effects of this GPO are. Sites, domains, and OUs that are linked to the GPO you've selected are listed at the top of the window. You can change the listing of pertinent links using the drop-down box, where you can choose to list links at the current domain, the entire forest, or all sites. At the bottom of the window, any security filtering done by ACLs is listed. Clicking the Add button brings up the standard permissions window, as you would expect from the Group Policy Object Editor.

At the very bottom, you can see any WMI filters to which this GPO is linked. You can choose to open the WMI filter for editing by clicking the Open button. You can associate only one WMI filter with any particular GPO, and WMI filters work only with Windows XP and Windows Server 2003. We'll get to these in a bit—for now, let's move on.

The next tab, Details, simply shows the domain in which the current GPO is located, the owner of the GPO, when the GPO was created and modified, the version numbers for the user and computer portions, the GUID of the object, and whether the GPO is fully enabled or fully disabled, or whether just the computer or user configuration portions are enabled.

Of particular interest is the Settings tab, as shown in Figure 6-2.

The Settings tab is one of the most useful tabs in the GPMC. The GPMC will generate HTML-based reports of all the settings in a particular GPO, and you can condense and expand portions of the report easily for uncluttered viewing. You can print the report for further reference, or save the report for posting to an internal web site for your IT administrators. It's a much, much easier way to discern what settings a GPO modifies than the Group Policy Object Editor. To edit the GPO that is displayed in the report, simply right-click it and select Edit. To print the HTML report, right-click it and select Print; to save the report, right-click it and select Save Report.

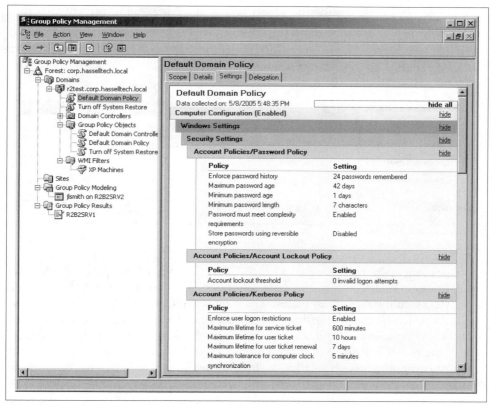

Figure 6-2. Examining a standard GPO via the Settings tab

Finally, the Delegation tab lists in a tabular format the users and groups that have specific permissions for the selected GPO, what those permissions are, and if they're inherited from a parent object. Clicking Add brings up the common Select User, Computer, or Group dialog box that you are familiar with from reading this chapter. You can remove a delegated permission by clicking the appropriate user or group in the list and then clicking the Remove button. The Properties button will bring up the standard Active Directory Users and Computers view of the selected user and group.

You'll see more of this interface in action as we proceed through the chapter.

Creating and editing Group Policy Objects

To start off, you need some GPOs to work with. Use the tree in the left pane to navigate through the various forests and domains on your network. Then, when you've settled on a location, right-click on that location and select Create and Link a GPO Here. In the New GPO box, enter a name for the object, and then click OK. You'll see the new GPO listed in the righthand pane; the GPO creation process is finished.

To edit the object, right-click the object and select Edit. You're presented with a screen much like that shown in Figure 6-3.

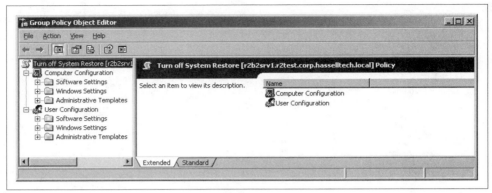

Figure 6-3. The Group Policy Object Editor screen

You'll note there are two branches to each GPO: Computer Configuration and User Configuration. Each contains the same sub-trees: Software Settings, Windows Settings, and Administrative Templates. The Computer Configuration tree is used to customize machine-specific settings, which become effective when a computer first boots. These policies are applied across any users that log on to the system, independent of their own individual policies. Using computer policies, you can lock down a group of computers in a lab or kiosk situation while still maintaining an independent set of user policies. The User Configuration tree, as you might suspect, contains user-specific settings that apply only to that user regardless of where she is on the network.

Administrative templates

Microsoft has kindly chosen to provide sample sets of GPs, located in the *%SystemRoot%\Inf* directory, which you can apply to domains or OUs to establish a standard configuration for certain aspects of Windows functionality. Table 6-1 shows the policies included and their respective functions.

Table 6-1. Administrative templates with Windows Server 2003

Template	Function
Common.adm	Sets Windows 95, 98, and NT 4.0 policies
Conf.adm	Sets policies for Microsoft NetMeeting
Inetcorp.adm	Sets policies to restrict Internet Explorer
Inetres.adm	Sets policies to restrict Internet activities
Inetset.adm	Sets policies for common Internet Explorer configuration
System.adm	Sets Windows 2000–specific policies

Template	Function
Windows.adm	Sets Windows 95– and Windows 98–specific policies
Winnt.adm	Sets Windows NT 4.0–specific policies
Wmplayer.adm	Sets policies to restrict and configure Windows Media Player
Wuau.adm	Sets the policy on automatic updates

You can access these templates through the Group Policy Object Editor (they are loaded automatically by the Group Policy Management Console the first time you run it) by navigating through each node, the Computer Configuration and User Configuration branches, and clicking Administrative Templates. Then you will see the categories of policies available to you under each template and can simply make the changes you want.

Once you make changes to one of these templates, the *registry.pol* files inside the GPT subfolders USER and MACHINE keep up with the changes and ensure that the proper policy versions are applied to the appropriate computers, depending on how you have assigned the GPO.

Disabling portions of policies

A GPO has the potential to be large because it can contain numerous computer and user settings. If you don't intend to populate either your computer or user settings, you can disable that portion of the GPO. By doing this, you're speeding up propagation time over the network and processing time on the computers that need to load the settings in the object. So, if you have a GPO that applies only to computers, you can disable the user configuration branch of the policy and significantly improve the performance of your network. To do so, follow these steps:

1. Open the Group Policy Management Console.
2. In the left pane, find the GPO in question and click on it to select it.
3. In the right pane, navigate to the Details tab, and under the GPO Status drop-down box, select User configuration settings disabled, as shown in Figure 6-4.
4. Click OK.

The portion of the policy you selected is now disabled. (Of course, you can disable the computer portion of policies using the same method.)

Refreshing computer policies

Speaking of changes to policies, it can take some time for modifications to propagate across domain controllers within a domain and finally to the objects for which they're destined. Policies are refreshed on a client when the computer is turned on, a user logs on, an application requests a policy refresh, a user requests a policy refresh,

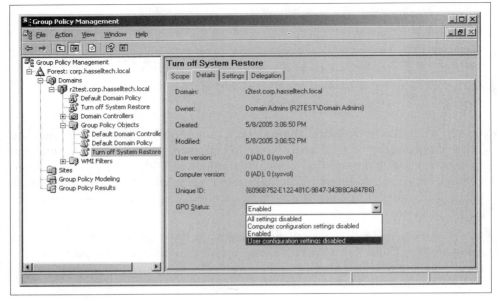

Figure 6-4. Disabling a portion of a policy

or the interval between refreshes has elapsed. The latter part of that sentence is key: there's a GPO you can enable that will allow you to customize the interval at which computer and domain controller policies refresh. It's best to make this change at either a domain or OU level for consistency.

To enable the policy refresh interval, follow these steps (I'll assume you're changing this on a domain-wide basis):

1. Within the Group Policy Management Console, find the Default Domain Policy in the left pane.

2. Right-click on Default Domain Policy, and choose Edit.

3. The Group Policy Object Editor window appears. In the Computer Configuration tree, navigate through Administrative Templates and System.

4. Click Group Policy.

5. In the right pane, double-click the setting Group Policy refresh interval for computers, or Group Policy refresh interval for domain controllers, whichever is applicable.

6. Select Enabled, and then enter an interval for the refresh. Be sure to make this a healthy interval; otherwise, you will degrade your network's performance with constant traffic updating policies across the domain. For smaller networks, 15 minutes should be an acceptable timeframe. Allow 30 to 45 minutes for larger networks.

7. Click OK.

You also can also manually force a policy refresh from the command line on client computers with the gpupdate command. To refresh all parts of a policy, issue this command:

```
gpupdate /force
```

To refresh just the Computer Configuration node of the policy:

```
gpupdate /target:computer /force
```

To refresh just the User Configuration node of the policy:

```
gpupdate /target:user /force
```

 Domain controllers make refresh requests every five minutes by default.

To manually refresh GPOs on Windows 2000, the syntax is a little different. To refresh only the computer policy:

```
secedit /refreshpolicy machine_policy
```

To refresh only the user policy:

```
secedit /refreshpolicy user_policy
```

You can force updates of objects, even if they haven't been modified since the last update, by adding the /enforce switch at the end of the command. Then Windows will enforce all policies, regardless of whether the actual policy objects have changed. This is useful if you are having network difficulties and want to ensure that every computer has a fresh application of policy, or if you have a large contingent of mobile users that connect to the network briefly and unpredictably.

For either clients or domain controllers, exercise extreme caution when modifying the default refresh interval. On large networks, altering the refresh interval can cause hellish amounts of traffic to be unleashed over your network—a costly move that's unnecessary for 95% of sites with domains installed. Although clients will pull down new policies only if those policies have changed, the increased traffic results from clients just contacting a domain controller every x minutes to get new policies and updates. There's very little reason to alter this value. Here's a good rule of thumb: if you don't know of a good justification to increase the refresh interval, it isn't necessary for your site.

 Folder redirection and software installation policies are not processed during a background policy refresh.

If you want, you also can elect to disable background policy refreshing completely. You might do this if you're having trouble tracking down an intermittent GPO problem, or if you don't want to have a GP applied during the middle of a client session because it might disrupt an application. Again, it's best to do this on a domain-wide or OU-wide basis for consistency and best performance.

To disable background processing, follow these steps:

1. Within the Group Policy Management Console, find the Default Domain Policy in the left pane .

2. Right-click on Default Domain Policy, and choose Edit.

3. The Group Policy Object Editor screen appears. In the Computer Configuration tree, navigate through Administrative Templates and System.

4. Click Group Policy.

5. In the right pane, double-click the setting Turn off background refresh of Group Policy.

6. Select Enabled.

7. Click OK.

In some situations, you might want a policy setting to be applied, even if no setting has changed. This goes against default GPO behavior because usually, only changes trigger a policy refresh and reapplication. For example, a user might change some Internet Explorer settings within his session. You might want that change to be reversed, but Windows won't trigger a refresh because the policy itself hasn't changed. To prevent this, you can use the configuration option called Process even if the Group Policy Object has not changed. (This is like the /enforce switch described a bit earlier.) You've probably caught on by now that it's best to do this on a domain-wide or OU-wide basis for consistency and best performance.

To do so, follow these steps:

1. Within the Group Policy Management Console, find the Default Domain Policy in the left pane.

2. Right-click on the Default Domain Policy GPO and choose Edit.

3. In the Computer Configuration tree, navigate through Administrative Templates, System, and Group Policy.

4. You'll see a list of options ending in "policy processing," such as Scripts policy processing and Wireless policy processing. These GPOs exist to allow you to tweak the functionality of these types of policies. Open the appropriate policy (which one is best for you depends on the type of policy that you're trying to trigger to change) to view its Properties.

5. Click the Enabled button.

6. Finally, check the Process even if the Group Policy Object has not changed checkbox.

Checking the box in step 6 provides the same functionality as issuing the command gpupdate /enforce from the command line.

Policy settings related to computer security follow a refresh policy that is a bit different from normal GPOs. The client computer still refreshes security policy settings even if the GPO has not been changed or modified. There are registry settings whose values indicate the maximum acceptable time a user or client computer can wait before reapplying GPOs, regardless of whether they are changed. They are as follows:

- To change the refresh interval for computers, set:

  HKEY_LOCAL_MACHINE\Software\Policies\Microsoft\Windows\System\GroupPolicyRefreshTime

  The type is REG_DWORD, and the valid range for data (in minutes) is 0 to 64,800.

- To change the offset interval for computers, set:

  HKEY_LOCAL_MACHINE\Software\Policies\Microsoft\Windows\System\GroupPolicyRefreshTimeOffset

  The type is REG_DWORD, and the valid range for data (in minutes) is 0 to 1,440.

- To change the refresh interval for domain controllers, set:

  HKEY_LOCAL_MACHINE\Software\Policies\Microsoft\Windows\System\GroupPolicyRefreshTimeDC

  The type is REG_DWORD, and the valid range for data (in minutes) is 0 to 64,800.

- To change the offset interval for domain controllers, set:

  HKEY_LOCAL_MACHINE\Software\Policies\Microsoft\Windows\System\GroupPolicyRefreshTimeOffsetDC

  The type is REG_DWORD, and the valid range for data (in minutes) is 0 to 1,440.

- To change the refresh interval for users, set:

  HKEY_CURRENT_USER\Software\Policies\Microsoft\Windows\System\GroupPolicyRefreshTime

  The type is REG_DWORD, and the valid range for data (in minutes) is 0 to 64,800.

- To change the offset interval for users, set:

  HKEY_CURRENT_USER\Software\Policies\Microsoft\Windows\System\GroupPolicyRefreshTimeOffset

  The type is REG_DWORD, and the valid range for data (in minutes) is 0 to 1,440.

Policy enforcement over slow network connections

Windows Server 2003 will detect the speed of a client's connection to the network and, based on its measurements, disable enforcement of certain policies that would bog down a slow connection. Policies that Windows will disable include disk quotas, folder redirection, scripts, and software installation and maintenance. By default, Windows considers a speed of less than 500 Kbps a slow link, but you can change this on a per-GPO basis.

To change the slow link threshold, follow these steps:

1. Edit the GPO for which you want to change the threshold in the Group Policy Management Console.
2. Navigate through Computer Configuration or User Configuration, as well as through Administrative Templates, System, and Group Policy.
3. Double-click the Group Policy Slow Link Detection policy in the righthand pane.
4. Click the Enabled option, and enter the connection speed you want to be the new threshold. Enter 0 to simply disable slow link detection.
5. Click OK when you're finished.

The Scope of Group Policy Objects

So, how far do these GPOs go? What types of objects can GPOs affect? To deploy a GP to a set of users, you "associate" a GPO to a container within Active Directory that contains those users. By default, all objects within a container with an associated GPO have that GPO applied to them. If you have a large number of GPOs or Active Directory objects, it can be confusing to track the scope and application of GPOs. Luckily, you can find out to which containers a specific policy is applied by selecting the GPO in the Group Policy Management Console and looking in the right pane at the Scope tab. The Links section will reveal the sites, domains, and OUs that are affected by the GPO. To adjust the view of links, you can use the drop-down list box under the Links section and choose the sites and domains you wish to see. You can see this section in Figure 6-5.

Of course, in practice there always are exceptions to any rule; for example, most likely there will be some computers within a container that shouldn't have a policy applied to them. The most straightforward way to limit the scope of a GPO within a specific container is to create security groups that contain only the objects that are to be included in the policy application. Once you've created the necessary groups, follow these steps:

1. Select the GPO you want to administer in the left pane of the Group Policy Management Console

2. On the Scope tab in the right pane, click the Add button under Security Filtering, and then add the groups that do not need the policy applied.

3. Verify the group was added to the Security Filtering list, as shown in Figure 6-5.

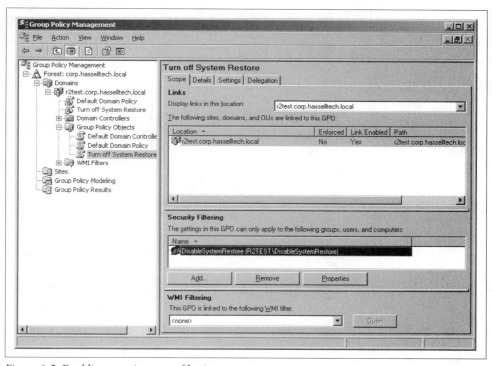

Figure 6-5. Enabling security group filtering

The GPMC makes it simple to limit the application of a GPO to a specific group, as you just saw. But what if you want more granular control than this? You also can play more tricks with groups and GPO ACLs to further limit the effects of policy application to objects, but you'll need to dive into the advanced security settings of the object itself to get more complex operations done. To get there, navigate to the Delegation tab in the right pane of the GPMC and click the Advanced button in the lower-right corner. The screen shown in Figure 6-6 will appear.

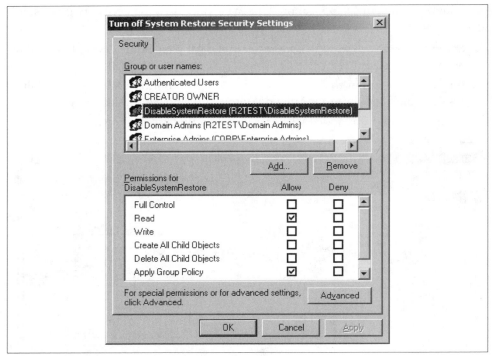

Figure 6-6. Manually setting security group filtering

The following is a list of appropriate ACL permissions to grant to obtain the desired result:

- If you do *not* want the policy to be applied to all members of a certain security group, add all the members to a group, add the group to the ACL for the object, and set the following permissions for the group: Apply Group Policy, deny; Read, deny. All members of the group will *not* have the policy applied, regardless of their existing memberships to other groups.

- If group membership (at least in a specific group) shouldn't play a part in the application of this policy, leave permissions alone.

Enforcement and Inheritance

Policies applied to parent objects are inherited automatically by child objects unless there are conflicts; if a child's directly applied policy conflicts with a general inherited policy from a parent, the child's policy will prevail, on the assumption that the administrator really wanted the result of the specifically applied policy and not one that is granted indirectly because of directory tree position. Policy settings that are currently disabled migrate to child objects in the disabled state as well, and policy settings that remain in the "not configured" state do not propagate at all. Additionally, if there are no conflicts, two policies can coexist peacefully, regardless of where the initial application occurred.

As with permissions, you can block GPO inheritance by using two options available within the user interface: Enforced, which instructs child containers to not replace any setting placed higher on the tree than they are; and Block Policy Inheritance, which simply eliminates any inheritance of parent object policies by child objects. If both of these options are set, the Enforced option always trumps the Block Policy Inheritance feature.

 Explicit permissions, be they Allow or Deny permissions, always will trump inherited permissions, even if Deny permissions on an object are inherited from a parent. Explicitly granting access to an object cannot be overridden by an inherited denial.

To set a GPO to not override parent GPO settings, you need to set the GPO status to "enforced." Follow these steps:

1. In the GPMC, select the domain in which the GPO resides in the left pane.
2. In the right pane, navigate to the Linked Group Policy Objects tab.
3. Right-click the object and select Enforced from the pop-up context menu. You'll receive a confirmation notice, which is shown in Figure 6-7.
4. Click OK to apply the changes.

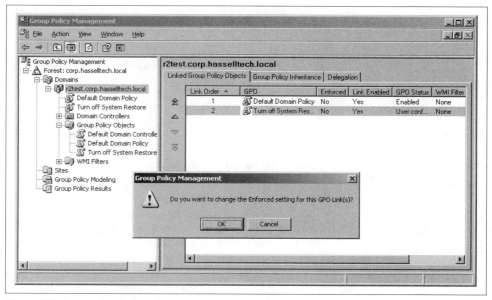

Figure 6-7. Setting the Enforced option on a GPO

To block any inheritance of parent policy settings for the current administrative container, first double-click the forest containing the domain or organizational unit for which you want to block inheritance for GPOs, and then do one of the following:

- To block inheritance of GPOs for an entire domain, double-click Domains, and then right-click the domain.
- To block inheritance for an OU, double-click Domains, double-click the domain containing OU, and then right-click on the OU.

Finally, click Block Inheritance, as shown in Figure 6-8.

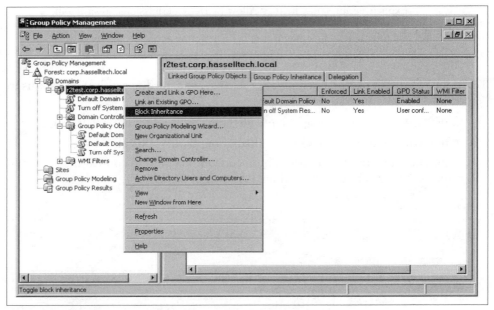

Figure 6-8. Setting the Block Policy Inheritance option

You'll see a small blue exclamation point in the icon beside the domain or OU for which you've blocked inheritance, indicating the operation was successful. To remove the inheritance block, use the aforementioned procedure, and simply uncheck Block Inheritance on the context menu.

 If multiple GPOs are assigned to an object, GPOs at the bottom of the list in the right pane of the GPMC are applied first, and objects at the top are applied last. Therefore, GPOs that are higher in the list have higher priorities.

WMI Filters

A new feature of Windows Server 2003 is the ability to filter how Group Policy is applied based on Windows Management Instrumention (WMI) data. Using WMI filters, you can construct a query with WMI Query Language (WQL) that will return various results onto which you can apply a GP. WMI allows you to pull various characteristics otherwise unavailable through the GPMC, such as a computer's manufacturer and model number, the installation of certain software packages, and other information. You might use WMI when applying policies using these criteria.

To create a WMI filter in the GPMC, right-click on the WMI Filters link in the left pane and select New. The New WMI Filter is shown in Figure 6-9. Enter a name and description for the filter, and then create the query that will represent the dataset against which the GPO will be filtered by clicking Add, selecting the namespace, and then entering the syntax of the query. Note that you can add more than one query to a filter. While constructing WMI queries is outside the scope of this book, you'll find that such queries are very similar in format to SQL queries. For this example, I'll use a simple query that retrieves machines running Windows XP on the network, as shown in the figure.

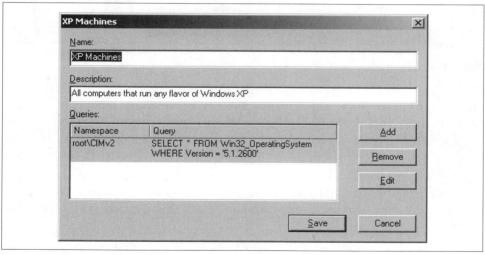

Figure 6-9. Creating a new WMI filter

Once you've entered the query and are satisfied with it, click Save.

To enable a WMI filter on a particular GPO, click the GPO in the GPMC and look at the bottom of the Scope tab in the right pane. There, you can select the WMI filter to apply to the GPO, as shown in Figure 6-10.

Keep in mind that if you set a WMI filter for a GPO, it's an all-or-nothing affair: you can't individually select certain policy settings to apply only to the filtered objects.

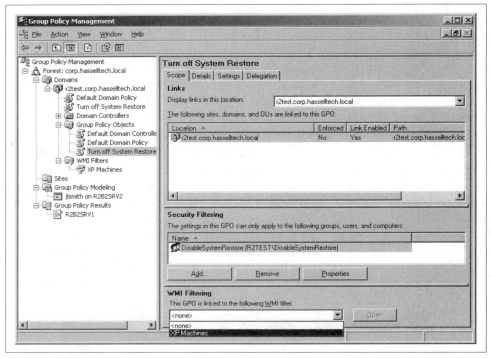

Figure 6-10. Adding a WMI filter to a GPO

Either the entire policy applies to the list of filtered objects, or the entire policy doesn't apply. This might unfortunately result in an inordinate number of GPOs in your directory, each servicing a different list of filtered objects. Keep this is mind when structuring policies. Also be aware that you can apply only one WMI filter per GPO, although each WMI filter can contain multiple WMI queries as I noted before.

If you're not familiar with WMI, Microsoft has provided a utility called Scriptomatic that, although unsupported by Microsoft, helps you construct and use WMI queries for many different Windows administration tasks. You can find the Scriptomatic utility at:

> *http://www.microsoft.com/downloads/details.aspx?FamilyID=9ef05cbd-c1c5-41e7-9da8-212c414a7ab0&displaylang=en*

If you're curious, here is a brief sample WMI filter from above that can reside as a simple XML file on a hard drive; these types of filters use a *.MOF* extension. This will give you an idea of the structure of a filter and how to create one:

```
<?xml version="1.0" encoding="utf-8" ?>
<filters>
<filter>
<description>XP Machines</description>
<group>MYDOMAIN\Windows XP Computers</group>
```

```
<query namespace="ROOT\CIMv2">
SELECT * FROM Win32_OperatingSystem
WHERE Version =
5.1.2600
</query>
<!-- More queries -->
</filter>
<!-- More filters -->
</filters>
```

If you have a lot of WMI filters in separate files, you can import them by right-clicking on WMI Filters in the left pane of the GPMC and selecting Import. You can browse for your MOF files and then import them for use in filtering.

Resultant Set of Policy

In Windows 2000, there was no easy way to see all the policies that were applied to a specific object, nor was there a way to easily project the potential changes to an object that a policy modification would make. However, Microsoft decided in Windows Server 2003 to include the Resultant Set of Policy (RSoP) tool, which can enumerate the following situations:

- Show policies in effect, in the "logging" mode. In the GPMC, this is called "results."
- Show the results of a proposed policy addition or change, in the "planning" mode. In the GPMC, this is called "modeling."

You can access each using the Group Policy Modeling and Group Policy Results items in the left pane of the GPMC. Right-click on the appropriate item and select the option that runs each wizard.

Planning mode

In RSoP planning mode, accessed through Group Policy Modeling, you can simulate the effects of the deployment of GPOs, change the GPO in accordance with those results, and then re-test. You can specify a particular domain controller, users, security groups, and user memberships within, the location of a machine or site, and any applicable WMI filters, and then model the results of applying a specific GPO.

To get started in planning mode, right-click Group Policy Modeling and, from the context menu, select Group Policy Modeling Wizard. Click Next from the introductory screen. The Domain Controller Selection screen appears, as shown in Figure 6-11.

Here, select the domain controller to use when processing the RSoP request. This domain controller must be running Windows Server 2003. You can choose a specific domain controller from the list, or let Windows choose a domain controller. You also can select a given domain to use its respective domain controllers using the Show domain controllers in this domain drop-down list. Click Next to continue.

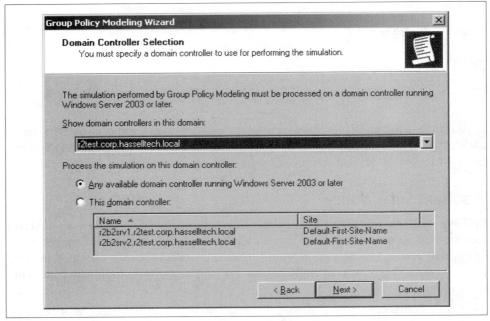

Figure 6-11. Modeling Group Policy: selecting a domain controller

The User and Computer Selection screen appears, as shown in Figure 6-12.

On this screen, you specify the user and computer settings you want to have analyzed when you apply GP. You also can choose a container if you want to analyze Group Policy objects that have been linked to a particular site, domain, or OU. Note also at the bottom of the screen the option to skip to the end of the wizard. If you have a simple query that is complete at any point during the wizard, simply select this option to bypass the remaining screens and go straight to the results of the query. Click Next to continue.

The Advanced Simulation Options screen appears, as shown in Figure 6-13.

On this screen, you can tell Windows to simulate a very slow link between domain controllers and clients, whether to merge or replace loopback processing, and the site to which these settings should apply. This is a very useful algorithm for testing real-world conditions. Click Next to continue.

You'll next see the Alternate Active Directory Paths screen, as shown in Figure 6-14.

On this screen, you can simulate the effects of moving your targets to different locations within your AD structure. You can use the default entries, which reflect the current location of the target objects, or change them using the Browse button to see what would happen if you moved the target to a new location. Click Next to continue.

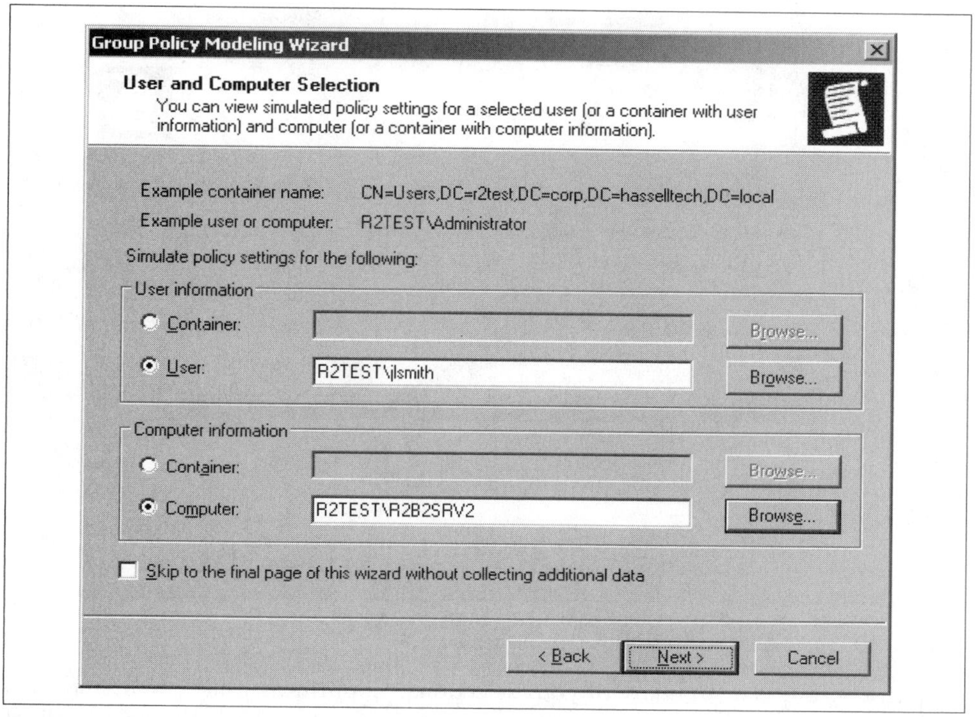

Figure 6-12. The User and Computer Selection screen

Next comes the User Security Groups screen, as depicted in Figure 6-15.

On this screen, you can see the results of applying Group Policy if you change the existing user or computer's security group memberships. The current group memberships are listed in the box, and you can add and remove them using the Add and Remove buttons. To undo your changes, just click Restore Defaults. Click Next when you have the list as you want it.

If you have selected a computer or container of computers in the initial step of the wizard, the Computer Security Groups screen will appear next. It operates exactly like the User Security Groups screen does, as just described. Click Next to continue.

The WMI Filters for Users screen appears next, as shown in Figure 6-16.

Here, you instruct Windows to assume that the user (or container of users) you've selected meets either all configured WMI filters or the specified WMI filter as shown in the box. Click Next when you've selected the appropriate filters.

If you selected a computer or container of computers in the first step of the modeling wizard, the WMI Filters for Computers screen appears next; this screen functions exactly like the WMI Filters for Users screen I just discussed. Click Next to continue.

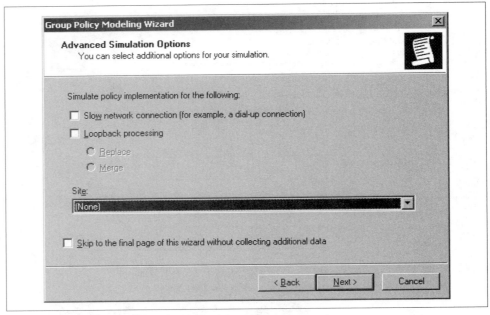

Figure 6-13. The Advanced Simulation Options screen

The next screen is a summary of your selections. Confirm that all is well, and then click Next to begin the simulation. When the process is complete, the wizard will let you know. When you click Finish, the results will appear. A sample results screen is shown in Figure 6-17.

The result is an HTML file that you can collapse and expand as needed. You can see each computer configuration and user configuration result, including GPOs that would be applied and denied, any WMI filters that would be used, how each GP component would survive the deployment, and general information about the query. You can right-click the report and either print or save it. And, if you change your GP settings and want to rerun the same query on the new settings, simply right-click the results page within the GPMC and select Rerun Query.

Logging mode

The RSoP logging mode with the GPMC, called Group Policy Results, operates in much the same way as the planning mode does. To get started, right-click Group Policy Results in the left pane of the GPMC and select Group Policy Results Wizard from the context menu.

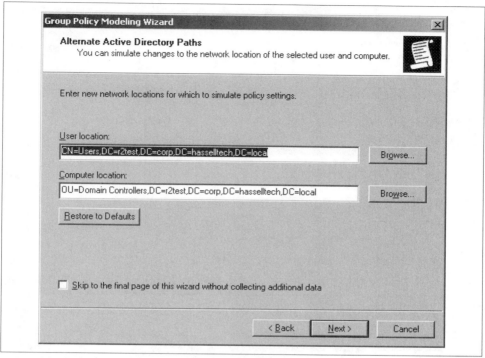

Figure 6-14. The Alternate Active Directory Paths screen

Click away from the introductory screen in the wizard, and the Computer Selection screen appears, as shown in Figure 6-18.

Here, select the computer for which you want to obtain results. You can analyze the current computer or another computer on the network. You also can limit the results to only the User Configuration portion of GP using the checkbox in the middle of the screen. Click Next to continue.

The User Selection screen appears next. This is reproduced in Figure 6-19.

On this screen, you can select which user to report the results of the User Configuration section for. The list is limited to those who have logged on to the computer at some point in time and for whom you have permission to read the results. You also can limit the results displayed to computer configuration information only by using the radio button at the bottom of the screen. Click Next to continue.

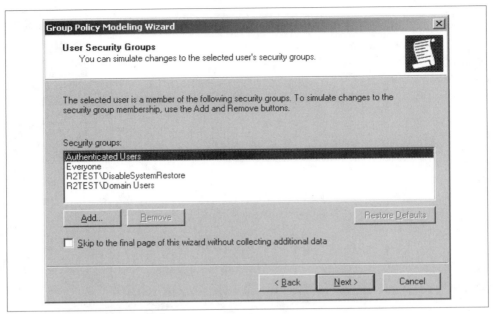

Figure 6-15. The User Security Groups screen

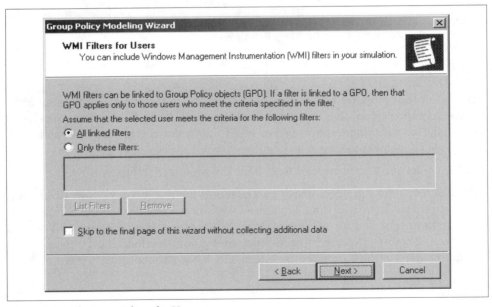

Figure 6-16. The WMI Filters for Users screen

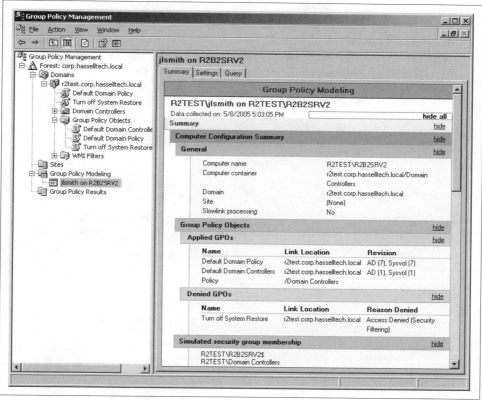

Figure 6-17. Group Policy Modeling results

The Summary of Selections screen appears. Confirm your choices, and click Next to perform the query. When the process is complete, the wizard will notify you. Click Finish to view the results; a sample result screen is shown in Figure 6-20.

Like the other GPMC reports, this one is HTML-based and can be saved and printed by right-clicking anywhere in the report and selecting the appropriate option. For each of the Computer Configuration and User Configuration portions of GP, the report shows the following:

- General information about the query
- GPOs that were applied and GPOs that were denied
- The user and/or computer's membership in security groups when GP was applied
- WMI filters that "catch" the user or computer
- The status of each component of GP, including GPOs themselves, EFS recovery, the registry, and security (permissions)

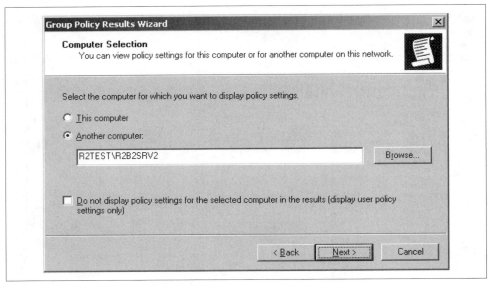

Figure 6-18. The Computer Selection screen

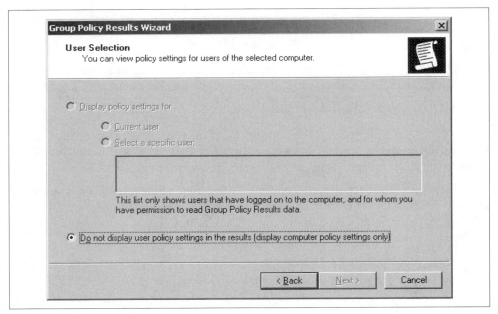

Figure 6-19. The User Selection screen

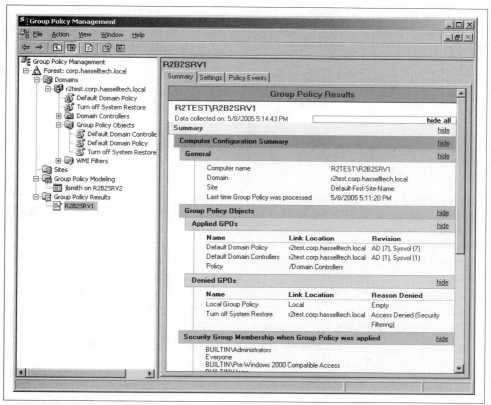

Figure 6-20. Results from the Group Policy Results Wizard

Using RSoP without the GUI

You also can script some functions using the RSoP APIs. The sample script provided in Example 6-1, courtesy of *http://ActiveDir.org* with some modifications, logs the user and computer objects being applied to a particular set of objects within Active Directory. To use it, copy and paste the following text into your favorite text editor, and save it using a *.vbs* extension. Then, run it from the command line using the following:

```
Cscript filename.vbs
```

Example 6-1. Creating an RSoP report with VBScript

```
'------------------------------------------------------------------------
ComputerName = InputBox("Enter the name of a computer running " & _
"Windows XP or Windows Server 2003", _
"Information","")
UserName = InputBox("Enter a user name under which to run the report", _
"Information","")
resultpath = InputBox("Enter a location to store the report", _
```

Example 6-1. Creating an RSoP report with VBScript (continued)

```
"Information", "c:\temp")
resultpath = resultpath&"\"&UserName&".HTML"
Set GPMC = CreateObject("GPMgmt.GPM")
Set Constants = GPMC.GetConstants( )
Set RSOP= GPMC.GetRSOP(Constants.RSOPModeLogging,"",0)
RSOP.LoggingComputer=ComputerName
RSOP.LoggingUser=UserName
RSOP.CreateQueryResults( )
RSOP.GenerateReportToFile Constants.ReportHTML, resultpath
msgbox("RSoP report complete! A full report has been placed at " & _
resultpath)
'-----------------------------------------------------------------------
```

You can retrieve information on the RSoP application in a few other ways as well. Microsoft includes a tool with the Windows 2000 Resource Kit, called *GPRESULT.EXE*, which you can run on a client computer. (Windows XP and Windows Server 2003 have this utility installed by default.) *GPRESULT* will return a listing of all policies applied to a user and computer, the OUs in which the computer and user are located, the site they are in, and a lot more information. You can find the *GPRESULT* executable and technical information on the tool at *http://www.microsoft.com/windows2000/techinfo/reskit/tools/existing/gpresult-o.asp*. The remote computers need to run Windows XP or Server 2003, however, for *GPRESULT* to return accurate information.

For example, to get information for the user jhassell on the remote workstation JH-WNXP-LTP using *GPRESULT*, run:

```
gpresult /s JH-WNXP-LTP /USER jhassell
```

Likewise, to get information for the user ljohnson on the remote workstation LJ-WNXP-DSK, run:

```
gpresult /s LJ-WNXP-DSK /USER ljohnson
```

You also can add the /V option to enable verbose logging, which will display detailed information and not just a summary view, or /Z, to enable extended verbose logging (even more details). Use the /SCOPE MACHINE option with /Z to look at only computer configuration policies; similarly, use /SCOPE USER to look at user configuration policies. You can redirect the output of *GPRESULT* to a text file using the standard > DOS redirect operator.

 New to the Windows Server 2003 Resource Kit is *WINPOLICIES. EXE*, a system tray tool that can show and troubleshoot client-side GPO processing.

Other Administrative Tasks

The GPMC also supports a few more functions, which I'll describe in this section.

Searching for GPOs

Using the GPMC, you can search for specific GPOs or for the values of properties of some GPOs. To do so, right-click a forest or domain in the lefthand pane of the GPMC and select Search from the context menu. The Search for Group Policy Objects screen appears, as shown in Figure 6-21.

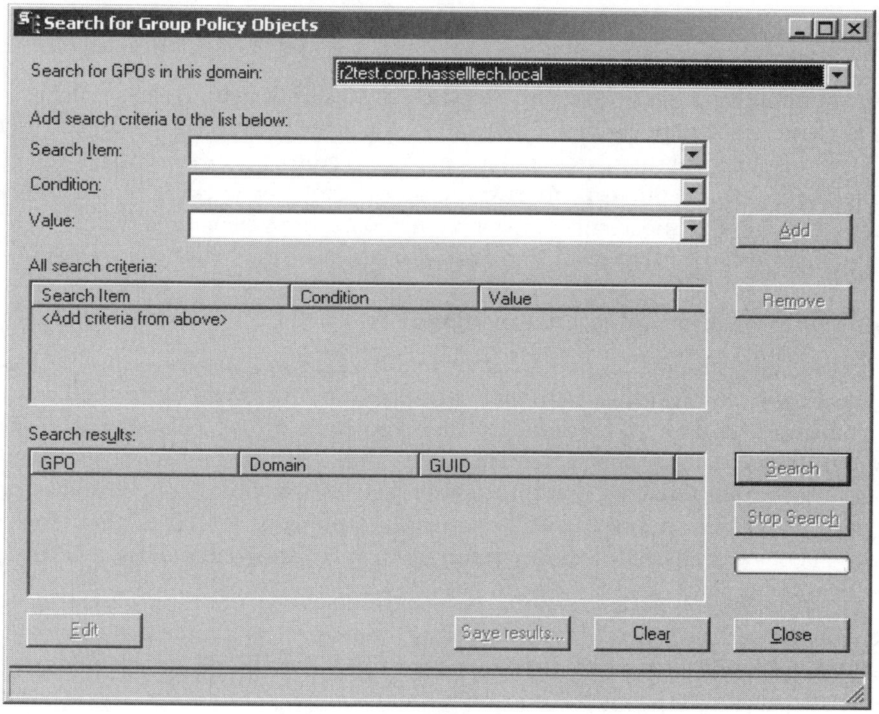

Figure 6-21. Searching for GPOs

You can select the scope of your search to be all domains within a forest, or within a specific domain that you select from the drop-down list at the top of the screen. Then you specify your search criteria by selecting the item to search, the condition to match, and the value that the condition should match. Here are the possible search terms:

- GPO name "contains," "does not contain," or "is exactly" your value.
- GPO links "exist in" or "do not exist in" certain sites or all sites.
- Security group; you simply select one or more security groups using the standard selection dialog.
- User configuration "contains" or "does not contain" folder redirection, Internet Explorer branding, registry, scripts, or software installation values.

- Computer configuration "contains" or "does not contain" EFS recovery, IP security, Microsoft disk quota, QoS packet scheduler, registry, scripts, software installation, or wireless GP values.
- GUID "equals" your value.

You can stack criteria to have multiple conditions in your search by selecting the appropriate query and clicking Add to add the current criteria to the query list. Then you can select more criteria and add them to create more complex searches. You can remove selected criteria from the query list by clicking the Remove button.

Click Search to start the search, and Stop Search to stop it before it has finished. The results of the search appear at the bottom of the screen. You can select a particular GPO that results from the search and go directly to editing it by selecting it and clicking the Edit button. You also can save the set of results by clicking the Save Results button, which puts the results in a text file of comma-separated values (CSVs). Finally, to clear the current results and perform a new search, click the Clear button.

Backing up, copying, importing, and exporting GPOs

The GPMC also supports copying, importing, backing up, and restoring GPO information. Previously, GPO backups were not possible unless you performed a system state backup of a domain controller. When you back up a GPO using the GPMC, only data pertinent to that particular GPO is backed up. Linked objects are not backed up because restoring that information becomes troublesome. However, when you restore, Windows automatically assigns the previous GUID of the backed-up GPO, which is wonderful for simply resurrecting an inadvertently deleted GPO.

It is not uncommon for administrators to spend a great deal of time configuring GPOs exactly as needed and then to find themselves having to repeat the process manually on several other OUs for which they are responsible. The GPMC can save hours upon hours with its copy capability. You simply can copy a GPO or set of GPOs and then paste them elsewhere into another OU. However, a copy isn't the same as a backup because the copy process doesn't replicate the information in a file that can be moved elsewhere for safekeeping. Also, a copy of a GPO has a different GUID than the original GPO. To perform a GPO copy, you need rights to create GPOs in the destination location and read access to the GPOs in the original location.

The GPMC also supports the ability to import and export GPOs—even to a separate domain with which no trust exists to the original domain. This is useful when you need to copy the same GPO settings to multiple domains or when moving between development and productions forests. You don't need to meticulously re-create all your GPOs on the other domains; simply export them using the GPMC and import them on the new domain. It's a faster and less error-prone procedure.

Importing GPOs across domains can be a bit complex because you'll need to create a migration table to specify how the GPMC should translate domain-specific data from one domain into the other. Most GPOs contain information such as users, groups, computers, and UNC paths that refer to objects available in a specific domain. These might not be applicable in the new domain, so you'll need to tell Windows how to translate these objects stored within the source GPO to other objects applicable to the destination GPO's location. Here's a more specific list of GPO aspects you can modify within the migration process:

- Security policy settings, including user rights assignments, restricted groups, services, filesystem entries, and registry keys and values
- Advanced folder redirection policies
- The ACL on a GPO itself, which can be preserved or discarded at your discretion
- The ACL on software installation GPOs (I'll discuss software installation later in this chapter), which relies on your selecting the option immediately preceding this one

Let's walk through several examples for backing up, copying, exporting, and importing GPOs with the GPMC. To back up a specific GPO, follow these steps:

1. Open the GPMC.
2. Expand the Forest and Domain trees in the left pane, and then select Group Policy Objects under your domain.
3. In the right pane, select the GPO you want to back up.
4. Right-click the GPO and select Back Up.
5. The Back Up Group Policy Object dialog box appears, as shown in Figure 6-22. Enter the location you want to store the backed-up GPO files in the first box, and then enter a helpful description for yourself so that you can identify the backed-up files later.
6. A progress box will appear, indicating how far Windows has progressed in the backup procedure. A message in the Status box will appear noting a successful backup when the procedure is finished.
7. Click OK to finish.

To copy a specific GPO, follow these steps:

1. Open the GPMC.
2. Expand the Forest and Domain trees in the left pane, and then select Group Policy Objects under your domain.
3. In the right pane, select the GPO you want to copy.
4. Right-click the GPO and select Copy.

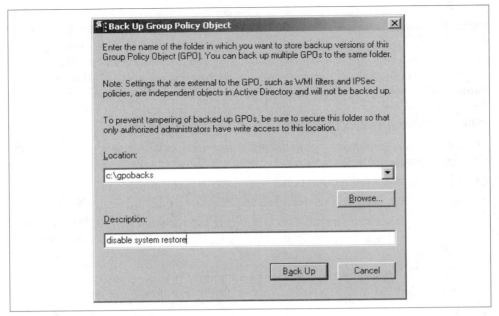

Figure 6-22. Backing up GPOs

5. Find the OU within Active Directory to which you want to paste the copied GPO and select it.

6. Right-click the OU and select Paste from the context menu. A message, shown in Figure 6-23, will appear asking you if you want to link the GPOs you copied to the destination OU. Click OK to continue.

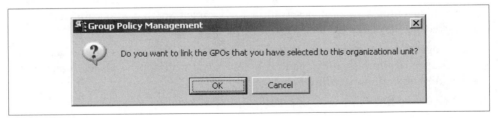

Figure 6-23. Copying GPOs

Your GPO has been copied.

To import a specific GPO, you need to create a new GPO in the location to which you want to import settings. For example, if you want to import the lockout policy from one domain into a new domain, you'll need to create a new GPO in the new domain. Then, follow these steps:

1. Open the GPMC.

2. Expand the Forest and Domain trees in the left pane, and then select Group Policy Objects under the new domain.

3. In the right pane, select the GPO you want to use.

4. Right-click the GPO and select Import Settings. The Import Settings Wizard appears.

5. The wizard will prompt you to back up the settings currently within the destination GPO. Click the Backup button to do so, and follow the procedure earlier in this section to step through that process. When you are done, click Next.

6. Select the location where the GPO that you want to import is located. Then, click Next.

7. The Source GPO screen appears. All the GPOs that are stored in the location you input in step 6 are listed on this screen. You can select an individual GPO and click View Settings to refresh your memory as to the settings the GPO contains. Select the GPO you want to use, and then click Next.

8. The Migrating References screen may appear (if not, skip to step 13). Depending on the settings contained within the GPO, you might need to "map" entries using a migration table. You can select to copy the existing entries directly from the source (using the first bulleted option), or you can create a new migration table by clicking New. This results in the Migration Table Editor window appearing.

9. From the Tools menu, select Populate from Backup, and then select the source GPO you are importing. Windows will populate the objects that need to be retranslated automatically.

10. In the Destination Name column, simply enter the correct name for the source property in its new location. Be sure these properties already exist within the destination location; the GPMC can't create them on the fly. Also, if some properties don't need to be changed, simply enter <Same As Source> in the Destination Name column.

11. You can save this migration table for use in other GPO import procedures by selecting Save from the File menu and specifying a location. This can be anywhere on your filesystem.

12. Close the Migration Table Editor. The Migrating References screen will reappear, and the migration table you just created will appear. Click Next to continue.

13. The Completing the Import Settings Wizard screen will appear. Confirm your settings are correct, and then click Finish. Your settings will be imported.

Managing GP across multiple forests

Using the GPMC, you can quite easily browse and set up GPOs in several distinct forests and domains. In fact, even the default setup of the GPMC allows you to select Add Forest from the Action menu and then to type the name of a forest you want to manage. The GPMC will add that to the list of available forests in the left pane.

Managing GP for multiple forests comes with a few requirements:

- To make everything work out of the box, you need to have a two-way trust between the target forest and the forest that the machine on which you are running the GPMC is in.

- If you have only a one-way trust, choose Options from the View menu, and then on the General Tab uncheck Enable Trust Delegation, a feature which allows permissions for managing GPOs to be assigned to the other forest for reciprocal management.

- If you don't have a trust, you'll need to use the Stored User Names and Passwords applet in the Control Panel of Windows Server 2003 or the User Accounts applet in Windows XP to keep your login information for the remote forest.

- Most likely you will need Enterprise Administrator credentials to manage GP in other forests.

Delegating administration of GPs

Windows 2000 introduced a feature that allowed you to delegate administrative authority for any number of privileges to certain users; this was an extremely useful and cost-effective way to spread out the workload and increase business unit responsibility for their own IT costs. In Windows Server 2003, Microsoft extended this ability to GPOs, allowing an administrator to extend supervisory privileges (to use old Netware terminology) over some actions with regard to GPOs. Here's how it works:

By default, the creation of GPOs is restricted to members of the Domain Admins or Enterprise Admins groups or to those users who belong to the Group Policy Creator Owners group. The key distinction between those security groups is that although those in an administrator group can create and edit any and all GPOs in a directory, the members of the Group Policy Creator Owners group (hereinafter referred to as the GPCO group) can edit only those policies they created themselves. (If you are familiar with LDAP terminology, this is the managedBy concept.) In addition, members of the GPCO group cannot link GPOs to containers within a directory unless a special permission, known as Manage Policy Links, has been explicitly granted to them.

If you take advantage of delegation in your organization and empower group or department managers to administer IT assets within their own scope of control, you might want to enable them to administer some GPOs for their group. It's likely that these managers aren't members of the Domain Administrators, Enterprise Administrators, or

Group Policy Administrators groups, so you'll need to delegate individual privileges—either the ability to create and edit GPOs themselves, or the ability to link GPOs to objects within Active Directory. The two privileges are independent; they are not required in tandem.

To delegate the ability to create and edit GPOs to a user or group, follow these steps:

1. Open the GPMC.
2. In the Tree view, select Group Policy Objects.
3. Navigate to the Delegation tab in the righthand pane.
4. Add the user or group to whom you want to delegate the privilege.

To delegate the ability to link GPOs to objects, follow these steps:

1. Open the GPMC.
2. Select the OU or other object for which you want to give the ability to link GPOs.
3. Navigate to the Delegation tab in the righthand pane.
4. Add the user or group to whom you want to delegate the privilege.

If you prefer to do this via scripting, a couple of sample scripts are included with a default GPMC installation, located in the *Program Files\Group Policy Management Console\Scripts* directory, that can delegate these two abilities. You can delegate GPO creation and ownership with the `SetGPOCreationPermissions.wsf` script, and you can link with the `SetSOMPermissions.wsf` script.

Local Group Policy

Now let's examine the two different types of GP, starting with local GP and moving to domain-based GP. Although local policies don't have the flexibility of domain-based GPs, as you will see, they still are a valuable tool for creating a deployable set of standards for computers in your organization. Local policies are most useful for creating a security configuration for either clients or servers that is appropriate for your company. With the Security Templates snap-in, you can create role-based templates that configure most security-related settings on your machines. And with the Security Configuration and Analysis Tool snap-in (covered in detail in Chapter 7), you can create a database of roles and policies for your organization's machines.

In this section, I'll look at local security policy and using the security templates features to create a consistent security configuration.

Security Templates

Microsoft wisely decided to ship Windows with a few predefined security settings files, hereafter referred to as "security templates." These files contain what are essentially recipes for configuring a machine's security policy based on its daily role. These templates, designed to be applied to new Windows installations that already have had a basic template applied, must be used on systems formatted with NTFS, at least on the boot partition (the one containing the operating system files). The incremental security templates are as follows:

- For workstations or servers in which users ought to be prevented from being in the Power Users group, apply the *compatws.inf* template. This template compensates for the lack of additional privileges afforded to members of the Power Users group by relaxing the rights restrictions on the normal Users group. But be careful: you should only use this template if you're dealing with non-certified software (programs that don't have the Windows logo affixed to them) that won't otherwise run.

- To further secure workstations or servers, the *securews.inf* template increases the overall security level of a machine by tightening areas of the OS not under the purvey of rights and restrictions. Areas that are more secured using this template include account policy settings, auditing controls, and registry keys that are prominent in security policy. The appropriate version of this template for Windows domain controllers is *securedc.inf*.

- For the ultra-paranoid and for those with the most stringent security requirements, the *hisecws.inf* (and for domain controllers, the *hisecdc.inf* file) can be used; however, because all network transmissions must be signed and encrypted by Windows machines, this template is appropriate only in pure Windows 2000 or greater environments.

- *Setup security.inf* restores the security settings of a machine to their default, out-of-the-box configuration. Use this if you have made modifications and want to completely reverse them and "wipe the slate clean," as it were.

- *Rootsec.inf* specifies the newer, more secure permissions for the root of the system drive, first introduced in Windows XP and carried over into Windows Server 2003. Most significantly, this removes the full control permissions from Everyone on the system drive. You also can use this template to reapply the more stringent root directory security on systems where the baseline security settings have been modified.

- *DC security.inf* refers to the default security template for domain controllers, which imposes more stringent requirements on network transmissions and secures more portions of the filesystem and registry. This template is created when a server is promoted to domain controller status.

- *Iesacls.inf* provides a tighter security configuration for Internet Explorer, restricting scripting activity in certain untrusted zones and providing a more stringent, but secure, web browsing atmosphere.

These convenient templates are designed to be used with the Security Templates snap-in. Using the snap-in, you can apply the basic and incremental security templates included with the product, or you can modify the templates to create your own easily distributable templates.

To begin using the Security Templates snap-in, follow this procedure:

1. Run `mmc /s` from a command line. This loads the MMC in author mode, allowing you to add a snap-in.

2. From the Console menu, select Add/Remove Snap-in. Then select Add. This raises a dialog box entitled Add Standalone Snap-in.

3. From the list, select Security Templates, click Add, and then click Close.

4. Click OK in the next box to confirm the addition of the snap-in.

Now you have the Security Templates snap-in added to a console. From this snap-in, you can expand the Security Templates section in the console tree on the left, and then expand the *C:\Windows\security\templates* folder to view the predefined security templates discussed earlier.

Creating a Custom Security Template

You might want to make your own customized policy modifications that go above and beyond those made in the templates shipped with Windows. Creating a custom security template affords you an easy way to package, deploy, and apply these modifications with a minimum of administrative headache. Best of all, you can use these templates in conjunction with a utility called the Security Configuration and Analysis Tool to assess the overall "hardness," or state of security, of your machines.

To create your own security template, follow these steps:

1. In the Security Templates console, expand Security Templates in the tree pane on the left, and right-click *C:\Windows\security\templates* (this is the default templates folder in the system).

2. Select New Template from the context menu that appears.

Now you can make any policy modifications you want in any one of the policy areas supported by the tool: account policies, local policies, the event log, restricted groups, system services, the registry, and the filesystem. Your additions, deletions, and other changes are saved directly into the template as they are made.

To take this one step further, you might decide to build on the basic policy settings provided by the basic and incremental templates shipped with Windows. In that case, it's quite simple to open the basic or incremental templates, resave to a different name, and make further modifications to create your own custom template. To do so, follow these steps:

1. Select an existing template inside the Security Templates console. In this example, I'll use the *securews.inf* file.

2. Right-click the existing template, and click Save as... from the context menu.

3. Give the new template a name.

4. Click OK. The new template is created with the settings from the old basic template.

Compiling the Security Database

The next step is to compile your templates into a security database using the Security Configuration and Analysis (SCA) tool. From within the MMC, add the SCA tool to the console. Then do the following:

1. Right-click Security Configuration and Analysis and select Open Database.

2. From the Open Database dialog, type the name of a new database.

3. Because no database exists with that name, you'll be prompted for the specific security template from which the database should be built. The choices in this box come from the *C:\Windows\Security\Templates* folder. Choose the template, and click OK.

Although you won't get any confirmation from the user interface, the template has been added to the database. Now you can right-click the SCA tool in the left pane and choose either Analyze Computer Now or Configure Computer Now. When you select Analyze Computer Now, the SCA tool looks at the new security configuration within the database, compares it with the current state of the computer, and reports on the differences; the report also is saved to a logfile in *\My Documents\Security\ Logs*. Alternatively, when you select Configure Computer Now, the changes will actually be committed to your system. You want to avoid using that option unless you're absolutely sure you want the results in production without seeing them first.

You also can script the application of templates across multiple computers, using a login script, Telnet server, or some other means, by taking advantage of the SECEDIT utility. SECEDIT takes a template file, adds it to the SCA database, and then applies the security settings to the machine on which SECEDIT is being run. To import a template named *Hassell-secure.inf*, compile it into SCA into a database called *securepcs* and overwrite any data already in the database, apply it to the current computer, and create a log for all of these actions named *apply.log*, for example, issue the following command:

```
secedit /configure /cfg Hassell-secure.inf /db securepcs /overwrite
/log apply.log
```

If you've already imported the template into SCA manually, and you just need to apply the settings to a computer, issue the following command:

```
secedit /configure /db securepcs /overwrite /log apply.log
```

Domain Group Policy

Domain-based GPs offer a much more flexible and configurable set of standards and settings for your organization than local GPs. In this section, I'll discuss the four most common methods of managing your IT assets centrally using domain GP: configuring a security standard, installing software using the IntelliMirror technology found in Windows Server 2003, redirecting folders present in the user interface to network locations, and writing and launching scripts triggered by events such as logons and logoffs.

Security Settings

As discussed earlier, one of the most useful aspects of GP is its ability to control security settings and configuration from a central location within the organization. Security policy is composed of three key components: restricted groups, registry settings, and filesystem settings. In this section, I'll take a look at each of them.

Restricted groups

The restricted groups option allows you to modify the current group configuration and membership on your client computers. When this policy is applied to workstations and servers, their individual group configurations are modified to match that configured inside the policy. The policy contains *members* and *members of* lists that overwrite any configuration on the target computers. For example, if you were to add the Administrator group to the policy but not add any users to the members of this group list, and then you applied the policy, Windows would remove any users currently in those groups on the client computers. However, the other facet of the policy, groups of which the added group is currently a member, is only additive: if the list is empty, no modifications are made to the client computers. Only additions are processed and changed.

Only the groups listed inside the Details window of the Restricted Groups policy branch can be modified using the policy, but it's a great way to keep individual users from modifying powerful groups on their own systems.

To modify the restricted groups policy, do the following:

1. Launch the GPMC, and then right-click on your target GPO in the left pane and select Edit.

2. Inside the Group Policy Object Editor, navigate through Computer Configuration, Windows Settings, and Security Settings.

3. Right-click the Restricted Group branch and select Add Group from the context menu.

4. Click the Browse button, and select any group currently inside your directory. Click OK.

5. Now, right-click the newly added group, and select Security from the context menu.

6. Add the users that belong to this group to the "Members of this group" list, and add the groups within which this group is nested to the This group is a member of list. Use the Add button in both cases. Figure 6-24 shows this screen.

7. When you're finished, click OK to close the boxes.

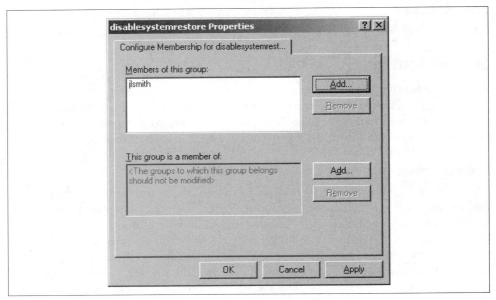

Figure 6-24. The Restricted Groups list screen

File system and registry policy

You also can use GPs to configure permissions on filesystem objects and registry keys. You can set entries on the ACLs of individual files, folders, and registry keys from a central location. If you make this change at the domain-wide level—one of the few changes I recommend and endorse at that level—registries are protected against meddling users all over the enterprise, which is definitely a benefit.

To add a registry key to be protected to a GPO, follow these steps:

1. Launch the GPMC, and then right-click on your target GPO in the left pane and select Edit.

2. Inside the Group Policy Object Editor, navigate through the Computer Configuration, Windows Settings, Security Settings, and Registry nodes. Right-click Registry and select Add Key from the context menu.

3. You can add one registry key at a time, and you can selectively apply permissions to each key. Figure 6-25 shows the screen.

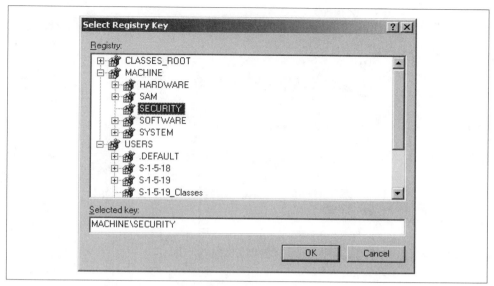

Figure 6-25. The Registry Key ACL editor screen

To add a file or folder to be protected to a GPO, follow these steps:

1. Launch the GPMC, and then right-click on your target GPO in the left pane and select Edit.

2. Inside the Group Policy Object Editor, navigate through the Computer Configuration, Windows Settings, Security Settings, and File System nodes. Right-click File System and select Add File from the context menu.

3. You can explore the entire directory structure, select a file, and then selectively assign permissions to files and folders. Figure 6-26 shows the screen.

Once you've selected the objects in question, you'll be prompted for their permissions just like I discussed in Chapter 3. After you enter the appropriate permissions, you'll be prompted to configure the properties of inheritance for these new permissions. This is shown in Figure 6-27.

If you select the configure option, you also will need to select how permissions are applied. If you choose to apply inheritable security to this file or folder and to its subfolders, the new permissions are applied to all child objects that do not have a permission or ACL entry explicitly set. This preserves your custom permissions on a tree but also automatically overwrites permissions simply inherited by default. If you choose to replace existing security for this file or folder and its subfolders, you overwrite all permissions on any child folders, including those permissions explicitly set.

If you'd rather not have any of these methods used to apply permissions, simply choose the following option: Prevent the application of security policies to this file or folder and its subfolders. Doing so will make child files and folders immune to the permissions assigned by this new policy.

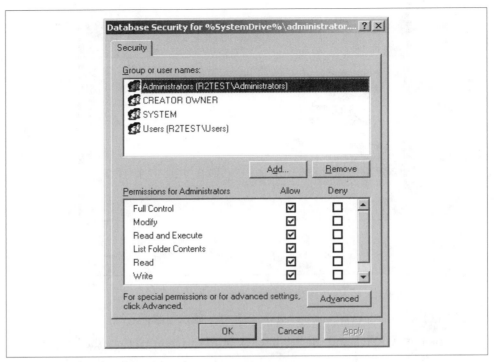

Figure 6-26. The File System ACL editor screen

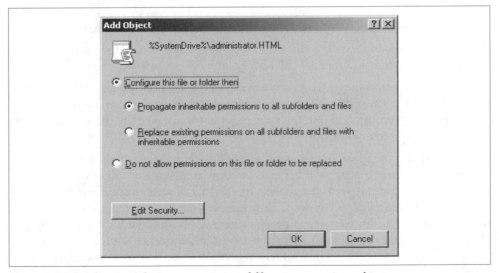

Figure 6-27. Configuring inheritance on protected filesystem or registry objects

IntelliMirror: Software Installation

In my opinion, software installation is one of the coolest and most useful features of GP, and I know many administrators who agree with me. Using Microsoft's IntelliMirror technology introduced in Windows 2000, administrators using GP can distribute software applications initially, using a push or pull method, and then upgrade, redeploy, or remove that software either wholesale or when certain conditions apply. IntelliMirror also offers intelligent application repair features so that when critical files for an application deployed through IntelliMirror are corrupted or deleted, Windows takes over and fixes the problem so that the application will still start and function correctly. This is a big timesaver.

You can distribute and install applications in your organization in two ways. You can assign a software package, which places a shortcut on the user's Start menu and loads the advertisement for the package into the computer's registry. Or you can publish an application, which simply places the program with the Add/Remove Programs applet in the Control Panel. The user can elect to install the software at his discretion and at a convenient time.

You also can distribute applications via the assign and publish functionality to a computer or a user. If you assign a package to a user, the application is installed on the local system the first time the user runs the software. Incidentally, you can also elect to install such an application when the user logs on, although this can make for long boot times and calls to the help desk. These user-assigned applications follow a user around the network to each computer to ensure that he has all the applications he should on each computer. If you assign a package to a computer, the application is installed on that system when booted up, and the software is installed only on the computer defined in the policy. Applications don't necessarily follow a user around. If you use the publish functionality of IntelliMirror, you can publish to only a specific user because computers can't choose how and where to install software. Published applications also are not quite as robust as assigned applications and the repair functionality of published applications is limited.

 Software installation cannot be accomplished using local policies.

Packaging software

The easiest way to publish and assign software is through the use of Microsoft Installer packages, or MSI files. Applications packaged in Installer format include a database of changes to make to files and registry keys, instructions on removing previous or outdated version of software, and strategies to install on multiple versions of Windows within one file. MSI files also allow intelligent repair functionality for use if installations become corrupted on individual computers, and their rollback function for removing or redeploying an application is useful as well. IntelliMirror and GP-based software distribution are designed to work with applications that install using an MSI package.

But all is not lost if your software isn't offered in MSI format. First, you can use the ZAP file method. You can use a *.ZAP* file when software isn't available with an MSI package to publish (but not assign) the application. A ZAP file is nothing more than a description of an application, its setup program, and any associated file extensions. A sample ZAP file for Adobe's Acrobat Reader 5.0 is shown here:

```
Line 1: [Application]
Line 2: FriendlyName = Adobe Acrobat Reader 5.0
Line 3: SetupCommand = \\deploy\adobe\rp505enu.exe
Line 4: DisplayVersion = 5.0
Line 5: Publisher = Adobe Corporation
Line 6: URL = http://www.adobe.com
Line 7:
Line 8: [Ext]
Line 9: PDF=
```

A few notes about this ZAP file: the `FriendlyName` section shows the application name, which will appear in the Add/Remove Programs applet within the Control Panel on the computers to which the package is published. It also contains the `Setup` directive, which tells Windows the network path of the file to install the package. The other tags, although offering more information on the version, manufacturer, and Internet address of the manufacturer, are optional. The `Ext` section lists file extensions to be associated with the program, each followed by an equals sign.

The ZAP file method has a few caveats. First and foremost, because ZAP file installations can only be published, you lose the robustness and intelligent repair features of software applications assigned to computers and users. You also can't set an application deployed via a ZAP file to install automatically on first use, and you can't upgrade or remove an application deployed via a ZAP file using a GPO. In addition, a specific user must have appropriate permissions to run the package's installer executable and to access the source files for the installation. And, the installation probably is not very automated, so the process likely would require user intervention to answer prompts such as the destination directory, installation options, and so forth, which is something we all try to avoid when possible. Finally, because the installer isn't granted sweeping administrative privileges during the setup process like an MSI installer is, you might have conflicts and problems to troubleshoot with a mass package deployment.

 If a program you want to deploy uses the InstallShield installation software, you can run `setup /r` to automatically make a scripted installation file, called *setup.iss*. Copy the *setup.iss* file to whatever deployment share you have set up (more on that in a bit), and then modify the ZAP file to contain the following setup command:

```
setup /r /setup.iss
```

If the ZAP file method doesn't appeal to you, you can use a repacking tool, such as Veritas WinInstall LE or the InstallShield deployment tools. These tools will take a snapshot of your current system configuration and prompt you to install the software you want to package. Once the installation is complete, these tools will take another snapshot, record what changed on the filesystem and registry, and prompt you with a list of what it detected. You go through the list, make sure the changes listed were due to installing the software and not to errant behavior on the part of Windows, and then confirm the list. The software will create an MSI with the program's installer and a database of filesystem and registry changes.

Using this method, you gain the robustness and rollback features of using an MSI installer as opposed to ZAP files. However, the repackaging tools can tend to be a bit flaky, and sometimes you'll have difficulty installing them on multiple platforms. There's not a good way around that, other than obtaining an MSI directly from the software vendor, but it's somewhat of a middle ground between the inflexible ZAP files and a true MSI from the manufacturer.

 If you still have a copy of a Windows 2000 distribution CD, you can find a limited version of WinInstall LE on that CD. However, for some reason Microsoft seems to have removed this program from the Windows Server 2003 CD, so if you don't have the Windows 2000 CD, you are unfortunately out of luck.

An example deployment

In this section, I'll step through an actual software deployment using GP, publishing an application for a user:

1. Copy the MSI file and other necessary files to a network share. This might require an administrative installation, if your software has one available. Consult the documentation and deployment instructions for more on this.

   The network share should have these permissions:

   - Authenticated Users should have Read permissions.
   - Domain Computers should have Read permissions.
   - Administrators should have Read, Change, and Full Control permissions.

2. Create a new GPO and open it, or edit an existing GPO that you've created for the purposes of distributing this software, using the Group Policy Management Console and Object Editor.

3. Within the Group Policy Object Editor, navigate through the User Configuration and Software Settings nodes in the left pane.

4. Right-click Software Installation, and select Package from the New menu.

5. In the Find File window, use the Browse button to find the package you copied to the network share. You can select either an MSI file or a ZAP file in this step;

if you select a ZAP file you need to ensure that its related installer file is located in the same folder as the ZAP file.

 If you are using a ZAP file, make sure the SetupCommand directive in the files points to the network path that contains the setup file and not to the local path. Otherwise, Windows won't translate the path to the file correctly, and if the software isn't present at the same local path on target systems, the installation will fail.

6. On the Deploy Software screen, select whether to publish the software or assign the software. (Skip the Advanced Publish and Assign option at this point, which allows you to use transform files to modify the installation process for an application. This is covered a bit later in this chapter.) For this example, I'll publish the software.

7. Click OK, and the software is added to the policy object and is saved to the directory.

Of course, to assign an application to a user, you can simply follow the preceding steps and select Assign instead of Publish in step 6. To assign an application to a computer, use the same process, but use Computer Configuration instead of User Configuration in step 3 and select Assign instead of Publish in step 6.

Deployment properties

You'll probably want to fine-tune the settings for deployment, and you can do this through the properties box for the software. Right-click the name of the software package inside the Group Policy Object Editor and then select Properties. The policy properties box contains the following six tabs.

General
> On this tab, you can modify the name of the package that will be displayed in Add/Remove Programs. You also can view the version, publisher, language, and platform of the software. Figure 6-28 shows the General tab.

Deployment
> The Deployment tab lets you configure the deployment type and user interaction methods for the software. Under Deployment Type, you can select whether to publish or assign this software. Under Deployment Options, you can choose to "Auto-install this application by file extension activation," which prevents or allows application installation when a user attempts to open a file with an extension associated with the application. You also can elect to "Uninstall this application when it falls out of the scope of management," which dictates whether to remove the application when the user or computer leaves the scope of the current GPO. Additionally, you can choose "Do not display this package in the Add/Remove Programs control panel," which simply hides the application's availability. The application still will be installed when the user opens a file with

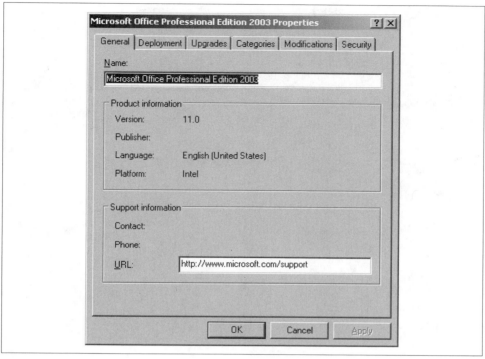

Figure 6-28. The General tab

the associated extension. The "Install this application at logon option" will allow applications assigned to computers to be installed once a user logs in to the computer and not during the computer's boot process, which is the default behavior. Finally, under the Installation user interface options, you can choose whether to eliminate most user intervention by installing the application using default values (with the Basic option) or to prompt the user for installation preferences and instructions (with the Maximum option). Figure 6-29 shows the Deployment tab.

Upgrades

On this tab you can specify that this new package will upgrade an existing installed package. You can make that mandatory by checking the Required upgrade for existing packages checkbox. To add a package to be upgraded, click the Add button and find the package to upgrade within the current object; alternatively, browse through your Active Directory structure by clicking a specific GPO and choosing a different GPO and software package. Then you can elect to uninstall the existing package and install the new package, or upgrade over the existing package. Figure 6-30 shows the Upgrades tab.

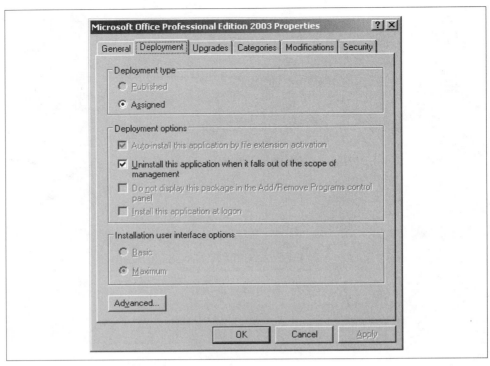

Figure 6-29. The Deployment tab

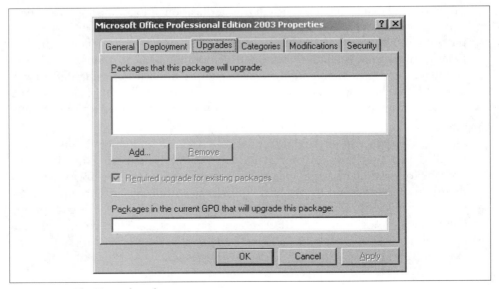

Figure 6-30. The Upgrades tab

Categories

In this tab you can create categories that will sort and filter the applications available through the Add/Remove Programs applet within the Control Panel. Users can more easily find the published application they want to install if they can click the type of software they need, rather than wading through a list of 100 possible applications. To add categories, simply click the Add button and enter a new category name. Once you've added the category, you can add packages under it. Choose a category from the Available categories pane and click Select to add the current package to it. Do this for each package you want to categorize. Figure 6-31 shows the Categories tab.

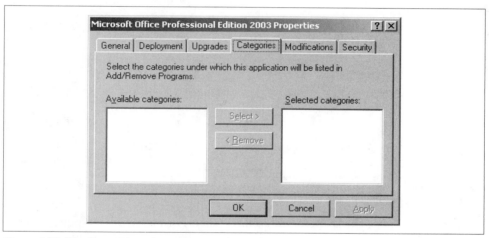

Figure 6-31. The Categories tab

Modifications

You can use a transform file (also called an MST file) to customize an MSI application's installation procedure; through the Modifications tab, you can use multiple MST files to ensure that various users, groups, and computers receive customized versions of a software package. To use a transform file for a particular GPO, click Add on this tab and browse the filesystem for the MST file to apply. There are two caveats: you must have deployed an application using the Advanced Publish or Assign method, selected when creating the software installation GPO. Also, once an MST has been applied and the software has been deployed, modifications cannot be added or removed. Figure 6-32 shows the Modifications tab.

Security

The Security tab, very similar to other ACLs on other objects within Windows Server 2003, allows you to specify permissions on the software installation package portion of the GPO for users, computers, and groups. You can use this tab in conjunction with the security group filtering strategy, discussed earlier in this

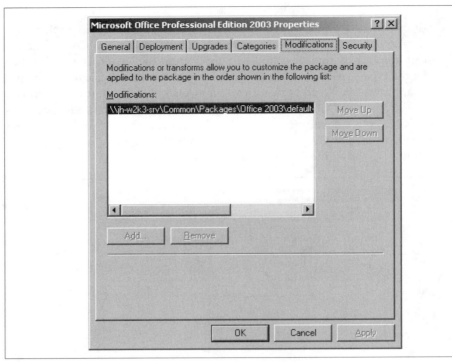

Figure 6-32. The Modifications tab

chapter, to limit the scope of an applied GPO. For example, one policy assigning Office to computers might apply only to sales, but a policy publishing Windows administrative tools might apply only to administrators. If you want to assign applications to computers, you need to add the Domain Computers group here, unless you already have a security group containing the computers you want. Figure 6-33 shows the Security tab.

Remember the following security settings guidelines when deploying software via security group filtering:

- If you want the policy to be applied to all members of a certain security group, then create security groups that contain only the objects that are to be included in the policy application. Then, select the GPO you want to administer in the left pane of the Group Policy Management Console. Next, on the Scope tab in the right pane, click the Add button under Security Filtering, and then add the groups that do not need the policy applied. Verify the group was added to the Security Filtering list.

- If you *do not* want the policy to be applied to all members of a certain security group, add all the members to a group, add the group to the ACL for the object by editing the GPO within the GPMC and accessing the ACL from within Group

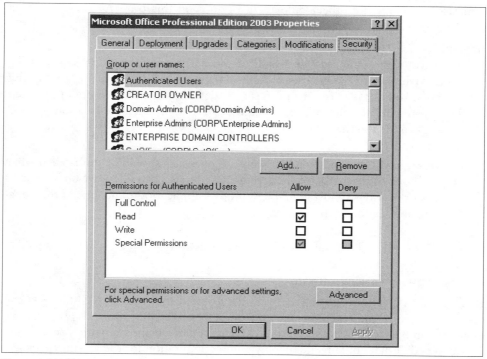

Figure 6-33. The Security tab

Policy Object Editor, and set the following permissions for the group: Apply Group Policy, deny; Read, deny. All members of the group will *not* have the policy applied, regardless of their existing memberships to other groups.

- If group membership (at least in a specific group) shouldn't play a part in the application of this policy, leave permissions alone.

Look back earlier in the chapter to the section "The Scope of Group Policy Objects" for a refresher on this.

You also can determine the order in which applications will be installed for a given file extension, a useful feature if your organization associates one file extension with multiple software packages. To do so, right-click the Software Installation node within the Group Policy Object Editor (in the lefthand pane) and select Properties. From there, navigate to the File Extensions tab. Select an extension from the dropdown list box, and then adjust the priority, from highest to lowest, of each application in the list box using the Up and Down buttons. If only one application in GP is associated with an extension, this feature will be grayed out because no priority needs to be established.

You also can configure other deployment options on this property sheet using the following tabs:

General
> Here, you can configure the default action when adding new packages to this GPO—whether to assign them, publish them, or display a dialog box asking which action to take. You also can set the default user interface options as well. Plus, you can indicate the path that will serve as the default location for new packages added to this GPO.

Advanced
> On this tab, you can indicate that software packages should be uninstalled when they fall out of the scope of management. You also can allow 64-bit Windows client workstations to install 32-bit Windows applications, and extend this capability to applications deployed via a ZAP file.

Categories
> The Categories tab was discussed earlier in this section.

Redeploying and removing software

If you need to patch an existing software deployment that uses an MSI file, you can take advantage of the redeployment functionality of IntelliMirror. Simply copy the new MSI and associated files over the existing copies on the network share. Then, inside the GPO that contains the deployment configuration for the existing package, right-click the package in the details window inside the Group Policy Object Editor and select Redeploy from the All Tasks menu. Click the Yes button to confirm your choice. The first time the application is started on client computers, regardless of whether the package was assigned or published, the new MSI will be installed.

Along the same lines, if you need to remove installed software, you can right-click the package inside the Group Policy Object Editor and select Remove from the All Tasks menu. You'll be presented with the window shown in Figure 6-34.

Figure 6-34. The Remove Software dialog box

You can choose to either forcibly remove the software immediately, which will uninstall the application no matter what, or simply remove the software from the list of available software, which will allow current installations to continue to use the software, but will prevent new computers from obtaining the software through GP.

Deploying service packs using GP

You also can distribute service packs for Windows 2000, XP, and Windows Server 2003 through the IntelliMirror software installation features of GPOs. Doing so can go a long way toward eliminating a tedious and time-consuming administrative task. You can assign the service pack to computers for mandatory deployment, or you can publish the service pack to a user so that he can choose to install it if his situation warrants it.

If you are assigning the service pack to computers, you simply can point a GPO to the *UPDATE.MSI* file included in the extracted portion of all current service packs from Microsoft. However, if you're publishing the service pack, you'll need to create a ZAP file and then point the software installation GPO to that ZAP file. Again, you can't publish MSI files.

To deploy a service pack using IntelliMirror, follow these steps:

1. Create a distribution share for the service pack and extract its contents there. This process is described in Chapter 2, or you can consult the *readme* files within the service pack distribution file for information.

2. If you are publishing the service pack to users, create a ZAP file pointing to *UPDATE.EXE* inside the folder containing the extracted service pack files.

3. Create a new GPO for the service pack. This isn't required—you can assign the service pack as part of default domain policy or any other level of policy—but it's best to keep software installations to their own GPOs so that changes can be reversed easily.

4. In the Group Policy Object Editor window for that GPO, navigate through Computer Configuration or User Configuration and then choose Software Installation.

5. Right-click Software Installation and choose Package from the New menu.

6. Find the network path to the service pack files and select either *UPDATE.MSI* if you're assigning to computers, or the *UPDATE.ZAP* file you created earlier if you're publishing to users.

7. Choose Assigned or Published in the Deploy Software dialog box.

8. Click OK.

The policy is set and the service pack will either be assigned or published, depending on your choices. Keep in mind that service packs are typically large files, so you should deploy them after considering the effect that process would have on both your network bandwidth and the time it would take to install locally on the client machines. Additionally, I would avoid automatically deploying service packs on your domain controllers. These machines are sensitive beasts that hold the keys to your Active Directory—manually install service packs on these machines one by one and test them to make sure there are no ill effects.

 It also makes sense in environments where you have multiple file servers to use Dfs as a method to store software installation points. Not only do you get fault tolerance through the use of Dfs, but also you can change the location of software installation points through Dfs without needing to change the configuration of the GPO.

Dfs is covered in detail in Chapter 3.

IntelliMirror: Folder Redirection

You can use the folder redirection functionality of GP to change the target location of many folders within a particular user's Windows interface. For example, you can specify custom locations for the Application Data, Desktop, My Documents (including the My Pictures subfolder), and Start Menu folders. Using folder redirection circumvents the nasty problem of roaming profiles: severe network traffic hikes caused by copying large My Documents and Desktop folders to workstations around the network when users log on. You also can back up the share where the folders are redirected using a normal network backup procedure, automatically protecting the contents.

To access the folder redirection functionality, launch the Group Policy Object Editor for a particular GPO and navigate through User Configuration, Windows Settings, and Folder Redirection. In the righthand pane you'll see the four folders you can redirect. Right-click each folder to bring up the Properties window. Figure 6-35 shows this screen.

On the Target tab, you can choose the type of redirection for this policy. For this example, choose the basic method, which simply redirects all users' folders to the same location. Next, enter the target folder at the bottom of the screen under Root Path, and select the option to create a new folder for each user underneath the root path. Then, move to the Settings tab, and choose the following settings.

Grant the user exclusive rights to My Documents
> If this setting is enabled, the user to whom the folder belongs and the local computer have administrative and exclusive rights to the folder, to the exclusion of all other objects. If this setting is disabled, the current permissions on the folder are kept.

Move the contents of My Documents to the new location
> If this setting is enabled, everything in the current My Documents folder will be moved to the new, redirected location. If this option is disabled, nothing will be moved and the new My Documents folder will be empty.

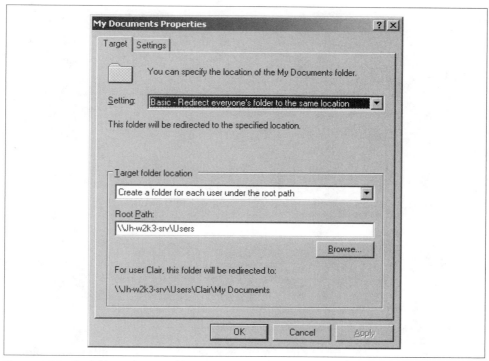

Figure 6-35. The folder redirection interface

Policy removal

> You can adjust the Windows default setting, which is to leave the folder in the redirected location if the redirection policy itself is removed. You also can choose to move the folder back to its initial location.

My Pictures preferences

> The default action for the My Pictures subfolder is to follow the My Documents folder to wherever it resides.

Redirecting folders based on group membership

If you want to redirect some profile folders to different locations based on the different groups to which a user belongs, you can use the Advanced method of redirection inside the redirect policy properties page, on the Target tab. When you select Advanced from the drop-down setting box indicating the type of redirection, click the Add button. The Specify Group and Location box will appear, as shown in Figure 6-36.

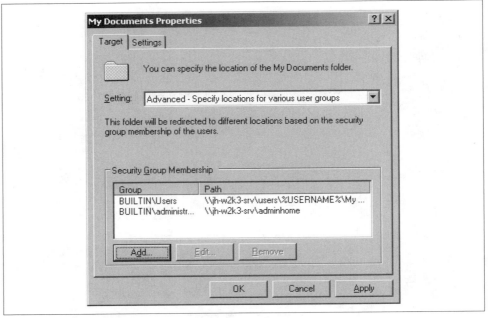

Figure 6-36. Redirecting folders based on group membership

Enter the name of a security group, and then enter the network path to the folders. Always use a UNC path, even if the folders are local to your machine, so that users taking advantage of roaming profiles will see the correct folders in an absolute path and not wrongly translate a local, relative path. Click OK when you're done, and then repeat the process for as many groups as you need.

If your users are creatures of habit, you even can turn on the Offline Files and Folders feature on the share where you've stored the redirected folders. This way, Windows will continue to display and use a customized environment even when the network is down and the share can't be reached.

Removing a redirection policy

It can be a bit difficult to track what happens to redirected folders if you decide to remove a redirection policy. It really depends on the appropriate setting on the Settings tab of the redirected folder's policy properties sheet.

If you've selected to redirect the folder back to the local user profile when the policy is removed, and the option to move the contents of the local folder to a new location is enabled, the folder will return to its original location and the contents of the folder will be copied back to the original location but not deleted from the redirected location. If the option to move the contents of the folder to a new location is disabled, the folder will revert to its original location, but the contents of the folder will not be copied or moved to the original location. This means the user is unable to access the contents of the redirected folder from the special folder's UI within the shell, but using a UNC path, she still can access the redirected folder and retrieve its contents manually. If you've selected to leave the folder in the new location when the policy is removed, the folder and its contents will remain at the redirected location, and the user will have access to it, regardless of whether the option to move the contents of the folder to the new location is enabled or disabled.

 It also is wise to use DFS in conjunction with folder redirection to make background changes to the location of files transparent to both the user and the GPO itself. Dfs is covered in depth in Chapter 3.

Software Restriction Policies

New to Windows Server 2003 are software restriction policies, which allow you to control the execution of certain programs. It's an excellent feature to use on terminal servers or machines serving as a public kiosk, so users are locked into one specific function and can't mess with administrative tools or Internet applications and utilities.

Windows can identify software to either restrict or allow in several different ways. For one, it can use hash rules, which are made by identifying characteristics of files and executables that come with a program and generating an algorithmic hash from them. Hashes are great for identifying specific versions of programs because the hash value would change when different files are used to compute the hash (which is a near certainty with newer version of a program). Certificate rules can identify software via a digital signature, which is a useful method to secure authorized scripts. Windows also can identify software via its path and the Internet zone (inside Internet Explorer) from which a particular piece of software is downloaded. Finally, Windows can create a rule that catches any software not explicitly identified either in a list or by any other rule. (Control for programs executed within a browser is lacking from the GP standpoint, but improvements to Internet Explorer in Windows XP Service Pack 2 pick up a bit of this slack.) Windows matches programs to rules in the order in which they're listed in the software restriction GPO, and if more than one rule identifies the same program, the rule that catches the program most specifically will trump any other rule.

You might be tempted to create a rule that disallows programs from running by default aside from those explicitly placed in an exception list. This seems like an easy way out, but it really can lobotomize a system unless you take great care to create an exception for every Windows executable a user might need, including his application programs. It can also step on the toes of any user logon scripts that might be necessary to create a secure environment. If you decide to go this route, it's imperative that you extensively test any restriction policies and exception lists in a lab. Also, when you do create the actual software restriction GPO, make sure to add the Domain Administrators group to the GPO's ACL and explicitly deny the Apply Group Policy permission to the GPO—this will enable an administrator to reverse the policy and not lock himself out.

Once you're ready to create the policy, follow this procedure:

1. Create a new GPO for each restriction policy. This makes it easier to disable a policy that might be overly restrictive.

2. Choose Computer Configuration or User Configuration to apply the restrictions to machines or users, and then navigate through Windows Settings → Security Settings → Software Restriction Policies.

3. Right-click Software Restriction Policies and choose New Software Restriction Policy from the context menu.

4. Set a default identifier rule: in the left pane, click Security Levels, and then right-click a specific security level and choose Set as Default from the pop-up context menu.

5. Now, create the actual rules that will catch software on which to enforce a restriction. Right-click Additional Rules in the lefthand pane. Choose New Certificate Rule and select the certificate to require or block, New Hash Rule and the file to allow or block, New Internet Zone Rule and the zone from which to allow or block programs, or New Path Rule and the file or registry key to allow or restrict.

6. In the righthand pane, double-click Enforcement. Here, indicate how these restrictions should be enforced. Use of the following options is recommended:

"All software files except libraries" will help you avoid blocking critical system and application function files.

"All users except local administrators" indicates that Windows should enforce the policy for everyone except those in the local administrator group.

7. Next, in the righthand pane, double-click Designated File Types. On this sheet, review and add file extensions associated with applications included in the software restriction policies. The list should be fairly complete, but ensure that any scripting languages you use in your organization have their associated file extensions included.

8. Finally, in the righthand pane, double-click Trusted Publishers. Here you can specify whether normal users, local administrators, or enterprise administrators are allowed to decide what certificates to trust when opening digitally signed programs and controls.

Scripts

Using GP, you can assign scripts to entire domains, organizational units, sites, and groups instead of repeatedly entering the same login script into multiple users' profiles. You can launch four types of scripts using a GPO: logon and logoff scripts, which apply to users, and startup and shutdown scripts, which apply to computers. Startup scripts are executed before logon scripts, and logoff scripts are executed before shutdown scripts.

You can write scripts in any number of languages. Windows Server 2003 is prepared to accept Jscript (*.JS*) and Visual Basic Scripting Edition (*.VBS*) files in addition to batch (*.BAT*), compiled command scripts (*.COM*), and application executables (*.EXE*). Scripts to be run through GP are stored on domain controllers in:

%SystemRoot%\SYSVOL\yourdomain.com\Policies\scripts

with *yourdomain.com* replaced with your fully qualified domain name.

You can assign startup and shutdown scripts in GP using the following procedure:

1. In the Group Policy Object Editor, navigate in the lefthand pane through Computer Configuration, Windows Settings, and Scripts (Startup/Shutdown).

2. In the righthand pane, click Startup and Shutdown to modify the scripts assigned to each.

You can assign logon and logoff scripts in GP using the following procedure:

1. In the Group Policy Object Editor, navigate in the lefthand pane through User Configuration, Windows Settings, and Scripts (Logon/Logoff).

2. In the righthand pane, click Logon and Logoff to modify the scripts assigned to each.

You can further define properties for these scripts under the Computer Configuration/Administrative Templates and User Configuration/Administrative Templates/System/Scripts nodes in the Group Policy Object Editor. For users running scripts, you have the following options (see Figure 6-37):

Run logon scripts synchronously
> Allows you to specify multiple scripts and have them run at the same time rather than in sequence as the default dictates.

Run legacy logon scripts hidden
> Tells Windows not to display the DOS window when using a *.COM* or *.BAT* logon or logoff script

Run logon scripts visible
> Indicates whether the actions and results of the logon script's execution should be displayed to the user

Run logoff scripts visible
> Indicates whether the actions and results of the logoff script's execution should be displayed to the user

For computers running scripts, you can configure the following options (see Figure 6-38):

Run logon scripts synchronously
> Allows you to specify multiple scripts and have them run at the same time, rather than in sequence as the default dictates, on a per-computer rather than a per-user basis

Run startup scripts asynchronously
> Allows to you to specify multiple scripts and have them run in sequence, rather than at the same time, as the default dictates

Run startup scripts visible
> Indicates whether the actions and results of the startup script's execution should be displayed to the user

Run shutdown scripts visible
> Indicates whether the actions and results of the shutdown script's execution should be displayed to the user

Maximum wait time for Group Policy scripts
> Sets a cutoff time for the execution of scripts specified in GP before Windows simply cuts them off and continues with the process at hand

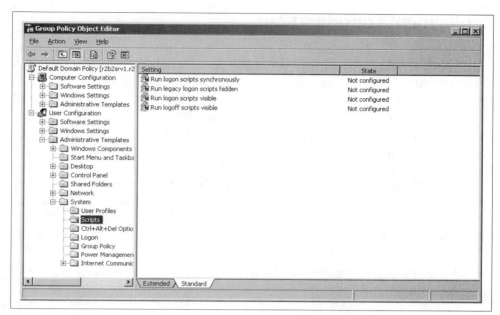

Figure 6-37. Logon and logoff script options

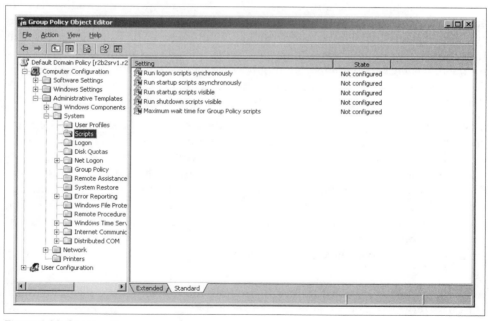

Figure 6-38. Script options

Deployment Considerations

You've learned a lot in this chapter about GP and how it works. Along with the exact mechanisms behind GP's magic, there is also an art to properly deploying it. You must account for several issues when using GP. In this section, I'll take a look at some common issues, and I'll offer suggestions about how best to deploy (in general terms) GPs in your organization.

First, you should keep the Default Domain Policy GPO clear of special exceptions. Remember that this policy is meant only for domain-wide, all-computer settings, and is not meant as a launching point for myriad policies of your own. Don't apply different settings to this policy and expect to use the inheritance blocking and security group filtering capabilities to limit the scope of a setting located here. It's a recipe for a troubleshooting nightmare. Instead, create individual GPOs applied to different containers, where your changes, even if blocked by certain properties of the GPOs, aren't as widespread and sweeping.

Also, try to favor creating several smaller GPOs rather than fewer large GPOs. Although the processing time will suffer, it won't suffer much; the benefit is that a GPO's scope is much easier to identify on certain computers when you have smaller GPOs affecting only a few objects.

Construct a naming structure for your GPOs that is clear and descriptive. Hardly anything is worse, especially during GP troubleshooting, than seeing a GPO called "Office" and not knowing whether it defines who receives Microsoft Office through IntelliMirror, who doesn't get Office, or whether the GPO contains security settings for the office worker computers and not for the factory floor. Of course, you want to document this in a safe place, too. Memories tend to fail us at the most inopportune times.

Design your directory structure intelligently. Make separate OUs to contain objects performing similar roles, and make different OUs for different types of users on your network. Separate client workstations from server computers, and differentiate normal users from power users and administrators through a logical, flowing directory. This makes it much easier to deploy GPOs effectively without a lot of inheritance "black magic." By the same token, however, make sure you have room for exceptions to this scheme—some clients might be servers and some servers might be clients, so it's best to have a plan for these oddballs. And along the same lines, try to create a shallow Active Directory structure to eliminate many levels of policies being applied to nested OUs.

Also, when looking at your directory, assess how you can use groups placed in different OUs to further define GPO scope through the security group filtering function. Placing groups in certain OUs can more clearly identify their function and members and can cut down on processing and application time because policy scope is more refined and less all-inclusive. At the same time, look at how WMI filtering can be used within the existing group and OU structure, and make modifications to streamline the effectiveness of RSoP and policy application functions.

Oh, and don't forget to document your GPOs and their links. What more needs to be said about that?

Troubleshooting Group Policy

The process of diagnosing what is going on with GP and why it's not doing what you want it to do can be infuriating at times. Use the steps recommended in the following sections to assist you in tracking down where your problem lies.

Resolving DNS Problems

DNS problems can plague your network and make it nearly impossible for GPOs to be applied. This problem manifests itself primarily in the requirements for logging on to a domain: without DNS, you still might be able to authenticate to a domain controller, but GPOs simply will break. That's because they require various types of DNS SRV records to know which computer has which service to manage. This is a good place to start looking if GP simply doesn't function.

Analyzing Inheritance

If you are a seasoned network professional, you'll be familiar with the concept of inheritance. This also can be a stumbling block with GP. Beware of a couple of options. The first is the No Override function, which does nothing more than cease the processing of any GPOs under the object on which the option is set. Conversely, also be wary of the Block Inheritance function, which stops the processing of GPOs that reside higher in the GPO processing hierarchy. This is a case of knowing what you set and properly documenting it, but it still can eat up hours upon hours of troubleshooting time.

GPO Distribution and Synchronization

Another issue you might see is that of GP distribution and synchronization. Distribution and synchronization both rely on a versioning system managed internally by Windows that keeps track of unique revisions of the two parts of a GPO: the GPC, which is associated with a particular organizational structure in Active Directory, and the Group Policy Template, which is a file located in the *C:\WINDOWS\SYSVOL\Policies* directory on domain controllers. Usually, these are pushed out from the domain controller that is in the PDC emulator role to all the other domain controllers in a given domain, but if the versioning system is wrong or somehow corrupted, this distribution might not finish completely, or it might not occur at all. Windows comes with a couple of tools that will help you fish out the nonstandard GPOs:

GPOTOOL, REPLMON, and the GPMC, which I covered earlier. Look at logs on the affected domain controllers and see if any errors can help you determine the cause. See the next section for more information on the GP logs.

Along the same lines is actually realizing when GPOs are distributed, retrieved, and applied. Earlier in this chapter I pointed out that the interval Windows Server 2003 uses to push out new GPOs is 90 minutes for workstations and regular member servers, and five minutes for domain controllers. But this is only for new or revised GPOs. If GP has not changed, nothing is pushed unless you manually push it, either from the command line or through another system-wide GPO that pushes policy regardless of whether a change has occurred. So, remember that GP won't necessarily correct local configuration changes unless the domain GPO changes or you force a refresh.

Getting More Detailed Logs

To troubleshoot GPOs more effectively, you can enable verbose logging, which will give you more data about how GPOs are retrieved and applied to a specific object. This does require a registry change on the client you're troubleshooting. Inside a registry editor, navigate to *HKEY_LOCAL_MACHINE\Software\Microsoft\Windows NT\CurrentVersion\Winlogon*. Select the value UserenvDebugLevel, of type REG_DWORD, and change the value of the key to 0x10002. Restart your system to make sure the change takes effect. Now, any GPO activities will be logged to a file called *userenv.log* in the *%SystemRoot%\Debug\Usermode* directory.

You also can enable direct logging to the application event log in much the same way. Inside your favorite registry editor, navigate to *HKEY_LOCAL_MACHINE\Software\Microsoft\Windows NT\CurrentVersion\Diagnostics*. Select the value RunDiagnosticLoggingGroupPolicy, of type DWORD, and change the value on the client you're troubleshooting of the key to 1. Restart to apply your changes and GPO activities will be logged in the application log.

Identifying Client Side Extension GUIDs

To troubleshoot problems pertaining to folder redirection, software installation, and other client-side difficulties, it can be useful to determine the GUID of the client-side extensions (CSEs) on each computer. The CSEs are simply "categories" for GPOs pertaining to different areas of the user interface. You can view all of these in one place inside the registry, under: *HKEY_LOCAL_MACHINE\Software\Microsoft\WindowsNT\CurrentVersion\WinLogon\GPExtensions*.

For reference, some common GUIDs for CSEs are included in Table 6-2. You can use these to match up information that you find in log files.

Table 6-2. Common CSE GUIDs

CSE	GUID
Application Management	C6DC5466-785A-11D2-84D0-00C04FB169F7
Folder Redirection	25537BA6-77A8-11D2-9B6C-0000F8080861
IP Security	E437BC1C-AA7D-11D2-A382-00C04F991E27
Scripts	42B5FAAE-6536-11D2-AE5A-0000F87571E3
Security	827D319E-6EAC-11D2-A4EA-00C04F79F83A

Locating GPT Files on Domain Controllers

For various reasons—for example, to diagnose a problem with available GPOs propagating in your domain to administrative workstations—you might want to inspect the directory structure of the GPTs for certain GPOs. First, you need to retrieve the specific GUID for the policy, and then you can find the folder that contains the hard files associated with that policy.

To actually match a specific policy within Active Directory to the specific GPT files on a domain controller inside its *SYSVOL* share, first you need to locate the GUID on the container in Active Directory where the GPO is applied. Using the GPMC, select the appropriate GPO, and then select the Details tab in the righthand pane. Copy the GUID from there. Then, open Explorer and navigate to *domainname.com*\ *sysvol*, which will open the *SYSVOL* share on the nearest domain controller. Open the *Policies* directory, and then open the folder whose name matches the GUID of the GPO you selected within the GPMC.

Hopefully, you probably will not need to do this very often, as the interface and propagation techniques for GP in Windows Server 2003 are resilient and efficient. But the information is indeed here, just in case.

Other Group Policy Management Tools

It's important to note that there are several paid third-party tools available to assist you in managing GPOs, their scope and effect, and their application, including the following:

FAZAM

> FAZAM tracks changes to GPOs, provides version control for GPOs, allows new or changed GPOs to move into production only after being tested and approved, eliminates the risk of making changes to a live production environment, handles multiple users making simultaneous changes, and enhances GPO administration delegation. However, there are reports that this tool does not work well with Windows 2000 and is fully functional only on Windows Server 2003. FAZAM is available at *http://www2.fullarmor.com/solutions/group*.

NetIQ Group Policy Administrator

NetIQ Group Policy Administrator handles change and release management to keep better track of GPO modification, creation, and deletion, and enhances change simulation and analysis of hypothetical GPO deployments above and beyond what Windows Server 2003 provides. NetIQ Group Policy Administrator is available at *http://www.netiq.com/products/gpa/default.asp*.

Quest ActiveRoles

Quest ActiveRoles allows junior-level administrators to securely make changes to important elements of Active Directory, including GP. Quest ActiveRoles is available at *http://www.quest.com/fastlane/activeroles/*.

Command-Line Utilities

Before we close up the chapter, I wanted to talk about the two most popular command-line management tools for GP. Although I've mentioned both of the utilities in this section earlier in the chapter, I wanted to give each of them a thorough treatment in this section for easier reference and use.

GPUpdate

GPUPDATE will refresh Group Policy settings that are stored either on individual machines or through Active Directory. It's fairly straightforward to use.

To refresh the GP settings on the current workstation, just issue the *GPUPDATE* command itself:

```
gpupdate
```

You can target either computer or user settings using the /target switch. If the switch is omitted, both computer and user settings are refreshed. To refresh computer settings on the current machine:

```
gpupdate /target:computer
```

You can force the refresh of GP settings with the /force switch:

```
gpupdate /target:computer /force
```

Finally, you can force a logoff and/or a reboot with the /logoff and /boot switches, respectively:

```
gpupdate /logoff
gpupdate /boot
```

GPResult

GPRESULT will return a listing of all policies applied to a user and computer, the OUs in which the computer and user are located, the site they are in, and a lot more information. The remote computers need to run Windows XP or Server 2003 for *GPRESULT* to return accurate information.

You can return a simple report using the currently logged on user at your workstation by simply issuing the command itself without any switches:

```
gpresult
```

The following is a sample of the report you'll receive:

```
Microsoft (R) Windows (R) Operating System Group Policy Result tool v2.0
Copyright (C) Microsoft Corp. 1981-2001

Created On 5/9/2005 at 12:15:16 PM


RSOP data for R2TEST\Administrator on R2B2SRV1 : Logging Mode
---------------------------------------------------------------

OS Type:                    Microsoft(R) Windows(R) Server 2003, Enterprise Edition
OS Configuration:           Primary Domain Controller
OS Version:                 5.2.3790
Terminal Server Mode:       Remote Administration
Site Name:                  Default-First-Site-Name
Roaming Profile:
Local Profile:              C:\Documents and Settings\Administrator
Connected over a slow link?: No


COMPUTER SETTINGS
------------------
    CN=R2B2SRV1,OU=Domain Controllers,DC=r2test,DC=corp,DC=haselltech,DC=local
    Last time Group Policy was applied: 5/9/2005 at 12:12:31 PM
    Group Policy was applied from:      r2b2srv1.r2test.corp.haselltech.local
    Group Policy slow link threshold:   500 kbps
    Domain Name:                        R2TEST
    Domain Type:                        Windows 2000

    Applied Group Policy Objects
    -----------------------------
        Default Domain Controllers Policy
        Default Domain Policy

    The following GPOs were not applied because they were filtered out
    ------------------------------------------------------------------
        Local Group Policy
            Filtering:  Not Applied (Empty)

        Turn off System Restore
            Filtering:  Denied (Security)

    The computer is a part of the following security groups
    -------------------------------------------------------
        BUILTIN\Administrators
```

```
    Everyone
    BUILTIN\Pre-Windows 2000 Compatible Access
    BUILTIN\Users
    Windows Authorization Access Group
    NT AUTHORITY\NETWORK
    NT AUTHORITY\Authenticated Users
    This Organization
    R2B2SRV1$
    Domain Controllers
    NT AUTHORITY\ENTERPRISE DOMAIN CONTROLLERS


USER SETTINGS
--------------
    CN=Administrator,CN=Users,DC=r2test,DC=corp,DC=hasselltech,DC=local
    Last time Group Policy was applied: 5/9/2005 at 12:02:32 PM
    Group Policy was applied from:      r2b2srv1.r2test.corp.hasselltech.local
    Group Policy slow link threshold:   500 kbps
    Domain Name:                        R2TEST
    Domain Type:                        Windows 2000

    Applied Group Policy Objects
    ----------------------------
        Default Domain Policy

    The following GPOs were not applied because they were filtered out
    ------------------------------------------------------------------
        Local Group Policy
            Filtering:  Not Applied (Empty)

        Turn off System Restore
            Filtering:  Disabled (GPO)

    The user is a part of the following security groups
    ---------------------------------------------------
        Domain Users
        Everyone
        BUILTIN\Administrators
        BUILTIN\Users
        BUILTIN\Pre-Windows 2000 Compatible Access
        NT AUTHORITY\INTERACTIVE
        NT AUTHORITY\Authenticated Users
        This Organization
        LOCAL
        Domain Admins
        Group Policy Creator Owners
```

To get information for the user jhassell on the remote workstation JH-WNXP-LTP using *GPRESULT*, run:

```
gpresult /s JH-WNXP-LTP /USER jhassell
```

Likewise, to get information for the user ljohnson in the domain R2TEST on the remote workstation 192.168.1.120, run:

```
gpresult /s 192.168.1.120 /USER R2TEST\ljohnson
```

You also can add the /V option to enable verbose logging, which will display detailed information and not just a summary view, or /Z, to enable extended verbose logging (even more details). Use the /SCOPE MACHINE option with /Z to look at only computer configuration policies; similarly, use /SCOPE USER to look at user configuration policies. You can redirect the output of *GPRESULT* to a text file using the standard > DOS redirect operator.

The Last Word

GP offers a flexible, compatible, and centralized way to obtain a consistent security and shell configuration across your organization. Through the use of security policies and IntelliMirror technologies, all discussed in this chapter, you can reduce your administrative burden and achieve nirvana.

In the next chapter, I'll take an in-depth look at the most popular security options within Windows Server 2003 and discuss how to make your machines and network more hardened and secure against threats.

CHAPTER 7

Windows Security and Patch Management

Entire books are devoted to Windows security—how to secure Windows clients, servers, headless machines, terminals, web servers, and more. In this chapter, however, I've chosen to highlight some of the useful tools for managing and for automating security on Windows Server 2003. I've also included some references to security policy settings that most organizations will find helpful.

In the interest of full disclosure, I must say I have not included an exhaustive reference to every security setting to be found in Windows. So many options are unique to different environments that I've found that the best option for this particular book is to give a broad overview of security policy management tools, along with some general settings that can increase security greatly, and then let you explore the Windows security features yourself. For a more in-depth treatment of Windows security, see *Securing Windows Server 2003* (O'Reilly).

Understanding Security Considerations

Most small- and medium-size businesses have several issues to keep in mind when securing their configurations. Some of these might include the following:

- The organization comprises multiple servers, and many have distinct and independent roles. It is difficult to be consistent and strict enough with a security policy when multiple machines are performing different functions, each with its own security requirements.

- Older operating systems and applications are in use. Older programs and systems often use programming and communication techniques that, although secure enough when they were developed, can be exploited easily by today's automated attacks. It can be problematic to ensure these older platforms are supported correctly and are protected adequately from a constant security threat.

- In some markets and professions, you must deal with legal procedures, protections, and consequences. For instance, in the medical profession, the Health

Insurance Portability and Accountability Act (HIPAA) has presented some challenges regarding data privacy and safekeeping that are making life more "interesting" (in the ancient-Chinese-curse sense of the term) for IT personnel. Such legislation and regulation can alter your security policy in specific situations.

- There might be a lack of physical security at the site, which makes moot any computer-based security configurations you plan to make. After all, if someone can make off with your domain controller, all bets are off.

- There might be a lack of security expertise among the technical employees at your company. Constructing and then implementing a security policy is a challenging task that requires patience and knowledge. Lacking these two qualities can make for a painful process. Of course, this chapter will help with the latter.

- There might be threats—internal, external, or even accidental—that could damage your systems or harm the valuable data contained therein. Take a hurricane, for example. What happens when looters grab the backup tape from the regional bank whose walls have collapsed during the storm? What kinds of bad things might those thieves do with that information?

- Finally, the most common scenario, there are limited resources—in terms of both money and labor—to implement secure solutions.

Of course, not all of these conditions apply to all businesses, but it's very likely that each is an obstacle that most organizations run into. In this chapter, I'll provide cost-effective ways to address some of these obstacles.

Principles of Server Security

Server security operates off the CIA principle, which is depicted in Figure 7-1.

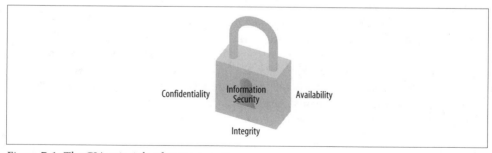

Figure 7-1. The CIA principle of server security

CIA stands for confidentiality, integrity, and availability. *Confidentiality* is the concept that information access is protected and restricted to only those who should have access. *Integrity* is the concept that information is protected from being tampered with or otherwise modified without prior authorization. And *availability* refers to ensuring that access to the information is available at all times, or at least as often as possible.

Keeping the CIA framework in mind, you can take a number of different security approaches at the server level. One of the most successful methods of preserving confidentiality, integrity, and availability is the layered approach, which both reduces an attacker's chance of success and increases his risk of detection. The layered approach comprises seven layers, each with its own methods and mechanisms for protection.

Data level

The data level guards against malicious activity performed on the actual data. Protection at the data level includes ACLs and encrypting file systems. Safeguards at this level cover the confidentiality and integrity levels of the CIA triangle.

Application level

Application-level security protects individual programs from attack. Security at this level can include hardening the applications themselves, installing security patches from the vendors, and activating antivirus software and performing regular scans. Safeguards at this level cover the integrity and availability levels of the CIA triangle.

Host level

Protection at the host level secures the computer and its operating system from attack, which nearly eliminates the potential for attack on the data and application levels. Protection at this level includes hardening the operating system itself (which is the primary focus of this chapter), managing security patches, authentication, authorization, and accounting, and host-based intrusion detection systems. Safeguards at this level cover the integrity and availability levels of the CIA triangle.

Internal network level

The organization's network is the next level, which protects against intruders entering at the perimeter and sniffing traffic, looking for keys to accessing levels higher than this one. Protection at this level includes segmenting your network into subnets, using IP Security (IPSec), and installing network intrusion detection systems. Safeguards at this level include all facets of the CIA triangle: confidentiality, integrity, and availability.

Perimeter level

The perimeter is where the internal network connects to other external networks, including those to other branches of the same corporation and connections to the Internet. Perimeter-level protections might include firewalls and quarantining virtual private network (VPN) and dial-up access. Safeguards at this level include all facets of the CIA triangle: confidentiality, integrity, and availability.

Physical security level

The physical security level involves protecting the real estate in which the business practices. Guards, locks, and tracking devices all comprise protection at this level. Safeguards at this level cover the confidentiality and integrity levels of the CIA triangle.

Policies, procedures, and awareness level

This level involves educating users as to best practices and acceptable and unacceptable methods of dealing with information technology. Safeguards at this level can include all facets of the CIA triangle: confidentiality, integrity, and availability.

Enhancements to Security in Service Pack 1

Windows Server 2003 Service Pack 1 includes not only all the security hotfixes and vulnerability corrections released to date, but also several enhancements to security operations. This particular release is akin to Windows XP's Service Pack 2, both in scope and in the degree of modification of the OS. Most of the security enhancements, including improvements in the user interface, of XP Service Pack 2 have been brought to Windows Server 2003.

The product contains the following fixes to some problems in the release version of Windows Server 2003:

- A correction to the way Certificate Services provides service to Microsoft Outlook clients, resolving the problem where clients are asked multiple times for their passwords.

- The ability to take advantage of the security of the Secure Sockets Layer (SSL) protocol while running IIS 6.0 in kernel mode. (Briefly, components running in kernel mode benefit from increased performance because the processes run closer to the core of the operating system and not in other "layers" of the OS.)

- Improvements to the way errors are logged when accessing the API for the HTTP protocol in Windows Server 2003.

- The Windows Firewall included in Windows Server 2003 SP1 includes support for IPv6.

- Terminal Services connections can take advantage of SSL for server authentication. This is disabled by default, but you can enable it through the GUI. To use this, the server must have an SSL-compatible certificate with a private key, and the client must trust the root of the server's certificate.

- On clean installations, inbound connections are blocked until an administrator acknowledges the status of Automatic Updates and the availability of updates on the Microsoft Update site.
- The Automatic Updates interface, as well as the Windows Firewall, now sports the XP-style interface.

The Security Configuration Wizard

The single most important new feature of Windows Server 2003 Service Pack 1 is the Security Configuration Wizard (SCW), which provides a roles-based way to lock down the surface of your Windows Server 2003 machines. It's a great way to navigate the maze of services found in the operating system and to safely decide which ones can be turned off without affecting functionality for you or your users.

In essence, the SCW uses a backend XML database that includes detailed configuration information about Windows Server 2003 and all of its associated products, including enterprise applications such as Exchange, ISA, Identity Integration Server, and the like. Using this data, the SCW can help you make intelligent decisions about which services need to be running and which can be turned off.

The SCW supports what is in effect an auditing mode, which begins by examining a machine and reporting the roles assigned to it (those roles being the ones assigned through the Manage Your Server Wizard). This is a great way to check the configurations of your servers. You can go a few steps further with the active configuration mode, which allows you to simply tell the wizard what roles should be assigned to the server. The SCW will then configure the server itself, turning services and ports on and off as needed.

The SCW creates files called security policies, which are simply reports of the results the SCW returns when analyzing a machine. The first machine to create a security policy is known as the baseline machine. These security policies can be exported and then applied to any server that matches the configuration of the baseline machine.

Another neat feature is the ability to import and export configurations, which makes it a lot simpler to deploy the same configuration to multiple servers nearly simultaneously. Additionally, you can add information about your custom, homegrown applications to the XML database, (third-party software companies can do likewise), so that the SCW can integrate with non-Microsoft applications as well.

Let's briefly walk through the SCW and see how to install it, open it, and apply a configuration.

Installing the SCW

It's quite simple to add the SCW software to a machine that's already running Windows Server 2003 SP1. To install the SCW, you must be an administrator—either a local administrator or a domain administrator. Follow these steps to complete the installation:

1. Open the Control Panel.
2. Double-click Add/Remove Programs.
3. Select Add/Remove Windows Components.
4. Select the Security Configuration Wizard checkbox, and click Next.
5. Click Finish when prompted.

Creating a Security Policy with the SCW

In this section, I'll describe the process of using the SCW to secure a machine running Windows Server 2003 and IIS 6.0 with a SMTP virtual server and POP3 services enabled. Of course, the results you get when running the SCW might differ depending on what roles your machine is assigned.

First, open the SCW itself. You'll be greeted with the introductory screen of the wizard. Clicking Next, the Configuration Action screen comes up. Here, choose to create a new security policy and then click Next to proceed through the wizard.

The next screen, the Select Server screen, asks you to select the server to analyze. This server will be used as the baseline for this new security policy, meaning that you can apply the file generated from the results of this analysis to any similarly configured machine. This is a great feature because it allows you to apply different security policies via the wizard to any number of machines from a single workstation. For the purposes of this example, choose the current server and then click Next.

The system will trundle for a bit, and then, when the processing is finished, you will be notified. Note that on that screen you can click the View Configuration Database button to be presented with the SCW Viewer application that reports the different roles, running applications, and open ports on that particular machine. This is handy to print and keep with your system configuration records. An example SCW Viewer report is shown in Figure 7-2.

To continue, click Next to view the roles assigned to this machine on the Select Server Roles screen. You'll note that some of the boxes are most likely prepopulated with checkboxes—in these cases, the wizard has detected that you are running some service or application associated with that role. Using the View list box at the top of the screen, you can toggle between seeing the roles currently installed on the machine, the roles not installed on the machine, all roles available, or the roles currently selected. It's a very granular, very thorough view of your system. Click Next to proceed.

The Select Client Features screen appears next. Because most every server also acts like a client in some situations, you'll need to allow the appropriate client services to run on the machine. Things like DNS client service, Active Directory domain membership,

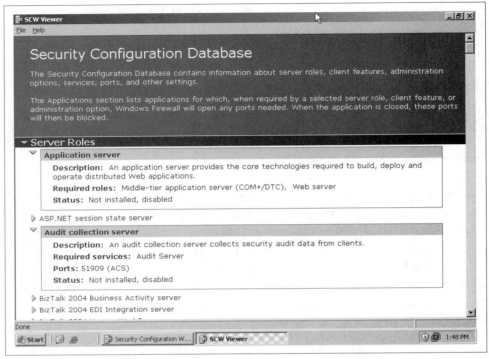

Figure 7-2. A sample SCW Viewer report

and Automatic Updates client software all need to be accounted for within this portion of the wizard. Note that on this screen, you also have the View menu available to customize the display of services and applications. Once you've finished making your selections, click Next.

The next screen, called Select Administration and Other Options, asks you to select and enable other services and open other ports. These are primarily used for remote administration services. Again, you can toggle what you see within the display box, using the View list box. Once your list is correct, click Next.

Next, on the Select Additional Services screen, the wizard lists the services it detected that it doesn't know about by default. You can choose to turn these on or off on this page. Clicking Next, the wizard will then ask you what to do when it finds other services that it doesn't know about. You can choose to either disable those services, or else leave them in their current state and deal with it later. Once you've made your selection, click Next to confirm. On the last screen in the section, the wizard wants you to verify the changes you've outlined in the SCW thus far. Click Next to continue.

The Network Security section allows you to configure ports and applications on a more granular basis than allowed earlier in the wizard. Figure 7-3 shows the first screen of this section, the Open Ports and Approve Applications screen.

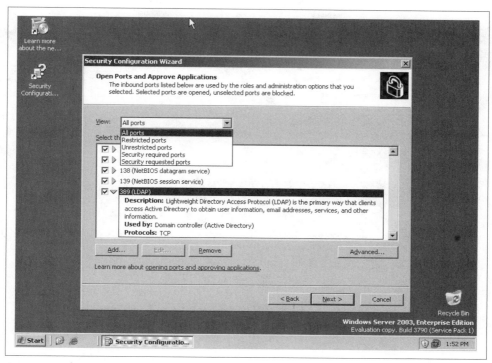

Figure 7-3. The Open Ports and Approve Applications screen

You can select inbound ports to open by clicking the checkbox beside each applicable port entry. If you do not select a port, it will be closed once the policy is applied to the machine. By clicking the Add button, you can add a port or application to the list that isn't already present. And by clicking the Advanced button, you can restrict certain ports on the list to certain subnets or further secure the port using an IPsec filter. Click Next to continue once you've selected the appropriate ports. Confirm the port configuration on the next screen, and then click Next.

The Registry Settings section allows you to set the behavior of certain communications protocols, directly in the Registry, that are used to pass data between machines. These modifications protect against password cracking and man-in-the-middle attacks. On the first screen, Require SMB Security Signatures (shown in Figure 7-4), you need to indicate what level of update the oldest client on your computer currently has installed. You also need to tell the wizard what sort of excess processor capacity you have, which has a direct relation to whether the wizard will recommend that you turn on signing and encryption for communications to and from this computer.

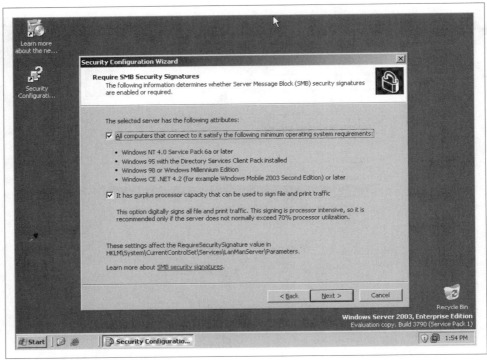

Figure 7-4. The Require SMB Security Signatures screen

The Require LDAP Signing screen is next. Here, simply tell the wizard if your clients all have Windows 2000 Service Pack 3 or later, which will enable LDAP queries to be signed to prevent spoofing a query's source address. The following screen, called Outbound Authentication Methods, allows you to tell the wizard how the computer authenticates itself to remote machines—either via domain or local accounts or simple file-sharing passwords for older, Windows 9x-based clients. You'll then be asked several questions about your selection, each involving the update level of those remote machines. The wizard in this case is simply making sure that the signing and encryption options it integrates into the policy won't break the ability to communicate with any important systems on your network.

At the end of this section, you'll have an opportunity to confirm the changes to the Registry that you want to make. Click Next to continue.

Next, in the Audit Policy section, you have the opportunity to tell the wizard what level of auditing you'd like (you have three choices—none, success auditing only, or complete auditing), and then the wizard will automatically enable and disable certain parts of the auditing system for you. Once you've made your choice of auditing level, you'll be presented with a screen much like Figure 7-5.

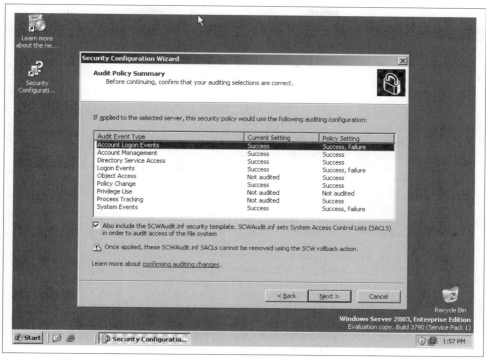

Figure 7-5. The Audit Policy Summary screen

On this screen, you can see how the wizard applied your auditing level preference to the system's various audit-enabled areas: logins to an account, account management, directory service access, logon events, object access, policy change, privilege use, process tracking, and system events. You can see what the machine's current setting is and compare it to the proposed policy's setting. You also have the option to include a security template, *SCWAudit.INF*, which would automatically audit access of the file system.

If you choose to include the *SCWAudit.INF* template, you will not be able to roll back the file system access audit policy. The wizard will warn you of this.

Once you have proceeded through the wizard and answered all the questions, you will be given an opportunity to review the proposed policy in the SCW Viewer applet described a bit earlier in the chapter. Confirm all of your changes, and then select the location to save the policy. You can also elect to apply the policy to the current machine now, or simply save the policy and wait to apply it to this machine or others until a later time.

Keep in mind that the policy itself is simply an XML file, which means that you can make changes directly to the file without necessarily loading the wizard and walking through all of its steps. An excerpt from a sample policy looks like this:

```xml
<?xml version="1.0" encoding="UTF-16" ?>
- <SecurityPolicy Version="1.0">
- <Rules>
- <Rule Name="Microsoft.OS.Services" Version="1.0">
- <Parameters>
- <Parameter Order="1">
  <Service Name="EDI Subsystem" StartupMode="Disabled" />
  <Service Name="ENTSSO" StartupMode="Disabled" />
  <Service Name="Microsoft.BizTalk.KwTpm.StsBizTalkAdapter.StsBizTalkAdapterService"
StartupMode="Disabled" />
  <Service Name="RuleEngineUpdateService" StartupMode="Disabled" />
  <Service Name="ListManager" StartupMode="Disabled" />
  <Service Name="DMLService" StartupMode="Disabled" />
  <Service Name="PredictorService" StartupMode="Disabled" />
  <Service Name="IMAP4Svc" StartupMode="Disabled" />
  <Service Name="RESvc" StartupMode="Disabled" />
  <Service Name="MSExchangeES" StartupMode="Disabled" />
  <Service Name="MSExchangeIS" StartupMode="Disabled" />
  <Service Name="MSExchangeMGMT" StartupMode="Disabled" />
  <Service Name="MSExchangeMTA" StartupMode="Disabled" />
  <Service Name="MSExchangeSA" StartupMode="Disabled" />
  <Service Name="MSExchangeSRS" StartupMode="Disabled" />
  <Service Name="MSPOP3Connector" StartupMode="Disabled" />
  <Service Name="UN2" StartupMode="Disabled" />
  <Service Name="DRDAResync" StartupMode="Disabled" />
  <Service Name="NVAlert" StartupMode="Disabled" />
  <Service Name="NVRunCmd" StartupMode="Disabled" />
  <Service Name="POoo5" StartupMode="Disabled" />
  <Service Name="SnaDdm" StartupMode="Disabled" />
  <Service Name="DDM001" StartupMode="Disabled" />
  <Service Name="DDM999" StartupMode="Disabled" />
  <Service Name="MngAgent" StartupMode="Disabled" />
  <Service Name="MQBridge" StartupMode="Disabled" />
  <Service Name="DDM6DB" StartupMode="Disabled" />
  <Service Name="SnaRpcService" StartupMode="Disabled" />
  <Service Name="SnaBase" StartupMode="Disabled" />
  <Service Name="SnaNetMn" StartupMode="Disabled" />
  <Service Name="SnaPrint" StartupMode="Disabled" />
  <Service Name="SnaServr" StartupMode="Disabled" />
  <Service Name="TN3270" StartupMode="Disabled" />
  <Service Name="TN5250" StartupMode="Disabled" />
  <Service Name="ISACtrl" StartupMode="Disabled" />
  <Service Name="ADAM_ISASTGCTRL" StartupMode="Disabled" />
  <Service Name="Fwsrv" StartupMode="Disabled" />
  <Service Name="ISASched" StartupMode="Disabled" />
  <Service Name="ISASTG" StartupMode="Disabled" />
  <Service Name="MSSQL$MSFW" StartupMode="Disabled" />
  <Service Name="SQLAgent$MSFW" StartupMode="Disabled" />
  <Service Name="MIIServer" StartupMode="Disabled" />
```

```
        <Service Name="MOM" StartupMode="Disabled" />
        <Service Name="SBCore" StartupMode="Disabled" />
   ...
```

As you can see, the SCW is a much-needed addition to Windows Server 2003 and appears at this point to be a worthy effort to help administrators harden their machines.

The rollback feature

If you applied a security policy with SCW that adversely affected some or all of the functionality of the machine, you can roll back the security policy that caused the problem and return the machine to an operational state. However, if you edit an SCW-applied policy in the Local Security Policy MMC after you apply it, the changes can't be rolled back to their preapplication state since the SCW has no way of tracking changes that were made through another interface. The server in question will remain in its current configuration.

For services and registry values, rolling back a policy restores settings that were changed during the configuration process. Windows Firewall and IPsec rollbacks consist of unassigning any SCW policy that is currently in place and reassigning the previous policy that was in place before the SCW policy was applied.

Also keep in mind that if you enabled file system access auditing, that policy cannot be rolled back. However, for most other policies, the rollback feature is a decent insurance policy that helps protect against recoverable mistakes.

 Do not end the Security Configuration Wizard either through Task Manager or by shutting down the machine while it's applying a policy. A policy should instead be rolled back after it has been completely applied to the system.

Best practices

To achieve best results from using the SCW, consider the following:

- Run the SCW on each of your unique role-based servers and save the policies. There's no need to go all-out when you first run the SCW—let it walk you through and help you decide the policies you want to set, and then simply save the file. You can reuse it later on an unlimited number of machines, and saving the file will also give you a chance to learn the XML format the wizard uses and to double-check the settings and changes the wizard wants to apply before actually committing them to production systems.

- Roll out saved policies one by one on the appropriate machines. Once you've tested the policies you created in the previous step, start applying them individually to servers that are performing like roles. Start with your file servers, and then move to domain controllers, Exchange machines, SQL Server boxes, and so on. A controlled but steady deployment is your best bet for success.

- Don't forget to include your existing security templates if necessary. Remember that the SCW has full support for any existing security templates that you may have created There's no need for the SCW to obsolesce this. On the last step of the Create a New Policy portion of the wizard is a button called Include Security Templates that you can click to select the template file to wrap into the manifest of your new policy. Unfortunately, there's not a way to intuitively roll these back once you've applied them.

 I'll cover security templates a bit later in the chapter—just remember the previous point for now.

- Finally, beg your service vendors for updates to their software that support configuration through the SCW since the SCW's XML database is extensible. Do you have third-party services that the SCW doesn't know about? Get in touch with your vendor and demand this support.

Creating and Enforcing Security Policies

If you haven't yet upgraded to Service Pack 1 and are still interested in distributing a comprehensive, consistent security policy to your machines, Windows Server 2003 comes with two basic tools that will help you do just that: security templates and the Security Configuration and Analysis tool. While they aren't as easy to use or as manageable as SCW-based policies, they are certainly as effective. Another bonus point: your investment of time and resources in creating these templates isn't wasted, as you can include them in any future SCW policies that you might create.

In this section, I'll discuss templates, how they're used, and how to create and manage them on your network.

Using Security Policy Templates

Security templates list all possible security attributes and settings for a given system and their associated configurations. By using the Security Templates snap-in, you can easily provision a standard collection of security settings across multiple systems using either remote registry editing or Group Policy. For administrators that have a large number of systems to manage, and for those who provision quite a few systems on a regular basis, security templates can save a lot of time: they can assist with setting up a new machine or rolling out a new organizational security policy to many systems. They're also helpful because you can define multiple templates, since few large organizations have a single security standard for all computers. Security policy templates are a tool your organization can use to implement the three facets of the CIA triangle, which I discussed earlier in the chapter.

You can begin using security templates by loading the Security Templates snap-in:

1. Run `mmc` from the command line to load the MMC in author mode. Author mode allows you to construct new consoles from scratch and add snap-ins to them.

2. From the Console menu, select Add/Remove Snap-in. Then select Add. This opens a dialog box entitled Add Standalone Snap-in.

3. From the list, select Security Templates, click Add, and then click Close.

4. Click OK in the next box to confirm the addition of the snap-in.

You now have the Security Templates snap-in added to a console. From this snap-in, you can expand the Security Templates section in the console tree on the left, and then expand the *C:\Windows\security\templates* folder to view the predefined security templates.

The Security Templates snap-in contains seven configurable areas, which you can display by double-clicking the label in the righthand pane inside the snap-in after selecting a template from the list in the lefthand pane. The areas are shown and described in Table 7-1.

Table 7-1. Template policy areas

Framework area	Description
Account policies	This area applies security configuration to user accounts, including passwords, account lockouts, and Kerberos ticket policies. Password and account lockout policies apply to workstations and servers; Kerberos ticket policies apply only to domain controllers.
Local policies	This area allows you to set auditing and event logging policies, user rights assignments, and registry keys that directly affect system security. It also controls auditing of events, including application actions and security notifications. Note that settings in this area apply to all Windows 2000 or later systems, and not to only a specific kind of system.
Restricted groups	This particularly useful area allows you to define policies regarding a user's membership into security groups that allow elevated privileges. It's simple to define a policy where domain users can never be a member of the local Administrators group; other policies are equally easy.
System services	This area contains startup options for services and access controls on them.
Registry	In this area, you can configure access permissions on specific keys in the registry. In addition, you can audit access and modification of registry entries.
File System	This area allows you to preconfigure access permissions on selected file system directories.
Event Log	In this area, you can specify how the Application, Security, and System event logs fill and rotate and what their maximum size might be. You also can configure who has access to view the logs.

Each template is nothing more than an ASCII text file with a *.INF* extension that contains a list of all settings therein. Looking at the file itself is often a more useful and quicker way to determine applicable settings. For example, the following is a portion of the *HISECWS.INF* file:

```
[Profile Description]
%SCEHiSecWSProfileDescription%
[version]
signature="$CHICAGO$"
revision=1
DriverVer=10/01/2002,5.2.3790.0
[System Access]
;-----------------------------------------------------------------
;Account Policies - Password Policy
;-----------------------------------------------------------------
MinimumPasswordAge = 2
MaximumPasswordAge = 42
MinimumPasswordLength = 8
PasswordComplexity = 1
PasswordHistorySize = 24
ClearTextPassword = 0
LSAAnonymousNameLookup = 0
EnableGuestAccount = 0
;-----------------------------------------------------------------
;Account Policies - Lockout Policy
;-----------------------------------------------------------------
LockoutBadCount = 5
ResetLockoutCount = 30
LockoutDuration = -1
;-----------------------------------------------------------------
;Local Policies - Security Options
;-----------------------------------------------------------------
;DC Only
;ForceLogoffWhenHourExpire = 1
;NewAdministatorName =
;NewGuestName =
;SecureSystemPartition
```

The compatible security template, *COMPATWS.INF*, is meant to allow non-Microsoft certified applications to run on a system without being inhibited by security features. It discerns between ordinary users, who can run only certified Windows applications (those earning the compatibility seal that's usually displayed on the software packaging), and power users, who can run uncertified and potentially problematic software. It also allows a certain subset of registry keys, initialization files, and other folders to be modified by otherwise unprivileged users. However, it's really not the most secure template to use, and I'd advise using another, more secure template (as I describe in a bit) unless you're running into impassable compatibility problems.

The secure security templates—*SECUREWS.INF* for workstations and ordinary servers and *SECUREDC.INF* for domain controllers—are designed to provide a middle-of-the-road level of security. The secure templates offer more stringent password policies, restricted guest access, audit policies that cover most important security events, and increased account lockout policies. However, files, folders, and registry keys and their security settings are not configured with this template because, for the most part, they are configured securely out of the box. For your environment, you might want to modify this to include custom permissions for certain directories and registry keys. You might use this if you have a sensitive application (say, a mortgage loan origination program) that has credit-report data stored locally. You can customize the template to secure this program's data directory by default.

If you are just starting to focus on security within your business, and you have applications that are up-to-date and in their latest release, try using these secure templates. They really batten down the hatches as opposed to the compatibility template, and they're a good place to start when tightening configurations on your network. Be aware that older applications that use insecure methods to communicate over the network might fail, though.

The highly secure template—*HISECWS.INF* for workstations and ordinary servers and *HISECDC.INF* for domain controllers—focuses on securing transmissions between workstations and servers running Windows Server 2003. It also removes the Authenticated Users group (and any other groups for that matter) from the Power Users group on all machines that use this template. Use this template only if you know your applications won't break with the stringent restrictions on network communications.

Finally, the default security template, *SETUP SECURITY.INF* (note the space), restores the default security settings for an initial installation of Windows. You can use this to restore the initial settings for a client computer or regular server if you have misapplied a template or you want to start "from scratch." However, you cannot do this for domain controllers. For more information on this, see:

> *http://www.microsoft.com/resources/documentation/WindowsServ/2003/standard/proddocs/en-us/Default.asp?url=/resources/documentation/windowsserv/2003/standard/proddocs/en-us/sag_SCEdefaultpols.asp*

Creating a custom security template

You might want to make your own customized policy modifications that go above and beyond those made in the templates shipped with Windows Server 2003. Creating a custom security template affords you an easy way to package, deploy, and apply these modifications with a minimum of administrative headaches. Best of all, you can use these templates in conjunction with a utility called the Security Configuration and Analysis Tool (SCA) to assess the overall "hardness," or state of security, of your machines.

To create your own security template, follow these steps:

1. In the Security Templates console, expand Security Templates in the tree pane on the left, and right-click *C:\WINDOWS\security\templates* (this is the default templates folder in the system).

2. Select New Template from the context menu that appears.

Now you can make any policy modifications you want in any one of the policy areas supported by the tool: account policies, local policies, the event log, restricted groups, system services, the registry, and the file system. Your additions, deletions, and other changes are saved in the template immediately.

To take this one step further, you might decide to build on the basic policy settings provided by the templates shipped with Windows Server 2003. In that case, it's quite simple to open one of the default templates, resave it to a different name, and make further modifications to create your own custom template. To do so, just follow these steps:

1. Select an existing template inside the Security Templates console. In this example, I'll use the *securews.inf* file.

2. Right-click the existing template, and click Save as… from the context menu.

3. Give the new template a name, as shown in Figure 7-6.

4. Click OK. The new template is created with the settings from the old basic template.

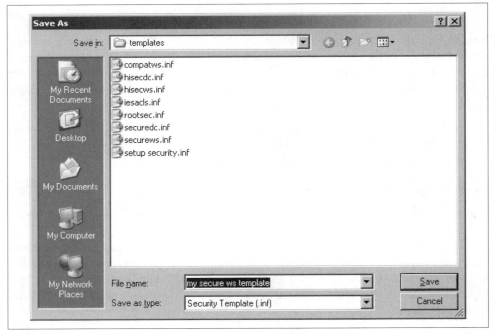

Figure 7-6. Creating a new security template

Importing a template into a GPO

One of the most common ways to apply a security template to many machines is by importing the template into a GPO. The following steps describe how to do it:

1. Select the GPO you want to use inside Group Policy Object Editor.

2. Navigate through Computer Configuration → Windows Settings → Security Settings.

3. Right-click Security Settings and select Import Policy from the context menu.

4. Select the appropriate security template from the list of *.INF* files, and then click OK.

Security Configuration and Analysis

The Security Configuration and Analysis (SCA) MMC snap-in lets you compare systems in their current configuration against settings specified within a security template, or within multiple templates. Using the report generated by that process, you can make wholesale changes to a system's security to bring it in line with an entire template, or you can modify configurations on an item-by-item basis. This is a great tool for initial system rollouts and deployments because you can have one template containing your business's entire security policy that you can apply using a simple tool. You also can save the current system configurations and export them to a template should a rollback be needed.

To begin using the SCA snap-in, you'll need to add it to a console. To do so, follow these steps:

1. Run `mmc` from the command line to load the MMC in author mode. Author mode allows you to construct new consoles from scratch and add snap-ins to them.

2. From the Console menu, select Add/Remove Snap-in. Then select Add. This raises a dialog box entitled Add Standalone Snap-in.

3. From the list, select Security Configuration and Analysis, click Add, and then click Close.

4. Click OK in the next box to confirm the addition of the snap-in.

Creating and using template databases with SCA

SCA uses databases, which have a *.SDB* extension, to store security templates for faster access and data retrieval. You can either create a new template database if this is your first time using SCA, or open an existing SDB file, by doing the following:

1. Right-click Security Configuration and Analysis in the left pane of your console and select Open Database from the context menu.

2. The Open Database dialog box appears. Type a name or select one from the list to open an existing database, or enter a name for a new database.

3. If you enter a new filename, you will be given the option of importing a base security template. Choose either a predefined template that ships with Windows Server 2003 or one that you've modified or customized.

4. Click OK.

Once you've created a database with an initial security template inside it, you can import any number of other templates into it as well. Simply right-click Security Configuration and Analysis, and from the context menu choose Import Template. From there, select the *.INF* file that is the template you want, and click OK. The settings are added to the database.

 In the case of templates whose settings conflict, the settings imported last will apply.

Keep in mind that when you make changes to a security policy from within SCA, those settings are saved to the database and not to a template file that you can import into a GPO or otherwise apply to other systems. You'll need to export any saved settings to another template to use the template in other systems. To do so, right-click Security Configuration and Analysis, and from the context menu choose Export Template. From there, choose a filename with a *.INF* extension for the exported template, and click OK.

Scanning system security

To analyze a system using SCA, right-click Security Configuration and Analysis in the console and select Analyze System Now from the context menu. The Perform Analysis dialog box will appear. Select a filename for the results and accompanying log and click OK.

Two reports will be generated. First, events will be written to a log file to correspond with each success and failure of a component analyzed by SCA. And second, SCA will write the current state of each component to the configuration trees within SCA, as shown in Figure 7-7.

To view the log file, right-click Security Configuration and Analysis in the left pane, then select View Log File. Windows will load the log file into the right pane and will show generally what portions of the computer's security policy don't match up to a certain baseline as set in the database. For a more exact analysis, you'll need to examine the policy tree itself. To do so, expand Security Configuration and Analysis and select one of the seven security areas to consider. Figure 7-8 shows the password policy tree under Account Policies.

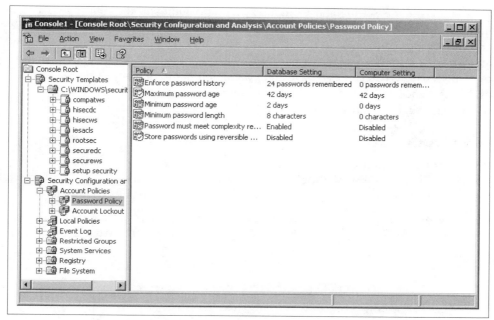

Figure 7-7. Using SCA to compare system status with a baseline

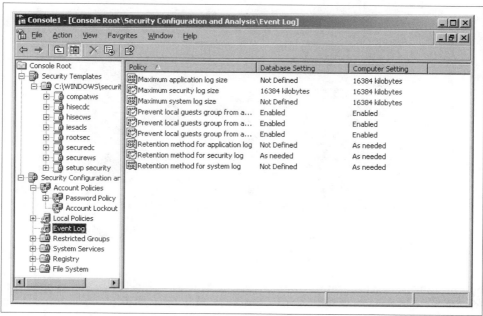

Figure 7-8. Examining the results of an SCA analysis

Note the Database Setting and Computer Setting columns in the right pane. These indicate exactly which configuration options match between the current computer and the settings configured in the SCA database. Settings that agree are preceded by an icon with a small green checkmark. Likewise, settings that disagree are preceded by a small red X. You can also have an exclamation point, depending on the severity of the difference and Windows' ability to comprehend what's going on. Settings that don't appear in the database are not analyzed and thus are not marked.

Correcting system security

If you want to make changes to a computer's security policy as specified by SCA in a wholesale manner, simply right-click Security Configuration and Analysis and select Configure Computer Now. The changes will be updated on the local computer.

If you want to make a change in the database based on an actual configuration object, you can right-click the attribute in question to raise the Analyzed Security Policy Setting dialog box, as shown in Figure 7-9.

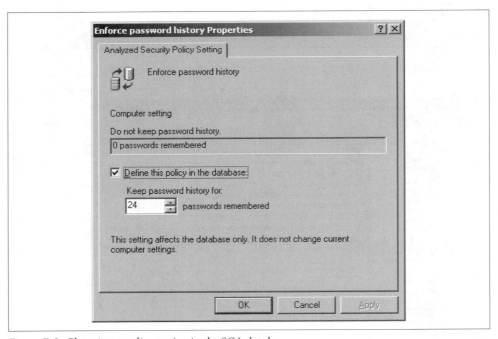

Figure 7-9. Changing a policy setting in the SCA database

Simply adjust the settings in the box and then click OK. The change will be committed to the database, but not to the local computer, and all future computers you examine with that SCA database will be analyzed with that change committed.

Microsoft Baseline Security Analyzer

The Microsoft Baseline Security Analyzer, or MBSA, is an excellent tool that you can use to assess your network and the effects of your security policy. MBSA works by scanning a machine or range of machines for specific policy problems, security updates that aren't present, Microsoft Office updates that aren't present, and other red flags that might indicate security risks. Then it lists all the problems in an easy-to-read report that you can use to rectify each problem.

The latest version as of this writing, Version 2.0, adds a better interface over the previous version with more informative screens and reports, and makes use of both the much-improved Microsoft Update catalog and Windows Update Agent detection engine. MBSA can scan for configuration problems in the following products out of the box:

- Windows NT 4.0
- Windows 2000
- Windows XP
- Windows Server 2003
- IIS
- SQL Server
- Internet Explorer
- Office

MBSA 2.0 also scans for missing security hotfixes in the following products:

- Windows NT 4.0
- Windows 2000
- Windows XP
- Windows Server 2003
- IIS
- SQL Server
- Internet Explorer
- Exchange Server
- Windows Media Player
- Microsoft Data Access Components (MDAC)
- MSXML
- Microsoft Virtual Machine
- Commerce Server
- Content Management Server
- BizTalk Server

- Host Integration Server
- Office

MBSA is an essential tool for ensuring the computers in your organization remain in compliance with any security policy you have in place. You can download the tool from the Microsoft web site at:

http://www.microsoft.com/technet/security/tools/mbsahome.mspx

Using the MBSA

Running a scan on a computer or set of computers using the MBSA is simple. In the following example, I'll assume we're scanning only a single computer. First, open the MBSA program. Then do the following:

1. Click Scan a computer to scan a single computer.
2. The Pick a computer to scan screen appears, as shown in Figure 7-10.

Figure 7-10. Scanning a computer using MBSA

3. Ensure the correct computer name is listed in the Computer Name field. You can also specify an IP address instead. Additionally, enter a name for the resulting report; you can use any of the options listed there—domain, IP address, date and time, or computer name.

4. Select the scope of the scan. You can choose to scan for Windows vulnerabilities, weak passwords, IIS vulnerabilities, SQL vulnerabilities, and security updates. (You can use a Windows Software Update Services [WSUS] server if you want. SUS is covered later in this chapter.)

5. Click Start Scan to begin the scan. The wizard will fetch the latest security update information from the Microsoft site and then commence the scan.

6. When the scan is complete, you'll see the View security report screen. A sample screen is shown in Figure 7-11.

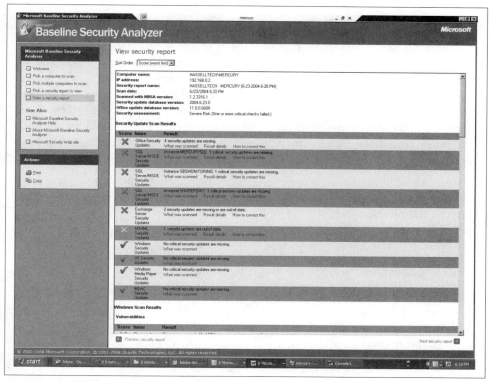

Figure 7-11. MBSA scan results

7. You can see each issue the scan identified, how serious the issue is, and a link to information on how to correct it.

A suggestion about security strategy: I recommend you use the MBSA before applying your security templates or SCW policies to know what issues to address, and then run it once again after your templates or SCW policies have been applied and tested to in order to identify what might have slipped through the cracks.

Locking Down Windows

Multi-user systems are security holes in and of themselves. The simplest systems—those used by only one person—are the easiest ones to secure because there's much less diversity and variance of usage on the part of one person than there is on the part of many. Unfortunately, most of our IT environments require multiple user accounts, so the following section focuses on some prudent ways to lock down

Windows systems, including Windows Server 2003 machines and associated client workstation operating systems.

Password Requirements

Long passwords are more secure, period. As you might suspect, there are more permutations and combinations to try when one is attempting to crack a machine via brute force, and common English words, on which a dictionary attack can be based, are generally shorter than eight characters in length. By the same token, passwords that have not been changed in a long time are also insecure. Although most users grudgingly change their passwords on a regular basis when encouraged by administrators, some accounts—namely the Administrator and Guest accounts—often have the same password for life, which makes them an easy target for attack.

To counter these threats, consider setting some basic requirements for passwords. To set these restrictions on individual workstations and Windows Server 2003 member servers, follow these steps:

1. Open the MMC and navigate to the Local Security Policy snap-in. You usually access this by selecting Start → All Programs → Administrative Tools.

2. Navigate down the tree, through Security Settings, to Account Policies.

3. Click Password Policy.

4. Enable the Passwords must meet complexity requirements setting.

5. Change the Minimum password length to a decent length. I recommend eight characters. (I must note here that I prefer passwords longer than 14 characters, but I predict that you will encounter serious user resistance to such a move.)

6. Change the Maximum password age setting to a conservative setting. I recommend 90 days.

You can accomplish the same through GP if you have a Windows domain by selecting an appropriate GPO and loading the Group Policy Object Editor as I explained in Chapter 6. Keep in mind that changes to the domain password policy will affect all machines within the scope of the GP. The configuration tree within the Group Policy Object Editor remains the same.

One final note on passwords: encourage your users to use passphrases and not just passwords. This is a great way to enforce a 14-character minimum password length while still making it easy for your users to remember their codes. For example, suggest that they use something such as "My dog is named Molly!" as a password instead of something such as "jsx8q6sv8qtr3r." Tell your users to type their passwords in the password entry box as though they were typing into Microsoft Word or another common word processing program. Windows can accept it, and your users are more likely to remember it.

Account Lockout Policies

Three old-fashioned methods of gaining unauthorized access to a system are to attempt authentication using the following:

- A well-known username (e.g., administrator)
- A username not known but derived logically (e.g., admin)
- A different password for the username on each attempt, repeating as often as possible

Windows can thwart these styles of attack using an account lockout policy, which will disable an account for a specified period after a certain number of unsuccessful logon attempts.

To set the account lockout policy, follow these steps:

1. Open the MMC and load the Group Policy Object Editor for an appropriate GPO, or navigate to the Local Security Policy snap-in.
2. Navigate down the tree, through Security Settings, to Account Policies.
3. Click Account Lockout Policy.
4. Set the Account lockout threshold to a reasonably small number. I recommend three bad login attempts.
5. Set both the Account lockout duration and the Reset account lockout after options to 15 minutes. This setting resists attack while not seriously imposing on users who just suffer from "typo syndrome."

 As with password policy, you can configure account lockout policy at the local computer or domain level. However, because the password policies are domain dependent, the "local" level is in affect only when the computer is not logged onto the domain.

Local Options

In addition to securing local accounts, the newer Windows platforms give you the ability to lock down certain rights and configurations on the local computer in addition to any domain security policy that might be configured. Several of the available options do little to thwart attacks, so in this section I'll cover the six most effective changes you can make to your local security policy.

You can enable all of the hardening suggestions in this section through the Security Options section of the Local Security Policy snap-in to the MMC. You usually can find this snap-in under Start, All Programs, and Administrative Tools. To get to the appropriate section, navigate the snap-in tree by selecting Computer Configuration, Windows Settings, Security Settings, and Local Policies. Then click Security Options, and the different configuration switches will appear in the righthand pane.

The instructions in this section assume that you have already loaded the snap-in and navigated to the appropriate section.

Anonymous access

Windows allows access by an anonymous user to many shares and files using a null user account; this is a security hazard, of course. You still can enable anonymous access to files and directories by explicitly granting rights to the ANONYMOUS USER account in Windows inside the appropriate ACL. This setting merely disables that access by default, so you know exactly where connections are being made.

To fix this hazard, set Additional Restrictions for Anonymous Connections to No access without explicit anonymous permissions.

Shutdown without logon

Windows 2000 and Windows XP Professional machines come in a default configuration that allows you to shut down the system using the Shutdown... button on the logon screen, so you might be familiar with this feature. However, Windows 2000 Server and Windows Server 2003 machines disable this out of the box. Despite the convenience factor that this feature affords, it's best to leave rebooting a machine to administrators.

Change Allow system to shut down without having to log on to Disabled to secure this.

Automatic logoff

Some users log on to the network and then don't log off for months. This is a prominent security hole, as when that user leaves her desk, she still is authenticated to the network with her credentials. Malicious people can use this to do destructive things: delete and transfer files, plant a "root kit" or backdoor program, or change passwords.

You can make automatic logoff work in two ways: first, each valid user needs to have a time when she is not permitted to log on. This can be sometime in the early morning, perhaps 3:00 to 3:30 a.m. Then, a change to the local security policy needs to be made so that when the user's logon time expires, she is not permitted to log on.

To set up a logon time restriction on a domain controller for an Active Directory-enabled domain, follow these steps:

1. Go to the Active Directory Users and Computers snap-in.
2. Expand the icon for your domain and click the Users container.
3. Right-click a user and select Properties.
4. Click the Account tab, and then click the Logon Hours... button.

5. Select the appropriate region of time in the calendar block, and click the radio buttons to the right to either permit or deny logons during that time.

6. Click OK, and then OK once more to exit the user property sheet.

This option is available only for members of an Active Directory domain.

Now, make the change to the computer's local security policy. Inside the Local Computer Policy snap-in, change Automatically log off users when logon time expires to Enabled. If you do not have a domain, instead change Automatically log off users when logon time expires (local) to Enabled. This will work even if users have locked their workstations.

Digitally signing communication

It's a good idea these days for a computer to authenticate itself to other computers during a communication. Otherwise, a technique called "spoofing" can be used, and a cracker's computer can pose as the remote end of a connection and receive potentially sensitive information. You can prevent this by using digital signatures. However, these are not pervasive; Windows compensates for this limited use by providing two options in the local policy: require it when possible, or require it, period.

I recommend requiring the signatures when possible on both ends of a connection (the RPC protocol refers to the requesting end as the "client" and the responding end as the "server," regardless of the systems' usual roles). Unsigned transmissions should occur only when signatures are not available, supported, or possible.

Be aware that this setting probably will break communications between Windows Server 2003 machines and older, less secure client operating systems, including Windows 95, Windows 98, and Windows ME. The SCW will set this policy for you and warn you of this.

To require digitally signed communication when possible, change "Digitally sign client communication (when possible)" to Enabled and "Digitally sign server communication (when possible)" to Enabled.

Requiring the three-keystroke salute at logon

The logon screen is one of the most trusted aspects of a computer to a normal user. He trusts it enough that he gives his password and username, and then the computer trusts him, too, if all of that is correct and verified. A cracker can take advantage of this mutual trust by writing a program that runs as a system service—in other words, it doesn't need user privileges. The program will mimic the logon box, grab the user's input, and do something with it such as email the password to the cracker, save the credentials to a backdoor program data file, or any number of other nefarious things. However, pressing Ctrl-Alt-Del brings Windows to attention, and you get the authentic Windows logon and not a shell of one that a cracker creates. This easy step makes your system much more secure.

To require this keystroke to begin, change Disable CTRL+ALT+Delete requirement for logon to Disabled. (Yes, that's right. Microsoft uses some questionable terminology.)

Last username display

By default, Windows displays the username of the last successfully authenticated person to use that particular system on the logon screen. This is giving away needless information, although some of your users are probably accustomed to it.

To disable the last username from being displayed, change the "Do not display last user name in logon screen" setting to Enabled.

Password expiration prompt

Earlier in this chapter, I discussed setting password policies to prevent brute force attacks. Of course, changing passwords is a problem for some users who'd rather not be bothered with IS minutiae and simply would like to use their computers to be productive. With this policy setting, you can tell the system to automatically remind a user when his or her password will expire and prompt him or her to change it. Setting this value to 14 days gives a user ample opportunity to change their password because that is in excess of most scheduled vacations and business trips.

To enable the password expiration prompt, change the Prompt user to change password before expiration setting to 14 days at minimum.

Network Options Via Group Policy

Windows Server 2003 and GP allow you to configure security options that reside inside GPOs that will apply to groups of computers. GP can manage security settings throughout an Active Directory environment in seven areas. They are shown in Table 7-2.

Table 7-2. GP areas and descriptions

Area	Description
Account area	This area applies security configuration to user accounts, including passwords, account lockouts, and Kerberos ticket policies. Password and account lockout policies apply to workstations and servers; Kerberos ticket policies apply only to domain controllers.
Local policies	This area allows you to set auditing and event logging policies, user rights assignments, and registry keys that directly affect system security. Settings in this area apply to all Windows 2000 or later systems.

Table 7-2. GP areas and descriptions (continued)

Area	Description
Restricted groups	This particularly useful group allows you to define policies regarding a user's membership into security groups that allow elevated privileges. It's simple to define a policy where domain users can never be a member of the local Administrators group; other policies are equally easy.
System services	Here you can set startup options for services and access controls on them.
Registry	In this area, you can configure access permissions on specific keys in the registry.
Public key policies	Here you can establish settings for encrypted recovery agents for the Windows EFS, certificate authorities for a specific Windows domain, trusted certificate authorities, and other public cryptography options.
IPSec policies on Active Directory	This area allows you to define IPSec configurations for any given unit in your Active Directory.

Viewing the default domain policy

When you install Windows Server 2003, a default domain security policy is created. The default domain security policy is simply a set of configurations that apply certain security settings to all members of the domain: these can include security settings for displaying the username of the last user that logged on to a system, how long a password should be, whether workstations should digitally sign transmissions to and from a server, and so on. It's a simple task to use this default policy as a base and customize settings based on your individual implementation. Let's look at this default policy first, and then work through customizing it.

To view the default domain security policy, follow these steps:

1. Open the Active Directory Users and Computers snap-in.

2. Expand the domain tree corresponding to your domain's name in the left pane.

3. Right-click the domain name and select Properties.

4. Click the Group Policy tab, select Default Domain Policy in the details box, and then click the Edit button. Windows opens the Group Policy Object Editor window.

5. To view each default domain policy, drill down through Computer Configuration, Windows Settings, and Security Settings, and click Account Policies.

6. Look at the right pane. You'll see Password Policy, Account Lockout Policy, and Kerberos Policy. By clicking each, you can view or change their default configuration.

Figure 7-12 shows the default domain policy on a standard, out-of-the-box installation of Windows Server 2003.

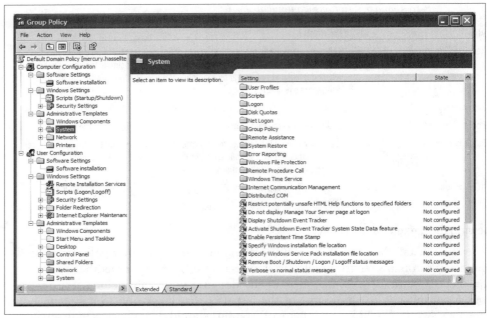

Figure 7-12. Default domain policy in Windows Server 2003

Viewing the default domain controller security policies

The default domain controller security policy, like the default domain security policy, applies a common configuration to a group of computers, but this time the focus is on only domain controllers. Domain controllers often have special security considerations that ought to be addressed separately, and this default policy does that. You will need to use the Group Policy Object Editor MMC snap-in to look at the default security policy on the Domain Controllers organizational unit. To do that, follow these steps:

1. Load the snap-in as described a bit earlier in the chapter. Ensure that in step 4, you selected the Domain Controllers.yourdomain.com object.

2. In the left pane, drill down through Computer Configuration, Windows Settings, and Security Settings.

3. Click Account Policies. In the right pane, you'll see the possible security options for this organizational unit.

Figure 7-13 shows the default domain controller security policy on a standard, out-of-the-box installation of Windows Server 2003.

There is a special way in which account policies are distributed to domain controllers which deserves comment. All domain controllers in a specific domain will apply security policies established at the domain level regardless of where the actual computer

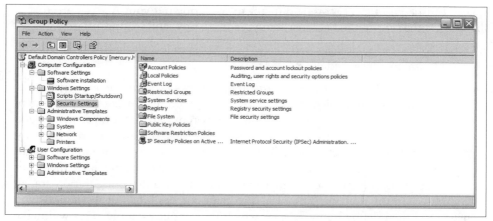

Figure 7-13. Default domain controller security policy in Windows Server 2003

object for that domain controller resides in Active Directory. This helps to ensure that consistent account policies apply to any domain account. All other policies are applied at the normal hierarchical level, both to domain controllers and to other workstations and servers in the domain. Only domain controllers are affected by this special exception. This is just a tip to remember when you're planning account policy distribution among your organizational units.

Viewing a domain controller's effective security policy

To view the effective security policy from a domain controller, complete the steps explained next.

1. Choose Start, click Run, and type **GPEdit.msc**. The Group Policy Object Editor will open.

2. In the left pane, drill down through Computer Configuration → Windows Settings → Security Settings, and click Local Policies.

Now you can view the domain controller's effective security policy. When you're finished, close the Group Policy/Local Computer Policy snap-in. (When prompted to save console settings, click No, unless you've done something you want to hold on to.)

At this point, you have all the tools you need to begin pushing automated security configurations to clients running Windows 2000 and later. Do note that all settings covered in this book, unless noted at the time each is presented, are fair game for distribution under GP.

Final words: organizing policy layout

With power comes complexity, and GP is no exception. Windows administrators have squandered away many hours of their lives on basic GP troubleshooting. Answers to quandaries such as, "Why isn't this policy in effect on this system?" or "I thought I turned *off* IPSec!" can be difficult to track down if your Active Directory is full of GPOs that are applied inconsistently, redundantly, and inappropriately.

To curtail your security policies and make them easier to locate, disable, change, and apply, try to follow these guidelines:

Organize your policies logically and define boundaries to contain them. Although your Active Directory might be organized by geographic location, your system management needs might revolve around a different paradigm: for instance, you might need IPSec for all company executives' laptops, but all of them might not be in your New York office. Or all middle managers in your corporation might require a customized version of Internet Explorer that doesn't lock them out from accessing the Internet, which might be the default configuration for all computers in the domain. The idea is to map out the kinds of restrictions you need, and then define boundaries to which those policies apply. This will make it easier to apply them to the target users and computers even if the geographical and managerial boundaries do not match.

Inside those boundaries configure policies that represent common values in your organization. Do you usually configure workstations in your finance department to lock a computer after three unsuccessful logon attempts? Does a particular domain in your forest need additional desktop restrictions—should they not be allowed to run the Control Panel, for instance? Change their wallpaper? Install software on their own? These are the kinds of policy sets that likely sound familiar. Group these together and create GPOs for each of these like sets of policy settings.

Configure organizational units inside Active Directory that contain machines grouped according to similar roles or functions within an organization. This gets further into the granularity of your security policies. For example, Windows comes by default with domain controllers residing in a separate organizational unit in Active Directory. You might consider putting desktops, laptops, and servers into their own organizational units, which makes it easier to apply policies, such as requiring use of the EFS, only to laptops.

Now I'll present an understatement: it can require some work to configure GP correctly and effectively. The most difficult parts of the process are planning and laying out the policy settings; Windows takes care of the actual deployment to client computers, which is one of the features that makes GP a compelling management tool. This ease of deployment is a double-edged sword, however: it is equally simple to misconfigure an ACL or change a setting (anybody who has played with the "require signed communications" settings knows this all too well) and wreak utter havoc on your domain. The process also is made more difficult by the lack of an API, so you can't write simple automation programs to help you out. You have to go the long way.

Even more difficult sometimes is getting the big picture. That is to say, it is hard to see how your Active Directory layout and structure—which logically and traditionally have likely mimicked your organization's hierarchical personnel structure—can co-exist with GPOs, which seem to cross hierarchy boundaries and rely on other scopes of application. With careful planning, however, GP can overlay your existing directory structure and complement it with its own management boundaries.

 GP configuration, structure, and operation are covered in detail in Chapter 6.

Using Auditing and the Event Log

Keeping track of what your system is doing is one of the most important, but tedious, processes of good IT security management. In this section, I'll look at the tools to audit events that happen on your system and the utilities used to view them.

Auditing controls and properties are modified through GPOs in Windows 2000, Windows XP, and Windows Server 2003. Assuming your computer is participating in an Active Directory domain, you can find the domain auditing policy inside the Default Domain Policy, in the Computer Configuration → Windows Settings → Security Settings → Local Policies → Audit Policies tree. Otherwise, you can view the Local Security Policy through the Administrative Tools applet in the Control Panel.

The settings for each GPO indicate on what type of events and on what type of result a log entry will be written. Here are the options for auditing policies:

Audit account logon events
   Writes an entry when domain users authenticate against a domain controller.

Audit account management
   Indicates when user accounts are added, modified, or deleted

Audit directory service access
   Audits when queries and other communications with Active Directory are made

Audit logon events
   Writes an entry when local users access a resource on a particular computer.

Audit object access
   Indicates when certain files, folders, or other system objects are opened, closed, or otherwise "touched"

Audit policy change
   Audits when local policies (such as the Local Security Policy) and their associated objects are changed

Audit privilege use

> Writes an entry when users make use of privileges assigned to them (such as "Take Ownership")

Audit process tracking

> Tracks program activation, when programs close, and other events that programs cause

Audit system events

> Audits when a user restarts a computer or when events are written to the security log or otherwise affect system security

You can configure individual objects to be audited by editing the system access control list (SACL) for any given object, which is much like assigning permissions, except it is indicating to Windows on what type of access an event log entry should be writing. You can access the SACL for an object by clicking the Advanced button on the Security tab of the object's properties sheet. On the Auditing tab, you can click Add to include new auditing events for an object, or click View/Edit to modify an existing auditing event. Figure 7-14 shows the SACL for an object.

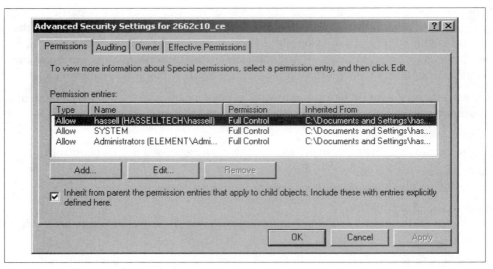

Figure 7-14. The SACL for an object

 Only NTFS files and folders can be audited. FAT partitions do not contain the necessary permission information to support auditing events.

Recommended Items to Audit

You'll want to take particular note of the following items from your event logs:

- Logon and logoff events are tracked by Audit account logon events and Audit logon events setting, which can indicate repeated logon failures and point to a particular user account that is being used for an attack.
- Account management is tracked by the Audit account management setting, which indicates users who have tried to use or used their granted user and computer administration power.
- Startup and shutdown events are tracked by the Audit system event setting, which shows that a user has tried to shut down a system as well as what services might not have started up properly upon reboot.
- Policy changes are tracked by the Audit policy change setting, which can indicate users tampering with security settings.
- Privilege use events are tracked by the Audit privilege use setting, which can show attempts to change permissions to certain objects.

You should be aware of a couple of things. First, too much auditing consumes large amounts of resources. Entries will be written every time a user moves a mouse (OK, that's an exaggeration, but not much of one). Second, too much auditing also tends to be overwhelming, and because auditing in general will do nothing for you if you don't view the audit entries, can you see a loop forming? You don't want to look at audits because there is so much to wade through, so effectively you're wasting resources and gaining no security advantage from it. Be aware.

Event Logs

Similar to auditing policies, the policies for configuring the event logs are found inside the Default Domain Policy, in the Computer Configuration → Windows Settings → Security Settings → Local Policies → Event Log tree. Here are the options for event log policies:

Maximum application log size
Sets the maximum size the log is allowed to reach before the oldest events in the log will be purged.

Maximum security log size
Does the same as the previous item but pertains to the security log.

Maximum system log size
Does the same as the previous two items but pertains to the system log.

Restrict guest access to application log
Disallows access to the application log from users logged onto the Guest account.

Restrict guest access to security log
> Disallows access to the security log from users logged onto the Guest account.

Restrict guess access to system log
> Disallows access to the system log from users logged onto the Guest account.

Retain application log
> Specifies whether to overwrite events or save them when the application log file reaches the maximum size.

Retain security log
> Specifies whether to overwrite events or save them when the security log file reaches the maximum size.

Retain system log
> Specifies whether to overwrite events or save them when the system log file reaches the maximum size.

Retention method for application log
> Specifies whether Windows should overwrite old application log events as it sees fit or only those older than *n* days; you also can choose to simply not overwrite files and clear the logs manually.

Retention method for security log
> Specifies whether Windows should overwrite old security log events as it sees fit or only those older than *n* days; you also can choose to simply not overwrite files and clear the logs manually.

Retention method for system log
> Specifies whether Windows should overwrite old system log events as it sees fit or only those older than *n* days; you also can choose to simply not overwrite files and clear the logs manually.

Shut down the computer when the security audit log is full
> Shuts off the computer until an administrator can clear the security log and new events can be written.

To configure the event logs locally on a computer that does not participate in a domain, load the Event Viewer console (which is within the Control Panel and Administrative Tools) and then right-click each log in the left pane. You can set the log size options on this screen, including the maximum size and the actions Windows should take when that limit is reached.

The Event Viewer

The Event Viewer allows you to look at events in three event logs by default. Other applications can add their own logs into the Event Viewer console. Figure 7-15 shows a typical Event Viewer console, with the three default logs.

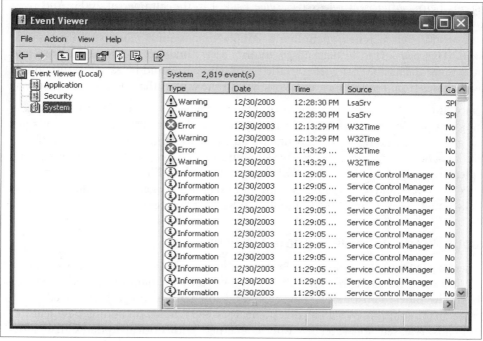

Figure 7-15. An Event Viewer console

First, the security log displays successes and failures with regard to privilege use, and classifies them into categories such as object access, account logon, policy change, privilege use, directory service access, and account management. The remaining event logs have three different classes of entries: errors, informational events, and warnings. The application log consists of information reported from programs running on the system. The system log consists of events and exceptions thrown by Windows itself. All users can see the system and application logs, but only members of the Administrators group can see the security log.

To clear all events from your Event Viewer console, choose Clear All Events from the Action menu.

Windows Server Update Services

The bane of every administrator's existence. The pain in the rear of system management. That never-ceasing headache that pounds at CIOs everywhere. You might have guessed by now that I'm speaking of patch management.

And I use the term "management" loosely. In 2003, there were more than 40 updates that needed to be applied to a new Dell computer running Windows XP. There were over 20 updates for Windows 2000 Service Pack 3 that needed to be applied to new systems before Microsoft released Service Pack 4 in the summer of 2003. And right now, machines running Windows XP Service Pack 2—released in summer of 2004—need around ten patches, including a couple that require reboots—to get up to speed. This ever-growing hairball of security fixes, bug fixes, critical updates, and patch revisions has almost gotten to the point where it would be easier to disconnect all machines from the Internet and work with stone tablets than deploy new systems.

It shouldn't be that way, and Microsoft realizes that. They've come out with a tool that's not perfect, that has limited functionality, and isn't very flexible. But it's got two great things going for it: It's timely, and it works fairly well. That product is Windows Server Update Services (WSUS), and this chapter will focus on installing, implementing, and administering WSUS on your network. I'll also cover a comparison between WSUS and a flagship network and system-management product (Systems Management Server), and how to monitor WSUS for failures.

About Windows Server Update Services

As part of its Strategic Technology Protection Program, Microsoft sought to leverage its Windows Update technology—the software that runs the universal update site for all but the oldest versions of Windows—and integrate it into a LAN-based patch management solution. WSUS at this point does NOT focus on adding new features to already released software; it's only concerned with critical updates that allow administrators to somewhat easily deploy critical updates to servers running Windows 2000 or Windows Server 2003, and desktop computers running Windows 2000 Professional or Windows XP Professional. It's designed to work especially in networks with an Active Directory implementation, but it will function without one.

Installing WSUS on your network requires at least one server, running either Windows 2000 Server or Windows Server 2003 (for the purposes of this chapter, I'll assume you're using the latter) connected to the Internet running the actual server component of WSUS. This server needs, for all practical purposes, at least a 1 GHz processor and 512 MB of RAM. This machine acts as a local version of the public Windows Update site, which contains critical updates and service packs for all supported operating systems. This server synchronizes with the public Windows Update site on a schedule that the corporate administrator selects. That administrator then approves or rejects the availability of certain updates on the WSUS server. You can also have multiple WSUS servers on an intranet and configure which client machines are directed to specific WSUS servers for updates.

On the client side, WSUS also requires the Automatic Updates feature of Windows 2000 Service Pack 3 and higher, Windows XP Professional at any revision level, or any edition of Windows Server 2003. Directed by a variety of methods, the client computers that are running this Automatic Updates feature are sent to the local network's WSUS server on a set schedule to download updates appropriate to their machines. The WSUS server will analyze the operating system, service-pack level, and any currently installed updates, and push only those updates that are both needed AND that have been approved by the administrator beforehand.

Using Windows Server Update Services: On the Server Side

There are a few phases to the WSUS installation. First, you should download and install the software, which includes the Windows SQL Server 2000 Desktop Engine (WMSDE):

1. Go to the WSUS web site at *http://go.microsoft.com/fwlink/?LinkId=24384*.
2. Download *WSUSSetup.exe* to a folder on the server where you want to install the product.
3. Double-click the file using the server on which you want to install or upgrade WSUS.
4. Click Next on the Welcome screen to continue.
5. Decide whether to accept or reject the license agreement, and click Next.
6. The Select Update Source screen appears. Here, you can choose where the client computers will get their updates. You can either allow the WSUS server to store update content locally by clicking the Store updates locally checkbox and selecting a location on your filesystem, or direct clients to the Internet-based Microsoft Update site by leaving it unchecked. Click Next to continue.
7. The Database Options page is next, where you select the software used to store information about the updates that are offered. Select the default option of using WSMDE, which the wizard will install for you, unless you have an available instance of a SQL Server 2000 database to use instead. Click Next.
8. Next comes the Web Site Selection page, where you specify the web site that WSUS will use. Be careful to note the two important addresses presented on this page: the URL that clients will use to get updates, and the URL for the administrative console. If you're installing WSUS on a computer that already has a web site running on port 80, you may need to create a custom web site running on a different port. You can use IIS Manager (in the Administrative Tools area of the Start menu) to accomplish this. Click Next to continue.
9. You should now see the Mirror Update Settings page, where you specify which management role this WSUS server should serve. For the purposes of this demonstration, you're installing the first WSUS server on your network, so you can skip this screen. (It comes in handy when you have multiple WSUS servers that should contain identical updates and approval records within their databases.) Click Next to continue.
10. On the Ready to Install Windows Server Update Services screen, confirm your selections, and then click Next.

The next step is to make sure that your WSUS server can receive update information from the Internet. If you restrict Internet access via your firewall to certain domains, be sure to add the following domains to your exceptions list:

- *http://windowsupdate.microsoft.com*
- *http://*.windowsupdate.microsoft.com*
- *https://*.windowsupdate.microsoft.com*
- *http://*.update.microsoft.com*
- *https://*.update.microsoft.com*
- *http://*.windowsupdate.com*
- *http://download.windowsupdate.com*
- *http://download.microsoft.com*
- *http://*.download.windowsupdate.com*
- *http://wustat.windows.com*
- *http://ntservicepack.microsoft.com*

The administrative console

To open the administrative console for WSUS, open the Start menu, point to All Programs, Administrative tools, and then select Microsoft Windows Server Update Services. You can also open this console from your web browser by surfing to *http://WSUSServerName/WSUSAdmin*. You can also navigate through Start, All Programs, Administrative Tools, and click Windows Software Update Services. You'll see something much like that in Figure 7-16.

You may need to set a proxy server configuration if you use such a system to connect to the Internet. To do so, on the console toolbar, select Options, and then click Synchronization Options. Select the Use a proxy server when synchronizing checkbox in the Proxy server box, and then enter the appropriate name and port number. (This form is used in much the same way that you would Internet Explorer's options.) You can also enter credentials should they be needed by clicking the Use user credentials to connect to the proxy server box. To apply these settings, click Save settings under Tasks, and then click OK to confirm this action.

Synchronizing content

When you start the content synchronization process, which actually retrieves the updates for you to configure and deploy, the WSUS server goes out to either the public Windows Update servers or another local WSUS server (as configured in the "Mirror Update Settings" section) and downloads the entire library of available critical updates and service packs for each language you've configured. This initial synchronization usually results in about 150 MB worth of data being transferred for just

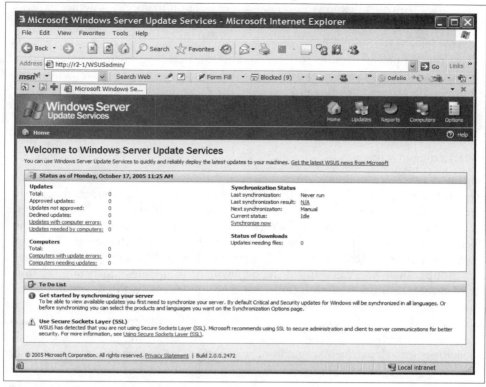

Figure 7-16. The WSUS administrative screen

English updates, or close to 600 MB of data for updates in every localization. After that, WSUS is able to determine if any new updates have been released since the last time you synchronized.

To synchronize content, surf to the WSUS administrative web site, and then do the following:

1. On the toolbar, click Options.

2. Click the Synchronize Now button under Tasks to begin the transfer.

There are also some advanced synchronization options that you can set, which can all be found under Options on the toolbar and Synchronization Options. Under Update Files and Languages, click Advanced, then read the warning and click OK. Then, select your preferred option or options:

- Use the "Download updates to this server only when updates are approved" option to determine if updates should be fetched from Microsoft Update during the synchronization process itself, or if updates should be downloaded only when an update is approved. This is a great bandwidth management feature.

- Use the "Download express installation files" option to specify whether express installation files should be downloaded during synchronization for faster installation on client computers.

- Use the Languages section to filter updates that are written in languages that aren't deployed on your network, so that when you synchronize, bandwidth and time isn't wasted downloading patches for those localized versions. You can choose to match the locale of the server, download all localizations regardless, or to download updates in languages that you specify in a list.

Creating a computer group

Computer groups are an important part of even the most basic WSUS systems. Computer groups enable you to target updates to specific sets of computers that likely share some common criteria. WSUS ships with two default groups, called All Computers and Unassigned Computers. When each client computer initially contacts the WSUS server (more on that process a bit later in the chapter), the server adds it to both these groups. Of course, it's likely that you'll want to create your own computer groups, since you can control the deployment of updates much more granularly with them. For example, you can create a group named Test that contains some lab machines. You can initially deploy a new patch to the test group, and then, once you've verified the patch works on those machines, roll it out to other groups. Since there's no limit to the number of custom groups you can create, you can also block off machines into departments, function, roles, or any other denominator you wish to use.

Setting up computer groups takes three steps. First, specify whether you intend to use server-side targeting, which involves manually adding each computer to its group by using WSUS; or client-side targeting, which involves automatically adding the clients by using either Group Policy or registry keys. Next, create the computer group on WSUS. Finally, move the computers into groups by using whichever method you chose in the first step.

In this section, I'll talk about server-side targeting, since it's the most likely method you'll use by far.

To specify that you'll use server-side targeting to select members of computer groups:

1. In the console toobar, click Options, and then click Computer Options.
2. Click "Use the Move computers" task in Windows Server Update Services in the Computer Options box.
3. Within Tasks, click Save settings, and then OK to confirm your selection.

Next, create a computer group. In this example, we'll create the Test group I mentioned earlier:

1. In the console toobar, click Computers.
2. Within Tasks, click "Create a computer group."
3. Enter **test** into the "Group name" box and then click OK.

Finally, add a machine to that group. Of course, you'll need to follow the instructions within the client-side portion of this chapter to get the Automatic Updates software deployed, which will populate the WSUS console with a list of available computers. Once that's done, though, follow these steps to add a machine to a group:

1. In the console toobar, click Computers.
2. In the Groups box, click the All Computers group, and then in the list, click the computer you want to move into the Test group.
3. Under Tasks, click "Move the selected computer," select the Test group, and click OK to perform the move.

And that's all there is to it. Lather, rinse, and repeat until you have a group structure appropriate to your network and deployment methodology.

Approving content

Now that you have an actual library of updates on or near your WSUS host machine, and you've defined a couple of computer groups, you can approve the updates individually for distribution to client machines within your network. The approval process makes it easy to withhold patches until further testing is done, which partly assuages the general fear that's caused by installing patches that might cause more problems than they fix. To begin the update approval process, do the following:

1. In the console toolbar, click Updates. On the resulting page, you'll see only critical and security updates that have been approved for use on client computers; this is by virtue of a filter that you can later adjust to view only updates relevant to what you're currently administering.

2. Within the update list, select the updates that you would like to approve. You can click the Details tab for more information about the updates, and you can select multiple updates at one time using the shift key.

3. When you've finished your selection, click "Change approval" under Update Tasks.

4. The Approve Updates dialog box appears. Click Install within the Approval column for the Test group, and then click OK.

WSUS will notify you when the approval is complete. In the righthand pane, where all the updates are shown, each patch's status is shown as one of five possible values. A new update is one that was just recently downloaded and hasn't been approved yet.

An approved update is available for distribution to each client machine. An update that isn't approved will not be distributed to clients, but the actual patch file remains in the library on the WSUS host machine. An updated patch indicates a new version of an earlier patch that currently exists in the library. And finally, a temporarily unavailable patch is one whose dependent files were downloaded incorrectly, could not be found, or were otherwise unable to be located by WSUS.

If, for some reason, you would like to clear the list of approved updates, you can clear all checkboxes on the list of available updates and then click Approve. This will remove any available updates from the WSUS catalog, and your client machines will stop downloading the updates until you approve more fixes. This will not, however, uninstall the patches from the client machines.

Checking the status of update deployments

Once a full 24 hours has passed, you can check the status of the approved update deployment. On the console toolbar, click Reports, and then on the resulting page, click Status of Updates. You can apply a filter by adjusting the settings under View, and you can change the view (perhaps to see the status of an update by computer group and then by computer, for example) by adjusting the controls on that page.

You can also print a status report by clicking "Print report" under Tasks.

Pushing out the automated updates client

Once your client computers first contact the WSUS server, the latest Automatic Updates software installed on your client computers will self-update to the latest version. There is one exception to this: the version of Automatic Updates included with Windows XP without any service packs cannot update itself automatically. You'll need to manually push this out via Group Policy, a login script, or "sneakernet"-style management.

You can install the updated Automatic Updates client on your clients by using the MSI install package, self-updating from the old Critical Update Notification (CUN) tool, installing Windows 2000 Service Pack 3 or 4, installing Windows XP Service Pack 1 or 2, or installing Windows Server 2003.

You can download the Automatic Updates client from the Microsoft web site at the WSUS web page, located at *http://www.microsoft.com/WSUS*. On a standalone machine, the AU client can simply be added by running the MSI file on the machine.

Manually installing a file can quickly become a pain when you have more than just a few machines to handle. Fortunately, because the client installation program is in the form of an MSI, you can easily push the program to clients by using Group Policy.

To create a new GPO, assign it to your computers, and then have it installed automatically:

1. Open the Active Directory Users and Computers MMC snap-in.

2. Right-click the domain or organizational unit to which you're interested in deploying the client, and select Properties.

3. Click the Group Policy tab.

4. Click New to create a new Group Policy object (GPO). Type in a name for the GPO.

5. Select the new GPO from the list, and click Edit to open the Group Policy Object Editor.

6. Expand Computer Configuration, and then select Software Settings.

7. Right-click Software Installation in the left pane, select New, and then click Package.

8. Enter the path to the Automatic Updates MSI file you downloaded from the web. Make sure you use a network path and not a local path to ensure that your clients can find the file at boot time. Click Open.

9. Choose Assigned to assign the package to the computers in the domain or organizational unit, and then click OK.

10. Allow time for polices to replicate through the domain. Usually this is accomplished within 15 minutes.

11. Restart the client computers. The client software should be installed before the Logon dialog box is displayed, although on Windows XP machines you might need to reboot up to three times for the software installation policy to take effect (this is because of the fast logon optimization feature).

 The application will be installed in the context of the local computer, so make sure that authenticated users have rights on the source folders.

You can also deploy the client MSI through a logon script by calling MSIEXEC followed by the client software file name as an argument. The software will be installed as requested.

Configuring the automatic updates client

The Automatic Updates client doesn't have any user-interface options for determining the origin of updates to install. You must set this with either a Registry change on each of the client computers or through Group Policy, either locally or based through a domain. Once the changes take effect, you'll be able to see the machines within the Computers page of the WSUS console.

Through a domain-based Group Policy, direct clients to the WSUS server by using the following procedure:

1. Open the Default Domain Policy GPO in Active Directory Users and Computers and click the Edit button.

2. Expand Computer Configuration, Administrative Templates, and Windows Components.

3. Select Windows Update. The right pane will contain four options that pertain to the Automatic Updates client, as depicted in Figure 7-17.

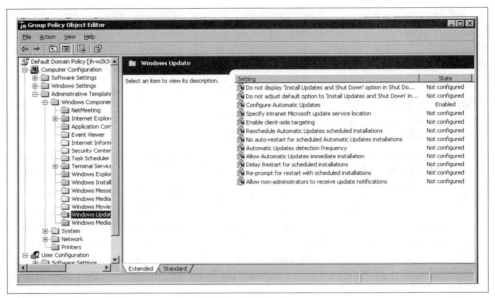

Figure 7-17. Group Policy options for WSUS and AU

These options are described here in more detail:

Configure Automatic Updates

This option specifies whether this computer will receive security updates and critical bug fixes. The first option makes sure that the currently logged-on user is notified before downloading updates. The user will then be notified again before installing the downloaded updates. The selcond option ensures that updates will automatically be downloaded, but not installed until a logged-on user acknowledges the updates' presence and authorizes the installation. The third option makes sure that updates are automatically downloaded and installed on a schedule that you can set in the appropriate boxes on the sheet. The fourth option, which will only appear if the AU software has updated itself to the version compatible with WSUS, allows local administrators to use AU in Control Panel to select their own configuration. To use this setting, click Enabled, and then select one of the options.

Specify Intranet Microsoft Update Service Location

This option designates a WSUS server from which to download updates. To use this setting, you must set two server name values: the server from which the Automatic Updates client detects and downloads updates, and the server to which updated workstations upload statistics. You can set both values to be the same server.

Enable Client-Side Targeting

This option enables client computers to automatically populate groups on thw SUS server. To use this option, click the Enabled option and then type the name of the group to which this computer should belong on the WSUS and then click OK. Keep in mind that you need to actually create the group on the WSUS server for this to take effect.

Reschedule Automatic Updates Scheduled Installations

This option specifies the amount of time to wait after booting before continuing with a scheduled installation that was missed previously for whatever reason (power outage, system powered off, network connection lost, and so on). If the status is set to Enabled, a missed scheduled installation will occur the specified number of minutes after the computer is next started. If the status is set to Disabled or Not Configured, a missed scheduled installation will simply roll over to the next scheduled installation.

No Auto-restart for Scheduled Automatic Updates Installations

This option designates whether a client computer should automatically reboot or not when an update that's just installed requires a system restart. If the status is set to Enabled, Automatic Updates will not restart a computer automatically during a scheduled installation if a user is logged in to the computer. Instead, it will notify the user to restart the computer to complete the installation. If the status is set to Disabled or Not Configured, Automatic Updates will notify the user that the computer will automatically restart in five minutes to complete the installation.

Automatic Update Detection Frequency

This option details the hours that Windows will use to figure out how long to wait before contacting the WSUS server to see if new updates are available. This time is actually determined by using the hours specified in this option and subtracting anywhere from zero to 20% of the hours specified. This offset helps to manage load. If the status is set to Enabled, you need to specify the number of hours; if it's set to Disabled or Not Configured, AU will check for new updates every 22 hours.

Allow Automatic Update Immediate Installation

This option specifies whether AU should automatically install updates that don't interrupt Windows or need a reboot. If you enable this option, AU will auto-install such updates; if you disable it, they will not be immediately installed.

Delay Restart for Scheduled Installations
This setting defines the amount of time AU will wait before executing a scheduled reboot. If this setting is enabled, the scheduled restart will happen after the number of minutes you specify. If this setting is disabled or not configured, the default waiting period is five minutes.

Re-Prompt for Restart with Scheduled Installations
If this setting is enabled, a scheduled restart will occur in the specified number of minutes after the prompt for restarting was postponed by the user. If this setting is disabled or not configured, the scheduled restart will take place ten minutes after the first prompt.

Allow Non-Administrators to Receive Update Notifications
If this setting is enabled, all users can receive notifications that updates are ready for download and/or installation. If this setting is disabled or not configured, AU will notify only logged-on administrators that pending update action is necessary.

Remove Links and Access to Windows Update
If this setting is enabled, end users cannot get updates from a Windows Update web site that you have not approved. If this policy is not enabled, the Windows Update icon remains in place for local administrators to visit. Such local administrators can in fact install unapproved updates.

You will want to allow 10 to 15 minutes for the changes to the domain's policy to replicate among all domain controllers. To manually initiate detection of these client machines, on the client, open a command prompt and type **wuauclt.exe /detectnow**.

To adjust the Group Policy on a machine that isn't managed by Active Directory, you need to load the appropriate templates into the Microsoft Management Console. Follow these steps:

1. Click Start, select Run, and type **GPEDIT.msc** to load the Group Policy snap-in.
2. Expand Computer Configuration and Administrative Templates.
3. Click Add/Remove Templates, and then click Add.
4. Enter the name of the Automatic Updates ADM file, which you can find in the *INF* subdirectory within your Windows root. In addition, you can find it in the *INF* subdirectory within the WSUS server machine's Windows root.
5. Click Open, and then click Close to load the *wuau.adm* file.

You can now adjust the policy settings as described in the previous subsection.

Finally, to adjust some of these behavior settings through Registry changes, use the appropriate key for each of the following settings:

- To enable or disable Automatic Updates: Create the value NoAutoUpdate in the key:

  HKEY_LOCAL_MACHINE\SOFTWARE\Policies\Microsoft\Windows\ WindowsUpdate\AU

The value is a DWORD with possible values zero (enabled) or one (disabled).

- To configure the update download and notification behavior: Create the value AUOptions in the key:

    HKEY_LOCAL_MACHINE\SOFTWARE\Policies\Microsoft\Windows\WindowsUpdate\AU

    The value is a DWORD that includes integers 2 (notify of download and notify before installation), 3 (automatically download but notify before installation), 4 (automatically download and schedule the installation), and 5 (let the local administrator choose the setting).

- To schedule an automated installation: Create the values ScheduledInstallDay and ScheduledInstallTime in the key:

    HKEY_LOCAL__MACHINE\SOFTWARE\Policies\Microsoft\Windows\WindowsUpdate\AU

    The value for each is a DWORD. For ScheduledInstallDay, the range is from 0 to 7, with 0 indicating every day and 1 through 7 indicating the days of the week, Sunday through Saturday. For ScheduledInstallTime, the range is from 0 to 23, signifying the hour of the day in military time.

- To specify a particular WSUS server to use with the Automatic Updates client: Create the value UseWUServer in the key:

    HKEY_LOCAL_MACHINE_SOFTWARE\Policies\Microsoft\Windows\WindowsUpdate\AU

    The value is a DWORD; set it to 1 to enable the custom WSUS server name. Then, create the values WUServer and WUStatusServer in the same key, of types Reg_SZ, and specify the name (with the http://) as the value.

- To specify how long to wait before completing a missed installation: Create the value RescheduleWaitTime in the key:

    HKEY_LOCAL_MACHINE_SOFTWARE\Policies\Microsoft\Windows\WindowsUpdate\AU

    The value is a DWORD that ranges from 1 to 60, measured in minutes.

- To specify whether to restart a scheduled installation with a currently logged-in nonadministrative user: Create the NoAutoRebootWithLoggedOnUsers value in the key:

    HKEY_LOCAL__MACHINE\SOFTWARE\Policies\Microsoft\Windows\WindowsUpdate\AU

    The value is a DWORD that can be 0, which indicates that a reboot will indeed take place, or 1, which indicates the reboot will be postponed while a user is logged on.

Using WSUS: On the Client Side

To configure Windows XP to work with WSUS, first enable the Automatic Updates feature. In Windows XP, do the following:

1. Open the Control Panel. Navigate to the System applet and open it.
2. Click the Automatic Updates tab.

In Windows 2000, do the following:

1. Open the Control Panel.
2. Navigate to the Automatic Updates applet and double-click it to open it.

You'll see the System Properties dialog box for the feature, as shown in Figure 7-18.

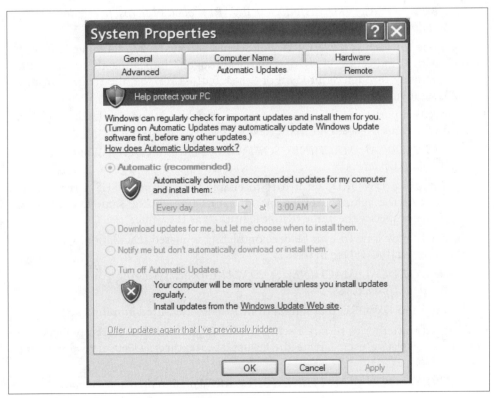

Figure 7-18. Configuring Automatic Updates on the client side

As the administrator, you select how updates are downloaded, signaled to the user, and subsequently installed on client machines. The currently logged-on user, if that person happens to have administrator credentials, is notified through a small update icon in the system tray as well as an information "bubble" that pops up when the download is complete. In addition, an administrator can determine if updates have been downloaded by looking at the system log. If the current user isn't an administrator, Windows will wait until one logs on to offer the notification that updates are available for installation.

Update download and installation

Updates are downloaded in a background thread by the Background Intelligent Transfer Service (BITS), which is an extension to Windows. BITS detects inactivity over a network connection and uses it to download large amounts of data from remote sites. BITS will detect when a user initiates activity over a connection and then pause the download process, waiting for the next idle period to resume it.

On the Automatic Updates property sheet, click the first option to have the currently logged-on user notified before downloading updates. The user will then be notified again before installing the downloaded updates. Use the second option if you want updates automatically downloaded, but want to wait until a logged-on user acknowledges their presence and authorizes the installation. Finally, click the third option if you want updates automatically downloaded and installed on a schedule that you can set in the boxes.

The update installation process proceeds depending on what you select in the boxes. When updates have finished downloading, the notification bubble will appear in the system-tray area of the machine, and an administrative user can double-click the bubble to open the Ready to Install dialog box, shown in Figure 7-19.

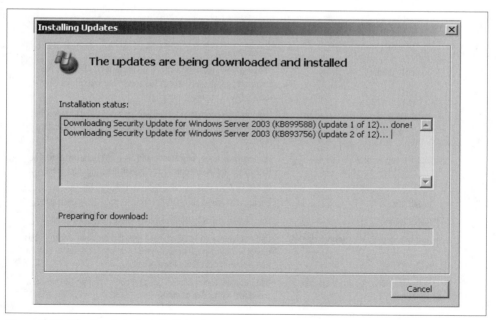

Figure 7-19. The Ready to Install dialog box

You can click the Remind Me Later button to defer the installation of updates for a set period of time, ranging from half an hour to three days from the current time.

If you've configured Automatic Updates to install fixes on a regular schedule, the updates will be downloaded in the background and automatically installed on that schedule. Automatic Updates installs the update and restarts the computer if an update requires that, even if there's no local administrator logged on. If an administrator is logged on, she will have the chance to cancel the process; if a normal user is logged on, he will receive a notification of the impending process and a countdown to its initiation. However, if updates have finished downloading between the configured install time and the current time, the notification will appear in the system tray as described earlier in this section. The user will not have the option to click Remind Me Later, but he can choose to install the updates at that time to have the process over with before the predetermined installation time.

Monitoring the client-side system

WSUS and the Automatic Updates client provide several event templates that are written to the system event log to describe the current status of the update process, any errors that are encountered, and a brief notation of what updates were successfully installed. You can program an event-log monitoring tool to monitor for certain event IDs that are specific to WSUS. This tool will give you a picture of your network's health with regards to updates. Table 7-3 lists these events and their meanings and contexts.

Table 7-3. WSUS and AU client event log messages

Event ID	Label	Description
16	Unable to connect	The client can't connect to either the Windows Update site, the Microsoft update site, or the WSUS server, but will continue trying indefinitely.
17	Install ready; no recurring schedule	Updates have been downloaded and are ready to be installed, but an administrator must log on and manually start the installation process.
18	Install ready, recurring schedule	Updates have been downloaded and are ready to be installed. The date this install is scheduled to occur is listed within the event description.
19	Install success	Updates have been successfully installed; these have been listed.
20	Install failure	Some updates didn't install correctly; these have been listed.
21	Restart required, no recurring schedule	Updates have been installed, but a reboot is required, and until this reboot is complete Windows cannot fetch more updates for installation. Any user can reboot the machine.
22	Restart required, recurring schedule	Updates have been installed, but a reboot is required and has been scheduled within five minutes.

Command-Line Utilities

In this section, I'll give an overview and some examples of various command-line utilities that pertain to Windows security that you can integrate into your scripts and programs.

SCWCMD

The Security Configuration Wizard (SCW) includes the Scwcmd.exe command-line tool. This tool is versatile and can perform many tasks that you might want to automate using scripts or batch files. Here, I'll briefly outline the most common tasks you will want to perform using SCWCMD.

Configuring servers with a policy

The most basic use of the command-line tool is to configure one or many servers with an SCW-generated policy. You can apply a policy to the local machine, to a remote machine using either its NetBIOS name or IP address, or to entire organizational unit's worth of machines. For example, to apply the machine.xml policy to the current computer, simply use this:

```
scwcmd configure /p:machine.xml
```

To apply the policy to all of the machines in the FileServers OU within company.com, you need to use the full LDAP name within the arguments of the command. It should look something like this:

```
Scwcmd configure /ou:OU=FileServers,DC=company,DC=com /p:machine.xml
```

Analyzing machines for policy compliance

You can also analyze a machine, a list of servers, or an entire organizational unit with an SCW-generated policy. For example, to analyze your SQL Server machine with the sqlserver.xml policy, use the following:

```
scwcmd analyze /m:SQLservername /p:sqlserver.xml /u:administrator
```

Or, to analyze the SQL Servers organizational unit, use the following: (Note that the entire LDAP name needs to be used when specifying Active Directory–based containers with this command.)

```
scwcmd analyze /ou:OU=SQLServers,DC=company,DC=com /p:sqlserver.xml /u:administrator
```

The results of running this command are returned to an XML file generated by the wizard, which you can view using another option in SCWCMD. I'll demonstrate that in a bit.

Roll back SCW policies

If you make a mistake and need to "undo" a policy application on either a local or remote machine, you can use the command-line tool to get the machine back up quickly. You can also use the /u switch to perform the operation using another user's credentials, if yours aren't sufficient on a remote machine.

For example, to rollback a policy on the machine R2B2SRV1, use the following:

```
scwcmd rollback /m:R2B2SRV1 /u:administrator
```

You can also use an IP address if you aren't sure of the friendly name of a machine:

```
scwcmd rollback /m:192.168.2.2 /u:localadmin
```

Viewing analysis results

You can use the scwcmd view command to render the raw XML results file that the wizard generates with an XML transform file that makes the results easier to read. The directory *%windir%\security\msscw\transformfiles* contains .xsl transform files which are applied to the .xml policy file for the rendering process.

To view a policy file, use the following syntax:

```
scwcmd view /x:policyfile.xml /s:policyview.xsl
```

MBSACLI

The Microsoft Baseline Security Analyzer has a command-line counterpart that will allow you to perform local and remote security scans and display reports from scans you conducted previously. You simply run MBSACLI from the directory in which the MBSA is installed.

It's fairly simple to perform a full scan of a single computer:

```
Mbsacli /target computername
```

You can also scan the computer for updates only and create a report of the missing updates:

```
Mbsacli /target CORP\lj-wnxp-dsk /wa
```

There's a great deal more syntax and options available, including the ability to create more customized reports that can be graphically displayed, sending reports in XML format for external parsing, scanning a list of computers, and using a custom update catalog file. Issue this command to learn more:

```
Mbsacli /?
```

The Last Word

In this chapter, I've taken you through the various considerations of security in a network environment and then shown you how to implement each using the tools bundled with Windows Server 2003, Service Pack 1, or additional utilities that are freely available for download. Recall that I mentioned in the introductory section of this chapter that I didn't intend to present an exhaustive list of tweaks and settings to adjust Windows Server 2003 to be at its most secure. Rather, I've given you a comprehensive foundation so that you can build on the concepts and procedures you learned in this chapter to create a secure infrastructure around your servers.

CHAPTER 8

Internet Information Services

Windows Server 2003 includes Internet Information Services (IIS) 6, a radically changed version of Microsoft's popular web server software. In this chapter, I'll look at the new features in IIS 6, the individual components and how to administer them, how to automate administration of IIS from the command line, and some general suggestions for improving the security of IIS and the machine on which it's running.

IIS Architecture

Because a picture is worth a thousand words, I'll start this section with a diagram (Figure 8-1) that shows the architecture and operation of IIS 6, and I'll describe the internal workings later in this section.

IIS begins with a *listener*, which detects requests for web services and pages; it's the foundation of IIS. The listener runs in kernel mode, meaning that it has more direct ties to the operating system than traditional programs running in user mode. This means requests are served much faster and much more efficiently.

When an HTTP request arrives at the HTTP Listener (*HTTP.SYS*, at the bottom of the figure), it verifies that the request is valid. If this check fails, the appropriate HTTP error and code number are sent back to the requester. If everything checks out, *HTTP.SYS* decides if it can handle the request from a cache of recently requested pages and operations. If the response is in the cache, *HTTP.SYS* sends the response immediately, without bothering any of the other parts of IIS. Otherwise, *HTTP.SYS* is forced to pass the request on, and places the request in a separate queue for each worker process—essentially a separate copy of IIS's listener running independently of all the other serving program copies. The worker process programs are called *W3WP.EXE*, as shown in the three partitions above *HTTP.SYS* in Figure 8-1.

This begs the question of how these individual worker processes are started. If a copy of *W3WP.EXE* is not listening on the request queue, *HTTP.SYS* signals the Web Administration Service (WAS), the W3SVC, to start and configure a worker process.

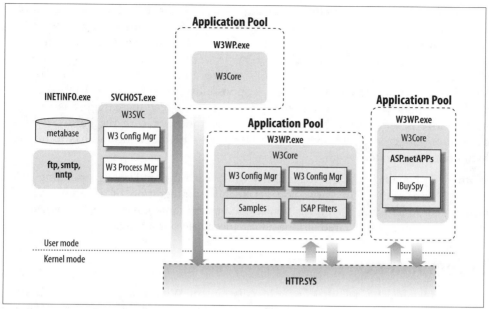

Figure 8-1. IIS 6 architecture

The W3SVC controls all the worker processes, bringing them up and shutting them down as load demands. This procedure is based on the configuration information stored in XML format in a file called the metabase, which is controlled by an over-arching process called *INETINFO.EXE*, shown to the very left in the above figure.

If a worker process or a group of worker processes (which Microsoft calls a web garden) is already started and connected to the request queue, the worker process pulls the request from the queue and processes it through any Internet Services Application Programming Interface (ISAPI) filter or extension and web application code. Then it returns the response to the *HTTP.SYS* and the requester.

The W3SVC also monitors the health of a worker process. For example, if a particular process does not respond or has exceeded some threshold, such as the number of hours running or number of requests handled, W3SVC coordinates with *HTTP.SYS* to hold requests in the queue while W3SVC stops the worker process and attempts to start it again.

But what does all this mean to the end user? After all, your customers measure how well you run your Internet business based on the speed of your web site. This structure of IIS also pushes the product to near the current limits of speed as far as a web server is concerned, according to the independent testing firm VeriTest. IIS 6 significantly overtakes Apache, the most popular web server at the time of this writing, as far as performance is concerned in both dynamic and static web serving, much to the chagrin of the open source community. To understand this, take a step backward and see how IIS 5 serviced requests: a single user process, called *inetinfo.exe*, took care of HTTP requests and acted as the traffic director, sending the requests on to worker processes using *dllhost.exe*. One problem was that *inetinfo.exe* operated in user mode rather than kernel mode, which made serving a lot slower just by virtue of where the process was residing in the OS architecture. Contrast this with IIS 6 in Windows Server 2003, which transfers responsibility for directing HTTP requests from a user mode process to a kernel mode driver. The speed increase just as a result of this move is remarkable, mainly because it can interact with the hardware at a lower, more direct level, listening for HTTP requests before Windows has to funnel them up to user mode.

Another big benefit is the interoperability of IIS with the underlying operating system and with Active Directory. You get seamless integration of all components, meaning administration is simpler (you're used to the same interfaces) and user data and information can be shared among all the pieces of your infrastructure.

IIS Components

IIS is not installed by default in new installations of Windows Server 2003, unlike previous versions. You can choose from several "subprograms" that each perform a different service and install them as you need them. IIS is the moniker that refers to all these services collectively. This section will highlight the individual components and provide a bit of information about each.

The Web Server

The web server, named W3SVC, is the part of the software that makes files available for web browsing using the HTTP protocol. You can support multiple DNS domains on one server by using either multiple virtual servers or a feature called *host headers*. Host headers examine the TCP/IP header of a web request, detect the intended destination of the packet, and route it to the appropriate process; this obviates the need for different domains to have unique IP addresses on one machine.

The FTP Server

This component of IIS (FTPSVC) enables you to transfer files from a server to a client. The FTP protocol dates back to the beginning of the Internet, and it's still one of the most efficient ways to transfer large amounts of data between hosts over a wide area. However, FTP is inherently insecure because it transfers all data—including the username and password for authentication purposes—in clear text.

The SMTP Server and POP3 Server

The Simple Mail Transfer Protocol (SMTP) is the protocol widely used to transport mail over the Internet. It's the actual component that pushes mail around from server to server. IIS 5, introduced in Windows 2000 Server, included a functional SMTP server (SMTPSVC) which supported the other parts of IIS and formed the basis of Internet email functionality in Exchange 2000. But out of the box it could only send mail. You couldn't set up a plain-vanilla Windows 2000 Server on the Internet and use it to send *and* receive email.

In Windows Server 2003, Microsoft has included a rudimentary but helpful and functional Post Office Protocol 3 (POP3) service. The POP3 service serves as the mechanism by which users can retrieve mail from their mailboxes. The POP3 service works, although its functionality is limited and its scalability is questionable. For a small business, it's a free alternative to more expensive commercial email software packages, such as Microsoft's Exchange Server 2003.

The NNTP Server

The USENET news service, full of newsgroups ranging in topics from music to cooking to computers to automobiles and everything in between, runs off the Network News Transport Protocol (NNTP). You can use the NNTP component of IIS (NNTPSVC) to implement a discussion board within your organization if you lack the time or knowledge to use a more complex solution such as Exchange or Share-Point Team Services.

What's New in IIS 6

It's fair to presume that everyone involved in computing now has surfed the Web at one point or another. The Web has become integrated into popular culture and many people now consider it a necessary utility, such as power and water. Microsoft recognizes this infiltration of the Web into everyday life and has capitalized on it. Of course, the company also believes web services are the foundation of its revenue base in the future, so one shouldn't find it too hard to believe that Microsoft would improve the product on which it is basing its existence. But no matter the impetus behind the revision, we all benefit from these improvements, as I'll discuss in this section.

In IIS 6 you can create multiple virtual servers on a single physical machine, with each virtual server acting as its own copy of IIS with its own properties and security configuration. The most popular use of this is among commercial web hosting companies that host tens or hundreds of individual web sites on one machine. By configuring multiple virtual servers, these companies can isolate each customer's traffic and configuration.

Although virtual servers are nice, perhaps the most important architectural improvement in IIS 6 is the new web service DLL that is independent from the web serving mechanism. The new DLL is called into memory by worker processes, which you know from the previous section are simply separate "threads" that work on requests from the kernel mode web server driver, *HTTP.SYS*. These worker processes load dynamic scripts and programs that use ISAPI. By separating the web server driver from the web service DLL, you achieve a more stable environment because a failure (such as a poorly written script, an exception fault, or other problem) that in previous versions of IIS could have brought down an entire web site now is isolated to only one specific application. If an application does break, the web service DLL creates an identical process that can finish service to any remaining requests. However, IIS still keeps track of failures, and if the application is brought down again, the process is ended permanently. (This feature is called rapid-fail protection and you can configure it through the Application Pools property page, which I'll cover in detail in a later section of this chapter.)

IIS uses application pools to manage all these requests. *HTTP.SYS* acts as a traffic director, sending requests to the individual application pools based on the addresses (URLs, to be specific) of the applications. Because multiple worker processes can serve a single application pool, there's better response time within an individual application. But what happens when you have worker processes that fail? Do all these processes "catch" the failure going down and bring them down, too? Fortunately, this is no longer the case because of *worker process isolation mode*, which simply isolates a memory segment for each application and its associated worker processes. An added bonus from this isolation is that you can limit CPU and memory use of individual applications to fine-tune once you have a very active server that's hosting sites and web applications.

IIS 6 also introduces the concept of *web gardens*, which are multiple worker processes serving a single application all on one server. For very basic but highly active applications, this is an effective technique for managing load and increasing speed, but complex applications still will need to be serviced across multiple physical servers (known as a *web farm*). But IIS 6 actually improves performance and process migration across all machines in a web farm, so there's quality in that arena as well.

Now you might assume that if a clever hacker manages to penetrate *HTTP.SYS*, he's got control of the entire operating system. You'd be correct in that assumption. However, Microsoft has done a thorough code review of IIS at all levels and assures everyone in the Internet community that IIS will be well-behaved. In fact, IIS is not even installed by default, which takes care of a big problem: previously, users would install a copy of Windows 2000 Server that happened to be connected to the Internet, and before they had a chance to install patches, Code Red and W32.Nimda would infect the machine. Further, even once IIS is installed it is set to serve up only static pages, not any dynamic content or script output. Even servers upgraded from previous versions of Windows server products have IIS disabled if the Setup program detects they are still operating with default settings intact. (This is because normally at least something is changed if IIS is in use on a particular machine, so even the deployment of Windows Server 2003 has a worm and virus "neutralizing" effect, disabling unused web servers that could be vulnerable to attack.)

There's also a laundry list of other minor improvements, some of which include the following:

- Furthering the discussion of isolation, the FTP server component of IIS runs in user isolation mode, so that when users log on they are restricted to their own home directory and cannot view or even realize that other directories on the server exist. If you're familiar with Unix systems, this is much like a CHROOT jail.

- IIS 6 comes prepackaged with a set of administration scripts, written in VBScript, that you can run from the command line. This is excellent if you have a custom program that you need to integrate with IIS to create and delete sites, make configuration changes, and so on.

- You can import configuration information, and export it as well, across the different aspects of IIS operation, from the directory to the site to the server level, so you can now create multiple servers that have identical setups.

- Configuration information—known as the *metabase*—is also stored in a set of two XML files, instead of a mysterious binary file that no one could look at. Now Microsoft Product Support Services can't get off easily telling you your problem is a corrupt metabase and that you need to reinstall—you can actually go inside the files and see what the problem might be.

- IIS 6 will now compress responses formed from dynamic content before sending them to the user, resulting in faster transmission times from the server to the client. Static content is stored in a disk cache as well that *HTTP.SYS* can access directly, which makes for rapid access to commonly requested files.

- IIS 6 supports IPv6 if it's installed on a Windows Server 2003 machine.

New in Windows Server 2003 Service Pack 1

Several enhancements to IIS have been made in Service Pack 1 and, by virtue of that, Windows Server 2003 R2. I'll briefly outline those here:

- There is no longer a default limit on simultaneous connections. In the original release of Windows Server 2003, that limit was 8,000 connections but it could be overridden by creating and setting the MaxConnections registry key. Like other Registry changes, when you install SP1, it won't remove that key if you have added it. If you've already created the key, however, you'll need to remove it to take advantage of the newly removed limit.

- The HTTP.sys "error" logging has also been enhanced; you'll see the headers that allow it to be parsed by standard log parsers, as well as more fields, and the ability to rollover based on date and time (as well as size).

- Service Pack 1 makes available kernel-mode SSL support. If that sounds like Greek to you, it mainly means that you'll see a substantial performance improvement in SSL-based operations. However, there are currently a number of restrictions and limitations that might prevent it from being a sensible choice—for example, there isn't any support for client certificates yet. (This will make more sense as you proceed through the chapter; just tuck that knowledge away for now.)

- There are a few changes to HTTP parsing as well which bring IIS more in line with the HTTP RFC standards.

If you're at all curious and want to go deeper into these changes, you can check out the whitepaper on Microsoft's site at:

http://www.microsoft.com/downloads/details.aspx?FamilyId=A3DA3D7F-18C7-45CE-A47A-ED747DACEF34&displaylang=en

All in all, there are few changes to IIS in Service Pack 1 that make it worth installing if your business depends on IIS.

Installing IIS

You can install IIS either from the Manage Your Server Wizard, which will set up IIS with default settings, or via the Add/Remove Programs applet in the Control Panel, which allows more granular control over what you install.

To install IIS using Add/Remove Programs, follow these steps:

1. Open the Control Panel, and double-click Add/Remove Programs.

2. In the left pane, click Add/Remove Windows Components.

3. Check the checkbox beside Application Server in the list. The Application Server selection box will appear.

4. Check the checkbox beside Internet Information Services (IIS), and click OK. For this example, we'll install just the basic components.

5. Click Next in the original dialog box to proceed to the file copy. You might be prompted to insert your Windows Server 2003 CD-ROM.

IIS is now installed on your computer. By default, IIS is set up with a basic HTTP service listening on port 80 of all IP addresses on your computer. This service will host only static web pages and text documents—no scripting is allowed out of the box as a security measure. A locked-down SMTP server is listening on port 25 of all IP addresses on the machine, ready to send mail. You get an NNTP server, without any feeds configured or local newsgroups set up, on port 119 of all IP addresses on your box. If you elect to install FrontPage Server Extensions during the setup process, you'll receive a default FTP site on port 21, and a specially created web site called Microsoft SharePoint Administration on a randomly assigned port on all IP addresses.

The port is randomly assigned for security purposes so that attackers can't target the software interface on all computers using just a single port number.

IIS Management Console

You configure IIS-related services in Windows Server 2003 through the IIS Manager snap-in, as pictured in Figure 8-2.

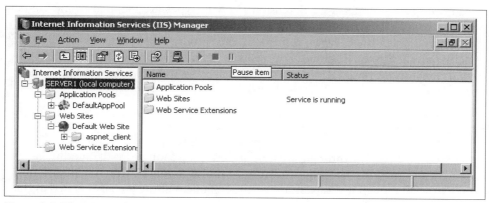

Figure 8-2. The Microsoft IIS Management Console

To access the console, select Start → All Programs → Administrative Tools, and click Internet Information Services (IIS) Manager. You also can load the snap-in into an existing management console using its filename, *iis.msc*.

You'll see the available resources aggregated into three different groups: Application Pools, which are available only when IIS is running in worker process isolation mode (described earlier in this chapter); web sites, which are the standard method of serving static web pages and simple dynamic HTML-based pages to clients; and web service extensions, which handle the more complex, dynamically loaded content, as well as runtime languages such as ASP.NET and other similar languages.

You can configure a few options that will affect the behavior of all sites and extensions across IIS, and you can edit these by right-clicking your server name in the left pane of IIS Manager and selecting Properties. A dialog box will open with the following options:

Enable Direct Metabase Edit
> Also called *edit-while-running*, this feature enables you to adjust the actual configuration of every aspect of IIS while the service is enabled. The metabase was previously an incomprehensible binary file that was subject to corruption very easily; in IIS 6, the metabase is now an XML file that the user can modify directly. With this feature enabled, you can edit the metabase directly with a text editor such as Notepad or Cooledit without having to stop the INETINFO service.

UTF-8 Logging

By selecting this option, you instruct IIS to write HTTP server logs in the UTF-8 character set rather than ASCII and/or the local character set as configured in the operating system. If you use Unix systems to process logs for your organization, this might be helpful for you. IIS does not support writing FTP log files in UTF-8 format.

MIME Types

Multipurpose Internet Mail Extension (MIME) types are mapped to individual file types and indicate what kinds of documents and data are served by the IIS machine. The MIME types defined in this box are served globally—that is, across all sites in the machine. You also can define specific MIME types for a virtual directory, a physical directory, and a specific web site. To configure these mappings, click the MIME Types button.

Managing Web Services

In this section, I'll walk through creating a new site, configuring it, modifying its properties, and securing it using certificates. I'll also assume you're creating a new web site as well, though if you want to use the Default Website already created in IIS, you can follow along through the explanation, too.

Creating a Site

First, open IIS Manager, and expand the tree in the left pane. Right-click the Websites folder, and from the New menu, select Website. The Website Creation Wizard appears. Click Next to continue, and then follow the procedure outlined here:

1. On the Website Description screen, enter some helpful text that represents the purpose or content of the web site you're creating. This is just for your or another administrator's reference. Click Next to continue.

2. The IP Address and Port Settings screen appears. Here, choose the IP address on which IIS will listen for requests addressed to this web site. You also can select All Unassigned to indicate to IIS to monitor all IP addresses that aren't reserved for the exclusive use of other web sites. Also, enter the TCP port number that requests to this web site will use. (The default is port 80.) Finally, enter the host header for this site if needed. I'll cover port numbers and host headers a bit later in this chapter. Click Next to continue.

3. On the Website Home Directory page, indicate where the pages you want to serve are located on your machine. You also can point IIS to a network location if you want your pages to be served from another machine. Windows by default creates a directory called *C:\Inetpub\wwwroot* that you can use as a starting point. Also, check the anonymous access checkbox if you want anonymous web

users to be able to browse to your site. If you uncheck this checkbox, users will need to authenticate to IIS before viewing the site. Click Next to continue.

4. The Website Access Permissions page appears. On this page, you can define what kinds of permissions users who access your web site will have on a general basis. If you disallow running scripts and executing files, for example, you'll be limited to serving static pages. The permissions you define here will trickle down to sub-directories and other files you create within the web site, though you can, of course, edit these permissions more granularly from IIS Manager or through the filesystem. Click Next once you've selected the appropriate set of permissions.

5. The confirmation screen appears. Click Finish to complete the process.

Now you need to add some web pages to the directory you specified in step 3—from here I'll call this your web root—so that your web site actually has content. You also can set filesystem permissions on the web root directory. This step deserves a bit of commentary: when an anonymous user connects to your web site, he or she actually *does* authenticate to your IIS machine; his or her browser automatically connects to the account named IUSR_*machinename*, which is created when you install IIS onto any machine. Anonymous users always use this user account, so if you want to deny anonymous access to a certain file in your web root, simply use the NTFS file permission modification utilities to deny the IUSR_*machinename* account read permissions.

Adjusting Server-Wide Site Properties

Much like you can configure global options for all sites in regard to direct metabase editing and MIME options, you also can set master properties for all web sites. The options that you set as master will trickle down to all web sites that currently exist, unless they have custom settings that were specified earlier, and to all new web sites as they're created. To access this functionality in IIS Manager, expand the computer name in the left pane, right-click Websites, and select Properties from the menu. The screen in Figure 8-3 will appear.

What you see is a replicated version of the property sheet for individual web sites, with properties that are appropriate to those specific sites grayed out. I'll cover most of these options when I discuss setting individual web site properties later in this chapter, but two properties, available only here, deserve some mention.

One is on the Service tab where you can configure the method in which IIS operates: either in worker process isolation mode, which I covered in the introductory section of this chapter, or in IIS 5 isolation mode, in which IIS emulates its previous version's behavior for legacy application compatibility. You need to use IIS 5 isolation mode if you have applications that are designed to be loaded by multiple worker processes and to be run simultaneously, if you have applications that delegate work to other processes, or if you have an application that manages state within a process. If you change this option from the default to IIS 5 mode, you will lose the security and stability benefits that IIS 6 brings you. You'll also need to restart IIS.

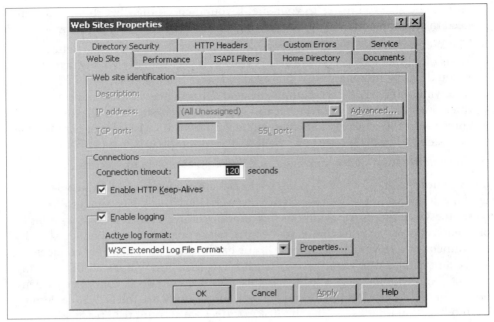

Figure 8-3. Default properties for all new IIS web sites

Alert your developers: ASP.NET is but one example of code that might not work on IIS 6 without some adjustment.

Those of you familiar with the venerable open source web server, Apache, might be familiar with its GZIP feature. GZIP is a plug-in for Apache that compresses data from the host machine to the client machine's browser before it is sent over the wire to reduce transfer time and make more efficient use of bandwidth. This functionality was available in IIS 5, although you had to write an ISAPI filter to use it. Fortunately, Microsoft has exposed this feature in IIS 6 directly through the UI so that you don't need to do any custom programming to use it. Under the HTTP Compression section, you can enable compression of either or both application files and static pages, and specify the location where these pages are cached temporarily. You also can restrict the size of that cache.

Finally, on the Directory Security tab, you can select to enable the Windows Directory Service Mapper. For IIS servers residing inside an Active Directory domain, this enables you to use client certificate mapping rather than one-to-one or many-to-one mapping (coverage of which is coming up later in this chapter), which would be required with traditional certificates.

Hosting Multiple Sites on One Physical Machine

It can be cost-efficient to host multiple web sites on a single machine. But the software gets in the way in this scenario: how does the web server sort and differentiate the requests for multiple sites, all coming to the same machine? IIS 6 provides three different methods by which you can host multiple virtual web sites on one set of physical hardware:

Multiple IP addresses

A "low-tech" solution is to configure Windows for several different IP addresses, and configure the individual web sites inside IIS to listen on each distinct address respectively. However, in recent times, the organizations that control the assignment of IP addresses worldwide have cracked down on issuing multiple IP addresses for this purpose, so you'll find it increasingly difficult to obtain multiple addresses from either your provider or directly from each organization. But if you have addresses to spare, this method certainly works.

Host headers

Using host headers, modern browsers will detect the name of the site to which a user wants to go, encapsulate that name inside the HTTP request's header, and send it on to the appropriate web server. Then, IIS will open the header, look for the name of the site for which the packet was intended, and serve up the pages from the designated virtual site. This is the easiest way, and the least costly service-wise, to provide multiple-site support, and the performance hit is negligible. You can configure this within the properties for a particular site.

Distinct port numbers

Much like the multiple IP addresses method, all virtual sites share a single hard-wired IP address on a physical machine, but the individual sites are listening on different TCP port numbers. This is a bit clunky on the users' side because they often need to remember a specific port number when surfing to a site that's configured like this, but for intranet use, it's a good way to conserve hardware. Some might argue that it is also a decent security improvement because the hackers have to search for the web service to crack it, instead of simply assuming it's on the standard port 80. Hackers commonly use port scanners, though, so you succeed only in keeping out the people interested in the easiest targets. You also can implement redirection solutions so that public-facing users don't have to enter a port number, although those programs and boxes are beyond the scope of this discussion.

During the process of setting up these new web sites with the wizard I stepped through earlier in this chapter, if you accidentally configure two distinct web sites to listen on the same ports and/or IP addresses, IIS will raise an error message alerting you to this.

Adjusting Individual Site Properties

Let's take a closer look at the configuration options for individual web sites and how you can adjust them. To look at the properties for one specific web site on your IIS machine, open IIS Manager, expand the node in the left pane that corresponds to your machine, expand the Websites tree, and right-click the appropriate web site. Select Properties from the menu and the properties sheet for that web site will appear.

Web Site

Figure 8-4 shows the Web Site tab.

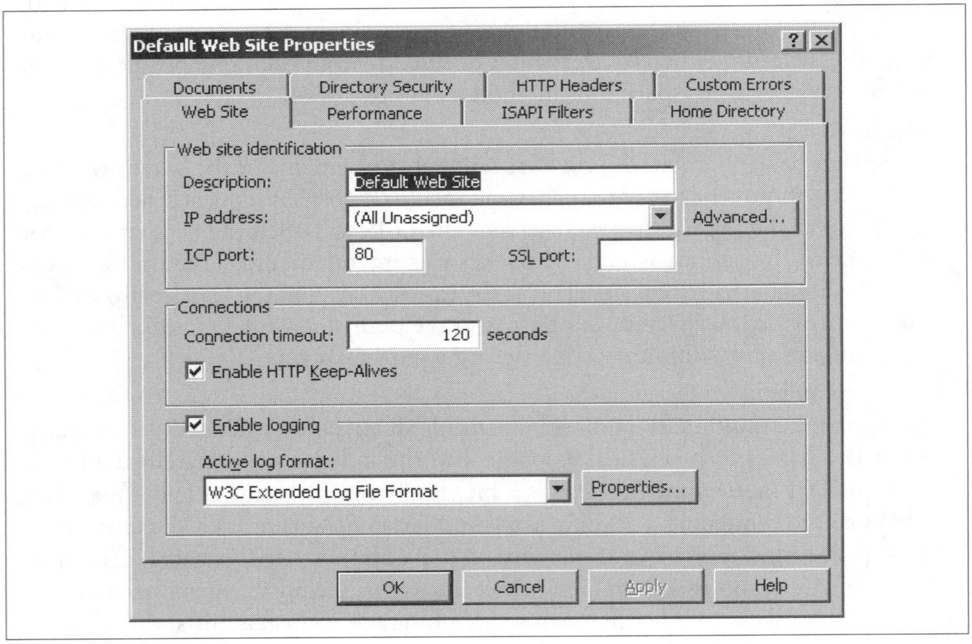

Figure 8-4. The Web Site tab

Under "Web site identification," you can enter a short description of the purpose of the site, the appropriate IP address for the site to listen on, and the port for normal and secure web requests. If you click the Advanced button, you can easily configure multiple identities for your site, each on different IP addresses and port numbers, and each with different host header values. You can do the same for the secure certificate-protected version of your site as well.

In the Connections section, you can configure how long a server will wait for a user and keep his connection alive while he is inactive. This serves to protect the server from multiple opened connections that clients have abandoned. You also can determine whether to enable *keepalive* functionality, a processor- and bandwidth-saving addition to the HTTP protocol standard. By using a keepalive, a client's browser has no need to redownload static images and content from a site as long as the browser can request to the server that the current session stay active. Most modern browsers are able to take advantage of this functionality, and it's enabled by default upon IIS installation. I recommend you leave it enabled, since disabling HTTP keepalives can degrade server performance and increase bandwidth usage significantly.

Finally, the Enable logging checkbox enables you to indicate whether IIS should record information about connections to the server in a file. Logs can include information on the origin of visitors to your site, the times they visit (in UTC form—Greenwich Mean Time), and information on the date of last viewing of certain content—all useful statistics for online marketing. You also can select the format in which you want the log to be written. Choose from the following:

Microsoft IIS Log Format

A fixed ASCII format. With this format, a single transaction can have multiple log file entries. A sample log file line might look like the following:

```
10.123.12.3, Nwtraders.com, 8/18/97, 13:17:37, SMTPSVC1, MAIL01,
10.200.200.1, 90, 42, 0, 250, 0, MAIL FROM,
-,FROM:<mariab@Nwtraders.com>,
10.123.12.3, Nwtraders.com, 8/18/97, 13:17:37, SMTPSVC1, MAIL01,
10.200.200.1, 0, 32, 0, 250, 0, RCPT TO, -, TO:<address@MSN.com>,
10.123.12.3, Nwtraders.com, 8/18/97, 13:17:37, SMTPSVC1, MAIL01,
10.200.200.1, 270, 480, 101, 250, 0, DATA, -, 0019E3517201287MAIL01,
10.123.12.3, Nwtraders.com, 8/18/97, 13:17:37, SMTPSVC1, MAIL01,
10.200.200.1, 81, 4, 52, 0, 541, QUIT, -, MAIL01,
```

NCSA Common Log Format

A fixed ASCII format. This format stores the following information for one web request/transaction: remote host; remote user identity (often found via a reverse DNS lookup); the authenticated user; the current date; the URL requested; the status of the request; and the number of bytes actually transferred.

ODBC Logging

A fixed format that has a connection to an external database and that writes data to that database. You design the fields that will be written to the database, and the location of the database that stores the information.

W3C Extended Log File Format

A user-modifiable ASCII format that supports process accounting. An example log file line might be:

```
#Version: 1.0
#Fields: date time c-ip sc-bytes time-taken cs-version
2004-05-01 02:10:57 192.0.0.2 6340 3 HTTP/1.0
```

Click the Properties button beside the log format selection box. On the General tab, you can select how often logs are rolled over—that is, how often IIS stops writing to one file and begins writing to a new file—and where to store the logs. On the

Advanced tab, you can select exactly which fields of data will be stored in the log file for each entry. The names of the fields are fairly self-explanatory. Click OK to exit the dialog box when you've finished making selections.

Performance

Figure 8-5 shows the Performance tab.

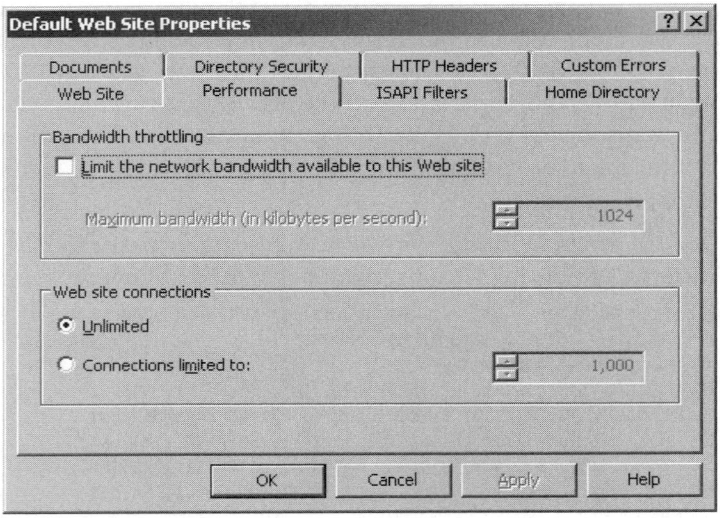

Figure 8-5. The Performance tab

The Performance tab contains settings that enable you to manage and restrict the bandwidth and physical connections that your IIS server uses in processing HTTP requests. The Bandwidth throttling section enables you to limit the sustained bandwidth allowed to an individual site so that you can retain a certain amount of bandwidth for the rest of the sites on a server—a cheap but effective method of load balancing. When you enable bandwidth throttling, IIS takes advantage of the native Windows Packet Scheduler service to determine when packets are transmitted over the wire. If the Packet Scheduler is not installed, IIS will install it the first time you enable bandwidth throttling. It also will default to a minimum transmission speed of 1KB per second. Adjust the actual restriction using the up and down arrows in the box on the sheet.

In the "Web site connections" section, you can restrict the number of incoming physical HTTP connections to an individual site, or you can allow an unlimited number of connections to a web site. This is a good way of managing load and keeping traffic and bandwidth usage patterns stable over an extended period of time. Simply enter the number of connections you want to allow using the up and down arrows. This value can vary largely based on the available bandwidth, the speed of your connection to the network, and the other duties your web server might be performing. The best way to determine a good value for your implementation is through trial and error.

ISAPI Filters

Figure 8-6 shows the ISAPI Filters tab.

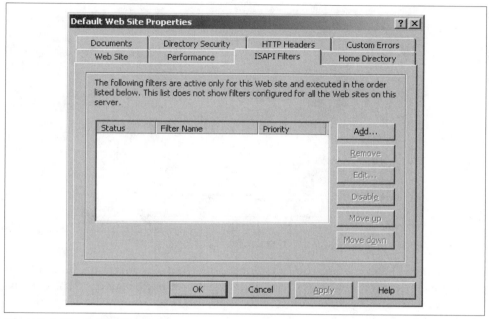

Figure 8-6. The ISAPI Filters tab

An ISAPI filter is a piece of executable code that is triggered by certain events inside a request to an IIS web server. On the ISAPI Filters tab, you can configure which of these filters are active for a particular web site, the order in which they'll be executed, and where the actual executable code resides in the filesystem. It's important to note that any change made on this tab at the server-wide (global) level requires a complete restart of IIS through IIS Manager on the affected machine. If you're managing filters on an individual web site, any filters added on the property sheet won't be activated until the first appropriate HTTP request is received.

You can use the Add, Remove, Edit, Disable, and Move Up/Down buttons to adjust the presence and priority of ISAPI filters.

Home Directory

Figure 8-7 shows the Home Directory tab.

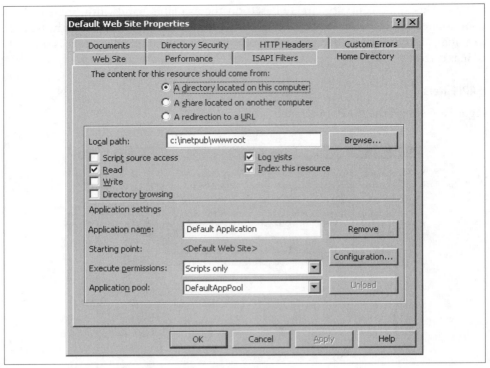

Figure 8-7. The Home Directory tab

On the Home Directory tab, you can configure the physical location where IIS will go to find content for a web site. You can use the three options under "The content for this resource should come from:" to locate home directory content in a folder on the current computer, on a file share somewhere over the network, or via a redirection from the current site to a completely different site. You can type the directory path in the Local Path box just beneath the radio buttons. If you're connecting via a network, you can click the Connect As button to enter credentials if they're required. If you need to redirect requests to another web site, type the name of the destination web site into the Redirect To box.

If your content is located on a directory on the IIS machine itself, you can select different permissions, outlined here:

Script source access

Enables users to view the source code to scripts and applications within the selected directory, assuming they have read or write permissions to that directory.

Read

Enables users to view or download files or directories, along with their individual properties.

Write

Enables users to upload files to the selected directory. It also enables them to change existing files within that directory. Browsers must support the PUT feature, implemented in HTTP Version 1.1, to take advantage of write access to a directory.

Directory browsing

Enables users to view an HTML page listing the contents of the selected directory, including any subdirectories. Note that the subdirectories listed in this view are physical filesystem directories, not IIS virtual directories. To access a virtual directory, a user will need to know its name.

Log visits

Specifies whether log entries should be created for visits to this directory. For this option to be functional, logging must be turned on for at least the current web site.

Index this resource

Allows the Microsoft Indexing Service to index the content of this web site. You'll need to enable the Indexing Service (through Add/Remove Programs inside the Control Panel) to begin using this feature.

You also have some options regarding web applications and how this individual web site should handle their behavior. You can safely ignore these settings if this web site is serving only static content, but if you have a complex web application, this is the place to customize it for IIS. In the Application name box, specify the name of the root directory that holds the files for the application. The Starting Point field shows where IIS thinks it should execute the application—usually this is where the application currently resides. You can set the level at which the program's application can actually execute within the server as well with the Execute permissions list box. Setting this to None renders any dynamic content unusable; setting this to Scripts allows only ASP scripts and other runtime noncompiled files to run; and setting this to Scripts and Executables allows scripts and application programs to run within IIS. Finally, the Application Pool option enables you to specify which pool of worker processes will serve this application.

The Remove or Create button enables you to delete an application from a web site or add an application to the current site. The Configuration page enables you to further customize an application's settings, including its own ISAPI filter mappings, how error pages are displayed, the default scripting languages, how session states are enabled and supported, and the like. The options under Application Configuration are beyond the scope of this overview and relate more to the programmatic side of web applications, so let's continue.

Documents

Figure 8-8 shows the Documents tab.

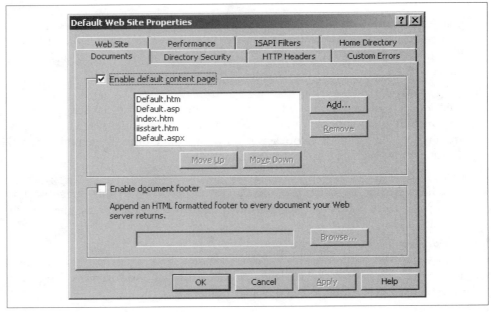

Figure 8-8. The Documents tab

This tab specifies the default page to be used when no page is specified in an HTTP request. You can specify the names of the default pages that will be returned, and you can configure the order in which IIS should search for a default page. All these files should be located in the web root. Click Add and Remove to add files to the list, and then use the Move Up and Move Down buttons to adjust their priority.

The Documents tab also enables you to configure a preformatted HTML footer to be inserted into every web page served by IIS, perfect for a disclaimer. Simply enter the path to the file that contains the footer, which should consist of enough HTML tags to describe the appearance and content of your footer, not an entire HTML document. An example disclaimer, with sufficient HTML coding, might look like this:

```
<p>This content does not necessarily represent the views of
<b>XYZ Corporation</b>. Please contact us with questions
at <a href="mailto:info@xyzcorp.com"> info@xyzcorp.com</a>.</p>
```

Directory Security

Figure 8-9 shows the Directory Security tab.

On the Directory Security tab, you can restrict the availability of content to certain users via a number of different methods.

First, you can enable or disable anonymous access and configure how IIS will authenticate nonanonymous (authenticated) users to the web site. Click the Edit button under the Authentication and access control section of the tab. You'll see a screen, called Authentication Methods, similar to that in Figure 8-10.

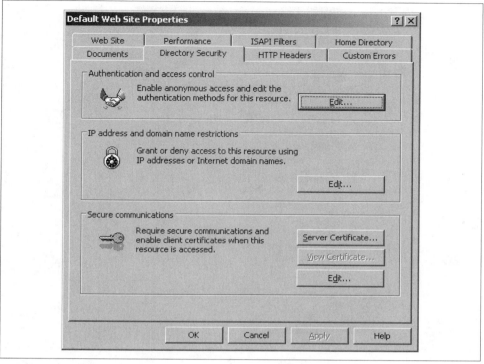

Figure 8-9. The Directory Security tab

Anonymous access to your web site is enabled here. You also can configure the user account under which anonymous users will automatically connect. Remember that there isn't a general open door for anonymous users to browse your IIS web sites: anonymous users actually use a real user account, to which you can grant NTFS filesystem permissions.

In the bottom part of the box, you can specify the method by which non-anonymous users will authenticate. These methods will be activated if anonymous access is not enabled for an individual web site, or if NTFS file or folder permissions prevent anonymous access to its contents. The four types of authentication are as follows:

Integrated Windows authentication
> Encrypts the username and password and sends it between the client and the server. This uses either the local SAM accounts database on the IIS server machine or Active Directory accounts.

Digest authentication
> This sends a hash of the password for an account, not the entire password, over the wire. The user's computer will then compute an identical hash, and the server will verify the two. This is available only when using Active Directory–based

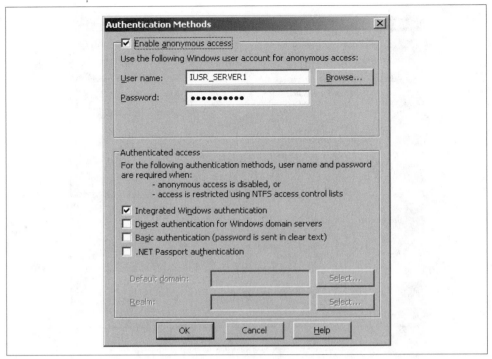

Figure 8-10. Authentication and access control in IIS

accounts, and the passwords must be available in clear text within the directory. You also can use it on proxy servers, firewalls, and WebDAV server machines. Note that you must identify a realm to use digest authentication.

 If your IIS machine also functions as a Windows Server 2003 domain controller, you can store the MD5 hash of passwords within Active Directory and not the entire clear-text password by editing the UseDigestSSP metabase key, which will enable a mode called advanced digest authentication.

Basic authentication

This is the most fundamental level of authentication, with the username and password traveling in clear text, unencrypted, across the wire. This is really suitable only on internal networks in this day and age unless you have a secure sockets layer (SSL)–encrypted connection in use. There is a great risk in letting passwords travel over the Internet in clear text.

.NET Passport authentication

This method uses the Microsoft .NET Passport identity management service to authenticate users. Using the .NET Passport service, a client can create a single sign-on ID and password to use across all sites that use the Passport authentication service. Although the Passport authentication service will verify a user's authenticity, it will not maintain lists of authorized files, folders, and resources on individual sites. So it's only a guard at the door; you must decide through NTFS permissions what Passport users can do once they're authenticated. You must enter a default domain when using .NET Passport authentication.

Enter a default Windows domain under which to authenticate users. You can click Select to browse the network for various available domains. Enter the default domain or another authentication control system in the Realm box. You can click the Select button here as well to select the appropriate machine. Click OK when you're finished configuring the authentication controls.

Next, you can grant or deny access to a site based on the client's IP address. This is useful if you have an abusive group of hosts that perhaps have been compromised, or if you want to restrict users of a site to only internal hosts. Click the Edit button under IP Address and Domain Name Restrictions, and you'll be greeted with a window of the same name, as shown in Figure 8-11.

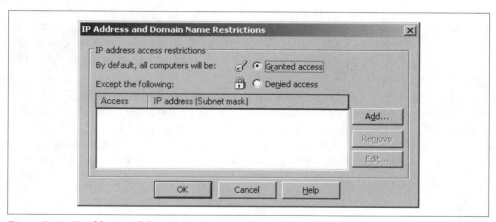

Figure 8-11. IP address and domain name restrictions in IIS

You first select whether all users will be granted or denied access to the site by using the radio buttons at the top of the window. Then you can configure individual exceptions to the rule you defined in the white list box. Click Add to include an address in the exceptions list. You'll be prompted with a box asking whether you want to exempt a single computer, a group of computers (an IP subnet), or an entire domain (DNS-based domain, that is).

Restricting or allowing access based on a DNS domain name is a very expensive operation because each HTTP request must be accompanied by a reverse lookup on the part of the IIS server. This can slow response time considerably and cause processor utilization to increase significantly. Enable this only if you're sure of the consequences or if you have a relatively lightly traveled web site to restrict.

Select the appropriate response, and then type in the actual IP address, network number and subnet, or domain name. You can click the DNS lookup button to perform a reverse lookup on a certain domain name to obtain its appropriate IP numbers.

If you want to restrict a web site to members in your organization only when they're at the office, and you have a proxy server, simply enter the proxy server's IP address in this box. All requests coming from a network behind a proxy server will display the proxy server's IP address.

When you're finished, click OK, and you'll be returned to the restrictions box. Now keep in mind that if you've configured default access for everyone to your site, the excepted addresses will be denied access. Conversely, if you've denied access by default to all IP addresses, the excepted addresses will be allowed access. This might seem obvious, but during a quick change it's easy to become a little confused at the quasi-backward logic. Click OK once you're finished.

The next section, Secure Communications, provides a way to ensure that data transmission sessions between a host and a client are made under proof that the server is who it says it is. This is done with certificates. If your server doesn't have a certificate yet, you'll need to create a request for one. Click the Server Certificate button to begin a wizard that will help you do this, and follow through this procedure as a guide:

1. Once the wizard starts, click Next to move on from the welcome screen.

2. You'll be prompted to create a new certificate, import one from a number of backup formats, or migrate a certificate from another computer onto the current one. For the purposes of this example, let's create a new certificate, so select that option and click Next.

3. On the Delayed or Immediate Request screen, choose whether to prepare the certificate signing request and save it for later transmission and purchase, or to prepare the request and immediately transmit it to a certification authority. In this example, we'll save the request and send it later. Click Next.

4. The Name and Security Settings page appears. Type a friendly, easy-to-identify name for the certificate. Also, select the bit length of the certificate. A shorter bit length results in faster transmission and decryption but has weaker security overall; a longer bit length is significantly more robust but involves a lot of transmission and

computing time during decryption. You also can choose to select a cryptographic service provider (CSP) for this certificate. Click Next to continue.

5. On the Organization Information page, enter the name of your organization and the division under which this server resides. It's best to get this information from your main corporate office, as identifying information corroborating what you enter here will most likely be required of you by the certifying authority. Click Next once you've entered the necessary information.

6. The Your Site's Common Name page is next. Here, enter the valid DNS domain name for your site (such as *order.enablehosting.com*) assuming it is visible to the Internet. If it's an internal site, simply enter the NetBIOS name of the computer (for example, LEAVETRACKER), but it's really better to hedge your bets and use a full DNS name even for an internal site. Click Next to continue.

7. Enter your country of residence, state or province, and city or locality. Do not use abbreviations. Click Next.

8. On the Certificate Request File Name page, specify a name for the certificate signing request and a location for the file. You can click the Browse button to create a new directory or to pick one graphically. Click Next.

9. The Request File Summary page appears. All your choices through the wizard are summarized here. Click Back to correct any information that's wrong, or click Next to create the signing request.

10. Click Finish on the acknowledgment screen.

The generated request will look something like this:

```
-----BEGIN NEW CERTIFICATE REQUEST-----
MIIGZjCCBE4CAQAwgYUxCzAJBgNVBAYTAlVTMRcwFQYDVQQIEw5Ob3JOaCBDYXJv
bGluYTEQMA4GA1UEBxMHUmFsZWlnaDEmMCQGA1UEChMdSm9uYXRoYW4gSGFzc2Vs
bCBUZWNObm9sb2dpZXMxETAPBgNVBAsTCE8nUmVpbGx5MRAwDgYDVQQDEwdzaG90
MS1kMIICIjANBgkqhkiG9w0BAQEFAAOCAg8AMIICCgKCAgEA4ACGd+bYrJ3koanc
OqWOSHhHj6HGU2cMWmFjxA9EEVsWrPZtdJ6IGvqZThxEB7uPQW3ywoEWBSegmceg
p3XzsPTC4LbqAgmymz/gE4ULRvCJNR3oPORaAQk3uJxdHNEDgIW3D2I+WeWk14Dq
BzoFPbVJb/pO92LZI4KDyDElloCs4QRSquf6Th8Bn9m2f2IRNx49xKGsVS7aP831
JVMoUaiT5LKkB7VHqT5QokJ69vPwPGG+PfyBRqPu5A8kdfHgiBhNpIei/mOPW7kn
oNpcVMvQNtnxePqJOBgx+J5ODPgVxg12Fuaa2DXvYFjOf4jHjGgXqyo3kuoo3RbM
knszTt+3OEvU3hBBk5M2dCTkcWQJxL3NuAbzVjIe6RPbOO7XUufUjznBdbl8dVVP
kOL9TgOZNA8VIRTteZhD8XGatSGrC95EI/lnr1UOpXqm6zLyjJVZbbJUacVjewNU
ptjSmGFKWdp6O8udUfVQslotMypraVOWaDFmA6acNcFFM7aI9SQEE6oQHVfQ9k11
q5bUPQG/RNiCfYwMas63BGzUzq2dslF4OAbLJQfkGTTKVOZ6rUU3eT8WQr1IO7yA
1lqJJMng6hQDgOKqeIcLztIRPOIJvsDWK5L9YmoAXyOwFdfZSpnDQ95HUJ8N8rMr
BygxL8QHAkt4xQJdGtpMEbSeDU8CAwEAAaCCAZkwGgYKKwYBBAGCNwoCAzEMFgo1
LjIuMzc5MC4yMHsGCisGAQQBgjcCAQ4xbTBrMA4GA1UdDwEB/wQEAwIE8DBEBgkq
hkiG9w0BCQ8ENzA1MA4GCCqGSIb3DQMCAgIAgDAOBggqhkiG9w0DBAICAIAwBwYF
Kw4DAgcwCgYIKoZIhvcNAwcwEwYDVR01BAwwCgYIKwYBBQUHAwEwgfOGCisGAQQB
gjcNAgIxge4wgesCAQEeWgBNAGkAYwByAG8AcwBvAGYAdAAgAFIAUwBBACAAUwBD
AGgAYQBuAG4AZQBsACAAQwByAHkAcABOAG8AZwByAGEAcBBoAGkAYwAgAFAAcgBv
AHYAaQBkAGUAcgOBiQAAAAAAAAAAAAAAAAAAAAAAAAAAAAAAAAAAAAAAAAAAAAAA
AAAAAAAAAAAAAAAAAAAAAAAAAAAAAAAAAAAAAAAAAAAAAAAAAAAAAAAAAAAAAAAA
```

```
AAAAAAAAAAAAAAAAAAAAAAAAAAAAAAAAAAAAAAAAAAAAAAAAAAAAAAAAAAAAAAAA
AAAAAAAAMAOGCSqGSIb3DQEBBQUAA4ICAQBFTI2csvyAMgm6qerhdLQD92KfiP4k
mXU8oOs7oQy1ohpkRIDeXtEPXiD5o2wSSwFe8X3+mmG/HqWfeXqILAfdxRZUQlCJ
bTPB8tFW+exODFzIzBpzrpzn1RVIgH35e8x/a9kZ9jZYy+uHtwcnumK1kvoG7Uwc
9uXdEA44GLkSpdQX4HUhw8T1D7KiwfXLycFVBtBpOLEI2VhpVoOgm8O+hILpYSom
8dGtdKzgPTOsN//wu1SRU9L7m9cAGo13Qc4KtmI/kDdNpfLGtyA46ObHNKJeL6Lo
gSgJmc5Npsfr4jZWqVuL9rxuE+fS/hHUQ6QLJObwKfYrconMoaWkpqgh2pYaf16Z
YdyGM/aBTycO2L2EXbP97g5XQvKgOjfFL4gb1xn4kHbjfXkOoqDXZqnm8TmyzYaw
8p/3/YWNywB7u3mA/9MChlx+P6sueHrMeyW4nu5oFYvtO1e/GMTJ1ieqhY/Cfm4y
oaVuEhLqxN/1eCElG82TKtl6SodjZ52KFw85/Ke3OHS2RFMeiWEB6VU1JmOacmDn
b3cDQS+nNWflAnt2Vn3vdHt5bFHBiElDJpbmZFRZKjZ9gg76bhEbPOv/4GUkVkeg
EnbEggH59mwEKCl2nlxsw5d2wZ/2prAjdJFwWnf96bHxdBb1VPQmTeNMmSgr/ssT
S9iTaY4ii2FaAg= =
-----END NEW CERTIFICATE REQUEST-----
```

You'll then submit this CSR to your certification authority, and receive a certificate after your submission and identification information has been verified. (All that material is covered in Chapter 11, so if you're not familiar with certificates and the associated processes, that's where to look.) When you receive the certificate, run the wizard again. It will detect an existing request and will ask you to match up your CSR with the actual certificate you were provided by the authority. You'll then have the certificate installed, and communications over SSL will be enabled.

Once your certificate is installed, you can adjust the behavior of IIS when it comes to client sessions over SSL. Click the Edit button under the Secure Communications section of the Directory Security tab. The Secure Communications dialog box appears, which is shown in Figure 8-12.

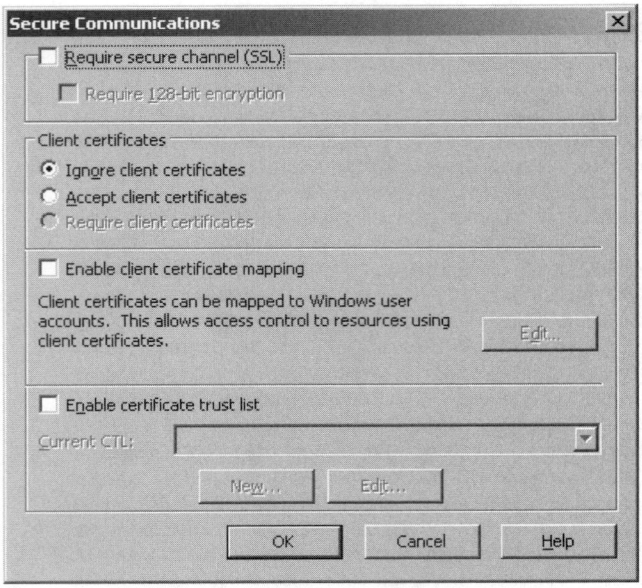

Figure 8-12. SSL and certificate behavior in IIS

First you can choose whether to require secure communications for a particular site. If you do require it, you can further secure communications by mandating 128-bit encryption of data exchanges between the client and the server. All data sent is encrypted using the web server's certificate. Under the client certificates section, you can choose whether to ignore certificates that clients present (to identify themselves to a server), to accept them without a mandate, or to require them. Depending on how security-conscious your organization is, I recommend either accepting them or requiring them.

You also can elect to enable client certificate mapping. In this scenario, you can map a client computer's certificates to actual Windows accounts—at that point, you can have more granular control over access to resources. Consider it almost a "grouping" of computers with their respective users, all configured to share one certificate. Click the Edit button to define these mappings. This will open the Account Mappings screen, shown in Figure 8-13.

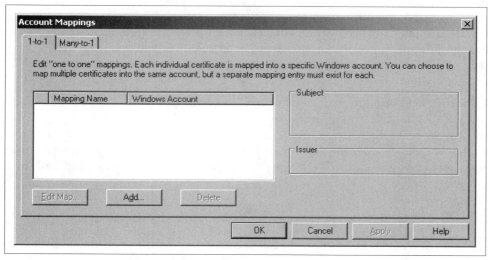

Figure 8-13. The client certificate mapping configuration screen

You can define two types of mappings—a one-to-one mapping, which maps one certificate to one Windows account, or a many-to-one mapping, in which you can match individual criteria about a client certificate to map to a group of Windows accounts. You could, for example, identify the division field of client certificates and log users in to a specific account because of their individual divisions. Each tab of the Account Mappings screen handles one of these types of mappings.

Let's look at a one-to-one mapping first. To create these mappings, IIS needs a text (ASCII) copy of the user's client certificate. IIS compares this copy of the certificate it has on file with the copy presented by the client during the initial HTTP request. The two must be absolutely identical—they cannot differ in any way—for the mapping to be successful. Certificates that are reissued to the client, even if they contain entirely the same information, must be remapped with IIS.

 Some client certificates need to be exported using Internet Explorer for use in one-to-one mapping with IIS.

Click the Add button to create a new mapping. You'll need to locate a copy of the client certificate, and select a Windows user account to which to map the certificate. You can then edit an existing mapping by clicking the Edit button, or delete a mapping by clicking Remove.

A many-to-one mapping is a little different. As I explained previously, many-to-one mapping employs sets of rules that match certain criteria within a client certificate, such as issuer or subject. With a many-to-one mapping, IIS doesn't actually compare any certificates. You don't even have to have a certificate on file for each client, which means exporting certificates is hassle-free. Instead, IIS simply accepts any certificate meeting a rule. New or reissued client certificates, as long as they still contain enough information to match an existing map rule, will still work. Of course, this method is a bit less secure because the extra step of certificate verification which is present in one-to-one mapping isn't built into the many-to-one mapping process.

Click the Add button to create a new many-to-one mapping. You can adjust the priority of existing rules using the Move Up and Move Down boxes. IIS will process rules in the order listed until a match is found; at that point, it will stop processing. If two rules conflict, the rule with the higher priority will be processed and the other will simply be ignored. Click OK when you're finished defining mappings and their priority.

 If the Windows Directory Service Mapper—the piece that connects certificates with Active Directory accounts—is enabled on a server-wide basis, you won't be able to configure one-to-one or many-to-one mappings.

Finally, you can enable or disable a certificate trust list (CTL) that IIS will look at to determine if it will treat a client certificate as valid. You can create a new CTL, which will involve importing certificates from root certifying authorities, or you can edit an existing store. The wizard for creating a new store is self-explanatory, so I won't cover it here.

HTTP Headers

Figure 8-14 shows the HTTP Headers tab.

Figure 8-14. The HTTP Headers tab

On the HTTP Headers page, you can customize the attributes and values of HTTP pages returned to a client's browser. (You can adjust these settings on a server-wide level; if an individual web site's settings conflict with the global header settings, the individual web site will win the conflict.) On this tab you also can rate your content so that users taking advantage of the corresponding feature in Internet Explorer will know the suitability of your content for viewing, and you can define additional MIME types that IIS can serve.

First, you can elect to have content expire after a set period of time, immediately after delivery, or on a certain date. Set this option by choosing the appropriate radio button and adjusting the date or length of time.

Next, customize the HTTP headers sent in a response to a client's request. You can use custom headers to send instructions that modify the behavior of the client browser from the IIS machine to the client, especially those that are not yet supported in the current revision of the HTTP protocol spec. Click Add, and enter the attribute and the value to be transmitted. Use the Edit button to modify an existing custom header, and the Remove button to delete it from the server.

Use the ratings modification tool to adjust the Recreational Software Advisory Council (RSAC) content rating of the material presented in your web site. RSAC-compliant browsers—which are prevalent in today's computing world—can detect this rating information and present it to the user before pages are loaded, enabling the client to specify whether he wants to see what Microsoft calls "potentially objectionable" web content. To edit the ratings for this web site, click the Edit button. Select the area of ratings, and drag the slider to adjust the actual score on that area. Enter your email address so that people who have questions about the suitability of the content can contact you, select a date on which these ratings will expire, and then click OK. If your organization is hosting a site that family-oriented surfers will browse to, it's to your advantage to configure these settings; many content-filtered browsers and proxy servers (NetNanny, anyone?) will look at RSAC ratings to determine if content is suitable for display.

Finally, define supported MIME types for this web site. MIME mappings register the types of files that IIS serves to client machines and browsers. IIS will serve only the types of files registered in this list. If a client requests a file with an extension that isn't mapped, an error page, specifically 404.3, will be returned. To add an extension, click the MIME Types button. Then click New, and define the attribute and its corresponding value. You also can modify existing mappings using the Edit button, and remove mappings using the Remove button.

 If you want IIS to serve all pages, regardless of their extension, input an asterisk as a wildcard in a MIME mapping.

Custom Errors

Figure 8-15 shows the Custom Errors tab.

On the Custom Errors tab, you can define the location and content of *custom error pages*, which are pages that are returned when you misspell a filename, or give out a bad link, or request a page for which you don't have adequate permissions. You can choose whether to use standard HTTP 1.1 error messages, the default IIS error pages (which give a bit more information about each error and some basic but useful troubleshooting information for the client), or completely custom error pages that you create on your own. You can also set these options on a server-wide level.

Server errors and messages are coded via four different strata of status types:

Codes 200-299
    These codes indicate successful HTTP transactions.

Codes 300-399
    These codes indicate that a protocol-based redirection to another site has occurred.

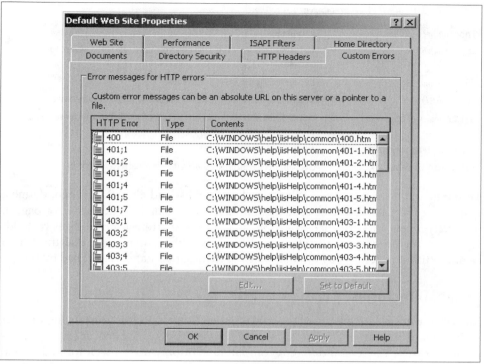

Figure 8-15. The Custom Errors tab

Codes 400-499

These are definite errors. Some of the most common include a 400 (a "bad request," used when the server can't decipher a message sent by a client), a 401 (an "unauthorized" error, whereby the user has no permissions to access a site), a 403 (a "forbidden" error, used when something other than a user's credentials prevents him from accessing a site), and a 404 (a "file not found" error, used when the file a client requests can't be located on the server).

These codes are errors to indicate there is a problem on the server side.

Table 8-1 lists some of the most common HTTP errors and what they mean.

Table 8-1. Common HTTP errors

Error number	Description
400 Bad Request	A syntax error has occurred in the URL, or the browser has sent a malformed HTTP request.
401 Unauthorized	You haven't submitted the proper credentials to access a certain site.

Table 8-1. Common HTTP errors (continued)

Error number	Description
403 Forbidden	You lack read privileges to the requested file, or you are not allowed to have access to that file.
404 Not Found	The page no longer exists at that location.
500 Internal Error	The server malfunctioned and was thus unable to send the requested file.
501 Not Implemented	Typically found with forms, this indicates a configuration error on the server side where new features are not fully set up.
502 Service Temporarily Overloaded	There is a high load on the server.
503 Gateway Time-Out	A routing error has occurred between the client and server computer.

To modify an error page, select the error from the list and click Edit. Then, define a custom location, set the error to its default behavior (using IIS's default error pages), or specify a new URL for the error. You also can select multiple error pages by holding down the Shift key and selecting the errors with your mouse. Use the Set to Default button to return custom mappings to their native state, as installed by IIS.

Virtual Directories

Virtual directories are great ways to make a site's structure easy to navigate for your users, even if the actual content stored on physical disks is located in several different locations or on several different computers. Not only does a well-formed virtual directory structure make a site easy to use for a web surfer, but it increases the flexibility of management for the web developer. It also provides a layer of security through obscurity because the virtual directory need not correspond directly to a physical directory on a hard disk.

To create a virtual directory, follow these steps:

1. Open IIS Manager and click the appropriate web site.

2. Right-click the web site and select Virtual Directory from the New menu. The Virtual Directory Creation Wizard will appear.

3. Enter a name for the alias that users will specify to refer to this virtual directory. This is the text that comes after the / in the URL.

4. Next, specify the location of the content that will populate this virtual directory. You can enter either a local path or a UNC network path, depending on whether you're mapping a local or remote path.

5. On the Security Credentials screen, specify the account and password used to authenticate to the network resources that hold the content for the virtual directory if necessary.

6. The Virtual Directory Access Permissions screen appears. Specify all the permissions you'd like to grant to the directory (the choices are the standard ones covered earlier in this chapter: read, run scripts, execute, write, and browse).

7. Click Finish to confirm the creation of the virtual directory.

You can adjust the properties of a virtual directory much like a web site itself: right-click the virtual directory inside IIS Manager and select Properties. You'll be presented with dialogs functionally equivalent to the ones covered earlier in this chapter, pertaining to web sites themselves.

FrontPage Server Extensions

Microsoft created the FrontPage Server Extensions as a way of ensuring that its Office-based web editor, Microsoft FrontPage, would become the de facto standard for web design in small and medium-size business. The extensions reside on a web server and make various web elements easier to include in a web site: such features as form design, a search engine, indexing service, and automated assistants called *bots* make life a tad easier for those with less web hosting experience. The extensions aren't required if you want to use FrontPage on a plain-vanilla site, but they do function as value-added bits.

To use the extensions with a site, you must, of course, install the extensions on the server—you can do this from the Add/Remove Programs applet in the Control Panel. Doing so creates a virtual server called Microsoft SharePoint Administration. Other requirements: the site that you want to enable FP extensions for must be its own virtual server, and you must explicitly enable extensions on the site, a process known as "extending" the web site.

To begin extending a site, follow these steps:

1. Open IIS Manager, and select the web site for which you want to enable the extensions.

2. Right-click the site, and from the All Tasks menu, select Configure Server Extensions 2002.

3. Your browser will open the Microsoft SharePoint Administration web site and prompt you to confirm the web site that you want the extensions installed on, and also the username of the administrator that will manage the web site.

4. Click Submit to acknowledge the extension of the web site.

When you install the extensions on a site, the procedure creates a tab on the properties of each web site, called Server Extensions 2002. On the tab is a button labeled Settings that will open a browser to the main administrative pages for the FrontPage Server Extensions. This page is shown in Figure 8-16.

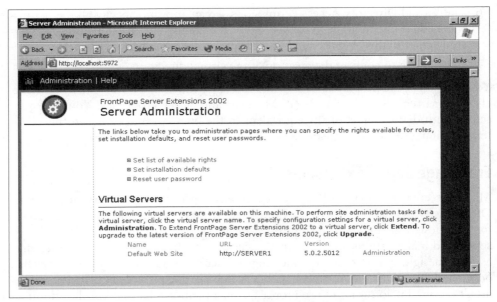

Figure 8-16. The main configuration page for Server Extensions 2002

Let's step through each configuration option on the page, broken down by section:

Enable authoring

> Check or uncheck this box to allow people to create or edit pages or scripts, using FrontPage, on this web site.

Mail settings

> Here, indicate the outgoing SMTP server to use subscriptions, invitations, and other email-based features. You can also customize the From and Reply To fields, and specify which mail-encoding scheme and character set should be used for the emails.

Performance tuning

> Specify the estimated traffic to the web site in the Tune For box. This will prepopulate the individual settings in the Tuning Properties section, and you can change the cache limits and size of the search indices as needed for your specific implementation.

Client scripting

> Here, you can indicate whether to allow users to use JavaScript, VBScript, to disallow scripting altogether, or to allow the default listed for the web site in IIS Manager.

Security settings

> You can indicate whether to write to the event log every time someone uses an authoring privilege, whether to mandate SSL for administration and authoring, and whether to allow authors to upload executable files.

Using Application Pools

As I discussed earlier in this chapter, application pools provide a measure of stability and reliability for high-volume web applications hosted with IIS 6. Although they provide greater predictability in behavior and several other side benefits, each application pool takes up a minimum of about 4MB of memory on your IIS machine, so it's best to accurately configure your application pools if you're to have multiple pools on one machine. In this section, I'll show you how to do that. Let's take a look at the application pool options available out of the box and then examine how to create custom application pools for your own services.

To examine the default settings for the "catch-all" existing application pool, open IIS Manager, right-click the Application Pools node, and select Properties from the context menu. Figure 8-17 shows the properties sheet that is opened.

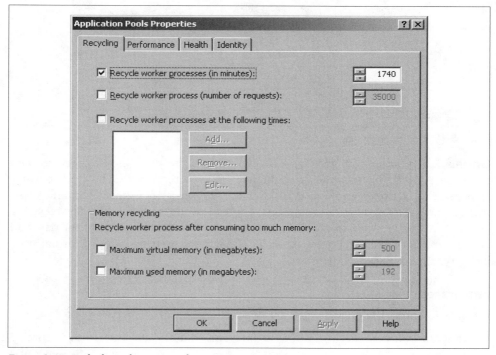

Figure 8-17. Default application pools properties

This page comprises four tabs, each with several different functions.

Recycling

Figure 8-18 shows the Recycling tab.

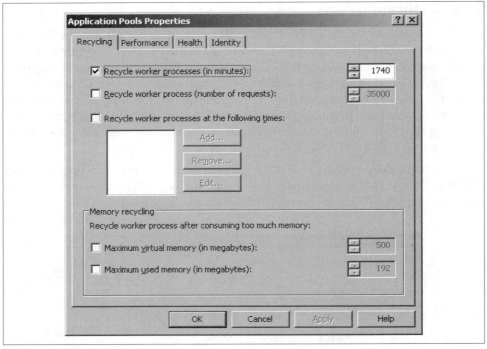

Figure 8-18. The Recycling tab

On this tab you can configure how IIS will handle the recycling of processes and memory. As discussed in the introduction, process recycling is how IIS ensures responsive processes by killing off old processes when they finish handling their requests and starting new ones to listen. You can configure how often this recycling occurs, whether at a certain cycle of time or at specific times throughout the day, and at what memory usage level (in terms of either total used memory or virtual used memory) a recycling will be triggered.

Performance

Figure 8-19 shows the Performance tab.

On this tab you can specify options to prevent your IIS machine from becoming overloaded with requests and worker processes. The first option, "Idle timeout," instructs IIS to kill off worker processes that have been sitting inactive for whatever period of time is specified. The Request queue limit option allows IIS to monitor the number of requests and place a restriction on the maximum number that can wait in line for servicing and distribution by the kernel. (When you reach this maximum, users see an HTTP 503 error, which indicates the server is too busy to handle the request.) The CPU monitoring section enables you to specify limits on the amount of processor time a specific application pool should get, how often these measurements should be taken, and what happens when the limits are exceeded by an application.

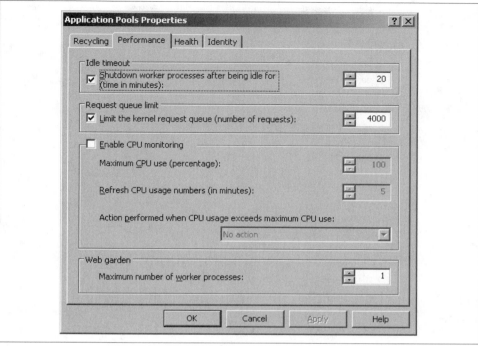

Figure 8-19. The Performance tab

Web gardens are basically application pools that are assigned more than one worker process. Adjust the number of worker processes assigned to this application pool here.

Health

Figure 8-20 shows the Health tab.

You can set various metrics to check the well-being of your server on the Health tab. These metrics are inspected by the WAS, which goes into the application pool, checks these parameters, and enforces any limits you set.

You can specify the default interval between pings to your worker process to tell if it's still alive. You also can configure a failure threshold—what Microsoft calls rapid-fail protection. In essence, you tell IIS that if a certain worker process fails x times within x minutes, shut it down for good so as to create less instability on the server. Lastly, you can specify a startup and shutdown time limit: if worker processes take too long to start or stop, they are assumed to be hung and are subsequently killed.

Identity

Figure 8-21 shows the Identity tab.

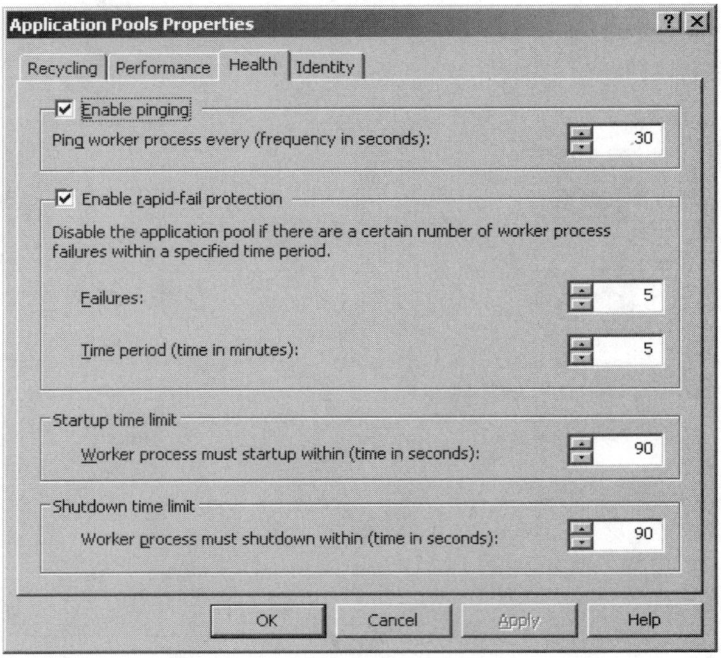

Figure 8-20. The Health tab

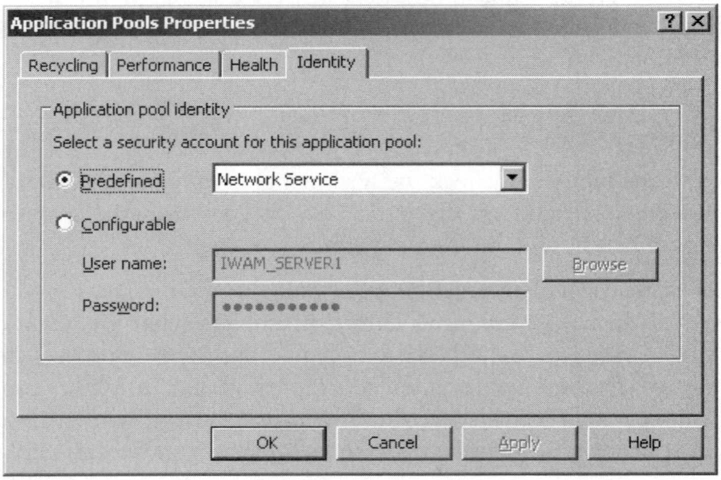

Figure 8-21. The Identity tab

On the Identity tab, you can configure the security context under which this application pool will run. You'll note the default is the Network Service account which doesn't grant very many permissions: only Read and Execute, List Folder Contents, and Read—a beneficial by-product of Microsoft's recent emphasis on security. You can specify a different account from the machine's local SAM database or from Active Directory, but the account must be in the IIS_WPG group on the local machine. The IIS_WPG group contains all worker process accounts and already contains the necessary permissions to interact with worker processes.

Creating a new application pool

If you need to create a new application pool and not host your worker processes in the existing DefaultAppPool, it's a two-step process: first you need to actually create the pool, and then assign your web sites to work inside the various pools.

To create a new pool, open IIS Manager, select the Application Pools node in the left pane, and right-click to select Application Pool from the New menu. The Add New Application Pool dialog box will be raised, as shown in Figure 8-22.

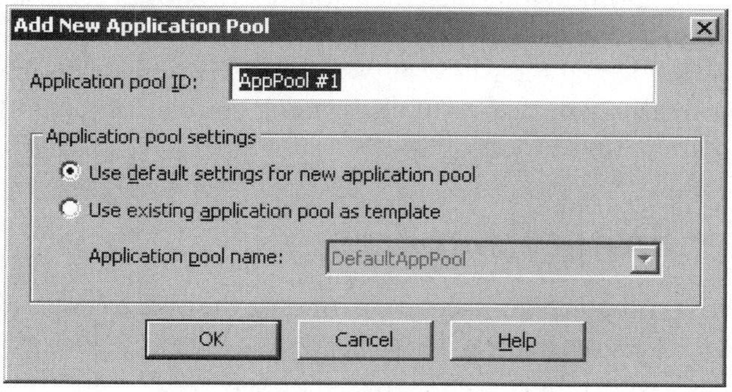

Figure 8-22. Adding a new application pool

Enter an identification tag for the new pool, and then specify whether to clone an existing pool's settings or to use IIS default settings. Click OK when you're finished, and the new pool will be displayed in IIS Manager.

The next step is to assign your web sites to the new pool. Right-click the appropriate web site within IIS Manager, select Properties, and then navigate to the Home Directory tab. At the bottom of the sheet, pull down the Application Pool menu, and select the pool in which this web site should operate. Click OK when you're finished. You don't need to restart or reboot anything; IIS will automatically migrate the site to the new pool itself seamlessly.

Using the Web Services Extensions Node

The Web Services Extensions node enables you to selectively enable and disable dynamic content based on the type of handlers for that content. By default, IIS 6 will serve only static content, which means that ASP.NET, server side includes, and FrontPage Server Extensions simply won't work unless they're enabled. You can tweak these settings using the Web Services Extensions node under IIS Manager.

When you click the Web Services Extensions node by default, it lists several different handlers for dynamic content and their current status on the server (allowed or prohibited). You can change the status by selecting the specific handler, and then clicking the Allow or Prohibit button on the left side of the righthand pane, depending on which action you prefer. If you want more information on a particular handler, you can right-click it and select Properties. The General tab will give you information on which services use the particular pages handled by that handler, and the Required Files tab delves down into more detail, enabling you to specifically enable or disable certain handler DLLs to enable the functionality.

You also can add new web service extensions by selecting the "Add a new Web service extension" link and filling in the extension name and its required files. In addition, you can specify which handlers will be enabled on an application-by-application basis by clicking the Allow all Web service extensions for a specific application link. And finally, you can turn all dynamic content off again by clicking the Prohibit all Web service extensions link.

File Transfer Protocol Services

The File Transfer Protocol (FTP) service is one of the most venerable Internet services in existence. Its presence on the Internet predates HTTP, and it's still one of the best options users have to transfer large files across a WAN. Indeed, some sites have begun offering HTTP-based downloads because of corporations that block both outgoing and incoming FTP ports, but FTP remains the more efficient transport mechanism of the two. However, FTP has some inherent security issues, the most prominent of which is its nature to transmit password information in clear text through the Internet—a huge security hole and a grab bag for packet sniffers. Beware of that, and use FTP when and where that problem is not severe or applicable enough for you to worry about.

IIS 6 comes complete with an FTP service and includes some new security features that harden FTP against unwanted access from the Internet. IIS 6 includes FTP user isolation mode, which restricts an FTP client's ability to move around in directory structures outside of his home directory. You need to set up an FTP site to either use isolation mode or disregard it, and in this section, we'll tackle both and discuss where it might be appropriate to use one or the other.

Creating FTP Sites

Let's create a new FTP site. Unfortunately, FTP does not support host header names, so if you need to distinguish between multiple FTP sites on one machine, you'll need to segregate content using either virtual directories (which are supported), multiple unique IP addresses, or unique TCP/IP ports.

To create a new site, follow these steps:

1. Open IIS Manager.

2. Select FTP Sites from the left pane. Right-click the node, and select FTP Site from the New menu.

3. The FTP Site Creation Wizard appears. First, enter a friendly name for the site so that you can recognize it easily within management tools.

4. Next, assign an IP address and TCP port number for this site, or use All Unassigned and the default of 21.

5. The FTP User Isolate screen appears. For this example, let's choose not to isolate users. (I'll cover the concept in a later example.) Click Next.

6. On the FTP Site Home Directory screen, enter the path on your local or network filesystem that will become the root directory of your FTP site. This is similar to the web root for an IIS web site.

7. Define permissions for the default user on an FTP site. You can choose from read and write permissions.

8. Click Finish once you've verified all your choices.

Your site is now created.

Master FTP Site Properties

Now that we have created a site, let's look at the default properties that can affect all sites on a machine. To access the master properties of all FTP sites, right-click the FTP sites node in the left pane on IIS Manager, and select Properties. You'll be greeted with the screen shown in Figure 8-23.

Some settings apply only to individual sites and not to all sites on a certain machine, and those options are grayed out. For the most part, all master settings work identically to those settings for individual sites, except that their scope is broader. In fact, configuring a setting inside the master properties means that all sites on the machine will inherit that setting except those that already have a value explicitly defined—in other words, no existing configurations will be overwritten.

The exception to this is the Service tab, on which you can throttle the bandwidth that all FTP sites use in total. This can be an effective way of restricting an FTP site from overtaking the total throughput of a leased line. You set the throttle based on KB per second. You can't set throttles on individual FTP sites; the option is available per machine only.

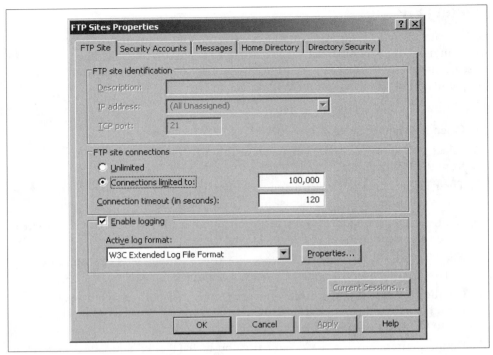

Figure 8-23. IIS FTP master properties

Individual FTP Site Properties

To open the properties sheets for an individual web site, select the site with IIS Manager under the FTP Sites node in the left pane. Right-click the site listing and select Properties. You'll see something similar to Figure 8-24 on your screen.

In this section, much like the discussion on web site properties, I'll step through each tab and show you the meaning of each setting.

FTP Site

Figure 8-25 shows the FTP Site tab.

On the FTP Site tab, you can specify the identification information for your site, including the friendly description, its assigned IP address if in use, and the port number on which the site operates. In addition, you can choose to limit connections to a certain number and forcibly end connections that don't generate activity for a certain number of seconds. Here, you also can enable logging, and choose the log format that best suits your needs. (I discussed these formats in the web site properties section earlier in this chapter.)

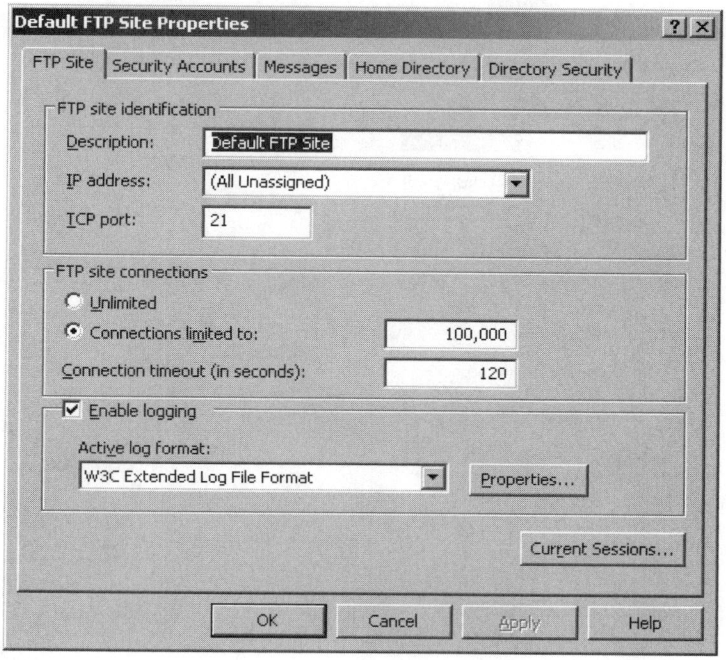

Figure 8-24. Individual FTP site properties

The Current Sessions button enables you to view who is currently connected to your FTP site, their login context if any, their source IP address, and how long their connection has been active. You also can click an active connection and disconnect it manually using the Disconnect button, or use Disconnect All to completely clear connections to your site.

Security Accounts

Figure 8-26 shows the Security Accounts tab.

On the Security Accounts tab, you can enable or disable anonymous access to your site and define what user account anonymous users will use when accessing your FTP site. Much like with the web server, anonymous users are actually logged on to your machine in the context of a specific user on the local computer or in Active Directory. This makes it easier to lock down filesystem content from external users and provides another layer of security—the NTFS permission system—on top of the basic IIS permissions available.

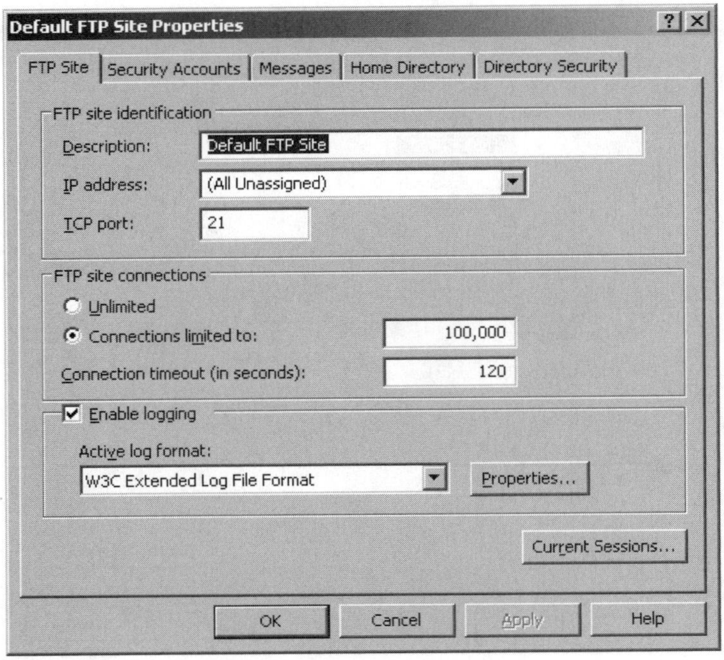

Figure 8-25. The FTP Site tab

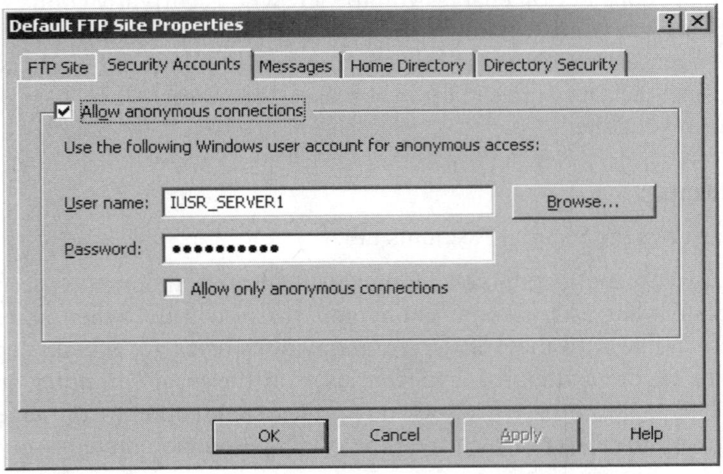

Figure 8-26. The Security Accounts tab

Keep in mind that FTP has no mechanism to encrypt passwords sent over the wire, so all passwords sent will be in clear text and subject to someone intercepting them while in transit.

The Allow only anonymous connections checkbox restricts normal users from logging on with an otherwise valid local or Active Directory account—perfect for a simple FTP site with small programs and documents. By doing so, you can completely disconnect the FTP site from Active Directory or your SAM database on the IIS machine itself, which adds an extra layer of security.

Messages

Figure 8-27 shows the Messages tab.

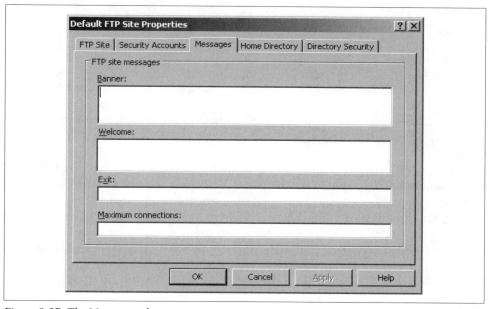

Figure 8-27. The Messages tab

The Messages tab enables you to define blocks of informational text that can be sent to a user's FTP client. Most browser-based FTP sites display the banner message, which is shown when users initially connect before logging in, and the welcome message, which follows a successful authentication. However, most people don't bother to display an exit message when the user disconnects properly. You also can specify a custom message to be displayed when the maximum connection limit has been reached.

Home Directory

Figure 8-28 shows the Home Directory tab.

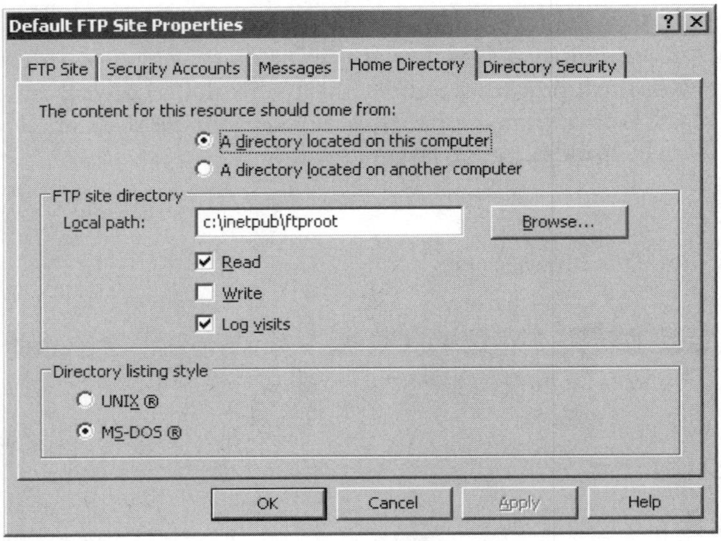

Figure 8-28. The Home Directory tab

On the Home Directory tab, you can configure the physical location where FTP content is stored. You can specify via the two radio-button options under "The content for this resource should come from:" that the home directory is located in a folder on the current computer or a file share somewhere over a network. You can type the local directory name or the network file share name in the Local Path or Network Directory box just beneath the radio buttons. If you're connecting via a network, you can click the Connect As button to enter credentials.

You can grant or deny the following permissions for the current FTP site:

Read
> Allows users to view or download files or directories, along with viewing their individual properties.

Write
> Allows users to upload files to the selected directory. It also allows them to change existing files within that directory.

Log visits
> Specifies whether log entries should be created for visits to this directory. For this option to be functional, logging must be turned on at least for the current FTP site as a whole.

You also can configure the style of the directory listing returned to a browser. Choose Unix to display a four-digit year when the date of the file differs from the year of the FTP server. Click MS-DOS to display a two-digit year in any case.

Directory Security

Figure 8-29 shows the Directory Security tab.

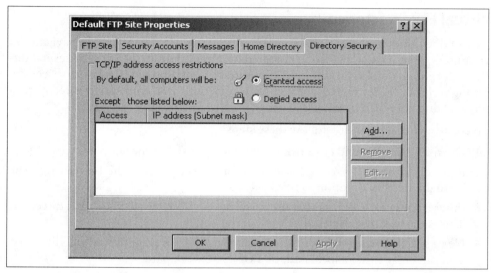

Figure 8-29. The Directory Security tab

On the Directory Security tab, you can grant or deny access to a site based on the client's IP address. This is useful if you have an abusive or compromised group of external hosts that continually attack your network, or if you want to restrict users of a site to internal hosts only.

First you select whether all users will be granted or denied access to the site by using the radio buttons at the top of the window. Then, you can configure individual exceptions to this rule in the white list box. Click Add to include an address in the exceptions list. You'll be prompted with a dialog box asking whether you want to exclude a single computer or a group of computers (an IP subnet). Select the appropriate response, and then type in the actual IP address or network number and subnet. You can click the DNS Lookup button to perform a reverse lookup on a certain domain name to obtain its appropriate IP range.

 If you want to restrict an FTP site to members in your organization only when they're at the office and you have a proxy server, simply enter the proxy server's IP address in the box shown in Figure 8-29. All requests coming from a network behind a proxy server will display the proxy server's IP address.

When you're finished, click OK, and you'll be returned to the restrictions box. Now, keep in mind that if you've configured default access for everyone to your site, the excluded addresses will be denied access. Conversely, if you've denied access by default to all IP addresses, the excluded addresses will be allowed access. This might seem obvious, but during a quick change it's easy to become a little confused at the quasi-backward logic. Click OK once you're finished.

Virtual FTP Directories

Virtual directories are great ways to make an FTP site's structure easy to navigate for your users, even if the actual content stored on physical disks is located in several different locations on several different computers. It also provides a layer of security through obscurity because the virtual directory need not correspond directly to a physical directory on a hard disk.

To create a virtual directory, follow these steps:

1. Open IIS Manager and click the appropriate FTP site in the left pane.
2. Right-click the FTP site, and select Virtual Directory from the New menu. The Virtual Directory Creation Wizard will appear.
3. Enter a name for the alias that users will specify to refer to this virtual directory. This is the text that comes after the / in the URL.
4. Next, specify the location of the content that will populate this virtual directory. You can enter either a local path or a UNC network path.
5. On the Security Credentials screen, specify the account and password used to authenticate to the network resources that hold the content for the virtual directory. You'll see this screen only if you entered a network path in step 4.
6. The Virtual Directory Access Permissions screen appears. Specify all the permissions you want to grant to the directory (the choices are the standard ones I covered earlier in this section: read and write).
7. Click Finish to confirm the creation of the virtual directory.

You can adjust the properties of a virtual directory much like an FTP site itself: right-click the virtual directory inside IIS Manager and select Properties. You'll be presented with dialogs functionally equivalent to the ones I covered earlier in this chapter pertaining to web sites.

One other issue with virtual directories deserves some commentary: any virtual directories you create will not show up inside a command-line FTP session, whether through a directory listing initiated by the user or any kind of transfer activity. They'll be displayed only when a graphical FTP client requests a directory listing because it interfaces directly with IIS: the dir or ls commands inside an FTP client interact directly with the physical filesystem, which virtual directories are not a part of (hence the term "virtual"). To use a virtual directory, the user needs to navigate directly to it. This is a bit of security through obscurity—certainly not impermeable, but still of value.

FTP User Isolation

User isolation is a new feature of IIS 6 in which users are sent directly to a home directory upon logging in that appears to them to be the root of the entire FTP server. In this scenario, users have no idea of any directory structures that exist outside of their own home directory. This is great for FTP sites used by multiple people, particularly those with privacy concerns over the data they would be uploading.

To set this up, you must take a few preliminary steps. First, determine where you want the location of the user home directories. This must be a directory named *LocalUser* (which can be hosted on a local or remote file server), the subdirectories of which will belong to each individual user. Do note that the previous name is not a variable for the user—it is actually the directory name you need to create. The specific name tells IIS where to look for subdirectories for the users, so it's important the name not change. Next, create the directories under *LocalUser*. The names must correspond to user accounts either in the local SAM database or inside Active Directory.

 Changing a site to user isolation mode cannot be undone. You must delete and recreate the site if you change your mind.

Continue by running the FTP Site Creation Wizard. This time when it prompts you for the user isolation configuration, choose Isolate Users. Then specify the path that you created earlier, grant the necessary read and write permissions (remember, this affects only the user's home directory and not any other directories), and finish the wizard.

If as with most networks you want a public area where anonymous users can get access, create a folder called *Public* under *LocalUsers*. Now, if you decide to allow anonymous access to a site, you can have authenticated users sent directly to their home directories and anonymous users sent to a single readable and (possibly) writeable directory. (This anonymous user uses the same account as anonymous web users: IUSR_*COMPUTERNAME*.)

Integrating Active Directory into user isolation

To extend the isolation functionality further, you can integrate the properties of a user account within Active Directory so that all user FTP directories don't need to reside in the same volume. IIS then reads a user's information from within Active Directory upon connecting to the server and, assuming he or she successfully authenticates, places him directly in their home directory as configured in his profile.

You'll need to make sure the user's home directory is explicitly defined with his or her Active Directory profile; redirection of a home directory only through Group Policies isn't sufficient. IIS looks for two attributes—FTPRoot and FTPDir—within the profile to enable this feature, so the value must be present with the Active Directory account itself. The best way to do this is to use a script included with IIS and located by default in *%SytemRoot%\System32* called *iisftp.vbs*. You can call it directly from the command line, and the syntax to set these properties is as follows:

```
iisftp /SetADProp
nameofuser
 FTPRoot
pathtodirectory

iisftp /SetADProp
nameofuser
 FTPDir
pathtodirectory
```

For example, to enable the home directory value for user ljohnson, you might use the following set of commands:

```
iisftp /SetADProp ljohnson FTPRoot \\mercury\users\ljohnson
iisftp /SetADProp ljohnson FTPDir \\mercury\users\ljohnson
```

Once these are set, you can run the FTP Site Creation Wizard one last time, and when prompted with the user isolation configuration, you can select Isolate Users using Active Directory. You'll then need to specify an account with credentials to read from the directory and the default domain to be used when users authenticate. (Keep in mind that users from different domains still can use their own domain by using the DOMAIN\username syntax.) Then, grant the appropriate access rights and finish out the wizard. Your user isolation mode is now integrated with Active Directory.

> If you decide to set the user's FTPRoot and FTPDir properties after you create an isolated FTP site, it can be helpful to restart the FTP site from within IIS Manager so that IIS can reread the changed user attributes.

One caveat when using Active Directory user isolation mode is this: once you've configured a site in that mode, you can't adjust any settings on the Security Accounts or Home Directory tabs of the site properties. The Site Creation Wizard will never prompt you to permit or deny anonymous access, so you'll never have a chance to explicitly set that option. So, what happens if anonymous access is actually turned on even though you never set it that way? Two events can occur: for one, if the IUSR_COMPUTERNAME account that is used for anonymous access does not have data for the FTPRoot and FTPDir attributes, anonymous access simply won't work—the user will be denied. If, however, the account contains that data, the user will be directed there, just as expected.

SMTP Services

Business today is conducted over Internet email in nearly the same volume as over the telephone network. The instantaneous nature of virtual communication has real advantages over playing phone tag, not to mention the fact that email is cost effective, more available, and easier to manage than a phone call.

IIS includes an SMTP component that allows your server to send and receive mail on the Internet with the big boys. The Windows Server 2003 Internet mail solution consists of two components: the SMTP server, which I'll discuss in this section, and the POP3 server, which is coming in the next section. The SMTP server acts as the switchboard, sending mail to different hosts based on different email addresses and receiving inbound mail routed for your domain. The POP3 server acts as a post office for your local organization, retrieving email that was delivered via the SMTP component and transferring it to individual users' mailboxes.

Like most other components of IIS, the default SMTP server created upon installation works as a virtual server. However, to dig deeper, let's create a new virtual server and then look at its configuration options.

Creating a New SMTP Virtual Server

During IIS 6 installation, a default SMTP virtual server is created that is sufficient for the most basic needs. The default server listens on TCP port 25, as a normal mail server would, and stores the mail it receives in a queue directory, which is, by default, *C:\Inetpub\Mailroot\Queue*. It also will accept outgoing mail for multiple domains without any reconfiguration.

However, if you want to create your own SMTP virtual server, a wizard exists to assist you. In IIS Manager, select your machine in the left pane, right-click it, and select SMTP Virtual Server from the New menu. The New SMTP Virtual Server Wizard appears. To complete it, follow these steps:

1. First, enter a friendly name that will be displayed in administrative tools to refer to this server. This generally should be the DNS name of the machine. Then, click Next.

2. Next, select an IP address on which the SMTP server will listen, or specify All Unassigned to listen on all addresses configured on the machine. Click Next to continue.

3. Now, select the path to the directory where the SMTP server will store its files. IIS uses four directories—*Badmail*, *Drop*, *Pickup*, and *Queue*—to store mail, and on this screen you can specify where this cluster of directories will be stored. Click Next.

You cannot store the SMTP server directories on a remote machine. They must be located directly on the SMTP server machine itself.

4. Specify the default DNS domain that will be used for the SMTP server. Click Next when you're finished.

5. Review your choices, and click Finish to create the virtual server.

The new SMTP virtual server has been created.

SMTP Properties

In this section, I'll look at adjusting the individual properties of an SMTP server. To modify the properties of a virtual server, right-click the SMTP Virtual Server listed in the left pane of IIS Manager and choose Properties.

General

Figure 8-30 shows the General tab.

Figure 8-30. The General tab

On the General tab, you can specify the IP address and port assignment. You also can limit the number of simultaneous connections, and use an idle timeout setting that will free up stale connections. Plus, you can enable logging in the formats detailed elsewhere within this chapter.

Access

Figure 8-31 shows the Access tab.

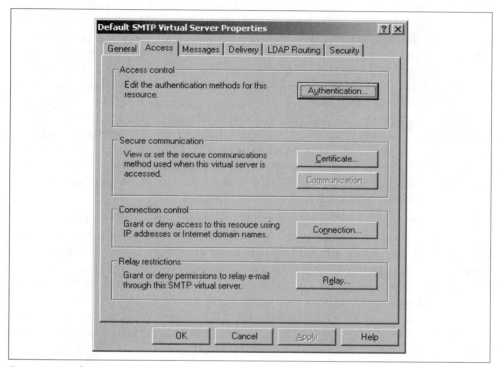

Figure 8-31. The Access tab

On the Access tab, you can specify how people can send email through your virtual server.

Click the Authentication button under the Access control section of the tab. You'll see a screen, called Authentication. Anonymous access to your SMTP server is enabled here by default. In the bottom portion of the box you can specify the method by which non-anonymous users will authenticate. The first option is basic authentication, which negotiates a username and password in clear text between the client and the SMTP server. There's also integrated Windows authentication, which encrypts the username and password and sends it between the client and the server. This uses either the SAM accounts database on the IIS server machine or Windows' built-in integration with Active Directory. Finally, there's SSL authentication, which uses certificates only to establish the identity of a client computer to a server. Either of the latter two options will work if you want credentials to be passed in a secure environment; basic authentication simply passes the credentials over the wire unprotected, leaving an open door for sniffers.

Back on the Access tab, you can grant or deny access to a site based on the client's IP address. This is useful if you have an abusive or compromised group of external hosts that are continually attacking your machine, or if you want to restrict users of a site to internal hosts only. Click the Edit button under IP Address and Domain Name Restrictions to configure this. You first select whether all users will be granted or denied access to the site by using the radio buttons at the top of the window. Then you can configure individual exceptions to the rule you just defined in the white list box. Click Add to include an address in the exceptions list. You'll be prompted with a box, asking whether you want to exempt a single computer, a group of computers (an IP subnet), or an entire domain (DNS-based domain, that is). Again, restricting or allowing access based on a DNS domain name is a very expensive operation because each SMTP request must be accompanied by a reverse lookup on the part of the IIS server. This can slow response time considerably and cause processor utilization to increase significantly. Enable this only if you're sure of the consequences or if you have a relatively lightly traveled web site to restrict.

Select the appropriate response, and then type in the actual IP address, network number and subnet, or domain name. You can click the DNS Lookup button to perform a reverse lookup on a certain domain name to obtain its appropriate IP numbers. When you're finished, click OK, and you'll be returned to the restrictions box. Now, keep in mind that if you've configured default access for everyone to your site, the excepted addresses will be denied access. Conversely, if you've denied access by default to all IP addresses, the excepted addresses will be allowed access. This might seem obvious, but during a quick change it's easy to become a little confused at the quasi-backward logic. Click OK once you're finished.

Finally, the Relay restrictions section of the Access tab enables you to lock down your server so that it can be used only by clients you approve and not by anonymous spammers that could take advantage of your open resource. This functions similarly to the connection control box, where you add IP addresses and allow or deny their access to the server. The difference is that with a relay restriction, you're only saying that these IP address are not allowed to send outgoing mail through this server. With the connection control, you are restricting the ability of a set of addresses to even communicate with the server—either to bring mail to the server *or* to send outgoing mail. This is an important distinction.

Usually, you add local IP addresses on your site to this list and allow only those addresses to talk. Also, you can specify whether computers that authenticate to the SMTP server can send outgoing email, regardless of whether they appear in the list. This is useful for Internet addresses—your clients, as long as they authenticate, still can use the SMTP server even though their address isn't local.

Messages

Figure 8-32 shows the Messages tab.

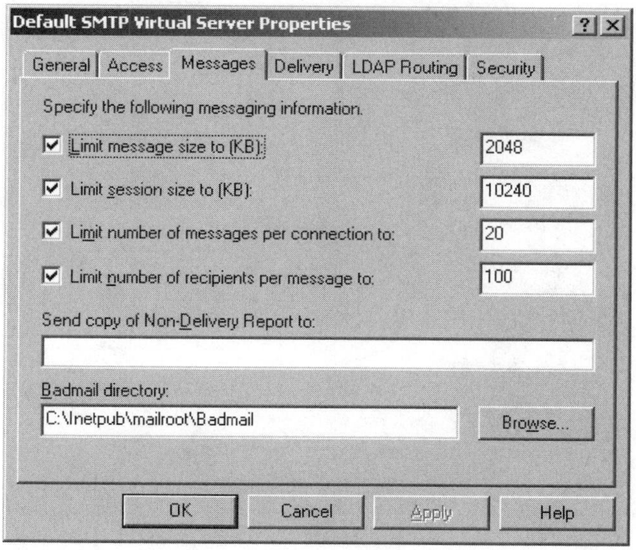

Figure 8-32. The Messages tab

The Messages tab enables you to specify policies on the types of messages to accept through the virtual server. You can limit message size in KB, the size of all messages transferred in a particular session in KB, the number of messages allowed in a particular session, and the number of addressees in a message. You also can specify a particular email address to which to send nondelivery reports (those dreaded bounce messages), and a directory to store mail that can't be delivered so that you can examine it for errors later.

Delivery

Figure 8-33 shows the Delivery tab.

The Delivery tab enables you to set options that relate to the actual transmission of messages to and from your server. You can specify the first three intervals for retrying delivery of a failed message, and then the interval at which further attempts are tried. You also can set how long the server should try to send a message before sending a notification to the sender, and how long the server should try to send the message before giving up (an "expiration timeout"). Plus, you can set the delay notification and expiration timeout values for messages sent between recipients local to the SMTP server.

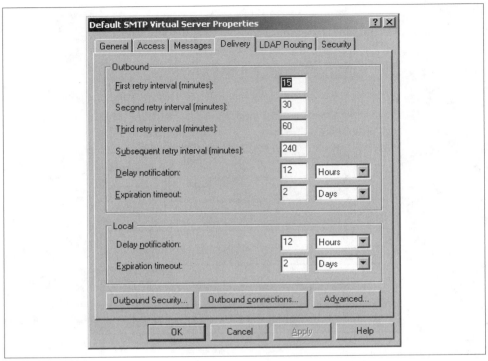

Figure 8-33. The Delivery tab

The Outbound Security button enables you to edit the settings used in conjunction with transmitting messages to other SMTP servers. You can set the levels of security used between two SMTP servers talking to each other—anonymous connections, basic authentication, and integrated Windows authentication, all of which I discussed previously in this section—and the option to perform the integrated Windows authentication using TLS encryption, which is very strong and hard to break.

 You can use integrated Windows authentication only if both servers involved in the transaction are Windows machines. If you are using Unix servers, you need to use basic authentication.

The Outbound connections button enables you to limit the number of outgoing connections from your virtual server, and to set a stale time limit for those connections. You also can restrict the number of connections per SMTP domain to a certain number. Plus, you can specify the port on which outbound SMTP transactions will be made; the default is 25.

Clicking the Advanced button brings up the Advanced Delivery screen, where you configure more complex settings to customize message transmission. The options include the following:

- You can set a maximum hop count, which counts the number of times a message is bounced around between SMTP servers, to avoid an interminable message loop. Usually I recommend setting this to 10 or less.

- You can set the DNS domain name with which all outgoing messages will be sent.

- You can configure the fully qualified domain name that your SMTP server will *masquerade* as. This is useful if your server's name is, perhaps, *server1.hasselltech.net*. The email address you want the public to see is *Hassell@hasselltech.net*, but according to the SMTP server you are *Hassell@server1.hasselltech.net*. By using the masquerade option, you can simply tell the SMTP server that it is *hasselltech.net* only and not *server1.hasselltech.net*.

- You can configure a "smart" host, which is a machine upstream on your Internet connection that relays outgoing messages on behalf of your server. In this case, your SMTP virtual server will toss all outbound messages to the smart host, who then becomes responsible for delivering them. You also can specify that the smart host option should be used only after failing to make a normal delivery.

- You can configure the server to find the domain name for the IP address of the server from which incoming mail is being transmitted. This can be an extra step to verifying that mail is legitimate and not spam. If the domain name is found via what's called a reverse lookup, it is placed inside the Received portion of the message's header.

LDAP Routing

Figure 8-34 shows the LDAP Routing tab.

On the LDAP Routing tab, you can instruct the SMTP server to access an LDAP server for more information on senders or recipients listed in messages coming through the server. Enabling LDAP routing automatically configures the SMTP server to access the currently available Active Directory by default if one is present. You also can specify other LDAP servers by supplying their hostnames, schema types, binding types, the account name and password for accessing it, and the naming context.

Security

Figure 8-35 shows the Security tab.

On this tab, you can specify the Windows accounts that should have operator privileges for the SMTP virtual server.

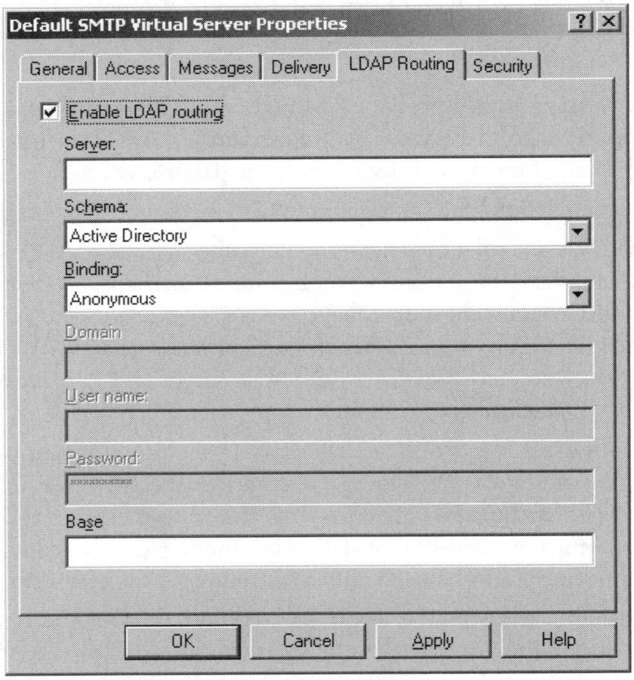

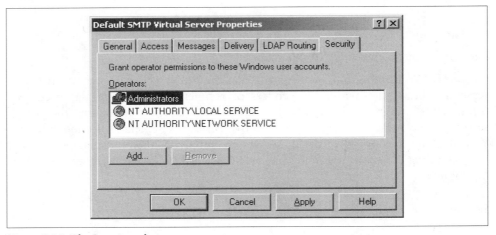

Figure 8-34. The LDAP Routing tab

Figure 8-35. The Security tab

Delivering for Multiple Internet Domains

If your company has more than one DNS domain, you can configure your SMTP virtual server to send and receive email for both domains. To make the server aware that you have multiple domains, you need to run the New SMTP Domain Wizard, which you can find inside IIS Manager by right-clicking the SMTP virtual server and selecting Domain from the New menu. Next, follow these steps:

1. On the first screen, tell the wizard whether the new domain you're adding is a *remote domain* (one hosted by another server elsewhere to which mail should be forwarded) or an *alias domain* (a domain that simply "sits on top" of a local domain). Click Next when you're finished.

2. Enter the actual domain name. Click Next to finish the process.

Your server is now configured for the new, additional domain. However, if you've selected the new domain to be a remote domain, some additional configuration remains. To access the properties for the remote domain, right-click the remote domain name in the right side of IIS Manager and select Properties. The sheet is shown in Figure 8-36.

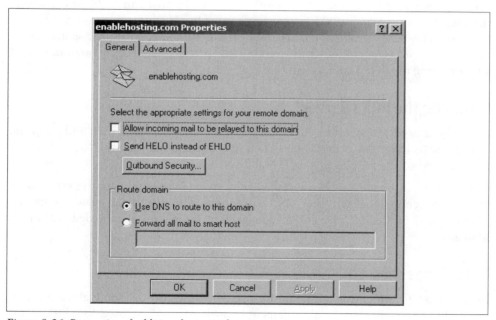

Figure 8-36. Properties of additional remote domain

You can configure whether email should forward from somewhere else to this domain (assuming the remote server is forwarding mail to your SMTP server) with the first check. The second option disables extended SMTP, or ESMTP, a useful troubleshooting step if you're having problems sending mail—disable this if your mail is bouncing or if you notice a lot of rejected requests in your log files. You also can specify whether to deliver mail using DNS or to forward this new domain's mail to a smart host, much like before.

On the Advanced tab of the new domain's properties, you can enable automatic dequeuing of mail using the TURN command in the SMTP protocol. This is useful if you have another server that gets its mail from this server that isn't permanently connected to the Internet. You also can specify the users that are allowed to trigger the dequeuing of mail.

The POP3 Server

Until the release of IIS 6, Windows Server products never included the software needed to retrieve mail that has been sent to a machine. Microsoft wisely decided in Windows Server 2003 to include a simple POP3 server that can make any machine running Windows Server 2003 into a server capable of sending and receiving Internet mail. The POP3 protocol enables users to log in and receive mail sent to them through the SMTP server. In this section, I'll look at installing, configuring, and administering the POP3 component of IIS.

Installing the POP3 Server

First, you'll need to install the POP3 server. Go to the Control Panel, and open the Add/Remove Programs applet; then click Windows Components. You'll find the POP3 checkbox by double-clicking E-Mail Services.

Once the POP3 service has been installed you can load the administrative console for the POP3 service through the MMC program. The specific console is named *p3server.msc*. By default, the POP3 management tools are not included within IIS Manager.

POP3 Properties

Before actually configuring a domain for use, you'll need to set some global properties within the POP3 Service management console that will be used for all domains receiving mail via the service. To access these properties, right-click the server name within the left pane of the management console and select Properties. You'll see something much like Figure 8-37.

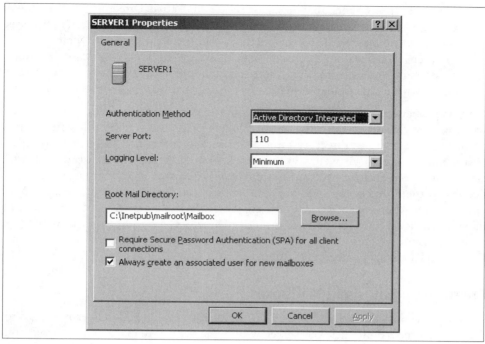

Figure 8-37. POP3 server properties

First, you should select the authentication method this server will use. Available methods are outlined in the following list:

Active Directory Integrated

If this authentication method is selected, the POP3 service will authenticate connecting users against Active Directory accounts on a domain controller. Any POP3 mailboxes created will correspond to Active Directory accounts. As an added bonus, Active Directory authentication supports multiple domains per POP3 server, and a user can retrieve mail from all of them using a single username and password—that of their Active Directory account.

Local Windows Accounts

This authentication method is designed for servers that aren't members of Active Directory domains. In this case, mailboxes must correspond to local user accounts, and authentication takes place against the SAM database local to the POP3 server. This option supports multiple domains, but usernames must be unique, even across domains, so it's impossible to make single sign-on available as you can with Active Directory integrated authentication.

Encrypted Password File

Use the Encrypted Password File method of authentication when you have lots of users—more than 1000 is a good delimiter—and you don't want to create and manage user accounts that actually reside in Active Directory or the POP3 server's SAM database. When you create an account (you also can refer to this as a mailbox) on a server using this method, you specify a password which is then stored encrypted within the user's mail directory. Although you can use multiple domain names with this authentication method, usernames have to be unique within a particular domain.

On this properties page, you also can specify the port number on which the service will run (the default is 110), the level of logging that the service will write to the event log, and the root directory on a server in which mailbox directories for each user should be stored. As well, you can choose to require Secure Password Authentication (SPA), a secure way to transmit passwords across a WAN, for each user connecting to the POP3 server, and you can instruct the POP3 service to create a new user account when mailboxes are created. The POP3 service will generate accounts in either the local SAM database or in Active Directory, depending on the method of authentication selected. This option is obviously grayed out on servers using Encrypted Password File authentication.

Creating Domains and Mailboxes

To add an email domain so that a POP3 server can receive and deliver messages to individual users, right-click the server within the service management console and select Domain from the New menu. The dialog box that appears asks you only for the domain name you want to add; enter it, and then click OK. Individual POP3 domains have no properties because the service handles properties only on a global basis for all domains managed by the service.

 Adding a domain to the POP3 service does not link the domain with Active Directory in any way. The POP3 service (and the SMTP service, for that matter) doesn't care what domain is used to deliver mail. The only time Active Directory is involved in a transaction is when a user authenticates—at that time it's expected that the credentials passed to the server will include an appropriate domain name for an Active Directory domain. Other than that, domain names are independent within the two services.

Now, add a mailbox to the domain by right-clicking the server name again and choosing Mailbox from the New menu. You'll be prompted for the mailbox name— here, supply either a new name or the login name of an existing user in the SAM or in Active Directory. If the user doesn't exist yet, also make sure the Create associated user for this mailbox checkbox is checked, and specify an initial password. That's all there is to it. Incoming user mail is stored in the *C:\Inetpub\Mailroot\Mailbox\USERNAME* folder.

Because this is a very simple POP3 server, you don't have any additional properties to configure. You can add and delete mailboxes and adjust the global properties of the POP3 server as described earlier in this section, but that's it. If you want a more full-featured mail solution, consider Microsoft Exchange or another POP3 or IMAP software package that runs on Windows.

 You can use a poor-man's disk quota system to limit the space available to each user by ensuring your mailbox directories reside on a partition or disk formatted with NTFS, and then enabling disk quotas on that volume. This will work only if you use Active Directory Integrated or Local Windows Accounts authentication because they're the only methods that actually create users on the system—you can assign quotas only to actual users. For more information on disk quotas, see Chapter 3.

Network News Services

The Network News Transport Protocol (NNTP) is a staple of the old-style Internet that continues to be useful today. The most popular newsgroup service, USENET, contains tens of thousands of groups dedicated to almost every subject imaginable, including car repair, hunting, computers, child development, travel, and the like. Some corporations have even begun establishing operations involving technical support for their products on private news servers. Microsoft has quite an extensive assisted community thriving on its news server at *msnews.microsoft.com*.

IIS 6 includes an NNTP server that you can install to create your own newsgroups for internal or external use. In this section I'll walk you through installing, configuring, and using your NNTP server.

Creating a Newsgroup Server

You can choose to install the newsgroup portion of IIS when you install IIS itself, so a default news server has already been created. But if you need a separate server, perhaps one for testing, the procedure is as follows:

1. Open IIS Manager.
2. Open the Action menu, and from the New menu, select NNTP Virtual Server.
3. The New NNTP Virtual Server Wizard appears. Click Next to skip the introductory text.
4. Enter a friendly name for the new news server that will appear on all administrative pages. Click Next.
5. Select the IP address on which the virtual server will live, and enter the port number on which the server will run. The defaults are All Unassigned and 119, respectively, unless you're creating a second server where the first server has

already accepted the default settings, in which case the default port won't be available.

6. In this step, tell IIS where to put and from where to read the files associated with the newsgroups carried on this virtual server. On the first screen, you tell IIS where it needs to store control and configuration information (called internal server files) for the news server.

7. On the next screen, you tell IIS where to store the actual contents of the newsgroups; this latter bit is called the storage medium. The default is *c:\inetpub\nntpfile*. This also can be a network directory; enter a UNC network path to take advantage of this. Click Next to continue.

8. Click Finish to confirm your choices on the wizard.

You have now created an NNTP server.

Modifying NNTP Server Properties

Once you've created a news server, you might find it helpful to customize its settings to suit your environment. In this section, I'll walk through the specific options available to mold your virtual news server into something that fits your business needs.

To get started, right-click the virtual NNTP server within IIS Manager, and select Properties from the context menu. The screen shown in Figure 8-38 will appear.

Let's step through each tab and discuss the available settings.

General

Figure 8-39 shows the General tab.

On the General tab, you can specify the IP address and port assignment of the news server. (You can use the Advanced button to specify multiple IP address assignments for this site.) You also can limit the number of inbound TCP connections to the server, and specify a *path header*, which is a string of data intended to allow upstream and downstream news servers to determine how to post a message. In addition, you can enable logging, which works in the same manner as the web and FTP logging that I covered earlier in this chapter.

Access

Figure 8-40 shows the Access tab.

The Access tab enables you to control who has access to your news server, and in what context that person has access—in other words, how to authenticate non-anonymous (authenticated) users to the web site. Click the Edit button under the Access Control section of the tab. You'll see a screen, called Authentication Methods. Anonymous access to your news server is enabled here by default, so anyone

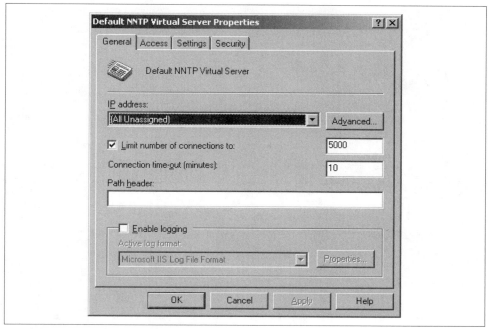

Figure 8-38. NNTP virtual server properties

can view the newsgroups on your server. You also can configure the user account under which anonymous users will automatically connect by clicking the Anonymous button on the appropriate tab.

The functionality on this tab is nearly identical to the properties sheet for the other types of services I covered in this chapter. See those other sections for information on the configuration options for this tab.

Specially, the Secure Communications section provides a way to ensure that data transmission sessions between a host and a client are created with proof that the server is who it says it is. This is done with certificates. See the web site portion of this chapter for more on using certificates to authenticate various entities.

Settings

Figure 8-41 shows the Settings tab.

The Settings tab includes options that pertain strictly to newsgroups and postings. You can enable or disable posting to the newsgroups from clients and set a limit on the size of a post the server will accept. You also can limit the size of a connection—actually, the bandwidth that a user will use when posting—so that he or she doesn't overload your machine with multiple small messages at small intervals.

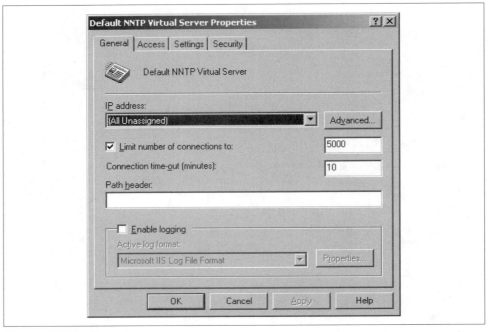

Figure 8-39. The General tab

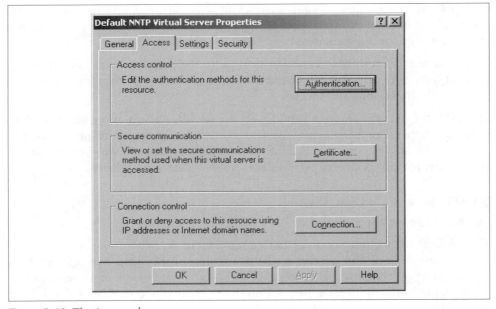

Figure 8-40. The Access tab

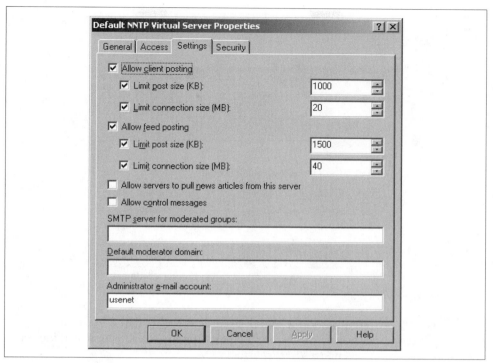

Figure 8-41. The Settings tab

The feed options currently have no function because the feature has yet to be implemented. This is definitely a limitation of the NNTP service in IIS. If you need newsfeed functionality—the pushing and pulling of articles from servers across the Internet—you should investigate Microsoft Exchange or another third-party solution.

> The preceding paragraph isn't entirely true: you can use a script called *rfeed.vbs* in *system32\inetsrv* to configure push and pull feeds with USENET servers. However, the mechanisms to allow the GUI to be used to administer newsfeeds certainly haven't been implemented yet, and on a personal basis, that makes me loathe to use the functionality in a production environment. It smacks of an un- or under-tested feature. Your mileage may vary, however.

You can allow control messages, which instruct the server how to post messages and create and delete groups within a hierarchy. Plus, you can specify the SMTP server to be used when a moderated newsgroup is used. In a moderated group, posts are sent to a specific person who then approves the post for publishing to the newsgroup. You need to set an outgoing mail server so that the moderator can be notified via email when a new posting is made. You also can set the default domain for the moderator's email.

Security

Figure 8-42 shows the Security tab.

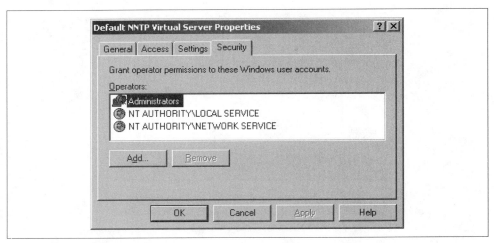

Figure 8-42. The Security tab

On the Security tab, simply add the Windows user accounts that correspond to users that should have operator privileges on this news server. These people can log on to and make configuration changes to the virtual server itself.

Virtual NNTP Directories

Virtual NNTP directories offer a way for you to distribute content among multiple servers in your organization. For example, one server can host the *accounting.** groups, while another can hold the *sales.** groups. By using virtual directories, you can specify which servers hold what parts of your group hierarchy.

To create a new virtual directory, open IIS Manager, expand the NNTP server node, right-click the server, and select Virtual Directory from the New menu. The New Virtual Directory Creation Wizard appears. On the first screen, enter the part of the hierarchy that the new virtual directory should serve. This can be as far up or down on the tree of groups that you have as you like. Once you've finished, click Next, and then select the storage medium on which the new virtual directory will store its content. Here, select a remote machine that should host these groups by using a network path. You'll also need to provide credentials so that IIS can authenticate to the remote machine. Click Next, and then Finish, and your new virtual directory will be created.

Modifying news directory properties

As you'll recall from the news server creation wizard, all news content—the groups and the postings—are stored within directories on the filesystem. The initial wizard makes a great deal of assumptions about how you want these directories configured, so it might be a good idea to review the settings in force and change them to suit your environment. To view the properties of individual directories, open IIS Manager, and under the NNTP Server node on the tree in the left pane, select the Virtual Directories section, right-click it, and choose Properties.

Now, you can edit the actual directory (which can be on a local or network filesystem) where the content will be stored. You also can require secure communications for only this virtual directory, and not all NNTP sites on the machine. Plus, there are options to enable or disable posting to the groups contained within the directory, to restrict the visibility of certain groups based on their NTFS permissions to the directory, and to log connections to the server. All these options should be familiar, and I've covered them elsewhere in this section or chapter.

Creating Newsgroups and Hierarchies

When IIS is installed, no newsgroups are present on the system by default. Because the feed functionality of the raw NNTP service in IIS is not yet implemented, to make your server really useful you'll need to create a hierarchy of newsgroups. You can do this by department, by division, by office location, or by any other division that makes sense. Some companies have internal help desks through a newsgroup, named `losangeles.helpdesk`, `Chicago.helpdesk`, and `newyork.helpdesk`, and others simply have newsgroups available by department—for example, `sales.products.widgets.presalequestions` and `customerservice.warranties.extended`.

To define new newsgroups, use the New Newsgroup Wizard, which you can find in IIS Manager under the NNTP Virtual Server node of the left pane. Right-click the node and select Newsgroups from the New menu. Then, follow these steps:

1. Enter the name of your new newsgroup, and then click Next.
2. Enter a description and friendly name for this group, and click Next.
3. Review the information you've entered, and click Finish to create the group.

Now, review the properties for the new group and customize it for your needs. In IIS Manager, right-click the group and select Properties. You can specify whether the group should be read-only, which is useful if you have information that shouldn't be edited or moderated, which is great for controlling the dissemination of information to the group.

Article Expiration

You might find it advantageous to have some articles in groups automatically expire or become unavailable at a certain point in time. The information contained in certain articles might be stale, or you might be concerned with the growing cost of storage for articles that no one reviews anymore. To set an expiration policy, expand the NNTP virtual server node within IIS Manager and select Expiration Policies. Right-click it, and select Expiration Policy from the New menu. Click through the introductory material to get started.

The first screen is where you define the groups to be affected by the policy. By default, the policy affects all configured groups. Click Add to include a specific group or hierarchy in the list, and click Remove to delete a group from the list. You can then move additional items up and down within the list to specify how the expiration policy is inherited. Groups that will be affected by the policy are denoted by a check, and groups that won't receive or enforce the policy have a red X beside them in the list. Move a group up to include it in a policy; move a group down to exclude it.

Next, specify the number of hours after which IIS will remove old articles. The default is 168, which indicates that the server will retain seven days' worth of postings.

Backing Up Your IIS Configuration

IIS has built-in functionality that enables you to take a snapshot of your configuration and save it to a file, which can later be restored in the event that something mucks with your production setup. The backups are time- and version-stamped, so you can create stepped snapshots to recreate your setup at any point in time. Keep in mind, though, that this backup function pertains to *only* the configuration of your IIS services—it does *not* back up files, directories, content, images, or anything of the sort. You'll need to use Windows backup, covered in Chapter 3, for that.

To back up your configuration, or to restore a setup from a previous backup, follow these steps:

1. Open IIS Manager, and select your server in the left pane.
2. Right-click your server, and select Backup/Restore Configuration from the All Tasks menu. Your screen will display something similar to Figure 8-43.
3. To back up your configuration, click the Create Backup button. You'll be prompted for a friendly name to identify the backup; enter one and click OK. You also can specify whether to require a password to restore. The backup file will be created in the *\Windows\System32\inetsrv\MetaBack* directory and cannot be used on another machine.
4. To restore your configuration, in the screen depicted in Figure 8-43, click the appropriate backup to select it, and then click the Restore button.

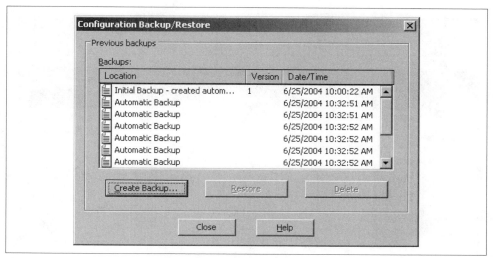

Figure 8-43. Backing up and restoring configurations in IIS 6

Remote Administration

The Remote Administration web site is a way to manage IIS functions and configurations from a web browser. You can administer most settings within IIS from a web browser anywhere in the world. Remote Administration is installed by default when you install IIS on a server running Windows Server 2003 Web Edition. This might not be the best security idea in the world, so I provide instructions for disabling it in the next section.

To use Remote Administration, you first need to find out the port on which it's installed. You can do this from within IIS Manager by opening the properties for the web site called Administration Website. Look on the General tab, note the port number—for non-secure connections, the default port is 8099, and for secure connections, it's 8098. You'll also want to lock down access to Remote Administration to a few specific IP addresses, so navigate to the Directory Security tab and proceed to lock out access via IP address. By default, everyone has access. Click Apply and then OK when you're done.

Once you've configured Remote Administration, you can access it from any web browser after authenticating. The default screen is shown in Figure 8-44.

Securing It All

Ever since a Gartner Report stated that anyone using IIS as a production web server should immediately migrate to Apache, the popular Unix web server, Microsoft's web platform has gotten quite a bad rap. And a lot of it was deserved: buffer overflows,

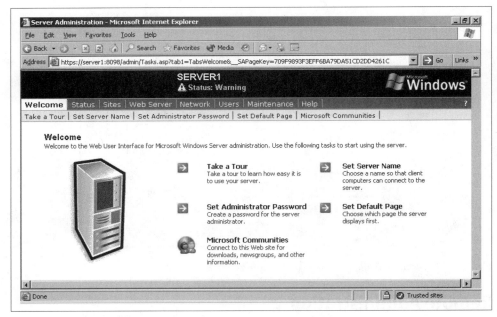

Figure 8-44. Remote administration web page

what seems like 10 security bulletins each week, worms that take over computers faster than they could be secured while on the network, and so on. Part of the problem was that the version of IIS included with Windows NT and Windows 2000, Versions 4 and 5, respectively, were lax in their default permissions: everyone could do everything at any given time. Even the fact that IIS was installed by default during a Windows 2000 installation was a bad move: it didn't matter if you didn't want a web server because you got one anyway.

Those who prey on insecure web servers rely on users who are lax, lazy, or unknowledgeable about keeping their servers hardened and updated. Essentially, the climate of the Internet has degenerated into a situation in which even innocent users that get penetrated are used as attack mechanisms against other innocent but open servers. The responsibility lies not just with the attackers who propagate these worms, but also with the administrators who allow their machines to be used like toys.

In this section, I'll look at nine simple steps you can take to make sure you're not a victim, and that you're not an accessory to the hackers.

Enable IIS Only if You Use It

Although it's probably the simplest suggestion in this section, it's also the most effective. It's a lot harder to attack a web server through a vulnerability in the web server software when a machine isn't functioning as a web server. Unfortunately, Windows

NT and Windows 2000 installed IIS by default for the most part and enabled it, too, so it was always running, waiting to serve either a legitimate HTTP request, or a message from a cracker.

IIS 6 fixes this problem somewhat: when you first install Windows, IIS isn't enabled at all, and even when you do enable it, it starts in a locked-down mode whereby dynamic content generation and script execution capabilities are disabled. In this default configuration, you can serve only static HTML pages. This is a big step in the right direction. In fact, when you upgrade a machine running Windows 2000 Server to Windows Server 2003, if it detects an IIS installation that still has the default settings engaged (a good sign it hasn't been modified or isn't in use), it will disable IIS upon the upgrade. You have to explicitly turn it back on.

If you do happen to be running IIS on a machine for any reason, and you want to decommission the machine as a web server but keep IIS on it anyway, you can do so by following these steps:

1. Open the Computer Management applet inside the Control Panel.
2. Double-click the Services icon to launch the Services console.
3. Scroll through the list and find World Wide Web Publishing Service, and select it.
4. Right-click the service, and select Stop.
5. If you don't intend to run the web server anymore, set the startup options to Disabled, and the service won't be restarted upon a reboot of the machine.

Better yet, get rid of IIS entirely if you're not using it anymore. Open the Manage Your Server console from the Start menu, and click Remove This Role under the Application Server heading. This is the most secure option.

Query All IIS Machines for Their Update Level

Given the number of patches released from 2001 to the present day, it can be tough to look at your network and determine the update level of each machine. Microsoft, sensing the need to remove a bit of egg from its face, purchased a license from Shavlik Technologies for the HFNetChk utility, short for Network Hotfix Checker. You can find *hfnetchk.exe* at:

> *http://www.microsoft.com/downloads/details.aspx?familyid=b13ebd6b-e258-4625-b0a3-64a4879f7798&displaylang=en*

 HFNetChk is exposed through the Microsoft Baseline Security Analyzer command-line interface through the following command: mbsacli.exe /hf. The latest version of the HFNetChk engine is available in Microsoft Baseline Security Analyzer (MBSA) v1.2.1.

HFNetChk is a command-line tool that scans Windows computers for installed updates and patches. The comparison is based on an XML file of all available updates and the criteria for those updates, and Microsoft updates the list constantly.

The first time you run the tool, the tool will download the signed XML file, verify its authenticity, and decompress the file. HFNetChk then scans the selected computers to figure out the level of the operating system, service packs, and programs installed on the systems. HFNetChk looks at three aspects of your system to determine if a patch is installed: the registry key that is installed by the patch, the file version, and the checksum for each file that is installed by the patch. By default, HFNetChk compares the files and registry details on the computer that is being scanned to the XML file that it downloads. If any of the three criteria discussed previously are not satisfied, the tool considers the associated patch to be absent and the results are displayed on the console. In the default configuration, HFNetChk output displays only those patches that are necessary to bring your computer up to date.

To use the tool, run the MBSA program and access HFNetChk from the command line with the -v option for verbose output, like so:

```
Mbsacli.exe /hf -v
```

The utility will scan your system and report on any missing patches, sorted by KB number. You also can scan with this command:

```
mbsacli.exe /hf -d HASSELLTECH
```

This will specify that all computers in the NetBIOS domain name HASSELLTECH should be scanned. It's a useful way to look at patch levels of multiple computers on the network at the same time.

Keep IIS Updated

Now that you know what hotfixes you need, you can update all your IIS boxes around your network. You can do this in a few ways, depending on how involved you as the administrator want to get. I'll look at two, with a tip for a third method.

Using Windows Update

Microsoft has recently improved its Windows Update web site utility. When you surf to *http://www.windowsupdate.com*, the site will search your system to see at what update level you are, and then list which hotfixes and service packs are applicable for your machine. This is a good, if not automated, way to ensure that you're completely recent in all code on your machine. The downside is that you are never quite sure what's been installed where because you don't actually go through the installation process yourself.

You also can set up the Automatic Updates utility in Windows by right-clicking My Computer and selecting Properties from the menu. Navigate to the Automatic

Updates tab, and you can indicate to Windows Server 2003 if you want updates to trickle down to your computer automatically and be installed on a set schedule. If you set patches to automatically download and install, you will never have to worry about not being up to date. Alas, some people don't trust Microsoft enough to come out with robust patches that simply can be installed on the day of their release; most administrators are in the habit of waiting a few days after a patch and letting other businesses be guinea pigs. But if you're a one-man shop and have eight other tasks to do at one time, the Automatic Updates solution might be good for you.

Using network-based hotfix installation

You also can download the individual security hotfixes and service packs one by one, save them to a central directory, and manually update each IIS machine on your network. Simply look at each security bulletin, or download the appropriate service packs (as of this writing, Windows Server 2003 is available), and store them in the same directory. Then, prepare a batch file.

Let's say you have two hotfix files to install. You surf the Web, find the files, and download them to *\\mercury\xd5fe*. Each hotfix is a separate executable. To simplify installation, I'll use two switches, -z and -m, that instruct the hotfix setup process to do so quietly (without raising dialogs to the user) and to not reboot at the end. Armed with this knowledge, I'll simply prepare a batch file similar to the following:

```
Set qfedir=\\mercury\qfe\
%qfedir%Q554147_wxp_sp2.exe -z -m
%qfedir%Q711041_wxp_sp2.exe -z -m
```

I'll type that text in Notepad and save it as a file called *UPDATE1.BAT*. The first line sets a variable for the path to the hotfix files, and the variables are used in the lines that call each hotfix. This way, if you decide to change the location of the hotfixes, you have to update only the first line, not each individual line.

Now, just run *UPDATE1.BAT* on all the computers that require those updates, or assign it via a login script through GP.

 If you deploy your Windows Server 2003 machines using RIS, you can automatically preinstall all hotfixes before actual Windows installation is complete, saving you the time and tedium of applying them manually after Setup finishes. See the latter half of Chapter 2 for a complete walkthrough of this.

Use Both IIS and NTFS Security

IIS has a bit of virtual directory security in that it has permissions for reading, writing, and executing scripts, as well as other basic privileges within a virtual directory;

these permissions also are independent of filesystem permissions. Here's a reminder of the available rights:

Script source access
> Enables users to view the source code to scripts and applications within the selected directory, assuming they have read or write permissions to that directory.

Read
> Enables users to view or download files or directories, along with their individual properties.

Write
> Enables users to upload files to the selected directory. It also enables them to change existing files within that directory.

Directory browsing
> Enables users to view an HTML page listing the contents of the selected directory, including any subdirectories. Note that these subdirectories listed in this view are physical filesystem directories, not IIS virtual directories.

As I mentioned earlier in the chapter, users browsing web content on your IIS machines are actually logging in to a guest-like IUSR account on your machine or directory service. Out of the box, Windows Server 2003 sets the following restrictions on the NTFS permissions given to the IUSR account:

- A user logged on through the IUSR account can only read and list the contents of the web root directory. No execute permissions are present, so scripts cannot run and no one can write files to the directory.

- The IUSR account has read, execute, and list contents permissions inside the Windows directory, just as the Authenticated Users group does.

Other than those exceptions, the IUSR account has no NTFS permissions across any file or folder on a disk. You can use the NTFS permissions, as covered in Chapter 3, to lock down IUSR's ability to further access content on your site.

Evaluate the Indexing Service

The installation process for Windows Server 2003 does not install the Indexing Service out of the box, so that ounce of prevention is a good step. However, indexing files on your hard disk or network opens up a whole host of issues that might be difficult to predict without careful planning. For example, what if you indicate to the Indexing Service that you want to index all files on your drive? The service would gladly do so, but it might also find angry letters to your users' superiors, love notes to their wives or girlfriends, salary information from the payroll department, memos from the boss on the latest round of layoffs, and so on. You can see that access to these bits of information by just anybody could create a disaster.

You can manage the Indexing Service using the MMC snap-in *ciadv.msc*. Loading the applet will present the dialog shown in Figure 8-45.

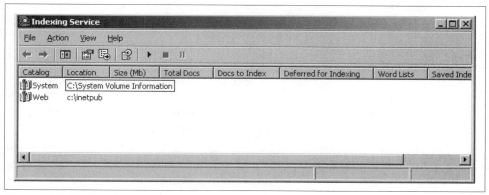

Figure 8-45. The Indexing Service management console

You can delete catalogs by simply right-clicking their names within the listing and selecting Delete. You can adjust the indexing properties for each catalog by right-clicking the name and selecting Properties. If you want the service *not* to index something, you can tell it directly (without the need for adjusting permissions) by right-clicking a catalog and selecting Directory from the New menu.

Now, bear with me for a moment as we delve into some seemingly backward logic: by default the Indexing Service takes a directory that you give it and indexes all its contents, including child files and subfolders. The key to excluding directories from indexing is to add a directory to the catalog, and then instruct the service *not* to index it. On the Add Directory dialog, you see an option to the right called Include in Index. This is where you can indicate whether to index a particular directory. So you can enter the base directory for the index—let's call it *C:\Documents*—and tell the Indexing Service to index it by clicking Yes to the option on the right. But for this example, suppose you have a folder in *C:\Documents* called *Top Secret*. Tell Indexing Service to ignore it by adding *C:\Documents\Top Secret* as a directory, but before you click OK switch the Yes to a No under Include in Index.

Of course, that's a very backward way of doing things, and it would have been a far better decision on the part of Microsoft to include an option that gives you the choice of which subfolders, if any, to index, within the management console of the Indexing Service. In true Microsoft form, you can indeed make these changes somewhat intuitively, albeit in a different place—the Advanced Attributes section of the Properties sheet of any file or folder. Just right-click any folder, select Properties, and then on the General tab click Advanced. The top section, archive and index attributes, contains an option that allows you to enable or disable the Indexing Service's access to this object. When you make a change and click OK, a dialog box will appear, asking if you want to apply the changes to subfolders and files within those subfolders.

So, with those points out of the way, consider the following suggestions about deploying the Indexing Service in your organization:

- Immediately remove the two catalogs the service creates upon installation by default, called Web and System. These index all web content and all files on your system, respectively.

- Understand the hierarchical nature of the indexing permission. If you give a top-level folder permission to be indexed, any subfolders contained within that folder will automatically have permission to be indexed as well.

- Explicitly enable the permission on only files and folders that you're sure you want indexed. It's easier to control what is being indexed when everything is *not* indexed by default.

The Indexing Service is a good thing, when kept under control. Unfortunately, a few worms have decided to take advantage of some flaws in its construction, so if you use the service you need to especially ensure you keep your IIS machines updated early and often.

You can find out more about the Indexing Service in Chapter 13.

Kill Unused Ports

This should really go without saying as firewalls become more pervasive, but you should protect your IIS machines by allowing traffic only on those ports that are required for its operation—by allowing traffic only on ports 80 and 443, for example. I know there are remote administration features that are great for internal servers, but with the continued security flaws that IIS has had, why take a chance exposing what amounts to root access to the outside world? Kill everything but ports 80 and 443 into your IIS machine and rest a bit easier at night.

You can disable these ports through a hardware or software firewall, or through an IPsec filter. I cover configuring IPsec filters in Chapter 11.

Delete Default Directories

Lots of web-based programs often come with sample files, instruction pages, and installation scripts that assist you in setting up and using the programs easily. When I was running my web hosting business, more than 75% of the scripts I used on a day-to-day basis, either that my customers needed installed or that I used to manage the systems, came with install scripts and default pages that left access to an account, a database, or even worse—a machine—nearly unguarded. These scripts don't advertise their presence, but it isn't hard for a nefarious person to look in standard places, such as a directory called *INSTALL* off of the web root, and wreak havoc on a machine.

IIS is no different from these other programs. Here's an action list of items to remove from the server, assuming none is being actively used:

- IIS comes with a web-based program so that you can remotely administer an IIS server from afar. I'll make my comment on that in as few words as possible: bad idea. Don't install it at all.

- FrontPage Extensions also expose a lot of functionality that might not be needed otherwise. If you're using FrontPage, by all means continue to use the bots, but if you've installed the extensions only because you don't feel like digging the Server 2003 CD out if you ever need it again, go ahead and uninstall it.

- If you're not using the extensions or any type of SharePoint site, be it from Team Services or the full-fledged Portal Server product, delete the Microsoft Share-Point Administration site.

- Get rid of web-based printing—does anyone actually use it anyway?—by deleting the folder called *Printers* from the web root.

The Ins and Outs of ISAPI

ISAPI is CGI's like-minded brother on the Windows platform. It allows for dynamic extensions to static HTML content, and new technologies such as Active Server Pages and other dynamic languages use ISAPI filters to interact with IIS. Of course, this opens up a potential security hole.

You need to make sure that the only ISAPI filters configured on your system are those that are in use. (You can find ISAPI filters in the Properties sheet for any web site.) For most systems, that would be the ASP.NET service. Look through your web root directory, and note the extensions on all your content. Do any differ from *.HTM*? If not, make sure any filters that are listed in the Properties tab are removed.

As a colleague points out, the entire Code Red virus could have been prevented had the IDA ISAPI filter been removed from IIS installations worldwide.

Command-Line Utilities

Many scripts are available for administering IIS from the command line, and they're detailed in this section. Most of these are located in the *\inetpub\adminscripts* directory; exceptions are noted within the individual command's discussion.

iisreset

You can control IIS using a command-line function called iisreset. Depending on the argument switches you use with the command, you can perform any number of tasks:

iisreset /restart
> Restarts all IIS-related services.

iisreset /start
> Starts IIS.

iisreset /stop
> Stops IIS.

iisreset /reboot
> Restarts the actual server machine, not just IIS.

iisreset /rebootonerror
> Use this to simply restart IIS—but, if errors are encountered during the process, reboot the server.

iisreset /noforce
> Doesn't forcefully terminate services that don't respond to requests.

iisreset /timeout:value
> IIS will wait for a service to respond for the number of seconds in the value field. If the service still doesn't respond, and /rebootonerror is used in the command as well, the machine will restart.

iisreset /status
> Lists the status of all IIS services.

iisreset /enable && iisreset /disable
> Toggles the ability to start or stop IIS services on the machine.

iisweb

iisweb can create new web sites from the command line. For instance:

```
iisweb /create e:\webcontent "Main Website" /d www.win.com
```

creates a web site named Main Website that can be addressed at *www.win.com* from content stored in the directory *e:\webcontent*.

By default, iisweb will start the new web site. To prevent this, add the /dontstart switch at the command line.

iisvdir

Using the utility iisvdir you can create virtual web directories from the command line. For instance:

```
iisvdir /create "Default Website" support e:\webcontent\support
```

creates a virtual directory named *support* in the web site named Default Website, deriving its content from the directory *e:\webcontent\support*.

If you specify a path that doesn't exist, IIS will create it.

iisapp

iisapp enables you to look at what process IDs (PIDs) are being used by which application pool. Simply type iisapp from the command line, and the result will display the worker PID and the application pool to which that process is assigned. This is a good way to monitor the health of worker processes and application pools.

iisftp

iisftp can create new FTP sites from the command line. For instance:

```
iisftp /create e:\webcontent "Main Website" /i 64.246.42.130
```

creates a web site named Main Website at the IP address 64.246.42.130 from content stored in the directory *e:\webcontent*.

iisftp contains a couple of other switches:

/b

This switch enables you to specify a port number other than 21, which is assumed when this switch is not present in the command.

/isolation

This switch creates new sites in one of the two isolation modes. Use Local as the argument for local user isolation or AD as the argument for Active Directory-integrated isolation.

The utility iisftp, as discussed earlier in this chapter, also explicitly defines a user's home directory with his Active Directory profile. This is for use with user isolation mode in FTP. You can call it directly from the command line, and the syntax to set these properties is as follows:

```
iisftp /SetADProp nameofuser FTPRoot pathtohomedirectory
iisftp /SetADProp nameofuser FTPDir pathtohomedirectory
```

iisftpdr

Using the utility iisftpdr, you can create virtual FTP directories from the command line. For instance:

```
iisftpdr /create "Default Website" support e:\webcontent\support
```

creates a virtual directory named *support* in the web site named Default Website, deriving its content from the directory *e:\webcontent\support*.

iisftpdr does not support UNC network naming. You need to either have content stored locally for use with the command or map a drive to the network share.

winpop

You can use winpop, located in *\Windows\system32\pop3server*, to automatically add mailboxes and create user accounts within Windows, depending on the authentication method you've chosen for the POP3 service. For instance:

```
winpop add lisa@divelover.net
```

simply adds the mailbox to the POP3 service. This command assumes a preexisting user account unless your authentication method is Encrypted Password File.

This command:

```
winpop add lisa@divelover.net /createuser luv2dive
```

adds a mailbox *and* creates a corresponding user within Active Directory with the password "luv2dive." There isn't any need to use this version of the command with the Encrypted Password File method of authentication.

The Last Word

IIS is a complex beast, and in this chapter you've walked through all of its major and most of its minor features. You also have been briefed on how to keep your IIS deployments secure. The bottom line: with IIS 6, it is safe to use Windows in an Internet-facing web environment.

CHAPTER 9

.NET Framework

Windows Server 2003 is the first operating system to include the .NET Framework preinstalled. Enhancements to IIS and COM+, along with security and stability improvements, have positioned Windows Server 2003 as the optimal operating system for the deployment of .NET applications. This chapter provides a guide to managing the .NET Framework and .NET applications.

What Is .NET?

.NET is two things: a state-of-the-art software platform, and a prime example of a marketing disaster. I'll try to focus on the former before I proceed, though, I would like to recommend that if you have been frequenting *Slashdot.org* or watching a lot of TV, please wipe your mind of all prior knowledge related to .NET. Most likely you are another victim of the Microsoft marketing department, which at one point had slated every Microsoft server product, including Windows Server 2003, to include the .NET name. Many months of disorder passed before Microsoft, probably inspired by a confused techie, finally reverted to a more sensible naming convention for its product line. Today only a few artifacts outside of the .NET software platform contain .NET in their names.

I've already stated that .NET is an amazing software platform. The next step is to actually define "software platform." A software platform is composed of the following elements:

Language
> A set of constructs and grammar the developer uses to convey logic into an application.

Libraries
> Modern software platforms provide a robust infrastructure of helpers to avoid the need to reinvent the wheel in each application. Libraries provide the functionality to accomplish tasks such as accessing the filesystem and talking to databases.

Tools

The digital equivalent of an administrative assistant, tools assist with automation and organization, leading to increased productivity.

Runtime

Modern runtimes provide a multitude of services to running applications. These include memory management and transaction support. The services provided free the application from having to explicitly perform tedious actions that seem to be common sense.

Now let's cover how .NET addresses each element.

Language

Prior to .NET, a single language defined a software platform. Examples of other platforms are Java, Visual Basic, and C++. Each platform corresponds directly to a language. Component Object Model (COM) and other technologies have made strides to allow interoperability between languages, but it's been at the expense of productivity and, most importantly, developer sanity.

.NET implements the concept of language interoperability from the bottom up. First it lays the ground rules: the Common Language Specification (CLS) and the Common Type Specification (CTS). Languages must abide by these rules to maintain interoperability with other languages. Currently Microsoft has incorporated several different languages into .NET, including C#, Visual Basic, Visual C++, Jscript, and J#. Microsoft recommends developers use C# and Visual Basic for general development and the other languages for ease of code migration or for rare scenarios that are beyond the scope of this chapter and book.

Microsoft also has opened the floodgates for anyone with a few spare hours to write a language compiler from scratch. .NET compilers for languages from COBOL to Perl have been developed and are freely distributed more often than not. You can find an up-to-date list at *http://www.jasonbock.net/dotnetlanguages.html*.

Libraries

Libraries provide building blocks for applications. You can accomplish tasks such as sending an email or updating a row in a database with minimal code by using a well-designed set of libraries. Traditionally, developers could depend on only a limited set of libraries to be present on a system before installing an application. Additional libraries required for an application would need to be packaged with the application before deployment. The concept of a robust class library in a PC environment began with the advent of Java.

.NET expands the idea of a class library with the .NET Class Library (sometimes referred to as the .NET Framework). The .NET Class Library includes thousands of different classes enabling the development of very complex applications without many dependencies outside of a base .NET Framework installation. Some of the most widely used libraries cover the following functionality:

Database access
> Drivers, or "managed providers," for a variety of different database platforms allow universal data access.

XML
> Virtually anything that you can do with XML you can perform using the base libraries in the .NET Framework. This includes parsing, generation, and SOAP web service interoperation.

Messaging
> MSMQ provides guaranteed delivery of messages to other applications in the enterprise.

Drawing
> Draw shapes and text dynamically onto images. Images can be displayed on the screen or saved to files.

Directory access
> Interact with any Active Directory– or LDAP-compliant directory.

Tools

A software platform requires a solid set of tools, such as code editors, help documentation, build tools, debuggers, and similar items, to support widespread adoption. Microsoft has continued the evolution of the Integrated Development Environment (IDE) with Visual Studio.NET. An IDE, as inferred by the name, is designed to provide the developer with all needed development functionality in a single application. Wizards, project templates, and database connectors are extras that make an IDE attractive.

Developers on a low budget or that like a little more control have not been forgotten with .NET. Microsoft distributes the .NET Framework and a Software Development Kit (SDK) free of charge. These two combined provide a crude subset of a full toolset, the most notable inclusions being documentation and compilers. Combine these with a favorite code editor and you're in business, as long as you can live without the wizards and other pizzazz of Visual Studio.NET.

Runtime

Not too long ago, software demands were quite simple and hardware resources were limited. With this in mind, developers could spend great amounts of time on simple tasks and focus heavily on efficiency. This mindset can be attributed to causing the Y2K hoopla, as developers trying to squeeze a little more data into a little less space decided that two digits were adequate to represent date years. Alas, times have changed. Software demands have become increasingly complex and the availability of hardware resources has increased by several orders of magnitude. This has allowed the developers to transfer a lot of the low-level, bit-twiddling work onto their new best friend, the runtime. Runtimes provide services to running code. Think of a runtime as your maid, your personal trainer, and your banker, combined digitally to serve your application. The runtime does all the dirty work that you had to do yourself, before you won the lottery. This includes cleaning up, managing performance, and making sure everything is correct along the way.

The Common Language Runtime (CLR) is the runtime for .NET. The name *Common Language Runtime* is somewhat deceptive. The name implies that code from each common language can be compiled and executed directly by the runtime. Actually, language code is not compiled directly. First it is compiled by the language compiler into Intermediate Language (IL) code. IL exists as a layer of abstraction to provide a common set of instructions in a very machine-efficient manner. The CLR operates exclusively with the IL code.

All types of .NET applications are hosted inside a CLR instance. The CLR provides a multitude of optimized services to application code. Automatic memory management, also known as "garbage collection," is arguably the most important service the runtime provides. The term *garbage collection* has earned itself quite a stigma because of some of the substandard implementations in the Java world. The implementation within .NET should alleviate the stigma. As well, just-in-time (JIT) compilation provides machine-based optimization to code at runtime. This allows the deployment of common code that you can optimize for future computer architectures.

What's New in .NET

The .NET Framework itself has not changed with the integration into Windows Server 2003. In fact, the default install looks as if Microsoft just slapped the .NET Framework 1.1 install on top of it. The tangible benefits of Windows Server 2003 include application hosting and infrastructure improvements:

- IIS 6 radically improves over IIS 5 in the hosting environment for ASP.NET web applications. The new concepts of application pools and web gardens enhance application stability, scalability, and performance. The new security measures further pull ASP.NET into the leading technology for enterprise web application development.

- Integrated UDDI provides a Yellow Pages of web services within secure company boundaries. This organization and publishing can help Department A avoid redeveloping the same services that Department B developed last week.

- COM+ adds features that align it with .NET. These include application pooling, application recycling, partitioning, and SOAP support.

Application Types

Table 9-1 outlines the many different types of applications that you can build on top of the .NET Framework.

Table 9-1. .NET application types

Type	Technology	Description
Web	ASP.NET	Web applications provide for a simple consistent user experience without all the geographical and system dependencies of thick client applications. ASP.NET, the successor to classic ASP, has been rewritten to abstract the complexities of the web environment to provide a simpler development environment.
Web service	ASP.NET	Web services are not directly exposed to users, but other applications do use them to access systems and data. Web services provide a standard method of inter-application communication across disparate systems.
Windows	Windows Forms	Windows applications provide a very rich, efficient user experience, but traditionally have been difficult to manage because of deployment and system dependencies. The .NET Framework with Windows Forms attempts to alleviate much of this hassle.
Component	COM+	Component applications, such as web services, are not exposed directly to users. An application running under COM+ can provide much of the same functionality as a web service, but COM+ provides more transactional and management capabilities.
Windows service	N/A	Windows service applications are long-running applications that do not require intervention from users. These applications can run without a user logged into the machine.
Console	N/A	Console applications are mostly useful as utility applications that require minimal user interaction. The input from the user is generally provided when the application starts in the form of command-line arguments.

These listed application types should encompass all incarnations of modern applications.

XML-Based Configuration

You'll primarily configure .NET applications through the use of XML files. This is replacing previous, more cryptic stores such as the Windows registry or a configuration database. If you are involved with .NET and are not yet familiar with XML, I recommend you purchase a good book to study it. I recommend *Microsoft ASP.NET Setup and Configuration Pocket Reference* (Microsoft Press). This work provides outstanding detail into the management of ASP.NET applications. It is a reference guide that covers ASP.NET along with a good amount of general .NET information.

Configuration Types

The .NET Framework defines two types of XML configuration files: Security Policy and Settings.

Security Policy

Security Policy files define the code access security policy, which specifies what type of actions code is allowed to perform. I will cover code access security in detail later in this chapter.

These files are far too big and ugly to display here. I strongly recommend using the .NET Configuration MMC, pictured in Figure 9-1, to administer these files.

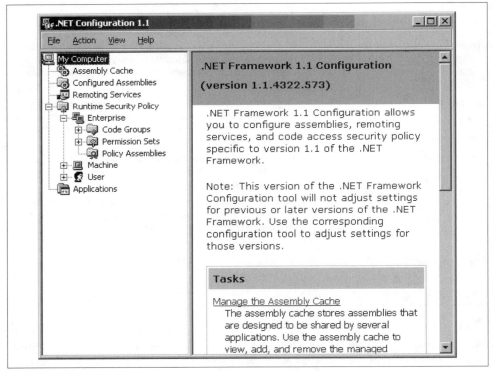

Figure 9-1. .NET Configuration MMC

Settings

Settings files are probably the most exciting breakthrough in .NET from a management perspective. These files have consolidated all application settings into a single repository, providing a well-defined bridge between system administrators and developers.

Example 9-1 shows a typical settings file for a web application. As you can see, the file is quite descriptive of itself through a well-defined hierarchy and semantics.

Example 9-1. Typical web.config file

```
<configuration>
<system.web>
<pages enableSessionState="false" enableViewState="false" />
<compilation defaultLanguage="C#" debug="false"/>
<customErrors mode="RemoteOnly">
<error statusCode="404" redirect="pageNotFound.aspx"/>
</customErrors>
<httpRuntime executionTimeout="240" maxRequestLength="8192" />
</system.web>
<appSettings>
<add key="application.name" value="Test Application" />
<add key="application.url" value="http://www.test.com" />
<add key="administrator.name" value="Mr. Administrator" />
</appSettings>
</configuration>
```

The .NET Framework defines sections of the file to configure everything from the runtime to cryptography through these files. The entire schema is far too complex to show here, however, Table 9-2 describes the core sections defined by the framework.

Table 9-2. Configuration file sections

Section	XML tag	Description
Startup	`<startup>`	Specifies the required and supported runtime versions. Typically used at the application level.
Runtime	`<runtime>`	Configures assemblies and garbage collection.
Remoting	`<system.runtime.remoting>`	Configures Remoting, the .NET remote procedure call (RPC) technology similar to DCOM.
Network	`<system.net>`	Configures network access. Can define proxy servers, limit connection count, etc.
Cryptography	`<mscorlib>` `<cryptographySettings>`	Used at the machine level to specify the cryptography providers on the system. Would not be specified at the application level unless custom cryptography providers were utilized.
Configuration Sections	`<configSections>`	This section defines other sections in the configuration file. At the machine level, the other core sections are defined. At an application level, custom sections can be defined.
Trace and Debug	`<system.diagnostics>`	Configures the level and output of tracing and debugging.

Table 9-2. Configuration file sections (continued)

Section	XML tag	Description
ASP.NET	`<system.web>`	The most in-depth section. Provides security, state, error handling, and many other configuration parameters for web applications.
Application Settings	`<appSettings>`	A list of name-value pairs to be used within an application. The application must be developed to look in this section for values.

Configuration Scopes

When an application is executed, the XML configuration files are arranged and evaluated in a chain starting with the widest scope, Enterprise, going down to the finest scope, Application. This allows a refined hierarchy of management starting with the system administrators, and extending to the users and developers, when allowed.

Enterprise

The Enterprise scope exists to define a security policy that is applicable to the entire enterprise, the widest scope. Despite the policy's scope, the configuration file must exist on each machine to be enforced. The configuration file is located at:

> *%SystemRoot%\Microsoft.NET\Framework\<version>\CONFIG\ enterprisesec.config*

By default, no security is defined in this scope.

Machine

The Machine scope has a settings file in addition to another level of security policy.

The Machine settings file, *machine.config*, is located at:

> *%SystemRoot%\Microsoft.NET\Framework\<version>\CONFIG\machine.config*

The *machine.config* provides a multitude of setting defaults, as it is the root of the settings hierarchy. This file is very well-commented, providing easy edit capability. You always should back up this file before editing, as there is no undo functionality.

The Machine security policy file, *security.config*, is located at:

> *%SystemRoot%\Microsoft.NET\Framework\<version>\CONFIG\security.config*

All code access security is applied in this file by default.

User

The User scope, like the Enterprise scope, defines security policy only. The configuration file is located at:

%UserProfile%\Application Data\Microsoft\CLR Security Config\<version>\ security.config

By default, no security is defined at this scope.

Application

The Application scope defines settings for the application. No code access security policy exists for the Application scope. The name and location of the configuration files depend on the type of application.

ASP.NET web applications use files named *web.config*. These files can be present in any directory within the application. As a page is executed, all *web.config* files within the page's directory structure are applied in the order of shallowest to deepest. For example, I'll use an application with the root *C:\Inetpub\wwwroot* and a page with the path *C:\Inetpub\wwwroot\subdirectory\page.aspx*. A *web.config* file is present in both the application root and the subdirectory with the page. The *web.config* file from the root directory is applied first. The *web.config* file from the subdirectory is applied next, overriding any conflicting settings in the *web.config* file from the root directory.

Executable-based applications use a configuration file in the same directory as the executable. The filename is the executable name with *.config* appended to it. An example is *application.exe.config*. Executable-based applications include Windows Forms, Windows Service, and Console applications.

Applications hosted inside Internet Explorer must specify the location of the configuration file through a `<link>` tag within the `<head>` tag of the web page. You can do this in the following format:

```
<html>
<head>
<link rel="application.dll.config" href="application.dll.config" />
...
```

Security

Despite the precedent I set earlier in this book, I'm going to discuss security toward the beginning of this chapter, for several reasons:

- Security is what you will encounter most often from a management perspective.
- The .NET Security model is probably the most radical shift from tradition among all elements of the Framework.

- Most other elements of the .NET Framework depend on security.
- It is just too darn important.

Code access security is an entirely new concept introduced by the .NET Framework. Traditional security models rely solely on the identification of the user in order to apply the appropriate permissions. .NET supplements this model with another model running in parallel, the code access security model. In code access security, the running code, not the user, is identified using "evidence" of its origin, and permissions are applied depending on that evidence.

This is very useful in many scenarios, but perhaps the most evident example is the case of spyware and viruses. In a code access security model, you can limit the functionality available to an application. This can prevent an Internet-based application from modifying the registry, accessing the network, accessing certain files, or performing virtually any action you choose to define.

As I mentioned earlier, code is identified based on evidence. Table 9-3 lists different types of evidence that can be exposed.

Table 9-3. Types of evidence

Evidence type	Description	Example(s) of condition
Zone	The zone that the assembly originated from. This is identical to the zone displayed on the Internet Explorer status bar.	My Computer Intranet Internet
Site	The site that the assembly originated from. When applying conditions, any URL starting with this value is valid.	http://microsoft.com/ http://test.com/public
URL	The URL that the assembly originated from. Similar to the site evidence type, but more granular. When applying conditions, exact locations of assemblies can be specified.	http://microsoft.com/* http://test.com/test.dll
Application directory	Indicates whether the assembly is located within the folder structure of the application.	N/A
Strong name	A strong name refers to the Public Key, Name, and Version of the assembly.	Public Key: A3AD... Name: Microsoft.Test Version: 1.1.0.0
Publisher	The publisher of the assembly. This will be exposed only if the assembly is digitally signed with a certificate.	Name: Microsoft Issuer Name: Verisign Hash: 23ASD3...
Hash	A simple MD5 or SHA1 hash of the assembly. When applying conditions, this ensures the exact binary assembly.	23ASD3...
Custom	Any other information needing to be interrogated about the assembly by the runtime.	

From the type of evidence exposed, the runtime places the code into one or more code groups. This is done by evaluating the membership condition of each defined code group. An example of a membership condition is Site = http://www.microsoft.com/. The default code groups correspond to zones in Table 9-4.

Table 9-4. Default permission sets for code groups

Code group	Permission set
All_Code	Nothing
My_Computer_Zone	FullTrust
LocalIntranet_Zone	LocalIntranet
Internet_Zone	Internet
Trusted_Zone	Internet
Restricted_Zone	Nothing

Each code group is associated with a single permission set, which is, as you might have guessed, a set of permissions. Each permission in the permission set is configured individually. Many different permissions exist, most corresponding to libraries within the .NET Class Library. There are too many permissions to list and describe here, so I recommend firing up the .NET Configuration MMC shown in Figure 9-2. By double-clicking a specific permission in the right pane, you can view the applicable parameters available for that permission and how the permission is configured for that permission set.

Figure 9-2. .NET Configuration MMC permission list

This is obviously a lot of information to digest, so I recommend diving into the configuration panel to get some hands-on experience. Also, keep in mind that the information presented is from a system administration perspective. Plus, the developers among us can utilize permissions within code and libraries, which introduces virtually limitless options for further levels of security.

Role-Based Security

.NET also provides a robust model for role-based security. This model relies on first identifying the user and the user's roles. Once the user is identified, access checks are made within the application to determine, based on the roles, whether a user is authorized to use a resource or perform an action.

A user is identified using a method of authentication. Three types of authentication are provided within the .NET Framework:

- "Windows" authentication can be used in any type of application. This will use local SAM or Active Directory credentials for the current user. To use this with a web application, you must configure IIS to allow Basic, Digest, Integrated Windows Authentication, or Certificates. See Chapter 8 for information on configuring IIS this way.
- "Forms" authentication is a custom scheme Microsoft built for web applications. In simple scenarios, forms authentication is configurable entirely within *web.config*. In more complex scenarios, forms authentication can be extended to interface with a database or directory for authentication.
- "Passport" is Microsoft's attempt at completely centralized authentication. .NET Framework provides authentication for web application users into Passport.

In addition to these authentication types, .NET provides a schema to implement custom authentication schemes, most likely using an organization's existing infrastructure.

Once a user is authenticated, authorization comes into play. You can implement authorization in different ways depending on the type of application. Windows applications typically perform authorization checks before a user attempts an action. Web applications often perform authorization checks before a user accesses a URL.

The security administration for web applications is much more flexible because of the introduction of security settings into *web.config*. Windows applications cannot be afforded this flexibility because of the obvious security risk of a user being able to manipulate the settings in the application configuration file.

Example 9-2 shows a very simple authentication and authorization scheme defined in *web.config*.

Example 9-2. Simple web application role-based configuration

```
<configuration>
<system.web>
<authentication mode="Forms">
<forms loginUrl="login.aspx">
```

Example 9-2. Simple web application role-based configuration (continued)

```
<credentials passwordFormat="Clear">
<user name="user" password="password" />
<user name="administrator" password="password" />
</credentials>
</forms>
</authentication>
<authorization>
<deny users="?" />
<allow users="*" />
</authorization>
</system.web>
</configuration>
```

The authentication element specifies forms authentication, and the forms parameters are defined within. In this case, the users are actually defined within the forms element. Keep in mind this would be practical only for the simplest of cases. Several pitfalls of this approach are as follows:

- No roles can be assigned to users. This allows only two levels of security, authenticated and anonymous, unless you explicitly name users in the authorization section, which is discouraged because of the maintenance involved.

- Changes made to *web.config* cause the application to restart. This is less than optimal in a high-traffic situation or when changes must be made very often.

- The user store is isolated from other applications, forcing a separate user store for each application.

The authorization section in Example 9-2 reflects the simplicity of the inline user store. The authorization section lists two conditions. The first condition specifies that all anonymous users, abbreviated as ?, are denied. The second condition, which is redundant with the default configuration, specifies that all users are allowed. By the configuration being applied top down, this would disallow anonymous users and allow authenticated users.

A more practical, but more system-dependent, *web.config* is shown in Example 9-3.

Example 9-3. Practical web application role-based configuration

```
<configuration>
<system.web>
<authentication mode="Windows" />
<authorization>
<deny roles="DOMAIN\Banned Users"
<allow roles="BUILTIN\Administrators,BUILTIN\Users" />
<deny users="*" />
</authorization>
</system.web>
</configuration>
```

This file specifies to use Windows security for authentication. The authorization section has several conditions, all based on roles. As the file is evaluated, first the user is checked to see if he is in the Banned Users group. If so, he is denied access immediately. Next, Windows checks to see if he is either an administrator or a user with a normal account, and he is admitted if either of these is true. Finally, all other users are denied access.

Both Examples 9-2 and 9-3 apply security to the entire directory structure in which *web.config* is located. For more granular security, you can place *web.config* files in subdirectories to specify different authorization logic. In this case, the authorization checks are merged between all *web.config* files in the hierarchy with the deepest subdirectory checks being evaluated first.

 The *machine.config* file defines a single authorization condition: `<allow users="*" />`. This effectively allows in any user that has not met a condition specified in the *web.config* file for the application. In a security-sensitive environment, I recommend to modify the *machine.config* file and change the authorization condition to `<deny users="*" />`. This denies all users by default.

Assemblies

Assemblies are file-based units of compiled code that compose .NET applications. An assembly can be an executable or library, named with the extension *.EXE* or *.DLL*, respectively.

You are probably thinking, "Hey, this sounds eerily familiar!" And it should. However, .NET has put quite a spin on things as they were, most notably eliminating the heartache associated with DLL hell. Two new options are provided, both without the complexity of traditional DLLs.

Private Assemblies

Private assemblies are designed to be deployed with a single application and shared with no other applications. They do not require signing or version information. Assemblies also do not need to be registered with the system; you can simply reference them by name. The runtime locates assemblies using a set of rules.

First, all `<dependentAssembly>` elements are loaded from the application configuration file. If the requested assembly is listed, the assembly is loaded from the location specified in the href attribute of the `<codeBase>` element. If this sounds a little complicated, don't worry about it. It's rare to have an assembly listed with this method in practice, but for the sake of completeness, I had to mention it.

Generally, we let the runtime do its job and probe for the assembly. The runtime uses the parameters listed in Table 9-5 to probe for the assembly. These parameters are mixed, matched, concatenated, appended, etc., until the runtime finds the assembly.

Table 9-5. Parameters used to probe for assemblies

Parameter	Description	Example
Assembly name	The name of the assembly, without the DLL.	`Hello`
Application base	The root directory, or URL, of the application.	`C:\Hello\`
Culture	The culture (language) in context. This is not always present.	`en-US`
Declared binpath	The binpath (path to binaries) that was declared in the application configuration file. Generally, no value is specified.	`declaredbin`
Program binpath	The binpath set by program code. Unless you have the source code, this is a mystery. Fortunately, this is rarely used.	`programbin`

Using the examples in Table 9-5, the runtime would probe the following locations:

```
C:\Hello\Hello.DLL
C:\Hello\Hello\Hello.DLL
C:\Hello\en-US\Hello.DLL
C:\Hello\en-US\Hello\Hello.DLL
C:\Hello\declaredbin\Hello.DLL
C:\Hello\declaredbin\Hello\Hello.DLL
C:\Hello\declaredbin\en-US\Hello.DLL
C:\Hello\declaredbin\en-US\Hello\Hello.DLL
C:\Hello\programbin\Hello.DLL
C:\Hello\programbin\Hello\Hello.DLL
C:\Hello\programbin\en-US\Hello.DLL
C:\Hello\programbin\en-US\Hello\Hello.DLL
```

Seems a little excessive, doesn't it? In reality, it is not. Usually the culture is neutral (not specified) and the declared and program binpaths are not specified, leaving only a fraction of the possibilities.

In web applications, the rules change a bit, and Microsoft doesn't do much to explain them. The Application Base becomes a *bin* directory off of the web application root. The rule is to place all assemblies in this directory, except for culture-specific assemblies which you should place in culture-named directories off of the *bin* directory.

Strong-Named Assemblies

Strong-named assemblies are intended to be used when more than a single application needs access to the assembly. They are used, for example, with the assemblies that contain the .NET Class Library. Strong-named assemblies contain several extension attributes to uniquely identify them:

Version
> This isn't your father's versioning scheme. The new scheme, major.minor.build. release (e.g., 1.1.4322.201), gives more precision than other development environments, providing the required uniqueness.

Culture
> This is used mostly when storing resources such as error messages. You can store an assembly for each culture, and only the assembly for the current culture is loaded into an application.

Public Key
> This prevents Joe Schmoe from camouflaging his assemblies as the ones by Microsoft, or your company. Assemblies are signed with a protected private key and subsequently can be verified with this public key.

Microsoft learned a hard lesson with its previous DLL registration technique. The previous model allowed a DLL to be registered once per system, and allowed any installer to update the DLL with a new version. In a perfect world, this would be optimal as you could keep things fresh and optimized, possibly providing a boost to existing applications as they would use the new version of the DLL. In the real world, it caused disasters. New versions of DLLs could break compatibility, interfering with applications that were sitting idly, minding their own business! Microsoft even had to introduce a feature into Windows 2000, System File Protection (SFP), to prevent its system DLLs from being overwritten in this fashion.

.NET takes a different approach to system assembly management. Rather than an application storing the name of an assembly, and being handed whatever version exists on the system, applications now must identify the assembly's name, version, and public key. This ensures that an application will use only assemblies that it has been tested with.

These system-wide assemblies are stored in the Global Assembly Cache (GAC). Called "the gack," this feature is included for those who still can't seem to keep their hands to themselves. The GAC is located in the *%SystemRoot%\assembly* folder. Assemblies are physically copied into the GAC when registered, providing a safe store for the assembly. You can manage the GAC in several different ways. The most obvious is to browse to the folder within Windows Explorer. Figure 9-3 illustrates an example of what you might find in the GAC. Notice the Explorer shell extension displaying the extended attributes.

The Windows shell extension supports delete operations and add operations via drag-and-drop. You can find a similar GAC management console in the .NET Configuration MMC under Assembly Cache.

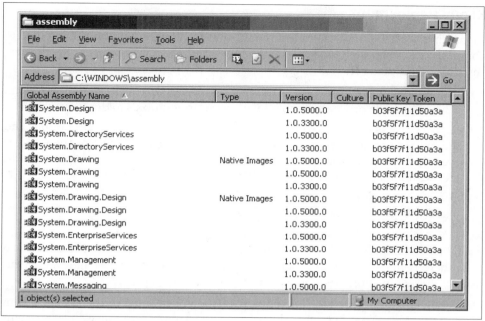

Figure 9-3. The GAC Explorer extension

You also can manage the GAC from the command line with the *gacutil.exe* utility, if the .NET SDK is installed. Basic usage is as follows:

- To install an assembly:

      gacutil /I <assemblyname>.dll

- To remove an assembly:

      gacutil /U <assemblyname>.dll

- To list all assemblies:

      gacutil /L

Deployment Models

Some of the most attractive features of .NET are the deployment options. Microsoft has realized the hectic nature of application deployment and provided several simple standards.

XCopy Deployment

Remember the DOS days when you could transfer applications from computer to computer via a simple XCOPY command? Well, those days are back. Several features make this possible:

- You no longer need to register DLLs (or assemblies) on the system to use them. You can include private assemblies within the application's folder structure.

- Registry access is discouraged. Because of the variety of deployment options and the limited permission set granted to code, in some situations registry access is even prohibited. You can store configuration information and settings in XML files within the application's folder structure.

- The runtime monitors web application files for changes. When changes are made, they are reflected live in the application.

XCOPY deployment does not require that you use the XCOPY utility. You should use Windows Explorer, FTP, batch files, or whatever suits you best. The concept to grasp here is that .NET applications have broken many of the system-level dependencies present in application builds on previous technology.

Occasionally, you'll have to take additional actions to configure the system for an application. This is needed when the application requires system-level environment changes. This can include actions such as creating a performance counter or an Event Log. In most cases you can perform these manually, but if you have some really slick developers, they might have embedded the configuration actions into the application's assemblies. In this case, meet *installutil.exe*, located in *%SystemRoot%\ Microsoft.NET\Framework\<version>*. This command-line utility can easily install and uninstall assemblies. You can invoke the utility on multiple assemblies, which causes it to operate in a transactional manner. This means that if one part of the installation fails, the entire installation will be "rolled back." The following example shows the commands for the installation and uninstallation of two assemblies:

```
installutil application.exe application2.exe
installutil /uninstall application.exe application2.exe
```

No-Touch Deployment

No-touch deployment is an effort to bring the simplicity of deploying a web application to thick client applications. This has been achieved by mimicking the web application deployment model.

In this model the only deployment is done to the server. The application assemblies sit within web server directories just as an HTML document would. When a user requests an executable assembly, either from a hyperlink or through manual entry, the web browser retrieves and examines the assembly. The assembly is launched if it's found to be a valid .NET assembly. The CLR is aware of the originating URL, and requests dependent assemblies and configuration files from the web server as needed.

Figure 9-4 demonstrates the deployment of a simple application.

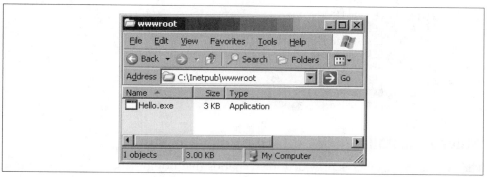

Figure 9-4. Deploying the assembly

Once deployed, you can run the application assembly simply by keying the URL into your web browser. You also can accomplish this from the Run menu or by creating a shortcut. Figure 9-5 shows the simple Hello application being run from your web browser.

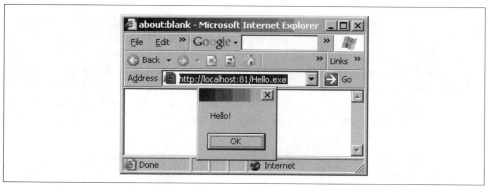

Figure 9-5. Running the assembly from the URL

The assembly is requested through Internet Explorer. After an initial examination, the control is passed to the .NET runtime. Example 9-4 is a fragment of the HTTP log file listing the requests the .NET runtime made to run and configure the assembly. As you can see, the process of interrogating the environment can be somewhat intense, especially with more complex applications that might require more assemblies. However, you can save a wealth of CPU cycles on the server by offloading the application processing onto the client machine, as opposed to a pure ASP.NET web application.

Example 9-4. Log file of activity used to run assembly

```
#Software: Microsoft Internet Information Services 5.1
#Version: 1.0
#Date: 2003-11-30 00:51:20
#Fields: time c-ip cs-method cs-uri-stem sc-status
00:51:20 127.0.0.1 GET /Hello.exe 304
00:51:20 127.0.0.1 GET /Hello.exe.config 404
00:51:21 127.0.0.1 GET /Hello.exe.config 404
00:51:21 127.0.0.1 GET /Hello.DLL 404
00:51:21 127.0.0.1 GET /Hello/Hello.DLL 404
00:51:21 127.0.0.1 GET /bin/Hello.DLL 403
00:51:21 127.0.0.1 GET /bin/Hello/Hello.DLL 403
00:51:21 127.0.0.1 GET /Hello.EXE 304
```

Windows Installer

The Windows Installer is provided for scenarios that do not lend themselves to one of the other deployment methods. These include times when complex tasks need to occur with the install or when deploying to users that would rather run a simple install package. Windows installer packages are simple *.EXE* or *.MSI* files that you can run from the Windows shell.

Diagnostics

The .NET Framework includes a wide variety of options for diagnosing different aspects of a running application. You can use diagnostics for many functions including auditing, logging, profiling, and debugging. You can use them to identify performance problems, resource usage, and security issues. Like many other management tasks, diagnostic work requires full cooperation between developers and the system management staff. This section will cover the diagnostics management and give you tips on what the development side of the house should do to keep their end of the bargain.

Debugging and Tracing

The debug and trace features allow an application to produce simple diagnostic information without interfering with the user interface. Developers can include statements within the application code to write information and failures to virtually any source, including the Windows Event Log.

Although the debug and trace features are exactly the same internally, they have different intended uses:

- Debug is used during the development and testing stages of an application. Debug statements are usually stripped out by the compiler in release builds of assemblies.
- Trace is used during the full life cycle of development, including production. Compilers typically leave Trace statements in release builds.

 If you're not a code monkey, you can safely skip the remainder of this section and move on to the next. I'll simply provide more detail for those interested in .NET Framework debugging and tracing features.

Example 9-5 shows a section of a configuration settings file that configures the debug and trace features. Most of the settings are self-explanatory, but a few of them are quite obscure. First, the <assert> element is actually the configuration for the DefaultTraceListener. If the DefaultTraceListener is removed, these settings have no effect. The other confusion within this section is the naming of the <trace> element. Despite the name of the element, all parameters and listeners defined also apply to the debug feature. You can see the first thing I did within the listeners was to remove the DefaultTraceListener. On the next line, I define a TextWriterTraceListener and in the initializeData, I define the name of the log file.

Example 9-5. Debug and Trace information in configuration settings

```
<configuration>
<system.diagnostics>
<assert assertuienabled="true" logfilename="test.log" />
<switches>
<add name="AuditSwitch" value="1" />
<add name="ErrorSwitch" value="4" />
</switches>
<trace autoflush="false" indentsize="0">
<listeners>
<remove name="Default" />
<add name="Text"
type="System.Diagnostics.TextWriterTraceListener, ..."
initializeData="realTest.log" />
</listeners>
</trace>
</system.diagnostics>
</configuration>
```

Keep in mind that, if necessary, you can override in the application code the listeners specified in the configuration file. This can provide additional levels of detail, such as sending the output of a TextWriterTraceListener through an encryption algorithm or over a network. It also can confuse administrators, so if you hear your developers around the corner snickering, that might explain why the trace output is being sent to the CEO's Inbox.

ASP.NET offers an additional form of tracing within web applications. Keep in mind that it is entirely different from the tracing functionality discussed earlier in that it isn't designed to be persistent. This form of tracing is designed to give real-time feedback on web page execution performance. Figure 9-6 is just a small sample of the information exposed through the trace request details.

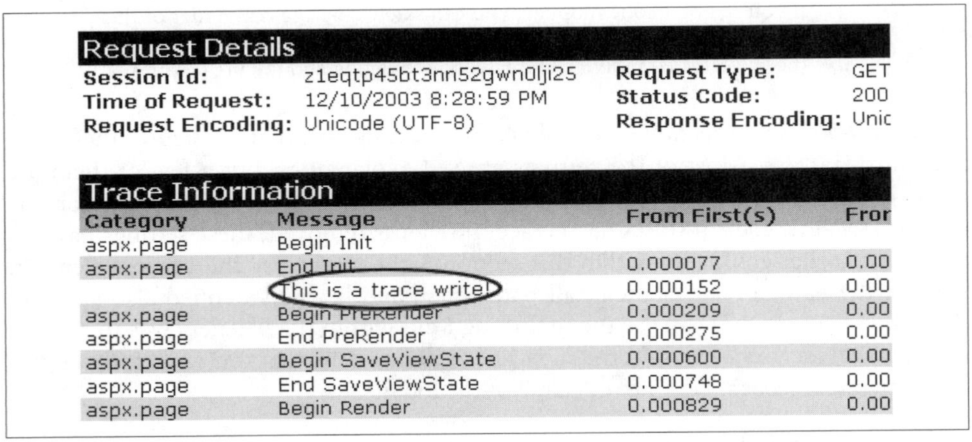

Figure 9-6. Details of a trace request

You can configure this information to be included at the end of every page, or store it in web server memory browsed with the *trace.axd* virtual page in your web application root. An example of the *web.config* configuration of tracing is shown here:

```
<system.web>
<trace enabled="true" localOnly="false" pageOutput="false"
requestLimit="50" />
</system.web>
```

The localOnly parameter defines whether the *trace.axd* page can be accessed from a machine other than the web server. The requestLimit parameter behaves a little oddly, as when it reaches this limit, all tracing stops. You must clear the trace or restart the application to begin tracing after the limit is reached.

Performance Counters

Performance counters provide an excellent interface to monitor activity within a Windows environment. The .NET Framework uses the performance counter infrastructure to report on its own performance and to allow applications to report on their custom performance characteristics.

Framework counters

The .NET Framework provides two categories of performance counters, CLR and ASP.NET. In these two categories are numerous different subcategories with counters within. You can apply the CLR counters on a per-process basis or on a global basis. These counters monitor the activity within the various services that the runtime provides. Although there is tremendous value in the outputs from these counters, they are very difficult to dissect without expert knowledge of the CLR. ASP.NET defines two subcategories for counters. The first category, *ASP.NET*, contains counters that aggregate all applications and system-level counters. The other category, *ASP.NET Applications*, contains counters that serve to report on individual web applications. Figure 9-7 illustrates the selection of .NET performance counters.

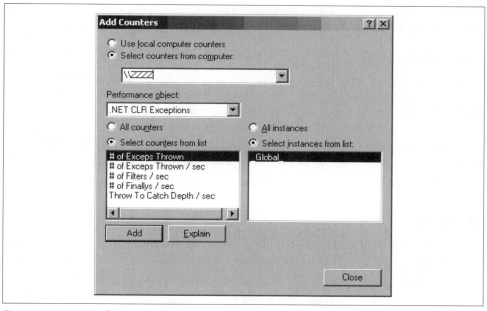

Figure 9-7. .NET performance counters

I won't cover all the counters here, as there are more than 100 in total, but I'd like to mention a few that provide easy-to-interpret results and can indicate bottlenecks:

- *# of Exceps Thrown* and *# of Exceps Thrown / sec* under the *.NET CLR Exceptions* subcategory can manifest problems within any application. Exceptions are errors that are not always propagated to the user interface. Exceptions are quite expensive for the runtime to create. This number should be low.

- *Current Queue Length* under the *.NET CLR LocksAndThreads* subcategory is useful in applications that are making a lot of long-running parallel calls. This number should be low.

- *Application Restarts* and *Worker Process Restarts* under *ASP.NET* can indicate memory usage problems or timeouts. Applications and Worker Processes restart periodically based on either of these two problems. This number should be low.

- *Requests Queued* under *ASP.NET* counts the number of requests waiting to be processed. This number should be low.

- *Cache API Hit Ratio*, *Cache Total Hit Ratio*, and *Output Cache Hit Ratio* under *ASP.NET Applications* are useful in determining the efficiency of cache usage. The caching features of ASP.NET allow applications to avoid invoking expensive operations every time data is needed. A low cache hit ratio indicates the cache is not being used efficiently.

The standard Windows performance counters grouped under the categories *System* and *Processor* also can be very important in monitoring .NET applications, but might not give the granularity that the .NET Framework counters provide.

Custom counters

Applications in need of specific performance monitoring can take advantage of custom performance counters. The .NET Framework provides a very simple set of libraries for developers to develop custom performance counters. Although the .NET Framework counters can indicate what type of performance problem exists, you can use custom counters to show what part of the application is causing the problems.

You also can use the counters to present business-related information. For example, a company could track the number of orders or shipments in real time.

Event Logs

The .NET Framework extends the integration into Windows management with event logging capability. Event logs provide a centralized store for reporting all types of application information.

Windows provides three default logs that applications can write to:

Application
> Applications report information and error messages here.

Security
> Audit records from system-level and application-level events are reported here.

System
> Like the Application log, this also is poorly described as "system error records." This log is used to report all system-level events.

In addition to the default logs, you can create an unlimited number of custom logs for any application. This is useful for events that do not fit into the other categories, or when the information needs to be segregated for management.

Use and configuration of event logs typically occur within the application code. .NET provides rich libraries to allow granular manipulation of many event parameters including the log name, the source, the type of entry, the event ID, the category, the raw data, and of course, the description. You can pass control of some of these parameters to system administrators in the form of parameters within the *appSettings* section in the configuration file, but developers would have to specifically code for this.

In the spirit of configuration-based applications, .NET does provide a method for administrators to enable event logging for an application. You can utilize this if the application implements tracing or debugging. You can configure the EventLogTraceListener within the application configuration file to send all trace and debug messages into the event log. However, the options are quite limited. The following XML placed within the <listeners> tag of the <trace> tag will register an EventLogTraceListener:

```
<add name="Event"
type="System.Diagnostics.EventLogTraceListener, System, ..."
initializeData="Hello Application" />
```

As the preceding XML shows, you can supply only one parameter, initializeData. This parameter sets the Source of the log entries. Figure 9-8 shows an actual log entry created using tracing. The Application log is used with an entry type of Information.

Management Tools

In this section, I'll look at both GUI and CLI management tools that you can use to administer the .NET Framework and your web applications with Windows Server 2003.

GUI Tools

The GUI tools included with the .NET Framework are fairly limited, but worth a mention. They consist of two tools, the .NET Framework Configuration MMC and the .NET Framework Wizards.

The .NET Framework Configuration MMC

This tool is apparently the greatest Microsoft has to offer in terms of graphical management of the .NET Framework. This is unfortunate, as this tool could use a lot of additions to the management of settings within XML configuration files.

You can find the tool in the Administrative Tools panel in Windows. Figure 9-9 shows a snapshot of the tool.

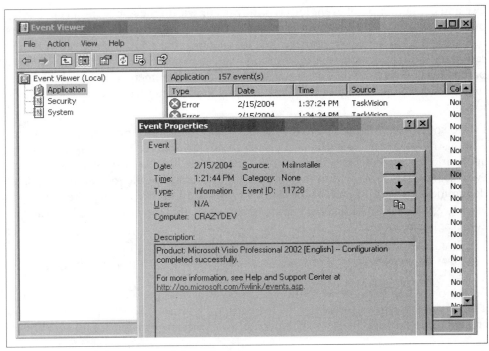

Figure 9-8. Event log entry created through tracing

Enterprise Instrumentation Framework

If you are really interested in diagnostics, I recommend you take a look at the Enterprise Instrumentation Framework (EIF). The EIF is a set of libraries designed to unify management and instrumentation in a .NET enterprise environment. Microsoft freely distributes the package as a separate download from the .NET Framework.

Think of the EIF as tracing on steroids. Instead of simple text messages, events are raised from applications. Events can be structured to include more information than can be contained in a sentence or two. You can create custom events that can be related to a specific business process. As events are raised, they are sent to one or more sinks. These sinks can be anything, including a new Windows Trace Session Manager that has been created for very high-frequency logging. You can configure all of this through a centralized XML configuration file.

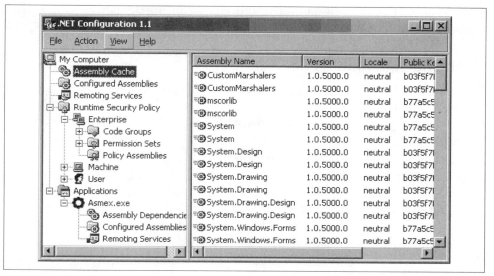

Figure 9-9. The .NET Framework Configuration MMC

I'll quickly cover the first level of the tree to give you a basic understanding of the tool:

- Assembly Cache is another view of the GAC Explorer extension that you also can find at *%SystemRoot%\assembly* in Windows Explorer, but without the drag-and-drop Add functionality. You can remove assemblies with it.

- Configured Assemblies is a summary of the assembly location and redirection settings from the *machine.config* XML configuration file. This provides a method to redirect references to an assembly on a machine basis.

- Remoting Services provides a very limited interface for manipulating the remoting section of *machine.config*. This interface does not allow you to add parameters, just edit those that exist.

- Runtime Security Policy is actually a nice interface for managing the security policy of the enterprise, the machine, or the current user.

- Applications allows graphical editing of an application's configuration file. The first time I saw this I thought it was a joke. Out of the hundreds of possible configuration parameters, this thing allows you to edit maybe 10 or 20 of the less important ones.

The .NET Framework Wizards tool

The .NET Framework Wizards tool is designed to streamline some of the common operations that are typically done with the .NET Framework Configuration MMC. You can also find this tool in the Administrative Tools panel. The most notable function is the Adjust .NET Security Wizard. This provides an Internet Explorer-like panel for adjusting security based on zones.

Command-Line Tools

The command-line tools provide a much more complete management solution for the .NET Framework. These tools are located in *%SystemRoot%\Microsoft.NET\ Framework\<version>* except where otherwise noted. I'll touch on a couple of the highlights here:

ASP.NET IIS Registration Tool (aspnet_regiis.exe)
> This tool is useful if you have web applications that need to use different versions of the .NET Framework on the same machine. Installing different versions might sound like a management nightmare, but it is actually fairly simple with this tool. To set a web application to a specific version of the framework, use the aspnet_regiis.exe included with the version as follows:
> ```
> aspnet_regiis -s W3SVC/1/ROOT/Application
> ```

Code Access Security Policy Tool (caspol.exe)
> Although this tool performs virtually anything involved with administering security policy, it is useful mostly for the quick and dirty little tasks such as trusting a single assembly. To do that using *caspol*, you'd run the following command:
> ```
> caspol -m -ft assembly.dll
> ```

Global Assembly Cache Tool (gacutil.exe)
> Use this to install, remove, and list items in the GAC. This tool is included with the .NET SDK and is located in the install directory. To install an assembly, use:
> ```
> gacutil /I assembly.dll
> ```

Installer Utility Tool (installutil.exe)
> Performs actions needed to run an assembly after an XCOPY deployment. To use on an assembly, use:
> ```
> installutil assembly.dll
> ```

Reference

Thousands of resources for .NET have surfaced since its introduction in early 2002, but very few of these are geared toward systems management. This frequently results in systems management being left to <gasp> the developers. This section covers what is out there, and how to find it.

You can find the most solid and up-to-date information directly at the source, the .NET SDK. MSDN publishes thousands of pages of SDK documentation online. I'll direct you to the 1% that deals with management. First, I'll throw out the URL to get you to the root of this thing:

> *http://msdn.microsoft.com/library/en-us/netstart/html/sdk_netstart.asp*

This will take you to a node in the tree view entitled .NET Framework. This is the root of the documentation included with the .NET SDK download. The following lists, in order of importance, the most notable sections covering systems management:

.NET Framework → Reference → Configuration File Schema
Covers top to bottom everything that can appear in a configuration settings file.

.NET Framework → Tools and Debugger → .NET Framework Tools
Description and usage examples for each tool included with the framework. Some of the tools pertain more to development.

.NET Framework → Configuring Applications
The title is self-explanatory. Very in-depth information regarding configuration.

.NET Framework → Reference → Performance Counters
Describes each .NET Framework performance counter.

.NET Framework → Getting Started → NET Framework System Requirements
If your organization is more diverse, you might want to look here first.

.NET Framework → Deploying Applications
Provides information on deploying assemblies and the .NET Framework redistributable.

The Last Word

Windows Server 2003 comes with the .NET Framework, and the enhancements to IIS and COM+, along with security and stability improvements, have ensured that the product is a credible offering in the world of application servers. In this chapter, you learned about the administrative sides of the .NET Framework and also pointed you to some other resources once your developers begin needing advanced services.

CHAPTER 10

Windows Terminal Services

In the old days of mainframe computing, employees typically used terminal equipment to connect to a big machine in a white room that ran all their programs and calculations. The terminal only showed the user interface while processing keystrokes and responses from the user; the mainframe in the back actually executed the programs and displayed the results to the end user so that very little processor intelligence resided at the client equipment end. This is largely why these terminal systems were called "dumb."

Although the move into the personal computing and desktop computing era made large inroads into corporate America, there are still some uses for dumb terminal (or in more modern terminology, "thin client") functionality. Windows Terminal Services (TS) is a set of programs and utilities that enable this functionality on a more intelligent, contemporary level. In fact, you might already be familiar with Terminal Services in a scaled-down mode. Both Windows XP's Remote Assistance and Remote Desktop Connection utilities are examples of Terminal Services in action. Terminal Services passes only the user interface of a program running on a server to the client computer, which then passes back the appropriate keyboard strokes and mouse clicks. The server running Terminal Services, which many clients can access simultaneously, manages the connections and the active programs seamlessly. It appears to the user that he's using his own computer, rather than one servicing other active applications at the same time.

Why is this useful? Many corporations, in an effort to reduce desktop support responsibilities for their help desks as well as equipment acquisition costs, are deploying thin client computers with limited client-side functionality. These thin clients provide users with a window into a server that is running the applications they need. Microsoft Office, many accounting applications, and multitudes of other programs work effectively under a Terminal Services environment, and the reduced management headaches are worth the extra initial setup effort for some businesses. Think about the reduced cost of applying patches, upgrading software, or removing outdated programs. You apply, upgrade, or remove once, and bingo: your entire enterprise IT environment is updated. It's hard to argue with that. This mode of using Terminal Services is known, very simply, as *Terminal Services.*

Terminal Services has another common use: remote administration. This is a hassle-free way that you can connect to machines running a Terminal Services-compatible operating system, and can use the machine's interface almost exactly as if you were sitting in front of it. Windows 2000, XP, and Server 2003 come bundled with a license to do this. This is quite a boon for administrators: you don't have to leave your cubicle to administer elements of Windows on servers in your machine room.

A Terminal Services connection uses TCP port 3389 to allow clients to log on to a session from their workstation. However, the Terminal Services Configuration applet and the Terminal Services Manager console, which I'll also cover in this chapter, enable you to change this port and a number of other properties about each connection.

Terminal Services has its own method for licensing clients that log on to terminal servers, separate from the licensing method for clients running one of the other flavors of Windows 2003. In addition to being enabled to use Terminal Services in their user account properties, clients must receive a valid license issued by a license server before they are allowed to log on to a terminal server. Later in this chapter I'll discuss in greater detail the subject of licensing issues when using Terminal Services.

 Terminal Services support is not included in Windows Server 2003 Web Edition, although you can use the Remote Desktop Connection applet in the Control Panel to remotely administer the server.

The Remote Desktop Protocol

The Remote Desktop Protocol (RDP) is the protocol that drives Terminal Services. RDP is based on and is an extension of the T.120 protocol family of standards. It is a multichannel-capable protocol that allows for separate virtual channels for carrying device communication and presentation data from the server, as well as encrypted client mouse and keyboard data. RDP provides a very extensible base from which to build many additional capabilities, supporting up to 64,000 separate channels for data transmission as well as provisions for multipoint transmission.

Figure 10-1 shows the structure of RDP and its functionality from a high-level perspective.

The new Terminal Services client software included in Windows Server 2003 (Remote Desktop Connection, or RDC) uses RDP 5.2, and many local resources are available within the remote session: the client drives, smart cards, audio card, serial ports, printers (including network), and clipboard. Additionally, you can select color depth from 256 colors (8-bit) to True Color (24-bit) and resolution from 640×480 up to 1600×1200.

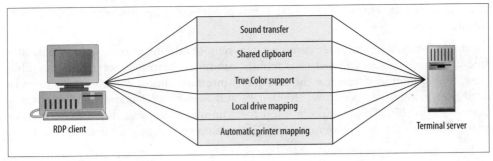

Figure 10-1. An overview of RDP

RDP basically takes instructions from a terminal server host machine on screen images and draws them onto a client's screen, refreshing that image about 20 times every second if there's activity on the client side. (To save bandwidth, if no activity is detected on the client side, it cuts the refresh rate in half.) It then notes any keyboard and mouse activity (among other things) and relays those signals to the terminal server host machine for processing. This two-way exchange of information is wrapped into what's called a *session*, which consists of the programs running on the host machine and the information being sent over RDP between the terminal server and the client machine.

Requirements for Terminal Services

Because most of the processing power that was traditionally on the desktop has moved to the server in a Terminal Services scenario, it follows that the machine hosting Terminal Services for your users should be significantly beefier than you might otherwise be used to. Perhaps the two most critical points as far as hardware requirements are CPU and RAM, followed by the network interface and links.

CPU Requirements

CPU requirements can be difficult to measure because individual users require different slices of processor time at different intervals. Two main factors determine CPU usage: intensity of the applications that users are running, and the number of simultaneous users. Table 10-1 gives a rough estimate for CPU requirements based on number of users and application intensity.

What Happened to Citrix?

When Microsoft introduced its revamped version of Terminal Services in Windows 2000, many predicted the demise of Citrix's venerable MetaFrame product. Citrix basically invented the idea of multiple sessions on one Windows host, and RDP is loosely based on Citrix's protocol, Independent Computing Architecture (ICA). MetaFrame has traditionally sat atop Terminal Services, using its basic functionality as a foundation and adding useful features on top. But many people have asked what with all the improvements to RDP, including bandwidth reduction, client-side caching, device mapping, sound redirection, and increased color depth, why a corporation would continue to buy Citrix's flagship product?

A feature known as Seamless Windows one-to-many connections is available with MetaFrame, but not with raw Terminal Services. For the client, this means applications you see are displayed without having to scroll or use full-screen mode. On the server, though, it's even better: all sessions on the same server that use Seamless Windows are operating out of the same physical instance of the program, saving on hardware resources.

Another hot item is application publishing, which uses a Citrix concept called Program Neighborhood to direct a user to applications via a menu of program options. The user doesn't have to know which servers run those applications with Citrix because he can just choose a program from the menu and be connected directly to it. To use native Terminal Services and RDP, the user would need to find the appropriate server and connect to it.

Additional core features of MetaFrame distinguish it from native Terminal Services. And as always, Citrix releases new features in its Service Releases. Larger organizations that use Terminal Services connections extensively might want to investigate how MetaFrame might improve their efficiency. However, most organizations, especially small businesses, will find that the initially free Terminal Services components of Windows Server 2003 (you pay only for licensing and not the initial software purchase) will suffice for their needs.

Table 10-1. Rough estimates of CPU requirements for Terminal Services

Simultaneous users	Intensity of application(s)	Recommended processor
20–25	Low	Pentium III 750 MHz+
	High	Dual Pentium III 750 MHz+ or Pentium IV Xeon any speed
35–40	Low	Pentium III or IV, 1 GHz+
	High	Dual Pentium IV Xeon 2 GHz+
50–55	Low	Dual Pentium IV Xeon 2 GHz+
	High	Not recommended

Amount of RAM

Here are some hard and fast facts about RAM usage with Terminal Services that you might find helpful:

- Each user takes up roughly 20 MB of the Terminal Services host machine's RAM just by logging in.
- A typical load of two to three Office applications per user will add approximately another 25 MB of RAM to the server's RAM usage.

Of course, additional applications on top of that consume more RAM, and power users typically will not run only Office applications, but rather, more powerful applications that require more hardware resources.

Network Interface Card

The Network Interface Card (NIC) is managed by Windows and should not require any configuration for use with Terminal Services. You should focus more on the available bandwidth and average latency on the network to which the card is connected, and not necessarily on the card itself.

Terminal Services does a surprisingly nice job of adjusting the bandwidth usage of the RDP client to the conditions of the link to which it's connected with the host. You can expect that most RDP connections will take up between 2 kbps and 7 kbps depending on the depth of color requested by the client, the amount of graphics being transmitted, whether sound is included, and other options.

Disk Space

The actual Terminal Services components inside Windows Server 2003 do not require any additional disk space on top of what is consumed by the normal system files. Around 15 MB is taken up for the file share that stores the client installation files for RDP. In addition, users store about half a megabyte of data for their Terminal Services profile information when they first log on to a server. (Remember that Terminal Services users' profiles are automatically roaming because their sessions follow them to whatever workstation is running the RDP client.) Other than this, not much disk space is required to support RDP.

Sizing for Scaling

Let's say, for instance, that you've built a server to run TS and now want to see how well it scales. Microsoft has released a group of scaling scripts and utilities that can be downloaded from:

http://www.microsoft.com/windows2000/techinfo/administration/terminal/
loadscripts.asp

The single download includes scripts that should be modified to fit your environment as necessary, and an Excel spreadsheet that will guide you through fine-tuning certain Registry settings to achieve best performance on a machine dedicated solely to hosting TS applications.

Adding the Terminal Server Role

Use the Configure Your Server Wizard to add the Terminal Server role to your machine:

1. Read the precautions and information in this section fully before proceeding.
2. Open the Configure Your Server Wizard as described earlier in this book. On the Server Role page, select Terminal Server, and click Next.
3. The procedure is very simple, so the Summary of Selections page immediately appears. Confirm that you want to install Terminal Services by clicking Next. You will be prompted to reboot to complete the installation.

The permissions to connect to a terminal server are simple to understand. Any user who wants to connect via Terminal Services must be a member of the Remote Desktop Users group on the computer he or she is connecting to. You can alter the access permissions, time-of-day requirements, and other properties for this group through the Active Directory Users and Computers snap-in as usual. (See Chapter 5 for more information on managing users and groups within Active Directory.) If your machine is not participating in an Active Directory environment, user accounts must be members of the Administrators group of the machine to which they're trying to connect.

You should install Terminal Services on an NTFS-formatted partition to take advantage of the superior security features of that filesystem.

Enabling Remote Desktop

As I mentioned earlier in this chapter, Remote Desktop mode is a special Terminal Services feature that enables you to open an RDP session as a single user to a specific machine and use its interface as though you were directly in front of it. This is useful if you're not looking to host applications for multiuser access but simply want a way to avoid walking to the server closet.

Windows Server 2003 comes installed with everything you need to use RDP to administer a server remotely, but as a security precaution, the service is turned off. It's easy to turn it back on, and it follows the same pattern that you use to turn on Remote Desktop in Windows XP versions as well. To turn it back on, follow these steps:

1. Open the System applet in the Control Panel.
2. Navigate to the Remote tab.

3. Under the section at the bottom called Remote Desktop, check the checkbox labeled Allow users to connect remotely to this computer.

4. Click Apply, and then click OK.

Windows will display a dialog box that reminds you that it disables RDP access to accounts that have no password. This is to protect your computer from being invaded by Internet crackers. You also might want to ensure that if you're using a firewall, port 3389 is open and port forwarding is configured if required by your router/firewall.

Once Remote Desktop mode is enabled, up to two administrative users can connect to the server simultaneously and use it as though they were sitting in front of it. The remainder of this chapter will focus on Terminal Services mode, where more users can connect and use the server as a true application server.

On the User's Side

In this section, we'll take a look at interacting with Terminal Services from the client's perspective.

Using the RDP Client

Windows XP comes with a built-in client that speaks RDP, called Remote Desktop Connection. You can find it by selecting Start → All Programs → Accessories → Communications → Remote Desktop Connection. Executing the program brings up a screen such as that shown in Figure 10-2.

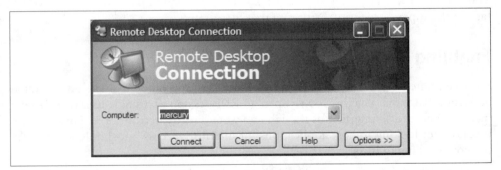

Figure 10-2. The basic Remote Desktop Connection screen

Enter a server name to establish a basic, no-frills connection to a machine. If you want to customize the environment you're working in, click the Options button at the lower right of the Remote Desktop Connection box. You're presented with a box with five tabs: General, Display, Local Resources, Programs, and Experience. Let's walk through each tab.

General

On the General tab, you can choose the Terminal Services machine to log on to, and you can prepopulate the username, password, and domain so that you're not prompted for this information over a slow link. You also can save the current settings to an RDP file that you can open later by clicking the Save As button, or you can open an existing RDP settings file by clicking Open.

Display

On the Display tab, you can select the resolution (up to full screen at your current resolution) in which the session window will be displayed. You also can choose your color depth. You will need to disconnect and then reconnect before changes to these settings will take effect. Finally, check the option to display the connection bar—a small panel centered at the top of the session window—during full-screen sessions. The connection bar provides an easy way to minimize, maximize, and disconnect from a session.

Local Resources

On the Local Resources tab, you can choose to redirect sound to the client machine, to not play sounds at all, or to play them on the remote machine (to the chuckle of some coworkers, perhaps). You also can set the application of standard Windows keyboard shortcuts, such as Alt-Tab, Ctrl-Esc, Ctrl-Alt-Del, and the like to the local computer, the remote computer, or the remote computer only if the display is set to full-screen mode. Finally, you can choose whether to make disk drives, printers, and serial ports on the client machine available to the Terminal Services session.

Programs

On the Programs tab, you can select one specific executable that will run automatically upon connection. This means that as soon as the user closes the program, the connection is terminated: there is no shell access to the session. You might choose to lock down Human Resources users by specifying that they can run only a PeopleSoft application; if they close PeopleSoft, their connection to the Terminal Services host machine is closed. You also can specify a working directory that the Open and Save dialog boxes will default to while the program is running.

Experience

On the Experience tab, you can adjust Microsoft's guesses as to your link quality and how bandwidth is managed during the session. You can choose your appropriate connection speed, and you can explicitly allow or deny the following to be transmitted: the desktop background, the contents of windows while they're being moved, animations of windows and menus (the scroll and fade effects), Windows desktop themes, and the caching of bitmaps.

Configuring a User's Environment

A few settings inside a user's Active Directory account can affect the behavior of a Terminal Services session. Open Active Directory Users and Computers and select a sample user from your directory. Right-click the user and select Properties. When the user's settings are opened, click the Sessions tab. You will see the box as depicted in Figure 10-3.

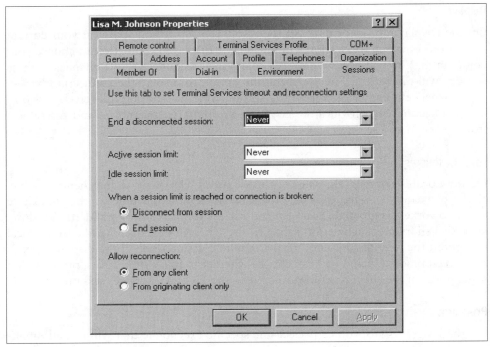

Figure 10-3. User properties in Active Directory for Terminal Services

Using the Sessions tab, you can configure Terminal Services' behavior when a user's session becomes inactive for a certain period of time. You can set the server to automatically log off a session that is disconnected after an interval of time you specify. You also can set a time limit on active sessions and idle sessions, and then configure the behavior when that limit is reached. (This is great if you have a central machine for checking email that's located in a kiosk or other publicly accessible location.) Finally, on this tab you can specify that reconnection to an existing session can occur either from any computer, or only from the computer that originated the session as an added security measure.

On the Environment tab, you can make many of the same modifications as on the Programs tab of Remote Desktop Connection. You can select one specific executable that will run automatically and exclusively upon connection. You also can specify a working directory that the Open and Save dialog boxes will default to while the program is running. Plus, you can map devices from the client machine to the Terminal Services session by default inside the user's properties, which then will carry forward into any future sessions.

On the Remote Control tab, you can specify whether an administrator can remotely control or observe a user's session. You also can configure whether doing that would require a user's permission. Plus, you can delineate how much control over the session is allowed—can the administrator just view the session, or can he or she also interact with the session?

On the Terminal Services Profile tab, you can enter a user profile to be used when connecting to a session. If you want to use a mandatory profile, be sure to enumerate the full network path down to the individual profile folder for that user. You also can determine if a drive is mapped to a user's home directory, which drive letter to use, and which network drive to map to. Finally, you can decide whether a specific user should be allowed to log in to a terminal server. This isn't the best place for this option, in my opinion, but we have a while to wait (until Longhorn Server is released) for this to be changed.

Alternative RDP Clients

You might wish to access TS sessions hosted on Windows 2000 Server and Windows Server 2003 machines from computers that run on alternative platforms, such as Linux or Mac OS X. In this section, I've compiled a brief list of available, reasonably robust RDP client utilities that are available for operating systems other than Windows:

RDesktop

rdesktop is an open RDP client, but unlike Citrix ICA, requires no server extensions. rdesktop currently runs on most Unix-based platforms with the X Window System. (This includes most commercially available Linux systems). As of this writing, the latest stable version of rdesktop is 1.4.0. You can download rdesktop from *http://www.rdesktop.org*.

Remote Desktop Client for Mac

Microsoft itself has released the Remote Desktop Client for Mac, which allows users of Mac OS X to open a TS session to their Windows XP or Windows Server 2003 machines from the comfort of their own environment. Download the client from Microsoft's Mac-oriented web site, located at *http://www.microsoft.com/mac/otherproducts/otherproducts.aspx?pid=remotedesktopclient*.

Installing an Application

If you want to install an application on the terminal server that is in Terminal Services mode so that users can access it from thin clients, the proper way is to install the application through the Add/Remove Programs applet inside the Control Panel and *not* through the application's default installation method. By using the Add/Remove Programs applet, Windows ensures that program files are installed to the Windows root directory on the server, as opposed to the Windows subfolder under the user's home directory. Windows also ensures the programs are installed properly for multiple use of the same memory space. Both of these steps make the programs available for multi-session access. Any program that displays the Certified for Windows logo will be able to handle the differences between normal local access and usage in a Terminal Services scenario. Other applications can cause problems, so be sure to test each application before deployment.

Also, it's prudent to check for prewritten scripts that help ensure an application is installed properly for multi-user execution. Microsoft tests some common applications for compatibility and releases templates and modifications so that these programs will install correctly for use with Terminal Services. You can find these scripts in *%SystemRoot%\Application Compatibility Scripts\Install*.

 Installing programs on the terminal server machine using RDC (for remote administration) works like any other software installation program, although depending on the application it might work only under the remote administration terminal and not other users' sessions.

To install a program using the Add/Remove Programs tool, follow these steps:

1. Open the Add/Remove Programs applet inside the Control Panel.

2. From the left bar, choose Add New Programs.

3. Click CD Or Floppy, which will raise a wizard. Click Next to continue.

4. Insert the program distribution media if it's external. Windows will attempt to look in your drives for a setup file. If Windows can't find the file, it will prompt you for its location. Click Next to complete this step.

5. Windows will begin the installation, but it will leave the After Installation dialog box open. Do not close that window until the installation is finished; otherwise, the program will not function correctly. Also, do not reboot the computer if the program's setup utility asks you to restart.

6. After the installation has completed, but before any necessary reboot, click Next in the After Installation dialog box and let Windows detect the changes and record the necessary data. Finally, click Finish.

7. Reboot at this point only if the setup program required it earlier.

Alternatively, you can go to the command line and use the change user command, which cycles through what Windows Server 2003 terms install modes and execute modes using switches attached to the command. Let's look at that in a bit more detail.

Executing change user /install before installing a new application places the system in install mode. Install mode also suspends .*ini* file mapping, which Windows normally uses to match .*ini* files to programs that use them and the associated users that actually install the program. The system also notes the way the setup routine initially installs the program. Running change user /execute when the installation finishes reverts the system to execute mode, reactivates .*ini* file mapping, and propagates specific data for each user to their respective home directories. In addition, when the user opens the program, user-specific registry setting files (.*ini*, .*dll*, .*ocx*, and so on) are propagated as needed to the user's home directory.

So, in brief, follow these steps from the command line to manually install a program:

1. Before installing a program, run change user /install from the command line.

2. Then, install the program using the application's native setup routine.

3. When installation is complete, run change user /execute to finish the process.

 Once you have begun installing programs for use on a terminal server machine, do not uninstall Terminal Services. The programs installed while Terminal Services was running might not function correctly at that point. If this happens, the easiest way to start over is with a clean slate: reformat the computer and reinstall the operating system.

Configuring Terminal Services Licensing

If you plan on using Terminal Services in a production environment to support thin client users, you must bring up a Terminal Services licensing server on your network within 120 days. Terminal Services licensing is independent of regular Windows Server 2003 licensing, meaning that a client license for Windows Server 2003 does not necessarily entitle a user to connect to a terminal server and use applications. (Connecting for administrative purposes using simply Remote Desktop mode is allowed without a separate license.)

Before actually placing a license server on your network, determine the type of license server you need. There are two types: a *domain license server*, which distributes licenses only within the Active Directory domain you select, or an *enterprise license server* (the default choice), which allocates licenses to any computer within the network. You'll be prompted for your choice upon initial licensing setup. When you actually install the license server, avoid installing Terminal Server Licensing on a terminal server computer unless you want to spend hours troubleshooting weird errors on your servers; use a separate machine instead. Also consider installing Terminal Services on a member server, not a domain controller. Domain controllers have their own load considerations, and the additional network, processor, and disk constraints of Terminal Services can adversely affect performance. If you must install on a domain controller, use the administration tools covered later in this chapter to restrict the number of allowed connections to Terminal Services.

 If you currently have a Windows 2000 Terminal Services Licensing server and you decide to add to your environment a Windows Server 2003 machine running Terminal Services, you also will need to add a Windows Server 2003 Licensing server. A Windows 2000 Licensing server cannot hold licenses for a Windows Server 2003 machine running Terminal Services.

You can officially license your Terminal Services capabilities on your network in one of three ways. (Keep in mind that to activate a licensing server, you need to be a member of the local Administrators group or a domain administrators group, or have delegated authority from an administrator to perform the task.)

To activate a Terminal Services license automatically, follow these steps:

1. Open the Terminal Services Licensing applet, found in the Administrative Tools group off the Start menu.
2. In the left pane, right-click the server you want to activate, and select Activate Server from the context menu.
3. Follow the prompts in the wizard to configure, license, and purchase the activation.

You also can use a web browser to activate a Terminal Services server. Follow the preceding steps, but select Web Browser from the Activation Methods list on the first page of the wizard. Finally, you can use a telephone to activate a Terminal Services server as well. Again, use the same procedure as before, but select Telephone from the Activation Methods list on the first page of the wizard.

After a Terminal Services Licensing server is activated, it becomes the repository for Terminal Server client licenses. A Terminal Services Licensing server can issue temporary licenses for clients that allow use of terminal servers for up to 120 days from the date of the first client logon. After this evaluation period ends, a terminal server can no longer allow clients to connect unless it locates a Terminal Services Licensing server to issue client licenses.

Terminal Services Administration

You can administer a Terminal Services machine from three points:

The Terminal Services Manager console
> You can run this console from any station to display and control Terminal Services connections on a network.

The Terminal Services Configuration console
> This console runs on each Terminal Services machine to adjust the individual Terminal Services configurations on each machine.

The Terminal Services Licensing console
> This console manages licensing across all Terminal Services machines in a domain.

I covered the Terminal Services Licensing applet in the previous section. In this section, I'll cover the basic administrative functions that the Terminal Services Manager applet can perform, and then I will focus on some common tasks using the Terminal Services Configuration applet.

Terminal Services Manager

Terminal Services Manager (TSM) is the focal point where all connections between client computers and Terminal Services machines come into view. Think of it as "mission control."

> TSM's full functionality only works when you run the console from a machine connected to Terminal Services through a TS session. Running TSM locally on the machine running Terminal Services will limit the functionality available to you.

Figure 10-4 shows the basic TSM layout.

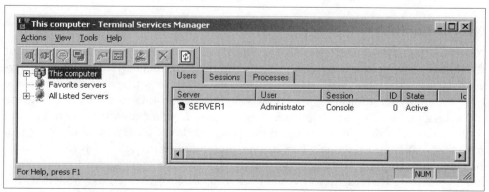

Figure 10-4. The default Terminal Services Manager window

By default, TSM shows all Terminal Services servers in your domain. You can connect to all of them at once if you so choose, but TSM looks at only one server at a time by default. To find servers, use the following procedures:

- To find all Terminal Services servers in your domain, in the left pane right-click the name of your domain, and select Refresh Servers in Domain.
- To find all Terminal Services servers on your network, in the left pane right-click All Listed Servers, and choose Refresh Servers in All Domains.
- To connect to any particular server, right-click its name in any list and select Connect.

Using TSM, you can perform a variety of network- and domain-wide session management functions. You can monitor a session, disconnect it, log it off, send messages to users, and take control of a session, among many other things.

Connecting to a session

Connecting to another session on a server is a useful tool for an administrator working remotely, for example, to fix a problem with a user's configuration in Microsoft Office while the user is at lunch. You always can connect to any active session or to a session that is disconnected. You can also connect to a session that is logged on inside your current security context (meaning basically your username), or if you have the appropriate permissions (Full Control or User Access permissions over Terminal Services sessions), you can connect to any session.

To connect to a session, follow these steps:

1. Right-click the appropriate session in the right pane of TSM. Alternatively, to connect to a session that is run by a user, right-click the appropriate user's name. Choose Connect in either case.
2. You are prompted for a password if needed. Otherwise, control is switched to the new session, and the active session is disconnected.

Disconnecting a session

A session that is disconnected is unique, in that it continues to run on the server, but the actual network link between the client and the Terminal Services machine is severed. Using a disconnected session, a user can return to a previous session at any time by simply reestablishing the connection, alleviating the need for either logging off or logging on. The catch to this is that, of course, server resources are finite, and if all users leave their sessions disconnected, everybody's copy of Outlook is still receiving mail, and everyone's PowerPoint presentations are still open to be edited. But disconnecting a session is still a handy way to clear your screen to take off to lunch, knowing that when you come back your desktop will be as you left it. It's sometimes useful to disconnect a session when Remote Desktop fails to pick up your old connection.

A user can disconnect any session of his own, and an administrator can disconnect any session over which he has Full Control rights.

To disconnect a session, follow these steps:

1. Right-click the appropriate session in the right pane of TSM, and choose Disconnect.
2. You are prompted to confirm your choice. Click OK, and the session will be disconnected.

You can select multiple sessions at a time in the right pane by pressing and holding the Ctrl key and clicking each session that you want to disconnect.

Logging off a session

Logging off a session ends that particular user's session on a host, thereby making available to other users any RAM and CPU resources that the particular session was using. Users must then log on the next time they connect to the Terminal Services server. A user can log off any session of his own, and an administrator can log off any session over which he has Full Control rights.

To log off a session, follow these steps:

1. Right-click the appropriate session in the right pane of TSM, and choose Log Off.
2. You are prompted to confirm your choice. Click OK, and the session will be disconnected.

Keep in mind that forcibly logging off users will result in data loss for those users, so always make them aware of any automatic logoffs before they happen.

You also can log off a session by issuing the LOGOFF command, followed by the session ID or name (which you can find inside TSM), at the terminal server's command prompt. To log off session number 8, for example, use the following command:

```
logoff 8
```

Resetting a session

When you reset a session, it forcibly terminates that session: programs are closed, open data is lost, and memory that those programs were occupying is immediately returned to the Terminal Services host. A user can reset any session of his or her own, and an administrator can reset any session over which he has Full Control rights.

To reset a session, follow these steps:

1. Right-click the appropriate session in the right pane of TSM, and choose Reset.
2. You are prompted to confirm your choice. Click OK, and the session will be reset.

You can select multiple sessions at a time in the right pane by pressing and holding the Ctrl key and clicking each session that you want to reset.

You also can reset a session by issuing the RESET command, followed by the session ID or name, at the terminal server's command prompt. To reset session number 8, for example, use the following command:

```
reset session 8
```

Viewing session information

Using TSM, you can get a wealth of detail about any particular session on a Terminal Services host machine, including the following:

- Originating computer
- Running process
- Session image resolution and color depth
- Data encryption level

To view this information, find the session in the left pane of TSM, and select it. Then, to view currently running programs and services, click the Processes tab. You'll see a listing much like that found in the Windows Task Manager. On the Information tab in the same pane, you find a listing of the username, client name, data encryption level, originating computer, and more.

But let's say you want information on all sessions, including their processes and logged-on users, for a particular Terminal Services machine, domain, or even an entire network. This is possible with TSM: simply select the machine, domain, or network in the left pane of TSM and use the Users, Sessions, or Processes tabs in the right pane to control the display of information.

Figure 10-5 shows this in action.

You also can view this information from the command line with the query process, query session, query termserver, and query user commands. These simple commands display a table or list of the desired information. Here is example output from the four commands:

```
C:\>query process
USERNAME SESSIONNAME ID PID IMAGE
>administrator rdp-tcp#10 1 4900 rdpclip.exe
>administrator rdp-tcp#10 1 4980 explorer.exe
>administrator rdp-tcp#10 1 3488 ducontrol.exe
>administrator rdp-tcp#10 1 5780 ctfmon.exe
>administrator rdp-tcp#10 1 3308 sqlmangr.exe
>administrator rdp-tcp#10 1 5056 cmd.exe
>administrator rdp-tcp#10 1 3088 query.exe
>administrator rdp-tcp#10 1 5844 qprocess.exe
C:\>query session
SESSIONNAME USERNAME ID STATE TYPE DEVICE
```

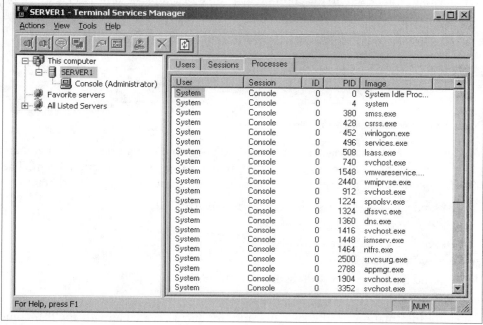

Figure 10-5. Viewing information on multiple sessions in TSM

```
console 0 Conn wdcon
rdp-tcp 65536 Listen rdpwd
>rdp-tcp#10 administrator 1 Active rdpwd
C:\>query user
USERNAME SESSIONNAME ID STATE IDLE TIME LOGON
>administrator rdp-tcp#10 1 Active .
7/15/2004 5:49 PM
C:\>query termserver
NETWORK NETWORK
mercury hasselltech.local
```

Sending a message to a user

Sometimes it's necessary to send a message to all users logged on to a specific host, whether to mention that there might be downtime that evening, or that a virus or worm (God forbid) has invaded the Terminal Services machine and it needs to be shut down immediately. To send a message to a user, follow these steps:

1. In the right pane of TSM, right-click either the sessions or users to whom you want to send a message, and select Send Message.

2. In the Send Message dialog box, enter the text for your message. If you want to use separate lines, press Ctrl-Enter to begin a new line.

3. Click OK when you've finished entering the message.

A notification will be sent to the appropriate people. A sample is shown in Figure 10-6.

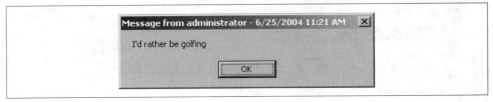

Figure 10-6. User messaging with Terminal Services

You also can send a message via the command line, which might be helpful if you are planning on scripting a message transmission that is triggered by a certain event. The MSG command is used to send these messages; some examples are presented here:

- To send a message to user lmjohnson on server WTS1:

      msg lmjohnson /server:WTS1 message

- To send a message to a particular session name:

      msg RDP-tcp#4 message

- To send a message that will display on a user's screen for 30 seconds:

      msg lmjohnson /server:WTS1 /time:30 message

For more information on the switches and arguments available with the MSG command, type **MSG /?** at any command prompt.

Taking control of a session

Have you ever been on a troubleshooting call that was an intensely frustrating exercise in walking a user through a procedure in Excel or Access? What if the user could watch you perform the actions on his screen, and what if you could show the user the steps without leaving your desk? If the user has a session on a Terminal Services machine, you as the administrator can take control of his session, giving you full access to whatever the user's screen displays. The user can watch whatever you do in his session, making the tool wonderful for quick problem solving. The user also can control his session while you have control so that both sides can interact.

> This is exactly like the Remote Assistance feature, which is available in Windows XP and Windows Server 2003 but recommended for use only with client computers running Windows XP. You shouldn't use Remote Assistance on servers for security reasons and should rely on the Terminal Services remote control feature instead.

To take control of a particular session, follow these steps:

1. In the right pane of TSM, right-click either the sessions or users to whom you want to send a message, and select Remote Control.

2. The Remote Control dialog appears. Here, select the appropriate key to be pressed along with the Ctrl key to end a remote control session.

3. By default, when you select OK, the user is prompted inside his session with a box asking him to confirm your request to take over his session. The user must acknowledge this prompt before remote control can begin.

It's possible to turn off the aforementioned user confirmation requirement through the user's properties inside Active Directory Users and Computers. On the Remote Control tab, uncheck the Require User's Permission checkbox, as shown in Figure 10-7.

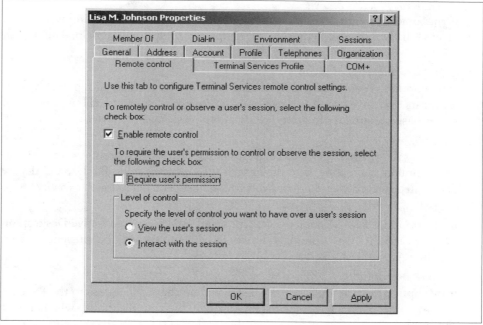

Figure 10-7. Disabling the user notification requirement for remote control

Later in this chapter, I will discuss a way to turn this notification on and off on a per-server basis.

You also can remotely control a user's session from the command line using the SHADOW command. You must know the session's name or identification number. For example, to connect to session 3 on the current server, issue the following command:

```
shadow 3
```

To connect to session 2 on server WTS2, and to have the SHADOW utility tell you exactly what it does, issue the following command:

```
shadow 2 /server:WTS2 /v
```

Terminal Services Configuration

The Terminal Services Configuration applet provides a way to configure settings that are relevant to a specific server. When you open Terminal Services Configuration, you'll note that the tree in the left pane of the console has two nodes: Connections and Server Settings. Let's focus on the Server Settings section in this part of the chapter.

When you select Server Settings, you're provided with either six or seven options in the right pane, depending on whether your terminal server machine is a member of a cluster. These options, and their intended purpose, are described here:

Delete temporary folders on exit
> If this option is set to Yes, any temporary folders created by Windows will be deleted. If the option is set to No, all temporary folders will remain. The default is Yes.

Use temporary folders per session
> If this option is set to Yes, each session will have its own set of temporary folders for its exclusive use. If this option is set to No, all sessions will use one set of server-based temporary folders. The default is Yes.

Licensing
> If this option is set to Per Device, Terminal Services CALs are given to each client computer that connects to the host. If this option is set to Per User, CALs are distributed to each user that connects to the host. The default is Per Device.

Active Desktop
> If this option is set to Enable, users will be allowed to enable Active Desktop on their sessions. If this option is set to Disable, users will be prevented from enabling Active Desktop. The default is Disable.

Permission Compatibility
> If this option is set to Full Security, users will not have full access to the Registry and to some parts of the filesystem through their applications, which might cause some older programs to fail. If this option is set to Relaxed Security, users will have access to these previously restricted areas, and older programs should still work. The default is Full Security.

Restrict Each User to One Session
> If this option is set to Yes, no user can log on more than once to a particular Terminal Services host machine. If this option is set to No, a user can log on multiple times to the same server. The default is Yes.

The following subsections will take you through common administrative tasks using the Connections node inside Terminal Services Configuration.

Creating a new connection listener

Use the Terminal Services Configuration applet to create a new Terminal Services connection by following these steps:

1. Open the Terminal Services Configuration applet.
2. In the console tree, select Connections.
3. Pull down the Action menu and select Create New Connection.
4. The configuration wizard starts. Follow the prompts on the wizard to configure your connection.

Windows permits only one RDP-based connection per network card in the machine running Terminal Services. Usually, administrators find that the preconfigured connection created when Terminal Services is installed is really the only one they need. However, if you need more RDP connections, you'll need to install an additional network adapter for each connection needed.

Restricting Terminal Services connections

You can restrict the total number of RDP connections to any given server, which can be helpful if you have bandwidth problems on your network or your Terminal Services server machine has limited hardware resources.

To restrict the total number of RDP connections to a server through the Terminal Services Configuration applet, follow these steps:

1. Open the Terminal Services Configuration applet.
2. In the console tree, select Connections.
3. In the Details pane, select the applicable connection, right-click it, and choose Properties.
4. Move to the Network Adapter tab and click Maximum Connections.
5. Enter the maximum number of sessions you want to connect to this server.
6. Click Apply to finish.

To do so using GP, which overrides and takes precedence over the settings specified in Terminal Services Configuration, follow the steps described next.

1. Open the Group Policy Object Editor snap-in.
2. Navigate through Computer Configuration → Administrative Templates → Windows Components in the tree in the left pane.
3. Select Terminal Services, and in the right pane, double-click the Limit Number of Connections setting.

4. Click Enabled.

5. Move to the TS Maximum Connections allowed box. In it, enter the maximum number of connections you want to allow, and then click OK.

You might want to restrict the number of Terminal Services sessions by server to improve performance and decrease load. This technique works especially well when you have a terminal server farm consisting of machines of various capabilities and configurations. You can adjust each server to the optimal number of connections to ensure a consistent response time across the farm for your users.

RDP connections, by default, are configured to allow an unlimited number of sessions on each server.

Encryption levels

Terminal Services supports multiple levels of encryption to secure communications between the client and the server. To change these levels through Terminal Services Configuration, follow these steps:

1. Open the Terminal Services Configuration applet.

2. Select Connections from the console tree.

3. Find the connection you want to modify in the righthand pane, right-click it, and select Properties.

4. Navigate to the General tab, and select the encryption level that best suits your needs. (I provide a description of the levels shortly.)

5. Check the Use standard Windows authentication checkbox if you want the connection to default to the standard authentication even if another authentication package exists.

You can also change the TS encryption level using Group Policy:

1. Open the Group Policy applet.

2. Navigate through Computer Configuration → Administrative Templates → Windows Components → Terminal Services.

3. Select Encryption and Security.

4. In the righthand pane, double-click the Set Client Connection Encryption Level setting, and then click Enabled.

5. In the Encryption Level list, click the desired security level.

6. Click OK to finish the procedure.

Use the following guide to determine which security setting is best for your environment:

FIPS Compliant

Encrypts client-to-server and server-to-client communications strongly enough to be in accordance with the Federal Information Processing Standard (FIPS). This method uses Microsoft-developed cryptographic modules.

 If you have already established FIPS encryption through a system cryptography policy object or through the Terminal Services Set Client Encryption Level option, you cannot change the encryption level through the Terminal Services Configuration applet or through a GPO.

High

Encrypts client-to-server and server-to-client communications using strong 128-bit encryption; useful only when the terminal server resides in an environment composed of 128-bit compliant clients only (i.e., one of the Windows Server 2003 operating systems). Other clients using non-compliant OSes will not be able to connect unless they download a separate Terminal Services client that supports high encryption from Microsoft's web site at:

> *http://www.microsoft.com/downloads/details.aspx?FamilyID=33AD53D8-9ABC-4E15-A78F-EB2AABAD74B5&displaylang=en*

Client Compatible

Encrypts client-to-server and server-to-client communications at the maximum possible level (key strength) supported on the client end. This option is best when the terminal server resides in a mixed client environment.

Low

Encrypts client-to-server communications only, using 56-bit encryption.

It's also important to note that the aforementioned GP procedure will work for local security policy configurations. However, if you have a domain environment and want to push this policy onto an existing domain or organizational unit, you need to connect to the domain controller using an account with administrator rights. Then you need to make the change through the Group Policy Management Console.

Also be aware that data sent from the server to the client (and not vice versa) is not encrypted.

Remote control permissions

You can adjust how administrators will be able to "shadow" a Terminal Services session. You can restrict a user to viewing a session only, or allow him or her to have full control of the keyboard and mouse. To adjust these settings through Terminal Services Configuration, follow these steps:

1. Open the Terminal Services Configuration applet.

2. In the console tree, click Connections.

3. Find the connection for which you want to configure remote control in the right-hand pane. Right-click the connection and select Properties.

4. Navigate to the Remote Control tab.

5. Click Use Remote Control with the Following Settings to configure remote control for the connection. Or, to disallow remote control, click Do Not Allow Remote Control.

6. To display a message on the client, asking permission to view or take part in the session, check the Require user's permission checkbox.

7. Under Level of Control, click View the Session to specify that the user's session can be viewed only, or click Interact with the Session to specify that the user's session can be actively controlled with your keyboard and mouse.

8. Click OK to complete the procedure.

To do so using GP, follow these steps:

1. Open the Group Policy applet.

2. Navigate through Computer Configuration → Administrative Templates → Windows Components.

3. Select Terminal Services.

4. In the righthand pane, double-click the Set Rules for Remote Control of Terminal Services User Sessions setting, and then click Enabled.

5. In the Options box, click the desired remote control permissions as described previously. Or, to disallow remote control, click No Remote Control Allowed.

6. Click OK to complete the procedure.

You should thoroughly test any changes you make to GP settings before applying them to users or computers. Use the RSoP tool to test new policy settings and confirm they will be applied as you intend. Chapter 6 contains detailed discussions and procedures for using this tool.

The aforementioned GP procedure also will work for local system policies. If you're using an Active Directory-based domain, though, and you want to push this policy onto an existing domain or organizational unit, you need to connect to the domain controller using an account with administrator rights and then make the change through the Group Policy Management Console.

Policies in effect are applied to and therefore are in full force for every client that connects to the terminal server.

Connecting to drives and printers

Terminal Services enables you to preserve mapped drives, mapped printers, and associated settings between sessions so that users don't have to recreate them each time they log on. To adjust the settings for this feature through Terminal Services Configuration, follow these steps:

1. Open the Terminal Services Configuration applet.
2. In the console tree, click Connections.
3. Find the connection for which you want to configure remote control in the right-hand pane. Right-click the connection and select Properties.
4. Navigate to the Client Settings tab.
5. In the Connections section, uncheck the Use connection settings from user settings checkbox. (This will ensure that any changes you make in this procedure will apply globally to all connections.)
6. Select one of the following options:

    Connect client drives at logon
    > Reconnects to all mapped client drives during the logon process.

    Connect client printers at logon
    > Reconnects to all mapped local client printers during the logon process.

    Default to main client printer
    > Prints to the default printer of the client. If one doesn't exist, the session reverts to the default printer of the server.

To do so through GP, follow these steps:

1. Open the Group Policy applet.
2. Navigate through Computer Configuration → Administrative Templates → Windows Components → Terminal Services.
3. Select Client/Server Data Redirections.
4. In the righthand pane, select the specific options you want to configure (as described previously) and select Enabled/Disabled as appropriate.
5. Click OK to complete the procedure.

These settings affect all clients that use the connection to log on to a terminal server. If you want to define settings on a per-user basis, use Terminal Services Group Policies or the Terminal Services Extension to Local Users and Groups.

Again, you can use these settings when configuring local security policy, but if you want to push them out throughout a domain, you need to change your domain's security policy through the Group Policy Management Console.

Session device mapping

One of the neat features of RDP is the ability to redirect local drives and local print-ers to your remote session so that through the remote computer's user interface you can still access the drives and printers on your personal machine. This is great when using hosted applications because Save As... and Open... dialog boxes work the same way as users expect.

To adjust the settings for this feature through Terminal Services Configuration, fol-low these steps:

1. Open the Terminal Services Configuration applet.
2. In the console tree, click Connections.
3. Find the connection for which you want to configure remote control in the right-hand pane. Right-click the connection and select Properties.
4. Navigate to the Client Settings tab.
5. Select one of the following options and enable or disable it as appropriate:
   - Drive mapping (enabled by default)
   - Windows printer mapping (enabled by default)
   - LPT port mapping (enabled by default)
   - COM port mapping (enabled by default)
   - Clipboard mapping (enabled by default)
   - Audio mapping (disabled by default)
6. Click OK to finish.

To do so through GP, follow these steps:

1. Open the Group Policy applet.
2. Navigate through Computer Configuration → Administrative Templates → Win-dows Components → Terminal Services.
3. Select Client/Server Data Redirections.
4. In the righthand pane, select the specific options you want to configure (as described previously) and select Enabled/Disabled as appropriate.
5. Click OK to complete the procedure.

As before, you can use these settings when configuring local security policy. How-ever, if you want to push them out throughout a domain, you need to modify your domain's security policy through the Group Policy Management Console.

Default Terminal Services permissions

You might want to give permission for specific users and groups to use Terminal Services.

You can accomplish this using the Terminal Services Configuration applet. The procedure is much like granting and revoking permissions on files and folders. To do so, follow these steps:

1. Open the Terminal Services Configuration applet.

2. In the console tree, click Connections.

3. Find the connection for which you want to configure remote control in the right-hand pane. Right-click the connection and select Properties.

4. Move to the Permissions tab and click Add.

5. The Select Users of Groups dialog box appears. Click Locations... to identify places to search, and click Object Types... to specify the types of objects you want to search for.

6. Click the Check Names button.

When the name is located, click OK. The name now appears in the Group or User Names list on the Permissions tab.

If you want to change the default permissions applied to users and groups that can access Terminal Services, follow these steps to use the Terminal Services Configuration applet to modify the default Terminal Services permissions assigned to users:

1. Open the Terminal Services Configuration applet.

2. In the console tree, click Connections.

3. Find the connection for which you want to configure remote control in the right-hand pane. Right-click the connection and select Properties.

4. Move to the Permissions tab and click the Advanced... button.

5. The Advanced Security Settings dialog box appears. In Permission Entries, select the user or group for which you want to change permissions. Click Edit... to open the Permission Entry dialog box.

6. Select or clear as appropriate the Allow/Deny boxes to grant or revoke privileges to the users you have selected.

Follow this procedure to remove a group from the list of users authorized to access Terminal Services:

1. Open the Terminal Services Configuration applet.

2. In the console tree, click Connections.

3. Find the connection for which you want to configure remote control in the right-hand pane. Right-click the connection and select Properties.

4. Move to the Permissions tab. In Group or User Names, select the user whose privileges you want to revoke and click Remove.

To change permissions and revoke permissions for specific users, you absolutely must use the Remote Desktop Users group, which is built-in and configured during the operating system installation, to manage remote access to Terminal Services and Windows' Remote Desktop for Administration features.

Ensuring RPC-based security

If you want to secure Terminal Services-based RPC traffic to and from the server, use Group Policies to accomplish this. Simply follow these steps:

1. Open the Group Policy applet.
2. Navigate through Computer Configuration → Administrative Templates → Windows Components → Terminal Services → Encryption → RPC Security Policy in the left pane.
3. In the righthand pane, double-click the Secure Server (Require Security) setting.
4. Click Enabled, and then click OK to finish.

You use the RPC interface to manage and configure Terminal Services. By setting the Secure Server (Require Security) option to Enabled, only RPC clients that support secure transactions are allowed to communicate with the server. If the setting is disabled, the terminal servers will always request a secure channel, but will allow connections that are unsecured if the client doesn't support secure transactions. The default status for this setting is not configured, which allows for unsecured transactions.

Command-Line Utilities

Several neat utilities that are sprinkled throughout this chapter, and some that I didn't cover in detail, enable you to perform much of the functionality you find in the graphical management interfaces for Terminal Services from the command line. I've collected them all in this final section of the chapter as a quick reference of sorts:

Change logon
> Enables logons (using the /enable switch) or disables logons (using the /disable switch) to a specific server. Use /query to find out what mode a machine is currently in.

Change port
> Modifies serial port mappings for programs that operate in DOS compatibility mode. Use /query to find out the current mappings.

Change user
> Changes the mode in which a Terminal Services machine operates. Using /install switches the machine into install mode to add applications of multi-session use, and using /execute disables the install mode for normal functionality. Use /query

to determine the current mode. See earlier in this chapter for detailed information on this command.

Cprofile

Cleans profiles for inefficient use of space, and removes from the Registry any file associations the user has configured. Profiles must not be in use to run this tool. Use /L to clean every local profile, /I to prompt you before cleaning each profile, and /V to display each action the program has taken.

Flattemp

Enables flat temporary directories—that is, enables the redirection of temporary directories to a location other than the default. /enable enables these directories obviously, /disable does the opposite, and /query displays the feature's current status.

Logoff

Logs off a session. Use logoff sessionname or logoff sessionid to identify the session to end, and specify a particular server using the /V switch if necessary. See earlier in this chapter for detailed information on this command.

Msg

Sends a message. See earlier in this chapter for detailed information on this command.

Query process

Displays a table listing processes by session. See earlier in this chapter for sample output of this command.

Query session

Displays a table listing sessions on a specific server. See earlier in this chapter for sample output of this command.

Query termserver

Displays a list of known terminal servers in a domain. See earlier in this chapter for sample output of this command.

Query user

Displays a list of users currently logged on to terminal services sessions. See earlier in this chapter for sample output of this command.

Register

Sets an application to operate as either a system global resource, with the /system switch, or a user global resource, with the /user switch. Include the executable file's name as an argument.

Reset session

Resets a session. Use reset sessionname or reset sessionid to identify the session to end, and specify a particular server using the /V switch if necessary. See earlier in this chapter for detailed information on this command.

Shadow

Views the display for another user's session. You must run this over a Terminal Services connection to the host machine. See earlier in this chapter for detailed information on this command.

Tscon

Connects to another session running on a server. See earlier in this chapter for detailed information on this command.

Tsdiscon

Disconnects from another session running on a server. See earlier in this chapter for detailed information on this command.

Tskill

Kills a certain process. Use `tskill processid` or `tskill processname`. To specify a server, use the `/server` switch, and to specify a certain session under which a process is running, use `/ID:sessionid`. To end a process running under all sessions, issue the `/a` switch.

Tsprof

Configures profiles for users connecting to a terminal server. See earlier in this chapter for detailed information on this command.

Tsshutdn

Shuts down a terminal server. You can specify an amount of time to wait before shutting down the machine by adding the number as an argument after the command name (i.e., `tsshutdn 120` to wait two minutes). You also can specify whether to simply restart the machine by using the `/reboot` switch, or to power it down completely with the `/powerdown` switch.

The Last Word

Windows Terminal Services is a useful inclusion to Windows Server 2003, allowing administrators to manage their servers without having to be directly in front of the console, and also allowing corporations to centrally host applications to reduce total cost of ownership and management and administrative requirements. In this chapter, I explored both the user and the administrator side of TS and how it can add value to your Windows infrastructure.

CHAPTER 11

Communications and Networking

In this chapter, I'll take a look at five major communications and networking services that are commonly used in Windows Server 2003 installations—the Dynamic Host Configuration Protocol, which helps administrators with IP address management, the Routing and Remote Access Service to manage inbound connections from VPN users, Certificate Services, to enable secure identity verification and transmission processes, the IP Security service to encrypt IP traffic between computers, and the Network Access Quarantine Control feature to protect your network from untrusted clients.

This chapter has a practical focus. Entire books can be (and have been) written on each of these topics, so I cannot possibly cover all of them in depth. Because of the vast amount of resources already available, I've chosen to focus on providing instructions for configuring these protocols and services to work under Windows Server 2003 rather than overwhelm you with page after page of theory. I discuss the mechanics a bit, but I place more emphasis on hands-on activities. At the end of the chapter I provide a comprehensive list of resources if you want more theory and background on these networking topics.

Let's begin.

Dynamic Host Configuration Protocol

The Dynamic Host Configuration Protocol (DHCP) assists administrators by automatically configuring computers with IP addresses, saving the hassle of assigning and tracking static IP addresses among multiple machines. When DHCP is coupled with dynamic DNS, a technique you learned about in Chapter 4, a lot of administrative headaches formerly encountered by network administrators are reduced and, in some cases, even eliminated. Let's take a look.

How It Works

The process is started by a client computer, which makes a request for an IP address to a DHCP server. If a client is new to the network, or currently has an invalid IP address, the client will broadcast a DHCPDISCOVER message over the local subnet. The responding DHCP server (or, in some cases, servers) will send an offer request in the form of a DHCPOFFER packet. Then the client will acknowledge receipt of that offer and officially ask for an address with a DHCPREQUEST packet. In return, the DHCP server will confirm the lease and send any additional options that are configured with the address inside a DHCPACK packet.

Leases are granted for a period of time known as the *lease duration*. After 50% of the lease duration has lapsed, the client will request an extension—officially, this is a lease renewal—from the DHCP server from which it originally obtained the lease. If the client doesn't receive a response from that server, it will wait until 87.5% of the lease duration to attempt to renew its current lease with any DHCP machine on the network. If no server honors the lease renewal request, the client will end its use of the current IP address and then behave like a new client, as described previously.

Options are attributes of a DHCP lease that define certain characteristics about the IP address and IP stack of the computer leasing the address. For example, DHCP options specify parameters such as the DNS connection suffix (e.g., client2.has-selltech.local), the default gateway for a particular computer (which is the router through which traffic outside the local subnet is sent), and other important traits of a connection. Using DHCP options saves you a lot of time in manually assigning these traits to all your client computers, and it also adds the element of consistency—all your computers leasing addresses within a certain scope get the same options and not a hodgepodge of configurations.

A Windows feature called Automatic Private IP Addressing (APIPA) overlaps DHCP functionality and can either be your best friend or drive you to insanity. Microsoft implemented this feature so that if a client is unable to lease an IP address from a DHCP server, it will resort to using a randomly chosen IP address from Microsoft's own Class B range (169.254.0.0 with subnet 255.255.0.0 and no default gateway assigned). The address is verified using an ARP request broadcast out to the network to ensure that no other client is using that address.

This feature is meant for convenience because most small businesses and home networks don't want to offer DHCP services from Windows itself and would like their networks to just work. However, if you have connectivity problems, Automatic Client Configuration (ACC) can really get in the way of troubleshooting at times. It's best to understand ACC's behavior under the following circumstances:

- If a client has a valid lease from a DHCP server but can't connect to that DHCP server, ACC will attempt to ping the default router/gateway entry defined by the lease. If the client receives a reply, ACC assumes the machine is still on the network where the original DHCP server is located, and it will continue to use its lease.

- If a router isn't answering at the gateway address in the lease, ACC will release the current IP address and pick an automatic address from the 169.254.0.0 range.

- In any event, when ACC is active, the client will continue to search every five minutes for a valid DHCP server to either renew its lease or obtain a new address and corresponding lease.

- You can also specify that the client use an alternate address in the event that the machine can't get an IP address from the DHCP server. You can view the settings and configure this in the properties of the network connection off the Start menu.

Installing a DHCP Server

Now that you know a bit about how DHCP works, let's move to installing an actual DHCP server. It's a fairly easy process. From the Manage Your Server page, click Add or remove a role. Then, on the Server Role page, click DHCP Server, and then click Next.

You'll be walked through a wizard that is outlined almost identically in the next section, so let's go there now.

Creating a New DHCP Scope

Creating a new DHCP scope involves selecting the range of IP addresses you want to make available to be leased out to clients who request them. This set of IP addresses is known as the *scope*.

The New Scope Wizard appears both when you first install a DHCP server and whenever you invoke it through the DHCP administration console, which you find off the Administrative Tools menu on the Start menu. To create a new scope on your DHCP server, follow these steps:

1. Open the DHCP administration console by selecting DHCP from the Administrative Tools folder.

2. Right-click the appropriate DHCP server in the lefthand pane, and select New Scope from the pop-up context menu.

3. The New Scope Wizard appears. Click Next to move off the introductory screen.

4. Enter a name and a friendly, useful description (for your purposes only) for the new scope and then click Next.

5. The IP Address Range screen appears, as shown in Figure 11-1. Enter a noninterrupted range of IP addresses that you want to offer to clients into the Start IP

address and End IP address fields. Then, enter the subnet mask to identify the network or subnet addresses you're using. (In most cases, you can accept the defaults.) Click Next to continue.

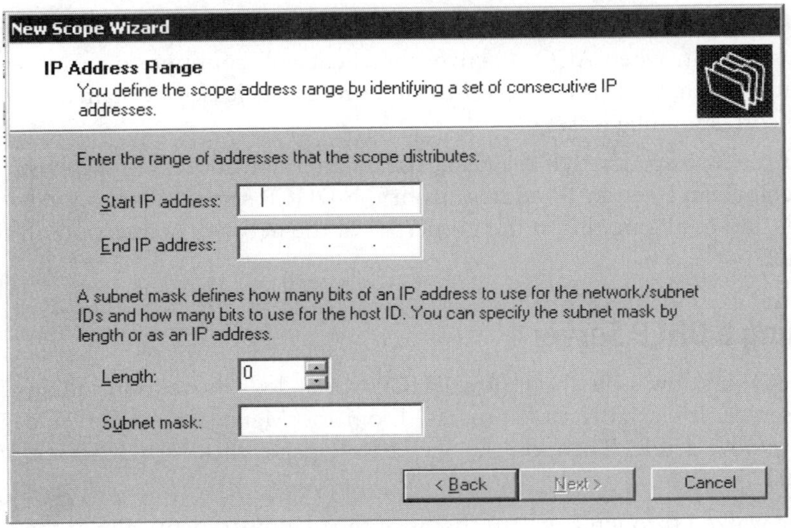

Figure 11-1. The IP Address Range screen

6. The Add Exclusions page appears next, depicted in Figure 11-2. On this page, you can enter a single address or range of addresses within your scope range that you want to exclude from client provisioning—for example, if you have a few servers with IP addresses within your chosen range, you can identify those addresses here so that DHCP won't give them out and cause a conflict. Click Next to continue when you've entered any relevant addresses.

7. The Lease Duration screen appears, which allows you to specify how long a DHCP-assigned address will be valid for a given scope. This is shown in Figure 11-3. Desktop systems can keep an IP lease for a long time; laptops and other mobile computers, however, should be given short lease durations so that when they are inactive their IP address becomes available to be reassigned to other machines. If you have a mix of both, I suggest favoring a shorter lease time. Adjust the time using the individual sliders for days, hours, and minutes, and then click Next when you're done.

8. The Configure DHCP Options screen appears. Here, you can specify whether to simply configure the scope with the options you've specified to this point, or further customize the data transmitted in response to each DHCP request. In this example, we'll proceed through the extended options to discuss each one. Select Yes, I want to configure these options now, and then click Next to continue.

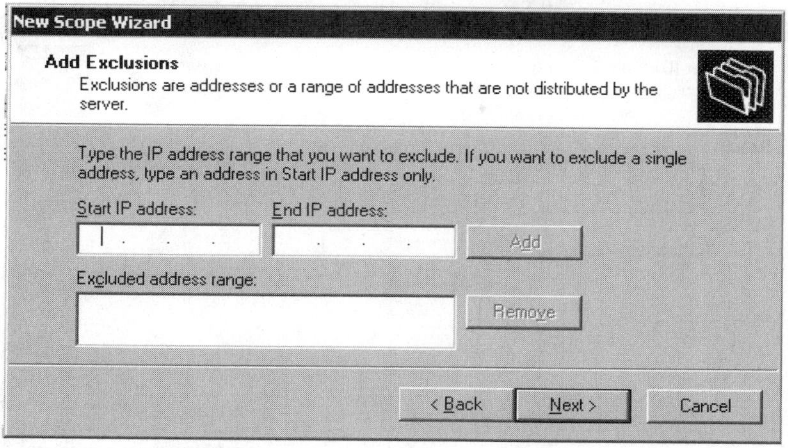

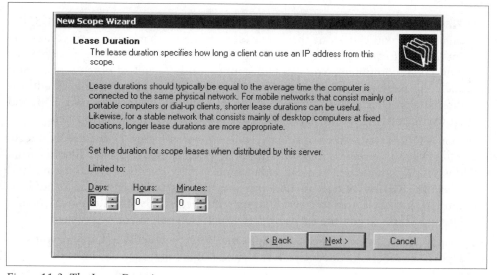

Figure 11-2. The Add Exclusions screen

Figure 11-3. The Lease Duration screen

9. The Router (Default Gateway) screen appears, as depicted in Figure 11-4. Here, you can specify a list of available network gateways or routers in the order of your preference. Add them using the Add buttons and adjust the list as needed using the Remove, Up, and Down buttons. Click Next when you've finished entering gateways.

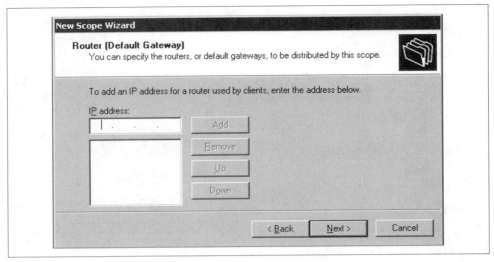

Figure 11-4. The Router (Default Gateway) screen

10. The Domain Name and DNS Servers screen appears, shown in Figure 11-5. On this screen, you can input the parent domain name that your client computers should use for this connection. You also can specify preferred DNS servers for your client computers. You can either input a fully qualified domain name and click the Resolve button to find out the IP address, or enter the IP address directly and click Add to insert a server into the list. Use the Remove, Up, and Down buttons to edit the list as needed. Click Next when you've finished.

11. The WINS Servers screen appears. This is shown in Figure 11-6. On this screen, enter the WINS servers for your enterprise that clients receiving addresses from this scope should use. You can either input a fully qualified domain name and click the Resolve button to find out the IP address, or enter the IP address directly and click Add to insert a server into the list. Use the Remove, Up, and Down buttons to edit the list as needed. Click Next when you've finished.

12. Finally, the Activate Scope screen appears. When you activate a scope, you start DHCP service for it. Choose your preferred option, and then click Next.

Once inside the DHCP console, which is shown in Figure 11-7, under the specific scope you can view the address pool, add a new exclusion range, view current IP addresses, enter reservations (more on this later), and reconfigure options for the scope. To view the current set of leases, simply click Address Leases underneath the node that represents the scope in which you're interested.

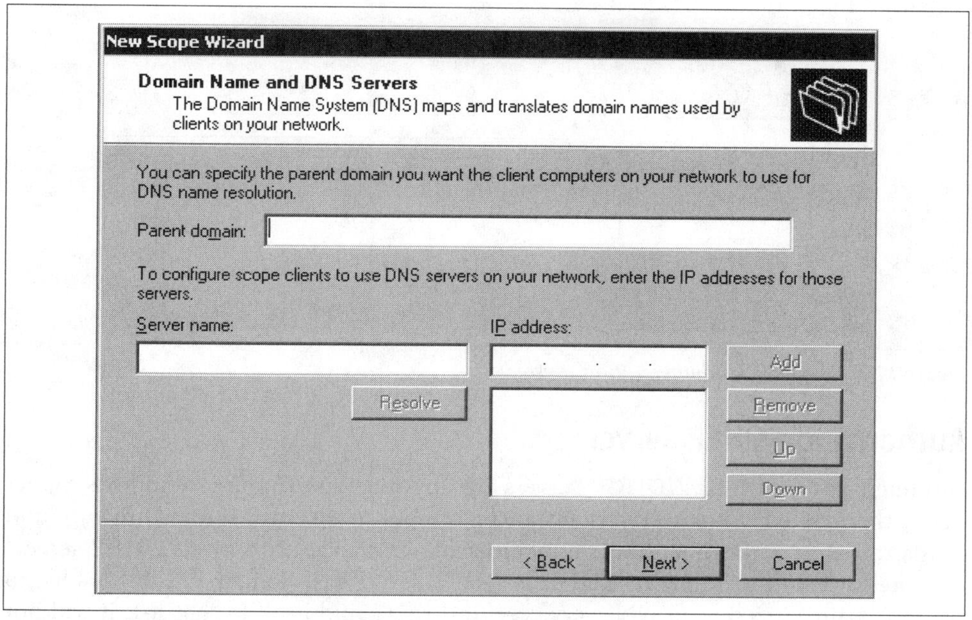

Figure 11-5. The Domain Name and DNS Servers screen

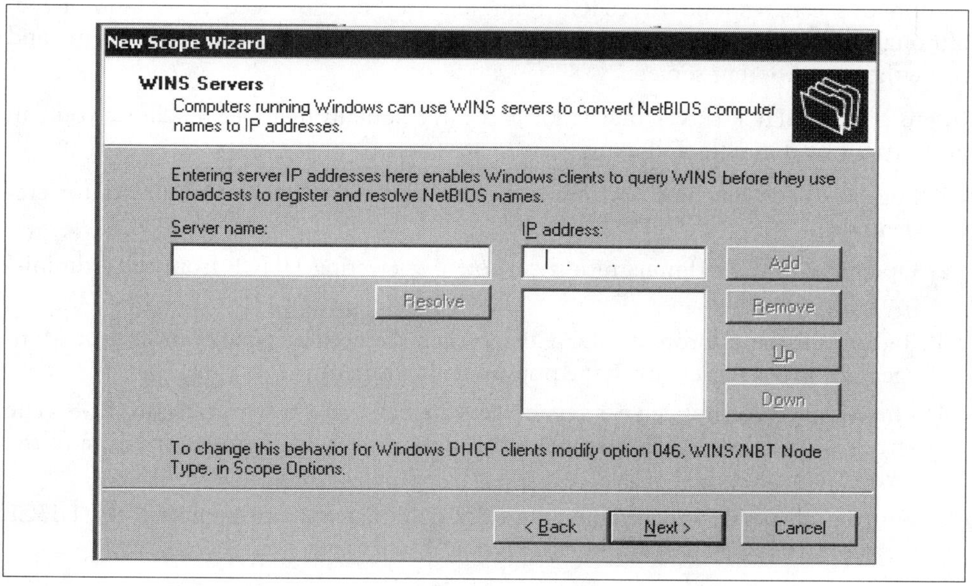

Figure 11-6. The WINS Servers screen

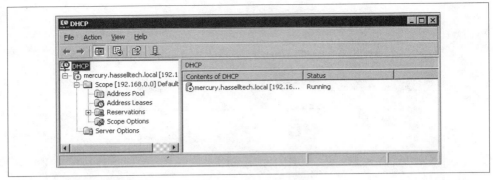

Figure 11-7. The DHCP administration console

Authorizing a DHCP Server

Although you can install DHCP servers on any machine running Windows Server 2003, the first DHCP server you install must hook itself into Active Directory and needs to be on a machine that is a member of a domain. Authorized DHCP servers are listed within the directory, and each DHCP server in a domain checks this list to see if it is authorized to provide service; if it doesn't find itself in that list, it will not respond to DHCP requests. DHCP servers on standalone servers that are not members of domains can respond to DHCP requests; they do not need to be authorized, although this can pose a security threat, since a rogue server could assist clients and route them to different servers.

If you have a DHCP server that is located on a domain member machine, you can authorize it by doing the following:

1. Log on to the machine with an account that has Enterprise Administrator credentials.

2. Open the DHCP administration console by selecting DHCP from the Administrative Tools folder.

3. Right-click the appropriate DHCP server in the lefthand pane and select Manage authorized servers from the pop-up context menu.

4. The Manage Authorized Servers screen appears, as shown in Figure 11-8. The screen lists all previously authorized DHCP servers. Click Authorize to add the server to this list.

5. On the following screen, enter the fully qualified domain name for the DHCP server or its associated IP address. Press OK.

6. Confirm your choice on the following dialog box.

Now the DHCP server is authorized and will begin serving IP addresses to clients who request them.

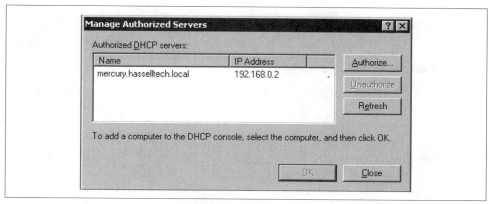

Figure 11-8. The Manage Authorized Servers screen

Reservations

Reservations allow you to effectively set static IP addresses through DHCP. Although a client using reservations still will be configured to obtain a dynamic IP address, the DHCP server has a reservation in its database for that client—which is identified using the MAC address of the network card—and thus always will receive the same IP address from the DHCP server.

To create a new reservation, right-click Reservations under the appropriate scope in the lefthand pane and select New Reservation. The New Reservation screen will appear. Here, enter a friendly name for this reservation as a reference, and then the IP address to reserve. Then, enter the MAC address of the network card inside the computer that you want to have the reserved address. (You can see this from the command line by issuing the `ipconfig /all` command and looking for the physical adapter address, or through the Control Panel and Network Connections by right-clicking the adapter and selecting Status.) Enter a description of the reservation if you want, and then click OK.

Figure 11-9 shows the reservations screen.

Understanding Classes

Classes are ways to distinguish between different systems and users for the purposes of assigning or allowing different options for them. Two types of classes are available within DHCP: vendor classes, which are set by the manufacturer and cannot be edited; and user classes, which are set at the client level on client computers and can be edited and used by administrators. Vendor classes can be used to send all computers matching a certain class a specific set of DHCP options—for example, to configure members of that class with a different set of DNS servers of gateways. And with

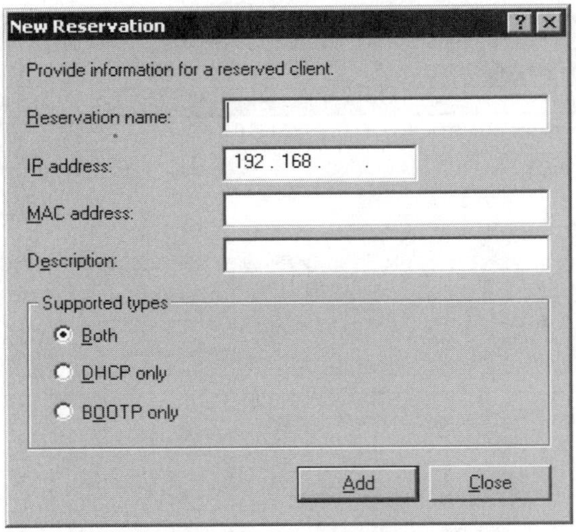

Figure 11-9. Making a DHCP reservation

the Windows Server 2003 vendor classes, you can offer specific systems the option of disabling NetBIOS, releasing its lease upon shutdown, and defining a metric for routing requests quickly and efficiently to network gateways.

> Vendors choose their own vendor classes, so you will need to consult with your vendor's documentation or support group to determine what vendor classes your adapters will listen for and respond to. Vendor classes also can represent the manufacturer of the network card and the manufacturer of the computer, whichever makes the most sense for your organization.
>
> Microsoft has created the MSFT prefix to provide classification of its DHCP clients in Windows 98 and higher.

User classes are set by administrators and are used to group users via means that aren't available via the vendor class. For example, you can set a user class for "Charlotte office" and another for "Raleigh office," for use in segregating the different groups to different IP resources. Identical classes need to be set on the client and on the DHCP server.

With user classes, it's possible to use predefined classes that can be used to support groups of clients with special needs, such as clients using the older BOOTP protocol, or clients connecting through the Routing and Remote Access Service. User classes really are meant for larger networks that need to manage DHCP option assignments based on different computer criteria and to assign and override the standard option assignments at the server, scope, or reservation level.

To create a user class on the server, follow these steps:

1. Open the DHCP administrator console.
2. Right-click the DHCP server and select Define User Classes from the pop-up context menu.
3. The DHCP User Classes dialog box appears. Click the Add button.
4. The New Class box appears, as shown in Figure 11-10.
5. Enter a name for the new class; this should be identical to the name you will use on a client. Also, enter a friendly description for your purposes if you want.
6. Enter the ASCII text of the class by clicking under the word ASCII and typing text. The binary version of what you type will be generated automatically.
7. Click OK.

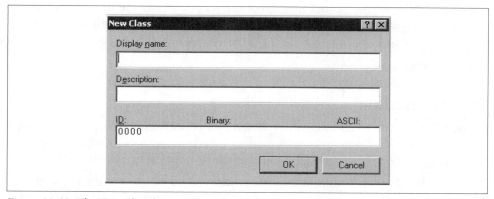

Figure 11-10. The New Class box

The new class has been created. Now, configure the DHCP options to send only to this class:

1. Under the server node in the left pane on the DHCP administrator console, right-click Scope Options and select Configure Options.
2. Navigate to the Advanced tab.
3. Under User Class, select the new class ID you just configured.
4. Finally, under Available Options, select the options you want to configure and enter the values for those options.
5. Click OK when you've finished.

Now the scope is configured to send certain options to your new class. On each client computer that will be members of that class, issue the following command:

```
ipconfig /setclassid "Local Area Connection" "Name of New User Class"
```

You will receive a message indicating the assignment was successful.

Superscopes

A *superscope* is a collection of scopes that can service requests from clients from multiple subnets over the same physical layer medium. By configuring a DHCP server with a superscope that encompasses several smaller scopes, you can provide DHCP service to multiple subnets simultaneously. Use superscopes when you need to provide leases to clients on more than one subnet with one DHCP server.

To begin configuring a superscope, follow these steps:

1. Load the DHCP administrator console.
2. Then, right-click the DHCP server node and select New Superscope from the pop-up context menu. Click Next off the introductory screen for the wizard.
3. Enter the name of the new superscope you're creating, and then click Next.
4. From the Available Scopes list, select the scopes to include in this new superscope. You can hold down the Ctrl button and click to select multiple scopes.
5. Click Next and confirm your settings. Then, click Finish.

The superscope is now active.

Conflict Detection

To ensure that one IP address is not leased to two different clients, the Windows Server 2003 DHCP service includes a conflict detection mechanism which involves a ping test to verify an IP address isn't in use before it is leased to a client.

You can verify that this feature is enabled, which you might want to do if you need to rebuild your DHCP server and ensure that when you bring the server back up it won't lease IP addresses currently in use. To do so, right-click the server name in the DHCP management console, select Properties, and navigate to the Advanced tab. Find the option called Conflict Detections Attempt, and set it to any value greater than 0 but less than 2 (performance issues arise with greater values). This number specifies the number of ping attempts the DHCP server will make before issuing an address.

DHCP Implications for DNS

The Windows Server 2003 DNS service supports updates from DHCP clients so that name-to-IP mappings continue to be accurate through the release and renewal process. On clients, you can configure this behavior by opening the properties of the local area connection (on Windows XP, you can find a list of network connections from the Connect to menu on the Start menu; in Windows 2000, this is done through the Network & Dial-up Connections applet in the Control Panel). Once you are inside the properties sheet, navigate to the DNS tab. At the bottom of the screen, select the option to Register this connection's addresses in DNS, as shown in Figure 11-11. This will instruct the client to transmit an updated A record to the primary DNS server.

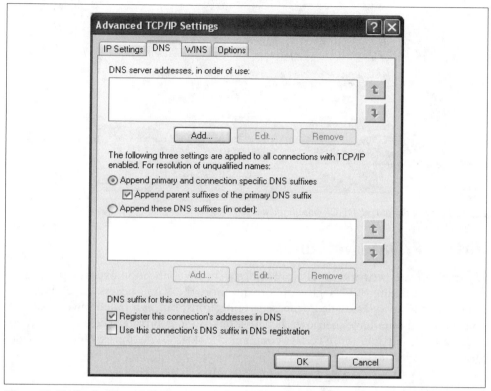

Figure 11-11. Registering a DHCP-assigned client address in DNS

If you want the DHCP server to handle these updates instead of the client, the first step is to make your DHCP server computer object a member of the DnsUpdateProxy group within Active Directory. If you have gone through the process of authorizing your DHCP server (described earlier in this chapter), this step has been completed automatically. If you haven't gone through this process, look at the DHCP administrators console—right-click the DHCP server node and click Properties. Navigate to the DNS tab, which is shown in Figure 11-12.

Here, you can instruct the DHCP service to automatically update DNS records for its clients at all times or only in instances where the client requests the update be pushed to the DNS server. You also can tell the service to expire the A records for a client when its current lease expires, and you can enable updates for clients that are unable to dynamically update their own records in DHCP.

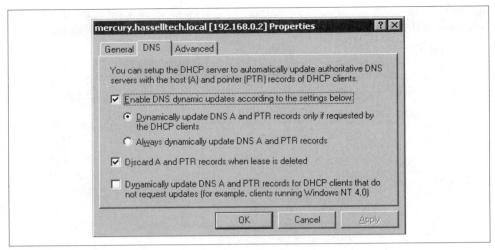

Figure 11-12. Configuring DHCP-based updates to DNS

Virtual Private Networks

A virtual private network, or VPN, provides a secure connection over the public network infrastructure. VPNs give an organization the same access capabilities for remote connectivity as owned or leased connections, but at a much lower cost. (Of course, leased lines have their own benefits, but as far as private access is concerned, VPNs are a good solution.) Today, companies look to VPNs for extranet and wide-area intranet services.

How It Works

VPNs encrypt data before sending it through the public infrastructure, and then decrypt the data at the receiving end of the network. For additional security, you can encrypt originating and destination network addresses. The VPN provides a point-to-point connection between the remote user's computer, the VPN client, and the organization's server, with data being passed through a "tunnel" that shields the data from the public network. In a sense, the public network's logistics don't matter because the data looks as if you sent it across a dedicated private link. Although the pathway doesn't matter to the VPN user, that pathway's performance does matter.

VPNs based on Microsoft technology first used the Point-to-Point Tunneling Protocol (PPTP) to create a secure environment in which to tunnel through the network, while VPNs on Cisco equipment used the proprietary Layer 2 Forwarding (L2F) protocol. However, as the popularity of VPNs grew, each company merged the best parts of its standard with the other, and the Layer 2 Tunneling Protocol (L2TP) was born. L2TP is the modern VPN protocol and will be used in all examples in the remainder of this section.

Configuring the Routing and Remote Access Server

To begin our exploration of VPNs, let's first set up the Routing and Remote Access Service (RRAS), which controls all remote connections attempting to connect to your server. The RRAS effectively serves as the endpoint to connections coming to and from your servers, routing them through the proper subnets and gateways, answering remote connection requests and sending authentication credentials to trusted sources, and enforcing encryption requirements. Think of RRAS as the manager for all things related to remote connectivity with your server.

Your server will need two network cards for a basic, automated VPN configuration: one for connectivity to your internal network, and another for basic IP connections to the Internet. You can configure a VPN with only one network adapter, but you must do so manually. In this section, I will cover the former method, which does require two network adapters.

Some of the most common setup scenarios for RRAS are:

NAT routing

> NAT (an acronym for Network Address Translation) allows for one public, routable IP address to be shared by clients behind a router or firewall. In this scenario, each client has a private, nonroutable IP address and sends all traffic to the gateway, which replaces the private IP address with the public address. This is an efficient and reasonably secure way to provide multiple clients with a shared Internet connection.

NAT routing with VPN access

> This scenario is the same as the previous configuration, with the exception that incoming VPN connection requests are supported. A private IP address is assigned to a successful VPN connection.

Secure private connection

> A secure private connection is simply an encrypted tunnel between two endpoint connections. It does not provide any sort of client IP address assignment or routing through gateways to the Internet; it simply exists to securely connect two endpoints to each other.

Remote access endpoint

> This scenario allows external clients to attempt to connect through dial-up or through a VPN to the current server. It simply functions as an "answering service," taking connection requests and providing remote access to the current server only.

Let's begin:

1. From the Administrative Tools folder, open the Routing and Remote Access console.

2. Right-click the server name in the lefthand pane of the console, and select Configure and Enable Routing and Remote Access.

3. The Routing and Remote Access Server Setup Wizard will appear. Click Next to move off the introductory screen.

4. The Configuration page will appear next, as shown in Figure 11-13. On this page, you can choose to configure a dial-up or VPN inbound connector, a NAT-based router, NAT with VPN, a secure connection between two remote sites, or a custom configuration consisting of any of the above. For our demonstration, select the first option, and click Next.

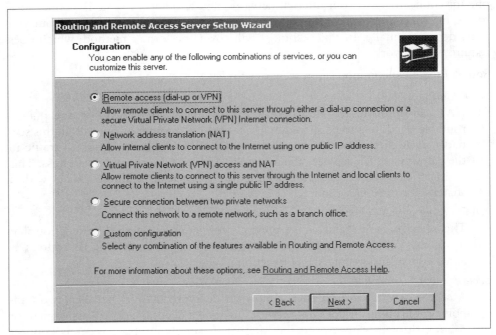

Figure 11-13. The Configuration screen

5. The Remote Access screen appears next. Choose to offer a VPN connection here by selecting the first option, and then click Next.

6. The VPN Connection screen appears next, as shown in Figure 11-14. Here, you select the network card that connects to the Internet—the public interface. You also can choose for the wizard to automatically set up packet filters that stop all traffic except for VPN traffic from coming into the network through that card. Check the appropriate card, and then enable the packet filters, and click Next.

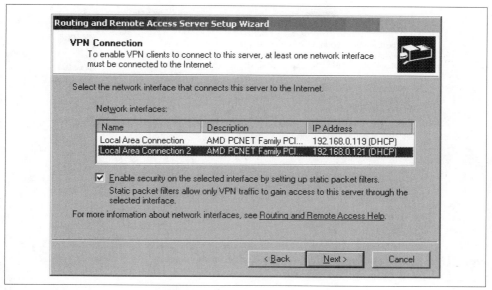

Figure 11-14. The VPN Connection screen

7. The IP Address Assignment screen appears next. Here, you select how to assign IP addresses to remote clients—either automatically from an existing DHCP server or a private address bank that RRAS generates itself (the first option), or from a select group of IP addresses that you specify (the second option). Use the first option, and click Next to continue.

8. The Managing Multiple Remote Access Servers screen appears next, as shown in Figure 11-15. Here, the wizard is asking if you want RRAS to be responsible for verifying usernames and passwords or if you want to delegate that to a RADIUS server. If you have multiple VPN connection points and use a RADIUS server to authenticate requests for these multiple points, choose Yes here. Otherwise, let RRAS handle authentication and choose the first option, No. Click Next.

9. The summary screen appears next. Verify your settings, and then click Finish.

The RRAS service will be stopped and then restarted, and your new settings will be in place. You'll be dumped back to the RRAS console with the service now started and ready for business.

Now, just make sure the virtual VPN ports are ready for use by your clients. From the RRAS console, expand the node with your server's name and right-click the Ports entry. Select Properties from the pop-up context menu and you'll see the screen shown in Figure 11-16.

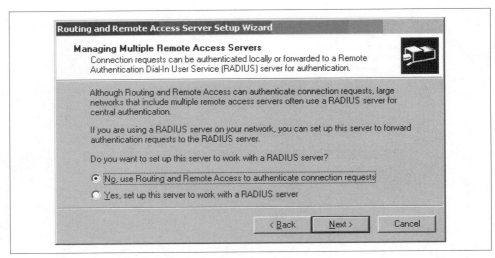

Figure 11-15. The Managing Multiple Remote Access Servers screen

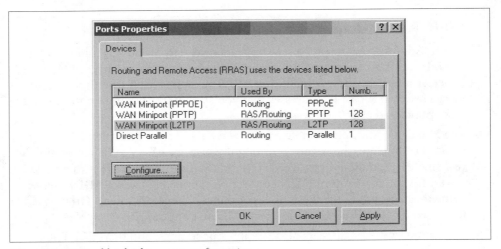

Figure 11-16. Double-checking port configuration

Select the WAN Miniport (L2TP) port, and then click the Configure button to ensure that inbound calls are allowed. You'll see the Configure Device screen appear, as shown in Figure 11-17.

Make sure the first option, Remote access connections (inbound only), is checked. Then, in the Phone number for this device field, enter the public IP address for this VPN server. This address is the one that clients will use from their remote locations to connect to your corporate network. You also can adjust upward or downward the number of connections you want to make available—anywhere from 1 to 128 simultaneous VPN tunnels. Click OK when you're finished.

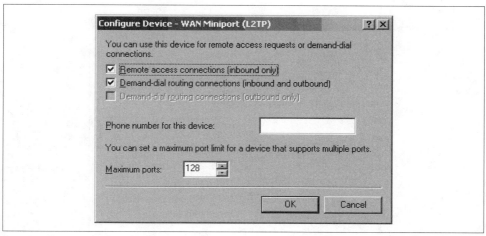

Figure 11-17. The Configure Device screen

Congratulations! Your RRAS server is set up to handle incoming VPN connections.

Granting access to users

Before your users can successfully use a VPN connection to your new RRAS server, you need to give them permission to dial in. You can do this through Active Directory Users and Computers. Simply open the tool and navigate through the console to the user for whom you want to enable access. Then right-click that user and select Properties.

Finally, navigate to the Dial-in tab. Click the Allow access option, which will grant access permission to the user. This is shown in Figure 11-18.

Authentication and Encryption Methods

VPNs in Windows Server 2003 support several different authentication and encryption methods, which you can configure on each RRAS server by right-clicking the server name in the left pane of the RRAS console and selecting Properties. The Security tab is command central for these settings, as you can see in Figure 11-19.

You can choose the different protocols by which to authenticate a user by clicking the Authentication Methods button. Doing so brings up the Authentication Methods screen, as shown in Figure 11-20.

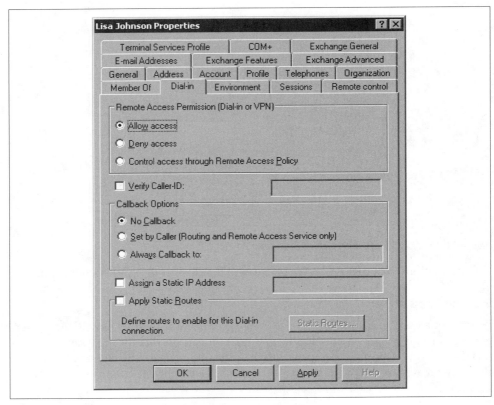

Figure 11-18. Granting permission to a user

On this screen, you can select the different authentication methods to use when a server is touched by a user attempting to connect. A short discussion of each method follows:

Extensible authentication protocol (EAP)
EAP is a protocol that allows you to "plug in" different schemes for authenticating a user. EAP in Windows Server 2003 supports the MD5-Challenge method, Smart Cards, Certificates (with TLS), Protected EAP (PEAP), and Secure Password (EAP-MSCHAPv2). The great aspect of EAP is that when newer, more secure authentication methods are developed, you simply can plug them into your existing architecture using EAP.

Microsoft encrypted authentication Version 2 (MS-CHAP v2)
MS-CHAP v2 allows you to encrypt an entire connection, not just the initial authentication portion, which provides a more robust way to transmit sensitive information over a VPN.

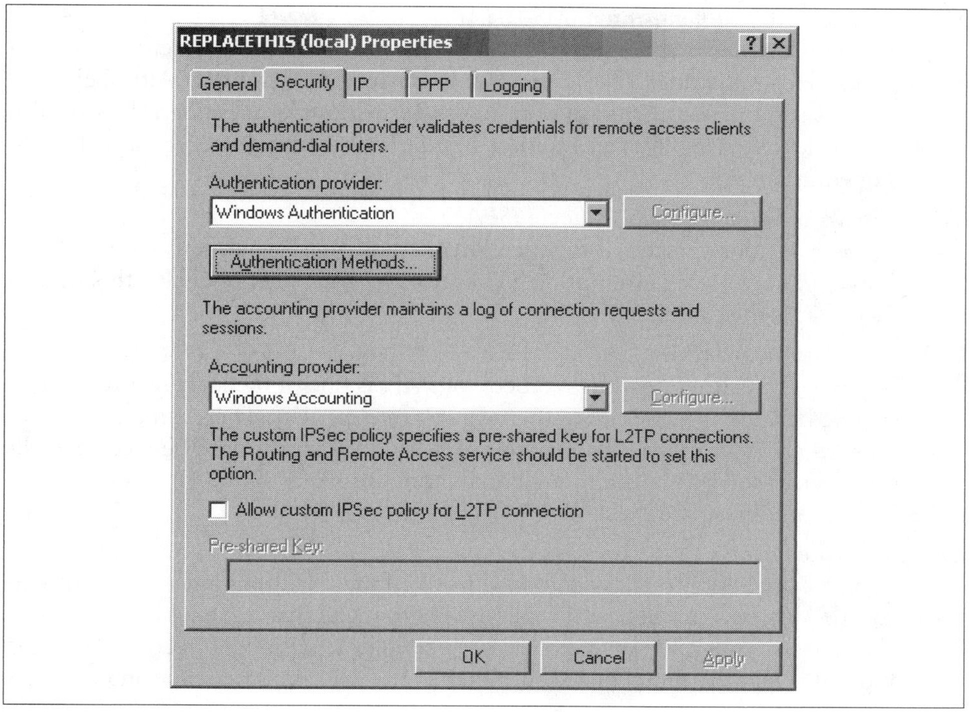

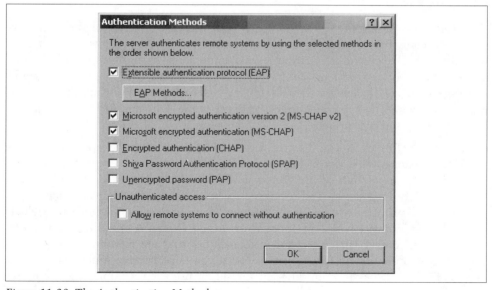

Figure 11-19. The Security tab

Figure 11-20. The Authentication Methods screen

Microsoft encrypted authentication (MS-CHAP)

Plain-vanilla MS-CHAP is simply a way to encrypt the initial authentication of a session. The remainder of the session is passed unencrypted. Although MS-CHAP v2 is more secure, its support across networking gear is not as broad; MS-CHAP is less secure but is an Internet standard and is supported by a wide variety of equipment.

Shiva Password Authentication Protocol (SPAP)

SPAP is a vendor-specific authentication method used when Shiva LAN Rover clients and servers are attempting to connect to your network. Use this option only if that is the case.

Unencrypted password (PAP)

The Password Authentication Protocol, or PAP, is one of the least secure options available because it passes all authentication in clear text. There isn't any sort of password encryption, so all someone needs to do is sniff traffic between the client and your server to obtain credentials that are likely valid. This isn't a good choice except in isolated test labs.

Unauthenticated access

You also can choose to allow any systems to connect without any sort of authentication. Although in the past it was possible to make this reasonably secure with some sort of caller ID or callback verification, I no longer recommend this option. It is just too much of a security hole in today's Internet environment.

Certificate Services

Certificates in Windows Server 2003 are primarily used for authentication purposes—to verify that the sender (and sometimes the receiver) of a message is indeed who that person says he is. Certificates are part of the broad-reaching public key infrastructure concept which mainly serves as a standard that manufacturers and developers can use to ensure their certificate-based authentication mechanism can interoperate with other manufacturers' equipment and software. PKI is important in a couple of key scenarios:

- The use of IPsec. As you'll learn in the next section of this chapter, IPsec provides a secure transport facility to send sensitive messages encrypted over the network. Part of that secure facility is the requirement that both ends of the transaction—the sender and receiver—must be able to authenticate each other. Microsoft provides two relatively hardened ways to do that: via Kerberos, which is the authentication system upon which Active Directory is built, or via certificates, which every machine, not just machines that are members of an Active Directory domain and forest, can use. So if you have two machines that need to use IPsec and they're from different forests, or not even members of AD in any fashion, then certificates are required for IPsec.

- The use of smart cards for user authentication. This is the wave of the future at this point—the ability to insert a card and start to work in the morning. In fact Microsoft itself requires all of its full-time employees to use smart cards, and they also double as electronic door keys, billing for cafeteria charges, and a score of other things. These smart cards contain certificates that serve as a sort of lingua franca for authentication. So smart cards require certificates.

Let's dig a little deeper into PKI before getting specifically into its implementation within Windows Server 2003.

Keys

There are two main types of keys that you'll hear when people speak or write about PKI—public keys and private keys. In PKI, keys are used in a scheme called asymmetric encryption, wherein one key is used to encrypt a message or some data and another, completely separate key is used to decrypt it. Such keys are generated by a computer and are based on a very long sequence of numbers that would be hard for an automated cracking program to guess. While the keys themselves are identical in format (but not content), users choose which one they will use to represent their public key; the remaining key becomes their private key. Messages can then be encrypted with a user's public key, and on the other side the associated private key—the only key that would work—would be used to decrypt it. (The process also works in reverse: you can encrypt something with a private key, and in that case only the public key can decrypt it.)

Keys are used with hashing algorithms that basically take an entire message or stream of data and condense it into a few bytes of data; this remainder is called a digest. For example, if I send an email and want to sign that email (thus authenticating that I indeed wrote the email myself) with my private key, the email client will assign a digest value to my message of, say, 1167. Note that the hashing function is one-way, in that you will always get the same digest coming out of the hashing function assuming you put the same data in, but from the digest you couldn't in any practical way figure out how the digest was computed—that is, you couldn't determine the formula or algorithm the hashing function was using. This is a cornerstone of PKI and encryption. To further secure the process, before the email is sent, the client program encrypts the digest, and then sends the message on with this encrypted digest embedded inside.

Let's dig a little further, taking the email example and moving to the receiver's end. The email client wants to ensure that the signature I put on the email was valid. So the receiving email client will run through its own hashing function, and it comes up with 1167 as the digest value. But the receiving client doesn't know what the digest value sent with the message was since it was encrypted. So it uses my public key—something freely available that I can give out through a number of avenues, which I'll talk about in just a bit—to decrypt the digest that was sent with the message. Then it discovers that that digest, with a value of 1167, matches its version of the digest, which is also 1167. The security and veracity of this authentication comes from this: if the message has been tampered with while in transit over the wire, the receiver's email client would have computed a different digest value from its hashing function (remember, different inputs in almost all cases means different digests). And since only the receiver's copy of my public key can decrypt something I've encrypted with my private key, the receiver can reasonably assume the digest is authentic and no one is faking him or her out.

So public keys and private keys, which are methods for asymmetric encryption, are useful for authenticating certain pieces of data. But making an entire communication series secure, and not just encrypting an individual a digest, is a bit more complicated. For example, when you use the secure socket layer (SSL) method of encryption as is primarily used between web servers, for the majority of the session you're actually engaging in symmetric encryption, which means that the same key is used at both ends of the transaction to encrypt and decrypt data. There's no public and private key in symmetric encryption: both sides agree on one key for use during that particular session only. The reasoning behind this lies primarily in the fact that symmetric encryption is significantly less processor-intensive than asymmetric encryption.

But how do the machines on both ends of the transmission agree on a key? After all, if you exchange the key in clear, unencrypted text before you begin encrypting things, it that really defeats the purpose of using encryption in the first place. The solution is through the use of asymmetric encryption to get a secure key exchange going. Here's how it works: one machine will have both a public key, which it will give out to anyone who asks for it, and a private key, which it of course keeps close to its chest. Let's assume the other machine is running a Web browser, and as part of its preparation to start conducting this secure session, has obtained the public key from the first machine. The browser then suggests a session key—the one both machines will use for that session only—and encrypts it with the public key of the first machine and sends it on. The first machine decrypts that message with its private key, which no one else knows, and finds the session key. Note that the key has never been transmitted across the wire in clear text. Now that both machines know the key, they can begin using symmetric encryption and drop the public/private key scheme. This process happens, of course, in mere milliseconds, and is known as a key exchange.

Certificates

There's a final element to this puzzle, and it addresses the problem of distributing and verifying the authenticity of public keys. I can give out public keys to anyone who asks, but the recipient could be easily duped into accepting a public key, supposedly from me, that was actually created by a nefarious person or group. Certificates themselves come into play in here: certificates are essentially a document containing someone's public key, some additional verification information, which is then signed by a trusted third party. This trusted third party, called a certificate authority, takes my public key, asks for some personally identifiable information from me (like a business license, state-issued identification, or some other legitimate documentation), assigns an expiration date, attaches their identifying information, and then puts the whole thing through a hashing function to compute a digest. The CA then uses its private key to sign that digest, and then it wraps all of this information into a convenient single "document," and that's the certificate. Recall that the certificate authority must have a public key if they have a private key, and this public key has been distributed about in various forms. For example, VeriSign, a commercial certificate authority, has its public keys installed in every modern web browser on the market today.

There are several different types of certificates that can be used in different scenarios. Consider some of them:

- Server certificates, which are certificates that are associated with a particular computer; these are used heavily in conjunction with IPsec communications

- User (email) certificates, which are tied to a specific person. There are actually two types of user certificates: a signing certificate which allows you to assert your identity, and the encryption certificate which allows you to decrypt mail and documents sent to you.

- CA certificates, which identify and authenticate a machine or an organization that verifies and signs other users' or machines' certificates

- EFS recovery agent certificates (you learned a bit about these in Chapter 3 during the discussion of the Encrypting File System), which allow certain users to recover files that were encrypted by someone other than themselves

Certificate Stores

These certificates need to be stored someplace on your system. In Windows client operating systems and Windows Server 2003, certificates are placed into a "certificate store," which is actually a part of the Registry. You will typically find both a user and a computer certificate store on any given machine, and you can add certificates to either store fairly easily simply by opening the certificate (either as a file or from a prompt your Web browser gives you when it encounters an unknown certificate) and telling Windows to place the certificate in the appropriate store. Note that if you have roaming profiles enabled, your user certificate store will roam with you. Certificates placed in the computer certificate store are available to any user who may log on to the machine.

There's also an MMC snap-in that makes it a bit easier to manage certificates and the certificate stores on Windows machines. You'll need to set up a custom console to see the snap-in, though, as it's not viewable by default with any of the console shipped with Windows Server 2003. To do so:

1. From the Start menu, choose Run.

2. Type **mmc** and then press Enter.

3. Within the MMC window, from the File menu, choose Add/Remove Snap-in.

4. Click Add, and select Certificates in the following window. Click Add once more.

5. The window will now ask which certificate store you'd like to manage with this particular instance of the snap-in. Choose Computer Account and click Next.

6. The window is now asking which computer store you'd like to manage. For the purposes of our example, choose Local Computer, and then click Finish. Now, it's time to add a snap-in instance to manage the user certificate store. Click Add in the Add Standalone Snap-in window. (Certificates should already have been highlighted.)

7. Leave the default option select to manage your current user certificate store, and click Finish.

8. Click Close, and then OK.

You've now created a custom MMC. It should look something like what you see in Figure 11-21.

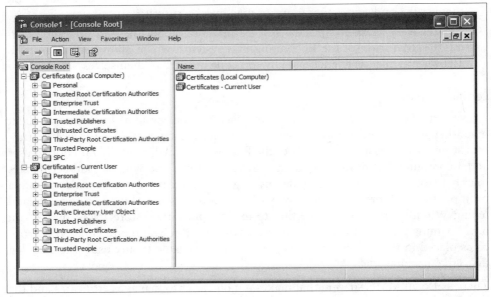

Figure 11-21. Viewing the user and computer certificate stores

Some folders in this console of which to take note:

- The *Trusted Root Certification Authorities* folder in both stores contains the certificates from the major certification authorities such as Thawte and Verisign. While it may appear that these certificates each reside in both the user and the computer certificate stores, in reality, when a user logs on to a machine, his or her user account inherits the certificates in the computer store. It just makes administration of certificates between users and computers a bit less of a headache than it otherwise would be.

- The *Intermediate Certification Authorities* folder has a folder underneath it called Certification Revocation List (also called a CRL), which contains a listing from each certification authority of invalid certificates that it has issued. If a CA improperly issues a certificate, it will list it in a CRL to alert other computers that the certificate is invalid.

Aside from its use to peek inside a machine's knowledge of certificates and organizational trusts, this MMC console will probably see little use from you, since this type of infrastructure tends to work fairly well for most uses. However, things begin to get less clear when you need to begin trusting other CAs besides those whose certificates are preloaded with Windows.

Trust, at least in this context, is somewhat of a complex issue, but the essence of it when dealing with PKI is the installation of a CA's certificate in a certificate store. Essentially, when you trust the decisions and the verification process of a CA, you are, by extension, trusting any certificate signed by that CA. By placing that CA's certificate in a certificate store, any valid certificate that comes along for inspection that is signed by that CA will be accepted. So if you place InstantCert.net's CA certificate in your store, you will accept at face value any validly formed certificate that comes your way that was signed by InstantCert.net's CA machines. The same works for your business partner: if you need to trust certificates signed by a partner's internal CA, then you would place that CA's certificate into the certificate store.

But what if your company needs to issue certificates internally to protect web servers or other machines that may pass sensitive information between themselves? What if you do business in a federated fashion with another firm and need to issue certificates to them?

Creating a Certificate Authority in Windows Server 2003

The answer is to run your own CA. The prospect sounds more formidable than the process actually is.

You'll find that certificates are a lot easier to request and distribute internally if you use Certificate Services' built-in web request feature; to enable this, you'll need to install IIS on your server and enable ASP.NET, which is turned off by default. Configure this prerequisite first through the Manage Your Server Wizard; see Chapter 8 for details. Once that's done, let's step through the procedure to actually get Certificate Services installed:

1. Open the Add/Remove Programs applet within Control Panel.

2. Click the Add/Remove Windows Components button toward the lefthand side of the window.

3. Check the box beside Certificate Services. You'll be prompted with a warning that you shouldn't rename the computer or change its domain membership once you've installed Certificate Services. Certificates that this CA will issue are tied to the computer's name and its current domain membership, and if you change this, all of the current certificates this CA issues would become void. Click OK to acknowledge.

4. The CA Type screen will appear, as shown in Figure 11-22. For the purposes of this example, choose the Stand-Alone Root CA option. Click Next.

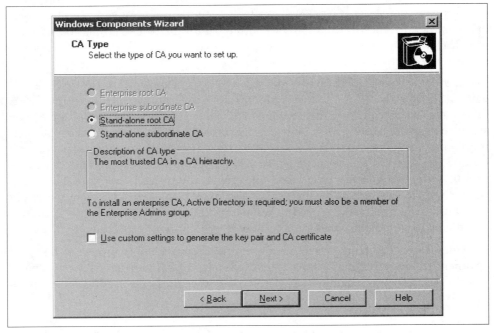

Figure 11-22. The CA Type screen

5. The CA Identifying Information screen will appear, which you can see in Figure 11-23. In the common name box, simply enter a friendly name that you'll recognize. In the distinguished name suffix, enter the DNS suffix of your computer in LDAP form: very simply, take the individual parts of your DNS name, precede them with DC= and replace the dots with commas. Thus, *corp.microsoft.com*

would become DC=corp,DC=microsoft,DC=com. You can choose the keep the default validity period. Click Next to continue.

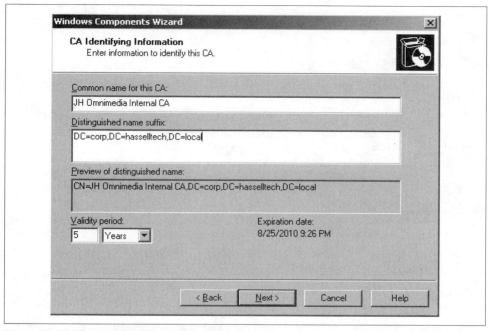

Figure 11-23. The CA Identifying Information screen

6. The Certificate Database Settings screen will appear, as you see in Figure 11-24. This screen is just asking for your preferences as to where the database of certificates will be stored; keep the defaults unless you have a better place in mind. You can also choose to store the database in a folder that's shared over the network; enter that folder in the box at the bottom of the screen, and click Next.

7. Click Finish to complete the installation.

The CA is now up and running, and we can now request a certificate from it for a machine. In this example, my machine, JH-WNXP-AUX, is going to ask for a plain server authentication certificate from the CA JH-W2K3-TST. First, I'll go to the Certificate Services web site at *http://jh-w2k3-tst/certsrv* and be greeted with the welcome screen shown in Figure 11-25.

I'll click the Request a Certificate link, and then since I don't want an email or web page certificate, I need to ask for the advanced certificate request page. This selection page is shown in Figure 11-26.

Next, I'll tell the wizard to create and submit a request to this CA and not another CA, as shown in Figure 11-27.

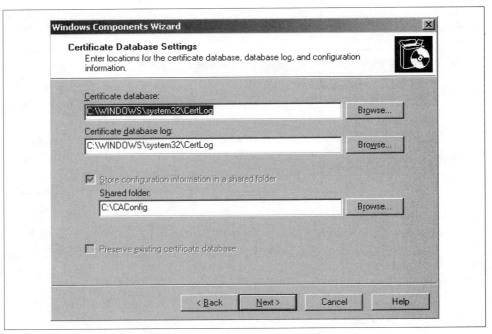

Figure 11-24. The Certificate Database Settings screen

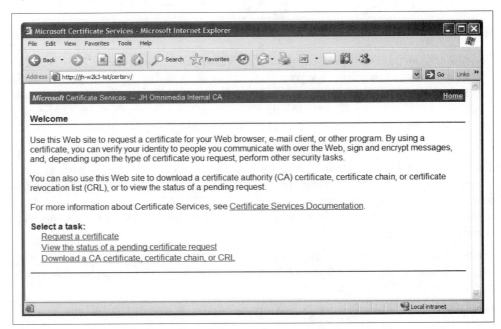

Figure 11-25. The Microsoft Certificate Services welcome screen

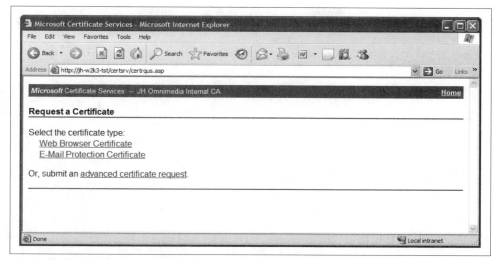

Figure 11-26. The Request a Certificate page

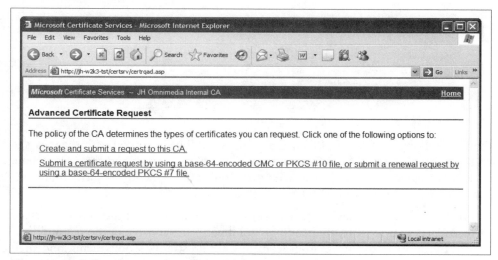

Figure 11-27. Telling the wizard to use this CA for requests and issuance

The Advanced Certificate Request screen appears. Since this is a long screen, I've captured the page in halves. Figure 11-28 shows the top half, and Figure 11-29 shows the bottom half.

I'll fill in the identifying information part of the page with my personal information, select Server Authentication Certificate from the Type of Certificate Needed list, and then accept the defaults—except that I'll check the option to store the certificate in my local store. (If you wanted only a signing key, or only an encryption [exchange] key, you can select the appropriate option in the Key Usage set of radio buttons.)

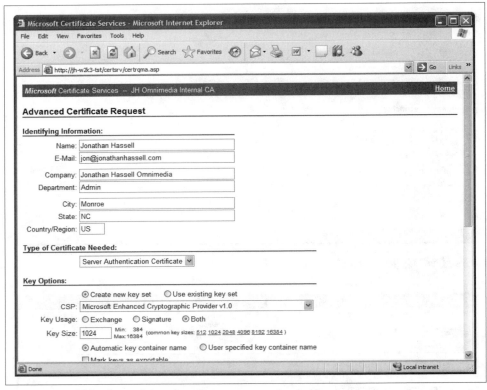

Figure 11-28. The Advanced Certificate Request screen (top half)

Once everything looks good, I'll click Submit, and I'll be rewarded with the message that the administrator of the CA needs to approve my request and that I can come back later to pick up the certificate. But that's only after a friendly security reminder, shown in Figure 11-30, to which I can safely say Yes.

So now that the key request has been submitted, as the administrator I need to issue the certificate that is currently pending. So I'll go to the console of the CA and load the Certification Authority snap-in from the Administrative Tools menu, and then click the Pending Requests folder in the left pane. The screen looks like that shown in Figure 11-31.

To issue the certificate, I'll simply right-click on the request, and from the All Tasks menu, choose Issue.

Now, back at the machine that's requesting the certificate, I'll return to the CA's web site and click View the status of a pending certificate. The next screen, shown in Figure 11-32, lists the requests I've made.

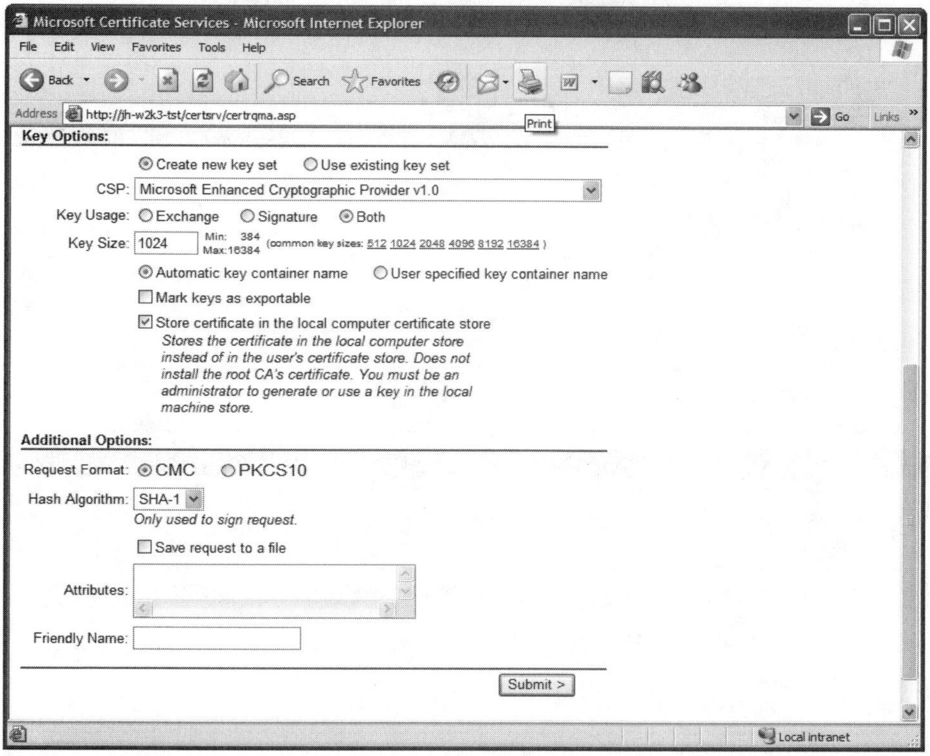

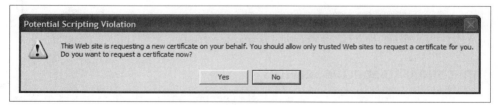

Figure 11-29. The Advanced Certificate Request screen (bottom half)

Figure 11-30. Finishing the certificate request process

I'll click the link, and then a page is returned with a link to the newly issued certificate. I can click on that link and Internet Explorer will automatically download that certificate into my store. You can see this in Figure 11-33.

And now the certificate request process is finished.

Note for your future reference that it's even easier for users to access this web site and download email or web page certificates since they won't need to submit an advanced certificate request for that; this example was the most complex certificate request to demonstrate.

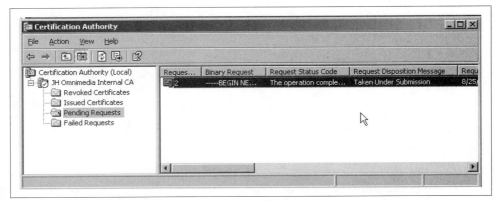

Figure 11-31. Pending requests

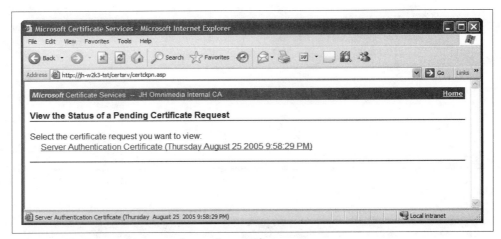

Figure 11-32. Viewing the status of a pending certificate request

Implications to Specific Services

Up to this point, you've taken a tour of PKI in general and certificate services in Windows Server 2003 in particular. In this section, I'll take a look at how this knowledge applies and relates to individual functions within the product.

IPsec

Using certificates with IPsec is easy—you'll first need to obtain the certificates from the CA. In the web interface that I just demonstrated, submit an advanced request, and then choose either an IPsec certificate or a client authentication certificate. Make sure to choose the option to store the certificate in the local store. You'll also need to ensure that all systems communicating through IPsec authenticated using certificates are using certificates signed by the same CA.

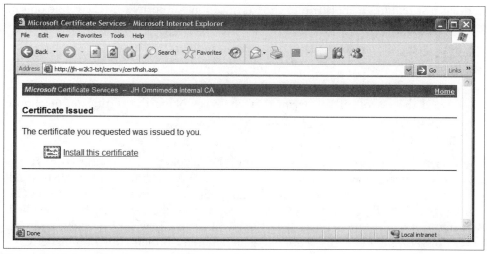

Figure 11-33. Installing the new certificate

It's recommended that you set up IPsec first using another, simpler form of authentication. There's ample guidance in the next section of this chapter. After you've gotten all the systems talking to each other, then you can elect to use certificates—it's a lot easier once the initial troubleshooting is over.

EFS

Remember from Chapter 3 that recovery agent certificates can allow another user to decrypt files, in an emergency situation, that a separate user encrypted. You can get this certificate from the web interface simply by submitting an advanced request and selecting the Recovery Agent option from the certificate type list.

Once you've downloaded the certificate, you'll need to install it on the machine where you need to decrypt files. Load the Local Security Policy applet from Administrative Tools, and navigate to the Public Key Policies and Encrypting File System folder. Right-click on that folder, and from the context menu, choose Add Data Recovery Agent, and follow the simple wizard from there. Of course, the usual caveat applies: the target machine must trust certificates signed by your CA.

Certificate Revocation

There may come a time when it's necessary to make a certificate null and void—for instance, in the event a notebook computer is stolen, or you've misidentified the credentials of someone after you've issued a certificate for him or her. This isn't difficult to do, it just requires a short trip to the Certification Authority MMC console on one of your CAs. Once that's loaded:

1. In the left pane, select the Issued Certificates folder.

2. In the right pane, right-click on the appropriate certificate and select Revoke Certificate from the All Tasks menu.

3. Record the reason, if you wish, that you're revoking the certificate, or choose Unspecified to ignore the question.

4. Click OK.

You'll then see the certificate you selected in the Revoked Certificates folder. To the CA, this certificate is now invalid, and the CA adds the certificate to its CRL (recall this list that I discussed earlier in the section). But if you have more than one CA, you'll probably find that they're not instantly aware of the certificate being revoked. By default, a Certificate Services-based CA will issue a new CRL weekly, and CAs lower down on the hierarchy chain will generally refresh their copy of a higher CA's CRL when the old one expires.

 You can also manually publish a new CRL. Check out:

> *http://www.microsoft.com/technet/prodtechnol/*
> *windowsserver2003/library/ServerHelp/56b47110-2ad2-4f66-a2fe-*
> *a89373b96425.mspx*

for details.

IP Security

IPSec is designed to secure traffic at the IP layer in a way that is transparent to the other layers and applications. By operating at such a low level, user applications and protocols that the OS uses need not be concerned with how security is applied; they can act normally, and the mechanics of IPSec are taken care of on an entirely separate level. IPSec addresses the weaknesses in the plain IP protocol by providing:

- Authentication of hosts before and during communications
- Confidentiality through encryption of IP traffic
- Integrity of IP traffic by identifying modified or spoofed traffic
- Prevention of replay attacks

You might be wondering how VPNs differ from the use of IPSec. If you are concerned only with securing traffic to and from a destination, there is little difference between the use of IPSec and the use of a VPN. VPN, however, comes with its own support burden, both on the end user and on the administrator, and in some cases VPNs are just too much to add to an administrator's current workload. On the other hand, VPNs also enable more complete functionality such as file sharing, browsing on the destination network, and other features that more closely mimic a "local" connection at the destination network. IPSec, meanwhile, supports only security features and does not add any of this type of functionality, and although the processor is pegged a bit more on both the client and server end because of the encryption and decryption routines, it has less of an effect on system resources than a VPN does. The bottom line comes down to whether you are considering using a VPN only for security purposes, in which case you might consider using a lighter-weight IPSec deployment instead, or if you want more localized features of the destination network, in which case a VPN would be a more logical choice.

IPSec in Windows consists of three main components: the policy agent, the Internet Key Exchange (IKE) module, and the IPSec driver. The policy agent collects the IPSec policies that the administrator has configured and then distributes the policies to the IKE module or IPSec driver. This component runs as the "IPSec Services" service in Windows Server 2003.

The IKE module negotiates security associations (SAs) for both the SA and key management systems and IPSec itself. It does this based on the authentication and security settings it receives from the policy agent. The IKE component is actually started (stopped and restarted, too) by the policy agent service.

And finally, the IPSec driver is responsible for executing the filters and monitoring connections to make sure they do not conflict with policy.

How IPSec Policies Work

Essentially, an IPSec policy consists of filter lists, which contain filters that match inbound and outbound traffic over a certain type of connection that has certain characteristics, such as IP address, port, or protocol. These filters have actions associated with them, which tell Windows what to do with the traffic that matches the filter. When traffic matches the filter and actions are taken with the traffic, actions consist of several methods of security that are used for authentication and key exchange between the two hosts that are exchanging the filtered traffic. All of these elements come together into an IPSec rule, which is the easiest unit of management when you're dealing with an organization full of security policies.

Filters can restrict traffic via one of four methods:

- Block the traffic and drop it before even processing it
- Encrypt the traffic before sending it on its way
- Sign the traffic to ensure its contents aren't changed during transmission and reception
- Permit the traffic to flow, untouched by IPSec

These filters can restrict that traffic:

- By the IP address, subnet, or fully qualified domain name of the source computer
- By the IP address, subnet, or fully qualified domain name of the destination computer
- By the port type (TCP, UDP, etc.) and number used in the transmission

Out of the box, Windows Server 2003 comes with three predefined security policies, which you can see in the default right pane of the IP Security Policy Management snap-in:

Client (respond only)
> This policy is used on computers that never need to transmit secure data but occasionally might need to respond to clients using secure transmissions.

Secure Server (require security)
> This policy, the strictest of the three, requires all inbound and outbound communications to be secure, and completely denies requests for insecure transmissions. This policy requires Kerberos.

Server (request security)
> Contrary to the popular definition of *server*, this policy can be used on machines acting in client or server roles that are required to protect all outbound transmissions but prefer to receive only secured inbound transmissions. This requires Kerberos.

 Only one IPSec policy can be in force (or "assigned") at a time. Assigning a new IPSec policy will automatically unassign the policy in effect immediately before the change.

Deconstructing an IPSec policy

Let's examine the Secure Server policy to see what components comprise it. Right-click Secure Server and select Properties to raise the Secure Server (Require Security) Properties box, as shown in Figure 11-34.

You can see the three rules that make up this policy; all are active, as indicated by the accompanying filled checkboxes. Note the filter list, action, authentication method, and tunnel setting of each rule. You can edit a particular rule by clicking it and then clicking the Edit button, which brings up the Edit Rule Properties dialog box, as shown in Figure 11-35.

Each of the five tabs—IP Filter List, Filter Action, Authentication Methods, Tunnel Setting, and Connection Type—allow you to edit the portion of the rule contained therein. You can use the Add and Edit buttons on each page to add new actions and methods to the rule. Click OK when finished.

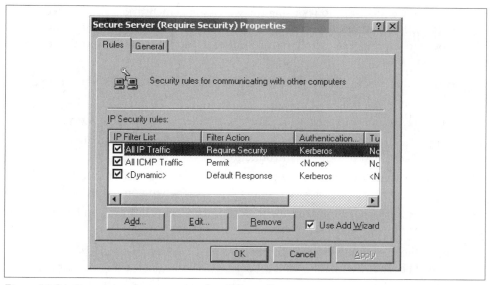

Figure 11-34. Examining the properties of an IPSec policy

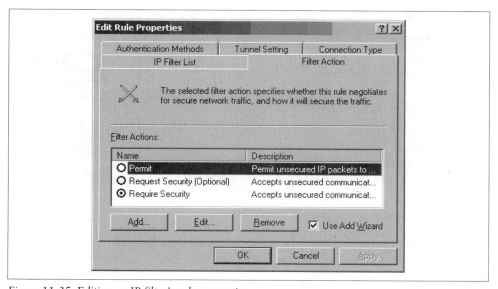

Figure 11-35. Editing an IP filter's rule properties

Creating an IPSec Policy

Now let's create an IPSec policy. In this example, I'll assume you want to block all traffic except that to ports 80 and 443, which is something you'd want to do for IIS web servers that operate on a standalone basis. (You would lose the ability to remotely manage these machines using the web management tools you learned about in Chapter 8, but I've already explained that it's a bad idea to use those, anyway.) Then you can modify the following procedure as appropriate for other rules you might want to create.

First, you need to create a filter action that describes what to allow and what to deny:

1. In the IP Security Policy Management snap-in, right-click IPSec Security Policies on Local Machine and then select Manage IP filter lists and filter actions.

2. Navigate to the Manage Filter Actions tab, and click Add to create a new filter action. Click Next to skip the introduction.

3. Type **LockDownWeb-Permit** as the name for the new filter action because we'll be using this action to permit web traffic. Click Next when you're finished.

4. The Filter Action General Options screen appears next, as shown in Figure 11-36. Select Permit, and then click Next.

5. Click Finish to complete the first filter action.

6. Create a second filter action called LockDownWeb-Block using the same procedure, except choose Block on the Filter Action dialog box this time.

7. Click Close once you're finished.

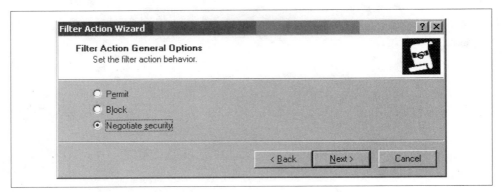

Figure 11-36. The Filter Action General Options screen

Now it's time to actually create the filters and lists based on the actions you just defined:

1. Right-click IPSec Security Policies on Local Machine and then select Manage IP filter lists and filter actions.

2. Click the Add button to create a new IP filter list.

3. Use AllTraffic for the filter list name.

4. Now, click the Add button again to create a new filter. Just select the default options through the IP Filter Wizard to create a filter that will catch all traffic.

5. Click Close when you're finished.

6. You'll be returned to the IP Filter List screen, shown in Figure 11-37. Now, click Add to create another filter list, and use CatchWebTraffic for the name.

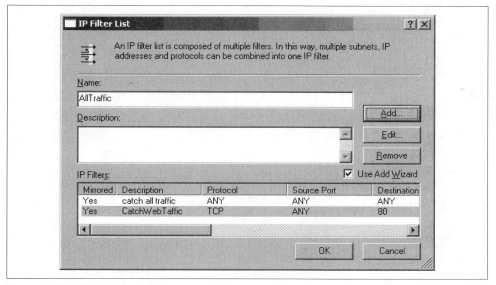

Figure 11-37. The IP Filter List screen

7. Select Any IP Address from the Source address drop-down list, and then click Next.

8. Select My IP Address from the Destination address drop-down list, and then click Next.

9. Choose TCP from the Select a protocol type drop-down list, and then click Next.

10. The IP Protocol Port screen appears which is depicted in Figure 11-38. Select To this port and then indicate port 80.

11. Click Next and then Finish.

At this point, you've filtered all traffic except that flowing to port 80. If you have an SSL site that needs access, click Add, and then repeat this procedure to create another filter that permits traffic to go to port 443. You might want to make a note of the values presented in Table 11-1.

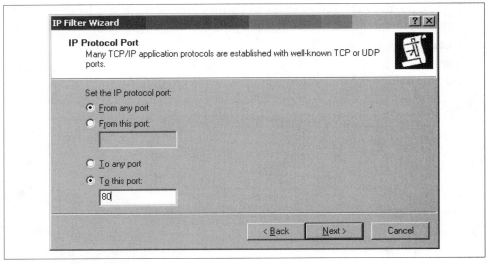

Figure 11-38. The IP Protocol Port screen

Table 11-1. Values to create IPSec rule for SSL web serving

Prompt	Information
Source Address	Any IP address
Destination Address	My IP address
Protocol	TCP
From Port	Any
To Port	443

IPSec Caveats

As with any technology, there are a few "gotchas" when it comes to using IPSec in production. For one, the protocol is supported only on Windows 2000 operating systems or later. And although the Microsoft version supposedly adheres to the IPSec protocol standard—the one all vendors are supposed to use when developing their implementations of a protocol—support for interoperability can be limited with some more obscure vendors. Always be sure to test your scenarios in a lab with identical equipment to make sure you have no issues with that.

With that said, foremost on the list of things to consider is that IPSec by default won't work with NAT-based connections. However, there is a modification of the IPSec protocol called NAT Traversal which will allow bridging of IPSec communications, intact, through a NAT router or firewall and back to the other side of the transmission. You do need a NAT machine that knows about this traversal feature, and you also need Windows Server 2003 to do the encrypting—previous versions of Windows simply won't cut it.

Since the first edition of this book was published, Microsoft has released an L2TP/IPSec NAT-T update for 2000 and XP, which you can find at the following location:

http://support.microsoft.com/default.aspx?scid=kb%3Ben-us%3B818043

Network Access Quarantine Control

One of the easiest and arguably most prevalent ways for nefarious software or Internet users to creep onto your network is not through holes in your firewall, or brute-force password attacks, or anything else that might occur at your corporate headquarters or campus. It's through your mobile users, when they try to connect to your business network while on the road.

Consider why that is the case. Most remote users are authenticated only on the basis of their identity; no effort is made to verify that their hardware and software meet a certain baseline requirement. Remote users could, and do everyday, fail any or all of the following guidelines:

- The latest service pack and the latest security hotfixes are installed

- The corporation-standard antivirus software is installed and running and the latest signature files are being used

- Internet or network routing is disabled

- Windows XP's ICF, or any other approved firewall, is installed, enabled, and actively protecting ports on the computer

You would expect your business desktops to follow policy, but in the past, mobile users have traditionally been forgotten or grudgingly accepted as exceptions to the rule. However, Windows Server 2003 includes a new feature in its Resource Kit, called Network Access Quarantine Control (NAQC), which allows you to prevent remote users from connecting to your network with machines that aren't up-to-date and secure. NAQC provides a different sort of security and addresses a different, but equally important, sector of communications than VPN or IPSec.

As of this writing, NAQC is supported only on Windows-based clients. Macintosh, Unix, and Linux-based systems can't use NAQC.

This section will detail how NAQC works and how to install and configure it.

How It Works

NAQC prevents unhindered, free access to a network from a remote location until the destination computer has verified the remote computer's configuration meets certain requirements and standards, as outlined in a script.

Figure 11-39 shows the pieces of this puzzle.

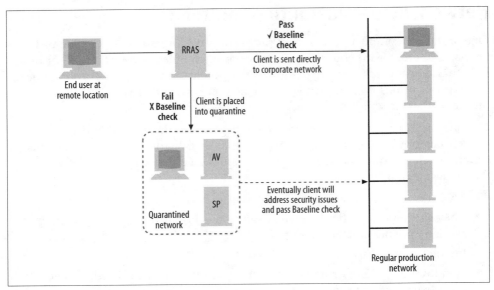

Figure 11-39. How NACQC works

To use NAQC, your remote access clients must be running Windows 98 Second Edition, Windows Millennium Edition, Windows 2000, or Windows XP Home or Professional. These versions of Windows support a *connectoid*, which is simply a dial-up or VPN connection profile located in the Network Connections element in the user interface, containing three essential elements:

Connection information
> Such as the remote server IP address, encryption requirements, and so on

The baselining script
> A simple batch file or program used to assess the suitability of the client computer (more on this in a bit)

A notifier component
> Talks to the destination network's backend machine and negotiates a lift of the client's quarantine

These elements are united into one profile using the Connection Manager (CM) Administration Kit (CMAK) in Windows Server 2003. Additionally, you'll need at least one Windows Server 2003 machine on the back end running an approved listening component; for the purposes of this chapter, I'll assume you're running the Remote Access Quarantine Agent service (called *rqs.exe*) from the Windows Server 2003 Resource Kit because that is the only agent available at press time. Finally, you'll need a NAQC-compliant RADIUS server, such as the Internet Authentication Service in Windows Server 2003, so that network access can be restricted using specific RADIUS attributes assigned during the connection process.

Under NAQC, when a client establishes a connection to a remote network's endpoint (a machine running RRAS), the destination DHCP server gives the remote, connecting computer an IP address, but an IAS server establishes a "quarantine mode."

In quarantine mode, the following restrictions are in effect:

- A set of packet filters is enabled that restricts the traffic sent to and received from a remote access client
- A session timer is enabled that limits the duration of a remote client's connection in quarantine mode before being terminated

Once the remote computer is in quarantine mode, the client computer automatically executes the baseline script. If Windows runs the script and is satisfied with the result, it contacts the listening service running on the Windows Server 2003 backend machine and reports this result. Then quarantine mode is removed and normal network access is restored. Otherwise, the client eventually is disconnected when the session timer reaches the configured limit, as described earlier.

A Step-by-Step Overview of NAQC

Here is a detailed outline of how the connection and quarantining process works, assuming you're using *rqc.exe* on the client end from the CMAK and *rqs.exe* on the back end from the Resource Kit:

1. The remote user connects his computer, using the quarantine CM connectoid to the quarantine-enabled connection point, which is a machine running RRAS.
2. The remote user authenticates.
3. RRAS sends a RADIUS Access-Request message to the RADIUS server—in this case, a Windows Server 2003 machine running IAS.
4. The IAS server verifies the remote user's credentials successfully and checks its remote access policies. The connection attempt matches the configured quarantine policy.
5. The connection is accepted, but with quarantine restrictions in place. The IAS server sends a RADIUS Access-Accept message, including the MS-Quarantine-IPFilter and MS-Quarantine-Session-Timeout attributes, to RRAS.

6. The remote user completes the remote access connection with the RRAS server, which includes leasing an IP address and establishing other network settings.

7. RRAS configures the MS-Quarantine-IPFilter and MS-Quarantine-Session-Time-out settings for the connection, now in quarantine mode. At this point, the remote user can only send traffic that matches the quarantine filters—all other traffic is filtered—and can only remain connected for the value, in second, of the MS-Quarantine-Session-Timeout attribute before the quarantine baselining script must be run and the result reported back to RRAS.

8. The CMAK profile runs the quarantine script, currently defined as the "post-connect action."

9. The quarantine script runs and verifies that the remote access client computer's configuration meets a baseline. If so, the script runs *rqc.exe* with its command-line parameters, including a text string representing the version of the quarantine script being used.

10. *rqc.exe* sends a notification to RRAS, indicating that the script ended successfully.

11. The notification is received by *rqs.exe* on the back end.

12. The listener component on the RRAS server verifies the script version string in the notification message with those configured in the registry of the RRAS and returns a message indicating that the script version was either valid or invalid.

13. If the script version was acceptable, the *rqs.exe* calls the `MprAdminConnectionRe-moveQuarantine( )` API, which indicates to RRAS that it's time to remove the MS-Quarantine-IPFilter and MS-Quarantine-Session-Timeout settings from the connection and reconfigure the session for normal network access.

14. Once this is done, the remote user has normal access to the resources on the network.

15. *rqs.exe* creates an event describing the quarantined connection in the System event log.

Deploying NAQC

In this section, I'll look at the actual deployment of NQAC on your network. Deployment comprises six steps, each outlined in separate subsections.

Creating quarantined resources

The first step is to create resources that actually can be accessed while the quarantine packet filters are in place for a remote client. Examples of such resources include DNS servers and DHCP servers, so that IP address and other connection information such as suffix addresses, DNS server addresses, and the like can be retrieved; fileservers to download appropriate software to update out-of-compliance machines;

and web servers that can describe the quarantining process or allow a remote user to contact IT support via email if any problems occur.

You can specify and use a quarantined resource in two ways. The first is to identify certain servers, which can be spread across your network, as these quarantine resources. This allows you to use an existing machine to host the quarantined resources, but you also have to create individual packet filters for quarantined sessions for each existing machine. For performance and overhead reasons, it's best to limit the number of individual packet filters for a session.

If you decide to go this route, you'll need to enable the packet filters shown in Table 11-2.

Table 11-2. Packet filters for distributed quarantine resources

Traffic type	Source port	Destination port	Alternatives (instead of specifying port information)
Quarantine Notifier	None	TCP 7250	None
DHCP	UDP 68	UDP 67	None
DNS	None	UDP 53	You also can specify the IP address of any DNS server.
WINS	None	UDP 137	You also can specify the IP address of any WINS server.
HTTP	None	TCP 80	You also can specify the IP address of any web server.
NetBIOS	None	TCP 139	You also can specify the IP address of any file server.
Direct Hosting	None	TCP 445	You also can specify the IP address of any file server.

You also can configure any other packet filters that are particular to your organization.

The other approach is to limit your quarantined resources to a particular IP subnet. This way, you need just one packet filter to quarantine traffic to a remote user, but you might need to readdress machines and, in most cases, take them out of their existing service or buy new ones.

Using this method, the packet filter requirements are much simpler. You just need to open one for notifier traffic on destination TCP port 7250, one for DHCP traffic on source UDP port 68 and destination IDP port 67, and for all other traffic, the address range of the dedicated quarantine resource subnet. And again, you can configure any other packet filters that are particular to your organization.

 Make sure the resources you make available to quarantined users are adequately hardened. Remember: you don't trust these machines, and they very well might be infected with worms, viruses, and other malware that can be detrimental to your quarantined resource machines. Ensure they are locked down tightly.

Writing the baselining script

The next step is to write a baselining script that will be run on the client. You can write this script in any scripting environment supported by your Windows clients, or even as a compiled EXE program. This script can check whatever you want—there is no standard level of baseline, as it's only what you feel comfortable with letting onto your network. You also can use any sort of interaction with any program that your scripting environment will allow. The baseline script is very flexible and can use whatever software resources you have available.

Here is an example batch file script:

```
@echo off
echo Your remote connection is %1
echo Your tunnel connection %2
echo Your Windows domain is %3
echo Your username is %4
set MYSTATUS=
REM Baselining checks begin here
REM Verify Internet Connection Firewall is enabled. Set CHECKFIRE
to 1-pass, 2-fail.
<insert your various commands to check the ICF>
REM Verify virus checker installed and sig file up. CHECKVIRUS is
1-pass, 2-fail.
<insert your various commands to verify the presence of antivirus
software and sig file>
REM Pass results to notifier or fail out with message to user.
if "%CHECKFIRE%" = = "2" goto :NONCOMPLIANT
if "%CHECKVIRUS%" = = "2" goto :NONCOMPLIANT
rqc.exe %1 %2 7250 %3 %4 Version1-0
REM These variables correspond to arguments and switches for RQC.EXE
REM %1 = %DialRasEntry%
REM %2 = %TunnelRasEntry%
REM RQS on backend listens on port 7250
REM %3 = %Domain%
REM %4 = %UserName%
REM The version of the baselining script is "Version1-0"
REM Print out the status
if "%ERRORLEVEL%" = = "0" (
set ERRORMSG=Successful baseline check.
) else if "%ERRORLEVEL%" = = "1" (
set ERRORMSG=Can't contact the RRAS server at the corporate
network. Contact a system administration.
) else if "%ERRORLEVEL%" = = "2" (
set ERRORMSG=Access is denied. Please install the Connection
Manager profile from http://location and attempt a connection
again.
) else (
set ERRORMSG=Unknown failure. You will remain in quarantine
mode until the session timeout is reached.
)
echo %ERRORMSG%
goto :EOF
```

```
:NONCOMPLIANT
echo
echo Your computer has failed a baseline check for updates on
echo your machine. It is against corporate policy to allow out of
echo date machines to access the network remotely. Currently
echo you must have Internet Connection Firewall enabled and
echo an updated virus scanning software package with the
echo latest virus signature files. For information about how to
echo install or configure these components, surf to
echo http://location.
Echo You will be permitted to access only that location until
Echo your computer passes the baselining check.
:EOF
```

Of course, this batch file is simple. I've added the necessary comments throughout the script so that you can follow the action. It's important to keep in mind that you can make the script as complex as you want; you even can compile a special program because the post-connect script option in CMAK allows a *.exe* file to be run.

The one requirement of every baseline script is that it must run *rqc.exe* if the baselining compliance check was successful and included the following parameters:

```
rqc ConnName TunnelConnName TCPPort Domain Username ScriptVersion
```

The switches and arguments are explained in the following list:

ConnName

> This argument is the name of the connectoid on the remote machine, most often inherited from the dial-in profile variable %DialRasEntry%.

TunnelConnName

> This argument is the name of the tunnel connectoid on the remote machine, most often inherited from the dial-in profile variable %TunnelRasEntry%.

TCPPort

> This argument is, obviously, the port used by the notifier to send a success message. This default is 7250.

Domain

> This argument is the Windows security domain name of the remote user, most often inherited from the dial-in profile variable %Domain%.

Username

> This argument is, as you might guess, the username of the remote user, most often inherited from the dial-in profile %UserName%.

ScriptVersion

> This argument is a text string that contains the script version that will be matched on the RRAS server. You can use any keyboard characters except /0 in a consecutive sequence.

Installing the listening components

The Remote Access Quarantine Agent service, known otherwise as *rqs.exe*, must be installed on the Windows Server 2003 machines accepting incoming calls using RRAS. RQS is found in the Windows Server 2003 Resource Kit Tools download, which you can find on the Microsoft web site at *http://www.microsoft.com/windowsserver*. Once you've run the installer for the tools, select the Command Shell option from the program group on the Start menu, and run RQS_SETUP /INSTALL from that shell. This batch file will copy the appropriate binaries to the *%SystemRoot%\System32\RAS* folder on your system and modify service and registry settings so that the listener starts automatically when the server boots up.

 To remove *rqs.exe*, type **RQS_SETUP /REMOVE** at a command prompt.

A bit of manual intervention is required, however, to finish the installation: you need to specify the version string for the baselining script. The listener service will match the version reported by the remote computer to the value stored on the RRAS computer to make sure the client is using the latest acceptable version of a script. This is a great way to enforce changes you make to your baseline scripts: if a user isn't using the latest version of the scripts (and therefore isn't making the latest analysis of the system based on your needs), he won't be released from the quarantine mode.

To make this change manually after you've run RQS_SETUP from the Tools download, follow these steps:

1. Open the Registry Editor.
2. Navigate to the key:

   HKEY_LOCAL_MACHINE/System/CurrentControlSet/Services/Rqs

3. Right-click in the right pane, and select New String.
4. Name the string **AllowedValue**.
5. Then, double-click the new entry, and enter the string that refers to an acceptable version of the script.

Alternatively, you can modify the RQS_SETUP batch file, so this step can be automated for future deployments. To do so, follow these steps:

1. Open the *rqs_setup.bat* file in Notepad.
2. Select Find from the Edit menu.
3. In Find what, enter **Version1\0**, and click OK. The text cursor should be on the following line:

   ```
   REM REG ADD %ServicePath% /v AllowedSet /t REG_MULTI_SZ /d Version1\0Version1a\
   0Test
   ```

4. To add just one acceptable version, delete REM from the beginning of the line.

5. Now, replace the text Version1\0Version1a\0Test with the script version string you want to be passed by *rqc.exe*.

6. If you want to add more than one acceptable version, you can replace the text Version1\0Version1a\0Test with the acceptable version strings, each separated by \0.

7. Save the file, and then exit Notepad.

RQS is set as a dependency of RRAS. However, when RRAS is restarted, RQS doesn't restart automatically, so you'll need to restart it manually if you ever stop RRAS manually.

 By default, *rqs.exe* listens on TCP port 7250. To change the default TCP port, navigate to the *HKEY_LOCAL_MACHINE\SYSTEM\CurrentControlSet\Services\rqs* key, create a new REG_DWORD value called Port, and set it to the desired port.

Creating a quarantined connection profile

The next step is to create a quarantined Connection Manager profile, which happens to be a normal profile you might create for any standard dial-up or VPN connection, with only a few modifications. For one, you need to add a post-connect action so that your baselining script will run and return a success or failure message to the RRAS machine. You also need to add the notifier to the profile.

Let's look at using the CMAK to create a custom connectoid including the necessary NAQC components. Because the process is somewhat involved, I will only include screenshots of the steps specific to configuring a quarantined connection.

1. Open the CMAK from the Administrative Tools menu, and then click Next off the introductory screen.

2. Select Create a new service profile, and then click Next.

3. In the Service name box, type a name that you want to use for the connection. This should be something familiar to users, such as "Connect to Corpnet" or something similar.

4. In the File name box, type a name that you want to use for the service profile. This name is used for the files that CMAK creates while building the service profile. Do not use any of the following characters in the filename: <SPACE> ! , ; * = / \ : ? ' " < >.

   Click Next.

5. I'll assume here that you do not have an existing CM profile to merge, so simply click Next to bypass the screen that appears that asks you to merge profile information.

6. If you want to add a line of support information to the logon dialog box, type it in the Support information box—for example, For customer support, email *support@hasselltech.net*. This is optional. Click Next when you've finished.

7. Specify whether the service requires a realm name, and then click Next.

8. If you want to configure custom Dial-Up Networking entries, click Add. In the Phone-book Dial-Up Networking entry dialog box, type the phonebook Dial-Up Networking entry that you want. Click Next.

9. Specify whether you want to assign specific DNS or WINS server addresses or a Dial-Up Networking script, and then click OK. Click Next.

10. If you want to add VPN support to the service profile, click to select the This service profile checkbox, and then click Next. Specify the server in the Server address box, specify whether you want to assign specific DNS or WINS server addresses and whether to use the same user credentials that are used for a dial-up connection, and then click OK. Click Next.

    (Here is where the quarantine steps begin.) The Custom Actions screen appears, and Figure 11-40 shows this.

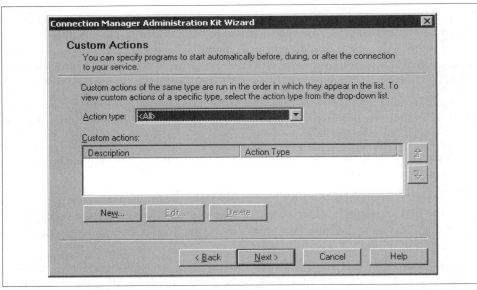

Figure 11-40. The Custom Actions screen of the CMAK Wizard

11. Select Post-Connect from the Action type drop-down box and then click the New button to add an action. The New Custom Action dialog box is displayed, as shown in Figure 11-41.

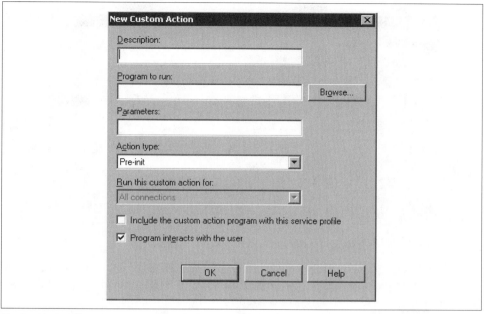

Figure 11-41. The New Custom Action dialog box

12. Type a descriptive title for the post-connection action in the Description box. In Program to run, enter the name of your baselining script. You also can use the Browse button to look for it. Type the command-line switches and their arguments in the Parameters box. Finally, check the two bottom boxes, Include the custom action program with this service profile and Program interacts with the user.

13. Click OK, and you should return to the Custom Actions screen. Click Next.

14. Continue filling in the wizard screens as appropriate, until you come to the Additional Files screen, depicted in Figure 11-42.

15. Click Add, and then enter **rqc.exe** in the dialog presented next. You can use the Browse button to search for it graphically. Once you're finished, click OK.

16. You'll be returned to the Additional Files screen, where you'll see *rqc.exe* listed. Click Next.

17. Complete the remainder of the wizard as appropriate.

Distributing the profile to remote users

The profile you just created is made into an executable file that you can distribute to your remote users so that they can run it on their systems automatically, creating a profile without any intervention after that. You have several options for actually getting that executable file to your users.

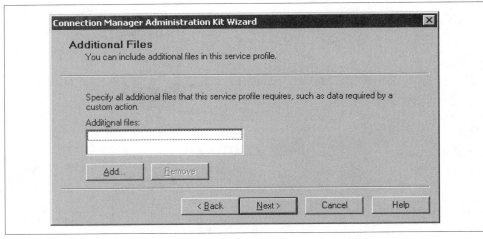

Figure 11-42. The CMAK Wizard Additional Files screen

You can transmit the executable file as an attachment to an email message, or better yet, as a link to the executable file hosted on a web server somewhere. In the email message, you can include instructions to run the file and use the new connectoids for all future remote access. You also can have the executable run as part of a logon or logoff script, but to do that, you need to either have your users log on through a dial-up connection, or wait until the mobile users return to the home network and are connected at the corporate campus to the network.

Regardless of which method you choose to initially transmit the profile installer to your users, you always should place the latest version of the profile installer on a quarantined resource somewhere, so client computers that don't pass your baselining script's compliancy checks can surf to a web site and download the latest version without compromising further the integrity of your network.

Configuring the quarantine policy

The final step in this process is to configure the actual quarantine policy within RRAS. In this section, I'll create a quarantine policy within RRAS that assumes you've posted the profile installer on a web server that is functioning as a quarantined resource.

 If RRAS is configured to use the Windows authentication provider, RRAS uses Active Directory or an NT4 domain (remember, the RRAS machine needs only to be running Windows Server 2003; it doesn't need to belong to an Active Directory-based domain) to authenticate users and look at their account properties. If RRAS is configured to use RADIUS, the RADIUS server must be a Server 2003 machine running IAS. Incidentally, IAS also uses Active Directory as an NT domain to authenticate users and look at their account properties.

1. Open the RRAS Manager.

2. In the left pane, right-click Remote Access Policies, and then select New Remote Access Policy from the context menu. Click Next through the introductory pages.

3. The Policy Configuration Method page appears. Enter **Quarantined remote access connections** as the name of this policy, as shown in Figure 11-43. Click Next when you're finished.

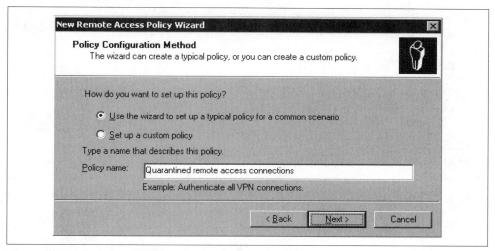

Figure 11-43. The Policy Configuration Method screen

4. The Access Method page appears next. Select VPN, and click Next.

5. On the User or Group Access page, select Group, and click Add.

6. Type in the group names that should be allowed to VPN into your network. If all domain users have this ability, enter **Everyone** or **Authenticated Users**. I'll assume this domain has a group called VPNUsers that has access to VPN capabilities. Click OK.

7. You'll be returned to the User or Group Access page, and you'll see the group name you added appear in the list box, as shown in Figure 11-44. Click Next if it looks accurate.

8. The Authentication Methods page appears. To keep this example simple, use the MS-CHAP v2 authentication protocol, which is selected by default. Click Next.

9. On the Policy Encryption Level page, make sure the Strongest Encryption setting is the only option checked. This is shown in Figure 11-45. Then, click Next.

10. Finish out the wizard by clicking Finish.

11. Back in RRAS Manager, right-click the new Quarantined VPN remote access connections policy, and select Properties from the context menu.

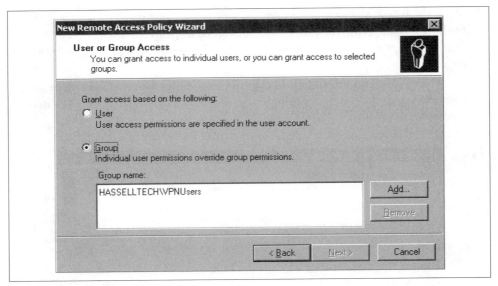

Figure 11-44. The User or Group Access screen

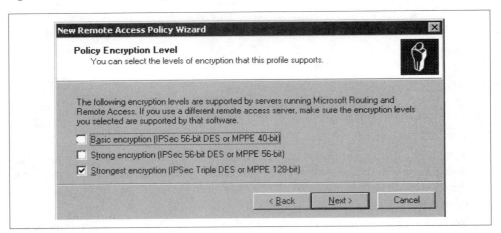

Figure 11-45. The Policy Encryption Level screen

12. Navigate to the Advanced tab, and click Add to include another attribute in the list.

13. The Add Attribute dialog box is displayed, as depicted in Figure 11-46.

14. Click MS-Quarantine-Session-Timeout, and then click Add.

15. In the Attribute Information dialog box, type the quarantine session time in the Attribute value box. Use a sample value of 60, which will be measured in seconds, for the purposes of this demonstration. Click OK, and then OK again to return to the Advanced tab.

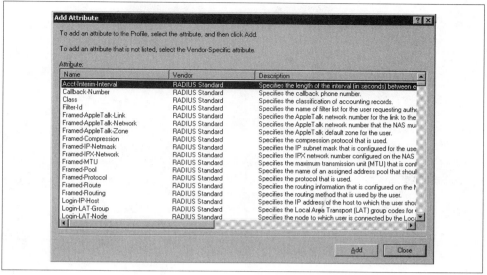

Figure 11-46. The Add Attribute dialog box

16. Click Add. In the Attribute list, click MS-Quarantine-IPFilter, and then click Add again. You'll see the IP Filter Attribute Information screen.

17. Click the Input Filters button, which displays the Inbound Filters dialog box.

18. Click New to add the first filter. The Add IP Filter dialog box is displayed. In the Protocol field, select TCP. In the Destination port field, enter **7250**. Click OK.

19. Now, back on the Inbound Filters screen, select the Permit only the packets listed below radio button. An example of the Inbound Filters screen is presented in Figure 11-47.

20. Click New and add the input filter for DHCP traffic, repeating the preceding steps and including the appropriate port number and type as described in Table 11-2. Follow the same directions to allow DNS and WINS traffic.

21. Click New and add an input filter for a quarantine resource, such as a web server, where your profile installer is located. Specify the appropriate IP address for the resource in the Destination network part of the Add IP Filter screen, as shown in Figure 11-48.

22. Finally, click OK on the Inbound Filters dialog box to save the filter list.

23. On the Edit Dial-in Profile dialog box, click OK to save the changes to the profile settings.

24. Then, to save the changes to the policy, click OK once more.

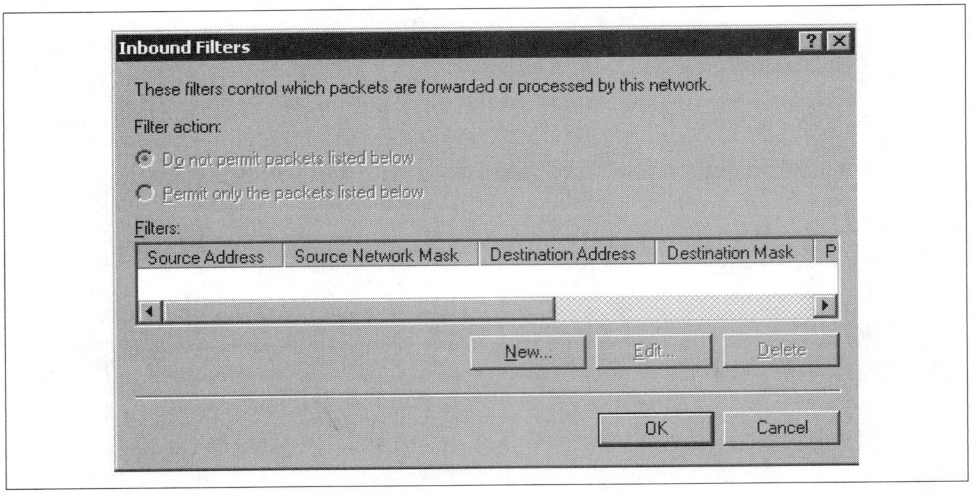

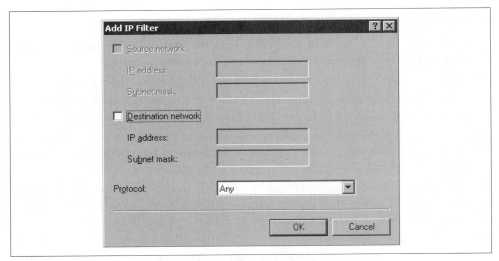

Figure 11-47. The Inbound Filters screen

Figure 11-48. The Add IP Filter box, adding a quarantined web resource

Creating exceptions to the rule

Although it is certainly advantageous to have all users connected through a quarantined session until their configurations can be verified, your organization might have logistical or political problems that force you to create exceptions to this requirement. If so, the simplest way to excuse a user or group of users from participating in the quarantine is to create an exception security group with Active Directory. The members of this group should be the ones that need not participate in the quarantining procedure.

Using that group, create another policy that applies to the exceptions group that's configured with the same settings as the quarantine remote access policy you created earlier in the chapter. This time, though, don't add or configure either the MS-Quarantine-IPFilter or the MS-Quarantine-Session-Timeout attributes. Once the policy has been created, move the policy that applies to the exceptions group so that it is evaluated before the policy that quarantines everyone else.

The Last Word

In this chapter, you've looked at a variety of different networking systems and techniques. DHCP combines with DNS to provide an automatic and self-managing way to provide IP services to your network. VPNs allow your remote users to use their client machines as if they were directly connected to a remote network, and IPSec offers a way to compensate for the lack of security built directly into the IP protocol. And finally, NAQC is a great way to assess the integrity and quality of remote client machines before they have a chance to potentially infect your network with malicious software.

In the next chapter, you'll see how you can scale your network services using software to provide load balancing and fault tolerance.

CHAPTER 12

Clustering Technologies

Clusters work to provide fault tolerance to a group of systems so that the services they provide are always available—or are at least unavailable for the least possible amount of time. Clusters also provide a single public-facing presence for a set of systems, which means end users and others who take advantage of the resources cluster members provide aren't aware that the cluster comprises more than one machine. They see only a single, unified presence on the network. The dirty work of spreading the load among multiple machines is done behind the scenes by clustering software.

Microsoft provides two distinct types of clustering with Windows Server 2003:

Network load-balancing (NLB) clusters
> These types of clusters allow for the high availability of services that rely on the TCP/IP protocol. You can have up to 32 machines running any edition of Windows Server 2003 and Windows 2000 Server (with one minor exception, covered later in this chapter) participating in an NLB cluster.

True server clusters
> Server clusters are the "premium" variety of highly available machines and consist of servers that can share workloads and processes across all members of the cluster (with some exceptions, as you'll see later in this chapter). Failed members of the cluster are automatically detected and the work being performed on them is moved to other, functional members of the cluster. True server clusters are supported in only the Enterprise and Datacenter editions of Windows Server 2003.

Where might each type of clusters be useful? For one, NLB is a very inexpensive way to achieve TCP/IP high availability for servers that run web services or other intranet or Internet applications. In effect, NLB acts as a balancer, distributing the load equally among multiple machines running their own, independent, isolated copies of IIS. NLB only protects against a server going offline, in that if a copy of IIS on a machine fails, the load will be redistributed among the other servers in the NLB cluster. Dynamic web pages that maintain sessions don't receive much benefit from this type of clustering because members of the cluster are running independent, unconnected versions of IIS and therefore cannot continue sessions created on other machines. However, much web content is static, and some implementations of dynamic web sites do not use sessions. Thus, chances are that NLB can improve the reliability of a site in production. Other services that can take advantage of NLB are IP-based applications such as FTP and VPN.

If you have business-critical applications that must be available at all times, true server clustering is a better fit for that type of use. In true server clusters, all members of the cluster are aware of all the other members' shared resources. The members also maintain a "heartbeat" pulse to monitor the availability of services on their fellow members' machines. In the event of a resource or machine failure, the Windows Server 2003 clustering service can automatically hand off jobs, processes, and sessions begun on one machine to another machine. That isn't to say this swapping is completely transparent. When the application is moved or fails to another member in the cluster, client sessions are actually broken and reestablished on the new owner of the resources. Although this happens relatively quickly, depending on the nature of your application it probably will not go unnoticed by your users. Often, your clients could be asked to reauthenticate to the new cluster owner. However, the cluster effectively acts as one unit and is completely fault-tolerant, and if you design the structure of your cluster correctly, you can avoid any one single point of failure. This decreases the chance that a single failed hardware or software component will bring your entire business-critical application to its knees.

In this chapter, I'll deal with each type of clustering individually, introducing concepts and showing you how to accomplish the most common administrative tasks.

Network Load-Balancing Clusters

NLB in Windows Server 2003 is accomplished by a special network driver that works between the drivers for the physical network adapter and the TCP/IP stack. This driver communicates with the NLB program (called *wlbs.exe*, for the Windows Load Balancing Service) running at the application layer—the same layer in the OSI model as the application you are clustering. NLB can work over FDDI- or Ethernet-based networks—even wireless networks—at up to gigabit speeds.

Why would you choose NLB? For a few reasons:

- NLB is an inexpensive way to make a TCP/IP-dependent application somewhat fault tolerant, without the expense of maintaining a true server cluster with fault-tolerant components. No special hardware is required to create an NLB cluster. It's also cheap hardware-wise because you need only two network adapters to mitigate a single point of failure.

- The "shared nothing" approach—meaning each server owns its own resources and doesn't share them with the cluster for management purposes, so to speak—

is easier to administer and less expensive to implement, although there is always some data lag between servers while information is transferred among the members. (This approach also has its drawbacks, however, because NLB can only direct clients to back-end servers or to independently replicated data.)

- Fault tolerance is provided at the network layer, ensuring that network connections are not directed to a server that is down
- Performance is improved for your web or FTP resource because load is distributed automatically among all members of the NLB cluster

NLB works in a seemingly simple way: all computers in an NLB cluster have their own IP address just like all networked machines do these days, but they also share a single, cluster-aware IP address that allows each member to answer requests on that IP address. NLB takes care of the IP address conflict problem and allows clients who connect to that shared IP address to be directed automatically to one of the cluster members.

NLB clusters support a maximum of 32 cluster members, meaning that no more than 32 machines can participate in the load-balancing and sharing features. Most applications that have a load over and above what a single 32-member cluster can handle take advantage of multiple clusters and use some sort of DNS load-balancing technique or device to distribute requests to the multiple clusters individually.

When considering an NLB cluster for your application, ask yourself the following questions: how will failure affect application and other cluster members? If you are a running a high-volume e-commerce site and one member of your cluster fails, are the other servers in the cluster adequately equipped to handle the extra traffic from the failed server? A lot of cluster implementations miss this important concept and later see the consequence—a cascading failure caused by perpetually growing load failed over onto servers perpetually failing from overload. Such a scenario is entirely likely and also entirely defeats the true purpose of a cluster. Avoid this by ensuring that all cluster members have sufficient hardware specifications to handle additional traffic when necessary.

Also examine the kind of application you are planning on clustering. What types of resources does it use extensively? Different types of applications stretch different components of the systems participating in a cluster. Most enterprise applications have some sort of performance testing utility; take advantage of any that your application offers in a testing lab and determine where potential bottlenecks might lie.

Web applications, Terminal Services, and Microsoft's new ISA Server 2004 product can take advantage of NLB clustering.

 It's important to be aware that NLB is unable to detect if a service on the server has crashed but not the machine itself, so it could direct a user to a system that can't offer the requested service.

NLB Terminology

Before we dig in deeper in our coverage of NLB, let's discuss a few terms that you will see. Some of the most common NLB technical terms are:

NLB driver
> This driver resides in memory on all members of a cluster and is instrumental in choosing which cluster node will accept and process the packet. Coupled with port rules and client affinity (all defined on the following pages), the driver decides whether to send the packet up the TCP/IP stack to the application on the current machine, or to pass on the packet because another server in the cluster will handle it.

Unicast mode
> In unicast mode, NLB hosts send packets to a single recipient.

Multicast mode
> In multicast mode, NLB hosts send packets to multiple recipients at the same time.

Port rules
> Port rules define the applications on which NLB will "work its magic," so to speak. Certain applications listen for packets sent to them on specific port numbers—for example, web servers usually listen for packets addressed to TCP port 80. You use port rules to instruct NLB to answer requests and load-balance them.

Affinity
> Affinity is a setting which controls whether traffic that originated from a certain cluster member should be returned to that particular cluster node. Effectively, this controls which cluster nodes will accept what types of traffic.

NLB Operation Styles and Modes

An NLB cluster can operate in four different ways:

- With a single network card in each server, using unicast mode
- With multiple network cards in each server, using unicast mode
- With a single network card in each server, using multicast mode
- With multiple network cards in each server, using multicast mode

You cannot mix unicast and multicast modes among the members of your cluster. All members must be running either unicast or multicast mode, although the number of cards in each member can differ.

The following sections detail each mode of operation.

Single card in each server in unicast mode

A single network card in each server operating in unicast mode requires less hardware, so obviously it's less expensive than maintaining multiple NICs in each cluster member. However, network performance is reduced because of the overhead of using the NLB driver over only one network card—cluster traffic still has to pass through one adapter, which can be easily saturated, and is additionally run through the NLB driver for load balancing. This can create real hang-ups in network performance.

An additional drawback is that cluster hosts can't communicate with each other through the usual methods, such as pinging—it's not supported using just a single adapter in unicast mode. This has to do with MAC address problems and the Address Resolution Protocol (ARP) protocol. Similarly, NetBIOS isn't supported in this mode either.

This configuration is shown in Figure 12-1.

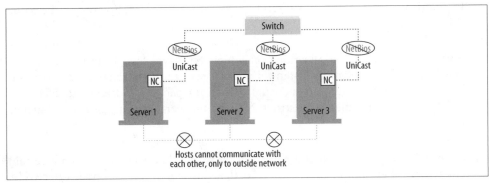

Figure 12-1. Single card in each server in unicast mode

Multiple cards in each server in unicast mode

This is usually the preferred configuration for NLB clusters because it enables the most functionality for the price in equipment. However, it is inherently more expensive because of the second network adapter in each cluster member. Having that second adapter, though, means there are no limitations among regular communications between members of the NLB cluster. Additionally, NetBIOS is supported through the first configured network adapter for simpler name resolution. All kinds and types and brands of routers support this method, and having more than one adapter in a machine removes bottlenecks found with only one adapter.

This configuration is shown in Figure 12-2.

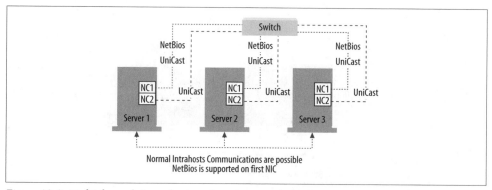

Figure 12-2. Multiple cards in each server in unicast mode

Single card in each server in multicast mode

Using a single card in multicast mode allows members of the cluster to communicate with each other normally, but network performance is still reduced because you still are using only a single network card. Router support might be spotty because of the need to support multicast MAC addresses, and NetBIOS isn't supported within the cluster.

This configuration is shown in Figure 12-3.

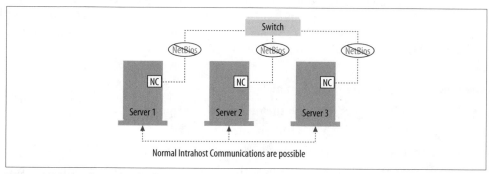

Figure 12-3. Single card in each server in multicast mode

Multiple cards in each server in multicast mode

This mode is used when some hosts have one network card and others have more than one, and all require regular communications among themselves. In this case, all hosts need to be in multicast mode because all hosts in an NLB cluster must be running the same mode. You might run into problems with router support using this model, but with careful planning you can make it work.

This configuration is shown in Figure 12-4.

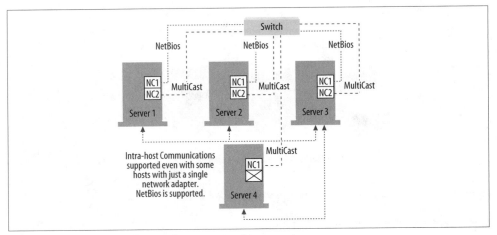

Figure 12-4. Multiple cards in each server in multicast mode

Port Rules

NLB clusters feature the ability to set port rules, which simply are ways to instruct Windows Server 2003 to handle each TCP/IP port's cluster network traffic. It does this filtering in three modes: disabled, where all network traffic for the associated port or ports will be blocked; single host mode, where network traffic from an associated port or ports should be handled by one specific machine in the cluster (still with fault tolerance features enabled); and multiple hosts mode (the default mode), where multiple hosts in the cluster can handle port traffic for a specific port or range of ports.

The rules contain the following parameters:

- The virtual IP address to which the rule should be applied
- The port range for which this rule should be applied
- The protocols for which this rule should apply, including TCP, UDP, or both
- The filtering mode that specifies how the cluster handles traffic described by the port range and protocols, as described just before this list

In addition, you can select one of three options for client affinity (which is, simply put, the types of clients from which the cluster will accept traffic): None, Single, and Class C. Single and Class C are used to ensure that all network traffic from a particular client is directed to the same cluster host. None indicates there is no client affinity, and traffic can go to any cluster host.

When using port rules in an NLB cluster, it's important to remember that the number and content of port rules must match exactly on all members of the cluster. When joining a node to an NLB cluster, if the number or content of port rules on the joining node doesn't match the number or content of rules on the existing member nodes, the joining member will be denied membership to the cluster. You need to synchronize these port rules manually across all members of the NLB cluster.

Creating an NLB Cluster

To create a new NLB cluster, use the Network Load Balancing Manager and follow the instructions shown next.

1. From the Administrative Tools folder, open the Network Load Balancing Manager. The main screen is shown in Figure 12-5.

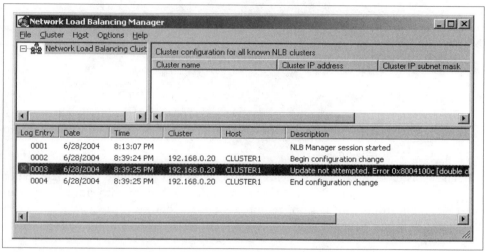

Figure 12-5. The Network Load Balancing Manager console

2. From the Cluster menu, select New.
3. The Cluster Parameters screen appears, as shown in Figure 12-6. Here, you specify the name of the cluster and the IP address information by which other computers will address the cluster. Enter the IP address, subnet mask, and full Internet name (i.e., the canonical DNS name). Also choose unicast or multicast mode, as discussed in the previous section. Click Next to continue.

 Enabling remote control of your cluster—meaning being able to load the NLB Manager client on other systems and connect remotely to the cluster—is not recommended because it is a large security risk. Avoid this unless absolutely necessary, and use other tools such as Terminal Services or Remote Desktop.

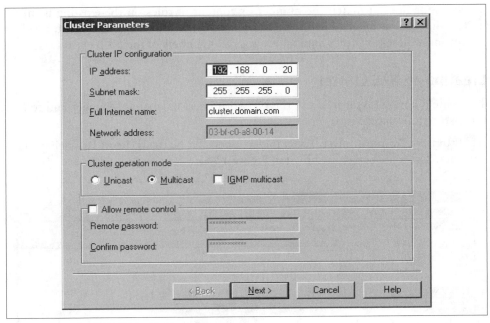

Figure 12-6. The Cluster Parameters screen

4. The Cluster IP Addresses screen appears, as shown in Figure 12-7. Here, enter any additional IP addresses the cluster might need. You might want this for specific applications, but it's not required for a standard setup. Click Next when you've finished, or if there are no other IP addresses by which this cluster will be known.

5. The Port Rules screen appears, as shown in Figure 12-8. Enter and configure any port rules you'd like, as discussed in the previous section, and then click Next when you're done.

6. The Connect screen appears, as shown in Figure 12-9. Here, enter the IP address or DNS name of the host that will be added to the cluster first. Then click Connect. The list in the white box at the bottom of the screen will be populated with the network interfaces available for creating a cluster. Click the public interface, and click Next.

7. The Host Parameters screen appears, as seen in Figure 12-10. On this screen, enter the priority for the host of the cluster, the dedicated IP that you'll use to connect to this specific member node, and the initial state of this host when you first boot up Windows Server 2003. Click Finish to complete the process.

The NLB cluster is created, and the first node is configured and added to the cluster.

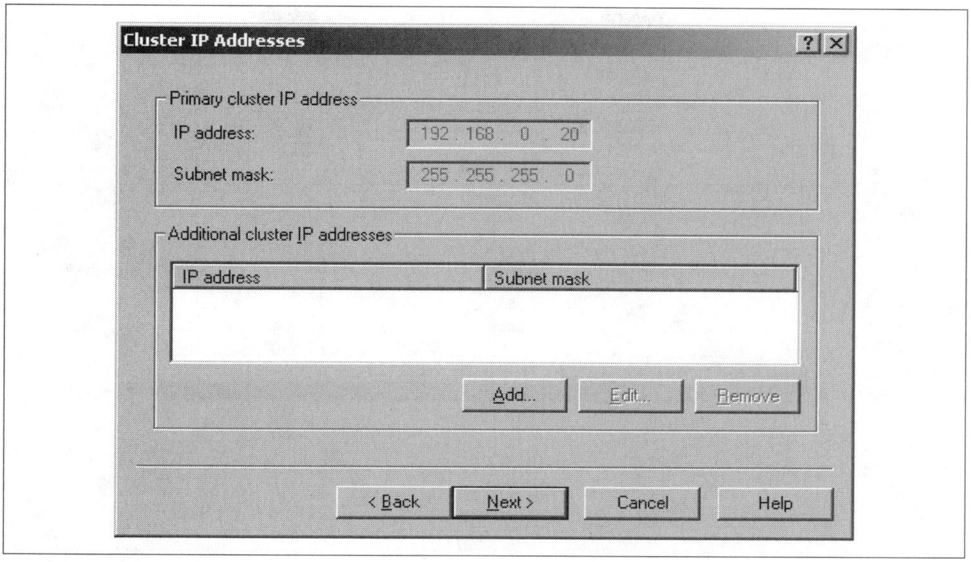

Figure 12-7. The Cluster IP Addresses screen

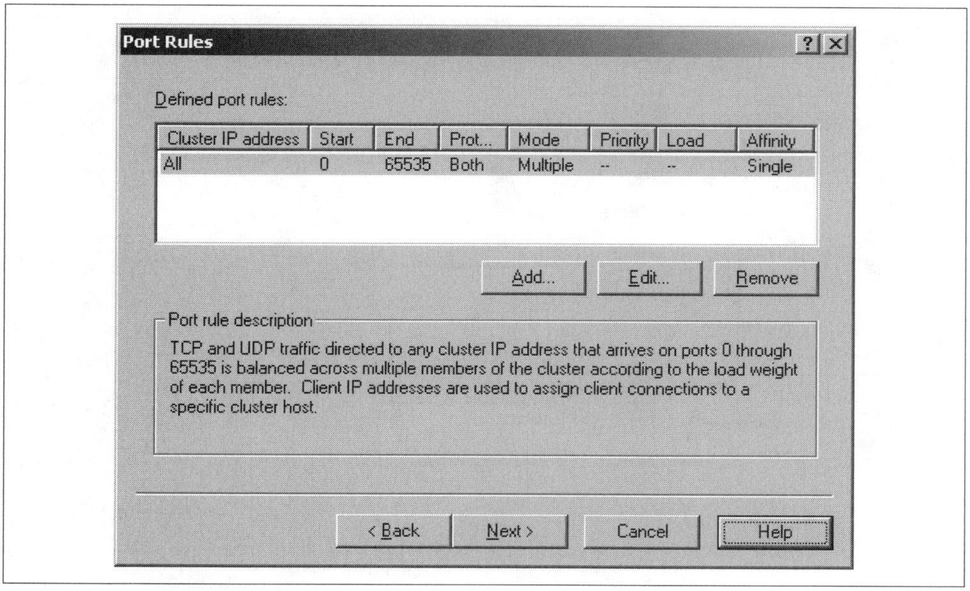

Figure 12-8. The Port Rules screen

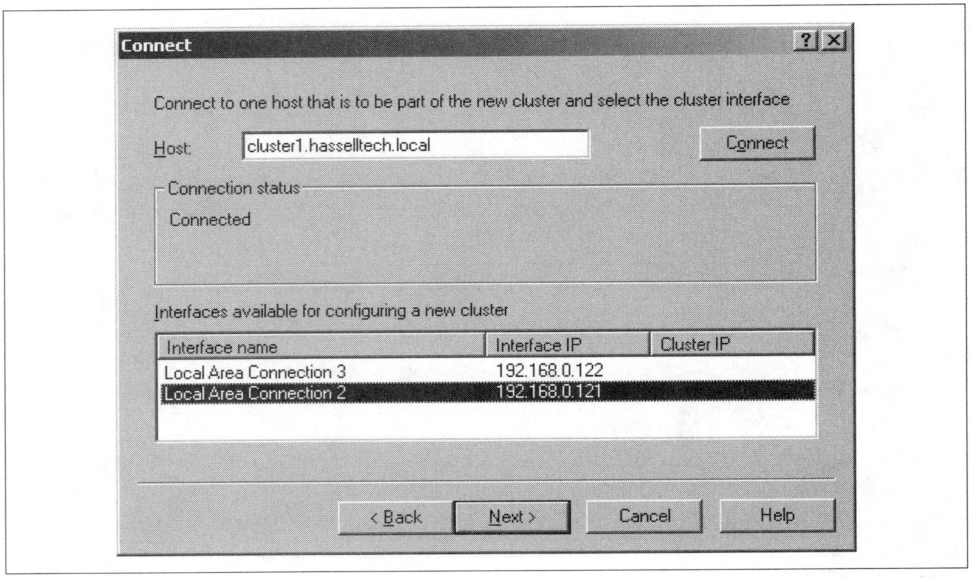

Figure 12-9. The Connect screen

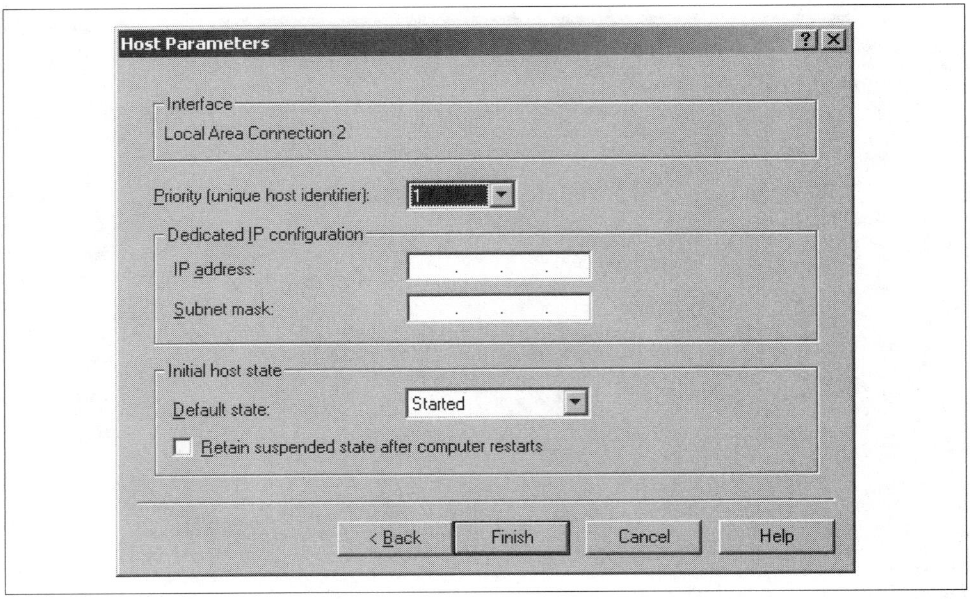

Figure 12-10. The Host Parameters screen

Adding Other Nodes to the Cluster

Chances are good that you want to add another machine to the cluster to take advantage of load balancing. To add a new node to an existing cluster, use the following procedure:

1. From the Administrative Tools menu, open the Network Load Balancing Manager console.

2. In the left pane, right-click the cluster to which you'd like to add a node, and then select Add Host to Cluster from the pop-up context menu.

3. The Connect screen appears. Type in the DNS name or the IP address of the host to join to the cluster. Click the Connect button to populate the list of network interfaces on that host, and then select the card that will host public traffic and click Next.

4. The Host Parameters screen appears. Enter the appropriate priority of the host (a setting which allows you to specify which machine should get the largest number of requests—useful if you have two machines in a cluster and one is more powerful than the other), the dedicated IP address of this member of the cluster, and the initial state of the potential member node when Windows Server 2003 first boots. You can set the initial state to Started, Stopped, or Suspended.

5. Click Finish to complete the procedure.

The node is then added to the selected NLB cluster. You can tell the process is finished when the node's status, as indicated within the Network Load Balancing Manager console, says "Converged."

Removing Nodes from the Cluster

For various reasons, you might need to remove a joined node from the cluster—to perform system maintenance, for example, or to replace the node with a newer, fresher, more powerful machine. You must remove an NLB cluster member gracefully. To do so, follow these steps:

1. From the Administrative Tools menu, open the Network Load Balancing Manager console.

2. Right-click Network Load Balancing Clusters in the left pane, and from the pop-up context menu, select Connect to Existing.

3. Enter the host to connect to, and then click Connect. Then, at the bottom of the Connect screen, select the cluster on the host, and click Next.

4. Finally, back in the console, right-click the node you want to remove in the left pane, and select Delete Host from the pop-up context menu.

This removes the node.

If you are only upgrading a node of the cluster and don't want to permanently remove a node from a cluster, you can use a couple of techniques to gradually reduce traffic to the host and then make it available for upgrading. The first is to perform a *drainstop* on the cluster host to be upgraded. Drainstopping prevents new clients from accessing the cluster while allowing existing clients to continue until they have completed their current operations. After all current clients have finished their operations, cluster operations on that node cease.

To perform a drainstop, follow these steps:

1. Open a command-line window.
2. From the command line, type **wlbs drainstop <*IP Address*>:<*hostID*>**, replacing the variable with the cluster IP address and the HostID with the unique number set in the Host Parameters tab in NLB properties.

For example, if my cluster was located at 192.168.0.14 and I wanted to upgrade node 2, I would enter the following command:

```
Wlbs drainstop 192.168.0.14:2
```

In addition, you can configure the Default state of the Initial host state to Stopped as you learned in the previous section. This way, that particular node cannot rejoin the cluster during the upgrade process. Then you can verify your upgrade was completed smoothly before the cluster is rejoined and clients begin accessing it.

Performance Optimization

NLB clusters often have problems with switches. Switches differ from hubs in that data transmission among client computers connected to a hub is point-to-point: the switch keeps a cache of the MAC address of all machines and sends traffic directly to its endpoint, whereas hubs simply broadcast all data to all connected machines and those machines must pick up their own data. However, switches work against NLB clusters because every packet of data sent to the cluster passes through all the ports on the switch to which members of the cluster are attached because all cluster members share the same IP address, as you've already learned. Obviously, this can be a problem.

To avert this problem, you can choose from a few workarounds:

- Use a premium hub to connect the NICs of all cluster members, and then use the uplink feature on the hub to link the hub to the switch.
- Enable unicast mode as opposed to multicast mode. Remember, you need to make this change on all members of the cluster.

- If possible, have all hosts on the same subnet, and then connect them to an isolated switch or configure them to connect in a single VLAN if you have that capability.
- Disable the source MAC masking feature in the Registry. The source MAC masking feature is used to change the MAC address of traffic originating from the cluster from the individual cluster node's MAC address to the MAC address of the server. In multicast mode in switching environments, this can flood switching ports, so disabling this feature will work around that problem. Change the Registry value of:

> *HKEY_LOCAL_MACHINE\System\CurrentControlSet\Services\WLBS\ Parameters\MaskSourceMAC*

from 1 to 0. Restart all mllembers of the cluster after making this change.

Server Clustering

If an NLB cluster is too limited in functionality for you, you should investigate a true server cluster. In a true server cluster, a group of machines have a single identity and work in tandem to manage and, in the event of failure, migrate applications away from problematic nodes and onto functional nodes. The nodes of the cluster use a common, shared resource database and log storage facility provided by a physical storage device that is located on a hardware bus shared by all members of the cluster.

The shared data facility does not support IDE disks, software RAID (including Windows-based dynamic RAID), dynamic disks or volumes, the EFS, mounted volumes and reparse points, or remote storage devices such as tape backup drives.

Three types of clusters are supported by Windows Server 2003 in the Enterprise and Datacenter editions of the product: single node clusters, which are useful in test and laboratory environments to see if applications and resources function in the manner intended but do not have any sort of fault-tolerant functionality; single quorum device clusters, which are the most common and most functional type of cluster used in production because of their multiple nodes; and majority node set clusters, which function as a cluster but without a shared physical storage device, something required of the other two types. Majority node set clusters are useful if you do not have a SCSI-based SAN or if the members of a cluster are spread out over several different sites, making a shared storage bus unfeasible. The Enterprise Edition supports up to four cluster nodes; the Datacenter Edition supports up to eight.

Clusters manage failure using failover and failback policies (that is, unless you are using a single node cluster). Failover policies dictate the behavior of cluster resources when a failure occurs—which nodes the failed resources can migrate to, the timing of a failover after the failure, and other properties. A failback policy specifies what will happen when the failed node comes back online again. How quickly should the migrated resources and applications be returned to the original node? Should the migrated objects stay at their new home? Should the repaired node be ignored? You can specify all of this behavior through policies.

Cluster Terminology

A few specific terms have special meanings when used in the context of clustering. They include the following:

Networks
> Networks, also called interconnects, are the ways in which clusters communicate with other members (nodes) of the cluster and the public network. The network is the most common point of failure in cluster nodes; always make network cards redundant in a true server cluster.

Nodes
> Nodes are the actual members of the cluster. The clustering service supports only member nodes running Windows Server 2003 Enterprise Edition or Datacenter Edition. Other requirements include the TCP/IP protocol, connection to a shared storage device, and at least one interconnect to other nodes.

Resources
> Resources are simply anything that can be managed by the cluster service and that the cluster can use to provide a service to clients. Resources can be logical or physical and can represent real devices, network services, or file system objects. A special type of physical disk resource called the *quorum disk* provides a place for the cluster service to store recovery logs and its own database. I'll provide a list of some resources in the next section.

Groups
> Resources can be collected into resource groups, which are simply units by which failover and failback policy can be specified. A group's resources all fail over and fail back according to a policy applied to the group, and all the resources move to other nodes together upon a failure.

Quorum
> A quorum is the shared storage facility that keeps the cluster resource database and logs. As noted earlier in this section, this needs to be a SCSI-based real drive with no special software features.

Types of Resources

A variety of resources are supported out of the box by the clustering service in Windows Server 2003. They include the following:

DHCP
> This type of resource manages the DHCP service, which can be used in a cluster to assure availability to client computers. The DHCP database must reside on the shared cluster storage device, otherwise known as the quorum disk.

File Share
> Shares on servers can be made redundant and fault-tolerant aside from using the Dfs service (covered in Chapter 3) by using the File Share resource inside a cluster. You can put shared files and folders into a cluster as a standard file share with only one level of folder visibility, as a shared subfolder system with the root folder and all immediate subfolders shared with distinct names, or as a standalone Dfs root.

> Fault-tolerant Dfs roots cannot be placed within a cluster.

Generic Application
> Applications that are not cluster-aware (meaning they don't have their own fault tolerance features that can hook into the cluster service) can be managed within a cluster using the Generic Application resource. Applications managed in this way must be able store any data they create in a custom location, use TCP/IP to connect clients, and be able to receive clients attempting to reconnect in the event of a failure. You can install a cluster-unaware application onto the shared cluster storage device; that way, you need to install the program only once and then the entire cluster can use it.

Generic Script
> This resource type is used to manage operating system scripts. You can cluster login scripts and account provisioning scripts, for example, if you regularly use those functions and need their continued availability even in the event of a machine failure. Hotmail's account provisioning functions, for instance, are a good fit for this feature, so users can sign up for the service at all hours of the day.

Generic Service
> You can manage Windows Server 2003 core services, if you require them to be highly available, using the Generic Service resource type. Only the bundled services are supported.

IP Address

The IP Address resource manages a static, dedicated IP address assigned to a cluster.

Local Quorum

This type of resource is used to represent the disk shared by the cluster for activity logs and the cluster resource database. Local quorums do not have failover capabilities.

Majority Node Set

The Majority Node Set resource represents cluster configurations that don't reside on a quorum disk. Because there is no quorum disk, particularly in instances where the nodes of a cluster are in separate, geographically distinct sites, there needs to be a mechanism by which the cluster nodes can stay updated on the cluster configuration and the logs each node creates. Only one Majority Node Set resource can be present within each cluster as a whole. With a majority node set, you need 1/2n + 1 functioning nodes for the cluster to be online, so if you have four members of the cluster, three must be functioning.

Network Name

The Network Name resource represents the shared DNS or NetBIOS name of the cluster, an application, or a virtual server contained within the cluster.

Physical Disk

Physical Disk resources manage storage devices that are shared to all cluster members. The drive letter assigned to the physical device is the same on all cluster nodes. The Physical Disk Resource is required by default for all cluster types except the Majority Node Set.

Print Spooler

Print services can be clustered using the Print Spooler resource. This represents printers attached directly to the network, not printers attached directly to a cluster node's ports. Printers that are clustered appear normally to clients, but in the event that one node fails, print jobs on that node will be moved to another, functional node and then restarted. Clients that are sending print jobs to the queue when a failure occurs will be notified of the failure and asked to resubmit their print jobs.

Volume Shadow Copy Service Task

This resource type is used to create shadow copy jobs in the Scheduled Task folder on the node that currently owns the specified resource group hosting that resource. You can use this resource only to provide fault tolerance for the shadow copy process.

WINS

The WINS resource type is associated with the Windows Internet Naming Service, which maps NetBIOS computer names to IP addresses. To use WINS and make it a clustered service, the WINS database needs to reside on the quorum disk.

Planning a Cluster Setup

Setting up a server cluster can be tricky, but you can take a lot of the guesswork out of the process by having a clear plan of exactly what goals you are attempting to accomplish by having a cluster. Are you interested in achieving fault tolerance and load balancing at the same time? Do you not care about balancing load but want your focus to be entirely on providing five-nines service? Or would you like to provide only critical fault tolerance and thereby reduce the expense involved in creating and deploying the cluster?

If you are interested in a balance between load balancing and high availability, you allow applications and resources in the cluster to "fail over," or migrate, to other nodes in the cluster in the event of a failure. The benefit is that they continue to operate and are accessible to clients, but they also increase the load among the remaining, functioning nodes of the cluster. This load can cause cascading failures—as nodes continually fail, the load on the remaining nodes increases to the point where their hardware or software is unable to handle the load, causing those nodes to fail, and the process continues until all nodes are dead—and that eventuality really makes your fault-tolerant cluster immaterial. The moral here is that you need to examine your application, and plan each node appropriately to handle an average load plus an "emergency reserve" that can handle increased loads in the event of failure. You also should have policies and procedures to manage loads quickly when nodes fail. This setup is shown in Figure 12-11.

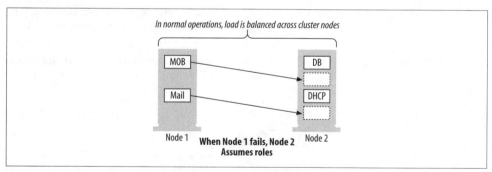

Figure 12-11. A balance between load balancing and high availability

If your be-all and end-all goal is true high availability, consider running a cluster member as a hot spare, ready to take over operations if a node fails. In this case, you would specify that if you had *n* cluster nodes, the applications and resources in the cluster should run on *n-1* nodes. Then, configure the one remaining node to be idle. In this fashion, when failures occur the applications will migrate to the idle node and continue functioning. A nice feature is that your hot spare node can change, meaning there's not necessarily a need to migrate failed-over processes to the previously failed node when it comes back up—it can remain idle as the new hot spare. This reduces your management responsibility a bit. This setup is shown in Figure 12-12.

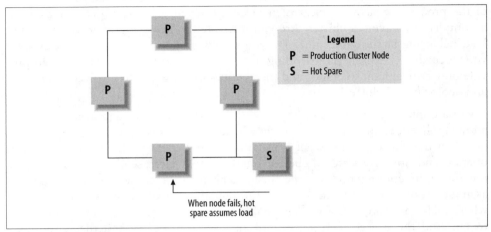

Figure 12-12. A setup with only high availability in mind

Also consider a load-shedding setup. In load shedding, you specify a certain set of resources or applications as "critical" and those are automatically failed over when one of your cluster nodes breaks. However, you also specify another set of applications and resources as "non-critical." These do not fail over. This type of setup helps prevent cascading failures when load is migrated between cluster nodes because you shed some of the processing time requirements in allowing non-critical applications and resources to simply fail. Once repairs have been made to the nonfunctional cluster node, you can bring up the non-critical applications and resources and the situation will return to normal. This setup is shown in Figure 12-13.

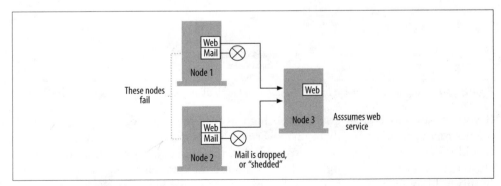

Figure 12-13. A sample load-shedding setup

Creating a True Server Cluster

With the background out of the way, it's time to create your first server cluster. Creating a new cluster involves inspecting the potential members of the cluster to ensure they meet a solid baseline configuration and then starting the cluster service on each so that resources are managed across the machines and not individually on each machine.

To create a true server cluster, follow these steps.

1. From the Administrative Tools folder, open the Cluster Administrator console.

2. The Open Connection to Cluster screen will appear automatically. From the drop-down list at the top of the box, select Create New Cluster. Click OK.

3. The New Server Cluster Wizard starts. Click Next from the introductory screen, and the Cluster Name and Domain screen appears. Enter the domain name and the name for the new cluster. Click Next to continue.

4. The Select Computer screen appears. Here, type in the name of the computer which will become the first member of the new cluster. Click Next.

5. The Analyzing Configuration screen will appear, as shown in Figure 12-14. Here, exhaustive tests will be done and the current configuration of the computer you identified in step 4 of this section will be examined for potential problems or showstoppers to its entrance into a cluster. The resulting progress bar will turn either green (indicating that no show-stopping errors were found) or red (indicating problems that must be rectified before continuing). You can examine the list in the middle of the screen for a brief explanation of any item encountered, or select the item and then click the Details button for a more thorough explanation. Correct any problems, and then click Next.

6. The IP Address page will appear. On this screen, enter the IP address that other computers will use to address the cluster as a whole. Click Next when you've entered an address.

7. The Cluster Service Account page appears. Here, specify either an existing account or a new account which will be given local administrator privileges over all machines that are members of the new cluster. Click Next when you've specified an account.

8. The Proposed Cluster Configuration screen appears next which summarizes the choices you've made in the wizard. Confirm the selections you've entered, and then click Next to build the cluster and add the first node to the new cluster.

9. Once the cluster has finished building, click Finish to end the wizard.

The new cluster is active, and the first member has been added to it. When the wizard exits, you're dumped back into the Cluster Administrator console, this time populated with management options and the new cluster node. A sample console is shown in Figure 12-15.

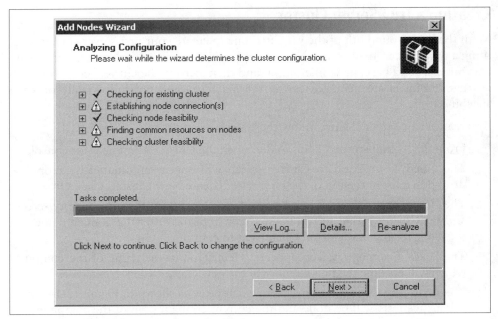

Figure 12-14. The Analyzing Configuration screen

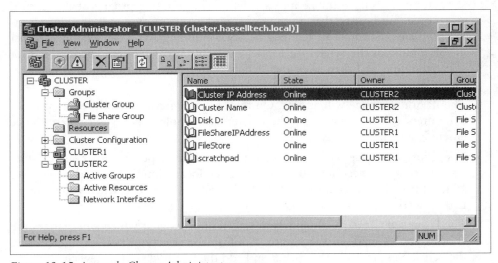

Figure 12-15. A sample Cluster Administrator screen

Adding a Node to an Existing Cluster

For a single-node cluster, you can leave your settings alone and the resulting cluster will function just fine. You can use this configuration in a testing environment, but it really provides no fault-tolerant functionality in production use. To get a more dependable, reliable solution, you need to move to single quorum device clusters and add a new node to the cluster. Then, resources and applications can fail over to other nodes in the cluster.

To add a new node to an existing cluster, follow these steps:

1. Within the Cluster Administrator console running on any current node of the cluster, connect to the cluster and then right-click the cluster name in the left pane. From the New menu, select Node.

2. The Add Nodes Wizard appears; click past the introductory screen and the Select Computers screen appears, as shown in Figure 12-16. Here, enter the names of any computers you'd like to join to the current cluster. Click Next when you're finished.

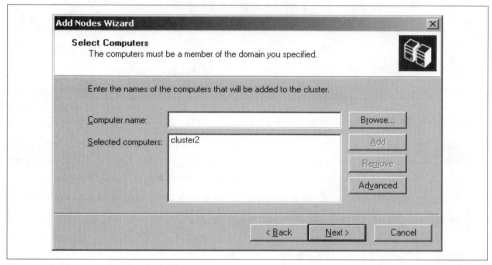

Figure 12-16. Specifying nodes to add to the cluster

3. The Analyzing Configuration screen will appear, as shown in Figure 12-17. Here, exhaustive tests will be done and the current configuration of the computer you identified in the previous step will be examined for potential problems or showstoppers to its entrance into a cluster. The resulting progress bar will turn either green (indicating no showstopping errors were found) or red (indicating problems that must be rectified before continuing). You can examine the list in the middle of the screen for a brief explanation of any item encountered, or select the item and then click the Details button for a more thorough explanation. Correct any problems, and then click Next.

4. The Cluster Service Account page appears next. Here, specify either an existing account or a new account which will be given local administrator privileges over the new member of the cluster. Click Next when you've specified an account.

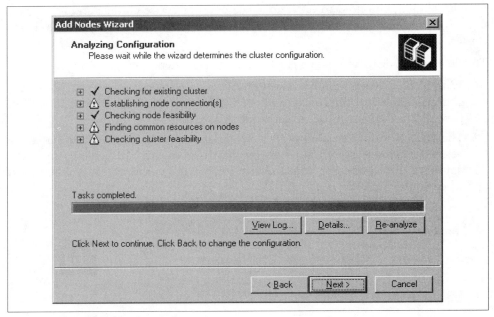

Figure 12-17. The Analyzing Configuration screen

5. The Proposed Cluster Configuration screen appears next, as shown in Figure 12-18, which summarizes the choices you've made in the wizard. Confirm the selections you've entered, and then click Next to add the node to the existing cluster.

6. Once the cluster has finished adding the new node, click Finish to end the wizard.

The machine in question is now a member of the cluster.

Creating a New Cluster Group

Recall that groups are simply containers of resources that have failover and failback policies applied to them. If you are creating a new set of resources, first create a group to store them.

To create a new group in an existing cluster, follow these steps:

1. Within the Cluster Administrator console, connect to the cluster that will host the new group.

2. In the left pane, right-click Active Groups under a node in the cluster and select Group from the New menu.

3. The New Group Wizard appears next, as shown in Figure 12-19. Enter a name and friendly description of the new cluster group, and then click Next.

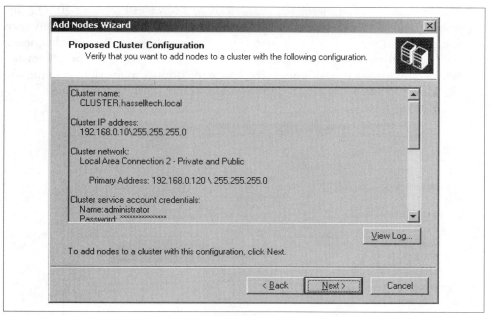

Figure 12-18. The Proposed Cluster Configuration screen

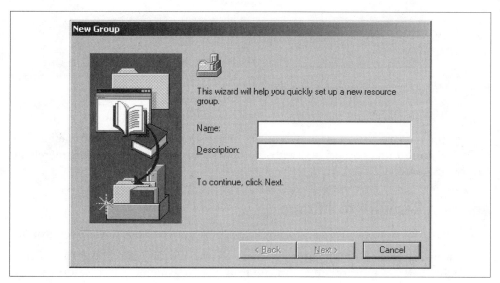

Figure 12-19. Creating a new group, phase 1

4. The Preferred Owners screen appears next, as shown in Figure 12-20. On this screen you can specify particular cluster nodes that you'd prefer to actually own the share and in what order those nodes fall in preference. The available nodes are listed on the right; use the Add and Remove buttons in the middle of the screen to adjust their positioning. To change the priority in the right column, use the Move Up and Move Down buttons. Once you're finished, click Finish.

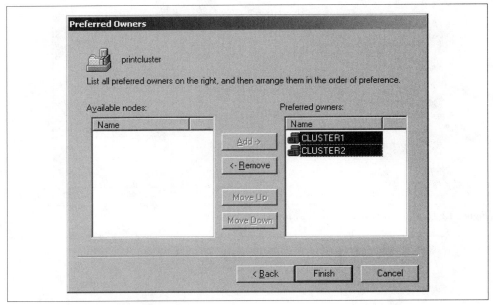

Figure 12-20. Creating a new group, phase 2

5. Click Finish to create the group.

The group is created for you. However, its initial state will be set to offline because you have no resources associated with the new group—at this point, it is merely an empty designator.

Adding a Resource to a Group

Continuing our example, let's add a physical disk resource to our new server group:

1. Within Cluster Administrator, connect to the cluster you'd like to manage. Right-click the appropriate group and from the New menu, select Resource.

2. The New Resource Wizard appears next, as shown in Figure 12-21. Enter a name and friendly description for the new resource. Then, from the Resource type drop-down box, select Physical Disk. Make sure the selection in the Group box matches the appropriate resource group you created in the previous section. Click Next to continue.

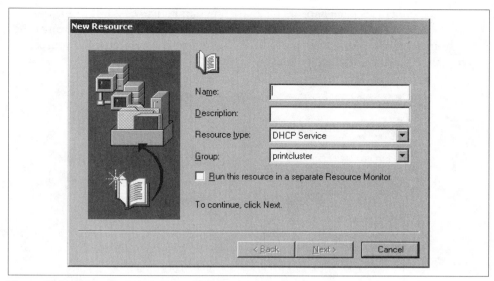

Figure 12-21. Creating a new resource, phase 1

3. The Possible Owners screen appears next, as shown in Figure 12-22. Here, specify the nodes of the cluster on which this resource can be brought online. Use the Add and Remove buttons to trade positions in the left and right columns on the screen. Click Next when you're finished.

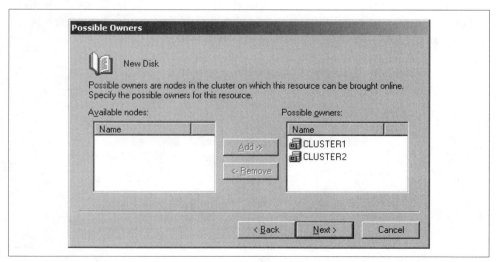

Figure 12-22. Creating a new resource, phase 2

4. The Dependencies page appears next, as shown in Figure 12-23. If this is the first resource in a group, leaving this screen blank is fine; otherwise, specify any other resources in the group that must be brought up first before this resource can function. Click Next when you've finished.

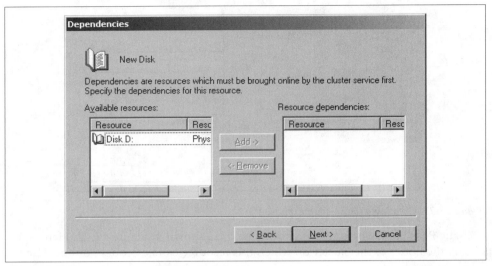

Figure 12-23. Creating a new resource, phase 3

5. The Disk Parameters page appears next, as shown in Figure 12-24. The drop-down list on this page shows all the disks available for use by the cluster. Select the appropriate physical disk, and then click Finish.

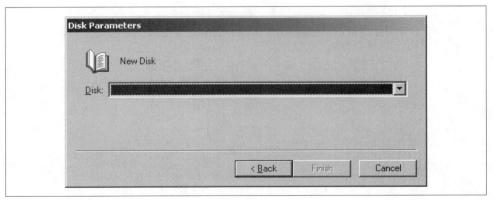

Figure 12-24. Creating a new resource, phase 4

The new physical disk resource is created.

Using the Cluster Application Wizard

You can use the Cluster Application Wizard to prepare your cluster for introducing an application. Part of the wizard's job is to create a virtual server for the application: essentially, virtual servers are simple ways to address a combination of resources for easy management. Virtual servers consist of a distinct resource group, a non-DHCP IP address, and a network name, as well as any other resources required by whatever application you want to cluster.

Once the virtual server has been created, you configure the path and directory of the application you want to cluster and then set advanced properties and failover/failback policies for the entire virtual server, automating the failure recovery process.

Let's step through the Cluster Application Wizard and configure our own fault-tolerant application, Notepad:

1. From within the Cluster Administrator console, select Configure Application from the File menu. The Cluster Application Wizard will appear. Click Next off of the introductory screen.

2. The Select or Create a Virtual Server page appears next, as shown in Figure 12-25. You can choose to create a new virtual server or select an existing one from the drop-down list box. Click Next to continue.

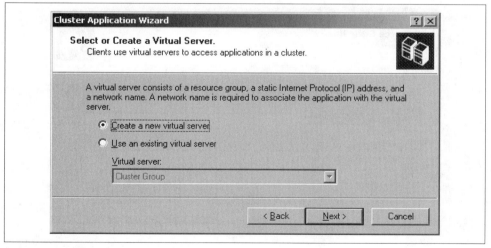

Figure 12-25. The Select or Create a Virtual Server screen

3. The Resource Group for the Virtual Server screen appears next, as shown in Figure 12-26. Identify the resource group by either creating a new one or selecting an existing one that will handle the resources needed by your application. In this example, we'll continue to use an existing one—if you elect to create a new one, the process is much like that described in the previous section. Click Next to continue.

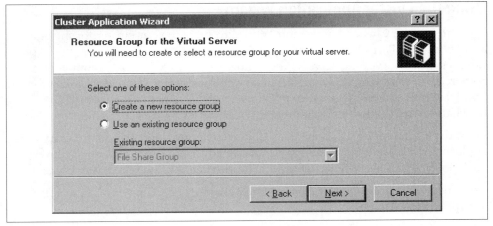

Figure 12-26. The Resource Group for the Virtual Server screen

4. The Resource Group Name screen appears next, as shown in Figure 12-27. This gives you an opportunity to verify the resource group selection you made on the previous screen. Confirm the information, make any necessary changes, and then click Next to continue.

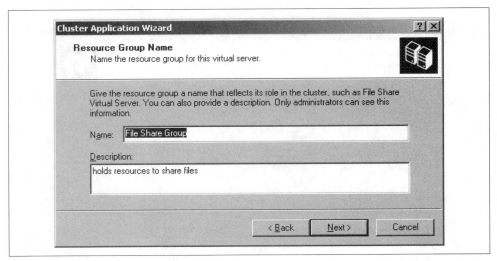

Figure 12-27. The Resource Group Name screen

5. The Virtual Server Access Information screen appears next, as shown in Figure 12-28. Here you specify a dedicated, static IP address for communicating with the new virtual server. Enter the name and IP address you like, and then click Next.

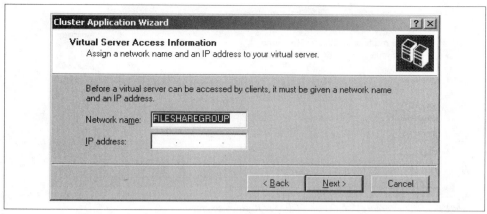

Figure 12-28. The Virtual Server Access Information screen

6. The Advanced Properties for the New Virtual Server screen appears next, as shown in Figure 12-29. On this screen, you can choose any element of the virtual server you've just created and modify its advanced properties. Select the item, and then click the Advanced Properties button to modify the properties. Otherwise, click Next to continue.

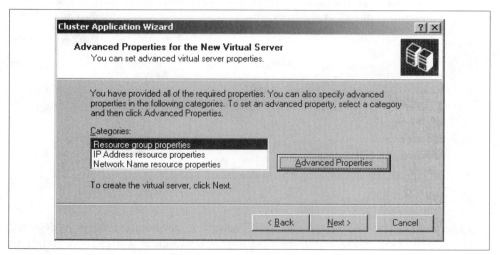

Figure 12-29. The Advanced Properties for the New Virtual Server screen

7. The Create Application Cluster Resource screen appears next, as shown in Figure 12-30. Windows needs to create a cluster resource to manage the fault tolerance of the resources contained in your new virtual server. Go ahead and allow Windows to create a cluster resource now by clicking the first option and then clicking Next.

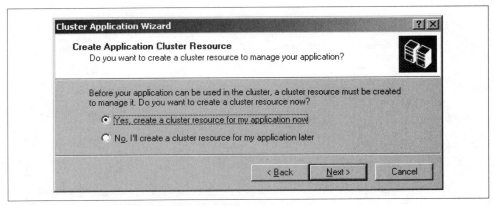

Figure 12-30. The Create Application Cluster Resource screen

8. The Application Resource Type screen appears next, as shown in Figure 12-31. Specify the resource type for your new application, as described earlier in this chapter, and then click Next. For this example, I'll just configure a Generic Application type resource.

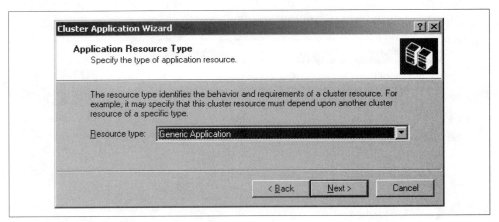

Figure 12-31. The Application Resource Type screen

9. The Application Resource Name and Description page appears next, as depicted in Figure 12-32. Here, name the new resource and enter a friendly description, which is used only for administrative purposes. Click the Advanced Properties button to configure policies on application restart, dependencies on resources, and possible owners of the application. Click Next when you've finished.

10. The Generic Application Parameters screen appears next, as shown in Figure 12-33. Enter the command that executes the application and the path in which the application resides. Choose whether the application can be seen at the cluster console using the Allow application to interact with desktop screen, and then click Next.

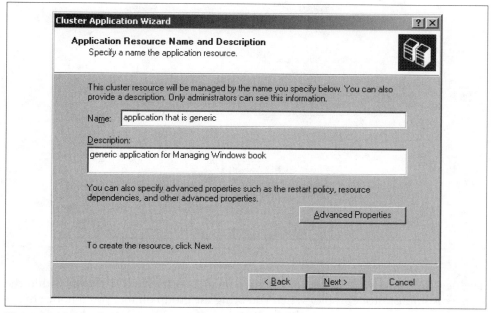

Figure 12-32. The Application Resource Name and Description screen

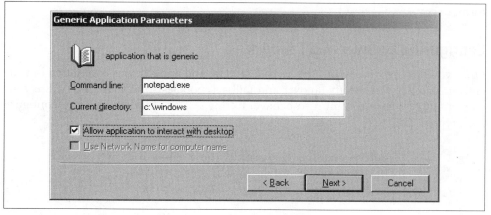

Figure 12-33. The Generic Application Parameters screen

11. The Registry Replication screen appears next, as shown in Figure 12-34. Enter any registry keys that are required by the application. These will be moved to the applicable active node automatically by the Cluster Service in Windows. Click Next when you've finished.

12. The Completing the Cluster Application Wizard appears next. Confirm your choices on this screen, and then click Finish.

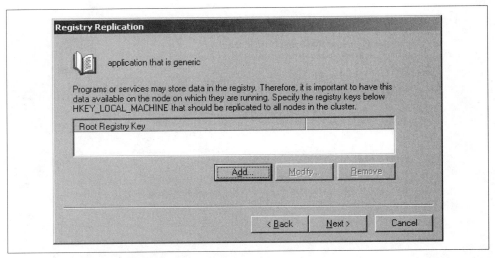

Figure 12-34. The Registry Replication screen

The new virtual server and cluster resource then is created and is shown within the Cluster Administrator console. When you bring the group online, you'll notice that a Notepad window is opened in the background. If you close Notepad, it will automatically relaunch itself. This is the power of the cluster, demonstrated in a simple form, of course.

Configuring Failover and Failback

Once you have resources, groups, virtual servers, and applications configured in your cluster, you need to specify failover and failback policies so that upon a failure your cluster behaves as you want it to behave. In this section, I'll detail how to configure each type of policy.

 Failover is configured automatically on a cluster with two or more nodes. Failback is not.

Failover

You can configure a failover policy by right-clicking any group within the Cluster Administrator console and selecting Properties from the pop-up context menu. Once the properties sheet appears, navigate to the Failover tab. A sample Failover tab for a group is shown in Figure 12-35.

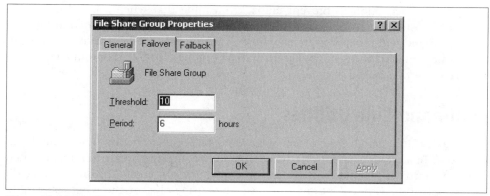

Figure 12-35. Configuring a failover policy

On this tab, specify the threshold, which is the maximum number of times this particular group is allowed to fail over during a specific timeframe, as specified by the period option. If there are more failovers than specified in the threshold value, the group enters a failed state and the clustering service won't attempt to bring it back to life.

Click OK when you've entered an appropriate value.

Failback

You also can configure a failback policy by right-clicking any group within the Cluster Administrator console and selecting Properties from the menu. Navigate to the Failback tab, a sample of which is shown in Figure 12-36.

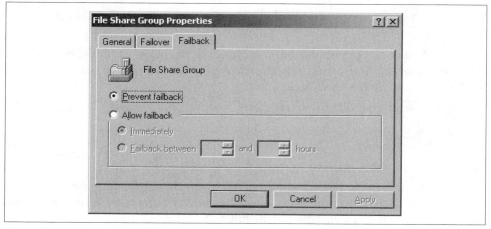

Figure 12-36. Configuring a failback policy

You can set the option to prevent failback, meaning that when a failed node that originally hosted the group returns to normal functionality, the migrated group will not return and will remain on its new host. If you decide to allow failback, you can choose how quickly the group will return to its original host—either immediately, or between a certain period of time.

Command-Line Utilities

The cluster utility enables you to manage almost all of the functions and administrative needs of a server cluster from the command line, making it easy to integrate such functions into scripts and dynamic web pages you might create. In this section, I'll take a look at the various options you have when using cluster and what you can do with the utility.

A couple of notes before I begin: When using cluster, the locale settings for the user account under which you're logged in must match the system default locale on the computer used to manage the cluster. It's best to match the locales on all cluster nodes and all computers from which you will use the command-line utility. Also, when you remotely manage a cluster using Cluster Administrator or *cluster.exe*, make sure that NetBIOS over TCP/IP (NetBT) is enabled on the client. See Chapter 11 for information on how to enable that setting.

With that out of the way, let's take a look at using the utility. You can create new clusters from the command line; for example, to create a new cluster called "testcluster" at the IP address 192.168.1.140 with the administrator account, use the following:

```
Cluster testcluster /create ipaddress:192.168.1.140 /pass:Password /user:HASSELLTECH\
admnistratior /verbose
```

The /verbose option outputs detailed information to the screen about the process of creating the cluster.

You can add a node or multiple nodes, as shown in the below example, by using the /add switch. In the next command, I'm adding three nodes, called test1, test2, and test3 respectively, to the testcluster cluster:

```
Cluster testcluster /add:test1,test2,test3 /pass:Password /verbose
```

You might also wish to change the quorum resource via the command line. You can do so as shown below:

```
Cluster testcluster /quorum:disk2 /path:D:\
```

One thing to note in the preceding command: if you change the location of the quorum resource, do not omit the drive letter, the colon, or any backslashes. Write out the path name as if you were entering the full path at the command line.

Managing Individual Nodes

The node option in cluster allows you to check on the status of and administer a cluster node. Some example commands include:

Cluster node test1 /status
> This command displays the cluster node status (for example, if the node is up, down, or paused).

Cluster node test1 /forcecleanup
> This command manually restores the configuration of the Cluster service on the specified node to its original state.

Cluster node test1 /start *(or* /stop *or* /pause *or* /resume*)*
> This command starts, stops, pauses, or resumes the Cluster service on the specified node.

Cluster node test1 /evict
> This command evicts a node from a cluster.

Cluster node test1 /listinterfaces
> This command lists the node's network interfaces.

Managing the Cluster Service Itself

There is also a command, called clussvc, that allows you to take action against a few things that might cause the cluster service to present trouble. You should only use this command if the cluster service fails to start, and it should only be run locally from the node which is presenting problems.

To enable the debugging of the resource dynamic-link libraries (DLLs) that are loaded by the resource monitor process, use the following:

    Clussvc /debug /debugresmon

To allow the Cluster service to start up, despite problems with the quorum device, issue the following command:

    Clussvc /debug /fixquorum

When the /fixquorum command is issued on a particular node, the Cluster service starts, but all the resources, including the quorum resource, remain offline. This allows you to then manually bring the quorum resource online and more easily diagnose quorum device failures.

If the quorum log file is not found or is corrupted, the following will create a new quorum log file based on information in the local node's cluster database file:

    Clussvc /debug /resetquorumlog

The new quorum file is created using information in the cluster database located in *%systemroot%\cluster\CLUSDB*. Be careful, however, as that information might be out of date; only use this if no backup is available.

Use the following command to disallow replication of event log entries:

```
Clussvc /debug /norepevtlogging
```

This command is useful in reducing the amount of information displayed in the command window by filtering out events already recorded in the event log.

And in the event that nothing else works, you can use the following command to force a quorum between a list of cluster nodes for a majority node set cluster:

```
Clussvc /debug /forcequorum node1,node2,node3
```

You might use that command in the case where all nodes in one location have lost the ability to communicate with nodes in another location.

The Last Word

As you've learned in this chapter, Windows Server 2003 supports two distinct types of clustering: NLB clusters, which simply provide load distribution capabilities to certain IP-based applications; and true server clustering, which provides fault tolerance capabilities to larger sets of machines.

NLB is quite useful if you have a web-based application and several machines that can be devoted to servicing that application. The hardware does not need to be terribly powerful, and NLB is a great way to put used machines into service while providing a faster end-user experience. True server clustering is a better fit for medium-size organizations that have business-critical applications that always have to be available, no questions asked. Of course, with the high availability aspect comes increased cost, and the hardware investment required for true fault-tolerant capabilities is significant and should not be overlooked.

CHAPTER 13

Other Windows Server 2003 Services

Throughout the previous chapters of this book, you've seen the bundled services most commonly used with Windows Server 2003. In this chapter, I'll review two more that are also popular: the Indexing Service and the Microsoft Message Queue. Then, I'll provide a brief, high-level overview of other applications and services from Microsoft, called "feature packs," that are either bundled with Windows Server 2003 R2 or available for download and might offer some value to your organization.

The Indexing Service

Windows Server 2003 includes Version 3.0 of the Indexing Service, which catalogs files stored on network drives, corporate intranets, and Internet sites, and provides a web-based query form for easy search and retrieval of those cataloged resources. The service is part of Internet Information Services (see Chapter 8 for a complete and detailed walkthrough of IIS).

Part of the power behind the Indexing Service is its ability to catalog documents without needing them reformatted to a special, proprietary format. The service understands most Microsoft Office file formats, including Word and Excel documents. This makes the service very useful, even beyond its basic premise of indexing plain web sites.

The Indexing Service works by identifying unique words within a document and establishing its location with that document, and then reporting that information back to a central database—the "index," as it were. You, as the administrator, can specify certain documents to either be indexed or be excluded from indexing. You also can include additional properties of a document in the catalog to expand the criteria on which your users can search, including title, author, creation date, date of last edit, and similar bits of information.

Of course, in some instances you might not want the Indexing Service installed. For example, on regular client workstations with no special needs, there would be no reason to have this service installed, only to occupy resources needlessly and present an additional security risk (that's not to say that the service is insecure, but that you should reduce the surface of attack for a machine as much as possible). On fileservers, however, the Indexing Service adds value and provides a service for your user community.

You can install the Indexing Service through the Add/Remove Programs applet within the Control Panel. Click Add/Remove Windows Components, and then check the box next to Indexing Service and click Next. That's all it takes to install it—a very easy process.

To confuse you further: by default, the Indexing Service is already installed, but it's just not started. If you open the Services console from the Administrative Tools menu and select Indexing Service, then set its startup type to Automatic and click Start, the service starts and functions properly even though it still doesn't show up as installed in Add/Remove Windows Components.

However, the only way to fully uninstall the service is to simply uncheck the box within Add/Remove Programs and click Next.

How the Indexing Service Works

The Indexing Service uses filters to extract information from documents. The CiDaemon process, which is initiated by the Indexing Service, runs in the background and filters documents for later indexing. It filters DLLs that actually extract words or property information from specific types of files such as Word documents or HTML pages. The Indexing Service comes with a standard set of filters that can index text, HTML, Microsoft Office documents created in Versions 95, 97, 2000, XP, and 2003, and Internet Mail and News posts. Filters are extensible and can be created by third-party vendors for their specific data types.

After using filters to extract data, the service compares the filtered data against an *exception list*, which mainly contains a list of commonly used prepositions, pronouns, articles, and other nonessential words. The exception list is called *NOISE.<XXX>*, where *XXX* represents the language of the document being indexed. After the filtered data has had words that matched entries on the exception list removed, the remaining data is moved to *word lists*, which are small, temporary, and volatile stores of index information that serve as holding bins. About once a day, a process called a *shadow merge* takes place to aggregate the information within shadow indexes and remove data from the "holding bin," to both free up memory occupied by volatile word lists and make filtered data persistent by saving it on a disk. Shadow indexes are created when word lists and other shadow indexes are combined into a single index.

At a separate time, the Indexing Service initiates *master merges*, which take place when individual shadow indexes are aggregated and infused into a current master index to create a single master index. The master index is a permanent index of a larger collection of documents. In a truer sense, the master index is the only index, containing pointers to resources within the *corpus* (a technical term for the body of work that is being indexed), much like the index of this book points you to certain words and phrases at specific points within the body. Picture a set of indexes, each for a certain chapter of this book. One could take these individual indexes (the "shadow indexes") and combine them into a master index, which would be placed at the back of this book—this is the process of master merging. These indexes are stored in the *catalog*, a specific folder that contains all indexes, either temporary word lists or more permanent shadow and master indexes.

Here are some additional terms you might run across while administering the Indexing Service:

Query
> Simply a certain request to the Indexing Service to retrieve files or data that match certain criteria.

Saved indexes
> Just highly compressed indexes that are stored on disk media and not simply placed in memory; thus, saved indexes persist after reboots. Saved indexes come in two flavors—shadow indexes and master indexes.

Scan
> Takes place when the Indexing Service wants to determine what files in a particular location have changed or otherwise been modified.

Scope
> Simply the range of documents and files to be searched when satisfying a query.

Virtual root
> An alias to a certain directory on a disk. The Indexing Service can index any location defined as a virtual root.

Performance Considerations

Obviously, the single largest requirement of any indexing service is its disk space— the service will need room to store its indexing files. Microsoft recommends that you allocate about 35% of the size of your corpus for the indexing service—I would allocate about 45%, simply to provide your service with room to grow. As more electronic information hits your disks you'll want to have ample space to index that data optimally. Master merges typically require large amounts of disk space on a temporary basis, as much as 50% of the corpus size.

Memory is also an important consideration. Table 13-1 shows the Microsoft minimum memory amounts and my recommended memory amounts for certain corpus sizes. Keep in mind that these recommendations are in excess of the current amount of memory in a machine for Windows Server 2003's general use—add the amount of memory you have plus the appropriate recommended amount from the table to obtain the correct total amount of memory for your machine.

Table 13-1. Corpus sizes and memory requirements

Corpus size	Minimum memory size	Recommended memory size
100,000 or fewer documents	64 MB	64 MB
Between 100,001 and 250,000 documents	64 MB	192 MB
Between 250,001 and 500,000 documents	64 MB	256 MB
More than 500,000 documents	128 MB	512 MB, or more if corpus size is considerably larger than 500,000 documents

Perhaps the greatest demand on your machine's CPU from the Indexing Service comes from master merges, which are very intensive and require large amounts of CPU time. Because of this, the Indexing Service schedules master merges automatically for midnight local time. However, if there is a better time when your machine's CPU load is low, you can change the time at which master merges will begin by doing some Registry editing. The `MasterMergeTime` value, located in *HKEY_LOCAL_MACHINE\System\CurrentControlSet\Control\ContentIndex*, allows you to specify the number of minutes after midnight local time that the master merge should commence. For this value, you can enter any number between 0 and 1439.

 One other performance note: the Indexing Service sometimes locks certain files that might be needed for other services. Be aware of any consequences this might have for these services and applications.

Common Administrative Tasks

In this section, I'll go through some common administrative tasks you will encounter with the Indexing Service. When performing most of these tasks, you'll find it easier to create a custom view within the MMC to access the Indexing Service controls because a clean default view of these options is not built into Windows Server 2003. To create a custom view, follow these steps:

1. From the Start menu, select the Run option.
2. Type **mmc** in the Run box and press Enter.
3. The MMC starts with an empty console, as shown in Figure 13-1.
4. From the File menu, choose Add/Remove Snap-in, and then click Add.
5. The Add Standalone Snap-in box appears. Select Indexing Service and click Add, as shown in Figure 13-2.

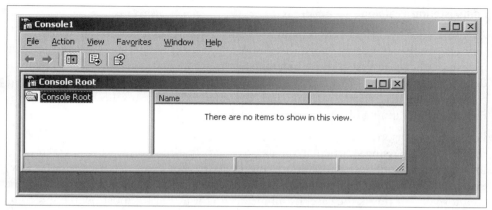

Figure 13-1. Adding a node to a blank MMC window

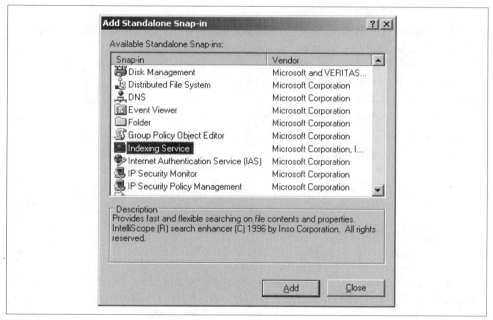

Figure 13-2. Adding the Indexing Service to an MMC window

6. Select Local Computer when prompted unless you're installing this set of tools to administer the Indexing Service on a remote machine; in that case, enter the name of the remote computer.

7. Click Close, and then click OK, and you'll be returned to the console with the Indexing Service node now added to the left pane.

Now you're ready to manage the service, as described in the next section.

Administering a catalog

As you read previously in this chapter, a catalog is a specific folder that contains all indexes; both temporary word lists and more permanent shadow and master indexes. When you first add the Indexing Service to a computer, the service creates a default index, named *System*, that includes all directories on all local drives attached to the system, and another default index, named *Web*, for any IIS-based web sites that might be running on that particular machine.

For security reasons, I recommend deleting both of these default catalogs. They are too all-encompassing, particular for web servers. It's best to create your own catalogs that index only certain data on your disk and not every file it can find. However, you might have a completely sanitized system and find that the defaults work well for you—if this is the case, by all means go for it. But for most people, I recommend deleting the default catalogs and enabling more specific, focused, and restrictive catalogs.

Creating a catalog. To create a custom catalog, use the custom MMC that you created with the Indexing Service snap-in and highlight the Indexing Service node in the left pane. Then, select the Action menu and choose Catalog from the New menu. The Add Catalog screen displays, as shown in Figure 13-3.

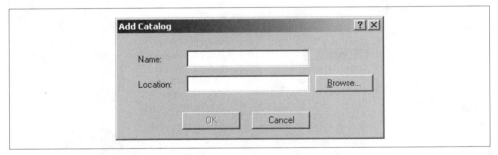

Figure 13-3. Creating a custom catalog

Enter a name for the new catalog in the Name box and then enter the path to the folder that will house the contents of the catalog in the Location box. You can use the Browse button to graphically navigate your directory structure. Click OK when you've entered this information. Keep in mind that if you're managing the service on a remote computer, that remote computer must have the default administrative shares (i.e., C$, D$, and the others, as discussed in Chapter 3) intact; otherwise, the operation will fail.

Avoid putting the catalog in the directory that you're cataloging. For example, if you're trying to catalog *D:\DOCS\WINSERVERBK*, do not put the catalog you create for that directory in *D:\DOCS\WINSER-VERBK*. You'll create a near-perpetual loop because the catalog is always changing, and the service will attempt to index the changing catalog and recatalog the catalog, and so on.

Also, avoid putting a catalog in the *WWWROOT* directory where IIS web sites live. It's fine to catalog the web sites; just don't put the actual catalog there.

Before the new catalog will become active, you must restart the Indexing Service. To quickly restart the service, right-click the Indexing Service node within the Console window and select Stop. Once the service has stopped, right-click in the same place again and choose Start.

Configuring a catalog. After catalogs are added, they need to be configured to act as you want. Within the Indexing Service console, right-click the catalog to be configured and select Properties. The screen shown in Figure 13-4 appears.

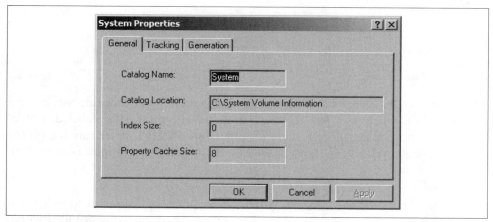

Figure 13-4. Adjusting the properties of an individual catalog

A discussion of the features available on each tab follows:

General

On the General tab is information about the catalog that cannot be modified, including the name and location of the catalog, the number of documents in its corpus, and the size of the property cache.

Tracking

Figure 13-5 shows the Tracking tab. On the Tracking tab, you can elect to automatically add and remove aliases for shared network drives and whether to inherit the setting for that option from the overall Indexing Service configuration.

Simply put, this means that if the service indexes data on a mapped drive, it will remember both the mapped drive and the full UNC path to the data. If you want to turn it off—to keep data private or to control the indexing of network drives and the traffic resulting from that process—you'll need to disable the inheritance feature with the second checkbox and then disable the automatic alias function by un-checking the first box. A lot of administrators turn this off to control and limit that resulting traffic.

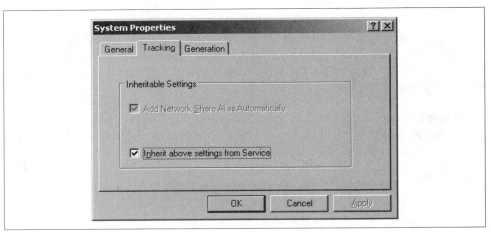

Figure 13-5. The Tracking tab

If you have IIS installed on the machine that is running the Indexing Service, you can select which web site to index from the drop-down list labeled WWW Server, and you can do the same for any news (NNTP) server running on the machine as well. If IIS is not installed on the machine, the option is grayed out and unavailable.

Generation

Figure 13-6 shows the Generation tab. On this tab, you can elect to index files that have extensions that aren't covered by the filters currently installed within the service. You also can specify whether the Indexing Service should generate abstracts for files returned from a query and present them on the results page. These two options are inherited from the overall Indexing Service configuration by default; to turn them off, uncheck the Inherit above settings from Service checkbox and then adjust the settings individually. Generally, administrators turn off the Index files with unknown extensions feature because of a marked increase in processor usage—it's just not worth it for a lot of situations.

You also can adjust the size of abstracts returned to the results page; because more time is needed for a query to be returned as abstracts increase in size, it's best to leave this at the default 320 characters unless you have a specific business need to change it.

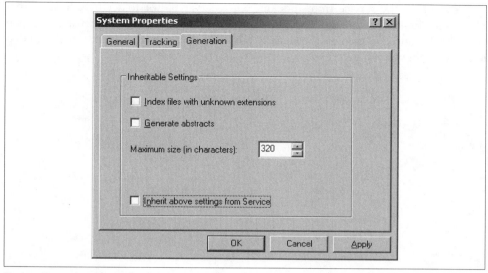

Figure 13-6. The Generation tab

Aside from the abstract generation setting, all the options on these tabs require a restart of the catalog to be recognized. To restart the catalog, simply right-click the appropriate catalog within the Indexing Service snap-in, select Stop and then Start. If you change the abstract generation setting, you need to stop and restart the Indexing Service itself; see the previous instructions for a procedure to do that.

Selecting a directory and location. Upon adding a new catalog and configuring its properties, you also need to define the directories to be included or excluded from its indexing activities. Specifying "included directories" encompasses any subdirectories of that particular directory. You can choose to exclude individual directories within an included parent directory, but you cannot include individual directories within an excluded parent directory—the directory will appear to be included, but it will not be indexed.

How does security play into the indexing process? The Indexing Service is completely compatible with any NTFS permissions you apply to files and folders; if a user's current security privileges won't allow him to see a file that is stored on a local NTFS volume, the Indexing Service won't return that file within the results of a query. If a catalog is configured to index a remote UNC share, it will show the protected files in the results of a search, but the user won't be able to access them. This is a moderate security risk of course, since a user knows of the existence of a file containing that sort of information. Additionally, encrypted files are not indexed at all. If a file included in a catalog is encrypted after it is indexed, it will be removed from the index.

You can block the service from indexing a particular file or folder by adjusting that object's attributes. Right-click the appropriate file or folder, choose Properties, and then click the Advanced button on the General tab. This opens the Advanced Attributes dialog box, as shown in Figure 13-7.

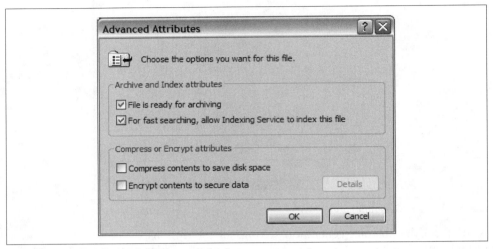

Figure 13-7. The Advanced Attributes dialog box

Under Archive and Index attributes, uncheck the second option, and the folder won't be indexed by the service.

Also, note that the operating system that hosts drives being indexed also affects the operation of the Indexing Service in the following ways:

- FAT volumes hosted remotely on machines running operating systems other than Windows NT, 2000, or Server 2003 will need to be rescanned periodically to detect modified files.

- Volumes on any filesystem hosted on Novell NetWare servers or Unix systems can be indexed, but there is no permission validation on files stored on those servers.

- Novell NetWare volumes will need to be rescanned periodically to detect modified files.

To include or exclude directories from a catalog's indexing processes, follow these steps:

1. Open the Indexing Service console.

2. Right-click the appropriate catalog in the right pane, and then from the New menu, select Directory.

3. The Add Directory dialog box appears, as shown in Figure 13-8. In the Path box, enter the location of the directory you're either including or excluding. This can be either a local path or a network (UNC) path.

4. If you are specifying a path to a remote computer, supply a valid username and password in the Account Information section.

5. Finally, select whether to include or exclude this particular directory in the index in the Include in Index? section to the right of the Account Information box.

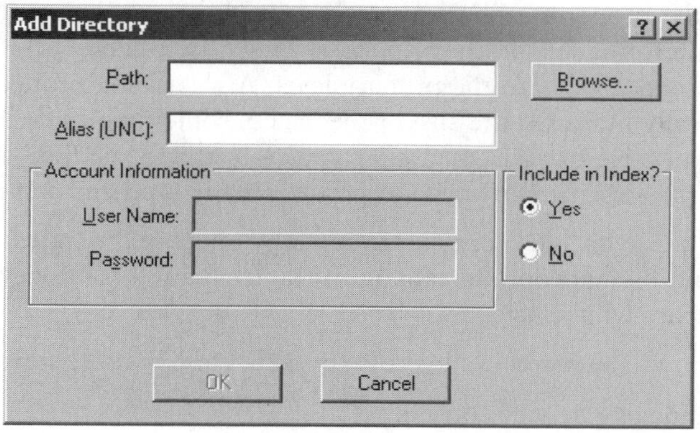

Figure 13-8. Specifying included and excluded directories

The property cache. The property cache is where the Indexing Service stores file property information for all documents and pages within each catalog. The cache is a dual-level cache, with the primary level containing property information that is accessed fairly regularly, and the secondary level holding information that is not accessed very often.

Table 13-2 shows the property values stored in the cache by default and their respective levels.

Table 13-2. Default property cache values

Descriptive identifier	Value	Function	Resident cache level
None	0 × 5	Unique identifier assigned to all NTFS volumes	Primary
None	0 × 6	Work ID of current directory's parent	Primary
None	0 × 7	Secondary storage ID	Primary
File Index	0 × 8	Unique ID of a document housed on an NTFS volume	Primary
Attrib	0 × d	Attributes of a document	Primary
DocTitle	0 × 2	Document's title	Secondary
Path	0 × b	Path of a document	Secondary

Table 13-2. Default property cache values (continued)

Descriptive identifier	Value	Function	Resident cache level
Size	0 × c	Size of a document	Secondary
Write	0 × e	Date and time the document was last modified	Secondary

You might find that you would like to track and include other properties within the index. For instance, your users might often search on the date a document was created, a property that is not tracked by default. You can definitely add properties to either level of the property cache and track them, but adding values to either level degrades the performance of the service overall—this effect is even more pronounced if you add a value to the primary level. Also, adding properties of variable length dramatically increases the size of the cache, something to be aware of if disk space isn't inexpensive to you. Also, after you've restarted the Indexing Service, the levels to which you assigned any new properties are finalized and cannot be changed.

You can see all the available properties to track by opening the Indexing Service console and clicking the appropriate catalog in the left pane. In the right pane, all the available properties will be listed.

To add a property to be saved in the property cache, follow these steps:

1. Open the Indexing Service console.
2. In the left pane, find the appropriate catalog, and then select the Properties folder underneath the node.
3. In the right pane, click the property you would like to add to the property cache.
4. Select Properties from the Action menu.
5. The property's Properties screen will appear. To include the property in the cache, check the Cached checkbox and then check the appropriate storage level in the drop-down checkbox. This is shown in Figure 13-9.
6. Click OK when you're finished.

The property has now been enabled for inclusion in the property cache. You will need to restart the Indexing Service for these changes to take effect. Also, only new documents added to the index will have these properties tracked and added to the cache; to include these specific properties of documents already in the index, you'll need to perform a full scan of the index (see the next section for details on that process).

To remove a property from being tracked, simply repeat the preceding process for the appropriate property, and on the Properties sheet, remove the check mark in the Cached checkbox. Then, restart the Indexing Service and again perform a full scan of the index to remove all traces of the property from the property cache.

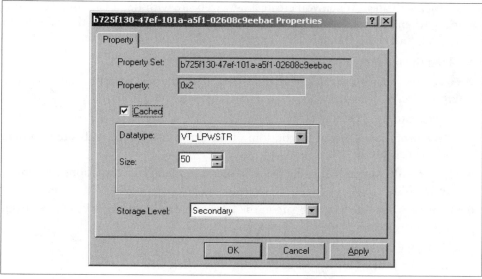

Figure 13-9. Adding a property to the property cache

Initiating scans. Full scans involve making a complete list of all documents contained in a catalog. When the Indexing Service is first installed it of course conducts a full scan, but these types of scans also are conducted when directories are added to a catalog and as part of the error recovery process. On the other hand, incremental scans—which only look for changed documents within a catalog—are done automatically upon a restart of the Indexing Service to determine what documents have changed while it was inactive.

If you have a heavy load on your server from a large amount of modified files, you might want to manually initiate either a full or an incremental scan. Here are the steps:

1. Open the Indexing Service console.
2. In the left pane, select the appropriate catalog.
3. In the right pane, double-click Directories.
4. Select the directory for which you want to initiate a scan.
5. From the Action menu, select All Tasks and then either Rescan (Full) or Rescan (Incremental), depending on which operation you want. (Obviously, you want to avoid a full rescan in the middle of the day.)
6. Confirm your choice by clicking OK.

The scan will proceed.

Indexing new web sites. When you create a new web site with IIS, it isn't indexed automatically when you create a catalog for it. If you want the contents of the web site to be indexed, follow these steps:

1. Open the Indexing Service console.
2. Select the relevant catalog and right-click it in the left or right pane. Choose Properties.
3. Navigate to the Tracking tab.
4. In the drop-down box at the bottom of the screen, select the web site to index, and then click OK.
5. Open the IIS Manager console (see Chapter 8 for detailed instructions on administering IIS).
6. Right-click the relevant web site in the left pane, and then select Properties from the context menu.
7. Navigate to the Home Directory tab.
8. Check the Index This Resource box, and then click OK.
9. Restart the Indexing Service.

The new catalog is active and will begin indexing the site you specified. I'll cover how to query this new catalog later in this chapter.

Indexing PDF files. Although the Indexing Service and Windows Server 2003 do not come bundled with a filter that can index the contents and properties of PDF files, Adobe—the manufacturer of Acrobat—has made available a free filter that you can install that will enable that functionality. You can find this filter at *http://www.adobe. com/support/salesdocs/1043a.htm*; you will need to have a login and password for the Adobe web site (both of which are free) to download it.

 Adobe doesn't officially certify this plug-in for Windows Server 2003—it guarantees it will work only on Windows NT and Windows 2000—but it definitely works in all of my test systems and I have no reports of it not working on other administrators' systems, too.

To install the PDF filter, follow these steps:

1. Open the Indexing Service console.
2. Stop the Indexing Service.
3. Double-click the *ifilter50.exe* file you downloaded from the Adobe web site.
4. The installation process will commence. You can accept the default location to install the filter product, unless you have a reason to change it.
5. Once the installation process finishes, start the Indexing Service.
6. Initiate a new scan, as described in the previous section.

If, for some reason, PDF files still are not being indexed after this procedure, check the Registry to make sure the Indexing Service knows the PDF filter is present and where it can find it. Stop the Indexing Service, and then open the Registry Editor and navigate to the key:

HKEY_LOCAL_MACHINE\SYSTEM\CurrentControlSet\Control\ContentIndex

In the right pane, double-click the *DLLsToRegister* key. Look to see whether *PDFFILT.DLL* is present, and make sure the path is correct. (If you accepted the default entries during the filter installation process, the path is *C:\Program Files\ Adobe\PDF IFilter 5.0*.)

Controlling merges

At some point within your organization a significant number of documents within your corpus might be modified. In this instance, it might be beneficial to initiate a master merge yourself, instead of waiting for the automatic master merge to occur in the evening.

To initiate a master merge manually, follow these steps:

1. Open the Computer Management applet within the Control Panel.
2. Expand the Indexing Service node in the left pane.
3. Right-click the appropriate catalog where the changed documents are represented, and select Merge from the All Tasks menu. This is shown in Figure 13-10.
4. Confirm your choice to merge the catalog by clicking Yes. Remember that this is a CPU- and time-intensive operation.

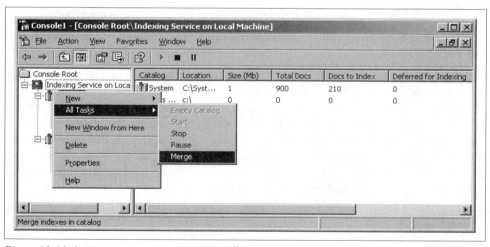

Figure 13-10. Initiating a master merge manually

You also might find it convenient to change the scheduled time for master merges to occur. Perhaps your lowest CPU load occurs at 3:00 a.m. and not at midnight when the service is preconfigured to perform merges. To change this time, you'll need to edit the Registry. Follow these steps:

1. Open the Registry Editor (selecting the Run command from the Start menu and entering **regedit** is an easy way).

2. Navigate to the key:

   *HKEY_LOCAL_MACHINE\SYSTEM\CurrentControlSet\Control\
   ContentIndex*

3. In the right pane, double-click the MasterMergeTime window.

4. In the Data box in the resulting DWORD Editor window, enter a value that represents the number of minutes past midnight that the master merge process should begin. This should be a number between 0 and 1,439. For our example—to begin at 3:00 a.m. instead of midnight—enter **180**. Be sure Decimal is selected.

5. Click OK.

Running and configuring queries

The Indexing Service has several interfaces. Perhaps the easiest and most accessible is simply through the Search command in the Start Menu, as shown in Figure 13-11.

When using this interface, choose the option to search for files and folders, and then enter a filename, a word, a string of text from a file, or some other criterion in the box provided. Then the Indexing Service will work its magic, displaying results as much as 10 times faster than a search done without the Indexing Service present.

The Indexing Service console also contains a Query the Catalog interface, as shown in Figure 13-12.

The main advantage of the Query the Catalog form is the wider availability of search criteria. Using this page, you can search for words and phrases, search for words and phrases that are near other words and phrases, search for strings within text properties (such as a document summary in Microsoft Word), search within certain document formats, use operators such as $<$, $<=$, $=$, $=>$, $>$, and $!=$ against a fixed data point (useful for comparing against a date, a time, a size, or the like), use Boolean operators, use wildcard operators, use regular expressions, and rank results by how close the match is to the query. It's certainly quite a list.

If you want to create your own custom query form, that's simple to do as well. A basic form might consist of the following:

```
<h1>Indexing Service Query</h1>
<p>Enter the term for your search, and then press Submit.</p>
<form method="POST" action="/scripts/querydemo.idq">
<p><input type="text" name="CiRestriction" size="75"><input
```

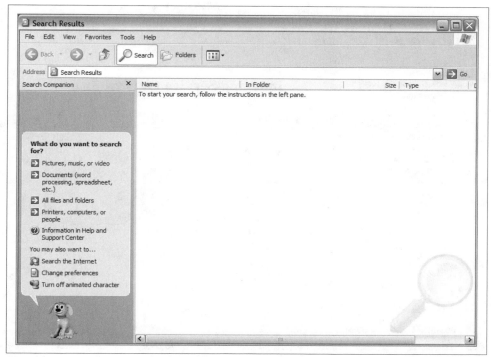

Figure 13-11. Accessing the Indexing Service via the Windows user interface

```
type="submit" value="Submit" name="B1">
<input type="reset" value="Reset" name="B2"></p>
</form>
```

A custom query form has one requirement: it must post back to the Internet data query (IDQ) file, which simply configures the correct query parameters for a search. (Head over to *http://msdn.microsoft.com* and search for "format IDQ" for a detailed reference on the formatting for these files.) The following code is a standard format for an IDQ file:

```
[Query]
# CiCatalog=d:\ <= COMMENTED OUT - default registry value used
CiColumns=filename,size,rank,characterization,vpath,DocTitle,write
CiRestriction=%CiRestriction%
CiMaxRecordsInResultSet=200
CiMaxRecordsPerPage=35
CiScope=/
CiFlags=DEEP
CiTemplate=/iissamples/issamples/ixtourqy.htx
CiSort=rank[d]
CiForceUseCi=true
```

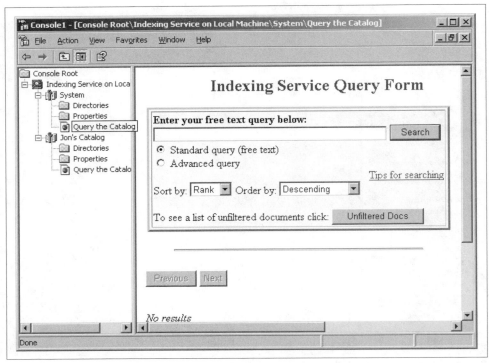

Figure 13-12. Accessing the Indexing Service via the Query the Catalog page

Let's take a closer look at each part of the IDQ file:

[Query]
> Identifies the following information as a query restriction.

CiCatalog=d:\
> Points to the index to use. In the previous case, the statement is commented out, so default is used.

CiColumns=filename,size,rank,characterization,vpath,DocTitle,write
> Indicates the kind of information to return in the result set.

CiRestriction=%CiRestriction%
> Indicates the query terms to search for. In this case, the CiRestriction form parameter is used, which matches the variable name of the text box used in the example form previously.

CiMaxRecordsInResultSet=200
> Sets the maximum number of results to be returned; in this example, 200.

`CiMaxRecordsPerPage=35`

Determines how many results are shown on each web page returned. In this case, 35 results will be shown per web page.

`CiScope=/`

Tells where to start the query. In this example, the query starts at the root of the virtual directory space. You can list more than one virtual directory in your scope by separating the directories with a comma (,). For example: `CiScope = /docs,/work,/school`.

`CiFlags=DEEP`

Instructs the query to search all subdirectories within the scope. Change `DEEP` to `SHALLOW` to search only the directory shown in `CiScope`.

`CiTemplate=/iissamples/issamples/ixtourqy.htx`

Indicates which file to use to format the results; in this case, *Ixtourqy.htx*.

`CiSort=rank[d]`

Tells how to sort the results. This example calls for results to be listed in descending (`[d]`) rank order; that is, the results are listed in order from the file with the most hits to the file with the least hits.

`CiForceUseCi=true`

This is an optional variable that, when set to `TRUE`, forces Indexing Service to search the content index even if it is out of date.

 If you use a sort method other than rank descending, you receive only a subset of the total set of matching documents, and that subset might be different with every successive query. The only surefire, consistent rank sorting method is rank descending, as described earlier.

If you are receiving an error such as "No documents matched the query" when using a custom query form, you can try a few things. For one, check the *.IDQ* file that is being used for the query, and make sure the line `CiCatalog` is pointing to the correct catalog location. If you are using a custom catalog, be sure to point this entry somewhere; otherwise, you are searching in the default catalog, which isn't what you want.

Also, if you are trying to search content on an IIS-hosted web site, make sure the Index this Resource checkbox is checked for that particular site. Open the IIS Manager console (see Chapter 8 for detailed instructions on administering IIS), and right-click the relevant web site in the left pane. Then select Properties from the context menu. Navigate to the Home Directory tab, check the Index This Resource box, and then click OK. Finally, restart the Indexing Service.

You also might be impeded from viewing some documents because of permissions. The Indexing Service scans and indexes using the System local account and must have at least Read permissions on the files you want indexed; otherwise, the service can't read them and they're not indexed. The service also needs Full Control permissions for the root folder of the drive that houses the catalog, and it needs Full Control on the *CATALOG.WCI* directory—this is located within the catalog directory. Additionally, if your users are attempting to search for documents, they might not be allowed to access them and thus those documents would not show up in the search results (if those documents are hosted on an NTFS volume).

Adjusting performance options

Trying to adjust performance for the Indexing Service and to issue recommendations is tantamount to aiming at a moving target: several variables significantly affect the performance of the service, including the obvious ones—corpus size, amount of memory available, and amount of physical disk space present. Testing on an informal basis has revealed that indexes with 150,000 documents or less tend to not require a special hardware emphasis: the stock hardware that runs Windows Server 2003 should be a sufficient base for such a small corpus. Above that "magic" number, however, you might need to look at expanding hardware on the machine running the Indexing Service to improve performance.

Configuring performance within the Indexing Service. You need to adjust a couple of knobs within the Indexing Service to configure a certain level of performance based on system load; these adjustments are sometimes a quick fix to avoid needing a hardware upgrade. However, it's important to realize that in the majority of cases, the service works in the background and configures itself to consume resources appropriately; these options will make a noticeable difference only in either very high- or very low-load situations.

With that disclaimer out of the way, let's turn to adjustments. For one, you can adjust the level at which the Indexing Service thinks it runs on the server—sometimes this can make the service a better player among the other processes jockeying for CPU time on your machine. To try this, do the following:

1. Open the Indexing Service console.
2. Right-click the Indexing Service node in the left pane, and select Stop.
3. Now, from the Action menu, select All Tasks and then choose Tune Performance.
4. The Indexing Service Usage screen appears, as shown in Figure 13-13.

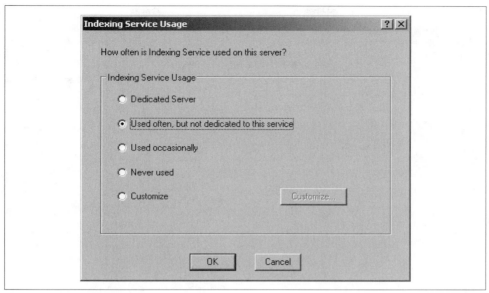

Figure 13-13. Adjusting Indexing Service usage

On this screen, simply select the options that adequately fit this machine's usage profile. Your options are as follows:

Dedicated server
Provides "instant" (quick) indexing and "high load" (good performance under stress) querying

Used often, but not dedicated to this service
Uses "lazy" (slower) indexing and "moderate load" (good performance under a modest load) querying

Used occasionally
Specifies "lazy" indexing and "low load" querying

Never used
Completely turns off the indexing service

Customize
Brings up a separate dialog, shown in Figure 13-14

The Desired Performance screen allows you to individually adjust the indexing and querying settings for the service to use. You can choose between lazy, moderate, and instant indexing, and low load, moderate load, and high load querying.

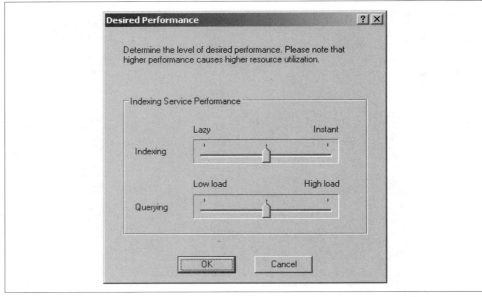

Figure 13-14. Customizing Indexing Server performance

Monitoring performance using the Performance Monitor. You might find that using the Performance Monitor bundled with Windows Server 2003 provides you with data on how the Indexing Service is performing. To call up the Performance Monitor, load the application from the Administrative Tools menu off the Start menu. Then, click the "+" icon in the middle of the toolbar in the right pane to open the Add Counters screen. Select the appropriate performance object as outlined in Table 13-3, which lists the relevant counters you can use to track this performance. Then, select the appropriate performance object and the appropriate counters on the right side of the screen, using Table 13-3 as a guide.

Table 13-3. Performance Monitor counters relevant to the Indexing Service

Object	Counter	Function
Indexing Service	Number of documents indexed	A tally of the documents indexed in the current session
	Deferred for indexing	Number of documents currently in use that require indexing
	Documents to be indexed	Least number of documents requiring indexing
	Index size (MB)	Size of the index, in megabytes
	Merge progress	Percentage of current merge process complete

Object	Counter	Function
	Running queries	Number of queries being processed at the moment
	Saved indexes	Number of saved indexes
	Total number of documents	Number of documents familiar to the Indexing Service
	Total number of queries	Number of queries that have been conducted in the current session
	Unique keys	Number of unique keys—words, properties, and other search criteria—present in the index
	Word lists	Number of word lists
Indexing Service Filter	Binding time (msec)	Average time, in milliseconds, for filter binding
	Indexing speed (MBph)	Speed of indexing the contents of a document, in megabytes per hour
	Total indexing speed (MBph)	Speed of indexing the contents of a document and its properties, in megabytes per hour

The Microsoft Message Queue

The Microsoft Message Queuing Service (MSMQ) provides you, as the system administrator, with a way to collect messaging transactions from various messaging-aware applications and queue them until applications are ready to process them. Messages, in this case, aren't like email messages between human users, but are functional messages or data exchanged between applications.

What is MSMQ used for? The MSMQ services come into play when one application wants to exchange a message with another application but that particular application isn't responding. When one person needs to communicate fairly quickly with another person, he typically uses a phone. If the person he is trying to reach isn't at his desk, and there is no voice mail or answering machine, the original caller needs to continue trying to reach the person—which can turn into a big waste of time. However, if he can leave a voice mail message in the other person's message "queue," the caller can go on about his other work and wait for the other person to deal with the message and take any appropriate action. MSMQ works the same way, providing a storage-and-retrieval service for applications that are available to accept messages sent to them. This allows sending applications to get on with their other processes without dedicating resources to continuing attempts to transmit programming and service messages to unavailable applications.

The queue—the holding bin for these messages—comes in different types and performs different functions:

Administration queues
> Established by the transmitting application and only serve to acknowledge sent messages

Public queues
> Available to any computer within your organization and are published within Active Directory and are replicated among the domain controllers in your domain or forest

Private queues
> Specific to only a few applications that have specific awareness of the existence of those queues—they are not published in Active Directory

Dead-letter queues
> Hold messages that can't be delivered

Response queues
> Hold messages sent in response to previous messages that are destined for the original sender

Report queues
> Detail the route taken by a message to its destination

System queues
> Combine other queues to orchestrate communication between the system and application

Journal queues
> Copy messages to make sure they are delivered correctly

The messages stored within these queues consist of a header, which contains the message identifier and other specific properties, and the body, which is the meat of the message and can be encrypted if it contains sensitive information. Messages cannot exceed 4 MB in size. There are four types of messages:

Normal messages
> Typical exchanges of information between applications, and can come from public, private, journal, or dead-letter queues

Report messages
> Customarily are test messages designed to determine what routing occurs for messages

Response messages
> Confirmations from the destination applications, such as responses to normal ping traffic on TCP/IP

Acknowledgement messages
> Like read receipts and acknowledge the receipt of messages on the part of the destination application

Communications with MSMQ

The basis of communications for MSMQ is the Active Directory site; thus, all message exchange between queues and applications is done within the context of your organization's Active Directory structure. MSMQ is a very chatty service and it uses a lot of network bandwidth, so make sure you place at least one MSMQ server in each Active Directory site or subnet to mitigate that effect. For traffic between sites, MSMQ uses routing links, which use the TCP/IP protocol to pass traffic to and from hosts.

Where direct connections cannot be established, the MSMQ software routes messages according to rules dictating how messages should be transmitted. Messages that are routed move from station to station—or "hop" to "hop," as it is formally known—until the destination is reached. MSMQ attempts to route messages along the least costly route, where the cost is derived from the available bandwidth divided by the actual currency cost of the connection. (This requires outside math on your part.) You specify the cost of the link, similar to how you specify the cost of an AD site link, to MSMQ, and it takes that into account when routing messages between MSMQ servers.

MSMQ Administration

Although much MSMQ detail is beyond the scope of this book, a lot of administrators find themselves administering MSMQ at least in part. With that in mind, the next section details some very common administrative tasks you can perform with the MSMQ. For a more detailed approach to MSMQ development and administration, consult a book or online resource dedicated to the topic. (I've listed one at the end of this section.)

Installing MSMQ

You can easily install MSMQ from the Add/Remove Programs tool within the Control Panel. Open the tool and then select Add/Remove Windows Components from the left pane. Select Application Server, and then click the Details button. Finally, check the checkbox next to Message Queuing, and click OK and then Next to install the components.

Some tips for best performance of MSMQ servers and links:

- If you have multiple Active Directory sites in your forest, try to install MSMQ on at least one server in every site. This way, messages will be more reliably delivered to their destinations between sites, and client broadcast requests will be acknowledged more efficiently.

- Try to install MSMQ on a Windows domain controller that is functioning as a global catalog server. This improves performance. In fact, installing MSMQ on multiple domain controllers will improve performance further.

- However, if you choose to install MSMQ on a domain controller, avoid installing it with routing enabled.

 MSMQ automatically will take on the identity of the site into which it's installed.

Finding an MSMQ server

To find a machine that is running the MSMQ software, open Active Directory Users and Computers, and then do the following:

1. From the View menu, select Users, Groups, and Computers as containers.
2. Again from the View menu, select Advanced Features.
3. In the left pane, select the relevant domain, and then expand the node and select Computers. Alternatively, select Domain Controllers if you have MSMQ installed on your domain controllers, as described earlier.
4. In the right pane, click each computer. Look for the MSMQ folder on each.

Setting a maximum message size

You might want to set a maximum message size for a particular system to compensate for disk space restraints or bandwidth concerns. To do so, take these steps:

1. Open Active Directory Users and Computers.
2. From the View menu, select Users, Groups, and Computers as containers.
3. Again from the View menu, select Advanced Features.
4. In the left pane, right-click MSMQ and choose Properties from the context menu.
5. Navigate to the General tab.
6. Under Storage limits, check the Limit message storage to (KB) option.
7. Enter a value, in kilobytes, that represents the maximum message size this system will accept.
8. Click OK to finish.

Enabling and disabling journals

Recall that journals are simply copies of messages to track their history. To enable or disable journals, follow these steps:

1. Open Active Directory Users and Computers.
2. From the View menu, select Users, Groups, and Computers as containers.

3. Again, from the View menu, select Advanced Features.

4. In the left pane, right-click the appropriate MSMQ queue and choose Properties from the context menu.

5. Navigate to the General tab.

6. Under the Journal section, check the Enable box.

7. Click OK to finish.

Limiting journal size

Like the maximum message size, you might want to constrain the amount of disk space available for journaling. To do so, follow these steps:

1. Open Active Directory Users and Computers.

2. From the View menu, select Users, Groups, and Computers as containers.

3. Again from the View menu, select Advanced Features.

4. In the left pane, right-click MSMQ and choose Properties from the context menu.

5. Navigate to the General tab.

6. Under Storage limits, check the Limit journal storage to (KB) option.

7. Enter a value, in kilobytes, that represents the maximum journal size this system will allow.

8. Click OK to finish.

Finding a queue

To find an MSMQ queue within your organization, do the following:

1. Open Active Directory Users and Computers.

2. From the View menu, select Users, Groups, and Computers as containers.

3. Again from the View menu, select Advanced Features.

4. In the left pane, right-click Computers, and select Find from the context menu.

5. Navigate to the Find MSMQ Queue tab.

6. Enter your search criteria in the Label or Type ID box, and then click Find Now.

Deleting a queue

At certain times, you might want to completely terminate a queue, which deletes all pending messages in the queue. To do so, follow these steps:

1. Open Active Directory Users and Computers.

2. From the View menu, select Users, Groups, and Computers as containers.

3. Again from the View menu, select Advanced Features.

4. Right-click the appropriate queue in the left pane, and select Delete.

5. Confirm your choice by clicking Yes at the prompt.

Viewing the properties of a message

To view the properties of a message, do the following:

1. Open Active Directory Users and Computers.
2. From the View menu, select Users, Groups, and Computers as containers.
3. Again from the View menu, select Advanced Features.
4. In the left pane, find the appropriate queue and select it.
5. Then, in the right pane, right-click the appropriate message and select Properties.

Deleting all messages

You might want to clear a queue of messages. To purge all messages in a queue, do the following:

1. Open Active Directory Users and Computers.
2. From the View menu, select Users, Groups, and Computers as containers.
3. Again from the View menu, select Advanced Features.
4. In the left pane, find the appropriate queue and select it.
5. Then, right-click Queue messages, and from the All tasks menu, select Purge.
6. Confirm your choice by clicking Yes at the prompt.

Creating routing links

Routing links are used to send messages between separate sites. Messages are routed through these links according to the cost of the link, a numeric identifier indicating the preference of the administrator as to how often a particular routing link is used. The lower the cost, the more often MSMQ will pass traffic over that routing link.

Only users in the Enterprise Admins group can create or modify links if there are multiple domains in your organization.

To create routing links, follow these steps:

1. Open Active Directory Sites and Services.
2. From the View menu, select Show Services Node.
3. In the console tree, right-click MsmqServices.
4. Select MSMQ Routing Link from the New menu.
5. In the screen that appears, select the site in the Site 1 list from which messages to be passed over this link should originate. In the Site 2 list, pick the destination site.
6. Enter the cost of the routing link in the Routing link cost box. Remember: the lower the cost, the more often the link will be used. Enter **0** to disable to link.
7. Click OK to finish.

There are a couple of issues to remember when creating routing links:

- Try to connect individual sites to each other using routing links and site gates. You should create a routing link to every new Active Directory site that is created.

- Tell MSMQ clients to use in-routing and out-routing servers for message routing to pass messages within a particular site.

Configuring routing links

Site gates represent individual MSMQ servers that service a routing link between sites. You might have occasion to add or remove servers that take care of a link—perhaps due to administrative maintenance or to decommission a particular machine.

To change the servers that coordinate the site link, follow these steps:

1. Open Active Directory Sites and Services.
2. From the View menu, select Show Services Node.
3. In the console tree, click MsmqServices.
4. In the right pane, right-click the appropriate routing link and select Properties from the pop-up context menu.
5. Navigate to the Site Gates tab.
6. To add a server to the link, select a server from the list in Site Servers and click the Add button. To remove a server presently servicing the link, select a server from the list in Site Gates and click the Remove button.
7. Click OK to finish.

You also might need to adjust the cost value you have assigned to a routing link for various reasons. To do so, follow these steps:

1. Open Active Directory Sites and Services.
2. From the View menu, select Show Services Node.
3. In the console tree, click MsmqServices.
4. In the right pane, right-click the appropriate routing link and select Properties from the pop-up context menu.
5. Navigate to the General tab.
6. In the Link cost box, specify a new cost.
7. Click OK to finish.

Creating foreign sites

Foreign sites are groups of computers that communicate with MSMQ servers that are apart from the current physical network. Much like Active Directory sites, which you learned about in Chapter 5, MSMQ sites are used to delineate the geographical positions of remote networks.

Here's how to create a new foreign site:

1. Open Active Directory Sites and Services.
2. From the View menu, select Show Services Node.
3. In the console tree, right-click MsmqServices.
4. From the context menu, click New Foreign Site.
5. Enter the name for the new site on the screen that appears, and click OK to finish.

Now you need to add foreign computers to the new foreign site. Follow the preceding steps, except in step 4, select New Foreign Computer. In the Name box of the resulting screen, enter the name of the foreign computer, and then select the foreign site to which that machine should belong. Click OK when you've finished the process.

Issues with MSMQ and Firewalls

MSMQ has certain requirements when communicating with machines on either side of a firewall. It is recommended that if MSMQ computers that reside externally to your firewall need to access your organization's Active Directory, you should configure a VPN for that communication that uses the point-to-point tunneling protocol (PPTP). VPNs are covered in detail in Chapter 11.

If you just need MSMQ traffic to be passed through your firewall without access to Active Directory, remote clients sending messages internally require only TCP port 1801 to be open on your firewall. Computers in this scenario cannot access Active Directory, nor can their messages be routed; hence, the destination computer must be directly reachable on the other side of the firewall.

More Resources

If administering MSMQ is a large part of your job, you might want to consult the following resources for more information:

- The MSMQ online documentation, which you can find at:

  http://windows.microsoft.com/windows2000/en/server/help/default.asp?url=/windows2000/en/server/help/sag_msmqconcepts3_3.htm

- The book *Designing Applications with MSMQ: Message Queuing for Developers* (Addison Wesley)

Extending Functionality

Microsoft released Windows Server 2003 in April 2003 and Windows Server 2003 R2 in November 2005, and has subsequently been developing extended functionality in the form of feature packs, some of which are free and some of which are available for a fee. Some of these feature packs may be integrated into the core Windows product at a later time, but for the most part you can pick and choose the feature packs you need at this point. This section provides a brief overview of the available feature packs. I'll note which ones ship in the box within Windows Server 2003 R2 within each section.

Note that in the body of this book, I have covered a portion of the available feature packs and I've noted that where the discussion of the product is given. The following list includes only feature packs which I haven't discussed already. The other feature packs covered in the book include the following:

- Active Directory Application Mode, detailed in Chapter 5
- The Group Policy Management Console, discussed in Chapter 6
- The Shadow Copy Client, covered in Chapter 3
- Windows Server Update Services, covered in Chapter 7

 The URL for all Windows Server 2003 feature packs is:
http://www.microsoft.com/windowsserver2003/downloads/ featurepacks/default.mspx.

Automated Deployment Services

Automated Deployment Services (ADS) include a new set of imaging tools and an infrastructure with improved security for rapidly deploying operating systems remotely onto new servers. ADS allows you to quickly install either Windows 2000 Server or Windows Server 2003 on new servers and customize their configuration, much like RIS functions for client computers, as discussed in Chapter 2.

ADS also offers a reliable, remote script execution framework that enables administrators to perform script-based administration with security on hundreds of servers as easily as they once did on a single server. However, there are reports that ADS is difficult to use on external drive arrays, which would appear to be a big limitation because external arrays would be an ideal place to store drive images.

You can download ADS from:

http://www.microsoft.com/windowsserver2003/technologies/management/ads/ default.mspx

DSML Services for Windows

DSML Services for Windows (DSFW) allows applications to access Active Directory using the SOAP protocol over standard HTTP, using the Directory Services Markup Language Version 2 specifications.

The DSML language is a way for you to represent the structure of your directory and operation performed against it in the form of an XML document. Because DSML is an open format, applications exchanging directory information using it can assure compatibility between themselves. Better still, DSML provides a common ground for specifying directory objects, attributes, and operations.

The DSML Services for Windows add-ons allow administrators to let many more applications access Active Directory using methods apart from the common standard, LDAP. Interoperability is the name of the game with DSFW.

You can download DSFW from:

> *http://www.microsoft.com/windows2000/server/evaluation/news/bulletins/dsml.asp*

Identity Integration Feature Pack

The Identity Integration Feature Pack (IIFP) for Windows Server 2003 keeps track of user identities and coordinates user details across Active Directory, ADAM, and Microsoft Exchange 2000 and Exchange Server 2003 implementations. Using the IIFP, you can combine property information for a given user or resource into a single, logical view for easy administration and modification. The IIFP also automates the provisioning of new and updated identity data in the event that you add, change, or delete users.

You can use the IIFP with a variety of directory services, including the following:

* Active Directory and ADAM
* Attribute value pair, delimited, and fixed width text files
* Directory Services Markup Language
* Global Address Lists (Exchange)
* LDAP Directory Interchange Format
* Lotus Notes/Domino 4.6 and 5.0
* Windows NT 4.0 Domains
* Exchange 5.5 Bridgeheads
* Exchange 5.5, 2000, and 2003
* SQL 7 and 2000 databases
* Novell eDirectory v8.6.2 and v8.7
* Oracle 8i and 9i databases
* SunONE/iPlanet/Netscape Directory
* IBM Informix, DB2, dBase, Access, Excel, and OLE DB via SQL DTS

You can download the IIFP from:

> *http://www.microsoft.com/downloads/details.aspx?FamilyID=d9143610-c04d-*
> *41c4-b7ea-6f56819769d5&DisplayLang=en*

Remote Control Add-on for Active Directory Users and Computers

Remote Control is a small add-on to Active Directory that enables you to right-click a computer account in the Active Directory Users and Computers console and choose Remote Control on that computer. Choosing that option will open a Remote Desktop connection to that computer.

Remote Control uses the Remote Desktop Connection software on both the target computer and the computer running the Active Directory Users and Computers console. This add-on works only with Windows 2000 Server, Windows XP Home and Professional, and Windows Server 2003. It does not work with Windows NT or Windows 2000 Professional.

You can download this add-on from:

> *http://www.microsoft.com/downloads/details.aspx?FamilyID=0a91d2e7-7594-4abb-8239-7a7eca6a6cb1&DisplayLang=en*

This ships on the second CD of Windows Server 2003 R2.

Windows Rights Management Services and Client

Microsoft Windows Rights Management Services (RMS) for Windows Server 2003 lets users and administrators control access and use of certain documents within the organization. Using RMS-enabled applications, users can specify certain documents as "for eyes only," "not for distribution," and the like to protect sensitive information.

RMS requires the purchase of CALs, so it is not a free solution. You can download RMS from:

> *http://www.microsoft.com/windowsserver2003/technologies/rightsmgmt/default.mspx*

Microsoft Services for NetWare 5.03a

Microsoft Services for NetWare 5.03a provides a cumulative set of updates and services that have been offered since the release of Services for NetWare 5.01 SP 1. The Services for NetWare (SFN) package offers a bridge between Windows servers and NetWare servers, allowing transitive file access, user and group security, and more.

You can download this add-on from:

> *http://www.microsoft.com/downloads/details.aspx?FamilyID=6c7f7c56-9298-4732-bf8a-7b771d27910a&displaylang=en*

Windows SharePoint Services

Windows SharePoint Services (WSS) allows administrators to create portal sites, such as that shown in Figure 13-15, that facilitate information access and worker collaboration. These sites can store documents, calendar information, and presentations, and can pull into a central location information on news and weather as well as on other current events.

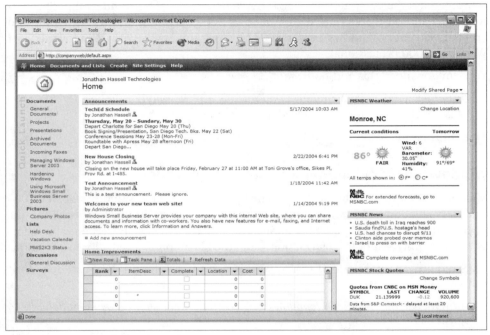

Figure 13-15. A sample Windows SharePoint Services site

You can download WSS from:

> *http://www.microsoft.com/windowsserver2003/technologies/sharepoint/
> default.mspx*

WSS ships on the second CD of Windows Server 2003 R2 and can be installed through Add/Remove Programs once you've installed the R2 components.

Windows Subsystem for Unix Applications

The Microsoft Windows Subsystem for Unix-Based Applications (SUA), previously known as Windows Services for Unix, now ships included with Windows SererServer 2003 R2. SUA provides a subsystem for programs brought over ("ported") from Unix environment, and serves as an interface between these applications and the Windows NT kernel itself.

How does SUA work, at least from a high-level perspective? For example, let's imagine that you have a order tracking and shipping system—one that's critical to your business—that runs on a Unix machine. While you're trying to integrate your back-end servers entirely to Windows Server 2003, and it's an on-going process, you don't have time to rewrite this application entirely in native Windows code. However, it would be great if you could host this application on a Windows machine for the time being to take advantage of advanced monitoring and management functions as you've seen throughout the book.

SUA acts as an interface through which to run your applications. You can compile your application's source code with SUA compiling tools, and install the finished application on computers running Windows operating systems.

Here are a few other scenarios in which SUA is likely to be useful for you:

- Many companies have custom scripts that take care of backup, host integration, and batch processing. You might want these scripts to run on Windows Server 2003 machines. SUA can handle these types of scripts.

- Perhaps you have an Oracle database environment on a computer running a flavor of Unix, and you have lots of Perl code supporting the database environment. SUA can help you make your scripts work across multiple platforms.

- You might also have some 64-bit Unix applications which you want to port to Windows. SUA can handle everything that needs doing for your 64-bit applications to be able to work on Windows.

Because the SUA subsystem is layered on top of the Windows kernel, it offers true Unix functionality without any emulation. For Unix junkies, this means that you get case-sensitive file names, job control, compilation tools, and the use of over 300 Unix commands and utilities and shell scripts within Windows itself.

A computer running Windows Services for Unix provides two different command-line environments: the Unix environment and the Windows environment. Applications run on specific subsystems and in specific environments. When you load the Interix subsystem, you get a Unix environment; when you run applications on the Windows subsystem, you get a Windows environment. You also get NIS capabilities, which allows directory services over Unix varieties, and password synchronization functionality to map Windows account to Unix identities and vice versa. In addition, the support for NFS allows you to share files and folders using a native Unix protocol.

Windows System Resource Manager

The Windows System Resource Manager (WSRM), an add-on feature for the Enterprise and Datacenter editions of Windows Server 2003, provides resource management and enables the allocation of resources, including processor and memory resources, among multiple applications based on business priorities. You can finely tune how resources are allocated to certain tasks to achieve the very best performance possible.

Previously, in Windows 2000 Server, this kind of control was available only in the Datacenter Edition of the product, but Microsoft kindly decided to make it available to users running the Enterprise Edition as well.

The WSRM is shown in Figure 13-16.

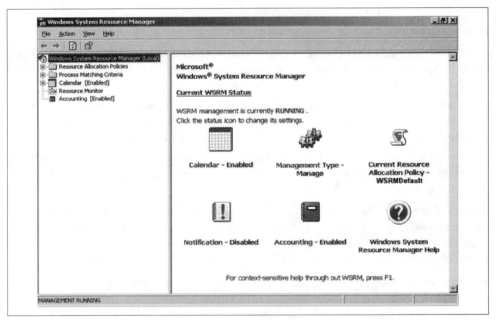

Figure 13-16. The WSRM

You can download the WSRM from:

http://www.microsoft.com/windowsserver2003/downloads/wsrm.mspx

The Last Word

In this last chapter of the book, I covered the Indexing Service—functionality that should prove useful in this search-oriented technology environment—and the Microsoft Message Queue. I also briefly surveyed the feature packs that are either bundled with Windows Server 2003 R2 or available for download.

Since this is the end of the book, I want to sincerely thank you for buying and reading this work! You now have a solid understanding of Windows Server 2003 and its various features and components. Good luck.

The Future of Windows Server

This rebook has focused on the currently available, released version of Windows Server 2003 and its R2 components. The next major revision to the Windows Server product, which Microsoft has codenamed "Longhorn Server," is expected to be released sometime in 2007.

In this appendix, I'll take a look at some of the improvements and fixes that will be integrated with Longhorn Server.

 This information is subject to change as Microsoft moves closer to the release date of Longhorn Server and further examines the software market. I include this preview here just for the curious; you shouldn't use it as a basis for long-range hardware or software investment planning.

General Notes

The first thing to note is that Microsoft will, more likely than not, significantly rearchitect the Windows server-based kernel in this release, which can mean compatibility problems and new security features that can break existing applications. Since the company is betting its future development over the next decade (give or take a few years) on Longhorn Server, it's prepared to break with compatibility, which heretofore has been the utmost priority for its new releases. So it's in your best interest to obtain a beta copy as soon as it's released so you can begin lab testing with the new offering. This change to the kernel certainly isn't set in stone, but most Microsoft watchers agree that the company has had its eye on such a radical reconstruction for a while.

When Longhorn Server rolls around, we can expect more of the same emphasis on security and a hardened exterior surface. Microsoft is purportedly experimenting with releasing different versions of the product targeted specifically at several different types of businesses, including small and medium businesses, high-performance computing, and storage. Of course, there will probably be others as well. There's even talk of a Home Server edition that would serve as a media and communications hub for a modern house—a burgeoning market that, if Microsoft takes advantage of it, could be served well by this proposed edition.

The Feature Roster

As I currently understand it, the following features will most likely make it into the final version of Longhorn Server:

Several enhancements to Active Directory
Including making AD run as a service, thus simplifying and hardening it, and the ability to make a domain controller read-only.

An upgrade to Terminal Services
Codenamed "Bear Claw," which changes the session paradigm that TS has used to date. Instead, users can access applications remotely as if they were running them locally—something Citrix MetaFrame users are already accustomed to. This application publishing feature was originally slated for inclusion in Windows Server 2003 R2 but was pushed out to Longhorn Server in late 2004.

An extension to network quarantine features
Currently present in Windows Server 2003, to be called Network Access Protection. Recall from Chapter 11 that quarantining is only supported (right now) for remote users. In Longhorn Server, notebooks and other hard-wired computers can be prevented from connecting to the network and shunted off into a quarantine area. The extension from remote users to all users is a big boon for security, and this is one of the biggest improvements you'll see in Longhorn Server.

Internet Information Services (IIS) 7.0
You'll find this new version to be modular and easily configurable, even from a text file, bringing it much closer to Apache in terms of its administrative model. Performance has also been significantly improved even over IIS 6. Version 7 will most likely position IIS as the best web server on the market for any application, assuming its security can be improved.

Windows SharePoint Services (WSS) 3.0
Will be included, although details are sketchy at this point.

Hot patching
With hot patching, all non-kernel updates can be applied without rebooting. According to Microsoft, this will reduce server reboots by up to 70 percent. Cool.

Limited user accounts (LUAs)
Prevents administrators from accidentally harming a system. Even when one logs on as an administrator, potentially detrimental actions will require one to enter one's password again as confirmation. The idea is to make people think twice before they issue commands that can hurt a machine.

A fully componentized architecture

Makes it a simple proposition to deploy servers that only include functionality that's absolutely required for a role. A core server OS component provides the very basic OS functionality and is the building block for more specific servers. So you can have a server that only supports DHCP, or just DNS, or is a very hardened Active Directory domain controller.

Improved image-based setup and deployment tools

You'll see these in the Longhorn client first.

A new roles-based management tool

Will be a mix of the current Manage Your Server and the Security Configuration Wizard.

All new versions of feature packs

Microsoft shipped these for Windows Server 2003.

Current Progress

As of this writing in September 2005, Longhorn Server is in beta 1 and is still very rough around the edges. At any time, Microsoft could decide to add or remove features. In fact, the user interface in the beta is very Windows 98–like, without the polish or finish of Windows Server 2003.

Longhorn Server will be a very interesting release, and while it may fall short of being worth the accolade of "revolutionary," it's shaping up to be the most significant release of Windows on the server since the move from NT Server to Windows 2000 Server.

Keep an eye on this release, folks. You'll like what you see.

Index

We'd like to hear your suggestions for improving our indexes. Send email to *index@oreilly.com*.

P

About the Author

Jonathan Hassell is an author, consultant, and speaker residing in Charlotte, North Carolina. Jonathan's previous published works include *RADIUS* for O'Reilly and *Hardening Windows* for Apress. His work is seen regularly in popular periodicals such as *Windows IT Pro Magazine*, *SecurityFocus*, *PC Pro*, and *Microsoft TechNet Magazine*, and he speaks around the world on topics including networking, security, and Windows administration.

Colophon

The animal on the cover of *Learning Windows Server 2003*, Second Edition is an American white pelican (*Pelecanus erythrorhynchos*). It inhabits the coastal regions, freshwater marshes, lakes, and rivers of North America, and it winters in the Gulf states of the southern United States and Mexico.

Sometimes confused with the whooping crane, the American white pelican is a huge white bird with black primary and outer secondary feathers, sporting a wingspan of over 9 feet and an average weight of 16 pounds. Unlike the brown pelican, which plunge-dives into water from the air, the white pelican feeds while swimming, straining fish, frogs, salamanders, and aquatic invertebrates in its pouch. White pelicans prefer to nest on low, bare islands, sandbars, or remote peninsulas, especially on freshwater lakes.

The cover image is a 19th-century engraving from the Dover Pictorial Archive. The cover font is Adobe ITC Garamond. The text font is Linotype Birka; the heading font is Adobe Myriad Condensed; and the code font is LucasFont's TheSans Mono Condensed.